THE COINTELPRO PAPERS

The COINTELPRO Papers

Documents from the FBI's Secret Wars Against Domestic Dissent

by
Ward Churchill and
Jim Vander Wall

Foreword by John Trudell
Preface by Brian Glick

South End Press   Boston, MA

Edited by the South End Press collective.
Design and layout by Saxifrage Publications Group.
Cover by Ty de Pas

Library of Congress Cataloging-in-Publication Data

Churchill, Ward
   The COINTELPRO Papers: documents from the FBI's secret wars against domestic dissent / by Ward Churchill and Jim Vander Wall; foreword by John Trudell; preface by Brian Glick.
      p. cm.
   Includes bibliographical references and index.
   ISBN 0-89608-360-8: $40.00 – ISBN 0-89608-359-4 (pbk.): $16.00
      1. United States. Federal Bureau of Investigation – Archives. 2.Political Crimes and offenses – United States – History – 20th century – Sources. 3. Political persecution – United States – History – 20th century – Sources. 4. Criminal investigation – United States – History – 20th century – Sources. I. Vander Wall, Jim. II. Title.

HV8144.F43C48 1990   90-40185
363.2'32 – dc20   CIP

South End Press/ 116 Saint Botolph St./ Boston, MA 02115

99 98 97 96 95 94 93 92 91 90   1 2 3 4 5 6 7 8 9

Table of Contents

Dedication

For Fred Hampton and Mark Clark, two brothers who paid COINTELPRO's ultimate penalty during the pre-dawn hours of December 4, 1969.

Acknowldgements

We would like to thank the following individuals without whose various contributions this book would not have been possible: Mike Albert, Maria del Pilar Arguellas, Chip Berlet, Maria Theresa Blanco, Kathy Boudin, Cindy Bowden, Paulette D'Auteuil-Robideau, Dan Debo, Vine Deloria, Jr., Bill Dunne, Bruce Ellison, Roger Finzel, Carmen Gautier, Sue Gegner, Larry Giddings, Merv Glass, Jr., Brian Glick, Lew Gurwitz, Jeff Haas, Candy Hamilton, Stuart Hanlon, Todd Jailer, M. Annette Jaimes, Bill Kunstler, Winona LaDuke, Tim Lange, Ken Lawrence, Larry Leaventhal, Jonathan Lubell, Peter Matthiessen, Russ Means, Nick Meinhart, Maria Merrill Ramirez, Jim Messerschmidt, Glenn Morris, Ahmed Obafemi, Sheila O'Donnell, Mary O'Melveny, Roz Payne, Geronimo Ji Jaga Pratt, Ellen Ray, Bob Robideau, Ricardo Romero, Susan Rosenberg, Lydia Sargent, Bill Schaap, Paul Scribner, Afeni Shakur, Standing Deer, Dan Stern, Jan Susler, Flint Taylor, John Thorne, Jennie Vander Wall, Bill Vornberger and Louis Wolf.

Certain of the documents reproduced herein have previously appeared in Harry Blackstock's *COINTELPRO: The FBI's Secret War on Political Freedom* (Pathfinder Press, 1987), Christy Macy's and Susan Kaplan's *Documents* (Penguin, 1980), Edith Tiger's *In Re Alger Hiss* (Hill and Wang, 1979) and Flint Taylor's and Margaret Vanhouten's *Counterintelligence: A Documentary Look at America's Secret Police* (National Lawyers Guild Task Force on Counterintelligence and the Secret Police, 1978). Portions of the material published herein have been published elsewhere by the authors in other forms. We would therefore like to express our gratitude to *Akwesasne Notes, Covert Action Information Bulletin, The Other Side, Propaganda Review, Rolling Stock* and *Zeta Magazine* for their various assistance and permission to reprint.

In terms of editing, technical assistance and general support we'd like to thank the entire South End Press Collective – Cynthia Peters, Steve Chase and Greg Bates in particular – as well as editor friends such as S.K. Levin and Bob Sipe. The Center for Studies of Ethnicity and Race in America at the University of Colorado/Boulder provided certain material assistance, as did the Educational Development Program at the same institution, and the Fourth World Center for Study of Indigenous Law and Politics at the University of Colorado/Denver. Thanks is also due the Saxifrage Publications Group (Boulder) for use of layout facilities. Finally, we would like to express our gratitude to the National Lawyers Guild Anti-Repression Project for its solidarity and financial support.

The book could never have been completed without the input and guidance of all of the above. Errors, factual or interpretive, however, remain solely the responsibility of the authors.

About the Authors

Ward Churchill (Creek/Cherokee *Métis*) is co-director, with Glenn Morris, of the Colorado Chapter of the American Indian Movement and coordinator of American Indian Studies with the Center for Studies of Ethnicity and Race in America at the University of Colorado/Boulder. He has served as a delegate of the International Indian Treaty Council to the United Nations Working Group on Indigenous Populations and the Inter-American Indian Congress, as well as to the nations of Libya and Cuba. His previous books include *Marxism and Native Americans* (1983), *Culture versus Economism: Essays on Marxism in the Multicultural Arena* (1984), and *Critical Issues in Native North America* (1989). He is also a regular columnist for *Zeta Magazine* and editor of *New Studies on the Left*.

Jim Vander Wall has been an active supporter of the struggles of Native Peoples for sovereignty since 1974 and has written several articles on FBI counter-intelligence operations. He is co-author, with Ward Churchill, of *Agents of Repression: The FBI's Secret Wars on the Black Panther Party and the American Indian Movement* (1988) and an editor of *New Studies on the Left*.

Brian Glick is an activist/attorney who has long been involved in the defense of those – notably Geronimo Ji Jaga Pratt – targeted for neutralization by federal counterintelligence operations. He is coauthor of *The Bust Book* (1969) and *The Jailhouse Lawyer's Manual* (1984), and author of *War at Home: Covert Action Against U.S. Activists and What We Can Do About It* (1989).

Chip Berlet is a long-time researcher on the workings of America's police state. Editor of a periodical, *The Public Eye*, devoted to exposing secret police and intelligence activities, he has also been a frequent contributor to journals like *Counterspy* and *Covert Action Information Bulletin*. He is presently associated with the National Lawyers Guild Anti-Repression Project.

John Trudell (Santee Dakota) was national chairman of the American Indian Movement from 1974-79, when the position was dissolved. On February 12 of the latter year, his entire family – his wife Tina, children Ricarda Star (age five), Sunshine Karma (age three) and Eli Changing Sun (age one), as well as his mother-in-law, Leah Hicks Manning – were murdered on the Duck Valley Paiute Reservation in Utah as part of a government anti-AIM counterintelligence operation. An accomplished poet, Trudell has authored a book of verse, *Living in Reality* (1982), and has recorded several tapes of his poetry with musical accompaniment. These include *Tribal Voice* (with Tribal Voice, 1983), *J.T./J.E.D.* (with Kiowa guitarist Jesse Edwin Davis, 1985), *A.K.A. Graffitti Man* (with the Graffitti Band, 1986), *Heart Jump Bouquet* (with the Graffitti Band, 1987) and *But This Isn't El Salvador* (with the Grafitti Band and Tribal Voice, 1987).

Living in Reality

...Living in Reality
we are targets
of your unwariness
With Warriors for targets
You Create
Your own destruction

This is how we
bring you down
target by target
You wound yourself
Using your greed
WE watch
Your spirit fade

Living in Reality
We can endure

> Your cages
> Your bullets
> Your lies
> Your confusion

We know
You have destroyed
> Your Peace
Living in Reality
You only exist.

> – *John Trudell*
> (Poem Fragment)

Preface

The Face of COINTELPRO

Regardless of the unattractiveness or noisy militancy of some private citizens or organizations, the Constitution does not permit federal interference with their activities except through the criminal justice system, armed with its ancient safeguards. There are no exceptions. No federal agency, the CIA, the IRS, or the FBI, can be at the same time policeman, prosecutor, judge and jury. That is what constitutionally guaranteed due process is all about. It may sometimes be disorderly and unsatisfactory to some, but it is the essence of freedom...I suggest that the philosophy supporting COINTELPRO is the subversive notion that any public official, the President or a policeman, possesses a kind of inherent power to set aside the Constitution whenever he thinks the public interest, or "national security" warrants it. That notion is postulate of tyranny.

– Congressman Don Edwards –
1975

The FBI documents collected in this book offer a unique window into the inner workings of the U.S. political police. They expose the secret, systematic, and sometimes savage use of force and fraud, by all levels of government, to sabotage progressive political activity supposedly protected by the U.S. constitution. They reveal ongoing, country-wide CIA-style covert action – infiltration, psychological warfare, legal harassment, and violence – against a very broad range of domestic dissidents. While prodding us to re-evaluate U.S. democracy and to rethink our understanding of recent U.S. history, these documents can help us to protect our movements from future government attack.

This is the final volume of what amounts to a South End Press trilogy on domestic covert action. Ward Churchill's and Jim Vander Wall's *Agents of Repression*[1] details the FBI's secret war on the Black Panther Party and the American Indian Movement. My *War at Home*[2] shows that such covert operations have become a permanent feature of U.S. politics. It analyzes the specific methods used against progressive activists and opens a discussion of how to respond.

Now Churchill and Vander Wall have reproduced many of the FBI files on which our books are based. Some of these documents illustrate recent FBI campaigns against the American Indian Movement (AIM) and the Committee in Solidarity with the People of El Salvador (CISPES). Others reveal early attacks on Marcus Garvey (1920s) and Alger Hiss (1950s). The bulk are from the counterintelligence programs (COINTELPROs) that the FBI mounted to "disrupt, misdirect, discredit or otherwise neutralize" the civil rights, black liberation, Puerto Rican independence, anti-war and student movements of the 1960s.

x

In this book, we see the actual directives that set in motion those infamous 1960s programs. Here, too, are action proposals that FBI field offices submitted in response to the COINTELPRO directives. FBI Headquarters teletypes back its approval or modifications. Agents report specific operations in which they took part. Supervisors summarize progress in neutralizing a particular target. Policy memoranda adjust Bureau tactics in light of new dangers and opportunities. Most illuminating are the book's facsimiles of some of the weapons the FBI actually deployed in its hidden war at home. From the Bureau's arsenal of psychological warfare, Churchill and Vander Wall show us:

- the letter the FBI secretly sent to Dr. Martin Luther King, Jr., in December 1964, in an attempt to provoke his suicide;

- other forged letters to activists and their supporters, families, employers, landlords, college administrators and church superiors;

- FBI-authored articles and editorials which "cooperative news media" ran as their own;

- cartoon leaflets that the FBI published in the name of certain radical groups in order to ridicule and antagonize others.

Although some of these documents have been published previously, the collections are hard to find and many are out of print. The most thorough and useful to date – the National Lawyers Guild's *Counterintelligence: A Documentary Look at America's Secret Police*,[3] – has been incorporated into *The COINTELPRO Papers*. The NLG Civil Liberties Committee generously donated its limited resources to subsidize publication of this book (and *War at Home*) instead of reprinting its earlier compilation.

The FBI documents reproduced here originated as confidential internal communications. They were for Bureau eyes only. They remained secret until March 1971, when a "Citizen's Committee to Investigate the FBI" removed boxes of files from an FBI resident agency office in Media, Pennsylvania, and released them to the press. Gradually, more files were obtained through the federal Freedom of Information Act (FOIA), which had been temporarily strengthened to help restore public confidence in government in the wake of Watergate and the exposure of official lies about the Vietnam War. A few agents and informers began to disaffect from the FBI and publicly confess their misdeeds. New senate and house intelligence committees held public hearings and published voluminous reports. These, in turn, enabled activists to get more documents through FOIA requests and lawsuits.

The full story of COINTELPRO has not yet been told. The Bureau's files were never seized by congress or the courts. Many have been destroyed. Others remain hidden or were released with such heavy deletion that only "the," "and," "or" and "but" remain (examples are reprinted in Chapter 1 of *The COINTELPRO Papers*, with a critique of the process which generates such absurdities). The most heinous and embarrassing counterintelligence actions were not committed to writing, and ex-operatives are now legally prohibited from disclosing them.

Still, an unprecedented wealth of detailed information has been amassed. That material is summarized in *Agents of Repression, War at Home* and elsewhere. What sets *The COINTELPRO Papers* apart is the number and scope of the FBI documents it reproduces. As the title indicates, these documents are drawn mainly from the FBI's formal counterintelligence programs, in place from 1956-1971. This is not because these were the FBI's only programs of domestic covert action. Rather, it is because they were the only ones to have their records substantially revealed.

COINTELPRO involved a unique experiment. Though covert operations have been employed throughout FBI history, the COINTELPROs were the first to be both broadly targeted and centrally directed. FBI headquarters set policy, assessed progress, charted new directions, demanded increased production, and carefully monitored and controlled day-to-day operations. This arrangement required that national COINTELPRO supervisors and local FBI field offices communicate back and forth, at great length, concerning every operation. They did so quite freely, with little fear of public exposure. This generated a prolific trail of bureaucratic paper. The moment that paper trail began to surface, the FBI discontinued all of its formal domestic counterintelligence programs. It did not, however, cease its covert political activity against U.S. dissidents. The documents show that the Bureau evaluated the COINTELPROs as "successful over the years." It disbanded them only "to afford additional security to our sensitive techniques and operations." Continued reliance on those same techniques and operations was officially authorized, only now on a case-by-case basis, "with tight procedures to insure absolute security."

By discontinuing use of the term "COINTELPRO," the Bureau gave the *appearance* of acceding to public and congressional pressure. In reality, it protected its capacity to continue precisely the same activity under other names. Decentralization of covert operations vastly reduced the volume of required reporting. It dispersed the remaining documentation to individual case files in diverse field offices, and it purged those files of any caption suggesting domestic covert action. The Bureau's "sensitive techniques and operations" have since been further insulated from public scrutiny. Scheduled congressional hearings into the Bureau's mid-1970s campaign against AIM were squelched by means of what turns out to have been yet another FBI covert operation. The FOIA has been drastically narrowed, with thousands of files reclassified "top secret." The Intelligence Identities Protection Act now makes it a federal crime to disclose" any information that identifies an individual as a covert agent."

This careful concealment of post-COINTELPRO domestic counterintelligence action is part of a broader effort to rehabilitate the U.S. political police. Central to that effort has been a sophisticated campaign to refurbish the public image of the FBI. The Bureau's egomaniacal, reactionary, crudely racist and sexist founder, J. Edgar Hoover, died in 1972. After interim directors failed to restore the Bureau's prestige, two federal judges, William Webster and William Sessions, were recruited to clean house and build a "new FBI." The new directors have cultivated a low-visibility managerial style and discreetly avoided public attack on prominent liberals. Anticommunism – the time-honored rationale for political police work – has been augmented by "counter-terrorism" and "the war on drugs," pretexts that better resonate with current popular fears. The old myth of the FBI as crime-busting protector of democratic rights has been revived in modern garb by films like *Mississippi Burning* and the television series, *Mancuso FBI*.

This repackaging seems to have sold the "new FBI" to some of the most prominent critics of earlier COINTELPRO. University professors and congressional committees that helped to expose the domestic covert action of the past now deny its persistence in the present. Because of their credentials, these respectable "objective" sources do more damage than the FBI's blatant right-wing publicists. Left uncontested, their sophistry could disarm a new generation of activists, leaving them vulnerable to government subversion.

The introduction to *The COINTELPRO Papers* refutes one such academic expert, Athan Theoharis, in his preposterous claim that the FBI's war on AIM during the 1970s was not a COINTELPRO-style "program of harassment." Equally treacherous is *The FBI and CISPES*, a 1989 report of the U.S. Senate Committee on Intelligence.[4] This is nothing more than a whitewash of the Bureau's covert and extralegal effort to wipe out domestic opposition to U.S. intervention in Central America.

That FBI campaign was first made public by a central participant, Frank Varelli. The Bureau admits it paid Varelli from 1981 to 1984 to infiltrate CISPES. Varelli has testified that the FBI's stated objective was to "break" CISPES. He recounts a *modus operandi* straight out of the annals COINTELPRO – from break-ins, bogus publications and disruption of public events to planting guns on CISPES members and seducing CISPES leaders in order to get blackmail photos for the FBI.[5]

Alerted by Varelli's disclosures, the Center for Constitutional Rights obtained a small portion of the Bureau's CISPES files and released them to the press. The files show the U.S. government targeting a very broad range of religious, labor and community groups opposed to its Central America policies. They confirm that the FBI's objective was to attack and "neutralize" these groups.[6] Mainstream media coverage of these revelations elicited a flurry of congressional investigations and hearings. Publicly exposed, the FBI tried to scapegoat the whistle blower. Its inhouse investigation found Varelli "unreliable" and held his false reports of CISPES terrorism responsible for the entire FBI operation. The Bureau denied any violation of the constitutional rights of U.S. citizens or involvement in the hundreds of break-ins reported by Central America activists. A grand total of six agents received "formal censure" and three were suspended for 14 days. The FBI moved its CISPES file to the national archives and Director Sessions declared the case closed, a mere "aberration" due to "failure in FBI management."[7]

The Bureau's slander of Varelli gave the congress an easy way out. The single congressional report, *The FBI and CISPES*, endorses the FBI's entire account, without any reservation or qualification. It legitimizes a cover-up of current covert operations by exploiting the past reputation of the Senate Intelligence Committee.

That committee – known initially as the "Church Committee," after its founding chair, Senator Frank Church (D., Idaho) – gained respect in the mid-1970s through detailed public documentation of FBI and CIA abuses. In truth, the committee never did play quite the heroic role claimed for it by liberal historians. Compromised from the outset, it allowed the agencies under investigation to turn over only sanitized versions of selected files and then to edit and censor the committee's reports before publication.[8] It colluded in the FBI's continuing concealment of a decade-long secret war on the Puerto Rican independence movement.

Church and his successor as committee chair, Senator Birch Bayh (D., Indiana), eventually were driven from office. They fell victim to the same combination of right-wing disinformation and Democratic Party passivity that later set up House Speaker Jim Wright.[9] Divested of its liberal populist leadership, the intelligence committee became – like so many other congressional and administrative bodies – an instrument of the very agencies it purports to oversee. It was this latter-day committee which ratified the FBI's coverup of its campaign against Central America activists without hearing from a single critic or victim. Relying exclusively on FBI and Justice Department testimony, the committee crudely reiterates the Bureau's own self-serving findings, often verbatim. It writes off Frank Varelli with the undocumented assertion that his "credibility...was called into doubt at a hearing before the House Judiciary Subcommittee on Civil and Constitutional Rights."[10]

The committee also ignores testimony that the reports submitted in Varelli's name, which provided the FBI's pretext for attacking CISPES, were actually dictated by FBI higher-ups.[11] It makes no reference to Varelli's repeated, detailed sworn statements – corroborated by the Bureau's own files – that the FBI used COIN-TELPRO methods against CISPES in order to achieve COINTELPRO ends. To rationalize its dismissal of the campaign against CISPES as a mere "aberration" from the FBI's "definite pattern of adherence to established safeguards for constitutional rights,"[12] the committee carefully avoids any reference to the sordid history of COINTELPRO. Neither the acronym nor the concept appear even once in its report.

Such a whitewash should not be allowed to obscure the reality of continuing COINTELPRO-type attacks on progressive activists. Ongoing domestic covert action is more than amply documented by *The COINTELPRO Papers*, *Agents of Repression* and *War at Home*. The targets are not limited to the opponents of U.S. intervention in Central America. They include virtually all who fight for peace and social justice in the United States – from AIM, Puerto Rican *independentistas* and the Coalition for a New South, to environmentalists, pacifists, trade unionists, homeless and seniors, feminists, gay and lesbian activists, radical clergy and teachers, publishers of dissident literature, prison reformers, progressive attorneys, civil rights and anti-poverty workers, and on and on. Consider the following examples drawn from 1989 alone:

- national leaders of Earth First! imprisoned on the word of an FBI infiltrator, Mike Tait;[13]

- the coordinator of the National Lawyers Guild's anti-repression task force, active in the defense of Puerto Rican *independentistas*, subpoenaed at the FBI's instigation before a gratuitous, punitive grand jury and faced with jail for refusing to testify against a former client;[14]

- more than 200 African-American elected officials in Alabama, Georgia and North Carolina victimized by FBI smear campaigns, false criminal charges and elaborate "sting" operations.[15]

These can be no more than the tip of the iceberg, given that the great bulk of COINTELPRO-type operations remain secret until long after their damage has been done. By all indications, domestic covert operations have become a permanent feature of U.S. politics. The implications of this are truly alarming: in the name of protecting our fundamental freedoms, the FBI and police systematically subvert them. They routinely take the law into their own hands to punish dissident speech and association without the least semblance of due process of law. Those who manage to organize for social justice in the United States, despite the many obstacles in their path, face country-wide covert campaigns to discredit and disrupt their con-stitutionally protected political activity.

The documents reproduced in this book reveal a U.S. political reality which is the antithesis of democracy. They also suggest an alternative reading of recent U.S. history. Memoirs and commentaries on "The Sixties" have recently become quite popular. COINTELPRO, however, receives little attention in these accounts. It is rarely mentioned, and even then it seems somehow not to affect the rest of the story. Otherwise responsible historians describe a systematic campaign to covertly dis-credit progressive movements without so much as considering the possibility that their own perceptions might be distorted as a result of that campaign.

Take, for instance, Todd Gitlin's often insightful and eloquent account of his experience in the 1960s. A sophisticated participant-observer and early president of Students for a Democratic Society (SDS), Gitlin is well aware of COINTELPRO. Yet, at least one pivotal incident reported matter-of-factly in his book turns out to have been an FBI covert operation. Recalling a 1969 telephone threat which helped split the emerging women's movement from SDS, Gitlin repeats a widely accepted account attributing the call to Cathy Wilkerson, a late-SDS and future Weather Underground militant. Gitlin was shocked to learn, at an SDS reunion in 1988, that neither Wilkerson nor any other SDS woman had made such a call. Who knows how many other incidents represented as historical fact by Gitlin (let alone in the writings of those lacking his integrity) are actually COINTELPRO fiction?[16]

COINTELPRO has been especially effective in distorting the public image of the Black Panther Party (BPP). The BPP was the most prominent African-American po-litical force in the U.S. during the late '60s, with chapters all across the country. Working from a 10 point socialist program for black self-determination, it formed (legal) armed street patrols to deter KKK and police brutality, gave out free food and health care, and fought against hard drugs. The BPP was instrumental in forging a broad-based "rainbow coalition" against U.S. intervention abroad and for community control of the police, schools and other key institutions at home. Its weekly newspaper, *The Black Panther*, brought a radical anti-imperialist perspective on national and international developments to over 100,000 readers.

These achievements have by and large been ignored by white historians, who present instead only the FBI's view of the BPP. Even books about COINTELPRO tend to regurgitate as scholarship the very lies and racist caricatures which the Bureau promoted through COINTELPRO. At best, such studies equate the government's violence with the BPP's, overlooking the fact that the FBI and police harassed, vandalized, beat, framed and murdered Panthers for years before finally provoking the party's retaliation. A prime example is Kenneth O'Reilly's *Racial Matters: The FBI's Secret File on Black America, 1960-1972*. Here we find the BPP identified as a gang of "preening ghetto generals spouting off-the-pig rhetoric and sporting black leathers, Cuban shades, and unkempt Afros." They were "peripheral characters...who never attained mass support." In a portrayal laced with the FBI's racist epithets – "monsters," "cold-blooded killers," "nihilistic terror" – O'Reilly argues that "the Black Panther Party invited the sort of FBI repression that typified Lyndon Johnson's last two years in the White House and Richard Nixon's first four." One such "invitation" consisted, we are told, of a "coloring book depicting Black children challenging white law and order in the ghetto." Only the most careful reader will discover, some 21 pages later, that this "outrageous Panther provocation" was actually a COINTELPRO forgery published by the FBI to discredit the BPP.[17]

Clearly, COINTELPRO and similar operations under other names work to distort academic and popular perceptions of recent U.S. history. They violate our basic democratic rights and undermine our ability to alter government policy and structure. They have done enormous damage to the struggle for peace and social justice. Though formidable and dangerous, such domestic covert action is not insurmountable. It can be overcome through a combination of militant public protest (as in recent "FBI Off Campus" campaigns) and careful internal education and preparation within progressive movements. The greatest gift of *The COINTELPRO Papers* is its potential for helping present and future activists grasp the methodology of this form of repression in order to defeat it. Read these documents with that in mind, and use them well!

Brian Glick
New Rochelle, New York
– March 1990 –

Guide to the Documents

by Chip Berlet and Brian Glick

Introduction

Understanding Deletions in FBI Documents

COINTELPRO – CP, USA

COINTELPRO – SWP

COINTELPRO – Puerto Rican Independence Movement

COINTELPRO Black Liberation Movement

COINTELPRO New Left

COINTELPRO – AIM

Conclusion

Introduction

Gee, but I'd like to be a G-Man
And go Bang! Bang! Bang! Bang!
Just like Dick Tracy, what a "he-man"
And go Bang! Bang! Bang! Bang!
I'd do as I please, act high-handed and regal
'Cause when you're a G-Man there's nothing illegal.

– Harold Rome –
from "The G-Man Song"
1937

Introduction

A Glimpse Into the Files of America's Political Police

The inescapable message of much of the material we have covered is that the FBI jeopardizes the whole system of freedom of expression which is the cornerstone of an open society...At worst it raises the specter of a police state...in essence the FBI conceives of itself as an instrument to prevent radical social change in America...the Bureau's view of its function leads it beyond data collection and into political warfare.

> – Thomas I. Emerson –
> Yale Law Professor
> 1971

A picture, as they say, is worth a thousand words. Actually seeing the visual representation of that which others describe, and from which they draw conclusions, can serve for many people as a sort of ultimate proof of the propositions at issue. The truth of this old adage seems quite pronounced in this instance, which leads us to reproduce secret FBI documents to allow the Bureau to document its own lawlessness.

In *Agents of Repression: The FBI's Secret Wars Against the Black Panther Party and the American Indian Movement* (South End Press, 1988), we endeavored to prove among other things that the Bureau has since its inception acted not as the country's foremost crime-fighting agency – an image it has always actively promoted in collaboration with a vast array of "friendly" media representatives and "scholars" – but as America's political police engaged in all manner of extralegality and illegality as expedients to containing and controlling political diversity within the United States. In essence, we argued that the FBI's *raison d'être* is and always has been the implementation of what the Bureau formally designated from the mid-1950s through the early '70s as "COINTELPROs" (COunterINTELligence PROgrams) designed to "disrupt and destabilize," "cripple," "destroy" or otherwise "neutralize" dissident individuals and political groupings in the United States, a process denounced by congressional investigators as being "a sophisticated vigilante operation."[1] Our case, it seemed to us, was rather plainly made.

Such clarity is, predictably enough, anathema to the Bureau and the more conscious apologists it has cultivated, both of whom wish to deny the realities we have sought to expose. For the FBI, as well as the broader politico-legalistic structure of which it is an integral part, there are matters of policy and outright criminal culpability to be covered up through systematic denial of truth and the extension of

1

certain countervailing mythologies. Many apologists have based their careers and professional reputations on shielding the Bureau from exposure while assisting in the perfection and perpetuation of its preferred myths.

On this score, a review of *Agents of Repression* written for the *Washington Post* by Athan Theoharis, a professor at Marquette University, serves as an instructive example.[2] The techniques employed in this attempt to discredit our theses afford virtual textbook instruction in how the facts of the Bureau's activities and agenda are obscured from the public by properly-anointed "experts" while the officially-approved image of the Bureau is reinforced, or at least maintained, through the mainstream media.[3] Consequently, the *Post* review bears detailed scrutiny.

Of Myths and Documentation

After accurately summarizing the main thrust of our conclusions regarding the nature, scope and duration of the FBI's domestic counterintelligence operations, Theoharis tries to bring about their dismissal out-of-hand. "Do the authors document these alarming charges?" he asks. "The answer is quite simply: They do not." Observe that he does not attempt to challenge the appropriateness of the documentation we offer, arguing that it is insufficient to our purposes or that we have somehow misinterpreted it. Instead, he asserts that we use no documentation at all, a claim intended to lead his readers to the false impression that *Agents* consists of nothing more than a lengthy stream of heavy-handed and unsupported accusations against the FBI.

In order to accomplish this gross distortion, he simply remains silent about the fact that we accompanied our 388 pages of text with 79 pages of notes (all in fine print), some 1,513 entries in all, hundreds of them citing more than a single source, and fully a third referring to specific FBI and/or other government documents. Having ignored the evidentiary record upon which we base our work, he contrives to extend a countering, essentially fictitious "record" of his own. Focusing on our main thesis, that rather than being suspended in anything other than name in 1971 (when the FBI says it was), COINTELPRO was actually continued and even escalated against the American Indian Movement over the next several years, the reviewer sets his stage.[4] The most serious problem with *Agents*, he says, is that "the authors seem indifferent to the uniqueness, and thus significance, of the FBI's COINTELPRO operations. They were unique because Bureau officials launched formal, action-oriented programs whose main purpose was not to collect evidence for prosecution, and in the process created a rather comprehensive written record of their actions."[5] He goes on to claim that:

> In contrast to its activities against the Black Panthers [before 1971], activities authorized and monitored exclusively by the Bureau, the FBI's activities involving AIM were designed to result in judicial prosecution [and] were subject to review by

Justice Department officials...The FBI files released on AIM do not document a program of harassment.

In this passage, Theoharis has carefully implanted another pair of serious pieces of disinformation in his supposedly factual rebuttal. One concerns the extent to which the Bureau has made available documents concerning its anti-AIM campaign, while the other centers upon what is allegedly revealed within this documentation. Both of these contribute directly to furtherance of the myth by which the FBI wishes to be publicly understood. Each element will be considered in turn, because both reveal much about the methods and functions of academic apologists in service to the Bureau propaganda system.

"The AIM Files"

After mentioning "the FBI files released on AIM," Theoharis sums up his point with a snide query: "Can we then read between the lines and conclude that by the 1970s FBI actions were not recorded in writing?" Leaving aside the possibility that by this point in its history agents might well have learned not to record certain things in written form, it is abundantly clear to anyone familiar with the material to which the reviewer refers that neither we *nor he* has had the opportunity to assess what the FBI did or did not commit to paper with regard to its actions against AIM. Still less have we been forced to "read between the lines" of available documents in order to arrive at conclusions contradicted by such evidence. Contrary to Theoharis' smug remark about what his own perusal of these files shows, the fact of the matter is that the vast bulk of them have never been released.

Although the Bureau acknowledges having compiled hundreds of thousands of "investigative" documents during the course of its major anti-AIM activities, only 17,000-odd pages of this material have been declassified and made available to researchers at the "reading room" facility in FBI headquarters, and most of these show extensive deletions. The reviewer is being deliberately misleading when he casually juxtaposes the veritable mountains of paper available through the FBI on its Black Panther COINTELPRO with the paucity of documents made available on AIM – pretending these are equivalent data-bases – and then suggests he had predicated his conclusions upon a comparison of the two sets of files. Nor is he more forthcoming about why such a disparity in the availability of these records exists.

In essence, the FBI was quite literally forced to divulge most of its Panther files by the Senate Select Committee to Study Government Operations during hearings held in 1974 and 1975. Conversely, the Bureau was able to avoid being compelled to do this with regard to its anti-AIM operations, under circumstances which bear recounting.[6] Concerning the Panther documents, the Senate committee itself found its hand forced by a seemingly endless series of revelations about governmental transgressions during the early '70s. There was a "credibility gap" engendered by the federal executive branch having been caught lying too many times, too red-handedly and over too many years in its efforts to dupe the public into supporting the U.S. war in Southeast Asia. This had reached epic proportions when Daniel Ellsberg leaked the "Pentagon Papers," a highly secret government documentary history of official duplicity by which America had become embroiled in Indochina, and caused particularly sensitive excerpts to be published in the *New York Times*.[7] The situation was greatly exacerbated by the so-called Watergate Scandal, which followed immediately, in which it was publicly revealed that virtually the entire Nixon administration had been, as a matter of course, engaging in exactly the same sort of behavior on many other fronts, both at home and abroad. To compound the crisis even further, a citizen's action group raided the FBI's Media, Pennsylvania resident agency, appropriated its files, and exposed the long-secret existence of COINTELPRO in the *Washington Post*.[8] As a result of all of these factors, public confidence in government was at an all-time low, and showed signs of unraveling even further.

In this peculiar and potentially volatile set of circumstances, a government-wide effort was undertaken to convince the citizenry that its institutions were fundamentally sound, albeit in need of "fine-tuning" and a bit of "housecleaning." It was immediately announced that U.S. ground forces would be withdrawn from Vietnam as rapidly as possible. Televised congressional hearings were staged to "get to the bottom of Watergate," a spectacle which soon led to the resignations of a number of Nixon officials, the brief imprisonment of a few of them, and the eventual resignation of the president himself. Another form assumed by this high-level exercise in (re)establishing a national consensus favoring faith-in-government was the conducting of a series of well-publicized and tightly-scripted show-trial-type hearings with regard to the various police and intelligence agencies which had been exposed as complicit in the Vietnam and Watergate "messes."

For its part, the FBI was cast as an agency which had "in the past" (no matter how recent) and "temporarily" (no matter how long the duration) "gotten out of control," thus "aberrantly" but busily trampling upon citizens' civil and constitutional rights in the name of social and political orthodoxy. To add just the right touch of melodrama to the whole affair, the Bureau was made to "confess" to a certain range of its already completed COINTELPRO operations – such as the not-directly-lethal dimensions of its anti-Panther activities – and to provide extensive portions of its internal documentation of these misdeeds. As a finale, Bureau officials were made to appear properly contrite while promising never to engage in such naughty things again. The FBI's *quid pro quo* for cooperating in this charade seems to have been that none of its agents would actually see the inside of a prison as a result of the "excesses" thereby revealed.[9]

The object of all this illusory congressional muscle-flexing was, of course, to instill in the public a perception that congress had finally gotten tough, placing itself in a position to administer "appropriate oversight" of the FBI. It followed that citizens had no further reason to worry over what the Bureau was doing at that very moment, or what it might do in the future. This, in turn, would allow the *status quo* sufficient breathing room to pass laws and executive orders gradually converting the FBI's COINTELPRO-style illegalities into legal, or at least protected, spheres of endeavor.[10] The selling of this bill of goods was apparently deemed so important that congress was willing go to to extreme lengths in achieving success.

Hence, in 1975 the Senate Select Committee concluded that in order to complete its (re)building of the required public impression, it might be necessary to risk going beyond exploration of the Bureau's past counterintelligence practices and explore *ongoing* (*i.e.*: ostensibly post-COINTELPRO) FBI conduct *vis à vis* political activists. Specifically at issue in this connection was what was even then being done to AIM, and hearings were scheduled to begin in July. But this is where the Bureau, which had been reluctantly going along up to that point, drew the line. The hearings never happened. Instead, they were "indefinitely postponed" in late June of 1975, at the direct request of the FBI, and on the basis of what by the Bureau's own admission turned out to have been a major disinformation ploy designed to win it widespread public support.[11]

The FBI's AIM files have thus ended up, not in the public domain as Theoharis would have his readers believe, but amongst the Bureau's most secret archives. While it is true, as the reviewer states, that the relatively few AIM files the FBI has chosen to release "do not document a program of harassment," what he intentionally leaves *un*stated is even more true: the released files in themselves provide a vastly insufficient evidentiary base from which Theoharis or anyone else might conclusively determine whether a *de facto* COINTELPRO was conducted against AIM. And sheer common sense will warn that the Bureau has not so fiercely resisted producing its records in this matter because their content is neutral or serves to absolve it of wrongdoing.[12]

"Judicial Prosecution"

The obvious question at this point is whether the FBI's success in blocking access to AIM files makes it impossible to arrive at *any* legitimate conclusion concerning what the Bureau did to that organization. Are we guilty, as Theoharis claims, of mere reliance upon "guilt by association – *i.e.*, that because the FBI launched a formal program to harass the Black Panthers, it adopted the same practices against AIM"? Hardly. Even disregarding such unofficial sources as eyewitness and victim accounts of various episodes of the Bureau's anti-AIM campaign – many of which we will always insist hold *at least* as much validity and integrity as any FBI teletype, field report or memorandum – there are still a great number of official sources which we could and did use to support the conclusions we reached in *Agents*.

These include several reports of the U.S. Commission on Civil Rights, a pair of reports of the Justice Department's Task Force on Indian Matters, a report of the Senate Committee on the Judiciary (Subcommittee on Internal Security), the findings of the federally-sponsored Minnesota Citizens' Commission to Review the FBI, a report from the General Accounting Office, transcripts of the 97th Congress' first session on FBI authorizations, several legal depositions, Bureau of Prison records, grand jury summaries, voluminous trial transcripts, an array of legal briefs and hearing transcripts, transcriptions of oral arguments on appeal and a number of judicial opinions. These sources, adding up to tens of thousands of pages of documentation, were all cited repeatedly, and most of them quoted, in *Agents*.

Theoharis avoids mentioning this extensive documentary base – consisting of the same sort of material he himself has drawn upon quite heavily in his own books on the FBI – while summarily dismissing our effort as "undocumented." And well he might. The conclusions reached in virtually every item of the *real* record correspond quite neatly with one or more of those drawn in *Agents*. This is to say that the tangible, officially available record of the FBI's anti-AIM campaign leads directly away from the sort of absolution of the Bureau Theoharis seeks to foist on his readers. It was, after all, the Civil Rights Commission – not Churchill and Vander Wall – which determined after extensive on-site investigation that the FBI had been complicit in rigging the 1974 Pine Ridge tribal election against AIM candidates.[13] And it was this same federal agency which officially reported that the Bureau was involved in perpetrating "a reign of terror" against AIM members and supporters on the same reservation, during the same period.[14]

Similarly, it was not the "tendentious" authors of *Agents*, but federal district judge Fred Nichol who noted that he was dismissing charges against AIM defendants because of the methods employed by the FBI and federal prosecutors. "The waters of justice have been polluted," said the judge, by the Bureau he had "revered so long," but which had "stooped so low" in its vendetta against AIM.[15] And again, it was not us but the foreman of a federal jury who, when acquitting other AIM defendants of murder charges the FBI had lodged against them, observed that aspects of the case assembled by the Bureau had been so obviously fabricated that not a member of the jury believed them.[16] We could, as we did in *Agents*, go on in this vein for hundreds of pages. But that book has already been written.

The last two examples are especially important, however, since they disprove Theoharis' argument that, "in contrast to its activities against the Black Panthers...the FBI's activities involving AIM were designed to result in judicial prosecution." The first untruth embedded in this proposition is that the COINTELPRO directed against the Panthers did not use false prosecution as a tactic.[17] The reality is, as is borne out in a Bureau document quoted verbatim in *Agents*, "key black activists" were repeatedly arrested "on any excuse" until "they could no longer make bail." As an illustration of how this worked, we examined in some detail the case of former Panther leader Geronimo Pratt, imprisoned in San Quentin for the past 18 years as a result of FBI actions causing him to be repeatedly prosecuted on bogus charges until he was finally convicted of a murder the Bureau had knew he never committed.[18]

As concerns AIM, the facts – which Theoharis opts to ignore – fit *precisely* the same pattern. After the 1973 siege of Wounded Knee, for instance, the FBI caused 542 separate charges to be filed against those it identified as "key AIM leaders." Russell

Means alone was faced with 37 felony and three misdemeanor charges. Organization members often languished in jail for months as the cumulative bail required to free them outstripped resource capabilities of AIM and supporting groups. Yet, when it came time for the trials, the transparency of the Bureau's evidence was such that hundreds of charges were simply dropped while the remaining defendants were acquitted in droves. The net result of this FBI "prosecution" effort was an absurdly low 15 convictions, all on such petty or contrived "offenses" as "interfering with a federal officer in the performance of his duty." *None* of the 40 charges leveled at Means held up in court.[19] But, while the juridical nature of what the Bureau was doing may be seen as ludicrous at best, this "prosecutorial" element of the anti-AIM campaign self-evidently served to "disrupt," "destabilize" and even "cripple" its target.

At another level, one might reasonably ask what sort of *bona fide* "investigation to facilitate prosecution" is involved in FBI agents bribing an individual, as they did with Louis Moves Camp, to testify as an "eyewitness" to the participation of others in felonious acts allegedly committed at a time when the witness was a thousand miles from the scene?[20] This is just one of the "Bureau activities involving AIM" which came out during the 1974 trial of Russell Means and Dennis Banks, the sort of activity which caused Judge Nichol to dismiss charges and write the opinion quoted earlier. The same query might be entered with regard to other of the FBI's efforts to secure conviction of AIM members. For example, what sort of legitimacy is it that attaches itself to the arrangement in which charges were dropped against Marvin Redshirt, confessed murderer of Los Angeles cab driver George Aird, in exchange for his admittedly perjured testimony against AIM members Paul "Skyhorse" Durant and Richard "Mohawk" Billings, men who were subsequently exonerated from having any part in the crime?[21]

We can easily go on framing such questions: What, exactly, is the difference between the way the FBI subverted the judicial system to "get results" during its COINTELPROs against "black extremists," and its well-documented kidnapping and raw coercion of a mentally unbalanced Indian woman, Myrtle Poor Bear, in order to force her to sign three mutually contradictory – and utterly false – affidavits; the Bureau's choice of the affidavits was, to be sure, duly submitted in court as an expedient to obtaining AIM member Leonard Peltier's extradition from Canada.[22] For that matter, what is the precise distinction between the COINTELPRO usage of phony witnesses such as Julio Butler in order to obtain the murder conviction of Geronimo Pratt on the one hand, and the FBI's later use of Poor Bear in the same capacity to secure a murder conviction against AIM member Richard Marshall on the other?[23] And again, what are we to make of FBI agents who went on the stand and testified to one thing in the murder trial of AIM members Dino Butler and Bob Robideau, only to reverse *completely* their testimony on the same events during the subsequent trial of Leonard Peltier on the same charge?

Obviously, the *documented* nature of the FBI's activities "designed to result in judicial prosecution" of AIM members was identical to those it employed under the rubric of COINTELPRO against the Black Panther Party and other black liberation organizations. For Theoharis to argue that the Bureau's "prosecutorial" tactics against AIM are normal FBI procedure not only tends to dissolve the very distinction between the COINTELPRO and "post-COINTELPRO" eras he seeks to establish, it bespeaks a very interesting view on his part of how the judicial process should be used.

Theoharis does make an important and serious point when he observes that the Panther COINTELPRO was "action-oriented" in ways which went beyond any conceivable definition of the judicial arena. We agree. So much so that, in *Agents*, we broke the tactical methodologies of COINTELPRO out into 10 separate categories, only one of which concerned manipulation of the judicial system, and demonstrated by example how each had been applied to the Panthers and other black liberation groups. This, however, hardly serves to validate either his assertion of a "contrast" between what was done to the Panthers and AIM, or his contention that the latter was not subjected to a comparable "program of harassment." To the contrary, we also demonstrated, on the basis of available documentation, that *each* of the remaining nine non-judicial COINTELPRO methods was utilized during the repression of AIM.

Take, for example, the category of "black propaganda." In the book, we quote verbatim one of the FBI's "Dog Soldier Teletypes," deliberately released to the press in 1976 under the guise of alerting the public to the "fact" that some "2,000 AIM warriors" were on the verge of launching an outlandish wave of terrorism throughout South Dakota. We cite a number of articles in major newspapers across the country in which this disinformation immediately and prominently appeared, as well as statements by local police authorities responding to the "menace." And we quote then-director of the FBI Clarence Kelley, on the witness stand shortly thereafter, admitting that he knew of no factual basis whatsoever to support these wild public allegations on the part of his typically close-mouthed Bureau. Several other instances of FBI activity *vis à vis* AIM in the propaganda area are also chronicled and substantiated with comparable documentation in *Agents*.[24]

Or, take the matter of the COINTELPRO tactic of infiltrating *agents provocateurs* into target organizations (*provocateurs*, as opposed to mere informants, are used to actively and illegally disrupt, entrap and otherwise neutralize their quarry). In *Agents*, we present an undeniable case that this was done to AIM in exactly the same fashion as it was done to the Panthers. The matter concerns the activities of one Douglass Durham, and is abundantly documented through such sources as the earlier-mentioned Skyhorse/Mohawk case (during which FBI undercover employee Durham went on the stand impersonating an "Iowa psychologist" in order to cause bail to be denied the defendants), the *provocateur's* own admission of what he'd done after he was unmasked as an infiltrator in 1975, and his subsequent testimony before the Senate Subcommittee on Internal Security. And so it goes, point by point, down the entire list of elements comprising the Bureau's COINTELPRO repertoire.

All of this disproves Theoharis' assertion that, when it came to AIM, the FBI's methods "were designed [only] to result in [legitimate] judicial prosecution." It also contradicts his accusation that, in concluding otherwise, we were forced to rely upon sheer "guilt by association." And, by rights, it should expose for what it really is the reviewer's allegation that "at no time do [we] substantiate [our] conjecture that an FBI-orchestrated conspiracy to harass AIM." Contrary to the fabricated version of reality presented in the *Post* review, it has been solidly demonstrated that the American Indian Movement was very much the victim of a *de facto* COINTELPRO operation.

Mythology

Merely being on the receiving end of a disingenuous review, while never pleasant, hardly warrants the assembly of an in-depth counter-critique such as we have provided here. At issue here, however, is not just the fact that Theoharis used his mainstream media forum as a vehicle with which to prevent accurate information from reaching the public, but the kinds of inaccuracies he seeks to promulgate as a replacement. It is not so much that he denies the validity of the way in which we used our documentation in *Agents*, for example, as that he denies such documentation exists. The upshot here is that he deliberately portrays the FBI – which in actuality went to extraordinary lengths to block disclosure of its AIM files in the 1970s, and which has clamped the tightest mantle of secrecy around them ever since – as a model of propriety, thoroughly forthcoming and above-board in the handling of these records, with nothing hidden about its anti-AIM campaign. The image projected by Theoharis' reference to a fictional "release" of AIM files is that the Bureau – which in reality has once again taken to treating the Freedom of Information and Privacy Acts as so much toilet paper, generally refusing to release *any* new document unless expressly required to do so by court order – is that of an "open" agency which typically makes its records available to researchers and the public at large. The resultant mis-impression is a building block in the reviewer's reasonably subtle construction of the real "contrast" he wishes to impart concerning what was done to the Black Panther Party and what was done to AIM. The locus of the false distinction Theoharis is after lies not so much within the experiences of the two groups as within the FBI itself.

In "the bad old days" of COINTELPRO, the story goes, the Bureau was proven to have committed criminal acts and used official secrecy to conceal them, but those days ended forever in the wake of the Church Committee investigations. When an FBI agent like Richard W. Held orchestrated a program in 1971 to disrupt and destroy the Los Angeles Black Panther Party, Theoharis agrees that this was a political counterintelligence program because FBI documents released to the Church Committee concerning these activities bore the caption "COINTELPRO." However, when the same agent was involved in the same type of program using exactly the same techniques against AIM on the Pine Ridge Reservation in 1975 or the Puerto

Rican independence movement in San Juan in 1985, Theoharis would have us believe this could not have been a COINTELPRO because the FBI has not released related documents bearing said caption. And, according to him, for us to assert otherwise is by definition simply "guilt by association."[25] The pacifying effect upon readers intended by the spooning up of this stale pabulum is unmistakable. And for the relative few who might remain skeptical in the face of this sort of reassurance, the reviewer offers a slightly different tranquilizer. They are calmly handed the option of sharing "the authors' outrage over some of the Bureau's [post-COINTELPRO] *investigative methods* and the fairness of the American legal system [emphasis added]," as if in the end we had somehow all agreed that it is only investigative rather than counterintelligence techniques which are at issue, and that the actions of the FBI in this quarter conform to some recognizable system of legality. The invitation extended to skeptics is thus no more than a final touch to the review's main purpose, a ruse designed not only to divert the last measure of attention away from what is contained in *Agents*, but to posit in its stead an impression of the reviewer's preferred version of reality.

We have arrived at the core of the myth, perpetuation of which constitutes the real purpose of reviews such as Theoharis'. This is, and has always been, the central myth of the FBI. Regardless of the variations and complexities of the lesser mythologies required to support it at a given moment or given context, it has remained remarkably consistent and ultimately reducible to the simplest terms: "Don't worry, *everything is OK now*." No matter when or in what circumstances the Bureau has been called to account, its official spokespeople and unofficial apologists can be counted upon to queue up and say whatever is necessary to pass along the idea that, while there may have been "problems" or "errors" in the past, these have been corrected. There has never been, in such recountings, any current reason for worry or concern. All has *already* been set right.

This theme prevailed in the 1920s, in the wake of the Palmer Raids. It was maintained in the '30s, after the worst of the Bureau's union busting had been completed. It continued in the '40s, when the true extent of the FBI's surveillance of the citizenry began to be apparent. During the '50s, it held up even as the Bureau's linkages to McCarthyism were exposed. In the '60s, those who would pose uncomfortable questions concerning FBI activities were, like Martin Luther King, dismissed as liars and "paranoids." Even during the 1970s, as the COINTELPRO revelations were ushered forth, the myth was used as the Bureau's major defense. And in the end, as always, it held sway. Meanwhile, through it all, the apparatus of political repression which the myth was created to shield continued, essentially unhindered by real public scrutiny of any sort, to be evolved, perfected and applied.

As we enter the '90s, the FBI's slaughter of "AIM militants" has long since been completed and hidden from view. CISPES (Committee in Solidarity with the People of El Salvador) and some 200 other domestic dissident groups have more recently found themselves monitored, disrupted and occasionally destabilized by Bureau operatives using many of the same COINTELPRO tactics employed against "New

Left" organizations two decades ago.[26] And still Professor Theoharis would have us believe the FBI no longer engages in political counterintelligence programs and when evidence emerges to the contrary, the Bureau (not the victims) should be given every benefit of the doubt.

We readily concur with his assessment that these are "important questions of decided contemporary relevance." Unlike him, however, we will continue to conclude that their importance lies in the fact that, concerning the form and function of the FBI, things have never been "OK." Further, we will continue to assert that things will never *be* OK in this regard until the realities both he and the Bureau seek so desperately to hide are brought fully into the open, until the whole pattern of FBI performance has at last been pieced completely together, called by its right name and placed before the public. Then, perhaps, real corrective action can occur. Unquestionably, the start of any such positive process must rest in destroying the myth Theoharis so clearly presents.

The COINTELPRO Papers

Citation of materials not readily accessible to the general public is not in itself sufficient to decide such issues, and this takes us right back to the proposition that a picture is worth a thousand words. Therefore, in this follow-up volume to *Agents* we will photographically reproduce a substantial selection of the FBI documents which led us to the conclusions expressed in *Agents*. Hence, when we say, for example, that the Bureau was engaged from its earliest moments in precisely the same tactics of political repression which later marked the COINTELPRO era *per se*, we do not intend to leave the matter open to debate or charges of "conjecture." Instead, we will provide the exact facsimile of a document – such as the accompanying 1919 letter written by FBI Director J. Edgar Hoover proposing a strategy which was ultimately used to neutralize black nationalist leader Marcus Garvey – allowing the Bureau itself to create a "word picture" concretizing our case for us.

As concerns the Garvey letter, readers should take careful note of the fact, clearly drawn by Hoover, that it is not written about an individual who is believed to have violated (or is planning to violate) any particular law. To the contrary, the FBI director is recommending – to the very sort of Justice Department officials whose "review" Theoharis would have us believe now safeguards us against such FBI activities – that the federal government devote its vast legal resources to contriving a case, *any* case, against Garvey, to make him *appear* guilty of a crime. In this way, the black dissident's eventual imprisonment could be made to seem a simple "criminal matter" rather than the act of political repression it actually was. The key to understanding what really happened in the Garvey case lies squarely in appreciation of the fact that the decision to bring about his elimination had been made at the highest level of the Bureau long before any hint of criminal conduct could be attached to him.

In the same vein, when we contend that upon approval of Hoover's plan the FBI

```
                        {                    }
                                             ?
    ADDRESS REPLY TO
 "THE ATTORNEY GENERAL"
   AND REFER TO
  INITIALS AND NUMBER           DEPARTMENT OF JUSTICE,
 J·III-3PO                         WASHINGTON, D. C.


                                        October 11, 1919.

              MEMORANDUM FOR MR. RIDGELY.

                  I am transmitting herewith a communication which has come
          to my attention from the Panama Canal, Washington office, rela-
          tive to the activities of MARCUS GARVEY.  Garvey is a West-
          Indian negro and in addition to his activities in endeavoring
          to establish the Black Star Line Steamship Corporation he has
          also been particularly active among the radical elements in
          New York City in agitating the negro movement.  Unfortunately,
          however, he has not as yet violated any federal law whereby
          he could be proceeded against on the grounds of being an un-
          desirable alien, from the point of view of deportation.  It
          occurs to me, however, from the attached clipping that there
          might be some proceeding against him for fraud in connection
          with his Black Star Line propaganda and for this reason I am
          transmitting the communication to you for your appropriate
          attention.

                  The following is a brief statement of Marcus Garvey and
          his activities:
                  Subject a native of the West Indies and one of the most
          prominent negro agitators in New York;
                  He is a founder of the Universal Negro Improvement Asso-
          ciation and African Communities League;
                  He is the promulgator of the Black Star Line and is the
          managing editor of the Negro World;
                  He is an exceptionally fine orator, creating much excitement
          among the negroes through his steamship proposition;
                  In his paper the "Negro World" the Soviet Russian Rule is
          upheld and there is open advocation of Bolshevism.


                              Respectfully,

                              J. E. Hoover
```

1919 letter from J. Edgar Hoover to the Attorney General, proposing to frame Marcus Garvey as a means of "neutralizing" the black nationalist leader's political effectiveness.

used infiltrators against Garvey's non-criminal United Negro Improvement Association (UNIA) in order to cast about for *some* kind of "evidence" through which a plausible case against its leader could be developed, we are prepared to back it up. For instance, we can reproduce the 1921 report to the Bureau from James Wormley Jones, code-named "Confidential Agent 800," a black man paid by the Bureau to work his way into a position of trust within UNIA. It should be noted that even with this highly-placed source of inside information, the FBI was unable to assemble any sort of case against Garvey in its first two attempts, both of which had to be abandoned for lack of even the appearance of substance. In the end, having charged him with everything from income tax evasion to conspiracy, the Bureau managed

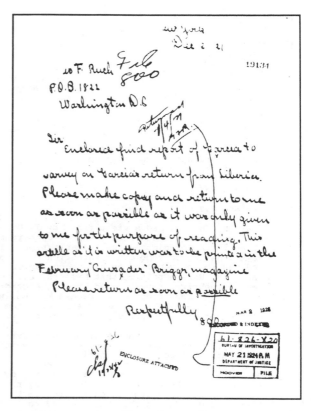

A report from James Wormley Jones, the "confidential agent 800" who infiltrated UNIA and helped finger Marcus Garvey for the FBI.

to obtain a conviction on only a single, relatively minor, count of mail fraud. This was enough, however, to take the black leader out of the political arena and into Atlanta federal prison, from whence he could be deported as an "undesirable alien" in 1927.[27]

Or, if we wish to leap three decades ahead and assert that comparable methods were utilized by the Bureau *vis a vis* "liberal" government officials such as Alger Hiss – an expedient in promoting McCarthyism and the Red Scare of the late 1940s and early '50s – we can produce documents to this effect. For example, consider the accompanying letter from Horace Schmahl to FBI agent Thomas Spencer. Schmahl, it should be noted, was an ostensible private investigator retained by Hiss defense attorneys to ferret out evidence which would exonerate their client from charges he'd used a position in the State Department to spy for the Soviet Union. In actuality, Schmahl was reporting directly to the Bureau on every nuance of the defense strategy, a matter which undoubtedly proved a great boon in the government's securing of a conviction.

The particular missive from Schmahl we reproduce is especially interesting because it shows him alerting the FBI to Hiss' attorneys' plans to argue on appeal that the key piece of evidence introduced by the government at the trial – a

HORACE W. SCHMAHL
TRIAL PREPARATION
TEL. DI4-1795
                                          62 William Street
                                          New York, New York
Robert S. Gilson,Jr.
Edward F. Gamber
              Associates
                                          22 November 1950

Mr. Thomas Spencer, Special Agent
Federal Bureau of Investigation
U. S. Court House
Foley Square
New York, N. Y.

Dear Mr. Spencer:

          Today I had a visit from Mr. J. Howard Haring, the hand-
writing expert who had been retained upon your suggestion by Mr.
McLean in the origional Hiss investigation. I had an occasion to
use Mr. Haring on some other matter, and he told me that Mr. Lockwood had recently called on him, accompanied by an attorney named
Lane. Mr. Haring told me that Messers. Lockwood and Lane had with
them a typewriter expert named Tytel. According to Mr. Haring,
Lockwood and Lane proposed to retain Mr. Haring to assist Mr. Tytel
in some task which he had undertaken upon the request of Messrs.
Lockwood and Lane in anticipation of a new trial in the Hiss case.

          It appears that Tytel had been retained by Mr. Hiss'
attorneys to reconstruct a Woodstock typewriter which would have
the identical type characteristics as the machine on which the
Whittaker Chambers papers had been typed. It seems furthermore
that Tytel is doing this work with the aid of typed records only.
He claims that he has not seen or had any physical contact with
the Woodstock typewriter which figured in the original trial.
Tytel told Mr. Haring that he expected to testify in this anticipated
new trial that he had been able to reproduce a machine having the
same type characteristics as the machine introduced in the course
of the original trial without ever having seen the machine. This
would appear to indicate that Hiss' new counsel might try to argue
that the Whittaker Chambers papers, on the basis of which Hiss was
convicted, were forgeries produced on a machine other than the
Fansler Woodstock typewriter which had been doctored up to match
the type of that machine. Mr. Tytel furthermore told Mr. Haring
that in the course of his efforts to produce a Woodstock typewriter
which would match the type characteristics of the original machine,
he went "form blind". Mr. Haring tells me that "form blindness"
is an occupational ailment that sometimes befalls handwriting or
typewriting experts when they concentrate strenuously on certain
types of print or writing over a period of time. Tyel wanted to

**Letter demonstrating that the private investigator supposedly working on Alger Hiss'
defense effort was actually reporting to the FBI.**

Woodstock typewriter once owned by Hiss, the type irregularities of which supposedly matched those appearing in alleged espionage correspondence – could have
been altered to produce the desired result. Schmahl's warning allowed the Bureau

Page 2 - Mr. Thomas Spencer

retain Haring to complete his work. Haring, who is a good patriotic American, said that he would have none of it and suggested that Messrs. Lockwood, Lane and Tytel leave his office.

Mr. Kenneth Simon left with my secretary an affidavit obviously prepared by Mr. Rosenwald, which he wanted me to sign. I refused to sign this affidavit. However, I am sending you herewith enclosed a copy of it for your files.

I expect to be pretty well tied up for the remainder of this week and therefore, find it difficult to drop-up and see you personally.

I would prefer that you destroy this letter after it has served your purpose. I remain, with my very best personal regards to yourself and Mr. McAndrews.

Faithfully yours,

Horace Schmahl

P.S. Needless to say that any other information that will come into my hands will be promptly submitted to you.

sufficient time to assemble a countering argument that no such modifications to a typewriter were possible. When we say the FBI was aware that its counter-argument – which served to keep the government's "proof of espionage" propaganda campaign alive (and Hiss in prison) was categorically untrue, we can make our case by reproducing the accompanying January 1951 memo from A.H. Belmont to D.M. Ladd in which the author admits the "FBI Laboratory advised that it would be possible for a person who is well versed in typewriter defects and similarities in type design to construct a typewriter so that it would make these defective characteristics appear on paper when the machine was used." Instructively, both documents were among the many thousands of pages in its Hiss files the Bureau kept secret for nearly three decades after the case was closed.[28]

Both of the examples used thus far have seemed to demonstrate that the reality of COINTELPRO greatly predates the formal adoption of the acronym during the mid-1950s. If, on the other hand, we wish to demonstrate that this reality has continued to exist after the FBI so pointedly abandoned the term in 1971, we can readily illustrate our point. We can, for example, simply reproduce the accompanying September 1983 teletype concerning the infiltration of an agent with "extensive UC [undercover] experience" into the Dallas chapter of CISPES. And lest the reader be persuaded the Bureau was doing this because it genuinely believed the organization was engaged (or planning to engage) in *bona fide* criminal activities – "terrorism," according to current FBI director William Sessions – attention should

B FORM NO. 64

~ *Office Memorandum* • UNITED STATES GOVERNMENT

TO   :   Mr. D. M. Ladd   DATE: January 30, 1951

FROM   :   A. H. Belmont

SUBJECT: JAY DAVID WHITTAKER CHAMBERS,
              was; ET AL
              PERJURY
              ESPIONAGE - R

PURPOSE

① His motion for new trial ④ Document examiner
② Horace Schmahl (p.2)
③ Ramos C. Feehan

To advise that the Hiss attorneys have attempted
to construct a Woodstock typewriter which will have the
same typing characteristics as the typing on the Chambers
documents used as evidence in this case; that by pure conjecture
they apparently intend to show that Chambers had constructed
a Woodstock typewriter on which Chambers typed these documents,
and that they, too, can construct a similar typewriter from
the typing characteristics on the Chambers documents; that they
are also endeavoring to prove that the film on which the "pumpkin
papers" were photographed was not manufactured in 1936, but
was manufactured at a later date. The FBI Laboratory advised
that it would be possible for a person who is well versed in
typewriter defects and similarities of type design to construct
a typewriter so that it would make these defective characteristics
appear on paper when the machine was used; that if the Hiss
attorneys have subsequently had a machine "doctored" to produce
the defects appearing in the 64 Chambers documents used by
the Laboratory technician in his testimony in court, and
those only, then they could easily have made a grave error,
inasmuch as every different character that makes its appearance
in the 64 documents would have to be studied carefully and the
type faces "fixed" on the typewriter; that not only would the
defects discovered by the Laboratory have to be identical,
but the reconstructed typewriter would have to have all of
its own characteristic letter defects eliminated and all of
the characteristics appearing on the 64 documents. SAIC
Donegan and USA Saypol have been fully advised of defense
tactics and they contemplate no action until such time as the
defense files a motion for a new trial based on newly-discovered
evidence.

BACKGROUND   EX. - 75   COPIED - 55

-4721.

FEB 8 1951

You will recall that Alger Hiss was convicted mainly
on the Government's presentation in evidence of 64 typewritten
documents produced by Whittaker Chambers, which he claimed were

FLJ:eas;(njs)

Ex.65A

CK

36 FEB 16 1951

**Although federal prosecutors in the case of Alger Hiss contended that it would be
impossible to alter Hiss' typewriter to match incriminating documents, here we find the
FBI acknowledging the reverse was true. Upon advice of the Bureau, the government continued to deny the possibility of alteration during Hiss' appeal.**

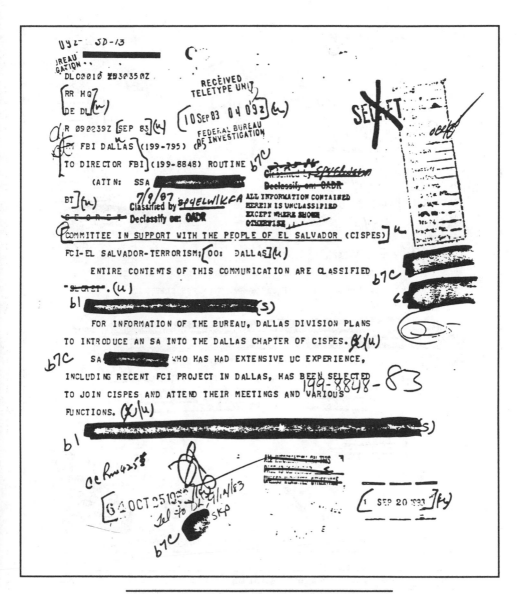

Teletype describing infiltration of CISPES, 1983.

be paid to the next reproduction, a November 1983 teletype originally classified as "secret." It explains rather clearly that the FBI found it "imperative to formulate some plan of attack against CISPES," not because of its suspected involvement in terrorism or any other criminal activity, but because of its association with "individuals [deleted] who defiantly display their contempt for the U.S. government by making speeches and propagandizing their cause." In plain English, CISPES was

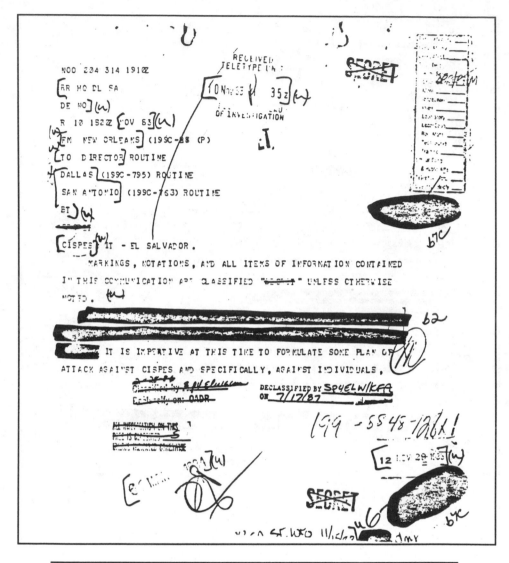

Teletype proposing actions against CISPES because of its "defiance," 1983.

politically objectionable to the Bureau – no more, or less – and was therefore deliberately targeted for repression. COINTELPRO by any other name is still COINTELPRO.[29]

The collection of FBI self-portraits contained herein is far from exhaustive. There are several reasons for this, beginning, of course, with the fact that so many of the Bureau's documents remain secret. Conversely, the material which has been released runs into hundreds of thousands of pages, most portions of which are

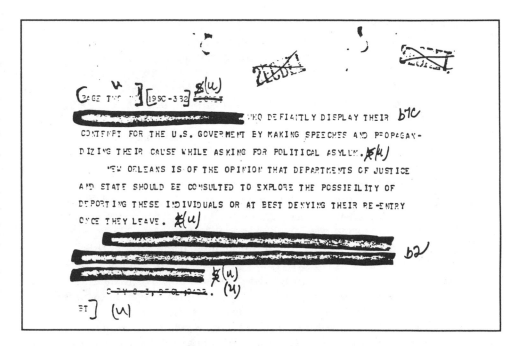

WHO DEFIAITLY DISPLAY THEIR b7c
CONTEMPT FOR THE U.S. GOVERMENT BY MAKING SPEECHES AND PROPAGAN-
DIZING THEIR CAUSE WHILE ASKING FOR POLITICAL ASYLUM. (u)

NEW ORLEANS IS OF THE OPINION THAT DEPARTMENTS OF JUSTICE
AND STATE SHOULD BE CONSULTED TO EXPLORE THE POSSIBILITY OF
DEPORTING THESE INDIVIDUALS OR AT BEST DENYING THEIR RE-ENTRY
ONCE THEY LEAVE. (u)

redundant, a seemingly endless repetition of the same theme. Many thousands of the documents released over the years were provided in such poor quality that they are simply impossible to reproduce with enough clarity to render them legible in book format. Still others were released in such deleted form as to be useless in any way at all (examples of this are provided in Chapter 1). A final problem presents itself in that the Bureau has run so many of these sorts of counterintelligence operations, and over such an extended period, that any attempt to offer a comprehensive, start-to-finish exposition would inevitably prove too bulky for a single volume, or even a dozen volumes.

Some means of not only organizing, but limiting the material we wish to present has therefore been necessary. The method we have employed has been to focus our attention on several of the entities the FBI itself has targeted for its fiercest attacks: the *Puertorriqueño* independence movement, the black liberation movement (particularly the Black Panther Party), and the American Indian Movement. Additionally, we will provide sections illustrating the tactics employed against a new left organization, Students for a Democratic Society (SDS), and two of the old left, the Communist Party, USA (CP,USA) and the Socialist Workers Party (SWP).[30] In each case, given constraints of available space, we will provide background narrative to "ground" our study, to provide readers with insights into the specific historical and topical contexts from which the COINTELPROs emerged and functioned, both socially and politically. In each instance, we also provide an overview of FBI counterintelligence operations *vis à vis* the Bureau's COINTELPRO targets since such things were supposedly stopped in 1971.

Most of the documentary material, with the exception of that concerning AIM, is drawn directly from the period when COINTELPRO reigned in its own name. This is partly because the documents are virtually crystalline in their representation of what the FBI's domestic counterintelligence operations are all about. It is also because, like the official non-Bureau sources we utilized in *Agents*, they provide so obvious a basis from which to understand the meaning underlying the FBI's AIM documents. The lines of continuity between the "pre-COINTELPRO," COIN-TELPRO and "post-COINTELPRO" eras are thereby dramatically underscored, and perhaps as a result an increasing number of activists can learn to recognize them from their own recent experiences. If so, this volume will have amply served its purpose, for in such recognition may be forged the means by which we may surmount the process of official political repression which has served for so long to abort the potential for positive social change in the United States. In our view, participation in the fostering of such change is the sole defensible motivation for anyone to engage in the acts of writing or publishing at the present time.

Clearly, there were many reasons for our doing this book, but it was the outlook expressed immediately above which ultimately proved decisive. In the end, we have assembled *The COINTELPRO Papers*, not simply to vindicate *Agents of Repression*, or to have another bibliographical entry in the *curriculum vita*, but to amplify the conclusions we reached in that volume. Simultaneously, we have sought to create a readily accessible mini-archive which will ultimately say more than we ever could. We have felt a responsibility to do this because the sad fact is that COINTELPRO lives. We must all learn its face. Only in unmasking it can we ever hope to destroy it and move forward to our more constructive goals and objectives.

Ward Churchill & Jim Vander Wall
Boulder, Colorado
– May 1990 –

The COINTELPRO Papers

The FBI, by infiltrating and spying on selected groups in American society, arrogated to itself the role of a thought police. It decided which groups were legitimate, and which were a danger – by FBI standards – to the Republic. It took sides in social and political conflicts...deciding, for example, that those who opposed the war in Vietnam, or whose skin was black, should be targets for FBI attention. Since the FBI acted secretly, it distorted the political process by covertly acting against certain groups and individuals. In short, the FBI filled the classic role of a secret political police.

– David Wise –
The American Police State

Chapter 1

Understanding Deletions in FBI Documents

We must be prepared to surrender a small measure of our liberties in order to preserve the great bulk of them.

- Clarence M. Kelley -
FBI Director
1975

Anyone having opportunity to review documents released by the FBI immediately encounters the fact that in most cases portions of the original document have been deleted. In some instances, this may consist of only a name or a few words; elsewhere, the entire text of documents has been obliterated (see accompanying examples) prior to their having been "made available" to the public. In such cases, Bureau censors will almost always scribble a code or series of codes – (b)(1)(b), for example – in the margins of each page, explaining the statutory basis upon which they decided to withhold particular bits of information. In order to understand not only the codes, but their underlying basis, it is necessary to review the evolution of such "exemptions."

"National Security"

The origins of the FBI's ability to declare its documents (or portions thereof) secret by reason that their release might "compromise the security of the United States" lie in two executive orders handed down during the early 1950s. The first was Harry Truman's EO-10290 (16 FR 9795, Sept. 25, 1951) which extended the military system of national security classification over certain nominally civilian police and intelligence agencies engaged in counter-espionage and counterintelligence operations directed at "agents of foreign powers hostile to the United States." The Truman order provided that the Bureau might withhold, even from courts of law, documents deriving from such pursuits under four classifications: "Security Information – Top Secret," "Security Information – Secret," "Security Information – Confidential," and "Security Information – Restricted."

Two years later, President Dwight D. Eisenhower effected EO-10501 (18 FR 7050, Nov. 10, 1953) which revised the classification system to include only three

The people's right to know. Information "released" by the FBI on the Rosenberg espionage case more than 30 years after the fact. Such extensive deletion in Bureau investigative documents is not at all uncommon. To the contrary, it has become normative under Ronald Reagan's E.O. 12356 if, indeed, documents are released at all.

categories: "Top Secret," "Secret," and "Confidential." The Atomic Energy Act of 1954 (68 *Stat.* 921) then added a fourth classification designated as "Restricted Data." Operating behind the shield of this series of headings, the Bureau also developed a sequence of internal classifications of its own: "Strictly Confidential," "Sensitive," "JUNE," and even "Do Not File." Taken together, this complex of security classifications was sufficient to hide virtually the entirety of the FBI's proliferating political action files for a full decade.

In 1964, congress passed the Freedom of Information Act (FOIA; 80 *Stat.* 250), designed and intended to provide citizen access to government files. However, in passing the act, congress failed to challenge the prerogative of the federal executive to simply declare whole bodies of information secret for reasons of national security. Instead, the act allowed agencies such as the FBI to exempt material they felt was:

(A) Specifically authorized under criteria established by an Executive Order to be kept secret in the interest of national security and (B) are in fact properly classified pursuant to such executive order.

This loophole allowed the Bureau to continue hiding its political files for another decade. With the COINTELPRO revelations of the early '70s demonstrating just what kind of documents the FBI was withholding, however, congress amended the FOIA in 1974 (P.L. 93-502) to provide that Bureau claims to national security exemption would be subject to *in camera* review by federal district courts to determine whether the classification assigned file materials in given cases was actually appropriate. This procedure may seem at first glance to represent a solution to the problem. But, as has been noted elsewhere:

The courts have shown reluctance to exercise their new power. Too often, despite notorious abuses by many agencies of the power to classify documents, courts have accepted at face value an agency's allegation that information has been properly classified, and have refused to examine the documents for themselves.[1]

Part of the problem may have been initially that as of the date the amended FOIA took effect (February 1975), even the lowest ("confidential") national security classification was still defined quite subjectively under Richard M. Nixon's EO-11652 (37 FR 5209, March 8, 1972) as material of which "unauthorized disclosure could reasonably be expected to cause damage to national security."[2] In 1978, President Jimmy Carter signed EO-12065 (43 FR 28950, July 3, 1978), defining the classification somewhat more stringently: "'Confidential' shall be applied to information, the unauthorized disclosure of which reasonably could be expected to cause *identifiable* damage to the national security [emphasis added]." Section 1-101 of this order also stipulated that, "if there is a reasonable doubt which classification ['Top Secret,' 'Secret,' or 'Confidential'] is appropriate, or whether the information should be classified at all, the less restrictive designation should be used, or the information should not be classified." Both points were reiterated in a separate directive to the recently-formed Interagency Classification Review Committee (43 FR 46280, Oct. 2, 1978).

In its amended form, the FOIA makes no allowance at all for restricting information on the basis of "national security," providing instead that classification must pertain to matters genuinely affecting "national defense" and "foreign policy." Carter's executive order and corresponding ICRC directive follow suit, at least to the extent that they define valid national security concerns as being only those matters clearly bearing on "the national defense and foreign policy of the United States." Section 1-601 of the order also specifies that "classification may not be used to conceal violations of the law, inefficiency, an administrative error, to prevent embarrassment to a person, organization, or agency, or to restrict competition."

As a domestic police agency, the FBI has – by definition – relatively little real role to play in either national defense or foreign policy. This is all the more true when the targets of the Bureau's attentions are U.S. citizens rather than "aliens" or "agents of foreign powers" supposedly operating within the country. Yet, anyone examining those documents the Bureau has "released" for public scrutiny will discover myriad instances in which text has been blacked out, with an accompanying "(b)(1)" notation indicating this was done for reasons of national security. The text of entire documents is often deleted on this basis, as was the case with some 95,000 pages pertaining to the Rosenberg case alone. Further, as Ann Mari Buitrago and Leon Andrew Immerman have pointed out:

> The FBI has also been known to "white" out classification markings entirely, so that the reader cannot tell whether the markings had ever been made. This is an unjustifiable practice unless – as is quite unlikely – the markings themselves are exempt under the FOIA.[3]

These deletion practices have been patently illegal sin 1975 when the amended FOIA took effect and were even more so in light of President Carter's instructions in 1978. Hence, although no FBI employees were ever penalized for their blatantly consistent violation of the law in this regard, occasional court victories forced selected batches of documents into the open. In April 1983, however, Ronald Reagan signed EO-12356 (48 FR 6304, April 9, 1983), effectively authorizing the Bureau and other U.S. intelligence agencies to withhold documents as they saw fit.[4] While this does not in itself legalize the FBI's documentary misconduct, it greatly confuses the issue, making it as difficult to force the Bureau to reveal its files as it was in the late 1960s.

Police Records

The FOIA offers another set of loopholes, collectively know as the "(b)(7) exemptions," through which the FBI has routinely passed *en route* to deleting information. The statutory language at issue allows the Bureau to withhold:

> ...investigatory records compiled for law enforcement purposes, but only to the extent that the production of such records would (A) interfere with law enforcement proceedings, (B) deprive a person of a right to a fair trial or impartial adjudication, (C) constitute an unwarranted invasion of privacy, (D) disclose the identity of a confidential source and, in the case of a record compiled by a criminal law enforcement authority in the course of a criminal investigation, or by any agency conducting a lawful national security investigation, confidential information fur-

nished only by the confidential source, (E) disclose investigative techniques and procedures, or (F) endanger the life or physical safety of law enforcement personnel.

Taken together, these provide an umbrella under which the Bureau can hide (and has hidden) many things. A particularly striking example concerns the use of the (b) (7) (a) category: the FBI has consistently sought to employ it, but has argued that FOIA applicants should not even be informed that it was being employed insofar as such notification might alert the subjects of investigations that there was (or had been) an investigation of them, and that the investigation was (or had been) in regard to suspected criminal activities. By the same token, says the Bureau, notifying applicants officially that there was no investigation of their activities might serve to allow them to continue criminal conduct "secure in the knowledge that the FBI is not yet on their trail." Thus, in simplest terms, the Bureau holds that it should be able to use the (b)(7)(a) exemption whenever it wants, but the exemption itself should be considered exempt within the "spirit" of the FOIA. As is usually the case, the FBI has simply proceeded to put its novel interpretation of the law into practice from time to time; hence, one finds occasional passages blacked out by Bureau censors without provision of accompanying code notations in the margins.

While struggling to prevent its reliance upon (b)(7)(a) from becoming a part of the record, the Bureau has, on the other hand, indulged itself spectacularly in the use of (b)(7)(c), ostensibly to "protect the privacy" of third parties mentioned in documents, but who were not themselves subject to the investigation in question. This tends to possess a certain appropriate sense until we note that the censors have often left many, even all, genuine third party names undeleted in the documents released while simultaneously blacking out the names of agents and FBI officials (including, in one document we have on file, the name of director J. Edgar Hoover himself). The latter, of course, are public officials rather than bona fide "third parties," and have never been legally entitled to "privacy" while in performance of their public duties. The Bureau's attempt to "reconcile" the situation has led censors to apply the (b)(7)(c) exemption to all names of third parties and FBI personnel alike in many documents. Bureau abuse of this exemption category was so flagrant that, in a memo dated May 25, 1977, the Justice Department set forth guidelines intended to curtail at least the worst manipulations:

> ...if the FBI has a file on John Doe – our requestor – and information has been deliberately placed in that file which pertains to Richard Roe, that Roe information is presumptively information about Doe as well and should not ordinarily be withheld from him on 7(c) grounds. If it does not pertain to Doe, one may well ask, why is it in the Doe file at all?...the routine excising/denial of all "third-party information" is to cease.

The Bureau didn't comply, of course, any more than it has ever conformed to the legal requirements that it restrict its (b)(7)(d) deletions with regard to "informer confidentiality" to appropriate instances. Despite a June 2, 1977 Justice Department memorandum emphasizing that the FOIA explicitly prohibited such exemptions to conceal unlawful activities on the part of the Bureau, the FBI has continued to conceal the fruits of its "black bag jobs" (burglaries) behind wording indicating they derive from "anonymous sources" and deleting material as if these sources were actually human beings. Similarly, the product of ELSURS (Electronic Surveillance) is typically referred to as coming from "confidential sources," with information carefully deleted in such a way as to make it appear that censors are protecting live informers.

One key to determining the type of activity at issue lies in the use of FBI internal informant identity codes left intact in the documents:

Permanent numbers are assigned to "sensitive" sources of information – for example "CSNY 1020-S*" ("a confidential source, New York") or "CNDI5" ("a confidential National Defense Informant"). Source numbers followed by "S" are "security" sources; by a "C," "criminal;" by an "R," "racial." Asterisked sources are unavailable to testify and are likely to be illegal investigative techniques...Electronic Surveillances and burglaries are often given "S*" numbers...[5]

The FBI has also contended that it is entitled to utilize the (b)(7)(d) exemption with regard to the identity of virtually any informant insofar as individuals performing such a "service" have done so only on the basis of a promise of confidentiality, either expressed or implied. For the most part, this is a categorically false contention. Former FBI agents have pointed out that standard Bureau procedure has always been to instruct informants from the outset that the FBI itself retained the option of calling upon them to testify in open court, an understanding by which promises of anonymity are effectively precluded.[6] The Bureau's convenient "interpretation" of the FOIA in this connection serves to retain its power in determining what (if any) information concerning informers will be released, and facilitates its hiding of illegal intelligence-gathering techniques within the framework of exemptions.

Another dubious use to which the Bureau has put the (b)(7)(d) clause has been to consistently delete the identities of government employees and agencies which have provided information during investigations. This is not only contrary to the intent of the FOIA, but in direct contravention of the guidelines laid down in the FBI's own manual, which states clearly that federal employees cannot be considered confidential sources. Bureau censors also habitually extend this lid of secrecy to cover the identities of state and local agencies and personnel, such as police departments, although they have absolutely no legal authorization to do so.

Finally, as with (b)(1) exemptions, there have always been serious questions about how the Bureau utilizes (b)(7)(d) to withhold information for reasons of "national security." Many of the FBI's more outrageous activities have been "reclassified" under national security headings in order to hide them. Although the (b)(7) cluster of exemptions is legally bound to the 1974 FOIA Amendments Congressional Conference Committee definition that national security considerations exist solely in "military security, national defense or foreign policy," as pertains to (b)(1),

> ...most "national security" investigations [have] had no connection to any national security interest. Investigations other than "criminal" or "applicant" were most often called "*subversive*," not "national security" cases. Such cases were conducted under headings such as "domestic intelligence," "internal security," "subversive matters," "racial intelligence," or "extremist." Such cases involved domestic dissenters almost exclusively, with no connecting strand to national defense or foreign relations. Yet these investigations are now, for concealment under FOIA exemptions, being justified in the name of "national security." The very term "investigation" is an euphemism when, as is often the case, it denotes a program to suppress lawful political action and speech.[7]

As with the primary (b)(1), "national security" escape mechanism, much of this transparently illegal Bureau manipulation of the classification system was shielded by Ronald Reagan EO-12356 in 1983.

Other Loopholes

One might think the preceding provided more than ample latitude for the Bureau to hide most anything it desired. Not in the view of the FBI. For instance, deletions have often been made on the alleged basis that they are authorized through the FOIA (b)(2) provision that reporting agencies might exempt information pertaining exclusively to "internal administrative procedures" such as "personnel's use of parking facilities or regulation of lunch hours, statements of policy as to sick leave and the like."[8] A 1976 Supreme Court ruling added that the "general thrust of the exemption is simply to relieve agencies of the burden of assembling and maintaining for public inspection matters in which the public could not reasonably be expected to have an interest."[9]

Notwithstanding these firm instructions, the Bureau has consistently "construed" (b)(2) to mean that it is free to excise such things as markings referring to file numbers, markings referring to type of investigation, records of document dissemination, case leads, agents' initials and notes synopsizing the contents of given documents. Self-evidently, all of this might well be of legitimate interest to the public. A May 25, 1977 Justice Department memo ostensibly ended the routine deletion of such material, yet the FBI has persisted in blacking out whatever in the sphere it considers "sensitive."[10] An indication of what is meant by this may be readily discerned in the fact that just one of the markings, "JUNE," refers exclusively to unwarranted electronic surveillance and surreptitious entries. Its very appearance would therefore provide *prima facie* evidence of illegal Bureau activity.

The notation (b)(3) seldom appears with reference to FBI deletions; when it does, it usually refers to information associated with secret grand jury proceedings. Although the secrecy surrounding such proceedings is objectionable in a number of ways, it is legally valid for the Bureau to withhold such material. Similarly, the (b)(5) exemption, allowing the withholding of documents originating in other government agencies (such as the military, CIA, or local police departments) is seldom used by FBI censors, although it does appear from time to time. Another occasionally used exemption notation, "(k)(5)," derives not from the FOIA but from the Privacy Act of 1974 (88 *Stat.* 1896). This allows withholding of:

> ...investigative material compiled solely for the purpose of determining suitability, eligibility, or qualifications for Federal civilian employment, military service, Federal contracts, or access to classified information, but only to the extent that the disclosure of such material would reveal the identity of a source who furnished information to the Government under an express premise that the identity would be held in confidence, or, prior to the effective date of this section [Sept. 27, 1975] under an implied promise that the identity of the source would be held in confidence.

Finally, as Buitrago and Immerman note, "One more 'exemption' must be considered: one which, though not mentioned by the FOIA or PA, enables the FBI to keep significant information from requesters. The FBI normally refuses to provide, or inform the requester of, information unilaterally determined to be 'outside the scope of' or 'not pertinent to' a request. Unfortunately, for the requester, information kept back as 'outside the scope' may be highly pertinent to a request. Yet this information will not be released and its existence will be difficult to discover."[11]

Conclusion

Despite the considerable range of means, both legal and illegal, available to the FBI to keep its documents (or portions of documents) secret, far more of this information has become public than the Bureau wanted. This is due only in part to such congressional actions as compelling disclosure of many of the Panther COINTELPRO files, processes which almost automatically propel the documents thus released into the FBI reading room. Large quantities of documents have also been released as the result of privately generated law suits – more than 100,000 pages in the Geronimo Pratt case alone,[12] another 100,000 as a result of litigation concerning the 1969 Hampton-Clark assassinations in Chicago[13] – and individual FOIA requests. Although each page of this material has been technically "declassified" and introduced into the public domain, the Bureau is not required to make any special public notice of the fact, or to make the items accessible through its reading room. To the contrary, many such documents, once "released," are denied to a different requester.

Many thousands of pages of material therefore remain isolated in the hands of individual recipients and – for FBI purposes – almost as secret as when lodged in Bureau archives. While much of this material is redundant, it still bears a certain research utility since FBI censors have proven amazingly erratic in what they delete. Material blacked out when a document is released pursuant to a given FOIA request or court order may well appear (although other information is usually censored) when the same document is provided with regard to a different request or order. In the same fashion, whole documents which are withheld in a given release often appear in the next. Comparison of multiple releases of the same document allow the assembly of a complete, or nearly complete, version. By using this comparison technique whole files can be assembled.

The task confronting those who wish to see as complete as possible a documentary record (and research base) on FBI activities is thus not simply to try to compel the Bureau to reveal more of its documents, although this is plainly an important and necessary enterprise. It is also to assemble as broad as possible a selection of those FBI materials which have already escaped from Bureau control in one place, where they may be properly catalogued, indexed, compared and rendered generally accessible to the public. Indeed, a need has long been recognized, and on at least one occasion seriously attempted, by progressives. The expense and sheer scale of such effort, however, greatly outstrips the resources and capabilities of even the most ambitious individuals and private political or legal organizations.

Still, the need is there. And it stands as mute testimony to the shallowness of established rhetoric on "scholarship," "openness," and "the public's right to know" that no element of government, or any major library or university, has ever undertaken to approach the task in anything resembling a systematic and comprehensive way. Until someone does, it is left to each of us to gather what we can, and to learn whatever is possible from what we gather.

Chapter 2

COINTELPRO – CP, USA

During the ten years that I was on the U.S. Intelligence Board...never once did I hear anybody, including myself, raise the questions: "Is this course of action which we have agreed upon lawful, is it legal, is it moral and ethical?" We never gave any thought to this realm of reasoning, because we were just naturally pragmatists. The one thing we were concerned with was this: will this course of action work, will it get us what we want, will it reach the objective we desire to reach?

> – William C. Sullivan –
> Former FBI Assistant Director
> 1975

The FBI's first formally designated COINTELPRO was directed against the Communist Party, USA (CP or CP,USA).[1] It was initiated by a closely guarded memorandum written by Director J. Edgar Hoover to a select group of officials within the Bureau's counterintelligence and internal security wings on August 28, 1956, bidding them to create extralegal "action programs" aimed at negating the CP's "influence over the masses, ability to create controversy leading to confusion and disunity, penetration of specific channels in American life where public opinion is molded, and espionage and sabotage potential."[2] With the exception of the last two areas mentioned, both of which seem to have been added on an almost *pro forma* basis, the stated objectives of COINTELPRO-CP,USA were all entirely legal modes of activity. The objective was thus plainly to "cripple or destroy" the CP as a *political* rather than "criminal" entity.

The immediate response to Hoover's concealed directive was a second secret memo, this one from Alan Belmont, head of the FBI's Internal Security Section, to L. V. Boardman of the Counterintelligence Division, recommending that these two legally separate units quietly collaborate to "foster factionalism" within the party and "initiate on a broader scale than heretofore attempted, a counterintelligence program against the CP." Belmont concluded that "[t]he Internal Security Section is giving this matter continuous thought and we are remaining alert for situations which could afford additional opportunities for further disruption of the CP, USA."[3]

FBI counterintelligence operations against the CP predate these memos. The party had been targeted for "special attention" from the moment it emerged under the leadership of Louis Fraina and Charles E. Ruthenburg as a left-wing splinter of the Socialist Party of America (SPA) during September 1919.[4] This was a period in

American history when ideologies for positive social change had made tremendous inroads into the country's popular consciousness.

> Talk of a major 'reconstruction' of American society was commonplace, and support for major and fundamental reforms was widespread...In a number of American cities, such as Butte [Montana], Portland [Oregon], Seattle, Toledo and Denver, Soldiers, Sailors and Workers' Councils were formed in conscious imitation of the Russian soviets, while thousands attended meetings in cities such as Denver, San Francisco, Seattle and Washington, D.C. to demand recognition of Bolshevik Russia, the freeing of political prisoners, and withdrawal of American troops from Russia...Even more ominous in the eyes of conservatives was the clearly increasing strength of radicalism within the labor movement.[5]

In response to this massive upsurge of public sentiment to alter the U.S. socio-economic and political *status quo*, on June 12, 1919 Attorney General A. Mitchell Palmer requested that congress appropriate $500,000 to "fight radicalism."[6] On July 19:

> Congress appropriated special funds for the Justice Department for prosecuting radicals, and on August 1 Palmer announced creation of the General Intelligence Division (GID), which had the sole function of collecting information on radical activities. Under the leadership of a twenty-four-year-old graduate of Georgetown University Law School named J. Edgar Hoover, the GID began a program of collecting information on radicals from private, local, state and military authorities, set up index files on hundreds of thousands of alleged radicals, began to heavily infiltrate radical organizations, and became a major agent fostering [a] red scare through its practice of sending out sensationalized charges against radicals to major organs of the media, including charges that strikes and race riots had connections to communist activity. The GID's program of general surveillance of radical activity was entirely without Congressional authorization, since money appropriated could only be used for "detection and prosecution of crimes," but the Justice Department got around this by authorizing the GID to secure evidence which might be of use under legislation "which may hereafter be enacted"...There is some evidence that Hoover...deliberately exploited the radical issue to enhance the power and prestige of the...GID, a tactic [he] would frequently use throughout his career.[7]

Actually, Hoover's prototype of the FBI did far more than "surveille" domestic dissidents. Indeed, it took a lead role in carrying out the so-called Palmer Raids, a draconian sweep of the nation designed to crush all manner of progressive expression in the U.S., from anarchism and radical unionism to socialism and communism. The first of these occurred on November 7, 1919, with GID agents raiding the offices of the Union of Russian Workers (URW) in twelve cities across the country. Although no evidence of criminal activity was ever linked to the URW, more than 650 warrantless arrests were effected; 250 more occurred in Detroit alone on November 8.[8] By December 21, 242 alleged "radical aliens," who had received no token of due process in the matter, were packed aboard the steamship *Buford* and arbitrarily deported to the USSR.[9] As concerns the CP:

The climactic event of the red scare occurred on January 2, 1920, when federal agents under the direction of Hoover and Palmer swooped down on radical hangouts in over thirty cities across the country and arrested somewhere between five and ten thousand persons believed to be alien members of the CP and the [closely related Communist Labor Party] CLP. Those arrested included virtually every local or national leader of the parties, and the raids disrupted the activities of practically every local communist organization in the country...The majority of arrests and break-ins were made without either search or arrest warrants.[10]

In New Jersey, "several 'bombs' were seized which turned out to be iron bowling balls. Throughout the country, only three pistols were seized in raids on what was [claimed] to be dangerous radicals actively plotting a revolution."[11] Nonetheless, the January 2 raids were followed up with "minor sweeping operations in various parts of the country during the next six weeks, with the last major raid in Seattle on January 20."[12]

The massive arrests completely overwhelmed detention facilities in many areas. In Detroit, eight hundred persons were detained for up to six days in a dark, windowless, narrow corridor in the city's federal building; they had access to one toilet and were denied food for twenty-four hours...Many of those arrested were beaten or threatened while in detention; in some cases persons coming to visit or bail out those arrested were themselves arrested on suspicion of being communists. Palmer explained such persons were "practically the same as a person found in an active meeting of the [CP] organization."[13]

Secretary of Labor William B. Wilson, meanwhile, announced on January 19 that mere membership in the CP would be considered sufficient grounds to warrant deportation of alien residents of the U.S., or bring about the denaturalization of those who had become citizens.[14] An unknown number of party members were shipped abroad before U.S. District Judge George Anderson finally put a stop to the practice in June of 1920, sharply rebuking Palmer and Hoover as having fomented virtual mob rule from the right: "A mob is a mob whether made up of government officials acting under instructions from the Department of Justice or of criminals, loafers and the vicious classes."[15]

Although the judge's ruling effectively ended the federal onslaught against progressive organizations, "by the mid-twenties, most liberals and social reformers had been thoroughly intimidated. But the more lasting significance of the red scare...was its devastation of all the organizations that had been built up so laboriously for twenty years which were capable of providing leadership for any sort of radical political or labor movement – the SPA, the IWW [Industrial Workers of the World, an anarcho-syndicalist union], the NPL [Non-Partisan League], the CP and the CLP...[And the] general climate of repression that prevailed throughout the twenties made it extremely difficult for rebuilding to occur."[16] With regard to the CP in particular, both party and FBI sources concur that this meant a drastic decline in membership over a span of barely more than six months; in October 1919, the CP ranks totaled 27,341, while by April of 1920 they had shrunk to 8,223.[17]

Hence, when Hoover was able to recast the GID as the FBI in 1924, he was very much in a position to sanctimoniously disavow any further "political activities" on the part of his Bureau, not because of any legal or moral considerations, but because he could feel he'd already destroyed radicalism as a viable force in American society. Throughout the 1920s and most of the '30s, the director was true to his word, at least insofar as placing a counterintelligence focus upon the CP *per se* was concerned. Rather, the application of such methods became situational, designed to "keep a lid on" party growth by destroying particular projects through which the CP hoped to bolster its shattered credibility. Examples of this include FBI collaboration in the brutal suppression of the party-backed textile workers' strikes in Passaic, New Jersey (1926); New Bedford, Massachusetts (1927); and Gastonia, North Carolina (1928).[18] Similar handling was accorded CP initiatives to support the Unemployed Movement and Bonus Army during the early '30s,[19] while pressure was maintained upon those – such as Eugene Dennis, Jack Barton, Sam Darcy, and Harry Bridges – identified as key party leaders.[20] CP forays into union activities in the '30s were also repressed quite harshly, and with Bureau complicity, as in the Imperial Valley, California agricultural workers' strike (1930) and the Harlan County, Kentucky coal miners' strike (1931-32).[21]

Still, the decade of the Great Depression provided rather fertile ground for CP recruitment, and by the late 1930s party membership was estimated to be as high as 40,000.[22] Hoover therefore appears to have determined that a resumption of counter-intelligence measures against the party would be in order. In this desire, he was aided to some extent by the formation of Representative Martin Dies' House Un-American Activities Committee in May 1938 and, briefly, by a wave of anti-CP sentiment following the signing of the nazi-Soviet "Mutual Non-Aggression Pact" in August of 1939.[23] Beginning at least as early as September 6, 1939, Hoover utilized a directive from President Franklin D. Roosevelt as the "authorizing basis" for illegal action against the party. The relevant portion of Roosevelt's instruction reads as follows:

> The Attorney General has been requested by me to instruct the Federal Bureau of the Department of Justice to take charge of the investigative work in matters relating to espionage, sabotage, and violations of the neutrality regulations...This task must be conducted in a comprehensive and effective manner on a national basis...To this end, I request all police officers, sheriffs, and other law enforcement officers in the United States promptly to turn over to the nearest representative of the [FBI] any information obtained by them relating to espionage, sabotage, *subversive activities*, and violations of the neutrality laws [emphasis added].[24]

Using the term "subversive activities" as a virtual synonym for the holding of any left-leaning ideological outlook, arch-reactionary Hoover began to devote an increasing proportion of the Bureau's energy and resources to "consideration" of organizations such as the CP and Socialist Workers Party (SWP; see next chapter). He encountered no resistance from the Roosevelt administration in such activities, and, as COINTELPRO architect William C. Sullivan would later recall, the methods of "investigation" included such anti-CP counterintelligence measures as "sending out anonymous letters and phone calls...in 1941."[25] Sullivan also recounted how one of his first assignments as an agent, in December 1941, was to bug and monitor party meetings in Milwaukee.[26] But, by late 1942, the situation had changed appreciably. With the U.S. engaged in World War II, and the Soviet Union a crucial ally in the campaign against nazi Germany, Roosevelt sought to "clarify" his earlier position. On January 3, 1943 he issued another statement:

> On September 6, 1939, I issued a directive providing that the [FBI]...should take charge of investigative work in matters relating to espionage, sabotage, and violations of the neutrality regulations, pointing out that the investigations must be carried out in a comprehensive manner, on a national basis and all information sifted and correlated in order to avoid confusion and irresponsibility...I am again calling the attention of all law enforcement officers to the request that they report all such information promptly to the nearest field representative of the [FBI].[27]

Despite the president's careful avoidance of using the words "subversive activities," a matter which can be construed as removing whatever authorization Hoover might previously have enjoyed in terms of placing a Bureau emphasis upon operations targeting "communists and communist sympathizers," the director consistently cited this 1943 directive as "further authorization" for his "war on Bolshevism." The FBI's anti-communist activities were thus continued without disruption. For instance, on February 27, 1946, Intelligence Division head D.M. Ladd suggested in a memo to Hoover that the Bureau undertake a campaign to influence public opinion by leaking "educational material" about the CP through "available channels." The purpose of this, according to Ladd, was hardly investigative or designed to stop criminal activity, either real or perceived. Rather, it was expressly to cause the political undermining of party support accruing from such "liberal elements" as churches and labor unions, and to "demonstrate the basically Russian nature of the Communist Party in this country."[28] Hoover approved, and Ladd turned to conservative columnists such as Walter Winchell as well as outright fascist sympathizers like Father John Cronin to carry the word.[29]

Finally, in 1948, the Bureau's role as a bastion of anti-communism, and as the primary vehicle for covert action against the CP, was concretized and to some extent legitimated. Attorney General Tom Clark formulated a Justice Department policy position, shortly after released as a public statement by President Harry Truman, which relied almost entirely upon J. Edgar Hoover's "interpretation" of Roosevelt's earlier posture:

> On September 6, 1939, and again on January 8, 1943, a Presidential directive was issued providing that the [FBI] should take charge of investigative work relating to espionage, sabotage, *subversive activities,* and *in related matters.*....The [FBI] has fully carried out its responsibilities with respect to the internal security of the United States under these directives...I wish to emphasize at this time that these directives continue in full force and effect...Investigations in matters relating to the internal

security of the United States must be conducted in a comprehensive manner, on a national basis, and by a single central agency. The [FBI] is the agency designated for this purpose. At this time again, I request that all information concerning activities within the United States, its territories or possessions, *believed to be subversive in nature*, be reported promptly to the nearest field representative of the Federal Bureau of Investigation [emphases added].[30]

After a lengthy review and consultation with his National Security Council, Truman issued a revised version of this statement, broadening his authorization of Bureau action against "subversives, and in related matters," on July 24, 1950.[31] Meanwhile, "During HUAC hearings in 1949-50, the FBI resumed its open collaboration with the now-Democratically-controlled committee. In fact, the major purpose of HUAC hearings during these years seemed to be that of 'publicizing information in FBI files.'"[32] As the matter has been put elsewhere:

[The FBI's] efforts to contain radicalism by [such techniques as] leaking derogatory information about prominent radicals and organizations did not constitute the sole political activities of FBI officials. They also sought to reduce the ability of radical organizations to function effectively or recruit new members. For a time, with the intensification of Cold War fears and the rise of McCarthyite politics, these informal efforts bore fruit. In 1948, for example, twelve Communist party leaders were indicted under the Smith Act of 1940 [18 U.S.C.A. § 2385]. Then, under provisions of the McCarran Internal Security Act of 1950 [66 *Stat.* 163] and the Communist Control Act of 1954 [68 *Stat.* 1146], Communist, Communist-front, and Communist-action organizations were required to register as foreign agents with the Subversive Activities Control Board and to label their publications as Communist propaganda. Beginning in 1947 and extending throughout the 1950s, moreover, through highly publicized hearings congressional committees (notably the House Committee on Un-American Activities and the Senate Subcommittee on Internal Security) relied directly or indirectly on FBI investigative reports to expose Communist influence in the federal government, in the entertainment industry, in labor unions, and in public schools and universities. Last, FBI investigative reports were employed during the conduct of federal loyalty/security programs to raise doubts about the loyalty of, and deny employment to certain ["subversive"] individuals."[33]

As a result of such harassment, J. Edgar Hoover was able to announce that the anti-communist crusade in which his Bureau was playing such a leading role had been able to bring about a reduction in overall CP membership to approximately 12,000.[34] Apparently realizing that his boast might be construed as an admission that there was "no longer a need" for the Bureau's services in "combatting subversion," he quickly offered a warning that although the number of party members might no longer be large, the public should not allow the information to be used "by the ignorant and apologists and appeasers of communism in our country as minimizing the danger of these subversives in our midst."[35]

The 1953 change from Truman's "liberal" Democratic administration to that of conservative Republican Dwight D. Eisenhower entailed no discernable alteration in the government's view of the FBI's self-defined mission of "fighting communism." To the contrary, on December 15, 1953, Eisenhower issued a statement in this regard which amounted to little more than a paraphrase of that offered by Truman in 1950.[36] Under Eisenhower, the bulk of FBI anti-CP activity was carried out under the heading COMINFIL (for **Communist Infiltration**). Within this program, the Bureau supposedly investigated party attempts to "influence" blacks, young people, women, veterans, religion, education, industry and other targets. But, as the Senate Intelligence Committee reported in 1976, although the COMINFIL investigations were supposed to focus only on the CP [in its alleged role as an "agency of a foreign power"] attempts to infiltrate various groups, "in practice the target often became the domestic groups themselves" and the COMINFIL investigations "reached into domestic groups in virtually every area of American political life."[37] There is no evidence that anyone in the Eisenhower administration ever expressed concern over the situation.

Cumulatively, all of these things laid a reasonably solid *post hoc* policy foundation under the Bureau's anti-CP counterintelligence "efforts [which dated from] the early 1940s,"[38] a flow of activity which congealed into COINTELPRO-CP,USA by the mid-'50s. That the new program was devoted *entirely* to extralegal (or clearly illegal) rather than prosecutorial initiatives was both because what the FBI had typically found objectionable about the Party was its politics rather than any defined (or definable) criminal behavior,[39] and even when this was not the case:

> High-level FBI officials had always been deeply concerned about prosecuting activities. These concerns increased after 1947 as FBI officials became troubled by the effect of prosecution on the FBI's intelligence-gathering capabilities. For example, over one hundred FBI informants had had to be exposed during the various Smith Act trials and Subversive Activities Control Board proceedings. Then, in a series of important rulings in 1956 and 1957, the U.S. Supreme Court imposed major restrictions on uses of FBI reports, challenged the premise that individual liberties must be sacrificed to safeguard the national security, and thereby threatened to close what for the FBI had been an effective means of propagandizing anti-radical fears.[40]

In any event, Hoover provided a briefing report on the progress of COINTELPRO-CP,USA on May 8, 1958. Although much has subsequently been made of the notion that the Bureau's COINTELPROs were conducted on an entirely autonomous basis, and without the knowledge of higher-ups, Hoover's missive to Attorney General William Rogers and Special Assistant to the President Robert Cutler spelled out quite plainly that for nearly two years the FBI had been engaged in an extensive program "designed to promote disruption within the ranks of the Communist Party." Specifically mentioned were tactics of using infiltrators to spark "acrimonious debates" and "increase factionalism" within the CP, and a campaign of anonymous mailings to generate "disillusionment [with] and defection" from the party.[41] This was followed, six months later, on November 8, by Hoover's provision of a personal briefing to Eisenhower's full cabinet concerning his anti-CP opera-

Office Memorandum · UNITED STATES GOVERNMENT

TO - Mr. L. V. Boardman   DATE: August 28, 1956

FROM : Mr. A. H. Belmont

SUBJECT: CP, USA - COUNTERINTELLIGENCE PROGRAM
         INTERNAL SECURITY - C

During its investigation of the Communist Party, USA, the Bureau has sought to capitalize on incidents involving the Party and its leaders in order to foster factionalism, bring the Communist Party (CP) and its leaders into disrepute before the American public and cause confusion and dissatisfaction among rank-and-file members of the CP.

Generally, the above action has constituted harrassment rather than disruption, since, for the most part, the Bureau has set up particular incidents, and the attack has been from the outside. At the present time, however, there is existing within the CP a situation resulting from the developments at the 20th Congress of the CP of the Soviet Union and the Government's attack on the Party principally through prosecutions under the Smith Act of 1940 and the Internal Security Act of 1950 which is made to order for an all-out disruptive attack against the CP from within. In other words, the Bureau is in a position to initiate, on a broader scale than heretofore attempted, a counterintelligence program against the CP, not by harrassment from the outside, which might only serve to bring the various factions together, but by feeding and fostering from within the internal fight currently raging.

We have been considering possible courses to implement such a program and, at the present time, we are actively working on the following four:

1) The Socialist Workers Party (SWP) is making an all-out effort to win over CP members who have become disillusioned with Stalinist communism. SWP members are distributing copies of "The Militant" (SWP publication) at CP rallies and meetings and are contacting individual CP members in an attempt to sell

Enclosures

Kickoff: The document which initiated COINTELPRO – CP, USA.

---

tions. Although the director's exposition could hardly be described as exhaustive, he utilized a classified ("Top Secret") 36-page booklet which described COINTELPRO-CP,USA as follows:

To counteract a resurgence of Communist Party influence in the United States, we have a...program designed to intensify confusion and dissatisfaction among its members. During the past few years, the program has been most effective. Selective informants were briefed and trained to raise controversial issues within the Party. In the process, they may be able to advance themselves to high positions. The Internal Revenue Service was furnished the names and addresses of Party functionaries...Based on this information, investigations have been instituted in 262 possible income tax evasion cases. Anticommunist literature and simulated Party documents were mailed anonymously to carefully chosen members.[42]

As Robert Justin Goldstein has observed, "Although the precise results of FBI efforts cannot be determined, between 1957 and 1959, what was left of the CP was virtually destroyed by factional infighting. Even as the CP collapsed into a tiny sect of a few thousand members, FBI COINTELPRO activities increased and expanded."[43] When the political winds blew liberal Democrats back into the executive, replacing Eisenhower's Republicans in 1961, the COINTELPRO *status quo* was maintained. On January 10, 1961 Hoover apprized the incoming Kennedy administration of the anti-CP COINTELPRO by sending identical letters to Secretary of State (designate) Dean Rusk and Attorney General (designate) Robert Kennedy. These read in part that some of the Bureau's "more effective" anti-communist counterintelligence operations included:

> ...penetration of the Party at all levels with security informants; use of various techniques to keep the Party off-balance and disillusion individual communists concerning communist ideology; investigation of every known member of the CPUSA in order to determine whether he should be detained in the event of a national emergency...As an adjunct to our regular investigative operations, we carry on a carefully planned program of counterattack against the CPUSA...In certain instances, we have been successful in preventing communists from seizing control of legitimate organizations and have discredited others.[44]

Neither Rusk nor Robert Kennedy – nor John F. Kennedy, for that matter – appear to have asked any questions on this matter, or suggested that perhaps the Bureau was exceeding its investigative mandate in launching intentionally disruptive direct action operations against a domestic political formation. The same may be said for President Lyndon B. Johnson. Under his administration, subsequently admitted COINTELPRO operations numbered 230 in 1964, 220 in 1965, 240 in 1966, 180 in 1967, and 123 in 1968.[45] As concerns the CP:

> COINTELPRO activities against the CP continued, with such tactics as informing the news media that the son of a CP couple had been arrested for drugs and that the wife of a CP leader had purchased a new car as an example of the "prosperity" of the CP leadership. In 1964, the FBI planted a document in the car of a leading New York CP official that made him appear an informer; subsequently the official (who had been convicted under the Smith Act and ordered to register as a communist by the [Subversive Activities Control Board]) was expelled from the party. A 1965 FBI memo reporting the expulsion stated that the affair "crippled the activities of the New York State communist organization and the turmoil within the party contin-

UNITED STATES GOVERNMENT

Memorandum

1 – Mr. DeLoach
1 – Mr. W.C. Sullivan
1 – Mr. Baumgardner

TO : Mr. W. C. Sullivan

DATE: October 4, 1966

FROM : Mr. F. J. Baumgardner

1 –

SUBJECT: HOODWINK
(INTERNAL SECURITY)

PURPOSE:

The purpose of this memorandum is to recommend a long-range counterintelligence program designed to provoke a dispute between the Communist Party, USA, and La Cosa Nostra under the code name of Hoodwink.

OBJECTIVES:

A dispute between the Communist Party, USA, and La Cosa Nostra would cause disruption of both groups by having each expend their energies, time, and money attacking the other. This would help neutralize the activities of both groups which are detrimental to this country.

BACKGROUND:

La Cosa Nostra has no sympathy for the communists. The Communist Party, USA, and La Cosa Nostra come in contact with each other in the labor field where hoodlums operate businesses under "sweatshop" conditions. By making it appear that the Party is attacking hoodlum labor practices, over a period of time we could provoke a bitter dispute between the two organizations.

The New York Office has recommended a specific technique to initiate this program. This technique consists of anonymously forwarding one leaflet to a local La Cosa Nostra leader attacking the labor practices of one of his enterprises. The leaflet would ostensibly be published by a local Party unit. A note with the leaflet would give the impression that it has received wide circulation.

REC 10

Enclosure Sent 10-6-66 17-MCT-41   100 – 14652?

1 – Special Investigative (Route through for review)

TJD:jes
(DELETED COPY SENT on H... policy   CONTINUED – OVER   18 OCT 19 1966
BY LETTER 12-4-75

Memorandum initiating Operation Hoodwink.

ues to this date." The FBI created a fictional organization in 1965 entitled the Committee for Expansion of Socialist Thought in America, which purported to attack the CP from the "Marxist right." As a result of other COINTELPRO activity, an FBI internal memo stated in 1965, "many meeting places formerly used on a regular basis by the Communists have been barred from their use"...Frequently actions which came under the CP COINTELPRO label were directed at non-CP groups and individuals. Thus, the FBI targeted the entire Unitarian Society of Cleveland in 1964 because the minister and some members circulated a petition

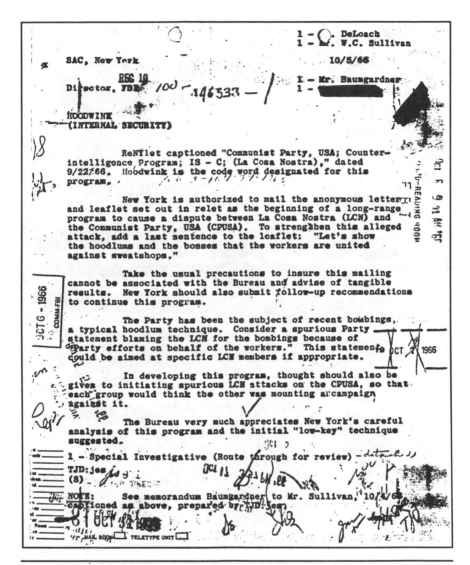

Memorandum authorizing Operation Hoodwink. Senior FBI officials could not have helped but be aware that the proposed plan could easily result in the murder of CP leaders and organizers. This became a standard COINTELPRO tactic.

calling for the abolition of HUAC and because the church gave office space to a group the FBI did not like. In 1965, the FBI tried to block a City Council campaign of a lawyer who had defended Smith Act defendants. In 1966, the FBI tried to get the Texas State Alcohol Beverage Control Commission to raid a Democratic Party fundraising affair because two Democratic candidates who would be present had participated in anti-war and anti-HUAC activities.[46]

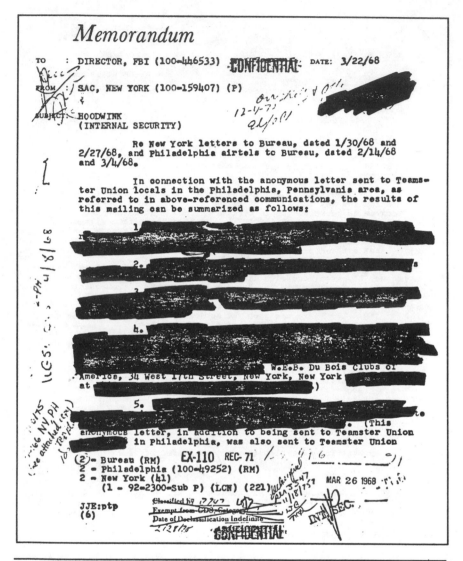

Memorandum

TO   : DIRECTOR, FBI (100-446533)   CONFIDENTIAL   DATE: 3/22/68

FROM : SAC, NEW YORK (100-159407) (P)

SUBJECT: HOODWINK
         (INTERNAL SECURITY)

        Re New York letters to Bureau, dated 1/30/68 and
2/27/68, and Philadelphia airtels to Bureau, dated 2/14/68
and 3/4/68.

        In connection with the anonymous letter sent to Teams-
ter Union locals in the Philadelphia, Pennsylvania area, as
referred to in above-referenced communications, the results of
this mailing can be summarized as follows:

        1.

        2.

        3.

        4.
                        W.E.B. Du Bois Clubs of
America, 34 West 17th Street, New York, New York
at   )

        5.
                            . (This
anonymous letter, in addition to being sent to Teamster Union
            in Philadelphia, was also sent to Teamster Union

(2)- Bureau (RM)   EX-110 REC-71
2 - Philadelphia (100-49252) (RM)
2 - New York (41)
   (1 - 92-2300-Sub P) (LCN) (221)   MAR 26 1968

JJE:ptp   Classified by
(6)   Exempt from CDS, Category
                    Date of Declassification Indefinite
                                CONFIDENTIAL

**Operation Hoodwink continues. As can be seen in this document the FBI was not
content with attempting to use only "La Cosa Nostra" to do its dirty work against
the CP. From the Bureau perspective, reactionary unions would do just as well.
(Memo continues on pages 45 and 46.)**

Hence, having received what amounted to concurrence from at least four suc-
cessive presidents that illegal operations against the CP were "justified," and would
therefore be condoned and hushed up, Hoover escalated the level of tactics employed within COINTELPRO-CP,USA to include attempts to orchestrate the assas-

NY 100-159407

~~█████████~~ in Philadelphia.)

Inasmuch as ~~██████████████████████~~

York Office (NYO) proposes that another anonymous letter be sent to the same above-mentioned Philadelphia Teamster Union Locals.

The NYO requests Bureau permission to prepare the following anonymous letter, Xerox copies of which would be mailed to the same Teamster Union locals in the Philadelphia, Pennsylvania area which were sent the first anonymous letter:

"March 22, 1968

"Dear Union Boss:

"I'm the loyal union man who wrote you around the end of January and I've got more news for you.

"You'll remember that I told you then that I heard from my Commie brother-in-law that the leaders of his party had been in Moscow and among the instructions they came back with was to try to get rid of the hoodlums in truck and dock unions in this country.

"Well, I was talking with my brother-in-law a few nights ago and he asked me how things were going in my Teamster local and I said O.K. He told me he knew that there were a lot of gangsters in my union but he said things would be changing for the best shortly. He told me that in February some of the leaders of his party were in Hungary meeting party people from other countries and it came up again about how his party is going to clean up the gangster controlled unions in the United States. I told him he was all wet but I didn't use those words.

"I'm afraid these Commies mean business so watch out.

"Thanks to the free use of a copy machine I can get the word around about this.

- 2 -

~~CONFIDENTIAL~~

sination of "key communist leaders." By 1964, this took the form, as is revealed by the accompanying October 4, 1966 memo from counterintelligence specialist Fred J. Baumgardner to Bureau Assistant Director William C. Sullivan, of "Operation Hoodwink." The plan was to provoke a "dispute" between organized crime and the CP and, as the means by which "La Cosa Nostra" tended to resolve conflicts was rather well known (even to FBI officials), the desired outcome of the scheme is not mysterious. As is readily apparent in the following memo, from Hoover and dated October 10, 1966 the concept was quickly approved and implemented. Finally, as is demonstrated by the third document in this series, from the SAC New York to

NY 100-159407   ~~CONFIDENTIAL~~

"Don't let the Commies take over."

"A Patriotic American and Union Man"

With respect to the above letter, it is a fact that three leaders of the Communist Party, USA (CP,USA) were in Budapest, Hungary in February and March, 1968 to attend an International Consultative Meeting of Communist and Workers Parties, and accounts of their scheduled attendance appeared in newspaper articles. Two of these three leaders have since returned to the United States. However, the information in the letter that in Hungary "it came up again about how his party is going to clean up the gangster controlled unions in the United States" has no basis in fact. A few typing errors would also be inserted into this letter.

Should the Bureau approve of this letter for anonymous mailing, it will be typed on commercial stationery, updated, and Xerox copies of this letter would be made on commercial stationery, and it will be mailed from New York City to the same Teamster Union locals in Philadelphia to which the first anonymous letter was sent. The original of this letter would not be sent and it would be retained in instant file.

The NYO is again hopeful that the above letter, though it contains some information without basis in fact, will reach criminal elements in the Teamsters Union and it might serve to start a dispute between these criminal elements and the CP,USA.

- 3 -

~~CONFIDENTIAL~~

Hoover, dated January 22, 1968, Operation Hoodwink was not only continued over a sustained period, but broadened to include a range of entities outside organized crime as well. Although, unlike COINTELPROs directed against other organizations (see Chapters 4, 5 and 7), there is no evidence that any CP member was actually killed as a result of Operation Hoodwink, this is obviously not for lack of the FBI's having tried to make things turn out otherwise.

Perhaps ironically, it was Hoover's personal obsession with the CP – undoubtedly developed over more than four decades of trying unsuccessfully to destroy it while constructing his personal anti-communist empire – which led him to insist on

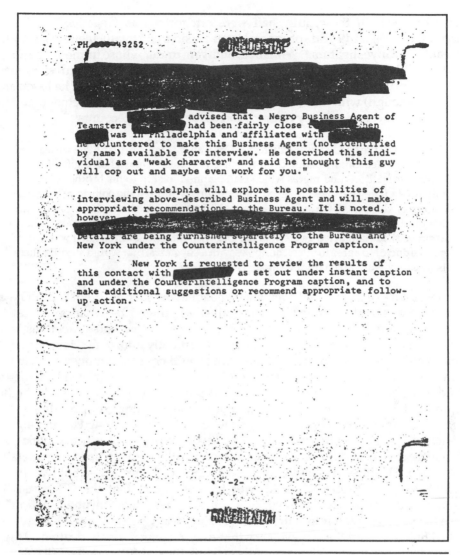

PH 9252

advised that a Negro Business Agent of
Teamsters   had been fairly close t   hen
         was in Philadelphia and affiliated with
he volunteered to make this Business Agent (not identified
by name) available for interview. He described this individual as a "weak character" and said he thought "this guy
will cop out and maybe even work for you."

Philadelphia will explore the possibilities of
interviewing above-described Business Agent and will make
appropriate recommendations to the Bureau. It is noted,
however

Details are being furnished separately to the Bureau and
New York under the Counterintelligence Program caption.

New York is requested to review the results of
this contact with   as set out under instant caption
and under the Counterintelligence Program caption, and to
make additional suggestions or recommend appropriate follow-
up action.

-2-

The cultivation of informers, usually of "weak character," was a staple of COIN-TELPRO – CP,USA and similar FBI undertakings.

going ahead with repression of CP,USA even after it had accomplished its objectives, and to thereby foster a bitter factionalism not only within the target organization, but within the FBI itself. By the second half of the 1960s, the CP had become so debilitated by the combination of unremitting counterintelligence operations aimed at it (in 1975, the Justice Department admitted the FBI had engaged in 1,388 separate COINTELPRO actions against the CP between 1956 and 1971) and its own ideological contradictions that its membership had shrunk from more than 80,000 in 1946 to less than 2,800. Of these, fully half were categorized as "inactive," while the remainder averaged 49 years of age and were considered "totally ineffectual" by the Bureau's own investigators.[47] William C. Sullivan, under whose immediate authority the COINTELPROs fell, therefore sought to reallocate his resources to focus upon "the mainstream of revolutionary action" in the U.S., a trend he associated (correctly enough) with the Black and *Puertorriqueño* liberation movements and the new left.[48] Hoover adamantly refused, and so, as Sullivan recounts:

> Even though the CPUSA was finished we kept after them. Early in 1969 we learned that the Soviet Union planned on sending [CP head Gus] Hall a gift of some expensive stallions and mares which Hall planned to ship to his brother's farm in Minnesota. They expected to breed thoroughbreds and sell the colts to help fill the coffers of the party. On learning about the impending gift to Hall, one of the imaginative men in my division came up with an idea [which Hoover quickly approved]. He contacted a veterinarian, and without telling him what it was about, got the doctor to agree to inject the horses with a substance that would sterilize them before they were taken off the ship in New York.[49]

It was not a disagreement over whether endeavors such as COINTELPRO were warranted or should be pursued, but against whom and by what prioritization. Sullivan had come to view such anti-CP activities as "the horse caper" as being largely childish, nonsensical or misdirected, eventually informing Hoover that, "if there is no longer a Communist problem we should not spend money on it. In fact, I have for some years been taking men off Communist work in the field and here at Headquarters and putting them on some important work."[50] Meanwhile, he had become actively involved in a Nixon administration planning group headed by Tom Huston and intended to bring about greater coordination among U.S. intelligence agencies, "upgrade the effectiveness" of domestic counterintelligence activities, and ultimately to depose "dinosaurs" such as Hoover (this is taken up in more detail in Chapter 6). The director sensed what was going on. Hence, when Sullivan finally went public on October 12, 1970 with his contention that the CP posed "no significant threat to national security,"[51] Hoover used this "insubordination" to force the younger man into retirement.[52] A significant portion of the Bureau supported Sullivan, and there is evidence that only Hoover's timely death on May 2, 1972 ended a process which was rapidly eroding the carefully crafted FBI cohesion the director had built up over the preceding half-century.

Chapter 3

COINTELPRO – SWP

As long as [anti-communism] remains national policy, an...important requirement is an aggressive covert psychological, political and paramilitary organization more effective, more unique, and if necessary, more ruthless than that employed by the enemy. No one should be permitted to stand in the way of the prompt, efficient, and secure establishment of this mission.

– The Doolittle Committee Report –
1954

As with the CP, "modern" FBI counterintelligence against the Socialist Workers Party (SWP, founded in 1938), began at least as early as the beginning of the 1940s. A result was that one of the two Smith Act prosecutions brought by the government on the basis of Bureau-assembled evidence during World War II was against this party.[1] As Howard Zinn frames the matter, "Only one organized socialist group opposed the war unequivocally. This was the Socialist Workers Party. The Espionage Act of 1917 [C 30 Title 1, 40 *Stat.* 217, *et seq.*], still on the books, applied to wartime statements. But, in 1940, with the United States not yet at war, Congress passed the Smith Act. This took Espionage Act prohibitions against talk or writing that would lead to refusal of duty in the armed forces and applied them to peacetime. The Smith Act also made it a crime to advocate the overthrow of the government by force or violence, or join any group that advocated this, or publish anything with such ideas. In Minneapolis in 1943, eighteen members of the [SWP] were convicted of belonging to a party whose ideas, expressed in its Declaration of Principles, and in the *Communist Manifesto,* were said to violate the Smith Act. They were sentenced to prison terms, and the Supreme Court refused to review their case."[2]

When the high court finally did get around to considering the Smith Act in 1950, it was in order to allow Justice Robert H. Jackson – fresh from a stint in Nuremberg prosecuting nazis for, among other things, their legalistic persecution of leftists during the 1930s – to articulate America's "liberal" philosophical alternative in handling "subversives." Utterly ignoring the act's proscriptions on anti-draft agitation, Jackson held that "it was no violation of free speech to convict Communists for conspiring to teach or advocate the forcible overthrow of the government, even if no clear and apparent danger [of such overthrow] could be proved. To await the danger becoming apparent, he argued, would mean that "Communist plotting is protected during the period of incubation; its preliminary stages of organization and preparation are immune from the law; the government can move only after imminent action is manifest, when it would, of course, be too late." Thus, for the supreme court,

49

"some legal formula that will secure [the] existing order against radicalism" was called for.[3]

The formula Justice Jackson sought was already at hand. In 1948, Republican congressmen Karl Mundt of South Dakota and Richard M. Nixon of California reported a draft bill out of Nixon's House Un-American Activities Committee, calling for the registration of all CP members as well as other radicals. Liberal Democrats in the Senate objected vociferously, and President Truman ultimately vetoed the legislation. As it turned out, the Democrats' problem was not with its clear totalitarian implications, but that it hadn't been heavy-handed *enough* in its original form. Among themselves, senate liberals such as Estes Kefauver and Hubert Humphrey supported an alternate version proposed by Nevada's reactionary Pat McCarran which included provisions for "the ultimate weapon of repression: concentration camps to intern potential troublemakers on the occasion of some loosely-defined future 'Internal Security Emergency.'"[4] As what became the Internal Security Act of 1950 (also known as the McCarran Act, after its sponsor) went through committee, Humphrey became obsessed that it might be "overly diluted," grousing openly that those herded into the planned camps might retain even the most elementary rights such as that of *habeas corpus*. Allowing the politically objectionable to retain *any* rights, he felt, would make for a "weaker bill, not a bill to strike stronger blows at the Communist menace, but weaker blows."[5] He needn't have worried; the act passed relatively intact, and was sustained over Truman's veto.[6]

In such a climate, the FBI was able to continue its *ad hoc* counterintelligence operations against the SWP throughout the 1950s.[7] Unlike the situation with the CP, however, these were never consolidated into a formal COINTELPRO during that decade, a situation which seems largely due to J. Edgar Hoover's personal assessment that the term "socialist" was somewhat less extreme (and therefore less of a priority) than the word "communist." Nonetheless, by 1961 – with a tacit green light from the newly-installed Kennedy administration on his anti-CP COINTELPRO already in hand – the director determined it would be both timely and appropriate to proceed in the same fashion against the SWP. Hence, on October 12 of that year he dispatched a memorandum to several field offices instructing them to begin the new "disruption program." The rationale for this, according to Hoover, was that the SWP:

...has, over the past several years, been openly espousing its line on a local and national basis through the running of candidates for public office and strongly directing and/or supporting such causes as Castro's Cuba and integration problems arising in the South. The SWP has been in frequent contact with international Trotskyite groups stopping short of open and direct contact with these groups...It is felt that a disruption program along similar lines [to COINTELPRO-CP,USA] could be initiated against the SWP on a very selective basis. One of the purposes of this program would be to alert the public to the fact that the SWP is not just another socialist group but follows the revolutionary principles of Marx, Lenin and Engels as interpreted by Leon Trotsky...It may be desirable to expand the program after the effects have been evaluated.[8]

One of the first "tasks" undertaken through COINTELPRO-SWP was to attempt to abort the judicial process in the case of the so-called Monroe defendants, a group of blacks and a white supporter who had followed the leadership of Monroe, North Carolina NAACP leader Robert Williams in adopting a posture of armed self-defense against ku klux klan terror in 1961.[9] The SWP extended its cooperation to the NAACP in establishing a multi-racial "Committee to Aid the Monroe Defendants" (CAMD) to put together a legal effort through which to obtain acquittals on the serious charges resultantly leveled against the accused. The initial expressed purpose of CAMD was "to fight the anticipated extradition order for [Williams' assistant Mae] Mallory, who was in Ohio, and Williams, whose whereabouts were unknown, and to raise bail money for the three defendants in Monroe."[10] As can be readily seen in the accompanying document, dated June 14, 1962, the Bureau immediately set out to break up this emerging support network, and thereby sought to destroy or at least seriously impair the defendants' right to mount an effective legal defense. This aspect of COINTELPRO-SWP was continued in full force after Mallory was extradited and the group went to trial facing capital charges in 1964. Under the circumstances, they were convicted, although this was later overturned on appeal.[11]

On other fronts, "The Bureau would investigate on the slightest pretext. When Lori Paton, a high school student in New Jersey, wrote to the Young Socialist Alliance (the youth branch of the Socialist Workers Party) for information as part of a project for her social studies class, agents visited the high school to ask about her."[12]

Some of the COINTELPRO activities against the SWP – revealed in Bureau documents that were released in 1975 in connection with a lawsuit filed by the Political Rights Defense Fund – were very inventive indeed. In one instance, the Bureau learned that Walter Elliott, scoutmaster of a Boy Scout troop in East Orange, New Jersey, whose wife was a member of the party, had said he considered the Scouts a better way of influencing young minds than joining the SWP. The Newark Field Office, although its files contained "no public source information of a subversive nature concerning Elliott," reacted by persuading the Boy Scouts not to renew his troop's charter.[13]

Overall, COINTELPRO-SWP seems to have focused itself in the educational and electoral arenas. For instance, as is reflected in the accompanying memo from the Special Agent in Charge (SAC), Denver to the Director, FBI, dated May 5, 1965, the Bureau produced and sent a phony letter ostensibly signed by "A Concerned Mother" as part of a disinformation campaign designed to ruin the candidacies of SWP members Barbara Taplin and Howard Wallace for the Denver School Board. Again, as is shown in the accompanying October 1, 1968 memo from the Phoenix SAC to the FBI director, the Bureau utilized similar disinformational techniques – in an effort the SAC confused with simultaneous operations being conducted under the rubric of COINTELPRO-New Left – to bring about the dismissal of Arizona State

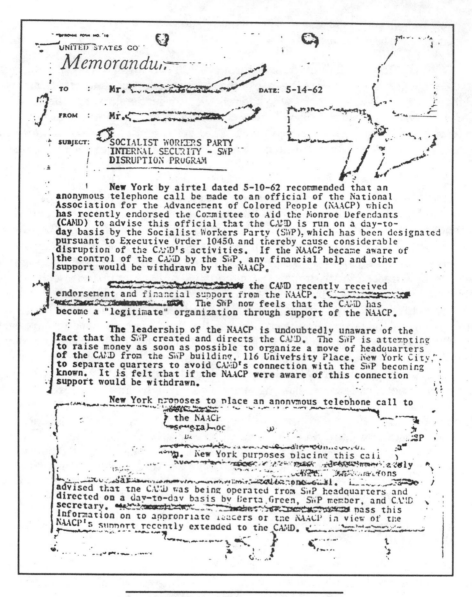

UNITED STATES GO

Memorandu...

TO   :   Mr.   DATE: 5-14-62

FROM :   Mr.

SUBJECT: SOCIALIST WORKERS PARTY
            INTERNAL SECURITY - SWP
            DISRUPTION PROGRAM

New York by airtel dated 5-10-62 recommended that an anonymous telephone call be made to an official of the National Association for the Advancement of Colored People (NAACP) which has recently endorsed the Committee to Aid the Monroe Defendants (CAMD) to advise this official that the CAMD is run on a day-to-day basis by the Socialist Workers Party (SWP), which has been designated pursuant to Executive Order 10450 and thereby cause considerable disruption of the CAMD's activities. If the NAACP became aware of the control of the CAMD by the SWP, any financial help and other support would be withdrawn by the NAACP.

the CAMD recently received endorsement and financial support from the NAACP. The SWP now feels that the CAMD has become a "legitimate" organization through support of the NAACP.

The leadership of the NAACP is undoubtedly unaware of the fact that the SWP created and directs the CAMD. The SWP is attempting to raise money as soon as possible to organize a move of headquarters of the CAMD from the SWP building, 116 University Place, New York City, to separate quarters to avoid CAMD's connection with the SWP becoming known. It is felt that if the NAACP were aware of this connection support would be withdrawn.

New York proposes to place an anonymous telephone call to
the NAACP
several oc
SP
New York purposes placing this call
tions
advised that the CAMD was being operated from SWP headquarters and directed on a day-to-day basis by Berta Green, SWP member, and CAMD secretary. pass this information on to appropriate leaders of the NAACP in view of the NAACP's support recently extended to the CAMD.

Memo initiating CAMD COINTELPRO.

University professor Morris Starsky (a matter which was not consummated until 1970).[14] On other fronts, as Noam Chomsky has pointed out:

Beginning in the late fall of 1971, some curious events took place in Detroit, Michigan. In late October, lists of supporters, contributors, and subscribers to the

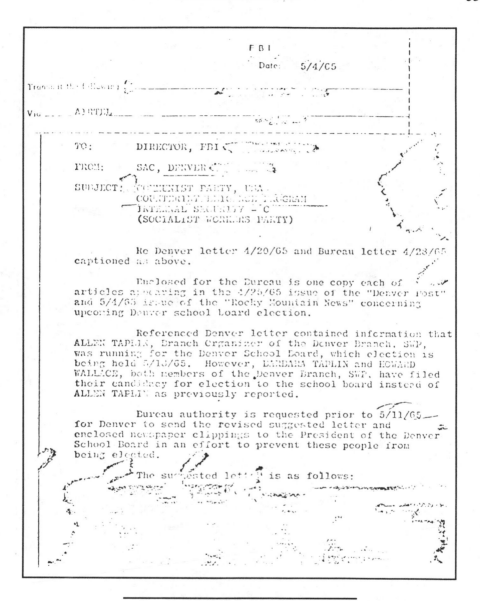

FBI

Date: 5/4/65

Transmit the following

Via   AIRTEL

TO: DIRECTOR, FBI

FROM: SAC, DENVER

SUBJECT: COMMUNIST PARTY, USA.
           COUNTERINTELLIGENCE PROGRAM
           INTERNAL SECURITY - C
           (SOCIALIST WORKERS PARTY)

           Re Denver letter 4/20/65 and Bureau letter 4/28/65
captioned as above.

           Enclosed for the Bureau is one copy each of
articles appearing in the 4/25/65 issue of the "Denver Post"
and 5/4/65 issue of the "Rocky Mountain News" concerning
upcoming Denver school board election.

           Referenced Denver letter contained information that
ALLEN TAPLIN, Branch Organizer of the Denver Branch, SWP,
was running for the Denver School Board, which election is
being held 5/18/65. However, BARBARA TAPLIN and HOWARD
WALLACE, both members of the Denver Branch, SWP, have filed
their candidacy for election to the school board instead of
ALLEN TAPLIN as previously reported.

           Bureau authority is requested prior to 5/11/65
for Denver to send the revised suggested letter and
enclosed newspaper clippings to the President of the Denver
School Board in an effort to prevent these people from
being elected.

           The suggested letter is as follows:

COINTELPRO against the SWP in Denver.

party newspaper were stolen from the headquarters of the Michigan [SWP]. A few
months later, the home of an [SWP] organizer was robbed. Valuables were ignored,
but membership lists and internal party bulletins were stolen. The burglaries
remain unsolved...If we ask who might be interested in obtaining the stolen
material, a plausible hypothesis suggests itself. The natural hypothesis gains

"Dear Sir:

"Recently while discussing with a friend the various candidates for the upcoming Denver School Board Election, I observed the names of Mrs. Barbara Taplin, 1631 Pearl Street, and Howard Wallace, 1980 Race Street, Denver, Colorado as candidates for the Denver School Board with their political parties listed as SWP.

"I vividly recall that Mr. Allen Taplin who is listed in the 'Post' article dated 4/25/65 as the husband of Mrs. Barbara Taplin, as the unsuccessful Socialist Workers Party candidate for the United States House of Representatives in 1964. In an article of the 'Denver Post' which I am enclosing for your information, this organization is listed as both subversive and on the Attorney General's list of subversive organizations. The article also hints that Mr. Taplin is a communist.

"Being a conscientious voter and mother of school age children, I feel that someone should do something to prevent persons of this sort from being elected to the school board.

"Although I am much in favor of publicly opposing these people, I feel it best for my family's sake that I withhold my name and leave this situation in your capable hands.

"A Concerned Mother"

If authority is granted to mail this letter, instructions concerning previous approved letter will be followed.

Text of bogus letter targeting Taplin and Wallace (above). Memo initiating action against SWP member Morris Starsky which cost him his faculty position at Arizona State University (facing page).

---

support from the fact that persons whose names appear on the stolen lists were then contacted and harassed by FBI agents, and a personal letter of resignation from the party, apparently stolen from the headquarters, was transmitted by the FBI to the

UNITED STATES GOVERNMENT

Memorandum

TO   : DIRECTOR, FBI ( ) (b)(7)   DATE: 10/1/63

FROM   SAC, PHOENIX ( ) (b)(7)

SUBJECT: COUNTERINTELLIGENCE PROGRAM
INTERNAL SECURITY
DISRUPTION OF THE NEW LEFT

Remylet, 7/1/68.

1. Potential Counterintelligence Action

MORRIS J. STARSKY, by his actions, has continued
to spotlight himself as a target for counterintelligence
action. He and his wife were both named as presidential
electors by and for the Socialist Workers Party when the
SWP in August, 1968, gained a place on the ballot in Arizona. In addition they have signed themselves as treasurer
and secretary respectively of the Arizona SWP. Professor
STARSKY's status at Arizona State University may be affected
by the outcome of his pending trial on charges of disturbing the peace. He is alleged to have used violent, abusive
and obscene language against the Assistant Managing Director
of Gammage Auditorium at ASU during memorial services for
MARTIN LUTHER KING last April. Trial is now scheduled for
10/8/68 in Justice Court, Tempe, Arizona.

A recommendation for counterintelligence action
as to STARSKY will be submitted by separate letter.

 (b)(7)

Bureau approval is requested to mail a copy of the
enclosed anonymous letter to each member of the faculty
committee which is hearing the charges against STARSKY. This
committee is sitting in the Law School on the ASU campus and
is composed of the following faculty members:

1. Dr. ROSS R. RICE, Chairman.

2. JOHN A. COCHRAN

3. RICHARD W. EFFLAND

4. JOHN P. DECKER

5. WALLACE ADAMS, Chairman of the Faculty Assembly.

ANONYMOUS LETTER TO MEMBERS
OF THE FACULTY COMMITTEE ON
ACADEMIC FREEDOM AND TENURE
ARIZONA STATE UNIVERSITY

Dear Sir:

It seems appropriate that you should be informed
of one of the most recent activities of Morris J. Starsky.
Starsky learned of a suicide attempt by one of his close campus
co-workers, David Murphy. Feeling that Murphy could no longer
be trusted as a member of the campus socialist group, Starsky
demanded that Murphy return all literature and other materials
belonging to the socialist group. Murphy refused to give Starsky
a quantity of socialist literature in his possession until Starsky
would pay him a sum slightly in excess of $50 which was owed for
telephone calls charged by Starsky to Murphy's telephone. Morris
Starsky was indignant at Murphy's independent attitude and at
2:00 A. M. on April 5, 1970 he, accompanied by his wife Pamela
and two young male associates, invaded Murphy's apartment and
under threat demanded return of the socialist literature. When
Murphy refused unless Starsky paid the phone bill, Starsky told
him that his two associates would beat him unmercifully. Murphy,
convalescing from a recent hospital stay, was under great fear
of bodily harm or death and surrendered the literature.

I find this episode interesting. Where did Starsky
learn of the effectiveness of smashing into a person's home at
2:00 A. M.? Also, of utilizing four persons to threaten the
health or life of someone? Is this an example of academic
socialism? Should the ASU student body enjoy the guidance of
such an instructor? It seems to me that this type of activity
is something that Himmler or Berit could accept with pride. If
Starsky did not enjoy the prestige and sanctuary of his position
he would be properly punished for such a totalitarian venture.
Unfortunately, Murphy is too terrified to testify against Starsky
and the other example of academic socialism.

/s/ A concerned ASU alumnus

Text of one of the bogus letters by which Starsky's dismissal was accomplished.

Civil Service Commission. Information that has since been obtained about FBI activities, including burglaries over many years, lends further substantiation to the conclusion that the FBI was engaged in one of its multifarious endeavors to undermine and disrupt activities that fall beyond the narrow bounds of the established political consensus...The Detroit events recall another incident which, with its aftermath, became the major news story of 1974. But it would be misleading to compare the Detroit burglaries to the Watergate caper...[T]he Detroit burglaries are a far more serious matter...[I]n Detroit it was the political police of the national government which, in their official function, were engaged in disrupting the "sanctity of the democratic process," not merely a gang of bunglers working "outside the system."[15]

The FBI's subversion of the electoral process through COINTELPRO-SWP has had a number of effects which go far beyond the question of who was allowed to win in a given race. A classic example concerns the 1966 candidacy of SWP member Judy White for governor of the state of New York. In a memo dated October 24, 1966, the SAC, New York informed Hoover that the New York field office had been successful in undertaking a disinformation campaign which resulted in the state legislature's changing of the New York election laws to preclude anyone under 30 years of age (which White was at the time) not only from being seated as governor, but from campaigning for the governorship as well. The intent of this, from the FBI point of view, was to block the SWP from having a forum.[16] The law, as altered by the Bureau, remains in effect a quarter-century later.

While COINTELPRO-SWP appears never to have entailed anything approaching the level of hoped for violence evident in COINTELPRO-CP,USA's Operation Hoodwink, or the concretely lethal dimension of several other COINTELPROs, there is at least one instance in which the FBI attempted to set an SWP candidate up to suffer physical harm. This concerns the Party's 1968 presidential candidate, Fred Halstead, who incorporated a trip to visit U.S. forces in Vietnam into his campaign. In a memo dated July 23, 1968, the SAC, New York proposed to the FBI director that the Bureau plant inflammatory information in the military press with the idea that this might cause G.I.s to physically attack Halstead upon his arrival.[17] Although the idea was approved on July 25, there is no indication service personnel responded in the desired manner. According to Halstead, he was instead "received in a friendly and courteous way. Never in a hostile way."[18]

Other anti-SWP efforts followed the pattern, established in the CAMD case, of attempting to foil alliances, real or potential, between the Party and other organizations. Notably, this included the spiking of a tentative association between the SWP in New York and the then-emergent Organization of Afro-American Unity (OAAU) headed by Malcolm X in 1965. In a memo dated June 15, 1965, the SAC, New York informed director Hoover that, "SWP influence on the followers of Malcolm X [can] be disrupted by emphasizing the atheism of the SWP as opposed to the basic religious orientation of the [OAAU]." Hoover quickly approved, and by August the New York SAC was reporting that, "It is believed probable that the disintegrating relations between the SWP and [the OAAU] can be attributed to the disruptive tactic authorized...and will result in a continued loss of influence by the SWP among this group of Negroes."[19]

As is evident from the accompanying memo from the SAC, New York to Hoover, dated February 13, 1970, the Bureau also went to considerable lengths – including the pornographic – in using disinformation to undermine coalitions between the SWP and new left anti-war organizations such as the New Mobilization to End the War in Vietnam ("Mobe" or "New Mobe") during the late 1960s and early '70s. As examples of the kind of activity involved:

In August 1968 the New York FBI office sent [an] anonymous letter to 68 "new left

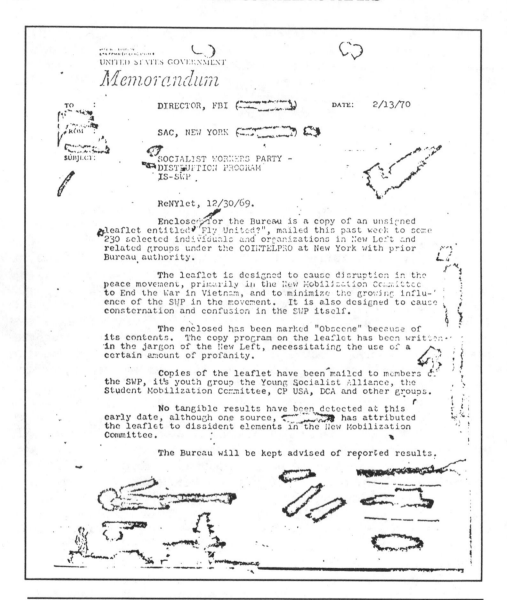

UNITED STATES GOVERNMENT

Memorandum

TO   :   DIRECTOR, FBI   DATE: 2/13/70

FROM   :   SAC, NEW YORK

SUBJECT: SOCIALIST WORKERS PARTY -
                DISRUPTION PROGRAM
                IS-SWP

ReNYlet, 12/30/69.

Enclosed for the Bureau is a copy of an unsigned leaflet entitled "Fly United?", mailed this past week to some 230 selected individuals and organizations in New Left and related groups under the COINTELPRO at New York with prior Bureau authority.

The leaflet is designed to cause disruption in the peace movement, primarily in the New Mobilization Committee to End the War in Vietnam, and to minimize the growing influence of the SWP in the movement. It is also designed to cause consternation and confusion in the SWP itself.

The enclosed has been marked "Obscene" because of its contents. The copy program on the leaflet has been written in the jargon of the New Left, necessitating the use of a certain amount of profanity.

Copies of the leaflet have been mailed to members of the SWP, it's youth group the Young Socialist Alliance, the Student Mobilization Committee, CP USA, DCA and other groups.

No tangible results have been detected at this early date, although one source,   has attributed the leaflet to dissident elements in the New Mobilization Committee.

The Bureau will be kept advised of reported results.

**Memorandum proposing action to drive a wedge between the SWP and "New Mobe,"
one of the New Left's array of anti-war organizations.**

groups" and "peace groups." The purpose of the FBI letter was to "widen the split" between the YSA and a prominent anti-war group called the Student Mobilization Committee to End the War in Vietnam ("SMC"). The letter accused the YSA of disrupting the SMC and of opposing the only really effective elements within the SMC. There is testimony to the effect that the letter caused great trouble within the YSA. The trouble related to the suspicion and worry as to who would write such a

Pornographic cartoon mailed to selected Mobe organizers in order to exacerbate tensions between them and the SWP.

letter and what its effects would be. In September 1968, to further embarrass the SWP and the YSA, the FBI sent a follow-up anonymous letter. This letter ridiculed these organizations for cowardice in the demonstration at the 1968 Democratic Party convention in Chicago. The letter implored the SWP and YSA to "stay home" on future occasions of this kind...The SWP and YSA participated in an anti-war group called the National Mobilization Committee ("MOBE"). In February 1969 the FBI's

New York office sent out an anonymous letter ridiculing MOBE's activities at the so-called "counter-inaugural" that took place in Washington, D.C. at the same time as President Nixon's inauguration in January 1969. The letter was sent to members of various anti-war groups, including the SWP and YSA. There is testimony that this letter aggravated certain problems within MOBE. MOBE ceased operation in February 1969...The next FBI effort involved an anti-war parade in New York City that took place on April 5, 1969. This parade was jointly sponsored by the SWP, YSA and SMC. Since it was to involve both civilians and military personnel, the sponsors of the parade considered it particularly important to keep the parade peaceful, so as not to draw the military personnel into trouble with the law. Just before the parade, the FBI's New York office distributed an anonymous leaflet entitled "Notes from the Sand Castle" (the latter term being slang for Columbia University), accusing the "SWP-YSA-SMC coalition" of cowardice in not being willing to fight the "pigs" (police) and to accumulate "battle wounds." The FBI's expressed purpose in creating the leaflet was to "disrupt plans for the demonstration and create ill-will between the SWP-YSA and other participating non-Trotskyist groups and individuals." The evidence shows that this communication created difficulties in managing the march...In December 1969 the New York FBI office sent an anonymous obscene leaflet to 230 individuals and organizations urging them to "flush" the SWP and YSA from the successor to MOBE, called New MOBE. From the scope and nature of the operation, the court concludes that it had a disruptive effect of the kind intended by the FBI...In February 1970 the New York FBI office sent a memorandum to various anti-war activists purporting to be written by a member of New MOBE. The FBI's purpose was to "create splits" between the SWP participants and other groups in the New MOBE coalition. The memorandum attacked "the Trotskyites" for taking control of the New MOBE and for resisting the recruitment of blacks. The FBI was aware, through its informant system, of criticism of the SWP about racial imbalance disfavoring blacks. The court concludes that this operation had a disruptive effect of the kind intended by the FBI...The SMC planned a conference at Catholic University, Washington, D.C. in February 1971. An internal FBI memorandum recommended efforts to bring the university's attention to the SWP/YSA's alleged domination of the SMC, and to disrupt the conference. The FBI distributed an anonymous leaflet in advance of the conference date, entitled "Trotskyists Welcomed at Catholic University!" The leaflet questioned whether the Catholic Church had been "duped again," in allowing its facilities to be used by the SMC...This operation was carried out under the COINTELPRO-New Left program. The evidence shows other instances of FBI operations designed to disrupt the SWP [in this regard].[20]

Although COINTELPRO-SWP had been officially terminated by the time its existence was revealed through a court-ordered release of documents to NBC reporter Carl Stern on March 7, 1974,[21] the *New York Times* reported two years later (*five* years after the "termination") that FBI infiltration and disruption of the Party was continuing unabated.[22] For instance:

An FBI report dated June 20, 1973 [*i.e.*: after COINTELPRO-SWP supposedly ended], refers to the FBI having obtained "items stolen from the YSA local office."

The reference is to certain file cards removed by [Timothy] Redfearn from a private file box. Redfearn regularly obtained confidential documents from the YSA, so that the FBI could copy them. Redfearn would then return the documents to their original location. In a report dated January 22, 1974, the FBI rated Redfearn as "excellent." On February 3, 1975, Redfearn was arrested by the Denver police for burglaries unrelated to his informant activities. Redfearn requested FBI assistance, but the FBI declined to help him [or so it says]. Redfearn then cooperated with local police and gave them information regarding other persons who were burglars or fences. Redfearn was [allegedly] discontinued as an FBI informant on April 17, 1975. Shortly thereafter he was [unaccountably] given a deferred prosecution [rather than a suspended sentence, or some such, which would be much more usual in the case of a snitch] on the local burglary charges...Redfearn then called the FBI, which reinstated him as an informant on May 28, 1975. Beginning in June 1976 Redfearn started to work at a book store in Denver that was operated by *The Militant*. Redfearn told the FBI that this would give him access to records of both the SWP and the YSA. On July 2, 1976, the SWP headquarters in Denver, located in the book store, was burglarized. A padlock on the door to the book store had been cut, and the contents of a file cabinet and a small box of petty cash were taken. On July 7 Redfearn called his FBI contact agent and showed him a group of SWP files [taken from the cabinet]...After the SWP burglary was reported in the local news media, the FBI claimed no knowledge of the matter. A local FBI agent was called before a grand jury in Denver and denied knowing how Redfearn had obtained the files.[23]

Given this, there is no particular reason to assume such anti-SWP activities on the part of the Bureau have ever really ended. Be this as it may:

[Between 1960 and 1971] the FBI approved and implemented forty-six disruptive COINTELPRO operations against the SWP; in addition, from 1960 to 1966, the FBI conducted over ninety burglaries of SWP offices, and photographed over eight thousand pages of SWP files, including financial records and personal letters.[24]

All of this undoubtedly was intended to quash:

...the threat of intellectual independence and uncontrolled political and social or-ganization [which] has been well contained...Alone among the parliamentary de-mocracies, the United States has had no mass-based socialist party, however mild and reformist [since 1920], no socialist voice in the media, and virtually no departure from centrist ideology within the schools and universities, at least until the pressure from student activism impelled a slight departure from orthodoxy [during the 1960s]. All this is testimony to the effectiveness of the system of controls that has been in force for many years, the activities of the FBI being only the spearhead for far more extensive, substantial, and effective – if more low-keyed – measures enforced throughout American society.[25]

Interestingly, as with its simultaneous operations against the CP, the FBI's COINTELPRO-SWP was probably self-defeating on its own terms. By the 1960s, both the CP and the SWP were, like most old left organizations, moribund. Left to themselves, they would undoubtedly have simply passed into a well deserved oblivion. Ultimately, "the only thing that seemed to keep organizations like the SWP going was the attention and concern of the FBI; just as their appeal would fade, the Bureau would issue a new warning about how dangerous they were and new recruits would flock to the cause."[26] The situation is made even more interesting by the fact that this largely useless (in its own terms) COINTELPRO ultimately resulted in the Bureau's losing a suit filed against it by the Political Rights Defense Fund on behalf of the SWP on July 18, 1973, under provisions of the Federal Tort Claims Act (28 U.S.C. § 2401 [b]).[27] After years of preliminary maneuvering, during which the government resisted plaintiff discovery motions and repeatedly moved for dismissal, the case came to trial in New York on April 2, 1981.[28] Five years after the trial, on August 25, 1986, U.S. District Judge Thomas P. Greisa ruled that the Bureau had indeed violated the basic rights of the plaintiff's over an extended period, through "the FBI's disruption activities, surreptitious entries and use of informants," he awarded the SWP a total of $246,000 in damages as a result.[29] This was followed, on August 17, 1987, by Judge Greisa's issuance of an unprecedented injunction against the FBI's use of the estimated 1,000,000 pages of investigative documents it had compiled on the SWP and its members since 1940 for any reason whatsoever, without the judge's personal consent, due to the illegal activity which had attended the gathering of the material; the injunction applies to all police and intelligence agencies – federal and local – within the U.S.[30]

Hence, even many of the "intelligence gathering" (as opposed to counterintelligence) activities which are associated with COINTELPRO – the use of infiltrators and informers against political targets, to take a notable example – have at last been declared unconstitutional in a court of law. As the celebrated constitutional attorney Leonard Boudin, who handled the case, has put it, "This lawsuit represented the first wholesale attack upon the entire hierarchy of so-called intelligence agencies that [have] attempted to infiltrate and destroy...lawful political part[ies]...The SWP and the Political Rights Defense Fund have carried to a successful conclusion a case whose victory materially advances the First Amendment rights of speech and association, and the Fourth Amendment Rights against invasion of privacy."[31]

Chapter 4

COINTELPRO - Puerto Rican Independence Movement

[Agents of the FBI's Domestic Intelligence Division] should bear in mind that the attitudes expressed by the President, the Director, and many legislators in Congress, have been to curtail the militant actions...on the part of a significant group of...people in the United States today. The thinking of the Supreme Court of the United States has been along the lines of suppressing the activities of those who openly advocate the overthrow of democratic authority in the United States. In addition the Internal Security Division of the Department of Justice has been specifically enlarged and strengthened to deal with these matters.

– J. Edgar Hoover –
1970

On February 27, 1946, D. Milton Ladd, head of the FBI's Intelligence Division, wrote a memorandum to J. Edgar Hoover recommending the Bureau cut back its operations in Puerto Rico, "specifically excepting" counterintelligence measures aimed at "communists and members of the Nationalist Party" on the island.[1] The memo emerged from the context of relations developed by the U.S. with its small Caribbean neighbor during the period since the former assumed direct "ownership" of the latter in 1899, after the Spanish-American War:

The United States had to make the Spanish feel their loss from the war. Because Spain had no cash left, as [U.S. plenipotentiary] Whitelaw Reid put it, "No indemnity was possible, save in territory." We thought of taking Cuba, but "desolated by twelve years of [its own anti-colonialist] war," the country wasn't worth much. That left Puerto Rico...[2]

Having acquired the island through conquest, the federal government set out to determine how the new possession should be managed:

The result of [more than a year of] congressional debate was the Foraker Act of 1900 [31 *Stat.* 77, named after Senator Thomas B. Foraker, its sponsor], which was Congress's first essay in crafting the so-called Organic Acts that were to govern Puerto Rico. Puerto Rico became a new constitutional animal, an "unincorporated territory" subject to the absolute will of Congress, a colonial status that was

63

recognized by the Insular Cases by the Supreme Court...Representative [James D.] Richardson's observations on Hawaii were quoted in the debate on the Foraker Act: "Nations have always acted and should govern themselves at all times upon principles which are entirely different from those which activate individuals...In looking at the question of any foreign territory the only question that should enter into consideration by us is one question: Is it best for the United States? The weal or woe, the misery or happiness, the poverty or prosperity of the foreigner or those to be annexed is not involved.[3]

With this self-enabling legislation in hand, the U.S. next installed a puppet government to administer its new colony. This consisted of "a governor and an Executive Council appointed by the president of the United States, who also appointed all the justices of the Supreme Court."[4] With a government under its total control in place, "the customs duty on Puerto Rican goods was removed [by congress]; dependent for export of its products, free of duty, to the mainland, the island became a regional economy of the United States. Thus, by 1901, the Foraker Act had set the essential framework of the U.S. connection. The political framework might be enlarged in the direction of home rule in an endeavor to remove the stigma of colonialism; the economic bond would work against any final severance of permanent political union with the metropolitan power."[5]

At first, the island response was to follow U.S.-stipulated procedural forms in attempting to alter the politico-economic equation. By 1916, however, *Puertorriqueño* sentiment against the nature of federal rule had risen to a point which caused Washington to reveal just how meaningless its "due process" really was. Concerned that a scheduled "referendum on the imposition of U.S. citizenship and the military draft" might result instead in an overwhelming vote for complete independence, President Woodrow Wilson arbitrarily suspended balloting until July 1917, *after* passage of the Jones Act (39 *Stat.* 951) unilaterally conferred citizenship and its attendant obligations upon the island populace, regardless of *Puertorriqueño* desires.[6] As to any prospect of eventual independence, the House Committee on Interior and Insular Affairs proclaimed that "*Our people* have already decided Porto Rico [*sic*] is forever to remain part of the United States [emphasis added]."[7]

Under such conditions, an increasing number of *Puertorriqueños* turned to non-electoral means of changing their circumstances. Following in the tradition of Ramón Emeterio Betances, one of the few island leaders who openly advocated complete separation from Spain prior to 1898, the Puerto Rican Nationalist Party (NPPR) was founded in 1922; Pedro Albizu Campos became its president in 1930, "injecting it with his radical nationalism."[8] Rejecting elections as "a periodic farce to keep the Puerto Rican family divided," Albizu called for a strategy of direct action to achieve full national sovereignty.[9] The federal response was to launch a campaign of repression against the *independentistas*, a matter for which the government was equipped with an on-site military (primarily naval) presence, the island's national guard, and the local colonial police apparatus working in direct liaison with the FBI (which maintained a field office in San Juan, as well as resident agencies in Ponce,

Aguadilla and Fajardo).[10] Although the Bureau's counterintelligence role in the events occurring in Puerto Rico during the '30s is sketchy at best, Ladd's memo provides firm indication that it was an active one, and that Albizu's followers were a particular target. The island's police commander, Colonel Frank Riggs announced that his men were in a state of "war to the death with all Puerto Ricans."[11]

In the face of this, Albizu proclaimed a *quid pro quo* of sorts: "for every Nationalist killed, a continental American would die."[12] Hence, when the police fired into a crowd of student demonstrators (killing five) from the University of Puerto Rico at Río Piedras on October 24, 1935, the NPPR replied by assassinating Riggs himself.[13]

> Albizu wanted revolution, but the United States tried to prevent one by holding the next face-off, not in the streets but in the courts. On March 7, 1936, federal authorities [read: the FBI] raided nationalist headquarters, collected "compromising evidence," and collected Albizu Campos and seven of his closest colleagues as well. The charge was sedition; the penalty, if convicted, was a long stretch in a mainland – never Puerto Rican – prison.[14]

As Ronald Fernandez has observed, "since eight Americans and four Puerto Ricans failed to reach a consensus, the first trial ended in a hung jury...[so] in the second trial, federal officials took no chances. They stacked the jury with twelve safe people. Ten were Americans, two were Puerto Ricans, and together they produced a verdict which federal prosecutors found 'satisfactory.'"[15] Official opinion held that the two-to-ten year sentences meted out to Albizu and most of the other NPPR leadership "ought to go far to restore order and tranquility on the island."[16] This assessment undoubtedly seemed all the more solid to the government insofar as the prosecution's "need to gather evidence" for the sedition trial had been used as the basis from which to undertake "the first use of Grand Jury proceedings to harass, intimidate, and cripple an organized national liberation movement."[17] Specifically at issue in this regard was the sentencing, on April 2, 1936, "to a year in federal prison of the then Secretary General of the Nationalist Party, Puerto Rican poet Juan Antonio Corretjer, for contempt...in refusing to surrender to [the grand jury] the minutes and list of members of the party."[18] However:

> Exactly the opposite occurred. Indeed, after the Federal Court of Appeals upheld Albizu's conviction in February 1937, Puerto Rico witnessed what is quite accurately referred to as a massacre of nationalist supporters. To show solidarity with Albizu, his followers planned a parade in Ponce...[H]eavily armed police blocked off every street in the vicinity...a shot rang out. Within minutes, twenty civilians, some just bystanders, had been killed and more than 150 wounded.[19]

Despite government contentions that the NPPR itself was responsible for the bloodbath, the American Civil Liberties Union (ACLU), after an exhaustive investigation, concluded "[t]he facts show that the affair of March 21, 1937, in Ponce was a massacre...due to the denial by police of the civil rights of citizens to parade and assemble. This denial was ordered by the [U.S. appointed] Governor of Puerto Rico."[20] Badly battered, the *independentistas* responded with a rapid series of reprisals before withdrawing into an extended period of regroupment:

> In June 1937, two nationalists tried to kill the federal judge who presided at Albizu's trial; during a rally at which Puerto Rico's resident commissioner defended the use of the American flag, two nationalists tried to kill him. And, on July 25, 1938, at a parade celebrating the fortieth anniversary of the American takeover, Albizu's followers tried to assassinate Governor Blanton Winship by firing more than eighty shots at the reviewing stand. Somehow Winship escaped injury, but his bodyguard was wounded and a colonel in the National Guard was killed by a stray bullet.[21]

With Albizu in prison – he ultimately served more than 18 years behind federal bars before dying of radiation-induced cancer in 1965[22] – the NPPR underwent a period of intense internal turmoil. The extent to which FBI infiltration facilitated its resultant fragmentation is unclear but, again, Ladd's memo suggests some such involvement. In any event, effectively leaderless and undoubtedly tired of incessant discord and infighting, a significant portion of the membership had, by 1945, drifted toward the softer and "more realistic" position of advocating commonwealth status rather than full independence for Puerto Rico, a posture advanced by the liberal Luis Muñoz Marin and his *Partido Popular Democrático* (PPD), founded in 1938.[23] This erosion was offset to some extent by the formation of a caucus calling itself the *Congresso pro Independentista* (CPI) which, by 1946, had largely merged with Concepcíon de García's *Partido Independentista Puertorriqueño* (PIP). The general flow away from the NPPR appears to have been what the federal government had in mind at a counterintelligence level, and Ladd's memo suggesting that pressure might be removed from all those other than active communists and/or nationalists should be viewed as a way of "encouraging defection."

By 1948, Muñoz Marin, posing himself as an "alternative to the violence of the *independentistas*," was able to win Puerto Rico's first elected governorship on the basis of a promise that he could negotiate a favorable resolution to the island's political status question with federal policy-makers.[24] "But Congress had absolutely no intention of letting Puerto Rico go. That the United States wanted to retain its colony was made clear to Muñoz on his frequent trips to Washington, and in the end he settled for what Congress was willing to give. Testifying before the House in March 1950, Muñoz [was reduced to] repeatedly telling congressmen what they wanted to hear," that he and the PPD would willingly bow to the authority of their colonizers in exchange for approval of a "constitution" which was itself utterly subordinate to the will of the U.S.[25] By this point, even the mainstream Puerto Rican press was attacking Muñoz as a sell-out.[26]

It was into this scene of perceived betrayal on the part of many *Puertorriqueños* that Pedro Albizu Campos returned after a full decade of incarceration. Immediately, he informed the *independentistas* that, "the Nationalist Party [which he sought to revitalize] is going to dynamite America and expel the Yankees from Puerto Rico...The day always comes when justice arms the weak and puts the giants to flight. Then another *Te Deum* shall be sung...but it will be preceded by armed struggle."[27]

On October 30, 1950, a group of approximately two thousand nationalists orchestrated uprisings throughout the island...in the mountains, the nationalists not only took over the town of Jayuya, they used it as a temporary capital for the sovereign republic of Puerto Rico...in San Juan, Muñoz was lucky to be alive. Armed with machine guns and Molotov cocktails, five nationalists had entered La Fortaleza, the governor's residence, intent upon killing him and blowing up the structure that had always been a potent symbol of colonialism.[28]

Muñoz Marin's would-be executioners were killed and the revolt put down (with considerable direct U.S. military involvement), but, "two days after the attack on La Fortaleza, two New York nationalists – Oscar Collazo and Grisilio Torresola – took a train to Washington. They meant to kill President Truman, but when they spotted guards at the entrance to Blair House (Truman's temporary residence), Collazo opened fire, and within seconds Terresola and a police officer were dead. Examining Terresola's body, police found letters from Albizu Campos. Although they said nothing explicit about an assassination...they led to Albizu's arrest and imprisonment."[29] This was followed, on March 4, 1954, by four *independentistas* managing to smuggle a gun into the House of Representatives, where they were able to wound five congressmen before running out of ammunition.[30]

As in the late 1930s, the momentum achieved by the NPPR could not be sustained. Exhaustion and factionalism once again took their toll during the late '50s, as the *independentistas* splintered into such smaller student organizations as the *Federación de Universários Pro Independencia* (FUPI) and *Federación Estudiantil pro Independencia* (FEPI, a high school level group), as well as a proliferating number of sectarian "grouplets" like the *Acción Patriótica Revolucionaria* (APR) and *Movimiento 27 de Marzo*, each committed to continuing the armed struggle on its own terms. As is the case with the 1940s, the precise role of FBI infiltration, disinformation, and so forth in helping this disintegration process along is murky, but subsequent Bureau memoranda allude to the fact that active counterintelligence operations were occurring at some level. Meanwhile, the PIP's increasingly legalistic strategy of "fighting the regime from within the regime," promulgated by party founder Gilberto Conception de García had come to seem largely irrelevant to a growing number of activists. The slack in radical party politics was taken up, to a certain extent at least, by recruitment of former NPPR members into the *Movimiento por Independencia Puertorriqueño* (MPIPR), headed by the avowed marxist-leninist, Juan Mari Bras, and the emergence of the *Partido Socialista Puertorriqueño* (PSP).[31]

It was at this juncture that the FBI implemented a formal COINTELPRO with the expressed intent of bolstering the U.S. colonial grip on Puerto Rico through the expedient of destroying virtually the entire spectrum of left opposition on the island. In a memorandum to the SAC, San Juan (accompanying text), on August 5, 1960, FBI director J. Edgar Hoover announced that the Bureau was "considering" the new

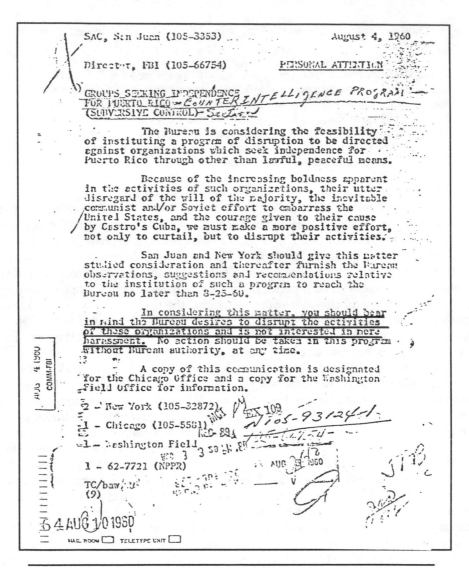

SAC, San Juan (105-3353) ...   August 4, 1960

Director, FBI (105-66754)   PERSONAL ATTENTION

GROUPS SEEKING INDEPENDENCE *INTELLIGENCE PROGRAM*
FOR PUERTO RICO — *COUNTER*
(SUBVERSIVE CONTROL) *Section*

            The Bureau is considering the feasibility
of instituting a program of disruption to be directed
against organizations which seek independence for
Puerto Rico through other than lawful, peaceful means.

            Because of the increasing boldness apparent
in the activities of such organizations, their utter
disregard of the will of the majority, the inevitable
communist and/or Soviet effort to embarrass the
United States, and the courage given to their cause
by Castro's Cuba, we must make a more positive effort,
not only to curtail, but to disrupt their activities.

            San Juan and New York should give this matter
studied consideration and thereafter furnish the Bureau
observations, suggestions and recommendations relative
to the institution of such a program to reach the
Bureau no later than 8-25-60.

            In considering this matter, you should bear
in mind the Bureau desires to disrupt the activities
of these organizations and is not interested in mere
harassment. No action should be taken in this program
without Bureau authority, at any time.

            A copy of this communication is designated
for the Chicago Office and a copy for the Washington
Field Office for information.

2 - New York (105-32872)
1 - Chicago (105-5581)
1 - Washington Field
1 - 62-7721 (NPPR)
TC/baw
(9)

MAIL ROOM ☐ TELETYPE UNIT ☐

Memo initiating COINTELPRO – Puerto Rican Independence Movement.

COINTELPRO, and stipulated he was no longer interested in operations which involved "mere harassment." San Juan complied, at least on the level of planting disinformation in the island press, as is indicated in the accompanying letter from Hoover to the SAC, dated November 14 (but referring to a October 26, 1960 communication from San Juan), in which the director critiques a fabricated news story. In the same missive, Hoover recommends gearing up the COINTELPRO, using *already existing* infiltrators within "groups seeking independence for Puerto Rico" in the

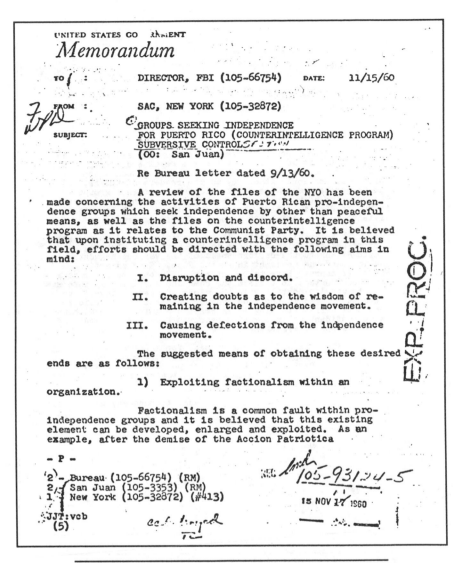

UNITED STATES GO ...hmENT

Memorandum

TO : DIRECTOR, FBI (105-66754)   DATE: 11/15/60

FROM : SAC, NEW YORK (105-32872)

SUBJECT: GROUPS SEEKING INDEPENDENCE
FOR PUERTO RICO (COUNTERINTELLIGENCE PROGRAM)
SUBVERSIVE CONTROL
(OO: San Juan)

Re Bureau letter dated 9/13/60.

A review of the files of the NYO has been
made concerning the activities of Puerto Rican pro-independence groups which seek independence by other than peaceful
means, as well as the files on the counterintelligence
program as it relates to the Communist Party. It is believed
that upon instituting a counterintelligence program in this
field, efforts should be directed with the following aims in
mind:

    I. Disruption and discord.

    II. Creating doubts as to the wisdom of re-
        maining in the independence movement.

    III. Causing defections from the independence
         movement.

    The suggested means of obtaining these desired
ends are as follows:

    1) Exploiting factionalism within an
organization.

    Factionalism is a common fault within pro-
independence groups and it is believed that this existing
element can be developed, enlarged and exploited. As an
example, after the demise of the Accion Patriotica

- P -

2 - Bureau (105-66754) (RM)
2 - San Juan (105-3353) (RM)
1 - New York (105-32872) (#413)
JJT:vcb
(5)

REC. 105-93124-5

15 NOV 17 1960

EXP. PROC.

New York field office response to COINTELPRO startup.

role of *provocateurs*. The director felt that "carefully selected informants" might be able to raise "controversial issues" within *independentista* formations such as the MPIPR, as they were even then doing within the CP, USA and preparing to do within the SWP. Further, he pointed out that such individuals might be utilized effectively to create situations in which "nationalist elements could be pitted against the communist elements to disrupt some of the organizations, particularly the MPIPR and...FUPI." He also instructed that "the San Juan Office should be constantly alert

SAC, San Juan (105-3353)   November 14, 1960

105-93124-4

Director, FBI (105-66754) 4 9

GROUPS SEEKING INDEPENDENCE
FOR PUERTO RICO
(COUNTERINTELLIGENCE PROGRAM)

Reurep 10-26-60.

After careful review of the proposed article, it is
believed that it would not achieve the results desired; namely,
to cause animosity between Juan Mari Bras and Juan Antonio
Corretjer, nor would it convey to the readers of the article
the dangerousness of the Puerto Rican independence groups.
The question of voting or not voting in the general elections
in Puerto Rico is not now the type of issue which is sufficiently
divisive to accomplish the purpose of this program.

As an alternative, it is suggested San Juan prepare
a brief article which would be in the nature of alerting
Puerto Ricans to the dangerousness of the various segments of
the independence movement in Puerto Rico. Such an article
would, of course, have to be interesting enough to interest a
newspaper contact to utilize the same and sufficiently informative to develop hostility in the minds of readers towards the
elements engaged in the independence movement. The article
should be self-sustaining in interest and informative without
using confidential information received from our sources, and
it should not embarrass the Bureau.

With regard to your request for information relating
to counterintelligence tactics and techniques employed against
the Communist Party, USA, (CPUSA) for possible use against
the Puerto Rican independence groups, it appears that the exact
same tactics would not be applicable.

Some varied forms of the same tactics may undoubtedly
be applied; for example;

1 - New York

NOV 14 1960
COMM-FBI

TC:djw
(6)

17 NOV 16 1960

The Bureau's first plan of attack against the *independentistas* .

for articles extolling the virtues of Puerto Rico's relationship to the United States as
opposed to complete separation from the United States, for use in anonymous mailings to selected subjects in the independence movement who may be psychologically affected by such information."

As can be seen in the next document, the New York field office (in cooperation
with San Juan) had responded with a concrete "action proposal" within 48 hours.
Within months, San Juan was reporting back regularly on the relative success of its
various counterintelligence operations (such as in the accompanying November

(1) Security informants operating inside the groups could, under certain circumstances, raise controversial issues at meetings, raise justifiable criticisms against leaders and take other steps which would weaken the organization. In the proposed article you furnished, the question of voting or abstaining from voting, as it was related by two of the top leaders of the Movimiento Pro Independencia de Puerto Rico (MPIPR), appears to be an issue which would be controversial within the MPIPR.

In connection with our counterintelligence program, any informant operating thereunder must be first approved by the Bureau for such operation and then carefully briefed by the Agent handling him before he engages in controversial discussions or criticisms inside the particular group. If you desire to initiate this type of action through selected informants you should furnish the identities of informants selected, basis for selection and the proposed manner you plan to use them. Our informants operating in the CPUSA have caused disruption without jeopardizing their informant status and, in fact, some have advanced inside the Party primarily because of their forceful acts in criticizing poor leaders and other weaknesses in the Party organization.

(2) The San Juan Office should be constantly alert for articles extolling the virtues of Puerto Rico's relationship with the United States as opposed to complete separation from the United States, for use in anonymous mailings to selected subjects in the independence movement who may be psychologically affected by such information.

(3) It appears the nationalist elements could be pitted against the communist elements to effectively disrupt some of the organizations, particularly the MPIPR and the Federacion de Universitarios Pro Independencia (FUPI), where we have determined there is communist influence. The nationalist elements in Puerto Rico prior to the time Castro obtained power in Cuba have indicated they were anticommunist. The CP in Puerto Rico has never been strong, and today it appears that the influence of international communism has a greater influence on the radical elements within Puerto Rico. In regard to the MPIPR and FUPI, it is noted that these two organizations apparently have the largest membership of any of the independence groups in Puerto Rico.

In the future, San Juan and New York should furnish the identity of the newspaper contact to whom you desire to furnish such articles at the time of the submission of the articles to the Bureau.

Because of the large number of Puerto Ricans residing in New York, and the fact that a number of Puerto Rican independence organizations are active in New York, New York and San Juan should exchange ideas relative to tactics and techniques which may be effective in your divisions.

The nationalists in Puerto Rico within themselves are a threat to the internal security of the United States, and nationalists influenced by international communism can be an even greater threat. The Bureau believes this program can be effective, and continuous attention must be given to it.

1960 memo describing the planting of an editorial in the San Juan daily, *El Mundo* and other actions), and receiving a steady flow of suggestions from Hoover as to how to improve the COINTELPRO's effectiveness (see accompanying document, dated November 21, 1962). By late 1967, the director was positively jubilant in his assessment to the San Juan SAC of the "benefits" accruing from such tactics:

> [The COINTELPRO has served to] confuse the independentist leaders, exploit group rivalries and jealousies, inflame personality conflicts, emasculate the...strength of these organizations, and *thwart any possibility of pro independence unity* [emphasis added].[32]

In achieving the results which so delighted the director, the San Juan SAC had first and foremost taken a tip from Hoover that, "the PSI [Public Security Index] is interested in publishing anticommunist articles, particularly those which could expose pro-Cuban and communist influence in the various national independence organizations in Puerto Pico...The purposes of this program are to disrupt the activities and lessen the influence of nationalists and communists who seek to separate Puerto Rico from the United States."[33] The COINTELPRO thus included a full-scale disinformation component by which agents systematically planted articles and editorials (often containing malicious gossip concerning *independentista* leaders' alleged sexual or financial affairs) in "friendly" newspapers, and dispensed "private" warnings to the owners of island radio stations that their FCC licenses might be revoked if pro-independence material were aired.

> The articles and editorials...were placed mainly in *El Mundo*, a Spanish language daily dating back to the early part of this century, and owned since the 1960s by Northamerican Mrs. Argentina Hills, the 1977-78 president of the Interamerican Press Association (a U.S. fomented association of newspaper owners in this hemisphere). *El Mundo* is also one of the Knight (U.S.) chain of newspapers...The *San Juan Star*, a Scripps-Howard (U.S.) chain newspaper, and *El Imparcial* in its latter days, after the death of its pro-independence owner, Sr. Ayuso, were also used to plant articles and editorials...Other less prominent newspapers like *El Vigía*, the University of Puerto Rico's Catholic Youth organ, and the so-called *Bohemia Libre Puertorriqueña* – well described by the Bureau as an "anticommunist and anti-Cuban publication" – were also used to disseminate the accusation that FUPI was communist and thus "scare other University students away from joining it."[34]

Concerning radio programming, there is clear evidence that agents "talked to" the owners of radio stations WLEO in Ponce, WKFE in Yauco and WJRS in San Germán about their licensing as early as 1963.[35] One result was cancellation of the one hour daily time-block allotted to "Radio Bandera," a program produced by the APU.[36] Such tactics to deny a media voice to *independentistas* accord well with other, more directly physical methods employed during the 1970s, *after* COINTELPRO supposedly ended:

> [There was] the bombing of *Claridad* [daily paper first of the MPIPR and then the

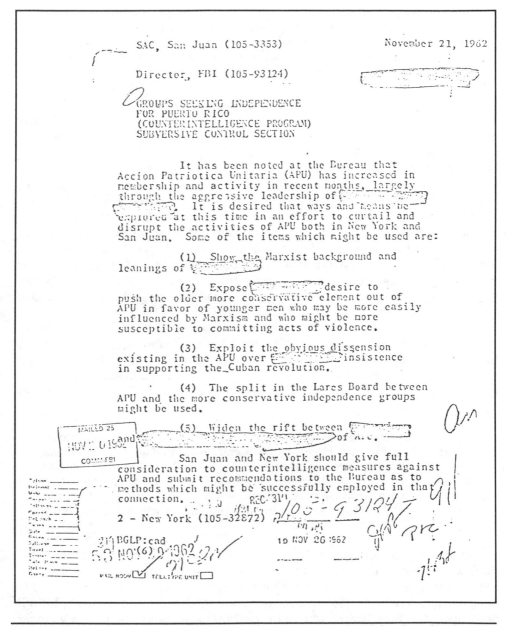

SAC, San Juan (105-3353)   November 21, 1962

Director, FBI (105-93124)

GROUPS SEEKING INDEPENDENCE
FOR PUERTO RICO
(COUNTERINTELLIGENCE PROGRAM)
SUBVERSIVE CONTROL SECTION

It has been noted at the Bureau that
Accion Patriotica Unitaria (APU) has increased in
membership and activity in recent months, largely
through the aggressive leadership of ⌐‾‾‾‾‾‾‾¬
⌐‾‾‾‾‾‾‾¬. It is desired that ways and means be
explored at this time in an effort to curtail and
disrupt the activities of APU both in New York and
San Juan. Some of the items which might be used are:

(1) Show the Marxist background and
leanings of ⌐‾‾‾‾‾‾¬.

(2) Expose ⌐‾‾‾‾‾‾¬ desire to
push the older more conservative element out of
APU in favor of younger men who may be more easily
influenced by Marxism and who might be more
susceptible to committing acts of violence.

(3) Exploit the obvious dissension
existing in the APU over ⌐‾‾‾‾‾‾¬ insistence
in supporting the Cuban revolution.

(4) The split in the Lares Board between
APU and the more conservative independence groups
might be used.

(5) Widen the rift between ⌐‾‾‾‾‾‾¬
and ⌐‾‾‾‾‾‾‾‾¬ of A.C. ⌐‾‾¬

San Juan and New York should give full
consideration to counterintelligence measures against
APU and submit recommendations to the Bureau as to
methods which might be successfully employed in that
connection.

2 - New York (105-32872)

RGLP:cad

The FBI's plan of attack against the *independentistas* is refined and developed in this 1962
memo, written when the COINTELPRO was approximately two years old. The tactics
involved have continued to be perfected over the years, but show every indication of still
being used by the Bureau and other police agencies at the present time (albeit, often
without a formal counterintelligence label).

PSP] printing presses which has occurred at least five times in the present decade. Although the MPI [now PSP] usually furnished the police with detailed information as to the perpetrators of these acts, not even *one* trial has ever been held on this island in connection with these bombings, nor even one arrest made. The same holds true for a 1973 bombing of the National Committee of the [PIP].[37]

Operating in this sort of curtailment in exposure of valid *independentista* views, the FBI was able to sow discord and factionalism within and between targeted groups much more effectively, "beginning with FUPI and the [NPPR] in 1960, through the [APU] in 1962 and 1963, [and later] *Ligua Socialista Puertorriqueña*, the MPI[PR] and...the PIP."[38] In order to accomplish this, as the accompanying June 12, 1961 memo from the San Juan SAC to Hoover indicates, the Bureau engaged in intensive investigation of *independentista* leaders both on the island and in New York in order to ascertain their (real or arguable) "weaknesses" in terms of "morals, criminal records, spouses, children, family life, educational qualifications and personal activities other than independence activities." The findings, however flimsy or contrived, were pumped into the media, disseminated as bogus cartoons or "political broadsides," and/or surfaced within organizational contexts by *provocateurs*, all with the express intent of setting the leaders one against the other and at odds with their respective organizational memberships.

The Bureau assessed such undertakings as being quite successful, a matter witnessed by the accompanying AIRTEL from Hoover to the SAC, San Juan, dated March 9, 1962, in which distribution of a bogus leaflet accusing the FUPI leadership of "secret links to communism" is discussed. When evidence to support such red-baiting contentions could not be discovered, the FBI's COINTELPRO specialists simply made it up:

> MPIPR leaders, cognizant of the basic antipathy of Puerto Ricans, predominantly Roman Catholic, to communism, have consistently avoided, at times through public statements, any direct, overt linkage of the MPIPR to communism...The [San Juan office] feels that the above situation can be exploited by means of a counterintelligence letter, purportedly by an anonymous veteran MPIPR member. This letter would alert MPIPR members to a probable Communist takeover of the organization.[39]

Such methods were routinely employed against all *independentista* organizations, as is shown in the accompanying memo from the San Juan SAC to Hoover, dated November 21, 1962 and targeting the APU. Things also assumed a highly personal tone, as when in 1966 an unidentified agent dummied up a letter to MPIPR head Juan Mari Bras "warning" him to "beware the ambitiousness" of a younger colleague.[40] By 1968, such tactics had evolved to the point that Mari Bras was being accused in Bureau-fabricated leaflets and cartoons of "sending young men out to die as members of the *Comandós Armados de Liberación* [CAL, an armed formation whose dedication was often misused by the FBI for such propaganda purposes] while he

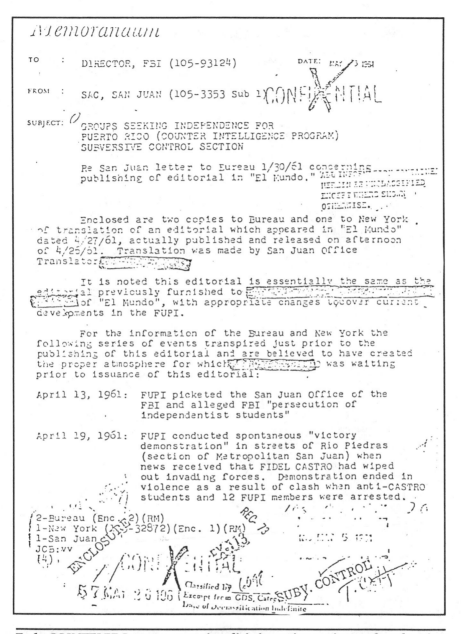

Memorandum

TO   : DIRECTOR, FBI (105-93124)   DATE: MAY 5 1961

FROM   : SAC, SAN JUAN (105-3353 Sub 1) CONFIDENTIAL

SUBJECT: GROUPS SEEKING INDEPENDENCE FOR
PUERTO RICO (COUNTER INTELLIGENCE PROGRAM)
SUBVERSIVE CONTROL SECTION

Re San Juan letter to Bureau 1/30/61 concerning
publishing of editorial in "El Mundo." ALL INFORMATION
HEREIN IS UNCLASSIFIED
EXCEPT WHERE SHOWN
OTHERWISE.

Enclosed are two copies to Bureau and one to New York
of translation of an editorial which appeared in "El Mundo"
dated 4/27/61, actually published and released on afternoon
of 4/26/61. Translation was made by San Juan Office
Translator.

It is noted this editorial is essentially the same as the
editorial previously furnished to of "El Mundo", with appropriate changes to cover current
developments in the FUPI.

For the information of the Bureau and New York the
following series of events transpired just prior to the
publishing of this editorial and are believed to have created
the proper atmosphere for which was waiting
prior to issuance of this editorial:

April 13, 1961:   FUPI picketed the San Juan Office of the
                  FBI and alleged FBI "persecution of
                  independentist students"

April 19, 1961:   FUPI conducted spontaneous "victory
                  demonstration" in streets of Rio Piedras
                  (section of Metropolitan San Juan) when
                  news received that FIDEL CASTRO had wiped
                  out invading forces. Demonstration ended in
                  violence as a result of clash when anti-CASTRO
                  students and 12 FUPI members were arrested.

2-Bureau (Enc. 2)(RM)
1-New York (105-32872)(Enc. 1)(RM)
1-San Juan
JCB:vv
(4)

REC-73

Classified by
Excempt from CDS, Cate
Date of Declassification Indefinite

**Early COINTELPRO memo recapping disinformation tactics employed against
Federación de Universitários pro Independencia (FUPI) and the results obtained
thereby. Such methods were used against *independentistas* throughout the duration of the COINTELPRO in Puerto Rico.**

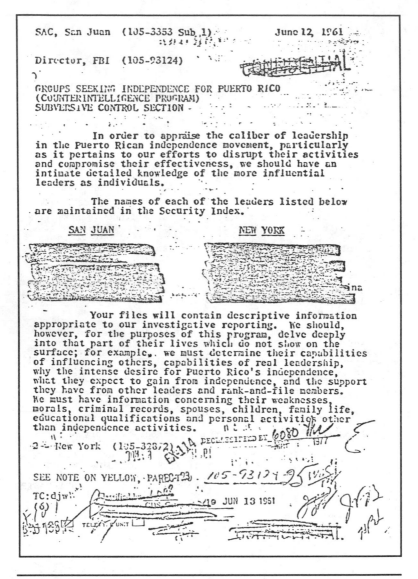

SAC, San Juan   (105-3353 Sub 1)   June 12, 1961

Director, FBI   (105-93124)

GROUPS SEEKING INDEPENDENCE FOR PUERTO RICO
(COUNTERINTELLIGENCE PROGRAM)
SUBVERSIVE CONTROL SECTION -

        In order to appraise the caliber of leadership
in the Puerto Rican independence movement, particularly
as it pertains to our efforts to disrupt their activities
and compromise their effectiveness, we should have an
intimate detailed knowledge of the more influential
leaders as individuals.

        The names of each of the leaders listed below
are maintained in the Security Index.

        SAN JUAN   NEW YORK

        Your files will contain descriptive information
appropriate to our investigative reporting. We should,
however, for the purposes of this program, delve deeply
into that part of their lives which do not show on the
surface; for example, we must determine their capabilities
of influencing others, capabilities of real leadership,
why the intense desire for Puerto Rico's independence,
what they expect to gain from independence, and the support
they have from other leaders and rank-and-file members.
We must have information concerning their weaknesses,
morals, criminal records, spouses, children, family life,
educational qualifications and personal activities other
than independence activities.

2 - New York (105-32872)   DECLASSIFIED BY 6080

SEE NOTE ON YELLOW, PAGE 22   105-93124

TC:djw
(6)
                                        JUN 13 1961

**Early document delineating plan to discredit selected *independentista*
leaders. Such tactics appear to still be in use today.**

---

remain[ed] protected by his foreign benefactor [supposedly Cuban premier Fidel
Castro]."[41]

These methods were used not only to divide *Puertorriqueños* among themselves,
but to forestall alliances between any of the various elements of the *independentista*
movement and progressive groups on the U.S. mainland. For instance, when the

```
[          ] supreme leader for many years
in the nationalist movement in Puerto Rico, often disavowed
communist influences in the nationalist movement. During
the United States war against communism in Korea,[          ]
specifically stated that the Nationalist Party of Puerto Rico
must avoid being considered in anyway communistic in its views.

        Whatever his relationship may have been with communist
individuals and regardless of how wrong or right he was,
[          ] was against Soviet communist ideology.

        Suppose [          ] could see his wife, [          ]
and so-called friend, [          ] together clinging to
Fidel Castro's Soviet-type communism like leeches.

        Suppose [          ] knew of the Federation of University
Students for Independence joining with international
communism, which, if we are indifferent, can eventually
destroy the Americas which [          ] loves.

        Suppose [          ] learns that Juan Mari Bras is
attempting to unite nationalists and communists under
the banner of the Movimiento Pro-Independencia. Always
opposite, the nationalists desire a republic and the
communists a socialist state like Soviet Russia.

        Suppose [          ] knew that the Accion Patriotica
Unitaria, contemporary descendent of his Nationalist
Party of Puerto Rico, is almost completely dominated
and controlled by the communist [          ]
who directs but never leads.

        [          ] is being betrayed, but more important
is the fact that Puerto Rico is being betrayed.

        The destiny of Puerto Rico must not include sub-
servience to an atheistic ideology.

        Puerto Rico, yes; communism, no!
```

Text of "anonymous leaflet" circulated in 1962 to discredit Juan Mari Bras.

black liberation journal *Soulbook* published an editorial entitled "The Puerto Rican Revolution" in 1965, arguing that *Puertorriqueños* and mainland Afro-Americans shared both a common heritage and a common oppressor,[42] COINTELPRO experts in New York saw to it that anonymous and thoroughly racist "letters of objection" were immediately dispatched to the MPIPR:

> We resent the implication that (name deleted) black nationalist allies in the editor's statement that our people are Negro as was our martyred leader Pedro Albizu Campos. We are proud of our Spanish heritage and culture. Although Negroes are welcome in our movement and may seek refuge in our nation, let it not be said that the majority of [*Puertorriqueños*] are Negro.[43]

On October 23, 1967, the New York SAC also came forth with a plan to

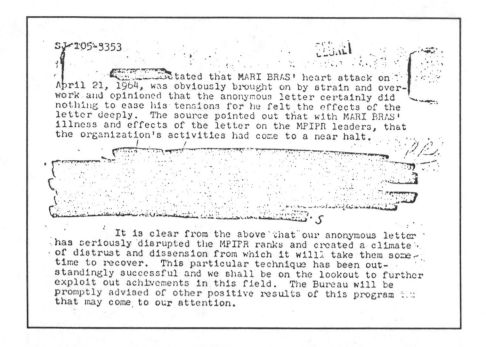

SI-105-3353

April 21, 1964, was obviously brought on by strain and overwork and opinioned that the anonymous letter certainly did nothing to ease his tensions for he felt the effects of the letter deeply. The source pointed out that with MARI BRAS' illness and effects of the letter on the MPIPR leaders, that the organization's activities had come to a near halt.

It is clear from the above that our anonymous letter has seriously disrupted the MPIPR ranks and created a climate of distrust and dissension from which it will take them some time to recover. This particular technique has been outstandingly successful and we shall be on the lookout to further exploit out achievements in this field. The Bureau will be promptly advised of other positive results of this program that may come to our attention.

Fragment of 1964 memo in which the FBI takes credit for the near-fatal heart attack of Juan Mari Bras. Such claims were repeated during the mid-70s in the wake of the assassination of the *independentista* leader's son.

disseminate a forged leaflet in the name of Juan Mari Bras and designed to misrepresent the MPIPR in such a way as to alienate a number of stateside organizations – Youth Against War and Fascism, the Progressive Labor Party, the Socialist Workers Party, *Movimiento por Independencia*, Casa Puerto Rico, the Worker's World Party and Young Socialist Alliance among them – with which Mari Bras had been attempting to forge a united front.[44] Similarly, the Bureau sought to thwart any possibility of a constructive relationship between *independentistas* and socialist countries or liberation movements located outside the U.S. By 1966, the FBI was preoccupied with "statements made by Mari Bras covering efforts to gain independence for Puerto Rico through the United Nations, support of the Cuban government and the South Viet Nam Liberation Front (Viet Cong)."[45] One response to this "threat" was the preparation and distribution of a cartoon (see page 89) purporting to show Mari Bras and other MPIPR leaders under the direct control of Castro.[46] Other efforts in this vein included a campaign of sexual slander targeting Doña Laura Meneses, wife of Albizu Campos, and Juan Juarbe y Juarbe, NPPR Delegate for External Affairs (both were living in Havana at the time) for purposes of "ridiculing the Puerto Rican independence movement, and the government of Fidel Castro."[47] By 1971, the Bureau was even undertaking COINTELPRO actions to

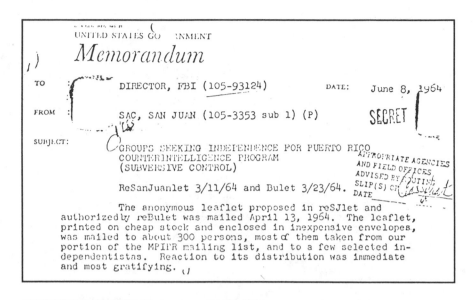

UNITED STATES GO   {RNMENT

Memorandum

TO   :   DIRECTOR, FBI (105-93124)   DATE: June 8, 1964

FROM   :   SAC, SAN JUAN (105-3353 sub 1) (P)   SECRET

SUBJECT: GROUPS SEEKING INDEPENDENCE FOR PUERTO RICO
                 COUNTERINTELLIGENCE PROGRAM
                 (SUBVERSIVE CONTROL)   APPROPRIATE AGENCIES
                                                     AND FIELD OFFICES
                                                     ADVISED BY ROUTING
                 ReSanJuanlet 3/11/64 and Bulet 3/23/64.   SLIP(S) OF
                                                           DATE

                 The anonymous leaflet proposed in reSJlet and
          authorized by reBulet was mailed April 13, 1964. The leaflet,
          printed on cheap stock and enclosed in inexpensive envelopes,
          was mailed to about 300 persons, most of them taken from our
          portion of the MPIPR mailing list, and to a few selected in-
          dependentistas. Reaction to its distribution was immediate
          and most gratifying.

Fragment of typical memo describing use of bogus leaflet to foster factionalism within the *independentista* movement.

prevent a link-up between the essentially defunct CP,USA on the basis that CP leader Gus Hall had traveled to Puerto Rico, "raised the priority of Puerto Rican independence" for his party, and promised to champion the cause when he traveled to "the USSR and other socialist countries."[48]

Predictably, the sorts of manipulations involved in the COINTELPRO against the Puertorriqueño independence movement entailed more than the fostering of confusion and infighting among *independentistas* and the public at large. There can be no doubt that lethal outcomes were acceptable to, even desired by, the FBI. For example, as the accompanying excerpt from a July 1964 memo from the San Juan SAC to Hoover bears out, the Bureau considered Mari Bras' near-fatal heart attack during April of that year to have been brought on, at least in part, by an anonymous counterintelligence letter. Far from expressing regret, or concern that perhaps the FBI was overstepping its intentions in light of these consequences, the SAC concludes by promising to "be on the lookout to exploit [our] *achievements* in this field [emphasis added]" in the future, and to "advise the Bureau of *other positive results* [emphasis added]" of the COINTELPRO in Puerto Rico.The pattern remained evident more than a decade later when, as Mari Bras subsequently testified before the United Nations Commission on Decolonization (after reviewing portions of the 75 volumes of documents the FBI had compiled on him), the Bureau undertook tactics apparently intended to cause him to suffer a second coronary:

[The documents] reflect the general activity of the FBI toward the movement. But some of the memos are dated 1976 and 1977; long after COINTELPRO was [suppos-

SAC, San Juan (105-3353)   8/25/64

-102-

Director, FBI (105-93124)

GROUPS SEEKING INDEPENDENCE FOR PUERTO RICO
COUNTERINTELLIGENCE PROGRAM
(SUBVERSIVE CONTROL)

ReBulet 8/5/64 which outlined a suggested
counterintelligence move against the Federation of
University Students for Independence (FUPI).

Your report of 8/7/64 concerning the
organization and activities of the Federation of Students
for Independence (FEPI) has been reviewed with interest.
It is believed that a counterintelligence program against
FEPI can be initiated along with the suggested activity
against FUPI. It is believed that copies of the flyer
which will be prepared showing FUPI's connection with
international communism can be effectively used along
with an attached flyer in the Spanish language showing
FUPI's connection with FEPI.

These documents could be distributed anonymously
to some of the school officials and parents and might tend
to reduce the influence of this budding youth organization.

Carefully review this matter with Agents of your
office handling investigations of FUPI and FEPI submitting
your recommendations to the Bureau regarding proposed
counterintelligence procedures.

NOTE:

FEPI is a new independence organization presently
existing in eight high schools in Puerto Rico. It is the
child of FUPI, college age independence group at the Universit
of Puerto Rico which has connected ties with international
communism as well as Puerto Rican independence groups.

1 - 105-123380 (FEPI) REC-43

BGLP:all (5)

EX-108   1 D AUG 24 1964

AUG 27 1964

MAIL ROOM ☐   TELETYPE UNIT ☐

Counterintelligence from cradle to grave. Document announcing FBI plans to add the high school organization *Federación Estudiantil pro Independencia* (FEPI) to its list of COINTELPRO targets in Puerto Rico. Indications are that the Bureau continued its operations against *Puertorriqueño* juveniles until at least 1971 and in all probability much longer, perhaps through the present moment.

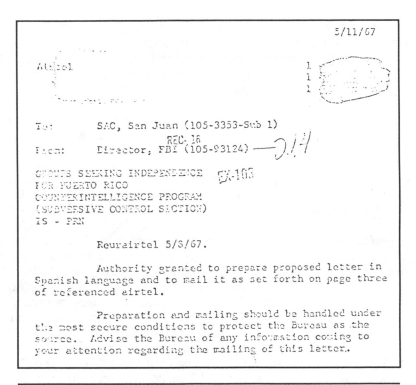

5/11/67

To: SAC, San Juan (105-3353-Sub 1)

From: Director, FBI (105-93124)

GROUPS SEEKING INDEPENDENCE
FOR PUERTO RICO
COUNTERINTELLIGENCE PROGRAM
(SUBVERSIVE CONTROL SECTION)
IS - PRN

     Reurairtel 5/3/67.

     Authority granted to prepare proposed letter in Spanish language and to mail it as set forth on page three of referenced airtel.

     Preparation and mailing should be handled under the most secure conditions to protect the Bureau as the source. Advise the Bureau of any information coming to your attention regarding the mailing of this letter.

Fragment of typical Airtel authorizing the sending of an anonymous letter to foment disputes within the *independentista* movement. Note the concern expressed that it not be discovered the letter originated with the FBI. Hundreds of such letters are known to have been sent.

edly] ended as an FBI activity...At one point, there is a detailed description of the death of my son, in 1976, at the hands of a gun-toting assassin. The bottom of the memo is fully deleted, leaving one to wonder who the assassin was. The main point, however, is that the memo is almost joyful about the impact his death will have upon me in my Gubernatorial campaign, as head of our party, in 1976.[49]

After this impact expressed itself in the form of an attack of severe depression the same year, the San Juan SAC noted in a memo to FBI headquarters that, "It would hardly be idle boasting to say that *some of the Bureau's activities have provoked the situation of Mari Bras* [emphasis added]."[50] Obviously, one possible interpretation of this language is that the FBI had a hand in orchestrating the murder of the MPIPR leader's son, or at least helped cover the trail of the assassin(s). Given the context established by the Bureau's own statements *vis à vis* Mari Bras, it also seems quite likely that one of the means by which the FBI continued to "exploit its achievements" in "provoking the situation" of the *independentista* leader was to arrange for the firebombing of his home in 1978,[51] in addition to maintaining such normal "investigative" harassment as obtaining copies of every single deposit slip and check written on his personal account for more than 20 years.[52]

Plainly, the lethal or near-lethal dimension of the Puerto Rico COINTELPRO expanded dramatically during the 1970s, *after* such operations had been allegedly terminated. As Alfredo López recounted in 1988:

> [O]ver the past fifteen years, 170 attacks – beatings, shootings, and bombings of independence organizations and activists – have been documented...there have been countless attacks and beatings of people at rallies and pickets, to say nothing of *independentistas* walking the streets. The 1975 bombing of a rally at Mayaguez that killed two restaurant workers was more dramatic, but like the other 170 attacks remains unsolved. Although many right-wing organizations claimed credit for these attacks, not one person has been arrested or brought to trial.[53]

This pattern of seeming ineffectuality on the part of the FBI and cooperating local police agencies when it comes to solving violent crimes against groups or individuals targeted by COINTELPRO is revealing in a way which will be explored more thoroughly in our chapter on the Bureau's anti-AIM operations. Suffice to say that there can be no question that "lack of manpower" accounts for such apparent ineptitude. By the 1970s, the FBI's San Juan field office was rostered with four squads (about 80 agents), with another squad posted to each of the three resident agencies (an additional 60 agents, overall), exclusive of a steady flow of technicians from the mainland brought in to perform one or another "special task," *all* interlocked tightly with the island's substantial local police force.[54] Further, the Bureau is known to have customarily shared information and coordinated activities on the island with the CIA, Secret Service, Naval Intelligence Service, 771st Military Intelligence Detachment, the State Department, and Office of Naval Intelligence, all of which maintain facilities and appreciable numbers of personnel on site in Puerto Rico.[55] All of this adds up to an incredible saturation of agents on a small Caribbean island with an aggregate population of only 3.5 million. And, while the Bureau can't seem to muster the wherewithal to apprehend *any* of the perpetrators of the beatings and bombings of *independentistas*, it has always had ample resources available to engage in anti-*independentista* gossip and editorializing, keeping track of Mari Bras' checkbook, and arresting numerous FUPI students engaged in distributing pro-independence literature on such weighty charges as "possessing marihuana cigarettes."[56]

In those few instances when the FBI did actually become involved in the investigation of the murders of *independentistas* during the '70s, the results have been bizarre. For example, when Teamster activist Juan Caballero disappeared in 1977, the Bureau atypically joined in the search for him. On October 25, a body was found in the El Yunque rain forest, badly decomposed and trussed up in electrical wire. This, the FBI announced, was Caballero, who had probably been killed by "associates" who suspected him of having been a "police informant." No such suspicion had existed prior to the Bureau's announcing it. Then, mysteriously, it was discovered that the dental structure of the corpse failed to match that of Caballero. Further

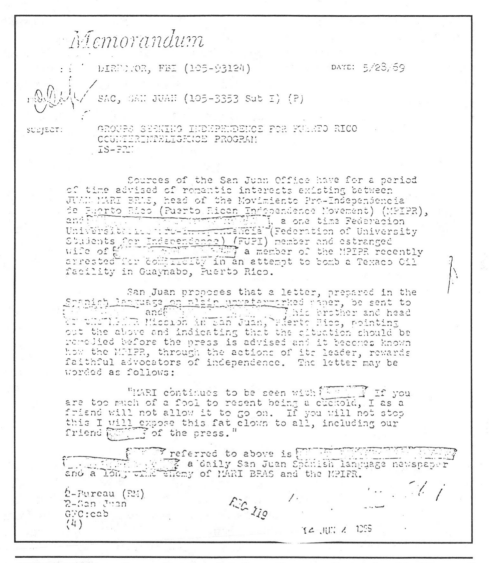

Memorandum

TO: DIRECTOR, FBI (105-93124)   DATE: 5/28/69

FROM: SAC, SAN JUAN (105-3353 Sub I) (P)

SUBJECT: GROUPS SEEKING INDEPENDENCE FOR PUERTO RICO
COUNTERINTELLIGENCE PROGRAM
IS-PR

Sources of the San Juan Office have for a period
of time advised of romantic interests existing between
JUAN MARI BRAS, head of the Movimiento Pro-Independencia
de Puerto Rico (Puerto Rican Independence Movement) (MPIPR),
and _____, a one time Federacion
Universitaria Pro-Independencia (Federation of University
Students for Independence) (FUPI) member and estranged
wife of _____, a member of the MPIPR recently
arrested for complicity in an attempt to bomb a Texaco Oil
facility in Guaynabo, Puerto Rico.

San Juan proposes that a letter, prepared in the
Spanish language on plain unwatermarked paper, be sent to
_____ and _____, his brother and head
of the MPIPR Mission in San Juan, Puerto Rico, pointing
out the above and indicating that the situation should be
remedied before the press is advised and it becomes known
how the MPIPR, through the actions of its leader, rewards
faithful advocators of independence. The letter may be
worded as follows:

"MARI continues to be seen with _____. If you
are too much of a fool to resent being a cuckold, I as a
friend will not allow it to go on. If you will not stop
this I will expose this fat clown to all, including our
friend _____ of the press."

_____ referred to above is _____
_____, a daily San Juan Spanish language newspaper
and a long time enemy of MARI BRAS and the MPIPR.

2-Bureau (RM)
2-San Juan
GFC:cab
(4)

REC 119

14 JUN 4 1969

**COINTELPRO continues. Ongoing disinformation operation against Mari Bras and
the MPIPR in 1969. Note sexual innuendos.**

---

tests revealed that the body lacked evidence of a bone fracture in the right hand the
ostensible victim was known to have suffered. The fingers of a hand were then
severed and shipped to the FBI crime lab in Washington, D.C., for fingerprint
identification. The lab promptly "lost" the fingers. The fate of Juan Caballero thus
remains unknown, as does the identity of the individual actually murdered in El
Yunque.[57]

Equally novel have been the techniques by which the Bureau has amassed "evidence" of alleged *independentista* violence. Take, for instance, the case of the "hopping fingerprint" after the shooting of North American attorney Allen Randall in September 1977.[58] Shortly after the killing, a communique was supposedly received from a "worker's commando," taking credit for the action and explaining the rationale underlying it. A follow-up communique was said to have been received within a matter of hours. Two days later, local police, acting on information provided by the FBI, arrested island Teamster head Miguel Cabrera and several other key union organizers. Cabrera's fingerprint, the Bureau said, had been found on the first communique. At a pretrial hearing during January of 1978, however, the prosecution produced Bureau-provided evidence that Cabrera's fingerprint was on the second communique rather than the first, thus producing the joke among the defendants that the print was busily hopping from document to document in the FBI crime lab. During the trial in 1979, police records were subpoenaed by the defense which showed that the Bureau had requested a set of Cabrera's prints prior to receiving *any* evidence in the case, a matter which strongly suggested the crime lab's conclusions had been predetermined. As a result, Cabrera and his colleagues were acquitted.[59]

A much clearer instance of direct FBI involvement in anti-*independentista* violence is the "Cerro Maravilla Episode" of July 25, 1978. On that date, two young activists, Arnaldo Dario Rosado and Carlos Soto Arrivi (son of the distinguished *Puertorriqueño* novelist, Pedro Juan Soto), accompanied a *provocateur* named Alejandro González Molavé, were lured into a trap and shot to death by police near the mountain village. Official reports claimed the pair had been on the way to blow up a television tower near Cerro Maravilla, and had fired first when officers attempted to arrest them. A taxi driver who was also on the scene, however, adamantly insisted that this was untrue, that neither *independentista* had offered resistance when captured, and that the police themselves had fired two volleys of shots in order to make it sound from a distance as if they'd been fired upon. "It was a planned murder," the witness said, "and it was carried out like that."[60] What had actually happened became even more obvious when a police officer named Julio Cesar Andrades came forward and asserted that the assassination had been planned "from on high" and in collaboration with the Bureau.[61] This led to confirmation of González Molavé's role as an infiltrator reporting to both the local police and the FBI, a situation which prompted him to admit "having planned and urged the bombing" in order to set the two young victims up for execution.[62] In the end, it was shown that:

> Dario and Soto [had] surrendered. Police forced the men to their knees, handcuffed their arms behind their backs, and as the two *independentistas* pleaded for justice, the police tortured and murdered them.[63]

None of the police and other officials involved were ever convicted of the murders and crimes directly involved in this sordid affair. However, despite several

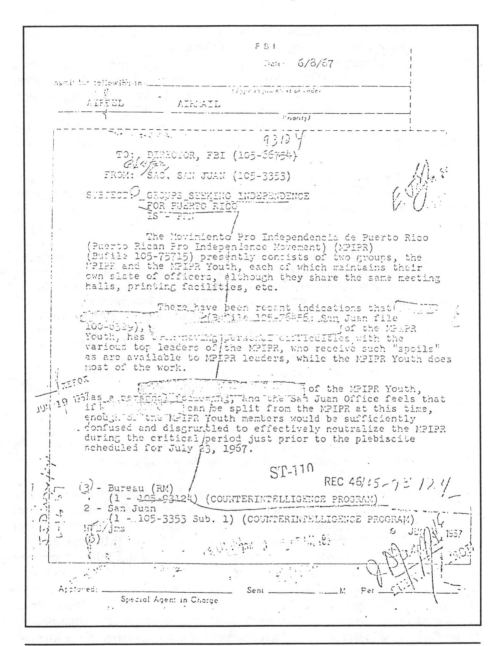

1967 Airtel from SAC, San Juan to J. Edgar Hoover describing a portion of the COIN-TELPRO methods to be used in subverting the 1967 United Nations plebescite to determine the political status of Puerto Rico.

years of systematic coverup by the FBI and U.S. Justice Department, working in direct collaboration with the guilty cops, ten of the latter were finally convicted on multiple counts of perjury and sentenced to prison terms ranging from six to 30 years apiece.[64] Having evaded legal responsibility for his actions altogether, *provocateur* González Molavé was shot to death in front of his home on April 29, 1986, by "party or parties unknown."[65] This was followed, on February 28, 1987, by the government's payment of $575,000 settlements to both victims' families, a total of $1,150,000 in acknowledgment of the official misconduct attending their deaths and the subsequent investigation(s).[66]

At about the same time that Dario and Soto were summarily executed (August 28 – September 1, 1978), the FBI was hosting an international conference on "counter-terrorism" in San Juan. Among the participants in this three-day event were:

Anthony Quainton (then head of the State Department's Office on Combatting Terrorism), British General Richard Clutterbuck (a specialist in counterinsurgency theory and author of several books on the subject), Uruguayan General Manuelo Querrolo (head of the 1960s campaign that destroyed the *Tupamaros* guerrillas), Reinhard Rupprecht (a head of the West German *Bundeskriminalamt* and responsible for pursuit of the Red Army Fraction [RAF]), Robin Borne (Canadian head of the campaign to repress the Québec Liberation Movement), Inspector Ronald McIntyre of the Royal Canadian Mounted Police (Canada's FBI), Jay Mallin (editor for "Terrorism and Latin America" with *Soldier of Fortune* magazine), Dr. Aaron Katz (of the Center for the Study of Human Behavior, a RAND-type think tank devoted to counterinsurgency research), and Louis O. Giuffrida (a "private sector" specialist involved in delivering counter-terrorist, counterinsurgency and SWAT training to law enforcement personnel). In addition, the meeting was attended by several high-ranking FBI men, including COINTELPRO specialist Richard Wallace Held, then Special Agent in Charge (SAC) of the Bureau's San Juan Field Office.[67]

One result of the conference seems to have been the designation of a mainland formation of the *independentista* movement, the *Fuerzas Armadas de Liberación Nacional* (FALN), along with three other national liberation organizations (the Republic of New Afrika [RNA], *Movimiento de Liberación Nacional Mexico* [MLNM], and the American Indian Movement) as "the most significant current internal security threats to the United States."[68] A more concrete outcome was a massive island-wide raid conducted by more than 300 SWAT-equipped agents, beginning before dawn on the morning of August 30, 1985. Operating out of the Roosevelt Roads Naval Base, the raiders invaded scores of homes and offices, arresting nearly 50 *independentistas* on "John Doe" warrants in which charges were not specified. Considerable personal property was destroyed, impounded or "lost."[69] The raid was initially "justified" by San Juan SAC Richard W. Held on the basis of "anti-terrorism" evidenced in the arrest of 11 *independentistas* – including Filiberto Ojeda Ríos, a leader of *Los Macheteros*, a clandestine organization – said to have been involved in

MUERTE DE REVOLUCIONARIO BORINQUEÑO

COINTELPRO cartoon distributed to discredit MPIPR leader Juan Mari Bras (depicted at left) just before the 1967 plebescite. The fraud was attributed to other *independentistas*.

the expropriation of $7.1 million from a Wells Fargo facility in West Hartford, Connecticut on September 12, 1983.[70]

The cover story, which in any event failed to explain why 37 other *independentistas* – none of whom were accused of specific criminal acts – had been rounded up in the raid, was quickly belied by the U.S. Attorney in Puerto Rico. "You have to remember," he said at a press conference, "there were two simultaneous investigations going on. There was the West Hartford investigation *and the one going on down here* [emphasis added]." His boss, U.S. Attorney General Edwin Meese, was even more straightforward: "We are sending a message to terrorists that their bloody acts will not be tolerated."[71] Thus mere public advocacy of independence for Puerto Rico was converted into "terrorism" and utilized as the basis for the continuation of COINTELPRO under the rhetorical veneer of "counter-terrorist" operations. What had happened was seen quite plainly on the island by nearly everyone, including relatively establishment-oriented politicians. PIP leader Rubén Berríos Martínez, for instance, termed the whole affair "a frontal attack on an entire movement and an entire set of ideals. It is virtually an act of war upon our people's will, determination and rights."[72] Even Governor Carlos Barceló Romero, no friend of the *independentistas*, formally protested the trampling upon Puerto Rico's constitution inherent to the Bureau's brand of counterintelligence activity.[73]

The governor was saying more than he intended. Inevitably, the FBI's concerted efforts to repress the *independentista* perspective in Puerto Rico's political life has served to deform the *Puertorriqueño* political process as a whole. And, as was the case with COINTELPRO-SWP, this appears to have been quite conscious and intentional. But, in Puerto Rico, the implications extend rather further. Not only did the Bureau's systematic denial of media access to, spreading of disinformation about, and fostering of factionalism within the *independentista* movement have the effect of negating much of the movement's electoral potential within the island arena itself, such tactics also subverted other initiatives to resolve the issue of Puerto Rico's colonial status in a peaceful fashion. This concerns in particular a plebescite called for July 23, 1967. During the ten months prior to the scheduled referendum to determine the desires of the *Puertorriqueño* public with regard to the political status of their island, the Bureau went far out of its way to spread confusion. The COINTELPRO methods used included creation of two fictitious organizations – *Grupo pro-Uso Voto del MPI* (roughly, "Group within the MPIPR in Favor of Voting to Achieve Independence") and the "Committee Against Foreign Domination of the Fight for Independence" – as the medium through which to misrepresent *independentista* positions "from the inside."[74] One outcome was that *Puertorriqueño* voters increasingly shied away from the apparently jumbled and bewildering *independentista* agenda and "accepted" continuation of a "commonwealth" status under U.S. domination which satisfied virtually none of the populace.

With this accomplished, the Bureau set about seeing to it the *independentistas* remained artificially discredited (and the overall *Puertorriqueño* option to mount a coherent effort to protest or reconvene the plebescite truncated) by shifting responsibility for the disaster onto its foremost victims:

> It might be desirable to blame the communist bloc and particularly Cuba for the failure of the United Nations and to criticize Mari Bras and others for isolating the Puerto Rican independence forces from the democratic countries.[75]

Since 1967, although Mari Bras and other *independentistas* have made an annual pilgrimage to the UN Committee on Decolonization, and in 1978 managed to achieve formal international recognition that the island remains a colony despite designation as a commonwealth,[76] the U.S. has been able to shunt off the issue. U.S. diplomats routinely argue that the 1967 referendum "permanently reaffirmed by popular consent" the "domestic status" of Puerto Rico accepted by Muñoz Marin in 1953. This, according to the diplomats, represents the "exercise of self-determina-

More Bureau art work. Cartoon purporting to show that Mari Bras (center) and other MPIPR leaders were under the control of Cuban premier Fidel Castro in 1967. The cartoon was distributed in the name of the *Grupo pro-Uso Voto del MPI*, a fictitious *independentista* entity invented by the FBI for such purposes. The fabrication was circulated immediately prior to the U.N. plebescite.

tion" by *Puertorriqueños*, and renders the island's affairs an "internal concern of the United States" rather than a matter of international jurisdiction.[77] And, just in case the utterly contrived nature of the U.S. position failed to prove sufficiently convincing to Third World nations, "[U.S. United Nations] Ambassador Jean Kirkpatrick made it clear to nonaligned nations that...a vote against the United States would carry penalties" when the *independentistas* finally managed to bring their questions to the General Assembly in 1981.[78]

With literally every avenue of "due and democratic process" sealed off by the extralegal methods of their colonizers, the *independentistas* have been left with essentially no recourse but armed struggle. Some realized this as early as the 1930s, others much later. For its part, the FBI seems to have understood from the outset that this would be the result of its mission in keeping Puerto Rico firmly within the U.S. orbit. Hence, the Bureau's early undertaking of counterintelligence operations against the NPPR and the evolution of these activities into the much more inclusive anti-*independentista* COINTELPRO beginning in 1960. Such an assessment also accounts for the apparent escalation of the sort of counterintelligence tactics used against the *independentistas* after 1971, when COINTELPRO was supposedly a thing of the past. As the events of 1985 abundantly demonstrate, in Puerto Rico the essentials of COINTELPRO remain very much alive. And, under the conditions which now prevail, its continuation promises to be more treacherous and violent than ever.

Chapter 5

COINTELPRO –
Black Liberation Movement

Predictably, the most serious of the FBI's disruption programs [between 1956 and 1971] were those directed at "Black Nationalists." These programs...initiated under liberal Democratic administrations, had as their purpose "to expose, disrupt, misdirect, discredit, or otherwise neutralize the activities of black nationalist, hate-type organizations and groupings, their leadership, spokesmen, membership, and supporters"...Agents were instructed to "inspire action in instances where circumstances warrant." Specifically, they were to undertake actions to discredit these groups both within the "responsible Negro community" and to "Negro radicals," and also "to the white community, both the responsible community and to 'liberals' who have vestiges of sympathy for militant black nationalists..."

– Noam Chomsky –
COINTELPRO

Although the FBI's COINTELPRO against the black liberation movement was not formally initiated until issuance of J. Edgar Hoover's August 25, 1967 memo quoted above by Noam Chomsky (see accompanying document), the roots of the Bureau's anti-black counterintelligence operations extend much deeper into U.S. history. As was documented in the introduction to this volume, Hoover was engaged at least as early as 1918 in plans to destroy black nationalist leader Marcus Garvey under the guise of "criminal proceedings." This occurred in the context of "the infamous race riot that first engulfed East St. Louis in July 1917, taking the lives of thirty-nine blacks and nine whites and the explosion that occurred less than two months later in Houston, Texas, in which two black soldiers and seventeen white men lost their lives."[1] Such violence was part of the process by which the U.S. national order, in which blacks as an overall population lived under near-total political disenfranchisement, economic prostration, and super-exploitation of their labor by the Euroamerican *status quo*, was intended to be preserved. In the aftermath of World War I, blacks had begun to mount the first serious challenge to such circumstances since the Reconstruction period immediately following the Civil War; Hoover and his proto-FBI organization, in kind with white vigilante formations, seem to have seen one of their primary missions as keeping blacks "in their place" by what ever repressive means were available.[2]

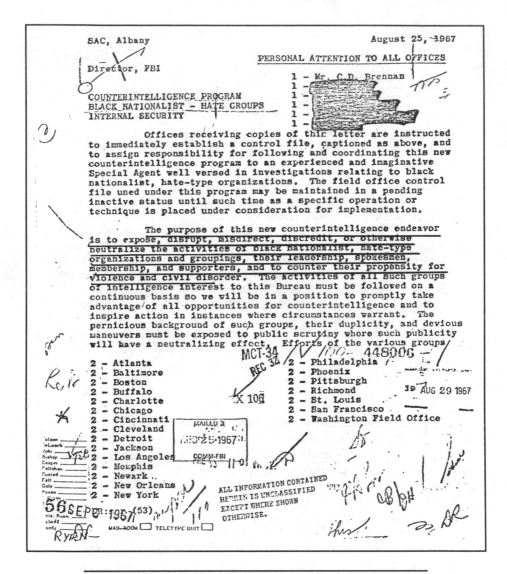

SAC, Albany   August 25, 1967

                        PERSONAL ATTENTION TO ALL OFFICES

Director, FBI   1 - Mr. C.D. Brennan
                                       1 -
COUNTERINTELLIGENCE PROGRAM   1 -
BLACK NATIONALIST - HATE GROUPS   1 -
INTERNAL SECURITY   1 -
                                       1 -
          Offices receiving copies of this letter are instructed
to immediately establish a control file, captioned as above, and
to assign responsibility for following and coordinating this new
counterintelligence program to an experienced and imaginative
Special Agent well versed in investigations relating to black
nationalist, hate-type organizations. The field office control
file used under this program may be maintained in a pending
inactive status until such time as a specific operation or
technique is placed under consideration for implementation.

          The purpose of this new counterintelligence endeavor
is to expose, disrupt, misdirect, discredit, or otherwise
neutralize the activities of black nationalist, hate-type
organizations and groupings, their leadership, spokesmen,
membership, and supporters, and to counter their propensity for
violence and civil disorder. The activities of all such groups
of intelligence interest to this Bureau must be followed on a
continuous basis so we will be in a position to promptly take
advantage of all opportunities for counterintelligence and to
inspire action in instances where circumstances warrant. The
pernicious background of such groups, their duplicity, and devious
maneuvers must be exposed to public scrutiny where such publicity
will have a neutralizing effect. Efforts of the various groups

2 - Atlanta   2 - Philadelphia
2 - Baltimore   2 - Phoenix
2 - Boston   2 - Pittsburgh
2 - Buffalo   2 - Richmond
2 - Charlotte   2 - St. Louis
2 - Chicago   2 - San Francisco
2 - Cincinnati   2 - Washington Field Office
2 - Cleveland
2 - Detroit
2 - Jackson
2 - Los Angeles
2 - Memphis
2 - Newark
2 - New Orleans
2 - New York

ALL INFORMATION CONTAINED
HEREIN IS UNCLASSIFIED
EXCEPT WHERE SHOWN
OTHERWISE.

Memo initiating COINTELPRO – Black Liberation Movement

It was into this disturbed atmosphere, further disturbed by the painful experiences of black soldiers during the [World War I] mobilization, that a new generation of radical black spokesmen, calling themselves "the New Negro" stepped...Buoyed by a wide array of spirited newspapers and militant journals that helped shape the black community's political consciousness, the New Negro radicals represented a new and startling breed...[offering] radical, some might even say revolutionary, prescriptions for overturning the status quo of white supremacy.[3]

Letter to SAC, Albany
RE: COUNTERINTELLIGENCE PROGRAM
     BLACK NATIONALIST – HATE GROUPS

to consolidate their forces or to recruit new or youthful
adherents must be frustrated. No opportunity should be missed
to exploit through counterintelligence techniques the
organizational and personal conflicts of the leaderships of the
groups and where possible an effort should be made to capitalize
upon existing conflicts between competing black nationalist
organizations. When an opportunity is apparent to disrupt or
neutralize black nationalist, hate-type organizations through the
cooperation of established local news media contacts or through
such contact with sources available to the Seat of Government,
in every instance careful attention must be given to the proposal
to insure the targeted group is disrupted, ridiculed, or
discredited through the publicity and not merely publicized.
Consideration should be given to techniques to preclude violence-
prone or rabble-rouser leaders of hate groups from spreading their
philosophy publicly or through various mass communication media.

         Many individuals currently active in black nationalist
organizations have backgrounds of immorality, subversive activity,
and criminal records. Through your investigation of key agitators,
you should endeavor to establish their unsavory backgrounds.
Be alert to determine evidence of misappropriation of funds or
other types of personal misconduct on the part of militant
nationalist leaders so any practical or warranted counterintelligence may be instituted.

         Intensified attention under this program should be
afforded to the activities of such groups as the Student
Nonviolent Coordinating Committee, the Southern Christian
Leadership Conference, Revolutionary Action Movement, the
Deacons for Defense and Justice, Congress of Racial Equality,
and the Nation of Islam. Particular emphasis should be given to
extremists who direct the activities and policies of
revolutionary or militant groups such as Stokely Carmichael,
H. "Rap" Brown, Elijah Muhammad, and Maxwell Stanford.

         At this time the Bureau is setting up no requirement
for status letters to be periodically submitted under this
program. It will be incumbent upon you to insure the program
is being afforded necessary and continuing attention and that
no opportunities will be overlooked for counterintelligence
action.

         This program should not be confused with the program
entitled "Communist Party, USA, Counterintelligence Program,
Internal Security – C," (Bufile 100-3-104), which is directed

                          -2-

Development of this "new racial awareness on the part of blacks led to a sharp increase in the number of lynchings after 1917 – seventy-six blacks were lynched in 1919 alone – and the simultaneous unprecedented wave of violent racial clashes, culminating in the summer of 1919 (known as 'Red Summer'), that must be seen largely as the attempt by whites to restore the racial *status quo ante*...In trying to contain the movement, the U.S. government chose to respond by launching a massive surveillance campaign to counter the influence of black leaders. Spear-headed by the Justice Department's Bureau of Investigation, forerunner of the

Federal Bureau of Investigation, the intelligence services tended to view the newly awakened black militancy through the tinted prism of the Red Scare (*i.e.*, as an off-shoot of communist agitation), leading them to adopt against blacks many of the same repressive measures employed against so-called subversives...What the official evidence now discloses is the apprehension by authorities of a parallel 'Black Scare.'"[4]

In this regard, Marcus Garvey and his Universal Negro Improvement Association (UNIA) were a primary target. When the FBI was able, after five solid years of intensive effort, to arrange for Garvey's indictment and subsequent conviction on extremely dubious "fraud" charges, "he was jailed without even one day to arrange for UNIA's future." Instead, he was surrounded by "heavily armed federal agents who conducted him to the Tombs prison [in New York City], from which he was taken [straight] to the Atlanta Federal Penitentiary in February 1925," as if he were a public menace rather than – at worst – the perpetrator of an offense devoid of physical violence.[5] As a result:

> By the summer of 1926 [UNIA] was no longer a coordinated unit, even though it still had hundreds of thousands of members, perhaps a million. The official Universal Negro Improvement Association was still there, and there was one last gigantic international convention in 1929, but the organization was no longer what it had been before Garvey entered prison.[6]

Nor was Garvey alone in being accorded "special attention" by the Bureau. For instance, during the massive railroad strikes in the 1920s, the FBI – as part of its much broader anti-labor and anti-black endeavors – went out of its way to topple A. Philip Randolph, black head of the Brotherhood of Sleeping Car Porters Union.[7] At about the same time, Hoover's agents initiated a "close surveillance" (a term usually associated with infiltration) of W.E.B. DuBois' National Association for the Advancement of Colored People (NAACP) in the name of knowing "what every radical organization in the country was doing."[8] The monitoring continued throughout the 1920s and '30s although it was not until 1940 that Hoover offered a definition of what the FBI meant by the term "subversive activities" with which he "justified" such activities. It included:

> [T]he holding of office in...Communist groups; the distribution of literature and propaganda favorable to a foreign power and opposed to the American way of life; agitators who are adherents of foreign ideologies who have for their purpose the stirring of internal strike [*sic*], class hatreds and the development of activities which in time of war would be a serious handicap in a program of internal security and national defense.[9]

This bald assertion of the political interests of the status quo was utilized as the rationale by which to step up investigation of possible CP "contamination and manipulation of the NAACP," a process which was "continued for twenty-five years despite FBI's failing to uncover any evidence of subversive domination of the [black organization]."[10]

> The [escalated] FBI investigation of the NAACP, begun in 1941, continued until 1966. Although the FBI prepared massive reports on the NAACP, including information on the group's political and legislative plans, the Bureau never uncovered any evidence of subversive domination or sympathies. In 1957, the New York field office of the FBI prepared a 137-page report on NAACP activities during the previous year, based on information supplied by 151 informers or confidential sources. From 1946 to 1960, the FBI used about three thousand wiretaps and over eight hundred "bugs," and obtained membership and financial records of [such] dissident groups.[11]

Notwithstanding its tangible lack of success in linking the NAACP to the CP or any other "foreign dominated" organization, the FBI lobbied to have it included among the groups covered by the Communist Control Act of 1954, and a cluster of corresponding state laws.[12] Only a series of Supreme Court decisions prevented the entire NAACP membership from being forced to register as "subversives," or going to prison for refusing to do so.[13] Meanwhile, the Bureau also began to focus its attention upon the recently-formed Southern Christian Leadership Conference (SCLC), an entirely reformist and philosophically nonviolent black civil rights advocacy organization established in 1957 by the Reverend Dr. Martin Luther King, Jr., and "several dozen other southern black ministers."[14]

The FBI and Martin Luther King

The stated objective of the SCLC, and the nature of its practical activities, was to organize for the securing of black voting rights across the rural South, with an eye toward the ultimate dismantlement of at least the most blatant aspects of the southern U.S. system of "segregation" (apartheid). Even this seemingly innocuous agenda was, however, seen as a threat by the FBI. In mid-September of 1957, FBI supervisor J.G. Kelly forwarded a newspaper clipping describing the formation of the SCLC to the Bureau's Atlanta field office – that city being the location of SCLC headquarters – informing local agents, for reasons which were never specified, the civil rights group was "a likely target for communist infiltration," and that "in view of the stated purpose of the organization you should remain alert for public source information concerning it in connection with the racial situation."[15]

The Atlanta field office "looked into" the matter and ultimately opened a COMINFIL investigation of the SCLC, apparently based on the fact that a single SWP member, Lonnie Cross, had offered his services as a clerk in the organization's main office.[16] By the end of the first year of FBI scrutiny, in September of 1958, a personal file had been opened on King himself, ostensibly because he had been approached on the steps of a Harlem church in which he'd delivered a guest sermon by black CP member Benjamin J. Davis.[17] By October 1960, as the SCLC call for desegregation and black voting rights in the south gained increasing attention and support across the nation, the Bureau began actively infiltrating organizational meetings and conferences.[18] In less than a year, by July of 1961 FBI intelligence on the group was detailed enough to recount that King had been affiliated with the Progressive Party in 1948 (while an undergraduate at Atlanta's Morehouse College), and that executive director Wyatt Tee Walker had once subscribed to a CP newspaper, *The Worker*.[19] Actual counterintelligence operations against King and the SCLC more generally seem to have begun with a January 8, 1962 letter from Hoover to Attorney General Robert F. Kennedy, contending that the civil rights leader enjoyed a "close relationship" with Stanley D. Levison, "a member of the Communist Party, USA," and that Isadore Wofsy, "a high ranking communist leader," had written a speech for King.[20]

On the night of March 15-16, 1962, FBI agents secretly broke into Levison's New York office and planted a bug; a wiretap of his office phone followed on March 20.[21] Among the other things picked up by this ELSURS surveillance was information that Jack O'Dell, who also had an alleged "record of ties to the Communist party," had been recommended by both King and Levison to serve as an assistant to Wyatt Tee Walker.[22] Although none of these supposed communist affiliations were ever substantiated, it was on this basis that SCLC was targeted within the Bureau's ongoing COINTELPRO-CP,USA, beginning with the planting of five disinformational "news stories" concerning the organization's "communist connections" on October 24, 1962.[23] By this point, Martin Luther King's name had been placed in Section A of the FBI Reserve Index, one step below those individuals registered in the Security Index and scheduled to be rounded up and "preventively detained" in concentration camps in the event of a declared national emergency;[24] Attorney General Kennedy had also authorized round-the-clock ELSURS surveillance of all SCLC offices, as well as King's home.[25] Hence, by November 8, 1963, comprehensive telephone taps had been installed at all organizational offices, and King's residence.[26]

The reasons for this covert but steadily mounting attention to the Reverend Dr. King were posited in an internal monograph on the subject prepared by FBI counterintelligence specialist Charles D. Brennan at the behest of COINTELPRO head William C. Sullivan in September 1963. In this 11-page document, Brennan found that, given the scope of support it had attracted over the preceding five years, civil rights agitation represented a clear threat to "the established order" of the U.S., and that "King is growing in stature daily as the leader among leaders of the Negro movement...so goes Martin Luther King, and also so goes the Negro movement in the United States."[27] This accorded well with Sullivan's own view, committed to writing shortly after King's landmark "I Have a Dream" speech during the massive civil rights demonstration in Washington, D.C., on August 28 of the same year:

> We must mark [King] now, if we have not before, as the most dangerous Negro in the future of this Nation from the standpoint of communism, the Negro, and

national security...it may be unrealistic to limit [our actions against King] to legalistic proofs that would stand up in court or before Congressional Committees.[28]

By 1964, King was not only firmly established as a preeminent civil rights leader, but was beginning to show signs of pursuing a more fundamental structural agenda of social change. Correspondingly, as the text of the accompanying memo from Sullivan to Joseph A. Sizoo makes plain, the Bureau's intent had crystallized into an unvarnished intervention into the domestic political process, with the goal of bringing about King's replacement with someone "acceptable" to the FBI. The means employed in the attempt to accomplish this centered in continued efforts to discredit King, maintaining a drumbeat of mass media-distributed propaganda concerning his supposed "communist influences" and sexual proclivities, as well as the triggering of a spate of harassment by the Internal Revenue Service (IRS).[29] When this strategy failed to the extent that it was announced on October 14 of that year that King would receive a Nobel Peace Prize as a reward for his work in behalf of the rights of American blacks, the Bureau – exhibiting a certain sense of desperation by this juncture – dramatically escalated its efforts to neutralize him.

Two days after announcement of the impending award, Sullivan caused a composite audio tape to be produced, supposedly consisting of "highlights" taken from the taps of King's phones and bugs placed in his various hotel rooms over the preceding two years. The result, prepared by FBI audio technician John Matter, purported to demonstrate the civil rights leader had engaged in a series of "orgiastic" trysts with prostitutes and, thus, "the depths of his sexual perversion and depravity." The finished tape was packaged, along with the accompanying anonymous letter (prepared on unwatermarked paper by Bureau Internal Security Supervisor Seymore F. Phillips on Sullivan's instruction), informing King that the audio material would be released to the media unless he committed suicide prior to bestowal of the Nobel Prize. Sullivan then instructed veteran COINTELPRO operative Lish Whitson to fly to Miami with the package; once there, Whitson was instructed to address the parcel and mail it to the intended victim.[30]

When King failed to comply with Sullivan's anonymous directive that he kill himself, FBI Associate Director Cartha D. "Deke" DeLoach attempted to follow through with the threat to make the contents of the doctored tape public:

> The Bureau Crime Records Division, headed by DeLoach, initiated a major campaign to let newsmen know just what the Bureau [claimed to have] on King. DeLoach personally offered a copy of the King surveillance transcript to *Newsweek* Washington bureau chief Benjamin Bradlee. Bradlee refused it, and mentioned the approach to a *Newsday* colleague, Jay Iselin.[31]

Bradlee's disclosure of what the FBI was up to served to curtail the effectiveness of DeLoach's operation, and Bureau propagandists consequently found relatively few takers on this particular "story." More, in the face of a planned investigation of

Date: December 1, 1964

To: Mr. W. C. Sullivan

From: J. A. Sizoo

Subject: MARTIN LUTHER KING, JR.

Reference is made to the attached memorandum DeLoach to Mohr dated 11/27/64 concerning DeLoach's interview with ▓▓▓▓ ▓▓▓▓▓ and to your informal memo, also attached.

▓▓▓▓▓▓▓▓ stated to DeLoach that he was faced with the difficult problem of taking steps to remove King from the national picture. He indicates in his comments a lack of confidence that he, alone, could be successful. It is, therefore, suggested that consideration be given to the following course of action:

That DeLoach have a further discussion with ▓▓▓▓▓ and offer to be helpful to ▓▓▓▓ in connection with the problem of the removal of King from the national scene;

That DeLoach suggest that ▓▓▓▓▓▓ might desire to call a meeting of Negro leaders in the country which might include, for instance, 2 or 3 top leaders in the civil rights movement such as James Farmer and A. Philip Randolph; 2 or 3 top Negro judges such as Judge Parsons and Judge Hasty; 2 or 3 top reputable ministers such as Robert Johnson, Moderator of the Washington City Presbytery; 2 or 3 other selected Negro officials from public life such as the Negro Attorney General from one of the New England states. These men could be called for the purpose of learning the facts as to the Bureau's performance in the fulfillment of its responsibilities under the Civil Rights statute, and this could well be done at such a meeting. In addition, the Bureau, on a highly confidential basis, could brief such a group on the security background of King ▓▓▓▓▓▓▓▓▓▓▓▓▓▓▓▓▓▓ The use of a tape, such as contemplated in your memorandum, together with a transcript for convenience in following the tape, should be most convincing.

The inclusion of U.S. Government officials, such as Carl Rowen or Ralph Bunche, is not suggested as they might feel a duty to advise the White House of such a contemplated meeting. It is believed this would give us an opportunity to outline to a group of influential Negro leaders what our record in the enforcement of civil rights has been. It would also give them, on a confidential basis, information concerning King which would convince them of the danger of King to the over-all civil rights movement. ▓▓▓▓▓ is already well aware of this. This group should include such leadership as would be capable of removing King from the scene if they, of their own volition, decided this was the thing to do after such a briefing. The group should include strong enough men to control a man like James Farmer and make him see the light of day. This might have the effect of increasing the stature of ▓▓▓ ▓▓▓▓▓ who is a capable person and is ambitious.

There are refinements which, of course, could be added to the above which is set forth in outline form for possible consideration.

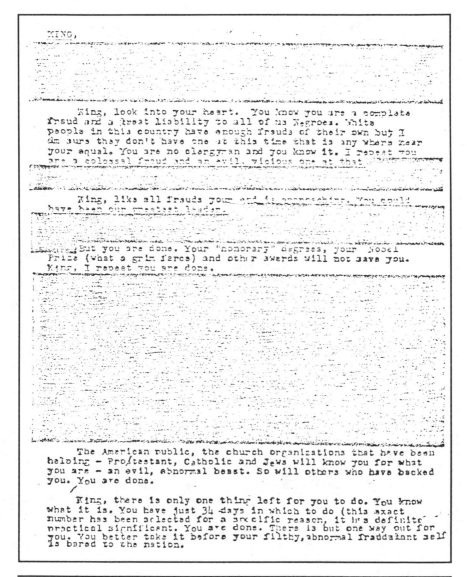

KING,

King, look into your heart. You know you are a complete fraud and a great liability to all of us Negroes. White people in this country have enough frauds of their own but I am sure they don't have one at this time that is any where near your equal. You are no clergyman and you know it. I repeat you are a colossal fraud and an evil, vicious one at that.

King, like all frauds your end is approaching. You could have been our greatest leader.

But you are done. Your "honorary" degrees, your Nobel Prize (what a grim farce) and other awards will not save you. King, I repeat you are done.

The American public, the church organizations that have been helping - Protestant, Catholic and Jews will know you for what you are - an evil, abnormal beast. So will others who have backed you. You are done.

King, there is only one thing left for you to do. You know what it is. You have just 34 days in which to do (this exact number has been selected for a specific reason, it has definite practical significant. You are done. There is but one way out for you. You better take it before your filthy, abnormal fraudulent self is bared to the nation.

Memo (left) proposing the sending of an anonymous letter (above) to Martin Luther King in an unsuccessful attempt to convince him to commit suicide.

electronic surveillance by government agencies announced by Democratic Missouri Senator Edward V. Long, J. Edgar Hoover was forced to order the rapid dismantling of the ELSURS coverage of both King and the SCLC, drying up much of the source material upon which Sullivan and his COINTELPRO specialists depended for "authenticity." Hoover's "weakness" on this matter appears to have infuriated Sulli-

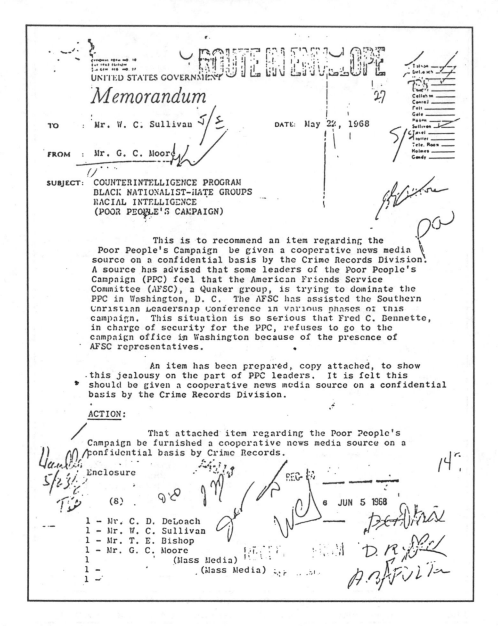

van, who seems to have felt that congress should simply have been defied, setting in place a permanent rift between the two senior FBI officials.[33]

Still, the Bureau's counterintelligence operations against King continued apace, right up to the moment of the target's death by sniper fire on a Memphis hotel balcony on April 14, 1968.[34] Indeed, as the accompanying memo from Sullivan to George C. Moore (head of the Bureau's "racial intelligence" squad) on May 22 of the

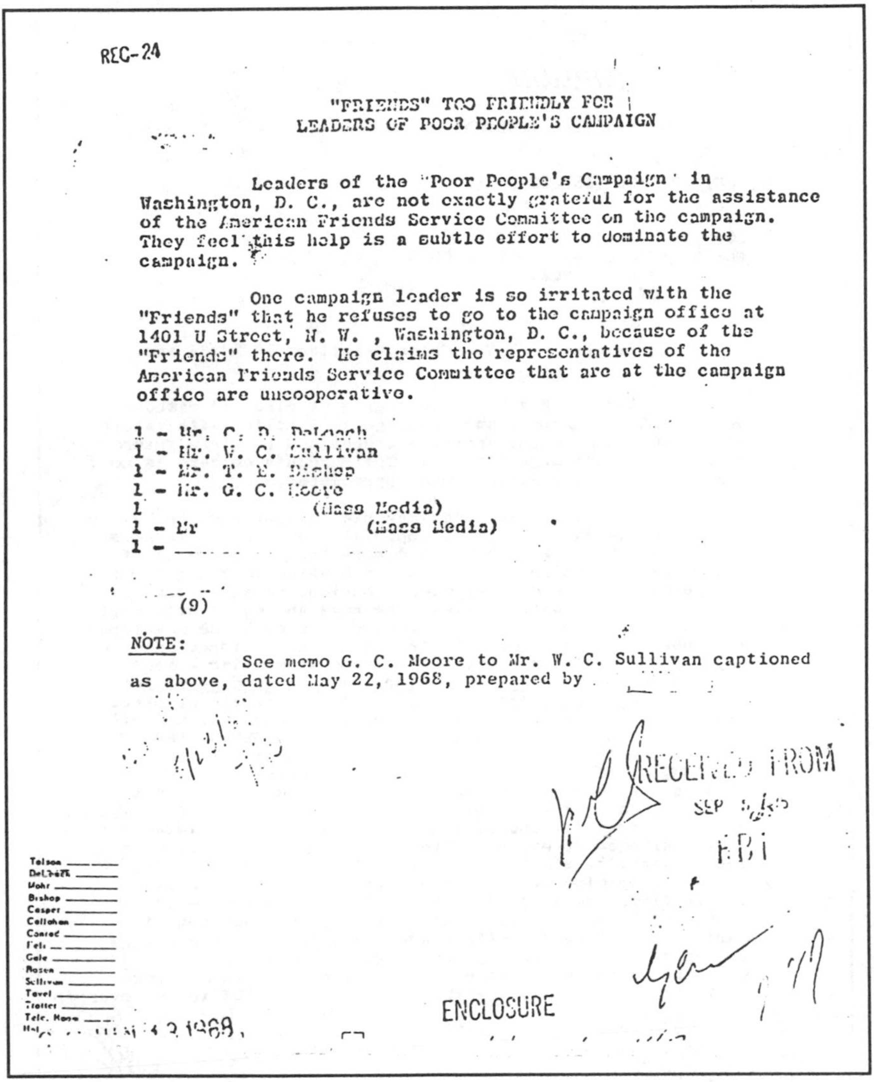

REC-24

"FRIENDS" TOO FRIENDLY FOR
LEADERS OF POOR PEOPLE'S CAMPAIGN

Leaders of the "Poor People's Campaign" in
Washington, D. C., are not exactly grateful for the assistance
of the American Friends Service Committee on the campaign.
They feel this help is a subtle effort to dominate the
campaign.

One campaign leader is so irritated with the
"Friends" that he refuses to go to the campaign office at
1401 U Street, N. W. , Washington, D. C., because of the
"Friends" there. He claims the representatives of the
American Friends Service Committee that are at the campaign
office are uncooperative.

1 - Mr. C. D. DeLoach
1 - Mr. W. C. Sullivan
1 - Mr. T. E. Bishop
1 - Mr. G. C. Moore
1   (Mass Media)
1 - Mr   (Mass Media)
1 - _____

(9)

NOTE:
        See memo G. C. Moore to Mr. W. C. Sullivan captioned
as above, dated May 22, 1968, prepared by _____

RECEIVED FROM
SEP ___
FBI

Tolson _____
DeLoach _____
Mohr _____
Bishop _____
Casper _____
Callahan _____
Conrad _____
Felt _____
Gale _____
Rosen _____
Sullivan _____
Tavel _____
Trotter _____
Tele. Room _____
Holmes _____   2 1969

ENCLOSURE

**Memo (left) proposing anonymous letter to disrupt the Poor People's Campaign.
Text of letter appears above.**

---

same year amply demonstrates, certain of King's projects – such as the Poor People's
Campaign – remained the focus of active COINTELPRO endeavors even after their
leader's assassination. By 1969, as has been noted elsewhere, "[FBI] efforts to
"'expose' Martin Luther King, Jr., had not slackened even though King had been
dead for a year. [The Bureau] furnished ammunition to conservatives to attack
King's memory, and...tried to block efforts to honor the slain leader."[35]

UNITED STATES OVERNMENT

Memorandum

TO : DIRECTOR, FBI (100-448006)   DATE: 1/22/69

FROM : SAC, CHICAGO (157-2209) (P)

SUBJECT: COUNTERINTELLIGENCE PROGRAM
BLACK NATIONALIST - HATE GROUPS
RACIAL INTELLIGENCE
(NATION OF ISLAM)

Reurlet, 1/7/69; Chicago letters 12/24/68 and 1/14/69.

ReBulet has been thoroughly studied and discussed by the SAC, the Supervisor, and Agents familiar with facets of the NOI which might indicate trends and possible future direction of the organization. The Bureau's concern is most understandable and suggestions appreciated.

Over the years considerable thought has been given, and action taken with Bureau approval, relating to methods through which the NOI could be discredited in the eyes of the general black populace or through which factionalism among the leadership could be created. Serious consideration has also been given towards developing ways and means of changing NOI philosophy to one whereby the members could be developed into useful citizens and the organization developed into one emphasizing religion - the brotherhood of mankind - and self improvement. Factional disputes have been developed - the most noteable being MALCOLM X LITTLE. Prominent black personages have publicly and nationally spoken out against the group - U.S. District Court Judge JAMES BENTON PARSONS being one example. The media of the press has played down the NOI. This appears to be a most effective tool as individuals such as MUHAMMAD assuredly seek any and all publicity be it good or bad; however, if the press is utilized it would appear it should not concentrate on such aspects as the alleged strength of the NOI, immoral activities of the leadership, misuse of funds by these officials, etc. It is the opinion of this office that such exposure is ineffective, possibly creates interest and maybe envy among the lesser educated black man causing them out of curiosity to attend meetings and maybe join, and encourage the opportunist to seek personal gain - physical or monetary - through alignment with the group. At any rate it is felt such publicity in the case of the NOI is not overly effective.

2 - Bureau (RM)
1 - Chicago
JRS:bab   *Buy U.S. Savings Bonds Regularly on the Payroll Savings Plan*
(3)

Memo taking credit for the assassination of Malcolm X, killed in an FBI-provoked factional dispute on February 14, 1965.

King and the SCLC were, of course, hardly the only objects of the Bureau's *de facto* COINTELPRO against the emerging black liberation movement during this period. As Manning Marable has pointed out, the FBI also went after the Student

Nonviolent Coordinating Committee (SNCC), an affiliated but rather more radical civil rights organization than the SCLC, very early on: "In late 1960, FBI agents began to monitor SNCC meetings. [President Lyndon] Johnson's Attorney General, Nicholas Katzenbach, gave approval for the FBI to wiretap all SNCC leaders' phones in 1965...Hoover ordered the extensive infiltration and disruption of SNCC."[36] Another instance concerns the Nation of Islam (NoI) or "Black Muslim" movement headed by Elijah Muhammad (s/n: Elijah Poole):

> The Bureau began wiretap surveillance of Elija Muhammed's [sic] Chicago residence in 1957...on the grounds that members of the NoI "disavow allegiance to the United States" and "are taught not to obey the laws of the United States"...When Elija Muhammed bought a winter home in Arizona in 1961, a wiretap and microphone were installed there. Both forms of surveillance continued for years...[The FBI] played assorted COINTEL tricks on the organization as early as the late 1950s.[37]

As was documented in Chapter 3, when Malcolm X, one of Elijah Muhammad's principle lieutenants, broke away from the NoI in March of 1964 to establish a separate church, the Muslim Mosque, Inc., and a consciously political black organization, the Organization of Afro-American Unity (OAAU), the Bureau undertook concerted COINTELPRO actions to block the development of alliances between the OAAU and white radical organizations such as the SWP. By the point of Malcolm's assassination during a speech in Harlem on the night of February 14, 1965, the FBI had compiled at least 2,300 pages of material on the victim in just one of its files on him, the NoI and the OAAU.[38] Malcolm X was supposedly murdered by former colleagues in the NoI as a result of the faction-fighting which had led to his splitting away from that movement, and their "natural wrath" at his establishment of a competing entity. However, as the accompanying January 22, 1969 memo from the SAC, Chicago, to the Director makes clear, the NoI factionalism at issue didn't "just happen." Rather, it had "been developed" by deliberate Bureau actions – through infiltration and the "sparking of acrimonious debates within the organization," rumor-mongering, and other tactics designed to foster internal disputes – which were always the standard fare of COINTELPRO.[39] The Chicago SAC, Marlin Johnson, who would shortly oversee the assassinations of Illinois Black Panther Party leaders Fred Hampton and Mark Clark, makes it quite obvious that he views the murder of Malcolm X as something of a model for "successful" counterintelligence operations.

Nor was it necessary for black spokespersons to be heading or forming political organizations in order to be targeted for elimination by the FBI's "informal" counterintelligence methods. As the accompanying May 15, 1968 memo from Director Hoover to the Chicago SAC reveals, even independent activists such as the writer/comedian Dick Gregory came in for potentially lethal treatment. In Gregory's case, these assumed the form – à la COINTELPRO–CP,USA's Operation Hoodwink (see Chapter 2) – of attempting to provoke "La Cosa Nostra" into dispensing with him. A considerable body of circumstantial evidence suggests – although docu-

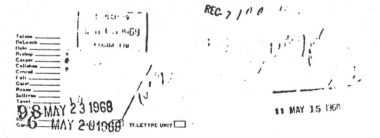

ROUTE IN ENVELOPE

SAC, Chicago

Director, FBI (100-448006)

May 15, 1968

1 —

1 —

PERSONAL ATTENTION

COUNTERINTELLIGENCE PROGRAM
BLACK NATIONALIST — HATE GROUPS
RACIAL INTELLIGENCE
(RICHARD CLAXTON GREGORY)

ReBulet 4/23/68.

Chicago airtel and LHM dated 5/2/68 and captioned "Richard Claxton Gregory" concern a speech by Gregory on 4/28/68 where he noted that "Syndicate hoods (are living all over. They are the filthiest snakes that exist on this earth." Referenced Bulet instructed you to develop counterintelligence action concerning militant black nationalist Dick Gregory.

Consider the use of this statement in developing a counterintelligence operation to alert La Cosa Nostra (LCN) to Gregory's attack on LCN. It is noted that other speeches by Gregory also contain attacks on the LCN. No counterintelligence action should be taken without Bureau authority.

TJD:pag/mrm
(5)

NOTE:

Teletype from New Orleans to Director, 5/30/68, captioned "Richard Claxton Gregory" reported speech by Gregory referring to the Director and FBI Agents in derogatory terms. The Director noted, on the informative note of 5/1 teletype which said we would recommend counterintelligence action against Gregory when indicated, "Right."

REC 7 100

Tolson
DeLoach
Mohr
Bishop
Casper
Callahan
Conrad
Felt
Gale
Rosen
Sullivan
Tavel

MAY 23 1968

MAY 20 1968   TELETYPE UNIT ☐

11 MAY 15 1968

Proposal to provoke the murder of comedian/activist Dick Gregory by "La Cosa Nostra" à la COINTELPRO – CP,USA's Operation Hoodwink.

---

ments have yet to be released – that the Bureau undertook comparably Machiavellian efforts to achieve the neutralization of a number of other black leaders during the late 1960s and early 1970s. These ranged from the Reverend Ralph Abernathy (King's replacement in SCLC) to Georgia Senator Julian Bond.

The War Against Black Liberation

As the 1960s unfolded, the true extent of official resistance to even the most moderate improvements in the status of blacks – and concomitant alterations in the balance of social, economic and political power in the U.S. – became increasingly apparent. This recalcitrance on the part of the *status quo* was signified but hardly encompassed by the repressive activities of the FBI *vis à vis* figures such as King. This official posture gave rise to a spiral of frustration on the part of those whose objectives had initially been merely the obtaining of such elemental rights as the ballot, equal pay for equal work, use of public facilities and the like. In turn, this frustration both led to broad acceptance of increasingly radical analyses of U.S. society on the part of black activists and theorists. By the mid-60s, the primacy of those such as King who had developed a mass following on the basis of appeals for "equal rights" was being rapidly supplanted by that of younger leaders such as SNCC's Stokely Carmichael and H. Rap Brown, who espoused a much more militant vision of "black power."[40]

At the same time, not only conscious black power adherents, but the black community as a whole, showed increasing signs of abandoning the posture of "principled nonviolence" which had all along marked the SCLC performance. This was manifested not only in Carmichael's and Brown's oversight of a change in SNCC's name from Student Nonviolent Coordinating Committee to Student *National* Coordinating Committee, but much more concretely, "in the streets."[41] This corresponded with the rise of a generalized perception among blacks that, far from being restricted to the former Confederate states of the "Old South," the problems they confronted were fully national in scope:

> Even before the assassination of Malcolm, many social critics sensed that non-violent direct action, a tactic of protest used effectively in the South, would have little appeal in the Northern ghetto. Far more likely were a series of urban social upheavals which could not be controlled or channeled by the civil rights leadership...In the spring and summer months of 1964, 1965, 1966, 1967 and 1968, massive black rebellions swept across almost every major US city in the Northeast, Middle West and California. In Watts and Compton, the black districts of Los Angeles, black men and women took to the streets, attacking and burning white-owned property and institutions. The [1965] Watts rebellion left $40 million in private property damage and 34 persons killed. Federal authorities ordered 15,000 state police and National Guardsmen into Detroit to quell that city's uprising of 1967. In Detroit 43 residents were killed; almost 2,000 were injured; 2,700 white-owned businesses were broken into, and 50 per cent of these were gutted by fire or completely destroyed; fourteen square miles of Detroit's inner city were torched; 5,000 black persons were left without homes. Combining the total weight of socio-economic destruction, the ghetto rebellions from 1964 to 1972 led to 250 deaths, 10,000 serious injuries, and 60,000 arrests, at a cost of police, troops, and other coercive measures taken by the state and losses to business in the billions of dollars.[42]

Given this, it is fair to say that, by 1967 at the latest, black Americans were in a state of open insurgency against the Euroamerican society to whose interests they had all along been subordinated. Established order in the U.S. was thereby confronted with its most serious internal challenge since the period of the First World War. The response of the *status quo* was essentially twofold. On the one hand, the government moved to defuse the situation through a series of cooptive gestures designed to make it appear that things were finally changing for the better. The executive branch, under President Lyndon B. Johnson, declared "war on poverty" and launched a series of tokenistic and soon to be forgotten programs such as "Project Build."[43] Congress cooperated in this exercise in damage control by quickly enacting bits of legislation like the Voting Rights Act of 1965 and revision of the Civil Rights Act in 1968, structured in such a way as to convey a superficial impression of "progress" to disgruntled blacks while leaving fundamental social relations very much intact.[44]

On the other hand, key government figures were astute enough to perceive that the ghetto rebellions were largely spontaneous and uncoordinated outpourings of black rage. Costly as the ghetto revolts were, real danger to the *status quo* would come only when a black organizational leadership appeared with the capacity to harness and direct the force of such anger. If this occurred, it was recognized, mere gestures would be insufficient to contain black pressure for social justice. Already, activist concepts and rhetoric had shifted from demands for black power within American society to black liberation from U.S. "internal colonialism."[45] The task thus presented in completing the federal counterinsurgency strategy was to destroy such community-based black leadership before it had an opportunity to consolidate itself and instill a vision of real freedom among the great mass of blacks. In this, of course, the FBI assumed a central role. President Johnson publicly announced, in the wake of the 1967 uprisings in Detroit and Newark, that he had issued "standing instructions" that the Bureau should bring "the instigators" of such "riots" to heel, by any means at its disposal,[46] while his attorney general, Ramsey Clark, instructed Hoover by memo to:

> [U]se the [FBI's] maximum resources, investigative and intelligence, to collect and report all facts bearing upon the question as to whether there has been or is a scheme or conspiracy by any group of whatever size, effectiveness or affiliation to plan, promote or aggravate riot activity.[47]

The attorney general's memo further suggested the FBI expand or establish "sources or informants" within "black nationalist organizations" such as SNCC, the Congress of Racial Equality (CORE) and "other less publicized groups" in order to "determine the size and purpose of these groups and their relationship to other groups, and also to determine the whereabouts of persons who might be involved" in their activities.[48] As was shown at the outset of this chapter, Hoover responded by launching a formal anti-black liberation COINTELPRO in August 1967. By early 1968, as the accompanying Airtel from G.C. Moore to William C. Sullivan demonstrates, the counterintelligence operation was not only in full swing across the

UNITED STATES GOVERNMENT

Memorandum

TO : Mr. W. C. Sullivan

FROM : G. C. Moore

SUBJECT: COUNTERINTELLIGENCE PROGRAM
BLACK NATIONALIST-HATE GROUPS
RACIAL INTELLIGENCE

DATE: February 29, 1968

1 - Mr. C. D. DeLoach
1 - Mr. W. C. Sullivan
1 - Mr. G. C. Moore
1 -
1 -

PURPOSE:

To expand the Counterintelligence Program designed to neutralize militant black nationalist groups from 23 to 41 field divisions so as to cover the great majority of black nationalist activity in this country.

BACKGROUND:

By letter dated August 25, 1967, 23 field offices were advised of a new Counterintelligence Program designed to neutralize militant black nationalists and prevent violence on their part. Goals of this program are to prevent the coalition of militant black nationalist groups, prevent the rise of a leader who might unify and electrify these violence-prone elements, prevent these militants from gaining respectability and prevent the growth of these groups among America's youth.

CURRENT DEVELOPMENTS:

In view of the tremendous increase in black nationalist activity, and the approach of summer, this program should be expanded and these goals should be reiterated to the field. Attached airtel also instructs the field to submit periodic progress letters to stimulate thinking in this area.

Attached airtel also reminds the field that counterintelligence suggestions to expose these militants or neutralize them must be approved by the Bureau.

ACTION:

6 MAR 11 1968

That attached airtel expanding this program, defining goals and instructing periodic progress letters be submitted be sent Albany and the other listed field offices.

Enclosure

TJD:rmm (6)

ALL INFORMATION CONTAINED
HEREIN IS UNCLASSIFIED
EXCEPT WHERE SHOWN
OTHERWISE.

Memorandum expanding COINTELPRO – Black Liberation Movement to fully National scope.

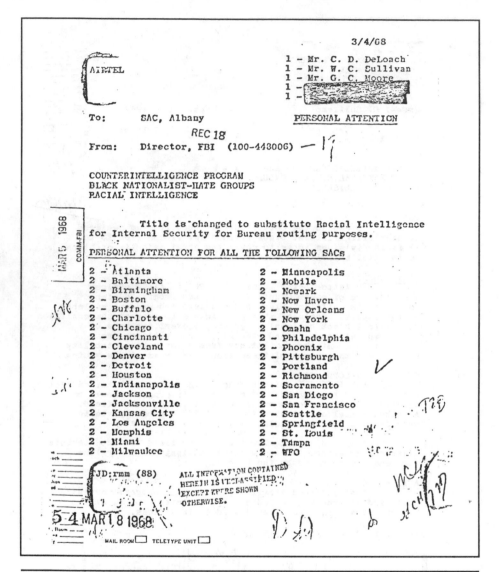

3/4/68

AIRTEL

1 - Mr. C. D. DeLoach
1 - Mr. W. C. Sullivan
1 - Mr. G. C. Moore
1 -
1 -

To: SAC, Albany   PERSONAL ATTENTION

REC 18

From: Director, FBI (100-443006) — 1?

COUNTERINTELLIGENCE PROGRAM
BLACK NATIONALIST-HATE GROUPS
RACIAL INTELLIGENCE

MAR 5 1968 COMM-FBI

          Title is changed to substitute Racial Intelligence
for Internal Security for Bureau routing purposes.

PERSONAL ATTENTION FOR ALL THE FOLLOWING SACs

2 - Atlanta   2 - Minneapolis
2 - Baltimore   2 - Mobile
2 - Birmingham   2 - Newark
2 - Boston   2 - New Haven
2 - Buffalo   2 - New Orleans
2 - Charlotte   2 - New York
2 - Chicago   2 - Omaha
2 - Cincinnati   2 - Philadelphia
2 - Cleveland   2 - Phoenix
2 - Denver   2 - Pittsburgh
2 - Detroit   2 - Portland
2 - Houston   2 - Richmond
2 - Indianapolis   2 - Sacramento
2 - Jackson   2 - San Diego
2 - Jacksonville   2 - San Francisco
2 - Kansas City   2 - Seattle
2 - Los Angeles   2 - Springfield
2 - Memphis   2 - St. Louis
2 - Miami   2 - Tampa
2 - Milwaukee   2 - WFO

JD:rmm (88)   ALL INFORMATION CONTAINED
                HEREIN IS UNCLASSIFIED
                EXCEPT WHERE SHOWN
                OTHERWISE.

5 4 MAR 8 1968

MAIL ROOM ☐   TELETYPE UNIT ☐

Airtel itemizing expanded list of FBI field offices participating in COINTELPRO – Black Liberation Movement. List of original participants and a description of this COINTELPRO's goals and targets appear as memo continues on the following pages.

country, but was being expanded from 23 to 41 cities. Both the initial and expanded lists of participating field offices are brought out in the accompanying March 4, 1968 memo from Hoover to the SAC, Albany, in which he shifts COINTELPRO-Black Liberation Movement from "Internal Security" to "Racial Intelligence" for purposes of internal Bureau classification, and describes the overall goals of the effort.

Airtel to SAC, Albany
RE: COUNTERINTELLIGENCE PROGRAM
BLACK NATIONALIST-HATE GROUPS

BACKGROUND

By letter dated 8/25/67 the following offices
were advised of the beginning of a Counterintelligence
Program against militant Black Nationalist-Hate Groups:

Albany	Memphis
Atlanta	Newark
Baltimore	New Orleans
Boston	New York
Buffalo	Philadelphia
Charlotte	Phoenix
Chicago	Pittsburgh
Cincinnati	Richmond
Cleveland	St. Louis
Detroit	San Francisco
Jackson	Washington Field
Los Angeles	

Each of the above offices was to designate a
Special Agent to coordinate this program. Replies to this
letter indicated an interest in counterintelligence against
militant black nationalist groups that foment violence and
several offices outlined procedures which had been effective
in the past. For example, Washington Field Office had
furnished information about a new Nation of Islam (NOI)
grade school to appropriate authorities in the District
of Columbia who investigated to determine if the school
conformed to District regulations for private schools. In
the process WFO obtained background information on the parents
of each pupil.

The Revolutionary Action Movement (RAM), a pro-
Chinese communist group, was active in Philadelphia, Pa.,
in the summer of 1967. The Philadelphia Office alerted
local police, who then put RAM leaders under close scrutiny.
They were arrested on every possible charge until they could
no longer make bail. As a result, RAM leaders spent most of the
summer in jail and no violence traceable to RAM took place.

The Counterintelligence Program is now being
expanded to include 41 offices. Each of the offices added
to this program should designate an Agent familiar with black

- 2 -

These last explicitly include the blocking of coalitions between radical black political organizations, the targeting of key leaders such as "Martin Luther King, Stokely Carmichael, and Elija Muhammed" for special attention by the Bureau, the "neutralizing" – by unspecified means – of both organizations and selected leaders, the undertaking of propaganda efforts to "discredit" targeted groups and individuals in order to deny them "respectability" within their own communities and, hence, "prevent the long-range growth of militant black nationalist organizations, especially among youth." Elsewhere, Hoover called upon his operatives to intervene directly in blocking free speech and access by black radicals to the media: "Consid-

Airtel to SAC, Albany
RE: COUNTERINTELLIGENCE PROGRAM
BLACK NATIONALIST-HATE GROUPS

nationalist activity, and interested in counterintelligence,
to coordinate this program. This Agent will be responsible
for the periodic progress letters being requested, but each
Agent working this type of case should participate in the
formulation of counterintelligence operations.

GOALS

       For maximum effectiveness of the Counterintelligence
Program, and to prevent wasted effort, long-range goals are
being set.

       1. Prevent the coalition of militant black
nationalist groups. In unity there is strength; a truism
that is no less valid for all its triteness. An effective
coalition of black nationalist groups might be the first
step toward a real "Mau Mau" in America, the beginning of
a true black revolution.

       2. Prevent the rise of a "messiah" who could
unify, and electrify, the militant black nationalist movement.
Malcolm X might have been such a "messiah;" he is the martyr
of the movement today. Martin Luther King, Stokely Carmichael
and Elijah Muhammad all aspire to this position. Elijah
Muhammad is less of a threat because of his age. King could
be a very real contender for this position should he abandon
his supposed "obedience" to "white, liberal doctrines"
(nonviolence) and embrace black nationalism. Carmichael
has the necessary charisma to be a real threat in this way.

       3. Prevent violence on the part of black
nationalist groups. This is of primary importance, and is,
of course, a goal of our investigative activity; it should
also be a goal of the Counterintelligence Program. Through
counterintelligence it should be possible to pinpoint potential
troublemakers and neutralize them before they exercise their
potential for violence.

       4. Prevent militant black nationalist groups and
leaders from gaining respectability, by discrediting them
to three separate segments of the community. The goal of
discrediting black nationalists must be handled tactically
in three ways. You must discredit these groups and
individuals to, first, the responsible Negro community.
Second, they must be discredited to the white community,

- 3 -

eration should be given to preclude [black] rabble-rouser leaders of these hate
groups from spreading their philosophy publicly or through the communications
media."[49]

Over the first year of its official anti-black COINTELPRO, the FBI developed a
network of some 4,000 members, assembled from what had previously been code-
named the TOPLEV ("**Top Level**" Black Community Leadership Program) BLACPRO
("**Black Program**") efforts as well as new recruits, called the "Ghetto Informant
Program."[50] It also used the information thus collected to go after the incipient black
liberation movement, hammer and tong:

Airtel to SAC, Albany
RE: COUNTERINTELLIGENCE PROGRAM
BLACK NATIONALIST-HATE GROUPS

both the responsible community and to "liberals" who have
vestiges of sympathy for militant black nationalist simply
because they are Negroes. Third, these groups must be
discredited in the eyes of Negro radicals, the followers
of the movement. This last area requires entirely different
tactics from the first two. Publicity about violent tendencies
and radical statements merely enhances black nationalists
to the last group; it adds "respectability" in a different
way.

     5. A final goal should be to prevent the long-
range growth of militant black nationalist organizations,
especially among youth. Specific tactics to prevent these
groups from converting young people must be developed.

     Besides these five goals counterintelligence is
a valuable part of our regular investigative program as it
often produces positive information.

TARGETS

     Primary targets of the Counterintelligence Program,
Black Nationalist-Hate Groups, should be the most violent
and radical groups and their leaders. We should emphasize
those leaders and organizations that are nationwide in scope
and are most capable of disrupting this country. These
targets should include the radical and violence-prone
leaders, members, and followers of the:

         Student Nonviolent Coordinating Committee (SNCC),
         Southern Christian Leadership Conference (SCLC),
         Revolutionary Action Movement (RAM),
         Nation of Islam (NOI)

     Offices handling these cases and those of Stokely
Carmichael of SNCC, H. Rap Brown of SNCC, Martin Luther King
of SCLC, Maxwell Stanford of RAM, and Elijah Muhammed of
NOI, should be alert for counterintelligence suggestions.

INSTRUCTIONS

     The effectiveness of counterintelligence depends
on the quality and quantity of positive information
available regarding the target and on the imagination and
initiative of Agents working the program. The response of
the field to the Counterintelligence Program against the
Communist Party, USA, indicates that a superb job can be
done by the field on counterintelligence.

     Counterintelligence operations must be approved
by the Bureau. Because of the nature of this program each
operation must be designed to protect the Bureau's interest
so that there is no possibility of embarrassment to the
Bureau. Beyond this the Bureau will give every possible
consideration to your proposals.

NOTE:
     See memorandum G. C. Moore to Mr. W. C. Sullivan
captioned as above dated 2/29/68, prepared by TJD:rmm.

In August 1967, FBI Director J. Edgar Hoover ordered the extensive infiltration and disruption of SNCC, as well as other...formations, such as the militant Revolutionary Action Movement, the Deacons of Defense, and CORE...FBI agents were sent to monitor [Stokely] Carmichael and [H. Rap] Brown wherever they went, seeking to elicit evidence to imprison them. Brown was charged with inciting a race riot in Maryland, and was eventually sentenced to five years in a federal penitentiary for carrying a rifle across state lines while under criminal indictment. [SNCC leader Ralph] Featherstone and...activist Ché Payne were murdered on 9 March 1970, when a bomb exploded in their automobile in Bel Air, Maryland. [SNCC leader Cleveland] Sellers was indicted for organizing black students in South Carolina and for [himself] resisting the draft.[51]

As has been noted elsewhere, "the FBI had between 5,000 and 10,000 active cases on matters of race at any given time nationwide. In 1967 some 1,246 FBI agents received...racial intelligence assignments each month. By [1968] the number had jumped to 1,678...Hoover [also ordered William Sullivan] to compile a more refined listing of 'vociferous rabble rousers' than provided by the Security Index. [He] hoped the first edition of the new Rabble Rouser Index of 'individuals who have demonstrated a potential for fomenting racial discord' would facilitate target selection for the new black nationalist counterintelligence program...Everything was computerized."[52]

Although Hoover contended the Bureau's COINTELPRO tactics were necessitated by the "violence" of its intended victims, his March 4 memo negates even this flimsy rationalization by placing King's purely pacifistic SCLC among its primary targets from the beginning, adding King himself in February 1968, shortly before the civil rights leader's assassination.[53] Similarly, he included SNCC, still calling it by its long-standing descriptor as a *nonviolent* entity. Even in the case of Maxwell Sanford's Revolutionary Action Movement (RAM), which had never offered professions of pacifist intent, Hoover was forced to admit that his agents had turned up no hard evidence of violence or other criminal activities. Rather, the director points with pride to an anti-RAM COINTELPRO operation undertaken during the summer of 1967 in which RAM members were "arrested on every possible charge until they could no longer make bail" and consequently "spent most of the summer in jail," even though there had never been any intent to take them to trial on the variety of contrived offenses with which they were charged.[54] Hoover recommended this campaign of deliberate false arrest as being the sort of "neutralizing" method he had in mind for black activists, and then ordered each of the 41 field offices receiving his memo to assign a full-time coordinator to such COINTELPRO activities within 30 days.

The nature of the actions triggered by Hoover's instructions varied considerably from field office to field office. In St. Louis, for example, agents undertook a series of anonymous letters – the first of which is proposed in the accompanying February 14, 1969 memo from the St. Louis SAC to the director, and approved in the accompanying reply from Hoover on February 28 – to ensnare the Reverend Charles

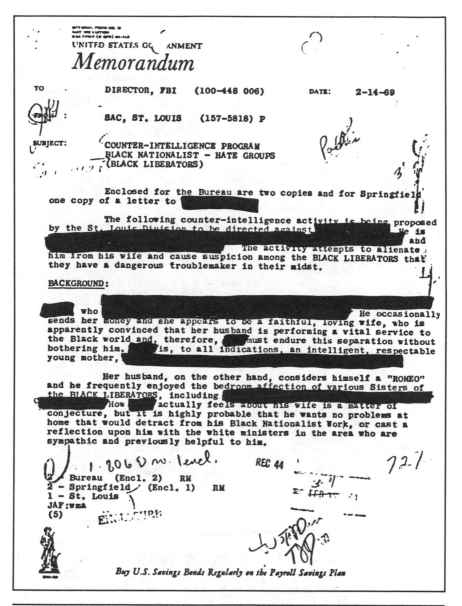

Memo proposing COINTELPRO against the Reverend Charles Koen in St. Louis

Koen, a long-time SNCC activist, in a web of sexual innuendo and/or outright slander (much the same approach as had been used against King). Koen was perceived by the Bureau, correctly enough, as the galvanizing figure in the then-occurring transformation of the Black Liberators, a black street gang in the St. Louis/

SL: ̲ 157-5818

EXPLANATION OF LETTER:

The enclosed letter was prepared from a penmanship, spelling, and vocabulary style to imitate that of the average Black Liberator member. It contains several accusations which should cause ████ great concern. The letter is to be mailed in a cheap, unmarked envelope with no return address and sent from St. Louis to ████ residence in Cairo. Since her letters to ████ are usually sent via the Black Liberator Headquarters, any member would have access to getting her address from one of her envelopes. This address is available to the St. Louis Division.

Her response, upon receipt of this letter, is difficult to predict and the counter-intelligence effect will be nullified if she does not discuss it with him. Therefore, to insure that ████ and the Black Liberators are made aware that the letter was sent, the below follow-up action is necessary:

St. Louis will furnish Springfield with a machine copy of the actual letter that is sent. Attached to this copy will be a neat typed note saying:

"A mutual friend made this available without ████ knowledge. I understand she recently recieved this letter from St. Louis. I suggest you look into this matter.

God Bless You! "

This note would give the impression that somehow one of ████ close friends, probably a minister, obtained a copy of the letter and made it available to ████ The above material is to be mailed by the Springfield Division at Cairo, Ill., anonymously in a suitable envelope with no return address to:

Although ████ is now living in E. St. Louis, Ill., he did use the above address when arrested in St. Louis in Jan., 1969, and it was printed in local newspapers. Mail will reach him at the above address since it is the residence of ████ a close associate of his.

ANTICIPATED RESULTS:

The following results are anticipated following the execution of the above-counter-intelligence activity:

1.   Ill feeling and possibly a lasting distrust will be brought about between ████ The concern over what to do about it may detract from his time spent in the plots and plans of the SNCC. He may even decide to spend more time with his wife and children and less time in Black Nationalist activity.

2.   The Black Liberators will waste a great deal of time trying to discover the writer of the letter. It is possible that their not-too subtle investigation will lose present members and alienate potential ones.

3.   Inasmuch as Black Liberator strength is ebbing at its lowest level, this action may well be the "death-blow."

ROUTE IN ENVELOPE

SAC, St. Louis (157-5818)   2/28/69

REC 44
Director, FBI (100-448006) -727   1 -
                                                    1 -
                                                    1 -

COUNTERINTELLIGENCE PROGRAM
BLACK NATIONALIST - HATE GROUPS
RACIAL INTELLIGENCE
(BLACK LIBERATORS)

         Reurlet 2/14/69.

         St. Louis is authorized to send anonymous letter
set out in relet and Springfield is authorized to send the
second anonymous letter proposed in relet. Use commercially
purchased stationery and take the other precautions set out
to insure this cannot be traced to this Bureau.

         The Bureau feels there should be an interval between
the two letters of at least ten days. St. Louis should advise
Springfield of date second letter should be mailed.

         St. Louis and Springfield should advise the Bureau
of any results.

2 - Springfield

TJD:ckl
   (8)

NOTE:

         The Black Liberators are a black extremist group
in St. Louis   of the Student Nonviolent Coordinating Committee
(SNCC) for the Midwest. SNCC is also a black extremist
group. St. Louis recommends anonymous letters be sent
and his wife regarding   extramarital activities.
                  The letters might cause Koen to spend more of
his time at home since   will know his wife is aware of
his activities. Since   and his wife are separated, the
letters cannot hurt the wife but might draw   back to
his wife.

         St. Louis also feels that the Black Liberators
will try to discover the writer within the organization
which will help neutralize new and potential members.
Since the letters are to be sent anonymously, there is no
possibility of embarrassment to the Bureau. St. Louis has
prepared the first anonymous letter using the penmanship and
grammar of the typical member of the Black Liberators.

         Based on data furnished by St. Louis, it appears this
separation is due to   organization work among black
extremists and not because of marital discord, however,
it is known   has had extramarital affairs.

MAILED 10
FEB 28 1969
COMM-FBI

The COINTELPRO against Koen continues (above) and, in a May 26, 1969 memo
(excerpt right) it is expanded to include a bogus underground newspaper, *The
Blackboard* to spread disinformation within the St. Louis black community.

BLACKBOARD UNDERGROUND NEWSPAPER

Pursuant to Bureau authority received in letter from the Bureau to St. Louis on 4/14/69, the St. Louis Division prepared 200 copies of BLACKBOARD, an alleged underground newspaper of the black students of Southern Illinois University (SIU). It was mailed anonymously by Special Agents of the St. Louis Division at Edwardsville, Ill., and copies of it were sent to virtually every black activist organization and Black Nationalist leader in the bi-state area.

The following results were noted by the St. Louis Division:

Page 10 of the 4/24/69 issued of the "St. Louis American", a weekly newspaper published in St. Louis, Mo., and oriented to the black community, contains a column by FARLEY WILSON, a black columnist for that newspaper. Midway through his column and recitation of various local events, WILSON said, "There is an absolutely scandalous 'underground' sheet floating around both sides of the river that devotes as entire section of its first page to some real dangerous allegations about a few of our 'blacker' black brothers and sisters and some so-called 'bad_mating' sure hope that whoever is printing that jazz is prepared to back it up."

▮▮▮▮▮▮▮▮▮▮▮▮▮▮▮▮▮▮▮▮▮▮▮▮ provided a Xerox copy of BLACKBOARD to the St. Louis FBI Office and advised that copies of it were all over St. Louis and East St. Louis. He stated that his sources have advised that ▮▮▮▮▮▮▮▮▮▮▮▮▮▮▮▮▮▮▮▮▮▮▮▮▮▮▮▮▮▮ He stated that although no one could publicly speak out against the ▮▮▮▮▮▮ "the word was out" that ▮▮▮▮▮▮▮ would be punished for his participation in it. ▮▮▮▮ also advised that ▮▮▮▮▮▮ was extremely angry about the newspaper, and he had told several people that he was going "to get" ▮▮▮▮▮▮ was so angry about it that he attempted to get a local Negro radio station to give him radio time to answer the charges in BLACKBOARD.

On 5/14/69, Detective ▮▮▮▮▮▮▮▮▮▮▮▮ advised that his sources stated that ▮▮▮▮▮▮ had been told to "get out of town" by several black leaders as a result of his tirades against the BLACKBOARD newspaper and his outburst at the ACTION meeting.

On 5/14/69, ▮▮▮▮▮▮▮▮▮▮▮ of the Springfield Division that ▮▮▮▮▮▮▮ is still very angry with ▮▮▮▮▮▮ for publicizing in BLACKBOARD ▮▮▮▮▮ previous connections with the Zulu 1200, a black extremist organization in St. Louis, Mo., which is now defunct. ▮▮▮▮▮ confronted ▮▮▮▮ in person about this recently, and although ▮▮▮▮ attempted to deny any connection with BLACKBOARD, ▮▮▮▮ did not believe ▮▮▮▮▮ denial. ▮▮▮▮▮ had no information as to any specific future action which black militants in the East St. Louis, Ill. area might take against ▮▮▮▮▮▮▮▮▮▮▮▮▮▮▮▮

The St. Louis Division feels, on the basis of the above, that the publication of BLACKBOARD was a most successful counterintelligence endeavor. It is felt that the effectiveness of ▮▮▮▮▮▮▮▮▮▮▮ has been blunted, and it is unlikely that they will ever be able to regain their former stature. ▮▮▮▮▮▮▮▮▮▮ have probably also lost some degree of influence as a result of BLACKBOARD's publication.

East St. Louis area, into a politicized social action organization. He was also known to be a key leader in black community attempts - through formation of a "United Front" – to resist Ku Klux Klan terror in nearby Cairo, Illinois. It was foreseen that his neutralization would lead to a virtual collapse of black political activity throughout southern Missouri and Illinois. By May 26, 1969, as the accompanying memo from the St. Louis SAC to Hoover shows, the letter campaign against Koen was not only well developed, but disinformation activities had been broadened to include production and distribution of *The Blackboard*, a bogus "underground" newspaper aimed mainly at spreading allegations of sexual impropriety about a broadening circle of black community leaders and activists. By 1970, the resulting interpersonal jealousies and animosities had sown a discord sufficient to cause a general disintegration of effectiveness within the black liberation movement in the target area.

Similarly, in New York, the Bureau "placed the fifteen or twenty members of Charles 37X Kenyatta's Harlem Mau Mau on the COINTELPRO target list."[55] Although the details of the operations directed against the group remain murky, they may well have played into the April 1973 murder of Malcolm X's brother, Hakim Jamal (s/n: Allen Donaldson), by a Roxbury, Massachusetts affiliate dubbed "De Mau Mau."[56] In any event, the death of Jamal prompted the Boston FBI office to file a request that headquarters "delete subject from the [Black] Extremist Photograph Album," indicating that he too had been a high-priority COINTELPRO target.[57]

Meanwhile, in southern Florida, as the accompanying August 5, 1968 memo from Hoover to the SAC, Albany, bears out, a more sophisticated propaganda effort had been conducted. Working with obviously "friendly" media representatives, local COINTELPRO specialists oversaw the finalization of a television "documentary" on both the black liberation movement and the new left in the Miami area. The program, which was viewed by a mass audience, was consciously edited to take the statements of key activists out of context in such a way as to make them appear to advocate gratuitous violence and seem "cowardly," and utilized camera angles deliberately selected to make those interviewed come off like "rats trapped under scientific observation." After detailing such intentionally gross distortion of reality – passed off all the while as "news" and "objective journalism" – Hoover called upon "[e]ach counterintelligence office [to] be alert to exploit this technique both for black nationalists and New Left types." Overall, it appears that most field offices complied with this instruction to the best of their respective abilities, a matter which perhaps accounts for much of the negativity with which the black liberation movement came to be publicly viewed by the end of the 1960s.

In Detroit, COINTELPRO operatives set out to destroy the recently-founded Republic of New Afrika (RNA) by targeting its leader, Imari Abubakari Obadele (s/n: Richard Henry). At first they used, as the accompanying memos dated November 22 and December 3, 1968 reveal, a barrage of anonymous letters in much the same fashion as those employed against Koen in St. Louis, albeit in this case they charged financial rather than sexual impropriety. When this approach failed to achieve the

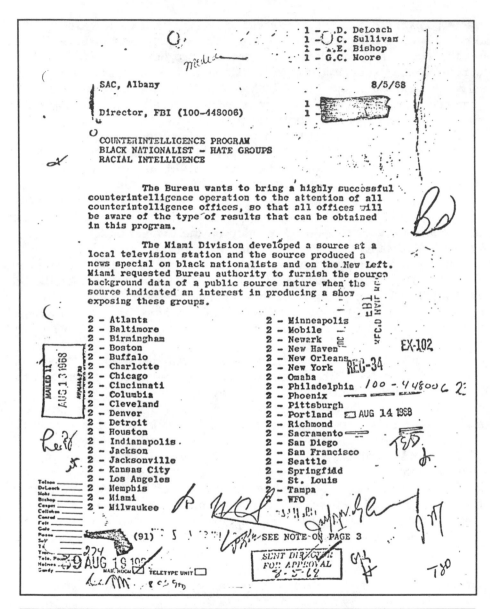

desired result, the Bureau escalated, setting out to bring about their target's imprisonment. In the view of involved agents, "If Obadele can be kept off the streets, it may prevent further problems with the RNA inasmuch as he completely domi-

Letter to SAC, Albany
RE: COUNTERINTELLIGENCE PROGRAM
100-448006

Show APPEARED 7/7/68

   The Bureau authorized ~~furnishing the source data~~
on a confidential basis and the ~~_____~~. A
great deal of research was done ~~by Miami Agents~~ and it
resulted in an excellent program. The show, which ended
with quotes from the Director on the nature of the New
Left, was so well received that the television station
received requests for a film of the show by local civic
groups.

   As you are aware publicity about New Left
and black nationalist groups, especially television
coverage, sometimes enhances the stature of these groups.
At the same time, Miami has demonstrated that a carefully
planned television show can be extremely effective in
showing these extremists for what they are. Local New
Left and black nationalist leaders were interviewed on
the show and seemed to have been chosen for either their
inability to articulate or their simpering and stupid
appearance.

   Miami furnished a film of this show for Bureau
review and it was apparent that the television source
used the very best judgment in editing comments by
these extremists. He brought out that they were in
favor of violent revolution without their explaining
why. But he also brought out that they, personally,
would be afraid to lead a violent revolution, making
them appear to be cowards. The interview of black
nationalist leaders on the show had the leaders seated,
ill at ease, in hard chairs. Full-length camera shots
showed each movement as they squirmed about in their
chairs, resembling rats trapped under scientific
observation.

   Each counterintelligence office should be
alert to exploit this technique both for black nationalists
and New Left types. Miami learned from sources that those
who appeared on the show realized that it presented them
in a most unfavorable light. One even complained to the
television station about it. This counterintelligence
operation will be of great value in the South Florida area
and the Bureau hopes these results can be duplicated in
other offices. Success in this case resulted from hard
work and acumen on the part of the Agents who handled
the matter. Especially important was the choice of
individuals interviewed as they did not have the ability
to stand up to a professional newsman. The fine job of
interviewing and editing done by the news people involved
was also most important.

   Each office should be alert to the possibility
of using this technique. No counterintelligence action
should be taken without Bureau authority. For your
information operations of this type must be handled
through reliable, established sources and must be set
up so that the FBI is not revealed as the source.

NOTE:

   See memorandum G.C. Moore to Mr. W.C. Sullivan,
captioned as above, dated 8/1/68, prepared by ~~_____~~

Memorandum

TO   :   DIRECTOR, FBI (100-448006)   DATE: 11/22/68

FROM   :   SAC, DETROIT (157-3214)

SUBJECT: COUNTERINTELLIGENCE PROGRAM
             BLACK NATIONALIST - HATE GROUPS
             RACIAL INTELLIGENCE
             (REPUBLIC OF NEW AFRICA)

               Re Bureau airtel to Detroit, dated
10/31/68.

               Per suggestion set forth in re Bureau
airtel, Detroit requests mailing letters prepared
on commercially purchased paper to various members
of the Republic of New Africa (RNA) with the
exception of RICHARD HENRY, signed by a concerned
RNA brother.

               The letter will read as follows:

               Dear Brother and Sister:

               Lately I have been concerned
about the lack of funds of the RNA.
I know that many brothers and sisters
have paid taxes and have donated on
various occasions to the Republic.
Where has the money gone, and why
haven't we purchased our land with
it?

               I do not make any direct
accusation at any brother or sister
but I would like to know how Brother
Imari owns a house, supports a family,
and travels all over the country when
he is not even working. I think we
all deserve an explanation of the use
of the RNA money, and I think we are
foolish to donate and pay taxes to
support one man, when the Republic
is in such dire need of money. I
think this question should be raised
at the next Wednesday meeting. I'm
not signing my name because I do not
want to create a personal conflict
among us.

                              A Concerned Brother

               This letter will be mailed to Detroit members
of the RNA only and if a favorable response is received,
a similar letter will be prepared for nationwide
RNA member circulation.

               Detroit requests Bureau approval.

Memo initiating COINTELPRO against the Republic of New Afrika by targeting its leader, Imari Abubakari Obadele (s/n: Richard Henry), shortly after the organization's founding in 1968.

ROUTE IN ENVELOPE

SAC, Detroit (157-3214)   December 3, 1968
            REC- 120
Director, FBI (100-448006)

                                        1 - Mr. Tunstall
                                        1 - Mr. Deakin
COUNTERINTELLIGENCE PROGRAM
BLACK NATIONALIST - HATE GROUPS
RACIAL INTELLIGENCE
(REPUBLIC OF NEW AFRICA)

          Reurlet 11/22/68.

          Detroit is authorized to send the anonymous letter
set out in relet to selected members of the Republic of
New Africa (RNA) using commercially purchased stationery.

          Insure this mailing cannot be traced to the Bureau
and advise of results. If results are favorable, consider
submitting a recommendation for circulating this letter
to other RNA members in other cities.

TJD:ekw
(5)

NOTE:

          This anonymous letter criticizes Richard Henry
(brother Imari), an RNA officer who allegedly is using
RNA funds for personal expenses. This has been a matter
of discussion with enough RNA members so as to protect our
sources. Criticism of leaders of black nationalist extremist
groups, such as the RNA, for misusing funds, is an effective
method of neutralizing these leaders. Since this is an
anonymous letter, there is no possibility of embarrassment
to the Bureau.

Memo authorizing COINTELPRO against Imari Obadele and the RNA.

nates the organization and all members follow his instructions."[58] Hence, when the
RNA leader moved south to consummate an organizational plan of establishing a
"liberated zone" in the Mississippi River delta, near Jackson, Mississippi, the FBI
moved to provoke a confrontation which could then be used to obtain a conviction.
First, as is shown in the accompanying December 12, 1970 memo from the SAC,

Since March, 1968, the Republic of New Africa (RNA)
has been attempting to start a separate black nation in five
southern states, starting with Mississippi. In this regard,
the RNA has been trying to buy and lease land in Mississippi
in the Jackson Division on several past occasions. (Counterintelligence measures has been able to abort all RNA efforts to
obtain land in Mississippi.)

In late July, 1970, RICHARD HENRY, aka Brother Imari,
leader of the RNA, came to Jackson, Mississippi, accompanied
by many out-of-state supporters to hold a national RNA meeting
"on the land of the nation in Mississippi". This conference was
disruptive and ineffective due to Jackson Division, Bureau-
approved counterintelligence measures.

In mid-September, 1970, Brother IMARI and a few close
associates of his came to look at land which was for sale in
rural Hinds County, Mississippi, near Jackson; this land was
owned by a Negro male who was retiring and owned over 560 acres.
Jackson informants advised Bureau Agents of developments regarding
this land and the fact that the owner of the land, [⎯⎯⎯⎯],
N/M, had advised Brother IMARI he will lease or sell him ten
to twenty acres. RNA leaders, including Brother IMARI, were
delighted over this land purchase or leasing prospect. Jackson
informants were directed by contacting Agents to approach [⎯⎯]
privately and indicate to him that his selling land to Brother
IMARI would not be a wise endeavor. Additionally, on 10/9/70,
[⎯⎯] was interviewed by Bureau Agents and advised of the true
nature and violence potential of the RNA and its leaders. The
interview lasted 1½ hours; following the interview, [⎯⎯]
indicated he would reconsider whether he would sell or lease
any land to the RNA; on 10/21/70, Bureau Agents interviewed
[⎯⎯⎯⎯⎯⎯⎯⎯⎯⎯⎯⎯⎯⎯] who was assisting the
RNA in their dealings with [⎯⎯⎯⎯] regarding the
land. The true nature and violence potential of the RNA
and its leaders was explained to [⎯⎯⎯]

As a result of the above counterintelligence
efforts, the land which the RNA had almost finalized plans
regarding purchasing or leasing in rural Hinds County,
Miss., has not been sold or leased to them. Jackson has
maintained contact with [⎯⎯⎯] and he has advised he has
no plans to lease or sell any land to the RNA in the immediate
future. There have been no recent visits by top officials
of the RNA to Mississippi regarding the land, it being noted
they made several visits in September, 1970, when their
prospects for the land purchase or leasing was good.

As a result of the above, intensive efforts
of the RNA to obtain land in Mississippi over the past
two and one-half years are still totally unsuccessful.

**Excerpt from a December 2, 1970 report detailing the COINTELPRO opera-
tions in Mississippi which resulted in the case of the RNA 11.**

Jackson (Elmer Linberg), to Hoover, agents intervened to block the perfectly legal
sale of a land parcel to Obadele. SA George Holder and his associates undertook by
word of mouth to foster a marked increase in anti-RNA sentiment in the Klan-ridden
Jackson area. Finally, they coordinated an early morning assault on RNA facilities
in the city involving some 36 heavily armed agents and local police headed by SAC
Linberg – as well as an armored car – on August 18, 1971.

In the resultant firefight, one police officer, William Skinner, was killed and an agent, William Stringer, was wounded. Imari Obadele and 10 other RNA members were arrested – thereby becoming the "RNA 11" – and charged with murder, assault, sedition, conspiracy, possession of illegal weapons, and "treason against the state of Mississippi."[59] Tellingly, the original charges, which had ostensibly provided a basis for the massive police raid, were never brought to court. In the end, eight of the accused were convicted, but only of conspiracy to assault federal officers, assault, illegal possession of a nonexistent automatic weapon, and having used weapons in the commission of these other "felonies."[60] This is to say they were imprisoned for having defended themselves from the armed attack of a large number of FBI agents and police who could never show any particular reason for having launched the assault in the first place. Obadele received a twelve year sentence, served seven, and the entire operation undoubtedly entered the annals of "successful" COINTELPROs.

COINTELPRO Against the Black Panther Party

By the fall of 1968, the FBI felt it had identified the organization most likely to succeed as the catalyst of a united black liberation movement in the U.S. This was the Black Panther Party (BPP), originally established as the Black Panther Party for Self-Defense in the San Francisco Bay area city of Oakland by Merritt College students Huey P. Newton and Bobby Seale (a former RAM member) during October of 1966. On September 8, 1968, J. Edgar Hoover let it be known in the pages of the *New York Times* that he considered the Panthers "the greatest [single] threat to the internal security of the country."[61] Shortly thereafter, William Sullivan sent the accompanying memo to George C. Moore, outlining a plan by which already-existing COINTELPRO actions against the BPP might "be accelerated."

Although Sullivan utilized the habitual Bureau pretense that targets of such attention were "violence-prone" and making "efforts to perpetrate violence in the United States," the party's predication – as evidenced in its Ten-Point Program – was in some ways rather moderate and, in any event, entirely legal.[62] Far from conducting "physical attacks on police," as Sullivan claimed, the Panthers were well-known to have anchored themselves firmly in the constitutional right to bear arms and effect citizen's arrests in order to curtail the high level of systematic (and generally quite illegal) violence customarily visited upon black inner city residents by local police.[63] More to the point, but left unmentioned by the FBI assistant director, was that the entire thrust of BPP organizing – reliance on the principle of armed self-defense included – went to forging direct community political control over and economic self-sufficiency within the black ghettos.[64] As has been noted elsewhere, "In late 1967, the Panthers initiated a free breakfast programme for black children, and offered free health care to ghetto residents."[65] By the summer of 1968, these undertakings had been augmented by a community education project and an anti-heroin campaign. The party was offering a coherent strategy to improve the realities

UNITED STATES GOVERNMENT

Memorandum

TO : Mr. W. C. Sullivan   DATE: 9/27/68

FROM : G. C. Moore

SUBJECT : COUNTERINTELLIGENCE PROGRAM
BLACK NATIONALIST - HATE GROUPS
RACIAL INTELLIGENCE
(BLACK PANTHER PARTY)

1 - Mr. C. D. DeLoach
1 - Mr. W. C. Sullivan
1 - Mr. G. C. Moore
1 -
1 -
1 -

PURPOSE:

        To obtain authority for the attached letter to
those field divisions having Black Panther Party (BPP)
activity instructing that the counterintelligence program
against this organization be accelerated and that each
office submit concrete suggestions as to future action
to be taken against the BPP.

        The extremist BPP of Oakland, California, is
rapidly expanding. It is the most violence-prone organization
of all the extremist groups now operating in the United States.
This group has a record of violence and connections with
foreign revolutionaries. It puts particular emphasis on not
only verbal attacks but also physical attacks on police.

OBSERVATIONS: REC-15

        The information we are receiving from our sources
concerning activites of the BPP clearly indicates that
more violence can be expected from this organization in the
immediate future. It therefore, is essential that we not
only accelerate our investigations of this organization
and increase our informants in the organization but that we
take action under the counterintelligence program to disrupt
the group. Our counterintelligence program may bring about
results which could lead to prosecution of these violence-prone
leaders and active members, thereby thwarting their efforts to
perpetrate violence in the United States.

        Enclosure
        100-448006   CONTINUED - OVER

        JGD:rmm (7)

Memo initiating COINTELPRO – BPP.

– both spiritual and material – of ghetto life. Consequently, black community perceptions of the BPP were radically different from those entertained by the police establishment (which the Panthers described as an "occupying army").

Memorandum to Mr. W. C. Sullivan
RE: ~COUNTERINTELLIGENCE PROGRAM
BLACK NATIONALIST - HATE GROUPS
RACIAL INTELLIGENCE
(BLACK PANTHER PARTY)

SCOPE OF PROPOSED COUNTERINTELLIGENCE PROGRAM:

As stated above, the attached letter will instruct
the field to submit positive suggestions as to actions to
be taken to thwart and disrupt the BPP. Instructions are and
will be reiterated that no action is to be taken without
prior Bureau authority.

These suggestions are to create factionalism between
not only the national leaders but also local leaders, steps
to neutralize all organizational efforts of the BPP as well
as create suspicion amongst the leaders as to each others
sources of finances, suspicion concerning their respective
spouses and suspicion as to who may be cooperating with
law enforcement. In addition, suspicion should be developed
as to who may be attempting to gain control of the organization
for their own private betterment, as well as suggestions as
to the best method of exploiting the foreign visits made by
BPP members. We are also soliciting recommendations as to
the best method of creating opposition to the BPP on the
part of the majority of the residents of the ghetto areas.

RECOMMENDATION:

That attached letter , in accordance with the above,
be approved.

A significant measure of the Black Panthers' success was described in racist terms by Sullivan who noted that membership was "multiplying rapidly." Beginning with a core of five members in 1966, the BPP had grown to include as many as 5,000 members within two years, and had spread from its original Oakland base to include chapters in more than a dozen cities.[66] This seems due, not only to the appeal inherent in the Panthers' combination of standing up for basic black rights in the face of even the most visible expressions of state power with concrete programs to upgrade inner city life, but to the party's unique inclusiveness. Although the conditions for acceptance into the BPP were in some ways quite stringent, Newton and Seale had from the outset focused their recruiting and organizing efforts on what they termed "the lumpen" – a cast of street gangs, prostitutes, convicts and ex-cons typically shunned by progressive movements – with an eye towards forming a new political force based upon this "most oppressed and alienated sector of the population" and activating its socially constructive energies.[67]

Also of apparent concern to the Bureau was the Panthers' demonstrated ability to link their new recruitment base to other important sectors of the U.S. opposition.[68] One of the party's first major achievements in this regard came when Chairman Bobby Seale and Minister of Information Eldridge Cleaver managed to engineer the merger of SNCC with their organization, an event signified at a mass rally in Oakland on February 17, 1968 when Stokely Carmichael was designated as honor-ary BPP Prime Minister, H. Rap Brown as Minister of Justice and James Forman as Minister of Foreign Affairs.[69] As is demonstrated in the accompanying October 10, 1968 memo from Moore to Sullivan, the FBI quickly initiated a COINTELPRO effort to "foster a split between...the two most prominent black nationalist extremist groups" through the media.

The SNCC leadership was also targeted more heavily than ever. H. Rap Brown was shortly eliminated by being "charged with inciting a race riot in Maryland," allowed to make bail only under the constitutionally dubious proviso that he not leave the Borough of Manhattan in New York, "and was eventually sentenced to five years in a federal penitentiary [not on the original charge, but] for carrying a rifle across state lines while under criminal indictment."[70] Stokely Carmichael's neutrali-zation took a rather different form. Utilizing the services of Peter Cardoza, an infiltrator who had worked his way into a position as the SNCC leader's bodyguard, the Bureau applied a "bad jacket," deliberately creating the false appearance that Carmichael was himself an operative.[71] In a memo dated July 10, 1968, the SAC, New York, proposed to Hoover that:

> ...consideration be given to convey the impression that CARMICHAEL is a CIA informer. One method of accomplishing [this] would be to have a carbon copy of an informant report supposedly written by CARMICHAEL to the CIA carefully deposited in the automobile of a close Black Nationalist friend...It is hoped that when the informant report is read it will help promote distrust between CARMICHAEL and the Black Community...It is also suggested that we inform a certain percentage of reliable criminal and racial informants that "we have it from reliable sources that CARMICHAEL is a CIA agent. It is hoped that the informants would spread the rumor in various large Negro communities across the land.[72]

Pursuant to a May 19, 1969 Airtel from the SAC, San Francisco, to Hoover, the Bureau then proceeded to "assist" the BPP in "expelling" Carmichael through the forgery of letters on party letterhead. The gambit worked, as is evidenced in the Sep-tember 5, 1970 assertion by BPP head Huey P. Newton: "We...charge that Stokely Carmichael is operating as an agent of the CIA."[73]

Meanwhile, according to the New York SAC, his COINTELPRO technicians had followed up, using the target's mother as a prop in their scheme:

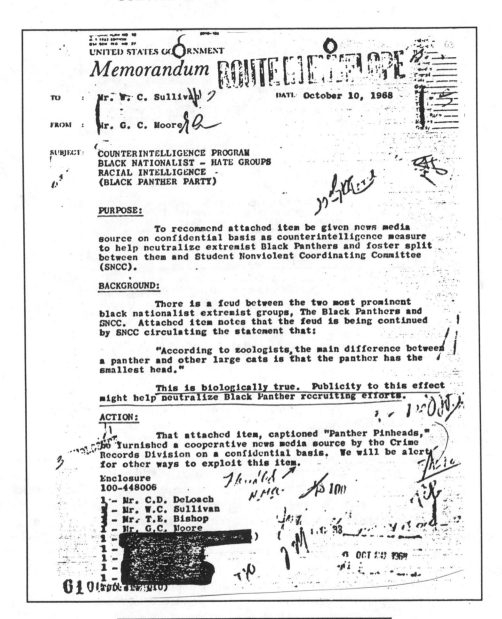

Memo outlining tactic to split the BPP and SNCC.

On 9/4/68, a pretext phone call was placed to the residence of STOKELY CARMICHAEL and in absence of CARMICHAEL his mother was told that a friend was calling who was fearful of the future safety of her son. It was explained to Mrs. CARMICHAEL the absolute necessity for CARMICHAEL to "hide out" inasmuch

> It is suggested that consideration be given to convey the impression that CARMICHAEL is a CIA informant.
>
> One method of accomplishing the above would be to have a carbon copy of informant report reportedly written by CARMICHAEL to the CIA carefully deposited in the automobile of a close Black Nationalist friend. The report should be so placed that it will be readily seen.
>
> It is hoped that when the informant report is read it will help promote distrust between CARMICHAEL and the Black Community. It is suggested that carbon copy of report be used to indicate that CARMICHAEL turned original copy into CIA and kept carbon copy for himself.
>
> It is also suggested that we inform a certain percentage of reliable criminal and racial informants that "we heard from reliable sources that CARMICHAEL is a CIA agent". It is hoped that these informants would spread the rumor in various large Negro communities across the land.

Excerpt from July 10, 1968 memo proposing the bad-jacketing of SNCC/BPP leader Stokely Carmichael.

as several BPP members were out to kill him. Mrs. CARMICHAEL appeared shocked upon hearing the news and stated she would tell STOKELY when he came home.[74]

Although there is no evidence whatsoever that a Panther "hit team" had been assembled to silence the accused informer, Carmichael left the U.S. for an extended period in Africa the following day, and the SNCC/Panther coalition was effectively destroyed.

As all this was going on, Cleaver was developing another highly visible alliance, this one with "white mother country radicals," which he and Seale had initiated in December 1967.[75] This was with the so-called Peace and Freedom Party, which planned to place Cleaver – not only in his capacity as a leading Panther, but as the celebrated convict-author of *Soul on Ice*[76] and parolee editor of *Ramparts* magazine – on the California ballot as a presidential candidate during the 1968 election; his vice presidential candidate was slated to be SDS co-founder Tom Hayden, while Huey P. Newton was offered as a congressional candidate from his prison cell.[77] The ensuing campaign resulted in a wave of positive exposure for the BPP which the authorities were relatively powerless to counteract. Hence, Cleaver – the powerful writer and speaker at the center of it all – was targeted for rapid elimination.

On April 6 [1968], two days after Martin Luther King was killed, Cleaver was in the *Ramparts* office in the late afternoon, dictating his article, "Requiem for Nonviolence." In a matter of hours he and other Panthers would be involved in a shootout with the Oakland police. Seventeen-year-old Bobby Hutton died, shot in the back moments after he and Eldridge, arms above their heads, stumbled out of the building where they'd taken refuge. Cleaver, who was wounded in the leg, was taken first to Oakland's Highland Hospital; then to the Alameda County Courthouse where police made him lie on the floor while he was being booked; and finally, that same night, to San Quentin Hospital where a guard pushed him down a flight of stairs. He was brought to the state medical facility at Vacaville and confined in the "hole."[78]

Although Cleaver was never convicted of any charge stemming from the firefight, and it soon became apparent that Ray Brown's Oakland Panther Squad had deliberately provoked the incident, his "parole was quickly revoked, and for two months he sat at Vacaville. The [California] Adult Authority had exercised its authority to suspend or revoke parole without notice or hearing, basing its actions solely on police reports. Three parole violations were listed: possession of firearms, associating with individuals of bad reputation, and failing to cooperate with the parole agent."[79] But, when Charles Garry, Cleaver's attorney, petitioned for a writ of *habeas corpus*, it was granted by state Superior Court Judge Raymond J. Sherwin, in Solano County (where Vacaville is located).

Judge Sherwin almost immediately dismissed the claim that Cleaver had associated with persons of "bad reputation," noting that the adult authority had been unable to even list who was supposedly at issue. The noncooperation claim was also scuttled when Garry introduced evidence that the parole officer in question had consistently assessed Cleaver in written reports as "reliable" and "cooperative" since his release from prison. The state's weapons possession claim also fell apart when the judge found that, "Cleaver's only handling of a firearm [a rifle] was in obedience to a police command. He did not handle a hand gun at all."[80] The judge concluded that:

It has to be stressed that the uncontradicted evidence presented to this Court indicated that the petitioner had been a model parolee. The peril to his parole status stemmed from no failure of personal rehabilitation, but from his undue eloquence in pursuing political goals, goals which were offensive to many of his contemporaries. Not only was there absence of cause for the cancellation of his parole, it was the product of a type of pressure unbecoming, to say the least, to the law enforcement paraphernalia of the state.[81]

With that, Judge Sherwin ordered Cleaver's release, a ruling which was immediately appealed by the adult authority to the state appellate court. The higher court, refusing to hear *any* evidence in the matter, simply affirmed "the arbitrary power of the adult authority to revoke parole."[82] Consequently, despite having been shown to have engaged in no criminal activity at all, Cleaver was ordered back to San Quentin as of November 27, 1968. Under such conditions, he opted instead to go into exile, first in Cuba, then Algeria and, eventually, France.[83] The immediacy of his talents, energy and stature were thus lost to the BPP – along with the life of Bobby Hutton, one of its earliest and most dedicated members – while the stage was set for a future COINTELPRO operation.

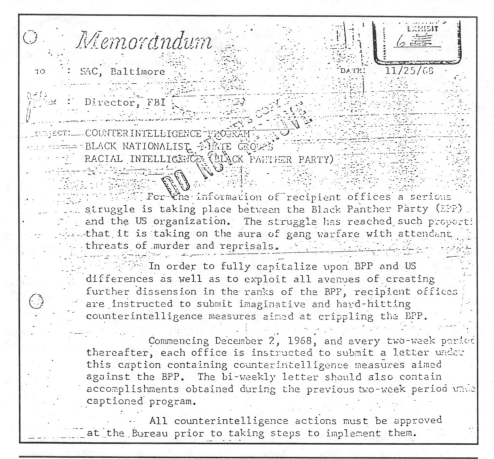

Memo initiating the lethal COINTELPRO which pitted the US organization against the BPP. Note the similarity in method to that of Operation Hoodwink.

Anti-Panther COINTELPRO activities were directed not only at blocking or destroying the party's coalition-building. They were, as the accompanying November 25, 1968 memo from Hoover to the SAC, Baltimore, bears out, also devoted to exacerbating tensions between the BPP and organizations with which it had strong ideological differences. In the case of the so-called United Slaves (US), a black cultural nationalist group based primarily in southern California, this was done despite – or because of – "The struggle...taking on the aura of gang warfare with attendant threats of murder and reprisal." What was meant by the Bureau "fully capitalizing" on the situation is readily attested by the accompanying November 29 memo to Hoover from the SAC, Los Angeles, proposing the sending of an anonymous letter – attributed to the Panthers – "revealing" a fictional BPP plot to assassinate US head Ron Karenga. The stated objective was to provoke "an US and BPP vendetta." A number of defamatory cartoons – attributed to both US and the

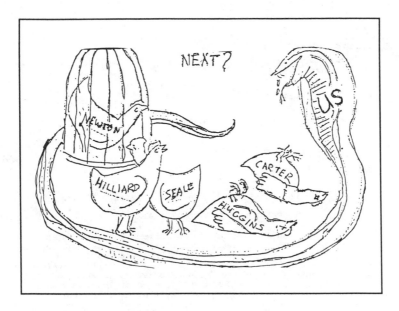

Samples of the sorts of cartoons produced and distributed by the FBI in southern California to provoke violence between US and the BPP.

BPP, with each side appearing to viciously ridicule the other – were also produced and distributed within local black communities by the Los Angeles and San Diego FBI offices.

OPTIONAL FORM NO. 10
MAY 1962 EDITION
GSA GEN. REG. NO. 27

UNITED STATES GOVERNMENT

Memorandum

TO: DIRECTOR, FBI (100-448006)   DATE: 11/29/68

FROM: SAC, LOS ANGELES (157-1751) (P)

SUBJECT: COUNTERINTELLIGENCE PROGRAM
BLACK NATIONALIST - HATE GROUPS
RACIAL INTELLIGENCE

          Re Los Angeles letter to Bureau dated 9/25/68.

          I. OPERATIONS UNDER CONSIDERATION

               The Los Angeles Office is currently preparing an
anonymous letter for Bureau approval which will be sent to
the Los Angeles Black Panther Party (BPP) supposedly from
a member of the "US" organization in which it will be stated
that the youth group of the "US" organization is aware of the
BPP "contract" to kill RON KARENGA, leader of "US", and they,
"US" members, in retaliation, have made plans to ambush
leaders of the BPP in Los Angeles.

               It is hoped this counterintelligence measure will
result in an "US" and BPP vendetta.

               Investigation has indicated that the Peace and
Freedom Party (PFP) has been furnishing the BPP with
financial assistance. An anonymous letter is being prepared
for Bureau approval to be sent to a leader of PFP in which
it is set forth that the BPP has made statements in closed
meetings that when the armed rebellion comes the whites in
the PFP will be lined up against the wall with the rest of the
whites.

               It is felt that this type of a letter could cause
considerable disruption of the association between the BPP
and the PFP.

               In order to cause disruption between the BPP of
Oakland, California, and the BPP of Los Angeles, an
envelope is being prepared for Bureau approval which appears

                              REC-9

② - Bureau (RM)
1 - Los Angeles

LWS/dlc
(3)

                                                    10 DEC

Portion of memo highlighting continuing efforts to foster violence between US
and the BPP. Note simultaneous operations being conducted to split the BPP from
its support base in the Peace and Freedom Party as well as to foment discord
among the Panthers themselves.

III.   TANGIBLE RESULTS

The BPP Breakfast Program appears to be floundering
in San Diego due to lack of public support and unfavorable
publicity concerning it. It is noted that it has presently
been temporarily suspended. Therefore, it was felt that .
placing the above mentioned anonymous call to the Bishop at
this particular time might be a significant factor in
precluding the resumption of the program. The information
to the Bishop appeared to be favorably received and he seemed
to be quite concerned over the fact that one of his Priests
was deeply involved in utilization of church facilities for
this purpose. This matter, of course, will be closely
followed for further anticipated developments concerning the
Breakfast Program.

Shootings, beatings, and a high degree of unrest
continues to prevail in the ghetto area of southeast San Diego.
Although no specific counterintelligence action can be
credited with contributing to this over-all situation, it is
felt that a substantial amount of the unrest is directly
attributable to this program.

In view of the recent killing of BPP member SYLVESTER
BELL, a new cartoon is being considered in the hopes that
it will assist in the continuance of the rift between BPP
and US., This cartoon, or series of cartoons, will be similar
in nature to those formerly approved by the Bureau and will
be forwarded to the Bureau for evaluation and approval
immediately upon their completion.

**Excerpt from an August 20, 1969 report summarizing the "accomplishments"
and plans for the BPP/US COINTELPRO in San Diego.**

On January 17, 1969, these tactics bore their malignant fruit when Los Angeles BPP leaders Alprentice "Bunchy" Carter and Jon Huggins were shot to death by US members George and Joseph Stiner, and Claude Hubert, in a classroom at UCLA's Campbell Hall. Apparently at the FBI's behest, the Los Angeles Police Department (LAPD) followed up by conducting a massive raid – 75 to 100 SWAT equipped police participated – on the home of Jon Huggins' widow, Ericka, on the evening of his death, an action guaranteed to drastically raise the level of rage and frustration felt by the Panthers assembled there. The police contended that the rousting of Ericka Huggins and other surviving LA-BPP leaders was intended to "avert further violence," a rationale which hardly explains why during the raid a cop placed a loaded gun to the head of the Huggins' six-month-old baby, Mai, laughed and said "You're next."[84] In the aftermath, southern California COINTELPRO specialists assigned themselves "a good measure of credit" for these "accomplishments," and proposed distribution of a new series of cartoons – including the accompanying examples – to "indicate to the BPP that the US organization feels they are ineffectual, inadequate, and riddled with graft and corruption."[85]

The idea was approved and, as is shown in the accompanying excerpts from an August 20, 1969 report by the San Diego SAC to Hoover, obtained similar results.

ROUTE IN ENVELOPE

SAC, Newark (100-49654)   10/2/69

REQ 17   EX-106
         Director, FBI (100-448006) /33 6

                                                      1 - ▓▓▓▓▓▓▓▓▓▓

         COUNTERINTELLIGENCE PROGRAM
         BLACK NATIONALIST - HATE GROUPS
         RACIAL INTELLIGENCE
         BLACK PANTHER PARTY (BPP)

              ReNKlet 9/18/69.

                   Authority is granted Newark to mail the cartoon
         submitted in referenced letter. The cartoon, which was
         drawn by the Newark Office, is satisfactory and needs no
         duplication. In reproducing this cartoon, Newark should
         insure that the paper and envelopes used do not contain
         any traceable markings. When mailing this cartoon, care
         should be taken so that the Bureau is not disclosed as the
         source and strict security is maintained. Newark should
         advise of any results received from this mailing.

The BPP/US COINTELPRO continued in the east.

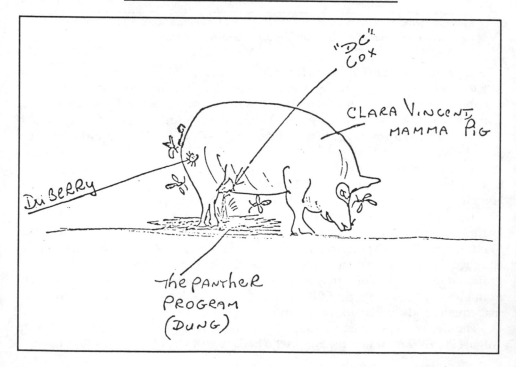

Among the "tangible results" which the SAC found to be "directly attributable to this program" were "shootings, beatings, and a high degree of unrest...in the ghetto area." At another point, he noted that one of the shootings had resulted in the death of Panther Sylvester Bell at the hands of US gunmen on August 14 (another San Diego Panther, John Savage, had also been murdered by US on May 23), and announced that, apparently on the basis of such a resounding success, "a new cartoon is being considered in the hopes that it will assist in the continuance of the rift between the BPP and US."

The Newark field office also joined in the act, as is attested by the accompanying October 2, 1969 memo from the SAC in that city to Hoover, and the cartoon which corresponds to it. Newark credited the COINTELPRO with three other Panther murders as of September 30, 1969, when it sent an anonymous letter to the local BPP chapter warning them to "watch out: Karenga's coming," and listing a national "box score" of "US – 6, Panthers – 0."[86] While this seems to have been the extent of the fatalities induced through the COINTELPRO operation – a bodycount which in itself would not have proven crippling to either side of the dispute – such FBI activities did, as cultural nationalist leader Amiri Baraka (s/n: LeRoi Jones) has pointed out, help solidify deep divisions within the radical black community as a whole which took years to overcome, and which effectively precluded the possibility of unified political action within the black liberation movement.[87]

As has been noted elsewhere, one "of the FBI's favorite tactics was to accuse the Panthers and other black nationalists of anti-Semitism, a tactic designed to destroy the movement's image 'among liberal and naive elements.' Bureau interest in anti-Semitism grew during the summer of 1967 at the National Convention for a New Politics, when SNCC's James Forman and Rap Brown led a floor fight for a resolution condemning Zionist expansion. The convention's black caucus introduced the resolution, and SNCC emerged as the first black group to take a public stand against Israel in the Mid-East conflict."[88] In New York, as is revealed in the accompanying September 10, 1969 memo, this assumed the form of sending anonymous letters to Rabbi Meir Kahane of the neo-fascistic Jewish Defense League in hopes that the "embellishment" of "factual information" within the missives might provoke Kahane's thugs "to act" against the BPP.

Comparable methods were used in Chicago, where BPP leader Fred Hampton was showing considerable promise in negotiating a working alliance with a huge black street gang known as the Blackstone Rangers (or Black P. Stone Nation). As is demonstrated in the accompanying January 30, 1969 letter from Hoover to Marlin Johnson, the Chicago SAC (see page 138), this "threat" prompted the local COINTELPRO section to propose – and Hoover to approve – the sending of an anonymous letter to Ranger head Jeff Fort, falsely warning that Hampton had "a hit [murder contract] out on" him as part of a Panther plot to take over his gang. What the Bureau expected to result from the sending of this missive had already been outlined by Johnson in a memo to Hoover on January 10:

It is believed that the [letter] may intensify the degree of animosity between the two

UNITED STATES ~~~~~~~ ~NMENT

Memorandum.

TO   :   DIRECTOR, FBI (100-448006)   DATE: 9/10/69

FROM :   SAC, NEW YORK (100-161140) (P)

SUBJECT: COUNTERINTELLIGENCE PROGRAM
                BLACK NATIONALIST - HATE GROUPS
                RACIAL INTELLIGENCE
                BLACK PANTHER PARTY (BPP)

   Re NY report of 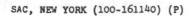, captioned
"JEWISH DEFENSE LEAGUE, RACIAL MATTERS", NY file 157-3463;
Bu letter to NY, 7/25/69.

   Referenced report has been reviewed by the NYO
in an effort to target one individual within the Jewish
Defense League (JEDEL) who would be the suitable recipient
of information furnished on an anonymous basis that the
Bureau wishes to disseminate and/or use for future counterintelligence purposes.

   NY is of the opinion that the individual within
JEDEL who would most suitably serve the above stated purpose
would be Rabbi MEIR KAHANE, a Director of JEDEL. It is
noted that Rabbi KAHANE's background as a writer for the
NY newspaper "Jewish Press" would enable him to give widespread coverage of anti-Semetic statements made by the BPP
and other Black Nationalist hate groups not only to members
of JEDEL but to other individuals who would take cognizance
of such statements.

   In order to prepare a suggested initial communication from the anonymous source to Rabbi KAHANE which would
establish rapport between the two, it is felt that this contact
should not be limited to the furnishing of factual information
of interest to the aims of JEDEL because the NYO does not
feel that JEDEL could be motivated to act as called for in
referenced Bureau letter if the information gathered by the
NYO concerning anti-semitism and other matters were furnished
to that organization without some embellishment.

Memo proposing anonymous letter to provoke conflict between the Jewish Defense League and the BPP. Text of letter appears on the next page.

groups and occasion Forte [*sic*] to take retaliatory action which could disrupt the
BPP or *lead to reprisals against its leadership*...Consideration has been given to a
similar letter to the BPP alleging a Ranger plot against the BPP leadership; however,
it is not felt that this would be *productive* principally because the BPP...is not believed
to be as violence prone as *the Rangers, to whom violent type activity – shooting and the
like – is second nature* [emphasis added].

  The FBI's concern in the matter was not, as Hoover makes abundantly clear in
his letter, that someone might be killed as a consequence of such "disruptive

For example it is felt that JEDEL is aware of the majority of information concerning the factual views of the BPP and other Black Nationalist groups through public sources of information such as the BPP newspaper, "The Black Panther", and to furnish such information from an "anonymous source" would either be dismissed by JEDEL as trivial or attributed to some other party who may have an interest in causing JEDEL to act against such groups as the BPP.

In view of the above comments the following is submitted as the suggested communication to be used to establish rapport between the anonymous source and the selected individual associated with JEDEL:

"Dear Rabbi Kahane:

I am a Negro man who is 48 years old and served his country in the U.S. Army in WW2 and worked as a truck driver with "the famous red-ball express" in Gen. Eisenhour's Army in France and Natzi Germany. One day I had a crash with the truck I was driving, a 2½ ton truck, and was injured real bad. I was treated and helped by a Jewish Army Dr. named "Rothstein" who helped me get better again.

Also I was encouraged to remain in high school for two years by my favorite teacher, Mr. Katz. I have always thought Jewish people are good and they have helped me all my life. That is why I become so upset about my oldest son who is a Black Panther and very much against Jewish people. My oldest son just returned from Algers in Africa where he met a bunch of other Black Panthers from all over the world. He said to me that they all agree that the Jewish people are against all the colored people and that the only friends the colored people have are the Arabs.

I told my child that the Jewish people are the friends of the colored people but he calls me a Tom and says I'll never be anything better than a Jew boy's slave. Last night my boy had a meeting at my house with six of his Black Panther friends. From the way they talked it sounded like they had a plan to force Jewish store owners to give them money or they would drop a bomb on the Jewish store. Some of the money they get will be sent to the Arabs in Africa. They left books and pictures around with Arab writing on them and pictures of Jewish soldiers killing Arab babys. I think they are going to give these away at Negro Christian Churchs.

I though you might be able to stop this. I think I can get some of the pictures and books without getting myself in trouble. I will send them to you if you are interested.

I would like not to use my real name at this time.

A friend"

It is further suggested that a second communication be sent to Rabbi KAHANE approximately one week after the above described letter which will follow the same foremat, but will contain as enclosures some BPP artifacts such as pictures of BOBBY SEALE, ELDRIDGE CLEAVER, a copy of a BPP newspaper, etc. It is felt that a progression of letters should then follow which would further establish rapport with the JEDEL and eventually culminate in the anonymous letter writer requesting some response from the JEDEL recipient of these letters.

SAC, Chicago (157-2209)   1/30/69

Director, FBI (100-448006) *597*
        REC-12

COUNTERINTELLIGENCE PROGRAM
BLACK NATIONALIST - HATE GROUPS
RACIAL INTELLIGENCE
BLACK PANTHER PARTY

        Reurlet 1/13/69.

        Authority is granted to mail anonymous letter
to Jeff Fort, as suggested in relet, in care of the
First Presbyterian Church, 6401 South Kimbark, Chicago,
Illinois.

        Utilize a commercially purchased envelope for
this letter and insure that the mailing is not traced
to the source.

        Advise the Bureau of any results obtained by
the above mailing.

WDH:ums
    (4)

NOTE:

        Jeff Fort is the leader of the Blackstone
Rangers, a black extremist organization. Chicago
advises that so long as Fort continues as the leader
of the Rangers, a working arrangement between the BPP
and the Rangers may be effected on Ranger terms.
Chicago has recommended the anonymous mailing of the
following letter in anticipation that its receipt by
Fort will intensify the degree of animosity existing
between these two black extremist organizations:

"Brother Jeff:

        "I've spent some time with some Panther friends
on the west side lately and I know what's been going on.
The brothers that run the Panthers blame you for blocking
their thing and there's supposed to be a hit out for
you. I'm not a Panther, or a Ranger, just black. From
what I see these Panthers are out for themselves not
black people. I think you ought to know what their up
to, I know what I'd do if I was you. You might hear from
me again."

                        "A black brother you don't know"

MAILED 10 JAN 29 1969 COMM-FBI

Tolson
DeLoach
Mohr
Bishop
Casper
Callahan
Conrad
Felt
Gale
Rosen
Sullivan
Tavel
Trotter

Letter authorizing sending of bogus letter to Chicago gang leader Jeff Fort in
hopes that it will provoke violent retaliation against city BPP head Fred Hampton.

activities," but that a properly nondescript envelope be employed in the mailing of
the bogus letter in order that "any tangible results obtained" could not be "traced
back to" the Bureau.[89] Similar tactics were employed to block or "destabilize"

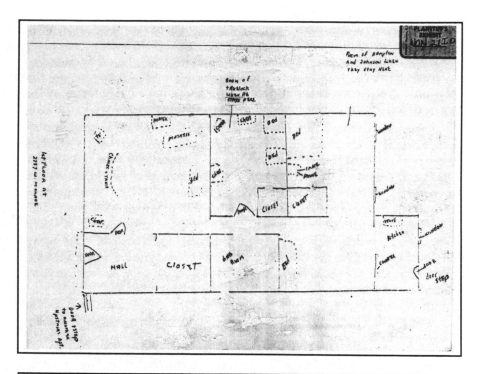

Floor plan of Hampton's apartment provided by FBI infiltrator William O'Neal in order to pinpoint targets during the Panther leader's assassination.

emerging alliances between the Chicago BPP and another black gang, the Mau Maus (unrelated to Kenyatta's Harlem-based organization), as well as the already politicized *Puertorriqueño* Young Lords, a white street gang called the Young Patriots, and even SDS, the white radical organization.[90] The letter-writing COINTELPRO had a significant impact in preventing Hampton from consolidating the city-wide "Rainbow Coalition" he was attempting to establish at the time, but it failed to bring about his physical liquidation.

Hence, in mid-November 1969, COINTELPRO specialist Roy Mitchell met with William O'Neal, a possibly psychopathic infiltrator/*provocateur* who had managed to become Hampton's personal bodyguard and chief of local BPP security, at the Golden Torch Restaurant in downtown Chicago. The agent secured from O'Neal the accompanying detailed floorplan of Hampton's apartment, including the disposition of furniture, and denotation of exactly where the BPP leader might be expected to be sleeping on any given night. Mitchell then took the floorplan to Richard Jalovec, overseer of a special police unit assigned to State's Attorney Edward V. Hanrahan; together, Mitchell and Jalovec met with police sergeant Daniel Groth, operational commander of the unit, and planned an "arms raid" on the Hampton residence.[91]

On the evening of December 3, 1969, shortly before the planned raid, infiltrator O'Neal seems to have slipped Hampton a substantial dose of secobarbital in a glass of kool-aid. The BPP leader was thus comatose in his bed when the fourteen-man police team – armed with a submachinegun and other special hardware – slammed into his home at about 4 a.m. on the morning of December 4.[92] He was nonetheless shot three times, once more-or-less slightly in the chest, and then twice more in the head at point-blank range.[93] Also killed was Mark Clark, head of the Peoria, Illinois, BPP chapter. Wounded were Panthers Ronald "Doc" Satchell, Blair Anderson and Verlina Brewer. Panthers Deborah Johnson (Hampton's fiancée, eight months pregnant with their child), Brenda Harris, Louis Truelock and Harold Bell were uninjured during the shooting.[94] Despite the fact that no Panther had fired a shot (with the possible exception of Clark, who may have squeezed off a single round during his death convulsions) while the police had pumped at least 98 rounds into the apartment, the BPP survivors were all beaten while handcuffed, charged with "aggressive assault" and "attempted murder" of the raiders, and held on $100,000 bond apiece.[95]

A week later, on December 11, Chicago COINTELPRO section head Robert Piper took a major share of the "credit" for this "success" in the accompanying memo, informing headquarters that the raid could not have occurred without intelligence information, "not available from any other source," provided by O'Neal via Mitchell and himself. He specifically noted that "the chairman of the Illinois BPP, Fred Hampton," was killed in the raid and that this was due, in large part, to the "tremendous value" of O'Neal's work inside the party. He then requested payment of a $300 cash "bonus" to the infiltrator for services rendered, a matter quickly approved at FBI headquarters.[96]

The Hampton-Clark assassinations were unique in that the cover stories of involved police and local officials quickly unraveled. Notwithstanding the FBI's best efforts to help "keep the lid on," there was a point when the sheer blatancy of the lies used to "explain" what had happened, the obvious falsification of ballistics and other evidence, and so on, led to the indictment of State's Attorney Hanrahan, Jalovec, and a dozen Chicago police personnel for conspiring to obstruct justice. This was dropped by Chicago Judge Phillip Romitti on November 1, 1972 as part of a *quid pro quo* arrangement in which remaining charges were dropped against the Panther survivors. The latter then joined the mothers of the deceased in a $47 million civil rights suit against not only the former state defendants, but a number of Chicago police investigators who had "cleared" the raiders of wrongdoing, and the FBI as well.[97]

The Bureau had long-since brought in ace COINTELPRO manager Richard G. Held, who replaced Marlin Johnson as Chicago SAC, in order to handle the administrative aspects of what was to be a monumental attempted cover-up. But even his undeniable skills in this regard were insufficient to gloss over the more than 100,000 pages of relevant Bureau documents concerning Hampton and the Chicago BPP he claimed under oath did not exist. Finally, after years of resolute perjury and

12/11/69

AIRTEL

TO: DIRECTOR, FBI ▓▓▓▓▓

FROM: SAC, CHICAGO ▓▓▓▓▓

SUBJECT: ▓▓▓▓▓▓▓▓▓▓

Re Bureau airtel 12/8/69 and Chicago letter 11/24/69.

Information set forth in Chicago letter and letterhead memorandum of 11/21/69, reflects legally purchased firearms in the possession of the Black Panther Party (BPP) were stored at 2337 West Monroe Street, Chicago. A detailed inventory of the weapons and also a detailed floor plan of the apartment were furnished to local authorities. In addition, the identities of BPP members utilizing the apartment at the above address were furnished. This information was not available from any other source and subsequently proved to be of tremendous value in that it subsequently saved injury and possible death to police officers participating in a raid at the address on the morning of 12/4/69. The raid was based on the information furnished by informant. During the resistance by the BPP members at the time of the raid, the Chairman of the Illinois Chapter, BPP, FRED HAMPTON, was killed and a BPP leader from Peoria, Illinois, was also killed. A quantity of weapons and ammunition were recovered.

It is felt that this information is of considerable value in consideration of a special payment for informant requested in re Chicago letter.

▓▓▓▓▓▓▓▓
1 - Chicago

Airtel recommending cash bonus be paid infiltrator O'Neal for services rendered in the Hampton-Clark assassinations. The money was quickly approved.

---

stonewalling by the FBI and Chicago police, as well as *directed* acquittals of the government defendants by U.S. District Judge J. Sam Perry (which had to be appealed and reversed by the Eighth Circuit Court), People's Law Office attorneys Flint Taylor, Jeff Haas and Dennis Cunningham finally scored. In November 1982, District Judge John F. Grady determined that there was sufficient evidence of a conspiracy to deprive the Panthers of their civil rights to award the plaintiffs $1.85 million in damages.[98]

The Hampton-Clark assassinations were hardly an isolated phenomenon. Four days after the lethal raid in Chicago, a similar scenario was acted out in Los Angeles. In this instance, the FBI utilized an infiltrator named Melvin "Cotton" Smith who, like O'Neal, had become the chief of local BPP security. Like O'Neal, Smith provided the Bureau with a detailed floorplan – albeit, in the form of a cardboard mock-up rather than a mere diagram – of the BPP facility to be assaulted. Forty men from the LAPD SWAT squad were employed, along with more than 100 regular police as "backup" in the 5:30 a.m. attack on December 8, 1969. This time, however, the primary target, LA Panther leader Elmer "Geronimo" Pratt, was not in his assigned spot. Unbeknownst to the police, he had decided to sleep on the floor alongside his bed on the night of the raid; consequently, the opening burst of gunfire which was apparently supposed to kill him missed entirely.[99] Another major difference between the events in Chicago and those in LA was that, in the latter, a sufficient number of Panthers were awake when the shooting started to mount an effective resistance:[100]

> The Panthers chose to defend themselves, and for four hours they fought off the police, refusing to surrender until press and public were on the scene. Six were wounded. Thirteen were arrested. Miraculously, none of them were killed.[101]

As in Chicago, the raiders were headed, not by a SWAT or regular police commander, but by a coordinator of the local police Red Squad. The Los Angeles raid was led by Detective Ray Callahan, a ranking member of the LAPD Criminal Conspiracy Section (CCS), a Panther-focused "subversives unit" tightly interlocked with the local FBI COINTELPRO section, headed by Richard Wallace Held, son of Chicago SAC Richard G. Held.[102] Also as in Chicago, the Panthers were immediately charged with "assaulting the police," an accusation which received considerable media play until it was quietly dropped when the matter was finally decided by a jury – and the defendants acquitted on December 23, 1971.[103] Pratt, meantime, spent a solid two months in the LA County Jail in the wake of the firefight, until his $125,000 bond money could be raised.[104]

As the U.S. Attorney in San Francisco put it at the time, pointing to a special "Panther unit" created by the Justice Department specifically to assist federal/local "cooperation" in "containing" the black liberation movement, "Whatever they say they're doing, they're out to get the Panthers."[105] Hence, although many anti-Panther actions around the country appeared to be purely local police initiatives, most were actually coordinated by the FBI's COINTELPRO operatives in each locality. By 1969, a uniform drumbeat of anti-BPP repression was readily apparent across the nation:

> From April to December, 1969, police raided Panther headquarters in San Francisco, Chicago, Salt Lake City, Indianapolis, Denver, San Diego, Sacramento and Los Angeles, including four separate raids in Chicago, two in San Diego and two in Los Angeles. Frequently Panthers were arrested during these raids on charges such as illegal use of sound equipment, harboring fugitives, possessing stolen goods and flight to avoid prosecution, and later released. In September, 1969, alone, police across the nation arrested Panthers in forty-six separate incidents [at least 348 were arrested during the whole year]...Police raids frequently involved severe damage to Panther headquarters. Thus during a raid in Sacramento in June, 1969, in search of

an alleged sniper who was never found, police sprayed the building with teargas, shot up the walls, broke typewriters and destroyed bulk food the Panthers were distributing free to ghetto children. Sacramento Mayor Richard Marriot said he was "shocked and horrified" by the "shambles" he reported police had left behind. During raids on Panther headquarters in Philadelphia in September, 1970, police ransacked the office, ripped out plumbing and chopped up and carted away furniture. Six Panthers were led into the street, placed against a wall and stripped as Police Chief [later mayor] Frank Rizzo boasted to newsmen, "Imagine the big Black Panthers with their pants down."[106]

Even in the "out back" of Nebraska, the story was the same:

> In August 1971, FBI agents and local police arrested two Black Panthers in Omaha...David Rice and Ed Poindexter, on charges of killing a local policeman. In subsequent investigations by Amnesty International and other human rights agencies, it was revealed that the FBI had collected over 2000 pages of information on the Omaha chapter of the Black Panthers, and that the actual murderer of the police officer was a former drug addict who was soon released by authorities, and who subsequently "disappeared." Both Rice and Poindexter were convicted, however, and still remain in federal penitentiaries.[107]

The pressure placed upon the party through such "extralegal legality" was enormous. As Panther attorney Charles Garry observed in 1970,

> In a period of two years – December, 1967 to December, 1969 – the Black Panther Party has expended in bail-bond premiums alone – just the premiums, that is, money that will never be returned – a sum in excess of $200,000! How many breakfasts or lunches for hungry children, how much medical attention sorely needed in the ghetto communities would that $200,000 have furnished?...In the same two-year period, twenty-eight Panthers were killed...Let me cite some additional statistics, though for a complete record, I would recommend you consult the special issue of *The Black Panther* (February 21, 1970) entitled, "Evidence and Intimidation of Fascist Crimes by U.S.A." Between May 2, 1967 and December 25, 1969 charges were dropped against at least 87 Panthers arrested for a wide variety of so-called violations of the law. Yet these men and women were kept in prison for days, weeks and months even though there was absolutely no evidence against them, and they were finally released. At least a dozen cases involving Panthers have been dismissed in court. In these cases, the purpose has clearly been to intimidate, to frighten, to remove from operation and activities the Panthers, and to hope the [resultant public] hysteria against the Black Panther Party would produce convictions and imprisonments.[108]

By 1970, what was occurring was evident enough that Mayor Wes Uhlman of Seattle, when his police were approached by agents in the local FBI office about rousting the city's BPP chapter, publicly announced that, "We are not going to have any 1932 Gestapo-type raids against anyone."[109] Even SAC Charles Bates in San Francisco had attempted to protest at least the extent of what the Bureau was doing

May 27, 1969

Airtel

1 - ▨▨▨
1 - ▨▨▨
1 - ▨▨▨
1 - ▨▨▨

To: SAC, San Francisco (157-601)

From: Director, FBI (100-448006)

COUNTERINTELLIGENCE PROGRAM
BLACK NATIONALIST - HATE GROUPS   PERSONAL ATTENTION
RACIAL INTELLIGENCE
BLACK PANTHER PARTY (BPP)
BUDED: 6/9/69

        ReSFairtel 5/14/69.

        A review has been made of referenced airtel which
contains your thoughts on the Counterintelligence Program (CIP).
Your reasoning is not in line with Bureau objectives as to our
responsibilities under the CIP.

        You state that while the Department of Justice con-
siders the BPP as a violence-prone organization seeking to
overthrow the Government by revolutionary means, "There seems
to be little likelihood of this." All information developed
to date leads to the obvious conclusion that this group is
dedicated to the principle of violent overthrow and will go
to any length to further this aim.

        You point out that the activities of the BPP have
reached the black and white communities as evidenced by their
weekly newspaper which has reached a circulation of 45,000.
You have previously been instructed to review your files
concerning this newspaper to determine whether we could disrupt
the mailings of the publication. Your answer stated that you
were not in a position to do this. You must immediately take
positive steps to insure that we will be in a position to
accomplish CIP objectives including the disruption of the mailing
of their publications. You must develop adequate informant
coverage to insure that we are in a position to accomplish all
of our objectives, which include steps to counteract the impact
this group has made.

        You state that local and national newspapers continue
to publicize information concerning the BPP. This fact automatical
lends itself toward mass media disseminations to capitalize on this
eagerness and to isolate the organization from the majority of
Americans, both black and white. The dissemination of mass media
information to selected and trusted newspapermen, pointing out the
violent and dangerous nature of a group, has contributed
measurably to the decline of the Ku Klux Klan in the United States.
Newspapers will print derogatory information much easier than
they will print commendatory information, especially if the
organization is by its nature violence-prone. For your informatio
the San Diego Office has waged an effective CIP against the BPP
which has measurably resulted in declining activities and
considerable disruption.

It is noted that BPP leader Bobby Seale speaks in schools and universities and receives fees of up to $1,000. This raises counterintelligence opportunities, among which are anonymous disseminations of derogatory information to universities and misuse of funds received.

As it concerns the BPP, you point out that results achieved by utilizing counterintelligence ideas such as publicizing the evils of violence, the lack of morals, the widespread use of narcotics and anonymous mailings, have not been outstanding. This is because a typical black supporter of the BPP is not disturbed by allegations which would upset a white community. You must recognize that one of our primary aims in counterintelligence as it concerns the BPP is to keep this group isolated from the moderate black and white community which may support it. This is most emphatically pointed out in their Breakfast for Children Program, where they are actively soliciting and receiving support from uninformed whites and moderate blacks. In addition, we have received information from San Francisco and other offices indicating that BPP officials are extremely suspicious of each other as to monies received. This also is a fertile ground for CIP and should be explored.

ReSFairtel states that nation-wide mailings to BPP chapter offices would automatically indicate that the FBI was the source. Mailings originating from Oakland, California, would logically be attributed to someone either at national headquarters of the BPP or a dissident who has recently resigned and had access to the records.

You state that the Bureau under the CIP should not attack programs of community interest such as the BPP "Breakfast for Children." You state that this is because many prominent "humanitarians," both white and black, are interested in the program as well as churches which are actively supporting it. You have obviously missed the point. The BPP is not engaged in the "Breakfast for Children" program for humanitarian reasons. This program was formed by the BPP for obvious reasons, including their efforts to create an image of civility, assume community control of Negroes, and to fill adolescent children with their insidious poison. An example of this is set forth in the May 11, 1969, issue of "The Black Panther." Page seven contains an article captioned "Black Panther Revolutionary Wedding." The article points out that two members of the Panthers were married at a church in Oakland, California, which is participating in the Breakfast Program. The crowd consisted mostly of Panther members and children from the Breakfast Program. Instead of a Bible, Bobby Seale used the "Red Book Quotations from Chairman Mao Tse-tung" to perform the marriage. After the ceremony, the children sang "We Want a Pork Chop Off the Pig."

The CIP in the San Francisco Office must be re-evaluated. During the reevaluation, give thorough consideration to the adequacy of the personnel assigned. Insure that you are utilizing the best personnel available in this program. Advise the Bureau of the results of your reevaluation by June 9, 1969.

Airtel from J. Edgar Hoover reprimanding the San Francisco office for its lack of vigor in pursuing COINTELPRO operations against the BPP.

to the Panthers. For his trouble, Bates received the accompanying May 27, 1969 Airtel from Hoover informing him that he had "obviously missed the point" and that his outlook was "not in line with Bureau objectives." The director also used the opportunity to order Bates to target the BPP Breakfast for Children Program in the Bay Area. Hoover then unleashed William Sullivan to pull Bates' office back in line:

> Sullivan gave Bates two weeks to assign his best agents to the COINTELPRO desks and get on with the task at hand: "Eradicate [the Panthers'] 'serve the people' programs...So [Charles] Gain, [William] Cohendet, and the other four agents assigned to the BPP squad supervised the taps and bugs on Panther homes and offices; mailed a William F. Buckley, Jr., column on the Panthers to prominent citizens in the Bay area; tipped off *San Francisco Examiner* reporter Ed Montgomery to Huey Newton's posh Oakland apartment overlooking Lake Merritt; disrupted the breakfast-for-children program "in the notorious Haight-Ashbury District" and elsewhere by spreading a rumor "that various personnel in [Panther] national headquarters are infected with venereal disease;" tried to break up Panther marriages with letters to wives about affairs with teenage girls; and assisted with a plan to harass the Panthers' attorney, Charles Garry...They carried out dozens of other counterintelligence operations as well.[110]

As should be obvious from the Rice, Poindexter and other cases already mentioned, spurious criminal prosecution was a favorite tactic used in neutralizing the BPP leadership. For instance, in 1969 Black Panther Chairman Bobby Seale was charged along with seven other Chicago conspiracy defendants, "although he had only the most tangential connection with the demonstrations during the Democratic Convention in Chicago during August of 1968 [which precipitated a major police riot in full view of national television, and for which the conspiracy charges were ostensibly brought], having been flown in at the last moment as a substitute speaker, given two speeches and left."[111] Predictably, the charges came to nothing, but not before Seale was denied the right to represent himself at trial, and the country was treated to the spectacle of a major Panther leader bound to his chair and gagged in open court.[112]

Meanwhile, on August 21, 1969 – before the Chicago trial even began – Seale was arrested in California in connection with the alleged New Haven, Connecticut torture-slaying of Alex Rackley, a Panther recruit from New York. Eleven other Panthers (mostly members of the New Haven BPP chapter) were indicted as well.[113] The main witness against Seale and the others turned out to be one of the defendants, George Sams, a police infiltrator and former psychiatric patient who had worked his way into a position in the Panther security apparatus before being expelled from the party by Seale.[114] As it turned out, Sams had accused Rackley of being an informer and had himself carried the bad-jacketing effort through a week-long interrogation during which the young recruit was chained to a bed and scalded with boiling water. Sams had then killed him, dumping the body in a swampy area where it was soon discovered by fishermen.[115]

In the aftermath, one New Haven Panther, Warren Kimbro, pled guilty to second degree murder, not for having killed Rackley, but for not having prevented his death; he was sentenced to life in prison.[116] A second, Lonnie McLucas, was tried alone, convicted of conspiracy to murder and sentenced to 15 years.[117] Sams, the actual killer, was also eventually given a life sentence, despite his various police connections.[118]

Although it was plain that the culprits in this ugly matter had been dealt with – even New Haven Police Chief James F. Ahern stated publicly that there was no evidence that Bobby Seale had been involved in Rackley's death[119] – the state proceeded to bring Seale, along with Ericka Huggins (widow of assassinated LA Panther leader Jon), another "notable," to trial. Apparently, the hope was that the earlier confession and convictions would have tempered public sentiment against the BPP to such an extent that these defendants would be found guilty on the basis of party membership alone. In this the government was disappointed when the "jury in the trial was ready to acquit Seale but...two jurors refused to vote for acquittal unless [Ericka Huggins] was convicted. [Judge Harold M. Mulveny then] ordered both cases dismissed [on May 24, 1971] when the jury reported it was hopelessly deadlocked."[120] State apologists promptly claimed "justice" had been served, but by then Seale had served more than two years in maximum security lockup without bail, much of it in solitary confinement, without ever having been convicted of anything at all, and was never really able to resume his former galvanizing role in the party.[121]

While this was going on, in "August, 1969, three Black Panthers were arrested while riding in a car with a New York City undercover agent, Wilbert Thomas, and charged with a variety of offenses including conspiracy to rob a hotel, attempted murder of a policeman and illegal possession of weapons. During the trial, it developed that Thomas had supplied the car, had drawn a map of the hotel – the only tangible evidence tying the Panthers to the robbery scheme – and had offered to supply the guns. The Panthers were eventually convicted only of a technical weapons charge, based on the fact that a shotgun, which the Panthers said had been planted by Thomas, was found in the car."[122]

Moving ahead, the "FBI pressured the Justice Department to get on with the conspiracy prosecutions," either in federal court or by assisting local prosecutors.[123] One result was that: "In May, 1971, the so-called 'Panther Twenty-One' were acquitted in New York City of charges of having conspired to bomb department stores, blow up police stations and murder policemen; a number of the defendants had been held in jail for over two years under $100,000 bails."[124] This was the 10% cash requirement associated with total bonds of $1,000,000 per defendant, making their aggregate bond a staggering $21,000,000! They had been indicted on April 2, 1969, largely on the basis of accusations tendered by three police infiltrators, Eugene Roberts, Carlos Ashwood (aka: Carl Wood) and Ralph White (aka: Sudan Yedaw). Their testimony literally fell apart in court.[125] The jury deliberated "less than an hour" in acquitting the defendants of all 156 charges levied against them by New York County District Attorney Frank Hogan and Assistant District Attorney Joseph

A. Phillips on the basis of "evidence" provided by "New York police officers and FBI agents."[126] But, as had been the case with Seale, the Panther 21 had been held under maximum security conditions – many in solitary confinement – for months on end, even though they were ultimately shown to have been innocent of the accusations leveled against them.[127] The New York BPP chapter virtually disintegrated during the extended mass incarceration of its entire leadership.

By the beginning of 1970, "the Black Panther Party had been severely damaged by arrests, trials, shootouts and police and FBI harassment which had jailed, killed or exiled most of the top leadership of the party. Nevertheless, in March 1970, the FBI initiated what the Senate Intelligence Committee has labelled a 'concerted program' to drive a permanent wedge between two factions in the party, one supporting Eldridge Cleaver [exiled in Algeria]...and the other supporting [Huey P.] Newton, then still in jail."[128] As can be seen in the accompanying May 14, 1970 memo from George C. Moore to William C. Sullivan, this was approached in a quite deliberate fashion through the use of forged and/or anonymous letters and the like. And, as is brought out clearly in the accompanying September 16, 1970 Airtel (see page 150) from the director to three SACs, the Bureau considered it "immaterial whether facts exist to substantiate" the sorts of charges it was introducing into the BPP communications network.

The sorts of repression which had already been visited upon the BPP had inevitably engendered among party members a strong sense of being in a battle for sheer physical survival, a matter lending potentially lethal implications to FBI-fostered rumors that given individuals or groups of Panthers were, say, police agents. That Hoover and his men were well aware these sorts of tactics could have fatal results for at least some of those targeted is readily discernable on the second page of the September 16 Airtel. As may be seen rather plainly, Hoover disapproved the sending of a particular anonymous letter only because, if it were traced back to its source, its wording might "place the Bureau in the position of aiding and abetting in a murder by the BPP." His instructions were simply to reword the letter in such a way as to accomplish the same result while leaving the FBI a window of "plausible deniability" in the event a homicide did in fact result. While there is no evidence that David Hilliard ever actually responded to COINTELPRO manipulation by attempting to have Newton killed, murders *did* result:

> [In New York] Robert Weaver, a Cleaverite, was shot dead on a Harlem street corner in early March [1971]. A month later persons unknown entered the Queens County office of the Black Panther Party, a Newtonite enclave, bound up Samuel Napier, circulation manager of *The Black Panther*, taped his eyes and mouth, laid him face down on a cot, and shot off the back of his head.[129]

At least three other murders, all in California, seem likely to have been directly related to this aspect of the FBI's anti-BPP COINTELPRO. These were the execution of LA-BPP member Fred Bennett at some point in early 1970 (Bennett's body was never found), Sandra Lane "Red" Pratt (Geronimo Pratt's wife) in LA on January 13,

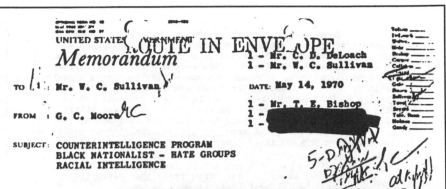

UNITED STATES GOVERNMENT

Memorandum

ROUTE IN ENVELOPE

1 - Mr. C. D. DeLoach
1 - Mr. W. C. Sullivan

TO : Mr. W. C. Sullivan

DATE: May 14, 1970

1 - Mr. T. E. Bishop
1 -
1 -

FROM : G. C. Moore

SUBJECT: COUNTERINTELLIGENCE PROGRAM
BLACK NATIONALIST - HATE GROUPS
RACIAL INTELLIGENCE

This is to recommend that the Counterintelligence Progra against black extremists be continued.

The Counterintelligence Program against black extremist organizations and individuals was initiated August 25, 1967, and on March 4, 1968, it was expanded from 27 to 42 participating field divisions. The goals of this program are to prevent violen by black extremists, to prevent the growth and/or unification of extremist groups, and to prevent extremist groups from gaining respectability in the Negro community. Some of the excellent results of counterintelligence action during the past year are se out below:

To create friction between Black Panther Party (BPP) leader Eldridge Cleaver in Algiers and BPP Headquarters, a spuric letter concerning an internal dispute was sent Cleaver, who accepted it as genuine. As a result, the International Staff of the BPP was neutralized when Cleaver fired most of its members. Bureau personnel received incentive awards from the Director for this operation.

To show the criminal nature of the BPP a write-up conce ing the convictions of its members was prepared and received publicity in a Robert S. Allen and John A. Goldsmith syndicated column of March 31, 1970. Previously we exposed the BPP Breakfa For Children Program in these writers' column of June 14, 1969.

Articles concerning the BPP based on information furni a news media source in Mississippi resulted in the closing of a BPP Chapter in Cleveland, Mississippi.

Counterintelligence action against other extremist org izations has also been effective. In San Diego, California, an anonymous telephone call to the landlord of the US organization resulted in the group being evicted from its Headquarters. In Florida, a television source was helped in the preparation of a gram exposing the Nation of Islam. The excellent results of thi program were contained in a memorandum from G. C. Moore to Mr. W Sullivan, October 21, 1969, on which the Director noted "Excelle

100-448006

CONTINUED - OVER

Memo reporting on the progress of a COINTELPRO utilizing disinformation and anonymous letters to foment a split between the international section of the BPP, headed by Eldridge Cleaver in Algiers, and Huey P. Newton's organization based in Oakland, California. The operation was continued with lethal results.

Concerning the first proposal submitted by Detroit, counterintelligence action by San Francisco to capitalize on Huey P. Newton's favorable stand toward homosexuals has already been authorized by the Bureau. The second Detroit proposal to consider directing an anonymous communication to Newton accusing David Hilliard of stealing BPP funds and depositing them in foreign banks does have merit and the Bureau does not concur with San Francisco's observation that this would have little effect since there is no record that Hilliard is skimming large amounts of money. Purpose of counterintelligence action is to disrupt BPP and it is immaterial whether facts exist to substantiate the charge. If facts are present, it aids in the success of the proposal but the Bureau feels that the skimming of money is such a sensitive issue that disruption can be accomplished without facts to back it up.

Accordingly, Detroit immediately furnish Bureau and San Francisco with specific suggestions and wording to this effect and San Francisco should then review same and submit specific proposal in this regard for approval by Bureau.

With respect to two anonymous letters proposed by Los Angeles, Bureau concurs with San Francisco that to include the card of a member of a rival black extremist group in a letter to Hilliard indicating Newton is marked for assassination could place the Bureau in the position of aiding or initiating a murder by the BPP. Accordingly, Los Angeles' proposal identified as "letter A" is not approved. Los Angeles should reword this letter to convey the same thought without directly indicating that it is from a specific member of a rival group. The letter could imply that the writer would soon get in touch with Hilliard to see what he would pay to have Newton eliminated. Resubmit the revised letter to the Bureau for approval.

Excerpt from a September 16, 1970 Airtel from Hoover informing his COIN-TELPRO operatives that outright lies were appropriate content for anonymous letters, and that murder was an appropriate outcome to such an operation so long as the cause could not be traced back to the Bureau.

1972, and the execution-style slaying of former Newton bodyguard Jimmy Carr by LA Panthers Lloyd Lamar Mims and Richard Rodriguez in San Francisco on April 6, 1972.[130] In the case of Fred Bennett, rather than conducting any serious investigation into his death the Bureau used it as a prop – as the accompanying February 17, 1971 teletype from the SAC, San Francisco to Hoover indicates – in the penning of a bogus letter to Panther Field Marshall Don Cox ("D.C.") in Algeria as a means to "further exploit dissension within the BPP." Bennett's murder remains "unsolved," as does that of Sandra Lane Pratt.

Such atrocities cannot be separated from the FBI's intervention to exacerbate the "Newton-Cleaver Split," a COINTELPRO initiative which was by then in full swing, as was made clear in a January 1, 1971 teletype from the San Francisco SAC to Hoover. The forged letter proposed in this teletype reads as follows:

FD-36 (Rev. 5-22-64)

F B I

Date: 2/17/71

Transmit the following in _____
(Type in plaintext or code)

Via TELETYPE _____ URGENT VITAL
(Priority)

TO: DIRECTOR (100-448006)

FROM: SAN FRANCISCO (157-601)

DECLASSIFIED BY _____
ON _____

COINTELPRO - BLACK EXTREMISTS, RM.

TO FURTHER EXPLOIT DISSENSION WITHIN THE BPP AND

SUSPICIONS REGARDING VARIOUS LEADERS, THE FOLLOWING LETTER

TO ▮▮▮▮▮▮▮ IN ALGERIA

IS PROPOSED BY THE SAN FRANCISCO OFFICE:

"D.C.

"BY NOW YOU HAVE HEARD ABOUT POOR FRED. I HAVE WARNED

HUEY OF THE POSSIBLE CONSEQUENCES. IT SEEMS TO BE GETTING

WORSE. J.B. AND ROBERT ARE NOW ALSO MISSING.

"IN VIEW OF THIS SITUATION YOU BETTER HAVE A LONG TALK

WITH ELDRIDGE BEFORE HE LETS KATHLEEN COME HERE. G. IS REALLY

UP TIGHT. BIG MAN IS JUST JIVING AND NO HELP AT ALL.

"A.C."

THIS LETTER IS ALSO SLANTED TO IMPLY THAT IT CAME FROM

▮▮▮▮▮▮▮ WHOSE EXACT WHEREABOUTS ARE NOT KNOWN TO THE

BPP AND IS IN THE FORM OF A WARNING TO ▮▮▮▮▮▮ IN VIEW OF

CLASSIFIED BY _____
EXEMPT FROM GENERAL DECLASSIFICATION
SCHEDULE OF EXECUTIVE ORDER 11652
EXEMPTION CATEGORY _____
AUTOMATICALLY DECLASSIFIED ON _____

JAC/jr
(1)

Approved: _____ Sent _____ M Per _____
Special Agent in Charge

100-448006-2270

Teletype proposing forged letter playing upon the murder of Fred Bennett as a means of widening the "Newton-Cleaver split." As the document continues (next page) it becomes clear that the gambit is also part of a COINTELPRO to isolate LA-BPP leader Geronimo Pratt (continued on next page).

FL 36 (Rev. 5-22-64)

F B I

Date:

Transmit the following in _____
                              (Type in plaintext or code)

Via _____ _____
                              (Priority)

SF 157-601   CONFIDENTIAL

PAGE TWO

THE SITUATION INVOLVING THE DEATH OF FRED BENNETT. THE
J.B. REFERRED TO IN THE LETTER IS ▓▓▓▓▓ AND ROBERT IS
▓▓▓▓▓▓ WHO TOGETHER WITH ▓▓▓▓ HAVE PREVIOUSLY WORKED
WITH ▓▓▓▓ AND ARE BELIEVED SYMPATHETIC TO THE DISSIDENT
BPP GROUP REPRESENTED BY GERONIMO. THE WHEREABOUTS OF
▓▓▓▓ AND ▓▓▓ IS UNKNOWN AT THE PRESENT TIME TO THE BPP.
INASMUCH AS THE FIRST A.C. LETTER COULD POSSIBLY HAVE BEEN
TAKEN BY NEWTON AS A WARNING FROM THE DISSIDENTS, THIS LETTER
WILL FURTHER THIS BELIEF IF THERE IS ANY DISCUSSION BY
NEWTON WITH BPP REPRESENTATIVES IN ALGERIA.

    THE LETTER ALSO CASTS REFLECTIONS ON ▓▓▓▓▓▓▓▓
CLEAVER STALWART.

    IF SUCCESSFUL, THIS MIGHT FURTHER SPLIT THE BPP AND
PREVENT THE POSSIBILITY OF THE RETURN TO THE U.S. OF KATHLEEN
CLEAVER WHO MIGHT ATTEMPT TO UNIFY THE DISSIDENT FACTIONS
IN THE PARTY IF SHE APPEARS.

                    CONFIDENTIAL

Approved: _____   Sent _____ M Per _____
          Special Agent in Charge   U. S. GOVERNMENT PRINTING OFFICE : 1988 O - 29-650 631

Eldridge,

I know you have not been told what has been happening lately. It is a shame
that a person, as well-placed as I am and so desirous of improving our Party, cannot
by present rules travel to or communicate with you. I really don't know where you
stand in relationship to our leaders and really am not confident you would protect
me in the event of exposure. Since this is my life-work, just let me say I have worked

long and well in your behalf in the past, and for the Party in many places on Planet Earth.

Things around Headquarters are dreadfully disorganized with the Comrade Commander not making proper decisions. The newspaper is in shambles. No one knows who is in charge. The Foreign Department gets no support. Brothers and sisters are accused of all sorts of things. The point of all this is to say I fear there is rebellion working just beneath the surface. You may know the story about "G" and his gang. I believe that people like "G" have many sympathizers who are not yet under suspicion but who should be. They have friends right in Headquarters where the Minister chooses to ignore them.

I am disturbed because I, myself, do not know which way to turn. While I think the Comrade Commander is weak, yet I do not like the evidences of disloyalty I see. I may be wrong but I think the core of this disloyalty (maybe you think what I consider disloyalty is actually supreme loyalty to the ideals of the Party rather than the leader himself) is with persons formerly close to the Field Marshall. If only you were here to inject some strength into the Movement, or to give some advice. One of two steps must be taken soon and both are drastic. We must either get rid of the Supreme Commander or get rid of the disloyal members. I know the brothers mean well but I fear the only sensible course that the Party can take is to initiate strong and complete action against the rebels, exposing their underhanded tricks to the community. Huey is really all we have right now and we can't let him down, regardless of how poorly he is acting, unless you feel otherwise. Remember he is still able to bring in the bread.

– Comrade C –

The letter was attributed by the Bureau to party member Connie Matthews ("Comrade C"), and designed – according to the text of the remainder of the teletype – not only to cause general "turmoil among the top echelon [of the BPP; *e.g.*: by casting doubt upon Field Marshall Don Cox, a Cleaver ally]," but to specifically target LA Panther leader Geronimo Pratt ("G") for suspicion by the Cleaver faction. Note the call for "drastic action" in the letter. This, after at least one Panther (Fred Bennett) was already thought to have been killed as a result of the Bureau's deliberate heightening of tensions attending "the split," and in the context of a lively internal dialogue among COINTELPRO planners concerning the probability that others would die if such tactics were continued. Under the circumstances, there can be little doubt as to the Bureau's intent in approving and sending the bogus missive.

Concerning Pratt, he had already been the target of a similar COINTELPRO operation which had led to his formal expulsion (as a "police agent" and/or a "Cleaverite") by the Newton faction on January 23, 1971.[131] This earlier operation, handled by LA COINTELPRO section head Richard W. Held and two subordinates, Richard H. Bloeser and Brendan Cleary, included the high priority targeting of Pratt – as one of the 100-odd "Key Activists" selected for inclusion in the Bureau's Black Nationalist Photo Album – and LA-BPP associate John William Washington for discrediting as part of the overall strategy to "deny unity of action" to the Panthers, a

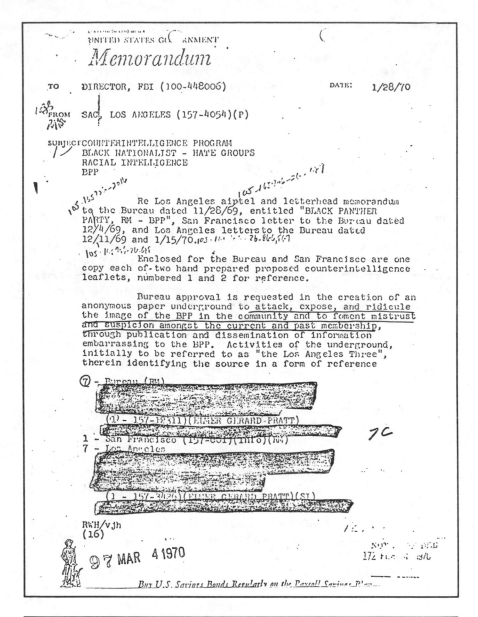

UNITED STATES GOVERNMENT

Memorandum

TO : DIRECTOR, FBI (100-448006)   DATE: 1/28/70

FROM : SAC, LOS ANGELES (157-4054)(P)

SUBJECT: COUNTERINTELLIGENCE PROGRAM
BLACK NATIONALIST - HATE GROUPS
RACIAL INTELLIGENCE
BPP

Re Los Angeles airtel and letterhead memorandum to the Bureau dated 11/28/69, entitled "BLACK PANTHER PARTY, RM - BPP", San Francisco letter to the Bureau dated 12/4/69, and Los Angeles letters to the Bureau dated 12/11/69 and 1/15/70.

Enclosed for the Bureau and San Francisco are one copy each of two hand prepared proposed counterintelligence leaflets, numbered 1 and 2 for reference.

Bureau approval is requested in the creation of an anonymous paper underground to attack, expose, and ridicule the image of the BPP in the community and to foment mistrust and suspicion amongst the current and past membership, through publication and dissemination of information embarrassing to the BPP. Activities of the underground, initially to be referred to as "the Los Angeles Three", therein identifying the source in a form of reference

⑦ - Bureau (RM)

(1) - 157-12311)(ELMER GERARD PRATT)

1 - San Francisco (157-601)(Info)(RM)
7 - Los Angeles

(1) - 157-3126)(ELMER GERARD PRATT)(SI)

RWH/vjh
(16)

97 MAR 4 1970

Buy U.S. Savings Bonds Regularly on the Payroll Savings Plan

Memo targeting Geronimo Pratt and his lieutenant John William "Long John" Washington for neutralization, denying "unity of action" to the LA-BPP.

matter brought out in the accompanying January 28 memo and June 26, 1970 teletype from the SAC, Los Angeles, to the director (see page 156).

This tied to a second dimension of a campaign to neutralize the LA party leader

LA 157-4054

common to Panther rhetoric, would be prepared to suggest
participation by active and past members of the Los Angeles
Black Panther Party (LA BPP). The selection of the
organization's name is an arbitrary one which lends itself
to a future display of the group's growth if the response
warrants. The necessity for the anonymity of the underground organization could be explained, if necessary, as
an imperative precaution in view of the past acts of violence
and retaliation executed by the LA BPP.

        It is anticipated that this counterintelligence
proposal could serve as one phase of a continuous attempt
to deny unity of action in the effort of the LA BPP by
calling to question the actions of the organization and the
legitimacy of its leadership.

        It is felt that the production and distribution
of these leaflets could be such that the identity of the
FBI as the source of the proposed organization could be
effectively concealed.

        In this respect, Bureau approval is requested in
the preparation and dissemination of leaflets similar to
the enclosed in the vicinities of 4115 South Central,
9818 Anzac, and 1810 East 103rd Street, locations of BPP
activities in Los Angeles. It would be the intention of the
Los Angeles Division to distribute leaflet No. 2 seven to
ten days following the introduction of leaflet No. 1, as
any follow up should not only make the effort a topical one,
but stimulate increased reaction within the Los Angeles BPP.

        Operation Number One is designed to challenge the
legitimacy of the authority exercised by ELMER GERARD PRATT,
BPP Deputy Minister of Defense for Southern California, and
JOHN WILLIAM WASHINGTON, an active member of the BPP in Los
Angeles.

        Operation Number Two is utilized to publicize the
illicit sexual activities allegedly encouraged and engaged
in by ▓▓▓▓▓▓▓▓▓▓▓▓▓▓▓▓▓▓▓▓▓▓▓▓▓▓▓▓▓▓▓▓▓ 7C

- 2 -

which saw him charged on December 16, 1970 with the so-called "Tennis Court Murder" (committed on December 18, 1968 in Santa Monica, California).[132] The "evidence" linking Pratt to the crime was primarily that of an FBI infiltrator, Julius C. "Julio" Butler, who was to perjure himself during the ensuing trial by testifying that he had had no paid association with any police agency since joining the BPP.[133] At trial, the FBI also denied the existence of ELSURS logs concerning its wiretapping and other electronic surveillance of the Panther national headquarters in Oakland, a record which would have established that Pratt was in the San Francisco Bay area, some 350 miles north of Santa Monica, on the evening the murder occurred. When the monitoring was later revealed, the Bureau claimed that its logs covering the two-week period which might have exonerated Pratt had been "lost."[134] The upshot of the Bureau's bad-jacketing COINTELPRO was that during the course of his trial, the

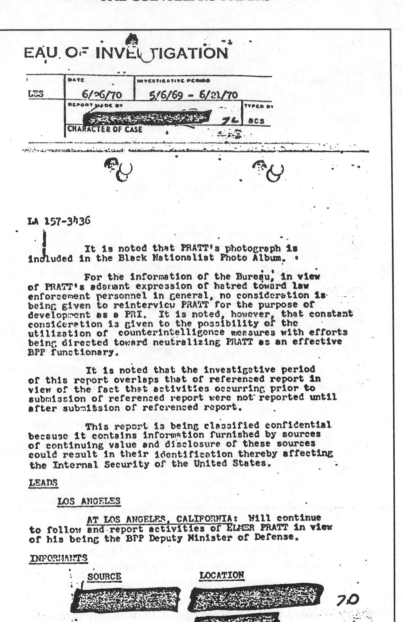

	DATE	INVESTIGATIVE PERIOD		
LES	6/26/70	5/6/69 - 6/21/70		
	REPORT MADE BY			TYPED BY
			JL	BCS
	CHARACTER OF CASE			

LA 157-3436

It is noted that PRATT's photograph is
included in the Black Nationalist Photo Album.

For the information of the Bureau, in view
of PRATT's adamant expression of hatred toward law
enforcement personnel in general, no consideration is
being given to reinterview PRATT for the purpose of
development as a PRI. It is noted, however, that constant
consideration is given to the possibility of the
utilization of counterintelligence measures with efforts
being directed toward neutralizing PRATT as an effective
BPP functionary.

It is noted that the investigative period
of this report overlaps that of referenced report in
view of the fact that activities occurring prior to
submission of referenced report were not reported until
after submission of referenced report.

This report is being classified confidential
because it contains information furnished by sources
of continuing value and disclosure of these sources
could result in their identification thereby affecting
the Internal Security of the United States.

LEADS

LOS ANGELES

AT LOS ANGELES, CALIFORNIA: Will continue
to follow and report activities of ELMER PRATT in view
of his being the BPP Deputy Minister of Defense.

INFORMANTS

SOURCE   LOCATION

Teletype denoting Geronimo Pratt's inclusion in the Black Nationalist Photo
Album, his refusal to cooperate with the FBI as a "Racial Informant," and the
Bureau's consequent intention to bad-jacket him.

target was isolated from the legal support which might have accrued from his former party associates, both within the Newton faction and – to some extent at least – the Cleaver faction as well. He was thus convicted, and sentenced to life imprisonment.[135] At present, he remains incarcerated at San Quentin.[136]

> An equally troubling case in New York involve[s] another COINTELPRO target, {Richard] Dhoruba Moore. A codefendant in the Panther 21 case who believed Newton had ordered his assassination, Moore jumped bail, fled the country, and was acquitted in absentia in March 1971. Police officers arrested him three months later at an after-hours club in the Bronx, booking him as a John Doe. The officers also confiscated a .45 calibre [sub]machine gun at the club. When they discovered Moore's identity, they charged him with the attempted murder of two patrolmen [Thomas Curry and Nicholas Binetti] who had been assigned to guard the Riverside Drive home of Panther 21 prosecutor Frank Hogan. Moore was indicted, tried, and convicted, with the court handing down a sentence of twenty-five years to life. The question that [goes] to the heart of the criminal justice system ha[s] less to do with Dhoruba Moore's guilt or innocence than whether he received a fair trial.[137]

A similar case is that of the "New York Three" – Herman Bell, Anthony "Jalil" Bottom and Albert "Nuh" Washington, members of the New York BPP chapter and alleged Black Liberation Army (BLA) members – sentenced to serve 25-year-to-life prison terms in 1975 for the 1971 shooting deaths of NYPD patrolmen Waverly Jones and Joseph Piagentini. Only much later, during the early '80s, did it begin to come out that the FBI had carefully concealed significant exculpatory material such as a ballistics report showing conclusively that the crucial piece of "physical evidence" introduced at trial – a .45 caliber automatic pistol in Bell's possession at the time of his arrest – was *not* (as prosecutors claimed) the weapon used to kill the policemen. Suppressed Bureau documents also record that a key government witness, Ruben Scott, was first tortured and then offered a deal on a pending murder charge against him in exchange for his "cooperation" against the three in court; Scott has subsequently recanted the entirety of his testimony. Two other witnesses were jailed for 13 months and threatened with loss of custody over their children to induce their testimony. Each woman was not only released from jail and allowed to retain custody, but also provided a rent-free apartment and $150 per week stipend for several years after her stint on the witness stand. At the time Bell, Bottom and Washington were tried, and during their subsequent appeals, the FBI falsely contended it had "nothing relevant" regarding their case. As is plainly shown in the accompanying January 24, 1974 memo from G.C. Moore to W.R. Wannall, this was no accident; the Bureau was quite concerned to insure that it could not be identified as the source of information being presented by the state. It thus avoided being compelled to disclose evidence which might have served to exonerate the defendants or bring about reversal of their convictions. As of this writing, all three men remain in prison after 15 years.[138]

Like the case of Geronimo Pratt, both the Dhoruba Moore case and that of the

UNITED STATES GOVERNMENT

Memorandum   1 - Office of Legal Counsel

TO   MR. W. R. WANNALL   DATE: January 21, 1974

                                         1 - Mr. W. R. Wannall
FROM   Mr. G. C. MOORE   1 - Mr. G. C. Moore
                                         1 - Mr. P. V. Daly

SUBJECT NEWKILL

PURPOSE:

   Purpose of this memorandum is to advise that the New York City Police Department (NYCPD) made available to defense attorneys copies of its investigative reports relative to captioned matter, pursuant to a court order, which reports contained information furnished by the Bureau. The New York Office advised, however, that the Bureau could not be identified in these reports as the source of the information.

BACKGROUND:

   Newkill is the code word used for the Bureau's investigation concerning the killing of two New York City police officers on 5/21/71. This investigation was initiated pursuant to request by President Nixon made of the Bureau on 5/26/71. Pertinent results of this investigation were made available to the NYCPD via letterhead memoranda (LHMs).

   The 1/8/74 issue of "The New York Times" reported that New York State Supreme Court Justice Roberts ordered the prosecution in captioned matter to make available any information contained in police files favorable to the defendants. According to this article, the Justice, after reviewing the police files, turned over most of this material to defense lawyers.

   We queried the New York Office as to whether any of the information furnished to the defense attorneys originated from the FBI and whether it could be clearly identified as such. New York Office, after contact with local authorities in New York, determined that the LHMs made available to the police by the Bureau concerning this matter were not turned over to the defense attorneys nor could the information furnished to the defense attorneys be clearly identified as originating from these LHMs. To date, there is no apparent indication that the defense attorneys may make a similar motion concerning information contained in Bureau files relative to our investigation on Newkill.

REG 45

ACTION: For information.

157-22002

PVD:ekw

57 JAN 28 1974

Memo showing the care taken by the FBI to hide the fact that it had gathered evidence which might have served to exonerate the New York Three. The coverup continued into the 1980s, and to an unknown extent goes on at present.

New York Three are bound up in the context of the FBI's COINTELPRO activities regarding the Newton-Cleaver split. These activities – as are partially reflected in the accompanying excerpt from a February 2, 1971 Hoover Airtel to 29 SACs (see next page) – left the BPP in divisive opposing factions, each utterly unable to provide coherent legal defense to its membership. That the FBI and cooperating police agencies capitalized upon this situation to the utmost has become increasingly apparent.

On other fronts, the Bureau engaged in a range of anti-Panther counterintelligence operations which ranged from the orchestration of murder to attempts to deny funding to BPP legal defense efforts. An example of the former may be found in the FBI's assistance to its allies in the LAPD's CCS to set up the celebrated prison author (and honorary BPP Field Marshal), George Jackson, for assassination inside San Quentin on August 21, 1971, and its subsequent use of the incident as the basis for accusations intended to neutralize Angela Y. Davis, head of Jackson's defense organization and a leading Panther-associated spokesperson.[139] On the latter count, as the accompanying May 21, 1970 memo from the New York SAC (see page 162) makes clear, efforts were undertaken (successfully, as it turned out) to utilize the earlier mentioned spurious information concerning BPP "anti-Semitism" to dry up legal defense contributions flowing from individuals such as Leonard Bernstein, wealthy conductor of the New York Philharmonic, to the Panther 21.[140]

According to the Senate Select Committee, other targets dealt with by the Bureau in a fashion comparable to that used against Bernstein included author Donald Freed (who headed the "Friends of the Panthers" organization in LA), Ed Pearl of the Peace and Freedom Party, the actress Jane Fonda, "the [unidentified] wife of a famous Hollywood actor," an unidentified "famous entertainer," and an employee of the Union Carbide Corporation, among others.[141] In each case, COINTELPRO actions were undertaken which "would be an effective means of combating BPP fund-raising activities among liberal and naive individuals."[142]

Elsewhere, the FBI utilized the services of an infiltrator to have the Sacramento chapter of the BPP print a racist and violence-oriented coloring book for children. When the item was brought to the attention of Bobby Seale and other members of the Panther leadership, it was immediately ordered destroyed rather than distributed. Nonetheless, the Bureau mailed copies to companies – including Safeway Stores, Inc., Mayfair Markets and the Jack-In-The-Box Corporation – which had been contributing food to the party's Breakfast for Children program, in order to cause the withdrawal of such support.[143] In the same vein, anonymous letters were mailed to the parishioners and bishop of a San Diego priest, Father Frank Curran, who had been allowing the Panthers to use his church as a Breakfast for Children serving facility, in order that use of the church be withdrawn and Father Curran transferred to "somewhere in the State of New Mexico for permanent assignment."[144]

Considerable COINTELPRO attention was also focused upon *The Black Panther* newspaper because, as was observed by FBI headquarters in 1970, "The BPP newspaper has a circulation of...139,000. It is the voice of the BPP and if it could be

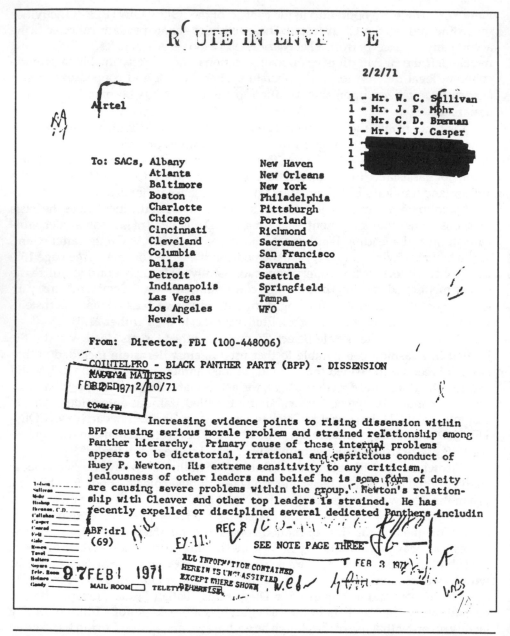

R UTE IN LNVE E

2/2/71

Airtel

1 - Mr. W. C. Sullivan
1 - Mr. J. P. Mohr
1 - Mr. C. D. Brennan
1 - Mr. J. J. Casper
1 -
1 -
1 -

To: SACs, Albany   New Haven
          Atlanta   New Orleans
          Baltimore   New York
          Boston   Philadelphia
          Charlotte   Pittsburgh
          Chicago   Portland
          Cincinnati   Richmond
          Cleveland   Sacramento
          Columbia   San Francisco
          Dallas   Savannah
          Detroit   Seattle
          Indianapolis   Springfield
          Las Vegas   Tampa
          Los Angeles   WFO
          Newark

From: Director, FBI (100-448006)

COINTELPRO - BLACK PANTHER PARTY (BPP) - DISSENSION
RACIAL MATTERS
2/10/71

COMM-FBI

Increasing evidence points to rising dissension within
BPP causing serious morale problem and strained relationship among
Panther hierarchy. Primary cause of these internal problems
appears to be dictatorial, irrational and capricious conduct of
Huey P. Newton. His extreme sensitivity to any criticism,
jealousness of other leaders and belief he is some form of deity
are causing severe problems within the group. Newton's relationship with Cleaver and other top leaders is strained. He has
recently expelled or disciplined several dedicated Panthers includin

ABF:drl
(69)   REC 8

                        SEE NOTE PAGE THREE

9 FEB 1971   ALL INFORMATION CONTAINED
                    HEREIN IS UNCLASSIFIED
MAIL ROOM☐ TELETYPE UNIT☐ EXCEPT WHERE SHOWN

Self-congratulatory Airtel describing the success of the COINTELPRO attending the
"Newton-Cleaver Split" in terms of "rising dissension within the BPP causing serious
morale problem and strained relationship among Panther hierarchy," which caused a
rapid disintegration of the Party.

Airtel to Albany et al
Re: COINTELPRO - Black Panther Party (BPP) - Dissension
100-448006

▬▬▬▬▬▬▬▬▬▬▬▬▬▬▬ and Newton's
▬▬▬▬▬▬▬▬ and companions who were involved
in BPP underground operation (see 1/23/71 edition of
"The Black Panther"); and the "New York 21" who were a
leading cause celebre of Pantherism.

This dissension coupled with financial difficulties
offers an exceptional opportunity to further disrupt,
aggravate and possibly neutralize this organization through
counterintelligence. In light of above developments this
program has been intensified by selected offices and should
be further expanded to increase measurably the pressure on
the BPP and its leaders.

San Francisco and New York are already involved
in counterintelligence actions and should continue to be
alert for further opportunities. All other recipients
should immediately devise at least two counterintelligence
proposals and submit same to Bureau by 2/10/71. First
proposal should be aimed strictly at creating dissension
within the local branch. Second proposal should be aimed
at creating dissension or problems between local branch
and/or its leaders and BPP national headquarters. Submit
each proposal in a separate airtel referencing this
communication and in first paragraph specifically indicate
whether proposal aimed at local dissension or national
dissension.

In order for these proposals to be effective it
is imperative that a close analysis be made of weaknesses
and problems within the local BPP branch and that all
proposals submitted be imaginative and timely. No proposal
should be implemented without specific Bureau approval.

effectively hindered, it would result in helping to cripple the BPP."[145] The methods employed for this purpose included an unsuccessful effort to use the IRS to close *The Black Panther* down and the sending of bogus cards and letters, attributed to the Minutemen organization, to the paper's staff purporting to show that the violent right-wing group intended to attack them physically (the operation was apparently intended to frighten the staff into quitting or at least suspending production of their publication).[146] The Bureau also attempted to bring about bankruptcy of the paper by convincing freight companies to shift from the general rate pertaining to printed material to the "full legal rate allowable for newspaper shipment."

Officials advise this increase...means approximately a forty percent increase. Officials agree to determine cosignor in San Francisco and from this determine cosignees throughout the United States so that it can impose full legal tariff. They believe the

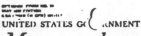

UNITED STATES GOVERNMENT

Memorandum

TO   : DIRECTOR, FBI (100-448006)   DATE: 5/21/70

FROM   : SAC, NEW YORK (100-161140) (P)

SUBJECT: COUNTERINTELLIGENCE PROGRAM
          BLACK NATIONALIST - HATE GROUPS
          RACIAL INTELLIGENCE

          ReNYlet to Bureau, 2/25/70.

1. Operations Under Consideration

          It is felt by the NYO that BPP operations can best be
disrupted by exposing them to individuals and groups who would have
a natural or conditioned animosity toward the BPP aims and ideals.

          The above can be accomplished through the continued use
of anonymous letters and handbills which would be directed toward
those who may be expected to act through economic or personal
means against the BPP thereby hindering BPP operations.

          The NYO realizes the importance of negating the financial
benefits coming to the BPP through the distribution of their official
newspaper "The Black Panther" and will continue to attempt to derive
a logical and practical plan to thwart this crucial BPP operation.

2. Operations Being Submitted

          On 2/27/70, correspondence was directed to individuals
known to have attended a BPP fund-raising function at the home of
the well known musician, LEONARD BERNSTEIN. This correspondence
outlined the BPP's anti-Semetic posture and pro-Arab position.

          On 3/5/70, mimeograph copies of a "BPP solicitation
letter" and a "Store owners letter" were sent to BPP headquarters
in NYC as per Bureau instructions dated 3/5/70.

          On 3/6/70, information was furnished to an established
newspaper contact concerning the source of monies used to raise
bail for one of the "Panther 21", a group of BPP members on trial
in New York City.

2- Bureau (RM)
1- New York (43)

JLL:tf
(3)

REC 17

EX-115

IO MAY 22 1970

-1783

ALL INFORMATION CONTAINED
HEREIN IS UNCLASSIFIED
EXCEPT WHERE SHOWN

RACIAL INT. SECT.

Buy U.S. Savings Bonds Regularly on the Payroll Savings Plan

Memo outlining plan to deny legal defense funding to the BPP in New York from
supporters such as Philharmonic conductor Leonard Bernstein. Note reliance upon the
"anti-Semitic" ploy and involvement of the JDL discussed earlier.

NY 100-161140

On 4/1/70, the NYO participated in the formulation of a Counterintelligence proposal submitted by San Francisco office and directed against black militant leader LEROY ELDRIDGE CLEAVER.

On 4/20/70, the NYO sent a letter to various individuals familiar with BPP activities in the New York area concerning STOKELY CARMICHAEL's views on the late ADOLPH HITLER.

3. Tangible Results

On 5/7/70, ▮▮▮▮▮▮▮▮▮▮▮▮ both of whom have furnished reliable information in the past, advised that on that date approximately 35 members of the Jewish Defense League (JDL) picketed the Harlem Branch of the BPP in NYC. The purpose of this demonstration was to show that the JDL feels the BPP is anti-Semetic in its acts and words.

Also on the above date approximately 50 members of the JDL demonstrated outside of the Bronx, New York BPP Headquarters for the aforementioned reasons.

In view of the above actions by the JDL it is felt that some of the counterintelligence measures of the NYO have produced tangible results.

4. Developments of Counter-
   Intelligence Interests

As the summer season approaches the NYO will be keenly aware of the activities of various racial and hate groups in New York City for the exploitation of such activities within the continuing counterintelligence program.

The NYO will immediately inform the Bureau of any situations or developments that occur where counterintelligence techniques may be used.

airlines are due the differences in freight tariffs as noted above for the past six to eight months, and are considering discussions with their legal staff concerning suit for recovery of deficit...[T]hey estimate that in New York alone [it] will exceed ten thousand dollars.[147]

When such actions failed to engender the desired results, the San Diego field office came up with the idea of utilizing a stink-bomb to close the paper's production facility; the San Diego SAC recommended using Skatol, "a chemical agent in powdered form...[which] emits an extremely noxiously [sic] odor rendering the premises surrounding the point of application uninhabitable."[148] This plan also failed, probably because a burglary was required to carry it out, and agents could not "achieve entry" into the "area utilized for production of 'The Black Panther'."[149] Overall, the Bureau's counterintelligence offensive against this element of "the free press" was undertaken because, in the words of the SAC, New York:

[The FBI] realizes the financial benefits coming to the BPP through the sale of this newspaper. Continued efforts will [therefore] be made to derive logical and practical plans to thwart this crucial BPP operation.[150]

The FBI has admitted that, during the COINTELPRO era proper (1956-71), it ran some 295 distinct COINTELPRO operations against individuals and organizations which – using a broad definition – may be considered as part of the black liberation movement. Of these, 233 were aimed at the BPP between 1967 and 1971.[151] The total number of fatalities resulting from these brutally illegal activities on the part of the nation's "top law enforcement agency" will probably never be known, nor will the number of years spent by innocent people railroaded into prison cells or the number of lives wrecked in somewhat more subtle ways. The government has, for obvious reasons, been loath to offer anything approximating a comprehensive study of what is known such things, even in the midst of such "housecleanings" as the Church Committee investigations of the mid-'70s.

Under the weight of such ruthless, concerted and sustained repression – and despite the incredible bravery with which many of its members attempted to continue their work – the Black Panther Party simply collapsed. Some of its survivors moved into the essentially militaristic Black Liberation Army, founded by BPP member Zayd Malik Shakur (s/n: James Costan) and others in New York as early as 1971.[152] Many others dropped out of radical activism altogether. By 1974, although there was still an Oakland organization bearing the name, the BPP could no longer be considered a viable political force by any standard of measure. With it, whatever its defects may have been, passed the best possibility of Afro-Americans attaining some real measure of self-sufficiency and self-determination which has presented itself during the 20th century.

Chapter 6

COINTELPRO – New Left

If [SDS] or any group was organized on a national basis to subvert our society, then I think Congress should pass laws to suppress that activity. When you see an epidemic like this cropping up all over the country – the same kind of people saying the same kinds of things – you begin to get the picture that it is a national subversive activity...[SDS and other new left activists] should be rounded up and put in a detention camp.

– Richard G. Kleindienst –
U.S. Deputy Attorney General
1969

The "new left" was a primarily white, campus-based, initially non-marxist oppositional movement which emerged in the aftermath of the 1950s ("McCarthyite") repression of "old left" political formations such as the CP,USA. Beginning with the establishment of Students for a Democratic Society (SDS) by a handful of college radicals including Al Haber and Tom Hayden during 1960-61, the new left had by the end of the decade come to encompass a multiplicity of organizations and literally hundreds of thousands of participants.[1] Along the way, it had engaged itself in a range of issues and activities including the pursuit of a vision of "participatory democracy," support to civil rights and black liberation groups like SNCC and the BPP, socio-economic reform in the inner cities, transformation of the educational process, attempts to hammer out a "new working class theory," anti-Vietnam war endeavors and, ultimately, a neo-marxian form of anti-imperialism.[2]

In his memoirs, COINTELPRO head William C. Sullivan claims that as of the spring of 1968 – when an SDS-led student action closed prestigious Columbia University – "we didn't know the New Left existed."[3] As Sullivan tells the story:

I teletyped the New York office and asked them what was behind all this and demanded to know what information they had. That afternoon I received a memorandum from New York that had attached to it a number of newspaper articles. I teletyped New York again, saying, "I don't want newspaper clippings. I want to know what you have in the files about the student uprising at Columbia University." New York got back to me again with the terse response, "We don't have anything."[4]

As with many of the assertions contained in the FBI assistant director's "history" of COINTELPRO, the account is less than truthful. At least as early as mid-1965, J. Edgar Hoover had asked for, and Attorney General Nicholas deB. "Katzenbach

[had] approved requests for taps on SDS."[5] There is also solid evidence that by this point, the Bureau had already begun to systematically infiltrate the student organization.[6] Such ELSURS and informant activity *vis à vis* SDS was an integral part of a more generalized FBI "political intelligence" emphasis during the period 1964-68 which saw the installation of more than 800 wiretaps and some 700 bugs (facilitated by at least 150 surreptitious entries), and an unknown number of informants and infiltrators, all utilized in "non-criminal investigations."[7] The Bureau had also been availing itself of the proceeds concerning SDS and other new left organizations deriving from CIA "mail covers" since at least as early as 1964.[8] Far from the Bureau's being unaware of the new left's existence until 1968, Hoover himself had gone on record in February 1966 describing SDS as "one of the most militant organizations" in the country and claiming that "communists are actively promoting and participating in the activities of this organization."[9] The same sort of perspective prevailed, albeit in somewhat less pronounced fashion, with regard to other new left individuals and organizations.

Friends of SNCC

Actually, the Bureau's interest in the new left had been lively since as early as 1961, when white activists, often referred to as "Friends of SNCC," began to accompany that group's civil rights workers on "Freedom Rides" into the Deep South. The objective of the rides was to integrate public transportation facilities coming under interstate transport regulations in states such as Alabama, Mississippi, Louisiana and Georgia, as well as to draw public attention to the Jim Crow laws still governing interracial affairs in the region and the lack of federal action to address the situation.[10] Kenneth O'Reilly recounts the performance of the FBI as the second of two buses arrived at Anniston, Alabama, about 60 miles from Birmingham, on May 13, 1961 (the first one, a Greyhound, having already been destroyed by local klansmen shortly before):

> The FBI watched as the second bus, the Trailways, pulled into Anniston within an hour. Eight toughs boarded, demanded the black riders move to the rear, and then beat two of the white riders, Dr. Walter Bergman and James Peck...The sixty-one-year-old Peck, a retired school administrator, suffered permanent brain damage. When the bus arrived at its terminal in Birmingham about fifty minutes later, a mob of about forty Klansmen and members of the National States Rights Party [a neo-nazi group] greeted the Freedom Riders. Most carried baseball bats or chains. A few had lead pipes. [The FBI looked on again as] one of them knocked down the unfortunate Peck once more.[11]

Although the Bureau had been "aware of the planned violence for weeks in advance, the FBI did nothing to stop it and had actually given the Birmingham police [headed by the notorious segregationist Eugene "Bull" Connor] details regarding the Freedom Riders' schedule, knowing full well that at least one law enforcement officer [Thomas H. Cook] relayed everything to the klan."[12] The Bureau, as journalist I.F. Stone observed at the time, "live[d] in cordial fraternity with the cops who enforce[d] white supremacy."[13] More, the FBI had a paid employee, Gary Thomas Rowe, among the klansmen who actually participated in the beatings administered at the Birmingham bus terminal. Such performance by the Bureau, which falsely claimed to be "neutral" and to lack "enforcement jurisdiction" in civil rights matters, remained consistent throughout the early '60s;[14] at best the FBI simply watched as activists were brutalized, at worst it assisted in orchestrating the brutalization.[15]

At the same time the Bureau was actively foot-dragging in its responsibilities to protect civil rights workers engaged in efforts to secure such fundamental social prerogativesfor black people as voting and using public restrooms, it was busily investigating the victims themselves:

> Under the pressure of events that began with the Freedom Rides and continued over the next two years, Hoover escalated FBI intelligence gathering activities. Earlier, in the mid-1950s, the Bureau conducted investigations of racial disturbances, particularly demonstrations and clashes arising out of school desegregation, but generally did not file reports with the [Justice Department] Civil Rights Division. Instead, the Bureau sent its reports to the Department's Internal Security Division, where the Division bumped them back over to Civil Rights after five or ten days. By organizing information from the FBI "around the requirements of internal security surveillance rather than civil rights protection," this procedure focused the Civil Rights Division's attention on the activities of the Communist party and not disenfranchisement, segregated schools and transportation, and other obstacles to black equality.[16]

Between March 1959 and January 1960, the FBI distributed 892 separate reports on "racial matters" – none having to do with the klan or other white racist organizations, but many of them dealing with support to the civil rights movement accruing from the budding new left – not only to the Justice Department, but to the various military intelligence agencies, as well as state and local police forces.[17]

> [FBI Section Head Courtney] Evans' [Special Investigation] Division ran the names of hundreds of individuals through the files at the request of Kennedy administration officials. The subjects of these searches ranged from the National Negro Congress, a communist front that had been dead for fourteen years, to James Baldwin, William Faulkner, and fifty other Nobel Prize laureates whose names graced a White House dinner invitation list – part of John and Jacqueline Kennedy's program to encourage and honor cultural and intellectual achievement. In Faulkner's case, the Bureau noted his statement to the Civil Rights Congress, another communist front and successor to the National Negro Congress, on behalf of Willie McGhee, convicted of raping a white woman in Laurel, Mississippi, in 1945. (McGhee exhausted all possible appeals by March 1951, when the Supreme Court refused to hear his case, and to the day the state executed him the FBI seemed most interested in exploring the "Communist connections" of one of his noncommunist lawyers, Bella Abzug). [18]

Under such circumstances, it is hardly surprising that when three young activists – James Chaney, Michael Schwerner and Andrew Goodman – disappeared in Neshoba County, Mississippi on June 21, 1963, the FBI had active "subversive" files open on one of the two whites, Schwerner, as well as Chaney, a 21-year-old black man. As it turned out, the three were in the area as part of a joint "Mississippi Freedom Summer" project being run by SNCC and CORE, registering voters in preparation for the sending of a black "Mississippi Freedom Democratic Party" (MFDP) delegation to the 1964 Democratic convention in Atlantic City, a significant step toward dismantling the Jim Crow structure of the "regular" state party hierarchy. On the fateful morning, they had driven from CORE headquarters in the sizable town of Meridian, Mississippi to the village of Longdale in order to investigate the beatings of three local blacks and burning of the Mt. Zion Church by the klan shortly before. On their return trip, they were arrested – ostensibly for speeding – by Neshoba County Deputy Sheriff Cecil Price and jailed in nearby Philadelphia, Mississippi. The deputy held them until approximately 10 p.m., released them, followed them out of town, and then stopped them again. This time, he turned them over to a group of klansmen who killed all three and then buried the bodies beneath a local dam construction project.[19]

The FBI had long since received informant reports that state klan leader Sam Bowers, Jr., had advised his followers – which included a high percentage of the state's law enforcement personnel – of how they might "legitimately" respond to the "nigger-commie invasion:" "catch [activists] outside the law, then under Mississippi law you can kill them."[20] The results of Bowers' suggestion had been immediately forthcoming. By the Bureau's own count, SNCC suffered some 1,000 arrests and at least 35 murders while engaged in constitutionally protected activities during Freedom Summer.[21] But the Bureau did absolutely nothing to protect the activists. Instead, it escalated its investigations of the intended *victims*, reporting many of the results of its intelligence gathering to the very police/klan amalgam which was perpetrating the violence. When the disappearance of Chaney, Schwerner and Goodman was reported to FBI agent Hunter E. Helgeson at the Jackson resident agency (nearest the murder scene), neither he nor his colleagues made any move to intervene.[22]

To the contrary, the FBI's sole agent in Meridian, John Proctor, is known to have accepted an invitation to drink contraband liquor with Deputy Price on the afternoon following the murders.[23] It was more than 48 hours, after heavy Justice Department pressure had been exerted because the potential for major negative publicity attending the case had emerged, that New Orleans SAC Harry Maynor finally sent a mere five agents to "see if we can find those guys."[24] Meanwhile, SNCC leader Robert Moses had already announced the obvious: "The kids are dead." Schwerner's wife, Rita, and Chaney's mother demanded to see both Mississippi Governor Paul Johnson and President Lyndon Johnson concerning the fate of their loved ones, a matter which prompted television anchorman Walter Cronkite to describe the case during the Six O'Clock News on June 25 as being "the focus of the whole country's concern."[25] Unsatisfied that the FBI's paltry performance would blunt the force of rising criticism, President Lyndon Johnson himself ordered Hoover to up the ante, dispatching FBI Assistant Director Alex Rosen to Mississippi, followed by Roy K. Moore (designated as SAC of a new field office in Jackson, established solely in response to the presidential ultimatum), Associate Director Cartha D. DeLoach and a total of 153 agents.[26] Finally, on July 10, Hoover himself put in a brief appearance to push things along.[27]

FBI Inspector Joseph Sullivan, who was named to head up the investigation in the field, ultimately commanded 258 agents and captioned his operation MIBURN (a contraction of "Mississippi Burning," in reference to the torching of the Mt. Zion Church which had led to Chaney, Schwerner and Goodman's fatal trip). While it may be true that Sullivan was well-intentioned, "FBI agents resigned rather than go to Mississippi" as part of the investigation, and those who did go could not overcome "the Bureau's prior performance, its deference to the rule of white over black and its indifference to the rule of law."[28] Most of the time was spent poking about in area swamps, trying to locate the bodies, a "process which turned up several black corpses and parts thereof – including a torso clad in a CORE t-shirt."[29] The remains were finally found on August 4, after the Bureau promised immunity from prosecution and paid $30,000 to Delmar Dennis, one of the klan participants in the murders. The Bureau, however, sandbagged even then, filing reports which contained "no evidence which [could] form the basis for an indictment for these murders."[30] As a result, on October 27, 1967, seven of the 19 remaining murderers (including klan leader Bowers and Deputy Price) were convicted only of conspiring to deprive their victims of their civil rights and sentenced to serve three-to-ten years in federal prison. Charges against the other twelve were dropped or they were acquitted altogether. As U.S. District Judge Harold Cox put it at the time of sentencing: "They killed one nigger, one Jew, and a white man. I gave them what I thought they deserved."[31]

The Bureau later claimed that, in the wake of MIBURN, a major COINTELPRO was mounted against the klan. As William Sullivan put it:

> Toward the end of the summer of 1964, Roy Wall, the special agent in charge of [the Philadelphia, Mississippi] office, called me. I told Roy, "Let's destroy these fellows, just utterly destroy them." I trusted Roy; he was an outstanding agent. He said that in Mississippi there were three different Klan organizations and that we were in a position either to keep them separated and have them compete and fight with each other for support, or to merge them into one organization. I asked Roy, "If we merge them into one, can you control it and if necessary destroy it?" Roy said, "Yes, we can do that." I told him to go ahead and merge them, through the use of informants. From that time on, the Klan never again raised its head in Mississippi.[32]

Sullivan's interpretation of events is novel, to say the least, insofar as each of the Mississippi klan organizations were part of a much larger apparatus, all of which was heavily infiltrated by the FBI and presumably under Bureau control by the end of 1964. The FBI claimed to have more than 2,000 informants, or some 20% of overall klan membership across the South, by 1965.[33] Yet, far from never again raising its head, the klan continued to perpetrate considerable violence – in Mississippi and elsewhere – during the latter year. In his autobiography, Friend of SNCC organizer Abbie Hoffman described the situation in McComb, Mississippi during the summer of 1965:

> The Ku Klux Klan was so strong they once held a rally in the middle of Route 80. Cars had to pass the meeting on side roads. It was hard to believe, but there they were: two hundred white sheets, flaming cross and all. [Twenty-four] years ago, the Klan was no outmoded joke. A faceless nightmare, they were furnished by police with a list of our license-plate numbers, and they patrolled the borders of each black community, gunning for organizers. "Coon huntin'," the local whites called it...Daily picket lines were scenes of vicious Klan beatings. Once I was thrown to the curb and kicked repeatedly. An FBI agent leaned over and asked sarcastically if my civil rights had been violated. No one ever got arrested except SNCC workers.[34]

A classic outcome of FBI assistance to the klan concerns Viola Liuzzo, a white mother of three and Friend of SNCC worker from Detroit, who was shot in the head and killed by a carload of klansmen near Selma, Alabama on March 25, 1965. One of the four men in the klan car was Gary Thomas Rowe, the FBI plant who had helped beat Freedom Riders in Birmingham during 1963, and who was a prime suspect in several bombings – including the infamous blast at Birmingham's 16th Street Baptist Church which killed four black children – during the same year.[35] The infiltrator was placed by the Bureau in its "witness protection program" rather than on trial, despite evidence that it was he who had actually fired the shot which killed Liuzzo.[36] Again, the FBI's investigation purportedly netted no evidence of use in a murder prosecution, and Rowe's colleagues – Collie Leroy Wilkins, Eugene Thomas and William O. Eaton – were sentenced only to ten-year sentences after being convicted of violating their victim's civil rights in December of 1965.[37]

While thus proving itself spectacularly unable or unwilling to come to grips with klan violence, the Bureau was simultaneously devoting its resources to harassing civil rights and new left activists, and in commissioning whitewashes of its conduct in the South. The former resulted in at least one major lawsuit against three FBI officials – Roy K. Moore, James O. Ingram and Hunter E. Helgeson– while the latter engendered such "authorized" (and celebratory) "historical works" as Don Whitehead's *Attack on Terror: The FBI Against the Klan in Mississippi* and its subsequent production as a television movie.[38] Meanwhile, the FBI helped to destroy the MDFP initiative at Atlantic City, an entirely legitimate effort into which thousands had poured their time and energy – and upon which they had pinned their best hopes for achieving some form of nonviolent, "due process" change in American society – and for which Chaney, Schwerner, Goodman and scores of others had died.

Even though the MDFP delegation had received the required votes to be seated at the convention, replacing Mississippi's Jim Crow delegation altogether, party regulars (headed by President Lyndon Johnson) contrived to block these legal rights, preserving the segregationist *status quo*. In accomplishing this, Johnson utilized a special 31-person task force of FBI agents – who infiltrated the convention floor itself, utilizing phony NBC press credentials – commanded by Bureau Assistant Director DeLoach to wiretap and bug such civil rights leaders as Martin Luther King and Fannie Lou Hamer, as well as CORE's James Farmer and Julius Lester, and SNCC's Stokely Carmichael, James Forman, Cleveland Sellers, and Ivanhoe Donaldson.[39] Not only were the Johnson forces thus made privy to the MDFP's external communications with Democratic Party dignitaries such as Robert Kennedy, but the group's internal communications – with each other, and with various new left advisors – as well.[40] Needless to say, the political process was aborted under such conditions, a matter which inculcated an increasing sense of futility within much of the civil rights movement.

Under this cumulative cloud of disillusionment with "the system," the arena of the new left moved northward, an adjustment which paved one of the major routes to Columbia. Also by early 1965, SNCC itself had shifted much of its focus from the rural South to organizing within the vast black ghettoes of northern cities such as New York, Newark, Washington, D.C., Detroit and Chicago. Correspondingly, SDS placed increasing emphasis upon its Economic Research and Action Project (ERAP), initiated during the summer of 1964, moving cadres into the inner cities and attempting to build "an interracial movement of the poor."[41]

Movement Against the War

The geographical change meshed nicely with developments which began on September 14, 1964, when the administration of the University of California at Berkeley, headed by Chancellor Clark Kerr, attempted to prohibit activities on campus concerning "off-campus political causes." The student response, galvanized by Friend of SNCC organizer Mario Savio (who correctly saw the administration rule as a move to deny new left support to civil rights groups), was to launch the "Free Speech Movement," a short-lived entity which forced a reversal of the institutional position as of January 3, 1965. Ultimately, Kerr was forced from his job as the result of the massive student refusal to forfeit their rights in the face of his arbitrary power. In the interim:

> [S]tudents carried confrontation with authority to the point of spontaneously surrounding a police car for thirty-two hours to prevent the young man inside [Jack Weinberg] from being taken to jail; the sit-in tactic was successfully transferred from Southern lunch counters...to the halls of ivy on three separate occasions, first with 200 students, then with 400, and finally with 1000; the police were called in, for perhaps the first time ever on a major university campus, to arrest, with proven brutality, 814 students who had engaged in a sit-in; undergraduates, joined by graduate students and a portion of the faculty, declared a successful strike of classes

that went on for five days, the first time that tactic had been used at a single university...Here, *ab ovo*, were all the elements of student protest that were to become familiar at so many campuses in the next six years.[42]

Within months, the events at Berkeley and their outcome had captured the imagination of student radicals across the nation and had been transformed into a generalized demand for "student power" within the institutional context. In simplest terms, the idea was that in redistributing power within the university, students would be taking a concrete step towards a much broader alteration of social power, an argument which could hardly be ignored in SDS circles.[43] Another of the primary tactical and emotional avenues leading to the insurrection at Columbia barely three years later had thus been paved.

As this was going on, moreover, the undeclared U.S. war in Vietnam heated up dramatically with the landing of a Marine expeditionary force at Danang on March 8, 1965.[44] Given the resulting upsurge in student anti-war sentiment, SDS elected to at least temporarily divert much of its energy to playing a key role in organizing the first mass demonstration protesting the U.S. role in Indochina; the event, held on April 17, attracted perhaps 25,000 people (the organizers had expected, at most, 5,000), and featured a landmark speech by SDS president Paul Potter.[45] In December, SDS co-founder Tom Hayden accompanied Yale historian/anti-war activist Staughton Lynd and CP theoretician Herbert Aptheker to North Vietnam to explore the extent to which "the other side" was inclined toward peace.[46] Although there was a distinct lack of consensus among SDS veterans as to whether and to what extent the organization should become permanently engaged in the "single issue" anti-war movement, an emphasis on such activity largely assumed a life of its own, at least at the local chapter level.[47] By December 1966, SDS had pledged itself to make opposition to the war a major agenda item and develop "anti-draft unions" on campuses throughout the country.[48] The third road to Columbia had been opened up.

Although it is unlikely the FBI director (or anyone else, for that matter; the nation had simply never before been confronted with increasing numbers of its youth actively rejecting the values and policies of the *status quo*) realized the full import of these events, he ordered intensified coverage of SDS as of April 1965 in order that the Bureau "have proper coverage similar to what we have...[on] the Communist Party." The directive shortly manifested itself in the large-scale infiltration of SDS chapters, a crudely ostentatious program of "interviewing" as many organizational members and supporters as could be identified, and the reinforcement of "cooperative arrangements" between the FBI and campus police and administrators. This was followed, in February of 1966, by a directive that agents investigate all "free university" activities associated with student power advocates insofar as the director had "reason to believe" these to be sponsored by "subversive groups" (mainly SDS). This led almost immediately (in April 1966) to distrinution of a Bureau study of such activities in Detroit to military intelligence, the Secret Service, the State Department and the Justice Department. Another report, prepared in Philadelphia at about the same time and based upon information provided by no less than thirteen infiltrators, was similarly disseminated. In May of 1966, Hoover ordered that such scrutiny of the new left be both intensified and expanded.[49]

No doubt contrary to Hoover's intentions, such overt FBI harassment seems if anything to have angered the "militants," stimulating them to higher levels of activity. The trend towards white radicals organizing around issues within their own rather than black communities also received sharp reinforcement in the spring of 1966 with the election of Stokely Carmichael as the president of SNCC, the formal articulation of that organization's black power position, its abandonment of nonviolence as a philosophical posture, and its determination that it needed henceforth to be "an all black project."[50] In clearest terms, Carmichael explained the need for new leftists (whom Carmichael described as "liberals") to transform their own home ground:

> I have said that most liberal whites react to "black power" with the question, What about me?, rather than saying: Tell me what you want and I'll see if I can do it. There are answers to the right question. One of the most disturbing things about almost all white supporters of the movement has been that they are afraid to go into their own communities – which is where the racism exists – and work to get rid of it. They want to run from Berkeley and tell us what to do in Mississippi; let them look instead at Berkeley. They admonish blacks to be nonviolent; let them preach nonviolence in the white community. They come to teach me Negro history; let them go to the suburbs and open freedom schools for whites. Let them work to stop America's racist foreign policy; let them press the government to cease supporting the economy of South Africa [and the war in Vietnam].[51]

Although SDS was never to abandon the priority it had maintained on collaborative relations with what was rapidly becoming the black liberation movement, it subsequently concentrated more and more of its energy upon campuses populated largely by white students, developing the notion of student power into the concept of "youth as a social class," and striving to create a truly massive popular opposition to the war.[52] As it did so, "activating" an ever-greater proportion of Euroamerican youth in dissident politics, the FBI homed in with increasing intensity, albeit with little ability to tell the new left from the old at this juncture. For instance, both the FBI and the "friendly journalists" to whom it habitually fed information at *U.S. News and World Report* persisted in confusing both the CP, USA's campus-based W.E.B. DuBois Clubs and the SWP's Young Socialist Alliance with new left organizations for some time.[53] Similar misidentifications concerned the Maoist Progressive Labor Party (PLP) and its anti-war "youth group," the May 2 Movement (M2M).[54]

Meantime, by the spring of 1967, SDS membership had mushroomed to at least 30,000, with active chapters on more than 250 campuses nationally.[55] The national SDS organization, in combination with an array of *ad hoc*, localized or special-focus organizations such as the Vietnam Day Committee in Berkeley, Spring Mobilization Against the War, and War Resisters League – most of which found local SDSers at the core – was proving that the new left could mount a steadily escalating campaign of opposition to the war effort while simultaneously developing a sense of "community self-empowerment." In April, some 200,000 people turned out for an anti-war march in New York City while at least 65,000 others marched in San Francisco; several hundred draft-age men burned their Selective Service cards in Central Park during the New York demonstration.[56] During the summer, more than 30,000 students fanned out into cities across the North to engage in a "Vietnam Summer" project of anti-war and draft resistance education in local communities.[57] By fall, as the Johnson administration made it clear that it intended to pursue the war regardless of the magnitude of "acceptable" forms of public protest – and with the Indochina theater commander, General William Westmoreland, requesting that the number of U.S. troops in Vietnam be increase to 543,000 – SDS tactics became more militant.[58]

On October 18, to kick off a national "Stop the Draft Week," several thousand demonstrators at the University of Wisconsin at Madison announced that representatives for the Dow Chemical Corporation – manufacturers of the napalm utilized by U.S. forces in Vietnam – would no longer be allowed to recruit on campus. Chancellor William Sewell, as part of his new "get tough" arrangement with the FBI, dispatched riot police to break up the previously peaceful demonstration. His police, apparently getting tough in turn, used tear gas to disperse protestors for the first time on a major college campus. Unexpectedly, the crowd fought back with fury, *growing* rather than diminishing as the day wore on. In the aftermath of the clash a general boycott of classes was proclaimed, and endorsed even by the conservative student government, until Dow recruiting at Madison was canceled. As with Kerr, Sewell was forced to resign.[59] The action in Madison was followed, on October 20, by a demonstration in which an estimated 10,000 people marched on the army induction center in Oakland, California. Finding themselves in a head-on confrontation with local riot police, the demonstrators forced them to retreat.[60] On October 21 and 22, the National Mobilization to End the War in Vietnam brought together the largest anti-war demonstration in the history of the nation's capital up to that point. Some 100,000 people marched to the seat of military authority at the Pentagon where many of them clashed physically with the large force of troops and federal marshals which had been assembled to "secure" the premises.[61]

A month later, on November 14, an action organized by the Fifth Avenue Peace Parade Committee was utilized by Columbia SDS leaders Ted Gold and Ted Kaptchuk to spark a confrontation designed to prevent Secretary of Defense Robert McNamara from speaking at the New York Hilton.[62] On at least 60 campuses, major demonstrations occurred during the remainder of 1967 and beginning of '68, all of them aimed at ending ROTC programs, or recruitment by the military, defense corporations and CIA.[63] Additionally, SDS chapters on some 50 campuses researched and made public the secret contracts obtaining between the defense/ intelligence community and the "neutral" scientists working on their campuses.[64] The ability of the U.S. government to conduct a war for reasons other than those provided to the public, and through a complex of other official lies and secret arrangements, was being seriously challenged.[65] One sign of how seriously the government had begun to take the anti-war opposition came in January 1968, when the

Justice Department under the "liberal" Attorney General [Ramsey] Clark initiated the single most repressive overt act of the Johnson administration – the indictment of William Sloane Coffin, chaplain of Yale University, nationally known pediatrician Dr. Benjamin Spock and three other anti-war leaders [Harvard graduate student Michael Ferber, writer/activist Mitchell Goodman and Marcus Raskin, director of the Institute for Policy Studies]...for conspiracy to "council, aid and abet" violations of the draft and to interfere with administration of the draft...There is very strong circumstantial evidence that the indictment was intended as a warning to all anti-war demonstrators and spokes[persons] that they might well face similar charges. All the overt actions cited in support of the indictment were public activities, such as signing statements and making speeches against the war, along with collecting draft cards turned in by *other* persons and forwarding them to the Justice Department. During the trial, the position of the Justice Department was that all twenty-eight thousand signers of an anti-draft statement, all persons who voiced support or even applauded at rallies where the defendants spoke, and even news[people] who reported the defendants' speeches could be indicted as members of the conspiracy. At one point, government prosecutors stated that the publishers and booksellers of a book which printed anti-draft statements could also be indicted...The outcome of the trial was that one of the defendants [Raskin] was acquitted and [the convictions of the remaining four set aside because of government misconduct during the trial; two were thereupon freed from further prosecution due to lack of evidence upon which charges might reasonably have been brought in the first place].[66]

For his part, J. Edgar Hoover – having deployed his agents to gather "evidence" for prosecution of those who had by then come to be known as the "Boston Five" – went on to sum up the Bureau perspective with the amazing contradiction of first announcing that "New Left organizations such as the Students for a Democratic Society work constantly in furtherance of the aims and objectives of the Communist Party throughout the nation," then describing SDS as "anarchistic and nihilistic."[67] In January of 1968, the FBI instituted its "Key Agitators Index," a roster in which SDS leaders and others in "anti-war groups" who were "extremely active and most vocal in their statements denouncing the United States and calling for civil disobedience" featured prominently. Field agents were instructed to maintain "high level informant coverage" of "key [new left] activists," with emphasis on their "sources of funds, foreign contacts and future plans."[68] By March 1968, the Bureau was routinely sending reports to the White House concerning new left demonstrations and demonstrators.[69] And *then* came Columbia. Obviously, contrary to Sullivan's version of events, by this point the Bureau's intelligence files on the new left were brimming, and the apparatus through which the FBI would undertake its COINTELPROs against that poorly-defined entity was well established.

The COINTELPRO Begins

The student explosion at Columbia University during April of 1968 incorporated all three strains of issues underlying new left activism: 1) institutional racism, as manifested in university construction of a gymnasium on land previously devoted to low-rent housing occupied by impoverished black and *Puertorriqueño* families, 2) institutional support to the U.S. "war machine," as specifically demonstrated in the relationship of the university to the Institute for Defense Analysis (IDA), and 3) student power concerns, as expressed in popular resistance to the university administration's arbitrary dispensation of "discipline" – probation, suspension, expulsion and the like – to student radicals.[70] When a series of meetings between the campus SDS chapter and University President Grayson Kirk, conducted through the spring semester, resulted in no change in policy, the students undertook direct action, first occupying the gym construction site on April 23, and then occupying several university buildings over the next few days.[71] Their action effectively brought Columbia to a standstill, a matter they announced would not change until a list of demands – including the university's severing its ties with the "military-industrial complex," halting its gym construction project, and allowing students a meaningful voice in institutional governance – were met.[72]

Although the Columbia administration ultimately resorted to the massive use of local rather than federal police force to "restore order,"[73] the FBI responded to the events at the university – as is shown in the accompanying May 9, 1968 memo from C.D. Brennan to W.C. Sullivan – by inaugurating a formal COINTELPRO campaign against the new left. As with other domestic counterintelligence operations, this one was designed to seize every opportunity to "expose, disrupt, and otherwise neutralize the activities of the various New Left organizations, their leadership and adherents" by frustrating "every effort of these groups and individuals to consolidate their forces or to recruit new and youthful members" by capitalizing "upon organizational and personal conflicts of the leadership," spreading disinformation through "cooperation of reliable news media," and to otherwise "inspire action where circumstances warrant." Another internal Bureau memo, written at about the same time, specified the justification for the COINTELPRO as being the fact that "certain New Left individuals" were "calling for revolution in America" and "for the defeat of the United States in Vietnam," and had upon occasion "viciously and scurrilously attacked the Director and the Bureau in an attempt to hamper our investigation of it and to drive us off the college campuses."[74]

The Bureau's new COINTELPRO effort was quickly linked to illegal (under its charter) CIA domestic surveillance programs such as Project MERRIMAC, Project RESISTANCE and Operation CHAOS, which collectively amassed and in some cases circulated "intelligence information" in the form of "watchlists" on "radical students, antiwar activists, draft resisters and deserters, black nationalists, anarchists and assorted 'New Leftists.'"[75] Before the last of these programs was allegedly terminated in 1974, they had caused "national security files" to be opened on at least

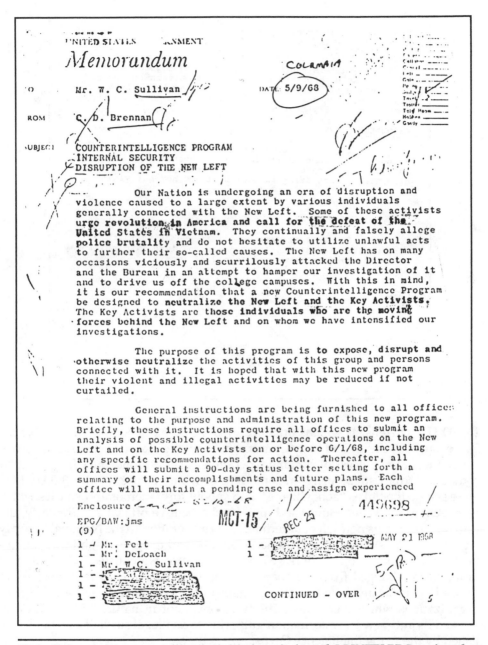

UNITED STATES   ...NMENT

Memorandum

COLUMBIA

O   Mr. W. C. Sullivan   DATE: 5/9/68

ROM   C. D. Brennan

UBJECT COUNTERINTELLIGENCE PROGRAM
        INTERNAL SECURITY
        DISRUPTION OF THE NEW LEFT

          Our Nation is undergoing an era of disruption and
violence caused to a large extent by various individuals
generally connected with the New Left. Some of these activists
urge revolution in America and call for the defeat of the
United States in Vietnam. They continually and falsely allege
police brutality and do not hesitate to utilize unlawful acts
to further their so-called causes. The New Left has on many
occasions viciously and scurrilously attacked the Director
and the Bureau in an attempt to hamper our investigation of it
and to drive us off the college campuses. With this in mind,
it is our recommendation that a new Counterintelligence Program
be designed to neutralize the New Left and the Key Activists.
The Key Activists are those individuals who are the moving
forces behind the New Left and on whom we have intensified our
investigations.

          The purpose of this program is to expose, disrupt and
otherwise neutralize the activities of this group and persons
connected with it. It is hoped that with this new program
their violent and illegal activities may be reduced if not
curtailed.

          General instructions are being furnished to all offices
relating to the purpose and administration of this new program.
Briefly, these instructions require all offices to submit an
analysis of possible counterintelligence operations on the New
Left and on the Key Activists on or before 6/1/68, including
any specific recommendations for action. Thereafter, all
offices will submit a 90-day status letter setting forth a
summary of their accomplishments and future plans. Each
office will maintain a pending case and assign experienced

Enclosure   449698

EPG/BAW:jms   MCT-15   REC-25
(9)
1 – Mr. Felt   1 –   MAY 21 1968
1 – Mr. DeLoach
1 – Mr. W. C. Sullivan
1 –
1 –
1 –   CONTINUED – OVER

Kickoff document: memo calling for initiation of a formal COINTELPRO against the new left and neutralization of its key leaders. Note these individuals are described as subject to ongoing investigation, contrary to the assertion of William C. Sullivan in his autobiography. Recommendations for action appear on next page.

Memo to Mr. Sullivan
Re: COUNTERINTELLIGENCE PROGRAM

personnel to this program. All proposed counterintelligence
action must be approved at the Seat of Government prior to
instituting it. This new program will be supervised at the
Seat of Government by a Special Agent supervisor in the
Internal Security Section.

RECOMMENDATIONS:

     1) That the Domestic Intelligence Division be
authorized to immediately initiate a coordinated Counterintelligence Program directed at exposing, disrupting, and
otherwise neutralizing the New Left and Key Activists.

     2) That the attached letter setting forth
instructions for the administration and immediate enactment
of the program be forwarded to all offices.

23,500 U.S. citizens, as well as organizations including SDS, Women's Strike for Peace, the BPP, Clergy and Laity Concerned About the War in Vietnam, and Grove Press, Inc. In the process of running Operation CHAOS alone, the CIA generated some 3,500 "domestic security" memos for its own internal use, another 3,000 which were sent to the FBI as "action items," and "about forty memos and studies which were sent to the White House and high level executive officials."[76] Similarly, the Bureau also tied its new left counterintelligence operation to the National Security Agency's (NSA's) illegal international telephone and telegram monitoring of citizens, code-named Project MINARET, which targeted watchlisted names of individuals who "ranged from members of radical political groups to celebrities, to ordinary citizens involved in protests against the government," and a number of organizations which were "peaceful and nonviolent in nature."[77] The FBI also hooked its anti-new left information-gathering to an illegal surveillance net established by the Army Intelligence Corps:

> According to Assistant Secretary of Defense Robert Froehlke, in testimony before a Senate subcommittee in 1971, Army directives called for information collection on "any category of information related even remotely to people or organizations

active in a community in which potential for a riot or disorder was present." Before the program was terminated in 1971 due to public exposure and criticism, Army intelligence had about fifteen hundred plainclothesmen assigned to collect political information on what the Senate Intelligence Committee later termed "virtually every group seeking peaceful change in the United States." Index cards were gathered on more than one hundred thousand civilian protesters and on more than seven hundred and sixty thousand organizations and "incidents." In addition to centralized Army intelligence files maintained at bases near Washington, D.C. local army units carried on their operations and investigations, with little central control. Thus, Fourth Army headquarters at Fort Sam Houston, Texas, had its own collection of one hundred twenty thousand file cards on "personalities of interest."[78]

Meanwhile, HUAC helped establish the tenor for severe repression by issuing a "report" claiming that new left and black liberation formations were "seriously considering the possibility of instituting armed insurrections in this country," and that SDS was actually planning "guerrilla-type operations against the government." Although the committee could come up with precious little by which to substantiate its allegations, it nonetheless proceeded to recommend utilization of the Internal Security Act's concentration camp provisions to effect the "temporary imprisonment of warring guerrillas."[79] HUAC's recommendations resulted in a formal review by a Justice Department committee headed by Attorney General Ramsey Clark of federal "emergency detention guidelines," intended to increase "flexibility and discretion at the operating level." The resulting revision of the 1950 statute's implementation procedures allowed for the "preventive detention" of anyone who evidenced "membership or participation in the activities of a basic revolutionary organization within the last five years," leadership or "substantive participation" in a "front organization" within the past three years, or anyone else who "could be expected" to utilize a national emergency as a format in which to engage in "interference with or threat to the survival and effective operation" of the government, whether or not they could be shown to have committed "overt acts or statements within the time limits prescribed."[80]

Within the context of such official sensibilities, among the activists designated by the Bureau as being "key" to the new left, and therefore targeted for rapid COINTELPRO neutralization, were – as the accompanying June 10, 1968 memo from Hoover to the Newark SAC reveals – SDS founder Tom Hayden and long-time pacifist organizer David Dellinger, a leader of the National Mobilization to End the War in Vietnam (Mobe). Hayden, Dellinger and a number of other new left activists were also subpoenaed by HUAC as a result of their FBI "extremist" designations.[81] Hayden himself was already being subjected to a concerted effort to bad-jacket him, as may be readily seen in the accompanying May 27, 1968 memo from the Newark SAC to Hoover. Such immediate attention was undoubtedly paid to the pair – as well as self-defined anarchists Abbie Hoffman and Jerry Rubin, who had recently founded a largely mythical organization dubbed Youth International Party (Yippie!) – not on the basis of their supposed "guerrilla" activities, but because of their

```
                                              1 - L . C. D. Brennan
                                              1 - Mr.
                                              1 - Mr.

   SAC, Newark (100-50166)                                  6/10/68
        EX-103
                                              PERSONAL ATTENTION
   Director, FBI (100-449698)-
             110-44969      31-1
                       REC-12
   COUNTERINTELLIGENCE PROGRAM
   INTERNAL SECURITY
   DISRUPTION OF THE NEW LEFT
```

                Reurlet 5/27/68.

                Bureau letter of 5/10/68 instructed all offices to
submit a detailed analysis of potential counterintelligence
action against New Left organizations and Key Activists
within their respective territories, together with specific
recommendations and necessary facts on any proposed action.
This letter also instructed that offices which have
investigative responsibility for Key Activists should
specifically comment in the initial letter to the Bureau
regarding these individuals.

                Your letter of 5/27/68 fails to provide the above
information, consists primarily of general observations and
indicates a negative attitude. It is also noted that this
letter contains proposed action against Key Activist
Thomas Emmett Hayden, now residing in Chicago, but makes
no mention of David Dellinger, a Key Activist of your office.
Specific comment on Dellinger should have been included as
instructed.

                The above-requested information should be submitted
by return mail and conform to the instructions contained in
Bureau letter of 5/10/68. It is imperative that this
Counterintelligence Program be assigned to an experienced,
imaginative Agent, and it is incumbent upon you to see that
it receives the proper emphasis.

```
   RLR:rsz
     (6)
```

   NOTE:

                Referenced letter from Newark failed to provide the
specific information requested by the Bureau.

Memo identifying Tom Hayden and David Dellinger as "Key Activists."

expressed intent to bring about massive street demonstrations during the Democratic Party's national convention, set for August in Chicago. The purpose of these

Memorandum

TO : DIRECTOR, FBI DATE: 5/27/68

FROM : SAC, NEWARK (100-50166)

SUBJECT: COUNTERINTELLIGENCE PROGRAM
INTERNAL SECURITY
DISRUPTION OF THE NEW LEFT

Re Bureau letter to Albany, 5/10/68.

It is believed that in attempting to expose,
disrupt, and otherwise neutralize the activities of the
"new left" by counterintelligence methods, the Bureau is
faced with a rather unique task. Because, first, the "new
left" is difficult to actually define; and second, of the
complete disregard by "new left" members for moral and social laws and social amenities.

It is believed that the nonconformism in dress
and speech, neglect of personal cleanliness, use of obscenities (printed and uttered), publicized sexual promiscuity,
experimenting with and the use of drugs, filthy clothes,
shaggy hair, wearing of sandals, beads, and unusual jewelry
tend to negate any attempt to hold these people up to ridicule. The American press has been doing this with no
apparent effect or curtailment of "new left" activities.
These individuals are apparently getting strength and more
brazen in their attempts to destroy American society, as
noted in the takeover recently at Columbia University, New
York City, and other universities in the U.S.

It is believed therefore, that they must be
destroyed or neutralized from the inside. Neutralize them
in the same manner they are trying to destroy and neutralize
the U.S.

It is Newark's opinion that this can possibly be
done in two ways:

MCT N100-449698-31-1

1. The U.S. Government must be convinced, through
the proper departments, that it must stop subsidizing its

2-Bureau (RM)
1-New York (INFO)(RM) REC-32
2-Chicago (THOMAS HAYDEN)(INFO)(RM)
3-Newark
(1-100-48095)(THOMAS HAYDEN)

US MAY 29 1968

Memo outlining plan to bad-jacket Tom Hayden (continued on next page).

demonstrations being to demand an end to the U.S. war in Southeast Asia, the FBI
appears to have viewed them as an insistence upon "defeat."[82]

By July 5, 1968 (the date of the accompanying letter from Hoover to the SAC,
Albany), therefore, the Bureau had assembled a 12-point "master plan" through
which it intended to destroy the new left opposition. This was coupled to a Justice

NK 100-50166

own destruction. Each field office should acquire the names
and backgrounds of all students of the new left", who have
been arrested for the very type of activity we are now trying
to curtail or halt. Any Government subsidization to these
individuals should be stopped.

They must be taken out of the ranks of this pre-
dominantly college-age movement; separate them and diminish
their power.

2.   Certain key leaders must be chosen to become
the object of a counterintelligence plot to identify them as
government informants. It appears that this is the only
thing that could cause these individuals concern; if some of
their leaders turned out to be paid informers. Attacking
their morals, disrespect for the law, or patriotic disdain
will not impress their followers, as it would normally to
other groups, so it must be by attacking them through their
own principles and beliefs. Accuse them of selling out to
"imperialistic monopoly capitalism".

THOMAS EMMETT HAYDEN
KEY ACTIVIST, NEWARK DIVISION

Newark believes that it might be possible to attach
the stigma of informant or Government "fink" to HAYDEN because
of the apparent unlimited finances at his disposal, enabling
him to take numerous trips in and out of the U.S., without any
job or other means of financial support. Also, the ease with
which he travels to communist countries, his reception there,
the privileges afforded him, and his eventual return with no
actual remonstrations by this Government.

Newark suggests that after HAYDEN visits a certain
city or country, that a news release, datelined Washington,
D.C., be prepared noting that "according to informed Government sources", etc., certain events happened in that certain
city or country which would reflect back on HAYDEN through
similarity of circumstances or events. It is suggested further
that these news releases be collected and when several promising items are collected, they be turned over to a representative
of a cooperative news media with a suggestion that a feature
writer be given the task of writing up a story pointing out
the coincidences of HAYDEN's visits to certain cities and
news stories emanating from Washington, D.C., pointing to
HAYDEN as the source. The connection may be spotlighted by
including certain sidelights or confidential bits of information which may only be known to HAYDEN and a Bureau source.

It is realized the above will take time, but in
order for the plan to be effective, it must have a solid
basis and a continual indictment.

One copy of this letter is being sent to Chicago
since THOMAS HAYDEN changed his residence to there.

One copy of this letter is being sent to NYO for
information because of available transportation facilities
which give "new left" demonstrators in this area the opportunity to choose either New York or New Jersey locations
for disruptive tactics.

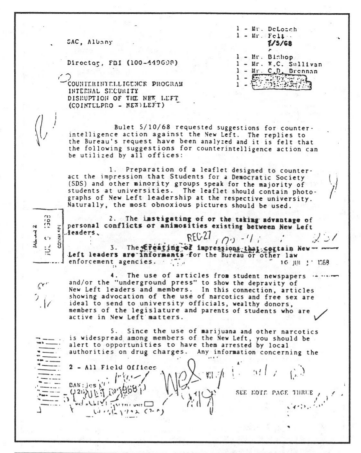

The FBI's 12 -point master plan for COINTELPRO – New Left (continued on next page).

Department initiative, spearheaded by Attorney General Clark, to consolidate what was called the Interdivisional Information Unit (IDIU) to coordinate "all information" on organizations and individuals "who play a role, whether purposefully or not, either in instigating or spreading civil disorders, or in preventing our checking them."[83] By 1970, the IDIU computer was being utilized to coordinate a flow of more than 40,000 intelligence reports per year concerning "civil disorders and campus disturbances" involving over 10,000 "anti-war activists and other dissidents." Organizations targeted for IDIU attention included groups ranging from the NAACP and Urban League to SDS and the BPP. Individuals included under its rubric spanned the range from United Farm Workers organizer Cesar Chavez to black entertainer Sammy Davis, Jr., from folk singer/activist Joan Baez to an unnamed "bearded militant who writes and recites poetry."[84]

fact that individuals have marijuana or are engaging in a
narcotics party should be immediately furnished to local
authorities and they should be encouraged to take action.

6. The drawing up of anonymous letters regarding
individuals active in the New Left. These letters should
set out their activities and should be sent to their parents,
neighbors and the parents' employers. This could have the
effect of forcing the parents to take action.

7. Anonymous letters or leaflets describing
faculty members and graduate assistants in the various
institutions of higher learning who are active in New Left matters.
The activities and associations of the individual should be
set out. Anonymous mailings should be made to university
officials, members of the state legislature, Board of
Regents, and to the press. Such letters could be signed
"A Concerned Alumni" or "A Concerned Taxpayer."

8. Whenever New Left groups engage in disruptive
activities on college campuses, cooperative press contacts
should be encouraged to emphasize that the disruptive
elements constitute a minority of the students and do not
represent the conviction of the majority. The press should
demand an immediate student referendum on the issue in
question. Inasmuch as the overwhelming majority of students
is not active in New Left matters, it is felt that this
technique, used in carefully selected cases, could put an
end to lengthy demonstrations and could cause embarrassment
to New Left elements.

9. There is a definite hostility among SDS and
other New Left groups toward the Socialist Workers Party
(SWP), the Young Socialist Alliance (YSA), and the
Progressive Labor Party (PLP). This hostility should be
exploited wherever possible.

10. The field was previously advised that New Left
groups are attempting to open coffeehouses near military
bases in order to influence members of the Armed Forces.
Wherever these coffeehouses are, friendly news media should
be alerted to them and their purpose. In addition, various
drugs, such as marijuana, will probably be utilized by
individuals running the coffeehouses or frequenting them.
Local law enforcement authorities should be promptly advised
whenever you receive an indication that this is being done.

11. Consider the use of cartoons, photographs, and
anonymous letters which will have the effect of ridiculing
the New Left. Ridicule is one of the most potent weapons
which we can use against it.

12. Be alert for opportunities to confuse and
disrupt New Left activities by disinformation. For example,
when events are planned, notification that the event has
been cancelled or postponed could be sent to various
individuals.

You are reminded that no counterintelligence
action is to be taken without Bureau approval. Insure that
this Program is assigned to an Agent with an excellent
knowledge of both New Left groups and individuals. It must
be approached with imagination and enthusiasm if it is to be
successful.

As an economy measure the caption "COINTELPRO - NEW LEFT"
should be used on all communications concerning this Program.

NOTE:

        See memo C.D. Brennan to W.C. Sullivan dated
7/3/68, captioned as above, prepared by BAW: jes.

COINTELPRO-New Left had, in the meantime, gotten well under way, as is
evidenced by the accompanying May 29, 1968 memo from Hoover to his Philadelphia SAC, calling upon that office to undertake specific counterintelligence activities – including the generation of cartoons *à la* the materials being circulated with
lethal results as a part of COINTELPRO-BPP at about the same time – to disrupt SDS
within its area of operations. By late July, as is indicated in the accompanying August
9, 1968 letter from Hoover to the SAC, Los Angeles, the sending of anonymous letters
had entered the arsenal of tactics being applied against SDS. All such efforts seem

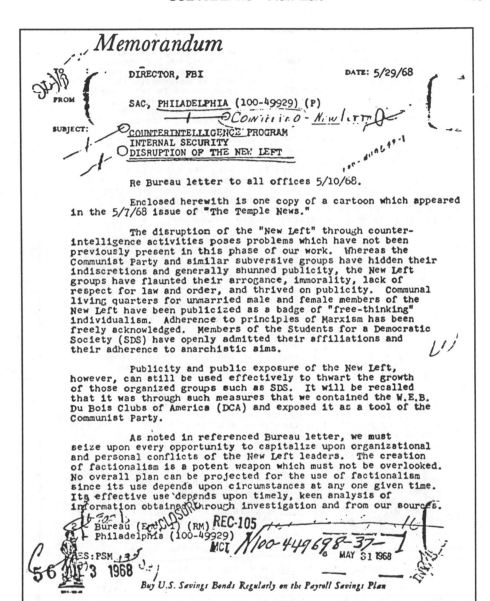

Memorandum

DIRECTOR, FBI   DATE: 5/29/68

FROM   SAC, PHILADELPHIA (100-49929) (P)

SUBJECT: COUNTERINTELLIGENCE PROGRAM
         INTERNAL SECURITY
         DISRUPTION OF THE NEW LEFT

Re Bureau letter to all offices 5/10/68.

Enclosed herewith is one copy of a cartoon which appeared in the 5/7/68 issue of "The Temple News."

The disruption of the "New Left" through counterintelligence activities poses problems which have not been previously present in this phase of our work. Whereas the Communist Party and similar subversive groups have hidden their indiscretions and generally shunned publicity, the New Left groups have flaunted their arrogance, immorality, lack of respect for law and order, and thrived on publicity. Communal living quarters for unmarried male and female members of the New Left have been publicized as a badge of "free-thinking" individualism. Adherence to principles of Marxism has been freely acknowledged. Members of the Students for a Democratic Society (SDS) have openly admitted their affiliations and their adherence to anarchistic aims.

Publicity and public exposure of the New Left, however, can still be used effectively to thwart the growth of those organized groups such as SDS. It will be recalled that it was through such measures that we contained the W.E.B. Du Bois Clubs of America (DCA) and exposed it as a tool of the Communist Party.

As noted in referenced Bureau letter, we must seize upon every opportunity to capitalize upon organizational and personal conflicts of the New Left leaders. The creation of factionalism is a potent weapon which must not be overlooked. No overall plan can be projected for the use of factionalism since its use depends upon circumstances at any one given time. Its effective use depends upon timely, keen analysis of information obtained through investigation and from our sources.

2 - Bureau (Enc. 1) (RM)   REC-105
1 - Philadelphia (100-49929)
                            MCT.
ES:PSM
(3)   1968

Buy U.S. Savings Bonds Regularly on the Payroll Savings Plan

Memo detailing plan to disrupt SDS at Temple University through use of cartoons, pamphlets and anonymous letters (continued on next page).

---

to have had the short-term objective of preventing the actualization of unified and coherent anti-war demonstrations in Chicago during early August. The longer term goal, of course, was to eliminate the new left as a factor in the U.S. political equation.

A most potent weapon not to be overlooked is the use of ridicule. In the past its use has been primarily restricted against individuals through cartoons and anonymous letters. Consideration should be given to greater use of this technique to discredit the entire New Left movement. An example is the cartoon attached which appeared in the "Temple University News," student newspaper at Temple University, Philadelphia, Pa. Photographs of student "sit-ins," such as that which occurred at Columbia University, with appropriate captions, such as "Give to the College of your Choice," could be prepared and anonymously circulated among appropriate legislators, prominent alumni members, and others.

Specifically, in Philadelphia, the main target for counterintelligence under this program will be the SDS. There are no Key Activists in the Philadelphia Division territory as of the date of this letter. No specific recommendations are being made at this time; however, the following avenues of action are open and under consideration for future use:

1. Cooperative news media representatives have been used in the past. Reliability and discreetness have been proven. Recommendations for specific action will include necessary assurances that the Bureau's interest will be protected.

2. Philadelphia has used cartoons to ridicule leaders of the CP. It is felt this method has the most potential for obtaining our goals. Under consideration is a proposal that a series of cartoons be prepared and that the anarchistic aims of the New Left be emphasized by labeling them "Mobocracy." It is apparent that "Mob" action is repugnant to the majority of college students and other serious-minded youth. Methods of distributing such cartoons can be done anonymously or through established sources in each Division.

3. Philadelphia has established contacts with the Catholic War Veterans (CWV). Through these contacts it was possible to prepare a series of leaflets exposing the DCA which were printed and published by the CWV on a national basis. It is felt similar arrangements can be made for the CWV to issue a pamphlet exposing the SDS. Such a project would require the assistance of the Bureau and Chicago. the Office of Origin in the SDS case.

4. A leading member of the CP youth was neutralized when the Philadelphia Office publicized his homosexual activity. Weaknesses and deficiencies of individual members of the New Left should be used by us to neutralize them. Anonymous letters to the parents of individual members of the New Left might very well serve the purpose, neutralizing them through parental discipline.

Although the foregoing is not intended to be all-inclusive, it represents the basic approach of the Philadelphia Division to this new program. Appropriate Special Agent personnel have been alerted to this program. Recommendations for specific counterintelligence action will be submitted to the Bureau by separate letter.

As at Columbia, during the convention itself the burden of physically and overtly repressing the demonstrators – who were, after all, merely exercising constitutionally protected rights to speech, assembly and petition – was passed to the tactical units of the Chicago police, a "duty" the CPD performed with a relish later described even by an official government commission as constituting a "police riot."[85] In the aftermath, however, with the election of Richard Nixon, the FBI and

First of the cartoons produced and distributed by the Philadelphia FBI office as part of its COINTELPRO to destroy SDS at Temple University. The caption, in a parody of the rhetoric of Sen. Joseph McCarthy reads: "I have in my hand a list of 200 names of people who don't advocate the violent overthrow of the government."

Justice Department moved in to "legally" eliminate their quarry by leveling at them an essentially baseless set of "conspiracy" charges. As Robert Justin Goldstein has observed:

> The Nixon administration instituted an extraordinary series of conspiracy trials against anti-war leaders – in fact, together with the Spock-Coffin trial of the Johnson administration, the Nixon administration prosecuted virtually every prominent anti-war leader. What was perhaps the most extraordinary thing about the prosecutions was that the major charges brought either all collapsed during the judicial process, or the cases were thrown out due to illegal government activities or refusal to disclose records of illegal wiretapping...While the prosecutions failed in one sense – historian William Manchester termed them "an unparalleled series of judicial disasters for the government" – they succeeded sensationally in another. Namely, they succeeded in tying up huge amounts of time, money and energy that the anti-war and radical movements could have used to expand rather than expend on protracted and costly defense struggles.[86]

Goldstein continues:

> The first major conspiracy trial, the so-called Chicago Conspiracy or Chicago Eight
> trial, resulted from indictments handed down in March, 1969 of eight anti-war
> leaders under the 1968 Anti-Riot Act for conspiring to cross state lines with intent
> to incite a riot...On March 20, 1969 [a] Chicago grand jury returned indictments
> against...eight demonstrators, six of whom were highly visible radical leaders,
> including pacifist David Dellinger, Black Panther Party Chairman Bobby Seale,
> [former] SDS leaders [now key members of the Mobe] Tom Hayden and Rennie
> Davis, and "Yippie" leaders Jerry Rubin and Abbie Hoffman [the other two
> defendants were little-known SDS members John Froines and Lee Weiner]...Seale's
> case was severed in mid-trial (and never retried) when Federal Judge Julius
> Hoffman found him in contempt of court and summarily sentenced him to an
> unprecedented four years in prison, as a result of repeated outbursts by Seale
> following Judge Hoffman's refusal to either allow Seale to defend himself or have
> the services of a lawyer of his own choosing. After a tumultuous trial – which at one
> point featured Seale tied to a chair with a gag in his mouth – the remaining seven
> defendants were found innocent of the conspiracy charge...two charged with
> teaching the use of incendiary devices were acquitted, and the other five were found
> guilty of crossing state lines with intent to incite a riot. Judge Hoffman...sentenced
> the five to five years in [prison] and $5,000 fines, and then added 175 contempt
> sentences ranging from two and a half months to over four years against all seven
> defendants and two of their lawyers [William Kunstler and Leonard Weinglass].
> Many of the contempt charges were based on the flimsiest possible grounds; for
> example, Dellinger was sentenced to six months for calling the judge "Mr." Hoffman,
> and Davis was sentenced to twenty-nine days for applauding at one point and
> laughing at another. Eventually both the contempt and substantive convictions
> were overturned by the Ninth Circuit Court of Appeals [but the damage had been
> done].[87]

Barely had the Chicago conspiracy trial ended than another began, in December
1970, in Seattle. In this case, eight leaders of an organization calling itself the Seattle
Liberation Front – predictably, they were described as the "Seattle Eight" – were
accused of having conspired to damage federal property, the result of a February
1970 demonstration protesting the contempt sentences handed down in the Chicago
trial which ended with windows broken and slogans spray-painted on the walls on
the Seattle federal building. Although it was obvious that the February demonstration was a purely local affair, the planning for which had begun barely ten days prior
to the event, four of the defendants were also charged under the 1968 anti-riot statute
used against the Chicago Eight with having crossed state lines with intent to incite
riot the preceding December, while a fifth was accused of having utilized interstate
telephone lines for the same purpose.[88] Although the presiding judge, George H.
Boldt, eventually declared a mistrial in these ludicrous proceedings, he followed the
lead of his Chicago colleague in meting out harsh contempt sentences, based on the
"totality" of the defendants' behavior during the trial. By this point, the once-vibrant
Seattle new left movement was completely wrecked.[89]
This was followed in 1971 by the leveling of conspiracy charges against Catholic

priests Phillip and Daniel Berrigan, along with six others, claiming that they had conspired to raid draft boards, blow up heating tunnels in Washington, D.C., and kidnap presidential advisor Henry Kissinger. The case had been devised by the Bureau, but upon review by Justice Department attorneys was deemed so weak that it could not even be presented to a grand jury. However, on November 27, 1970, J. Edgar Hoover personally testified before an "appropriations subcommittee" represented only by a pair of long-time Hoover admirers – Senators Robert C. Byrd (D., West Virginia) and Roman L. Hruska (R., Nebraska) – as to the existence of the "plot," thus forcing matters into court.[90] At trial, however, the Bureau's "case" turned out to be based exclusively on the testimony of a single infiltrator/*provocateur*, Boyd Douglass, who had been paid some $9,000 for his "services" by the FBI and certified by a federal psychiatrist as a "sociopath and pathological liar."[91] Although the defense declined to present a single witness, the jury deadlocked ten to two for acquittal on all major counts with which the Berrigans and their colleagues had been charged, voting to convict the accused only of having smuggled letters to one another during previous incarcerations.[92] Eventually, an appeals court overturned six of the seven convictions which were obtained even on this minor charge, given that Douglass had served as courier of the forbidden mail, and had done so on the express instructions of the FBI and at least one prison warden.[93] Ultimately, after all the smoke borne of sensational headlines had cleared, only Father Phillip Berrigan went briefly to prison, the only U.S. citizen ever sentenced by a court for sending or possessing "contraband" letters.[94]

Another conspiracy case brought in 1971 involved Daniel Ellsberg, a former high-level defense consultant with a government think tank, the Rand Corporation, who had shifted from staunch support of the Vietnam War to near-absolute condemnation of it, and his colleague, Anthony Russo.[95] The government charged that the pair had conspired to deny the government "its lawful function of withholding classified information from the public," by virtue of their removing several thousand pages of secret documentation (the so-called "Pentagon Papers") concerning the government's systematic deception of the U.S. public with regard to the country's Indochina policy from Rand facilities. They then passed the material along to *New York Times* reporter Neil Sheehan, who saw to it that selections appeared in the paper. Among other things, Ellsberg and Russo were charged with violating the 1917 Espionage Act, a wartime statute said to be in effect because President Harry Truman's invocation of it in 1950 – at the onset of the Korean War – had never been revoked (!).[96] Although the government was unable to establish that the Ellsberg/Russo "conspiracy" in any way jeopardized valid national security interests – to the contrary, federal prosecutors unsuccessfully argued at trial that no such jeopardy was required under the law – or even that the government possessed a statutory basis from which to contend that its classification and withholding of information from the public was "lawful," the case was taken to court.[97]

The Pentagon Papers trial was marked by a series of virtually unbelievable instances of government misconduct, including attempts by the government to suppress internal memoranda and studies casting doubt on the national security significance of the papers, an apparent government denial of any wiretaps and then an admission that Ellsberg and someone connected with the defense had both been overheard on taps directed at other persons, and the secret offer of the directorship of the FBI [Hoover being dead by this point] to presiding Judge Matthew Byrne by White House Domestic Advisor John Ehrlichman in the middle of the trial. The most sensational revelation was that persons associated with the White House Special Investigations Unit [the so-called "Plumbers," including former FBI agents G. Gordon Liddy and James McCord]...had burglarized the office of Ellsberg's psychiatrist [Dr. Louis Fielding] after the indictment was handed down...White House papers released in the course of the Watergate investigation revealed that the purpose of the burglary was to obtain information which could be used to create a "negative press image" of Ellsberg in an attempt to, as White House Counsel Charles Colson said, to "plumber" Howard Hunt in one telephone conversation, "put this bastard into one hell of a situation and discredit the New Left." With the final straw the government's temporary inability to uncover its wiretap records on Ellsberg, Judge Byrne ordered a mistrial and dismissed the case in April, 1973.[98]

The year 1972 witnessed yet another conspiracy extravaganza with the indictment of the so-called "Gainesville Eight" – thus designated as a result of the site of trial being set for Gainesville, Florida – all leaders of Vietnam Veterans Against the War (VVAW). The defendants were charged with conspiring to disrupt the 1972 Democratic and Republican Party national conventions in Miami through use of weapons ranging from "fried marbles" and ball bearings glued to cherry bombs (effectively constituting low-powered fragmentation grenades) to "wrist slingshots," crossbows, automatic weapons and incendiary devices. The timing of the federal grand jury which led to the indictments, and to which all eight defendants were called, was such as to effectively gut any VVAW demonstrations – including peaceful ones – at the Democratic convention, while the holding of four of the accused without bond for refusing to testify, and the arraignment of all eight during the Republican convention ruined their plans for that one as well. At trial, government witnesses broadened the array of weaponry the eight allegedly planned to use to include anti-tank weapons such as bazookas, but it emerged that police infiltrators rather than the defendants had been the primary discussants of higher-powered weapons such as machineguns. The only physical evidence prosecutors could produce in this regard were slingshots available at any sporting goods store.[99] The government's supposed star witness, an FBI infiltrator named William Lemmer, turned out to have been threatened with a psychiatric discharge by the army, and recently ordered held for a sanity hearing at the request of his wife after he wrote her a letter blaming VVAW for the breakup of his marriage explaining that if he decided to "get" the defendants, it would be silently, in "tennis shoes" and with a "length of piano wire."[100] He had also been only recently released by local police after they arrested him in possession of a loaded rifle and pistol, and an examining doctor recommended he receive psychiatric help. The jury deliberated less than three and a half hours before acquitting all eight defendants of all charges against them, but by then VVAW had ceased to function as an effective organization.[101]

Escalation

While the Justice Department was playing out its string of legal charades against the new left leadership, the FBI was quite busily engaged in more clandestine forms of repression. In the backwash of the Democratic convention in Chicago, it quickly set about fostering the divisiveness and fragmentation of dissident groups, a matter which is readily borne out in the accompanying August 28, 1968 memo from the director to the SAC, Detroit, calling for the employment of various COINTELPRO tactics against the Detroit Coalition Committee. Of particular interest to the FBI in the Detroit area was John Sinclair, head of a Yippie!-oriented organization called the White Panther Party, so much so that the Bureau provided considerable assistance to the local red squad in setting Sinclair up to receive an all but unprecedented nine-and-a-half year sentence for smoking marijuana at a rock concert in the presence of two undercover police officers.[102] In a number of other cases across the country, there was strong evidence that police had actually planted the "controlled substances" used to "judicially" effect political neutralizations.[103] As Frank Donner, an ACLU expert on political surveillance and counterintelligence was to put it in 1971, "The pot bust has become a punitive sanction against political dissent and the threat of prosecution [on drug charges] is a favorite method of 'hooking' student informers."[104]

Another favorite tactic was arrest and sometimes prosecution of student activists for "desecration of the flag." Despite clear first amendment protection, local police red squads working in collusion with FBI COINTELPRO desks habitually rousted demonstrators who incorporated the flag into their apparel, altered it to include peace signs or other movement symbols, burned it, or even flew it upside down (the international signal of distress). By May of 1971, the ACLU alone reported that it had at least 100 "flag cases" under consideration.[105] Eventually, defendants were tried and a number convicted in Hawaii, Minnesota, New York, Colorado, Washington state, Pennsylvania, New Hampshire and California before the Supreme Court finally ruled in *Spence v. Washington* (1974) that such prosecutions were unconstitutional.[106] Still, punishments on such grounds continued to occur through juvenile courts, as when in August 1974 an Ohio judge sentenced two teenaged girls to attend flag ceremonies for a week, observe a six-month curfew, and not to communicate with one another in any way for a year, all because they'd burned a flag during an anti-war demonstration.[107]

The "underground press," both "cultural" and political, was also a primary target during the early phases of COINTELPRO-New Left, as is made clear in the accompanying September 9, 1968 letter from Hoover to the SAC, New York, requesting a plan of attack; an October 7 proposal by the SAC; and Hoover's October 21 reply approving the operation. Focused upon is Liberation News Service (LNS), roughly the equivalent of Associated Press for the hundreds of alternative tabloids – mainly community-based – which had emerged across the country during the second half of the '60s. Between the point of inception of the COINTELPRO and late

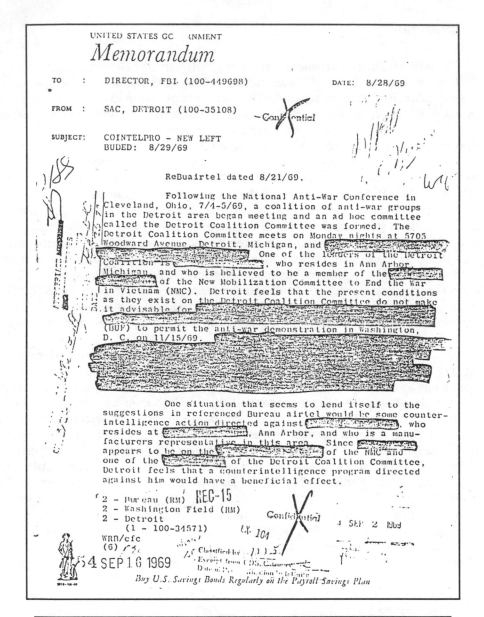

UNITED STATES GC   (NMENT

Memorandum

TO   :   DIRECTOR, FBI (100-449698)   DATE: 8/28/69

FROM   :   SAC, DETROIT (100-35108)   — Confidential

SUBJECT: COINTELPRO - NEW LEFT
            BUDED: 8/29/69

ReBuairtel dated 8/21/69.

Following the National Anti-War Conference in
Cleveland, Ohio, 7/4-5/69, a coalition of anti-war groups
in the Detroit area began meeting and an ad hoc committee
called the Detroit Coalition Committee was formed. The
Detroit Coalition Committee meets on Monday nights at 5705
Woodward Avenue, Detroit, Michigan, and ▓▓▓▓▓▓▓▓▓▓▓▓▓▓
▓▓▓▓▓▓▓▓▓▓▓▓▓▓▓ One of the leaders of the Detroit
Coalition is ▓▓▓▓▓▓▓▓▓▓, who resides in Ann Arbor,
Michigan, and who is believed to be a member of the▓▓▓▓▓
▓▓▓▓of the New Mobilization Committee to End the War
in Vietnam (NMC). Detroit feels that the present conditions
as they exist on the Detroit Coalition Committee do not make
it advisable for ▓▓▓▓▓▓▓▓▓▓▓▓▓▓▓▓▓▓▓▓▓▓▓▓▓▓▓▓▓▓▓▓▓▓
(BUF) to permit the anti-war demonstration in Washington,
D. C. on 11/15/69. ▓▓▓▓▓▓▓▓▓▓▓▓▓▓▓▓▓▓▓▓▓▓▓▓▓▓▓▓▓▓▓▓▓
▓▓▓

One situation that seems to lend itself to the
suggestions in referenced Bureau airtel would be some counterintelligence action directed against▓▓▓▓▓▓▓▓▓▓▓▓, who
resides at ▓▓▓▓▓▓▓▓▓▓, Ann Arbor, and who is a manufacturers representative in this area. Since ▓▓▓▓▓▓▓▓
appears to be on the ▓▓▓▓▓▓▓▓ of the NMC and
one of the ▓▓▓▓▓▓▓▓ of the Detroit Coalition Committee,
Detroit feels that a counterintelligence program directed
against him would have a beneficial effect.

```
2 - Bureau (RM)   REC-15
2 - Washington Field (RM)
2 - Detroit                    Confidential
    (1 - 100-34571)            EX. 101      4 SEP 2 1969
WRD/cfc
  (6)
54 SEP 16 1969        Classified by
                      Exempt from
                      Date of:
    Buy U.S. Savings Bonds Regularly on the Payroll Savings Plan
```

Memo describing plan to block emergence of a political coalition in Detroit.

1971, scores of alternative press workers were arrested (some repeatedly) on a
variety of thoroughly bogus charges.[108] In one notable example, Dallas police,
accompanied by FBI "observers," raided the offices of *Dallas Notes* in October of
1968, using a warrant which allowed them to search for "pornographic" material.

DE 100-35108   Confidential

     The specific suggestion is that a letter could be written from the BUF at Washington, D. C. to the White Panther Party (WPP), 1510 Hill Street, Ann Arbor, and also to the "Michigan Daily", University of Michigan student newspaper at Ann Arbor, pleading the BUF cause. The letter which could possibly be initiated by an informant in the BUF in Washington, D. C., or which could be a fraudulent letter could ask the WPP, a white militant group that strongly supports the Black Panther Party (BPP), to help the BUF collect the just and modest sum of $25,000.00 from the NMC by making a direct overture to ▓▓▓▓▓▓▓▓▓▓▓, an NMC leader in Ann Arbor. The letter could state that the BUF realizes that a substantial part of this sum could be easily raised by the NMC in Michigan because of the many professional and academicians supporting the anti-war demonstration scheduled for Washington, D. C. The letter could also state that a copy is being directed to the University of Michigan student newspaper to further publicize the very just nature of the BUF request.

     Detroit feels that the "Michigan Daily" would be delighted to publish this type of a letter. It is felt that such a letter would be of a disruptive nature if presented to the Detroit Coalition Committee by ▓▓▓▓▓▓▓ and could develop into a situation where ▓▓▓▓▓▓▓▓▓▓▓▓▓▓ ▓▓▓▓▓▓▓▓▓▓

     Such a letter would also be a disruptive factor to the amicable relations between the WPP and Black Nationalist supporters and groups in Ann Arbor, inasmuch as WPP would be forced to make a choice between BUF cause and the position of the white liberals in Ann Arbor who have been critical of the war and have to this point supported the WPP. The issue in the letter would be that the BUF knows that the white liberals, who are identified with the NMC, have unlimited sums of money available through their contacts and the sole issue is whether or not they want to give the $25,000.00 to the BUF.

     Comments of WFO are requested. If the Bureau approves of this suggestion, a draft of such a letter will be prepared by Detroit.

Confidential

The raiders left with more than two tons of items, including four typewriters and several credit cards, and ripped the electrical wiring out of the walls before leaving. The paper's editor was subsequently charged with "possession of pornography," an accusation which was thrown out as groundless by a local judge. He was then charged with "obscenity," resulting in another dismissal. Finally, he was brought into court, charged with "instigating a riot," convicted and sent to prison for three years. By this time, the paper was in a shambles.[109] The *Philadelphia Free Press*, for its part, found itself officially banned from all campuses of the Pennsylvania State University system, and thus denied much of its potential market.[110]

Nor is the case isolated. Shortly after the *San Diego Street Journal* had published

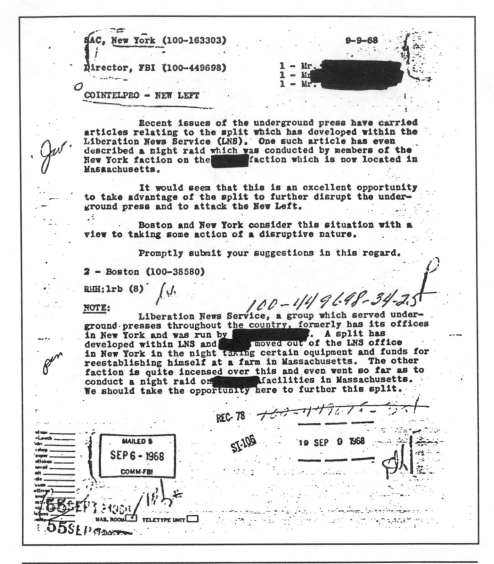

SAC, New York (100-163303)   9-9-68

Director, FBI (100-449698)   1 - Mr. ████
                                          1 - Mr. ████████████
                                          1 - Mr. ████████████

COINTELPRO - NEW LEFT

          Recent issues of the underground press have carried
articles relating to the split which has developed within the
Liberation News Service (LNS). One such article has even
described a night raid which was conducted by members of the
New York faction on the ████ faction which is now located in
Massachusetts.

          It would seem that this is an excellent opportunity
to take advantage of the split to further disrupt the underground press and to attack the New Left.

          Boston and New York consider this situation with a
view to taking some action of a disruptive nature.

          Promptly submit your suggestions in this regard.

     2 - Boston (100-38580)

RHH:lrb (8)

NOTE: 100-449698-34-25
          Liberation News Service, a group which served under-
ground presses throughout the country, formerly has its offices
in New York and was run by ████████. A split has
developed within LNS and ████████ moved out of the LNS office
in New York in the night taking certain equipment and funds for
reestablishing himself at a farm in Massachusetts. The other
faction is quite incensed over this and even went so far as to
conduct a night raid on ████████ facilities in Massachusetts.
We should take the opportunity here to further this split.

                    REC- 78

          MAILED 5
          SEP 6 - 1968
          COMM-FBI

Document outlining COINTELPRO action designed to disrupt Liberation News
Service in New England, using the standard tactic of sending anonymous letters.

an exposé on the practices of the local business elite during the fall of 1969, the paper
suffered an unwarranted raid of its offices coordinated by the local red squad while,
simultaneously, more than 20 of its street vendors were arrested for "littering" and
"obstructing the sidewalk." Not long afterward, an FBI operative named Howard
Berry Godfrey led a Bureau-financed group of right-wing thugs calling themselves
the "Secret Army Organization" (SAO) in a nocturnal entry of the paper's produc-

........And Who Got The Co▮ ▮e Jar?"

We see by the papers – New Left Notes, Guardian – that the Liberation News Service has been screwed into the ground while the peace movement has just been screwed. A real kindergarten performance by all concerned. See the cats run from the LNS office with the typewriters. See the girls dash away with the office supplies. See ▮▮▮▮▮ carrying the check for $6,000 skins. See SDS people weeping and grinding their teeth. (Scene change)

See the farm at Montague, Massachusetts. See the hip confrontation. What language! Now, all the men are fighting. Now the pigs are near. Will the State of Massachusetts charge ▮▮▮ with kidnaping? Will he be executed in public? Will LNS survive? Baby, at this point we wonder.....

New Left Notes described ▮▮▮ – one of the founders of LNS and onetime member of SDS – as suffering from megalomania. Could be. ▮▮▮ has always been a bit of a nut. Nice guy, understand, but just a little uptight where LNS was concerned. He has screamed charges of SDS take-over and conspiracy. He's named ▮▮▮ a traitor. With it all, he's managed to turn LNS from an efficient movement news service into a complete mess. The establishment of a bastard LNS at "Fortress Montague" is the most unrealistic bag of all. ▮▮▮ you've left the scene of the action in exchange for assorted ducks and sheep.

▮▮▮ as used the old bat "doctrinaire propaganda" to describe the monthly contribution of SDS to the LNS subscriber packets. It just ain't true, ▮▮▮ and you know it. SDS contributed meaningful ideas, yes. Maybe just a squib of intelligence. A little color. Some meat. How many of the 4CO-odd subscribers complained? One? Two? The office staff saw the response to the monthly mailing. Most was favorable, some not so hot. But not one letter was received by the New York office accusing LNS of engaging in SDS propaganda. Actually, after Chicago, what's wrong with a little SDS spiel?

"He saved LNS from withering away", says ▮▮▮ Not so. We say he killed it dead. Sort of a literary euthanasia. The New York Staff is trying to keep one limb alive at ▮▮▮ under the medical care of ▮▮▮ Will it live? Frankly, we don't know.

It's a bad scene when a good movement organization engages in civil war. Some of the details might be termed funny (We like the kidnaping bit), but dirty wash in public can only hurt. The situation was stupid, stupid, stupid.

What now? ▮▮▮ got the bread. Others got the office junk. ▮▮▮ got the finger. A fink ran off with the water cooler. And we got the cookie jar. LNS seems dead. Long live, LNS.

– A former Staffer

tion facility, stealing over $4,000 of its equipment and "putting it [temporarily] out of action."[111] In the South, things were just as bad:

Kudzu, produced in Jackson, Mississippi, served as a major organizational center for the New Left and counterculture in that area. The tenacity of the paper and its allies can be gauged by the fact that by 1968 the newspaper had survived a conviction on obscenity charges, the arrest of salespeople, the confiscation of cameras, and even eviction from its offices. On October 8, 1968, eighteen staff members and supporters of Kudzu were attacked and beaten by Jackson deputy sheriffs...In 1970, Kudzu was

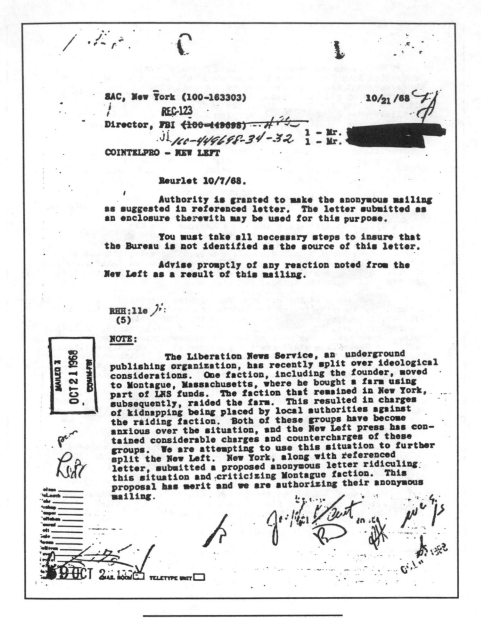

SAC, New York (100-163303)   10/21/68
          REC-123
Director, FBI (100-449698)
          100-449698-34-32   1 - Mr.
                                    1 - Mr.
COINTELPRO - NEW LEFT

          Reurlet 10/7/68.

          Authority is granted to make the anonymous mailing
as suggested in referenced letter. The letter submitted as
an enclosure therewith may be used for this purpose.

          You must take all necessary steps to insure that
the Bureau is not identified as the source of this letter.

          Advise promptly of any reaction noted from the
New Left as a result of this mailing.

RHH:lle
  (5)

NOTE:

          The Liberation News Service, an underground
publishing organization, has recently split over ideological
considerations. One faction, including the founder, moved
to Montague, Massachusetts, where he bought a farm using
part of LNS funds. The faction that remained in New York,
subsequently, raided the farm. This resulted in charges
of kidnapping being placed by local authorities against
the raiding faction. Both of these groups have become
anxious over the situation, and the New Left press has contained considerable charges and countercharges of these
groups. We are attempting to use this situation to further
split the New Left. New York, along with referenced
letter, submitted a proposed anonymous letter ridiculing
this situation and criticizing Montague faction. This
proposal has merit and we are authorizing their anonymous
mailing.

MAILED 2
OCT 21 1968
COMM-FBI

Letter approving action to split LNS.

put under direct surveillance by the FBI. For more than two months FBI agents
made daily searches without warrants...On October 24 and 25, *Kudzu* sponsored a
Southern regional conference of the Underground Press Syndicate. The night
before the conference the FBI and Jackson detectives searched the *Kudzu* offices
twice. During the search, an FBI agent threatened to kill *Kudzu* staffers. On the

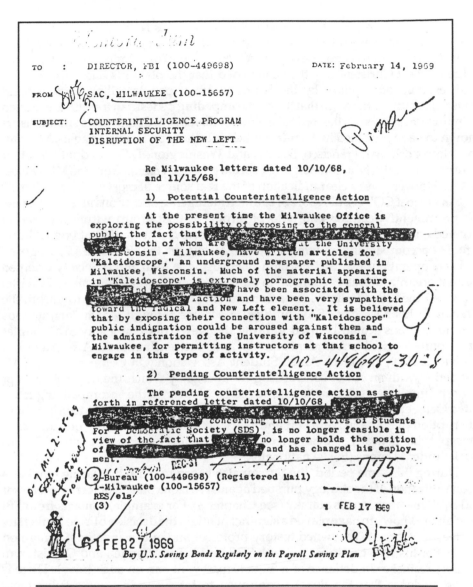

TO   :   DIRECTOR, FBI (100-449698)   DATE: February 14, 1969

FROM   SAC, MILWAUKEE (100-15657)

SUBJECT: COUNTERINTELLIGENCE PROGRAM
           INTERNAL SECURITY
           DISRUPTION OF THE NEW LEFT

              Re Milwaukee letters dated 10/10/68,
              and 11/15/68.

              1) Potential Counterintelligence Action

                   At the present time the Milwaukee Office is
              exploring the possibility of exposing to the general
              public the fact that ███████████████████████████
              ██████ both of whom are ████████████ at the University
              of Wisconsin - Milwaukee, have written articles for
              "Kaleidoscope," an underground newspaper published in
              Milwaukee, Wisconsin. Much of the material appearing
              in "Kaleidoscope" is extremely pornographic in nature.
              ████████ and ████████████ have been associated with the
              ████████████████ faction and have been very sympathetic
              toward the radical and New Left element. It is believed
              that by exposing their connection with "Kaleidoscope"
              public indignation could be aroused against them and
              the administration of the University of Wisconsin -
              Milwaukee, for permitting instructors at that school to
              engage in this type of activity.   100-449698-30-8

              2) Pending Counterintelligence Action

                   The pending counterintelligence action as set
              forth in referenced letter dated 10/10/68, ████████████
              ██████████████████ concerning the activities of Students
              For A Democratic Society (SDS), is no longer feasible in
              view of the fact that ████████ no longer holds the position
              of ██████████████████████ and has changed his employ-
              ment.

              2-Bureau (100-449698) (Registered Mail)   775
              1-Milwaukee (100-15657)
              RES/els
              (3)   FEB 17 1969

              FEB 27 1969
              Buy U.S. Savings Bonds Regularly on the Payroll Savings Plan

---

COINTELPRO plan aimed at the *Kaleidoscope* newspaper in Milwaukee.

morning of October 26, FBI agents again searched the offices. That evening local
police entered the building, held its eight occupants at gunpoint, produced a bag of
marijuana, then arrested them...A *Kudzu* staff member commented, "The FBI used
to be fairly sophisticated, but lately they have broken one of our doors, pointed guns
in our faces, told us that 'punks like you don't have any rights,' and threatened to
shoot us on the street if they see us with our hands in our pockets."[112]

In New Orleans, street vendors for the *New Orleans Nola Express* were repeatedly arrested on charges such as "vagrancy" and "peddling without a license." The harassment continued until the paper pressed a federal discrimination suit; District Judge Herbert Christenberry then concluded that the plaintiffs had "overwhelmingly established a policy by the police to arrest people selling underground newspapers under the guise that they were impeding pedestrian traffic," and issued an injunction against further official actions of this sort.[113] Comparable situations are known to have prevailed in Atlanta, Berkeley, Indianapolis, Los Angeles, Milwaukee, New York, San Francisco, Seattle, and Washington, D.C., no doubt a rather incomplete list.[114] The accompanying February 14, 1969 memo from the Milwaukee SAC to Hoover gives a clear indication of the real source of most such "problems."

As in most COINTELPROs, FBI counterintelligence operations against the new left prominently featured efforts to pit group against group within the overall targeted communities, often through production and distribution of bogus literature. The accompanying September 19, 1968 Airtel from the Newark SAC, proposed such an operation against Princeton SDS (using a John Birch Society-oriented student organization as a "counter" in the plan), and Hoover's September 24 Airtel approved the idea. Similarly, the accompanying October 17, 1968 Airtel from the director to his New York SAC outlined a scheme through which "anonymous communications" could be used to bring the New York University SDS chapter "into conflict" with black student organizations such as Katara, the Afro-American Student Society, and Black Allied Student Association. On October 21, the SAC responded with an Airtel concretizing the means by which the original concept could be implemented, a matter approved by Hoover in the accompanying letter dated October 25. As Hoover noted in his initial missive, the plan was to bring about "disruption of both the New Left and black student power forces" on campus, a concept tying in neatly with an ongoing Bureau effort to repress not only SDS but Black Student Unions (BSUs) nationally.[115]

During this same period, the Bureau also began to place increasing emphasis upon utilization of the strategy pursued against Arizona State University professor and SWP member Morris Starsky (see Chapter 3). For example, contacts from FBI officials are known to have played a significant role in the decision of Yale University trustees to terminate renowned history professor and anti-war activist Staughton Lynd after his 1966 trip to Hanoi with SDS leader Tom Hayden and CP historian Herbert Aptheker in defiance of a State Department ban on such travel. There is strong evidence that the Bureau continued to intervene in Lynd's subsequent attempts to secure a faculty position, notably in Illinois where the Board of Governors of State Colleges and Universities reversed decisions to hire him at the Chicago Circle Campus, Northern Illinois University, and even Chicago State College. The board, parroting J. Edgar Hoover's rhetoric, publicly stipulated its actions were predicated in the understanding that Lynd's travel, writings and speeches went "beyond mere dissent" (exactly how this was so, they didn't say). As a result, Lynd was forced out of academia altogether.[116]

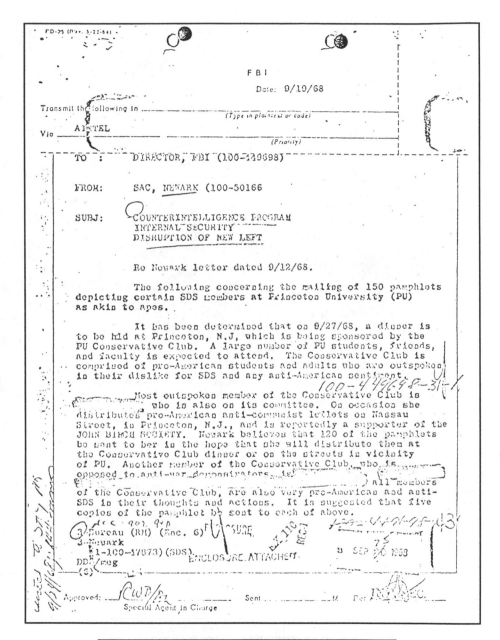

Airtel outlining COINTELPRO against Princeton SDS.

In another instance, Michael Parenti, a political scientist and anti-war activist at the University of Vermont, was denied renewal of his teaching contract – despite unanimous recommendations that he be retained from his dean, department and

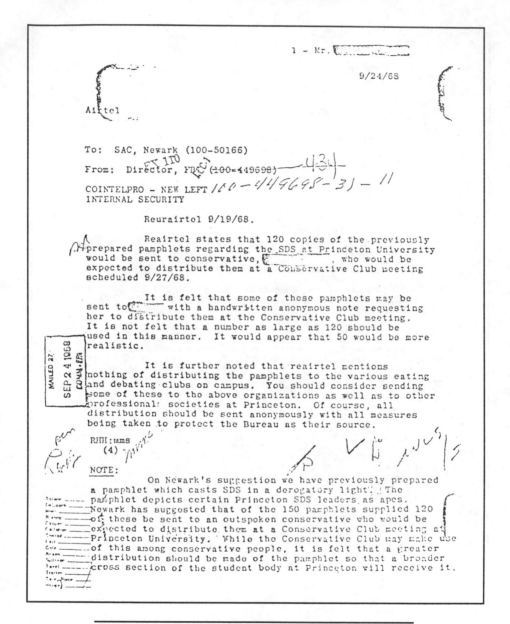

1 - Mr.

9/24/68

Airtel

To: SAC, Newark (100-50166)

From: Director, FBI (100-449698)

COINTELPRO - NEW LEFT
INTERNAL SECURITY

Reurairtel 9/19/68.

Reairtel states that 120 copies of the previously
prepared pamphlets regarding the SDS at Princeton University
would be sent to conservative, [   ], who would be
expected to distribute them at a Conservative Club meeting
scheduled 9/27/68.

It is felt that some of these pamphlets may be
sent to [   ] with a handwritten anonymous note requesting
her to distribute them at the Conservative Club meeting.
It is not felt that a number as large as 120 should be
used in this manner. It would appear that 50 would be more
realistic.

It is further noted that reairtel mentions
nothing of distributing the pamphlets to the various eating
and debating clubs on campus. You should consider sending
some of these to the above organizations as well as to other
professional societies at Princeton. Of course, all
distribution should be sent anonymously with all measures
being taken to protect the Bureau as their source.

RJH:mms
(4)

NOTE:

On Newark's suggestion we have previously prepared
a pamphlet which casts SDS in a derogatory light. The
pamphlet depicts certain Princeton SDS leaders as apes.
Newark has suggested that of the 150 pamphlets supplied 120
of these be sent to an outspoken conservative who would be
expected to distribute them at a Conservative Club meeting at
Princeton University. While the Conservative Club may make use
of this among conservative people, it is felt that a greater
distribution should be made of the pamphlet so that a broader
cross section of the student body at Princeton will receive it.

Airtel approving COINTELPRO against SDS at Princeton.

even the university administration – after the institution's trustees received a spate
of anonymous letters condemning his political activities. The trustees specified that,
although in no way questioning Parenti's "professional competence" or effectiveness as a teacher, they were nonetheless bound to "protect the image of the

Cartoon used in Princeton COINTELPRO.

University" from new left radicalism.[117] At UCLA in 1969, the regents fired philosophy professor Angela Y. Davis on the basis of her association with the Black Panther Party, CP and Soledad Brothers Defense Committee, as well as for having given political speeches "so extreme...and so obviously false," despite her endorsement by every relevant university official and by a blue-ribbon faculty committee formed by the regents themselves to pass judgment on Davis' academic competence.[118] The correspondence of the Los Angeles FBI office during this period suggests the Bureau played an active part in helping the regents' decision along.

Similarly, George Murray, an English instructor and BPP Minister of Education, was summarily suspended by Chancellor Glenn Dumke of the California State College system in 1969, after the BPP leader publicly advised black students to adopt principles of armed self-defense. Two other San Francisco State professors were also sacked for their political views at the same time as Murray, and two others denied tenure, one for protesting Murray's suspension and the other apparently for having participated in Murray's original hiring. Interestingly, Dumke's action sparked a sustained student strike which eclipsed those which had earlier occurred at Berkeley and Columbia – in perseverance and militancy, if not in publicity received – which paralyzed the institution for several months.[119] Perhaps the worst case of this sort involved Peter G. Bohmer, a radical economics professor at San Diego State

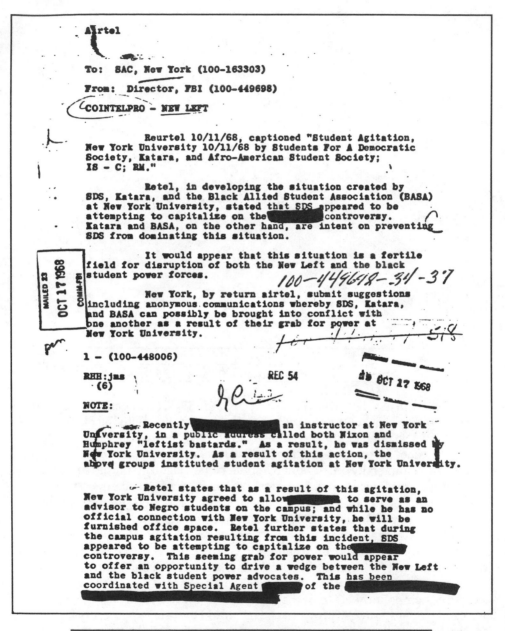

Airtel

To: SAC, New York (100-163303)

From: Director, FBI (100-449698)

COINTELPRO - NEW LEFT

Reurtel 10/11/68, captioned "Student Agitation, New York University 10/11/68 by Students For A Democratic Society, Katara, and Afro-American Student Society; IS - C; RM."

Retel, in developing the situation created by SDS, Katara, and the Black Allied Student Association (BASA) at New York University, stated that SDS appeared to be attempting to capitalize on the ███████ controversy. Katara and BASA, on the other hand, are intent on preventing SDS from dominating this situation.

It would appear that this situation is a fertile field for disruption of both the New Left and the black student power forces.

100-449698-34-37

New York, by return airtel, submit suggestions including anonymous communications whereby SDS, Katara, and BASA can possibly be brought into conflict with one another as a result of their grab for power at New York University.

1 - (100-448006)

RHH:jms
(6)

REC 54

NOTE:

Recently ████████████ an instructor at New York University, in a public address called both Nixon and Humphrey "leftist bastards." As a result, he was dismissed by New York University. As a result of this action, the above groups instituted student agitation at New York University.

Retel states that as a result of this agitation, New York University agreed to allow ████████ to serve as an advisor to Negro students on the campus; and while he has no official connection with New York University, he will be furnished office space. Retel further states that during the campus agitation resulting from this incident, SDS appeared to be attempting to capitalize on the ████████ controversy. This seeming grab for power would appear to offer an opportunity to drive a wedge between the New Left and the black student power advocates. This has been coordinated with Special Agent ████████ of the ████████

COINTELPRO to block student coalition at New York University.

University, who was arbitrarily fired by Chancellor Dumke in 1971, despite the fact that he was in contention for a teaching award (which he won, two weeks after his dismissal).[120] This was followed, on the night of January 9, 1972, by shots being fired

                    ████████ The Black Racist With
                    A Megaphone Mouth

     There are times when the movement - especially SDS - allows
itself to be sucked into backing rather dim causes. During the
recent confrontation with ████████ and NYU over the firing of
████████ a member of Katara was heard to say "This is a
black thing, man. Keep the Jew-boys in their own building".
He was referring to the occupation of the Gould Student Center
on the uptown NYU campus by the blacks and the ground floor
of the library by the whites, mostly SDS.

     Most students active in SDS consider the ████████ thing a
poor excuse to occupy anything. This man has uttered incredibly
stupid statements on Black - Jewish relations. In an article
written for the African - American Teachers Forum, ████████
stated that the minds of black students were being poisoned
by "anti-black Jewish teachers." As a result, black campus
organizations are busy biting the hands which have helped them
the most. ████████ continues to suffer from diarrhea of the
mouth. The pity of it all is that by operating alone at NYU,
Katara, Basa and other loose black organizations screwed up
the bit. ████████ Katara leader, led his followers out
of the student center shouting "Beep, beep, bop, bop, ungawa,
black power. We won. We won." ████████ would be retained by
NYU; black power would be served. Horseshit. It was a flop,
flop, not bop, bop. SDS knew it immediately. ████████ and
████████ were up against the wall, not NYU.

     SDS leaders on New York campuses should wake up. Put a
stop to unlimited concessions to demands of black organizations.
And this includes being called a "Jew bastard" to your face or
smiling while a militant informs us that the blame for the
ghettos rests on the heads of Jewish businessmen who have
"bled the blacks for two hundred years". For that matter, Mr.
████████ is the perfect example of a racist. He's a black
George Wallace. They are two of a kind; only the skin is
different.

     We think SDS should continue the fight for black rights,
but let's be a little choosy. Katara and Basa should be left
to go their own way. No support should be given until asked for.

     In the future many students in SDS will refuse to support
black racism in any form. My heritage (Jewish) is as precious
to me as that of any black. I'll not see it shit on, brothers.
We're with you but let's knock off racist stupidity.

                              SDS Member, NYU (Class of '71)

Anonymous letter used in the NYU COINTELPRO, proposed in an Airtel
dated October 21, 1968. Note the blatant racism employed.

through the windows of Bohmer's home, one of which struck the right elbow of one
of his friends, Paula Tharp, permanently disabling her. It turned out that the
attempted assassination had been performed by the FBI-sponsored Secret Army
Organization, and that Bureau infiltrator Howard Berry Godfrey had been in the car
along with gunman George M. Hoover who had fired the shots. Although Godfrey
immediately informed his handler, SA Steve Christianson, of what had happened,
it was more than six months before the Bureau took action in the matter.[121]

Some of the gambits employed by the Bureau in COINTELPRO-New Left were

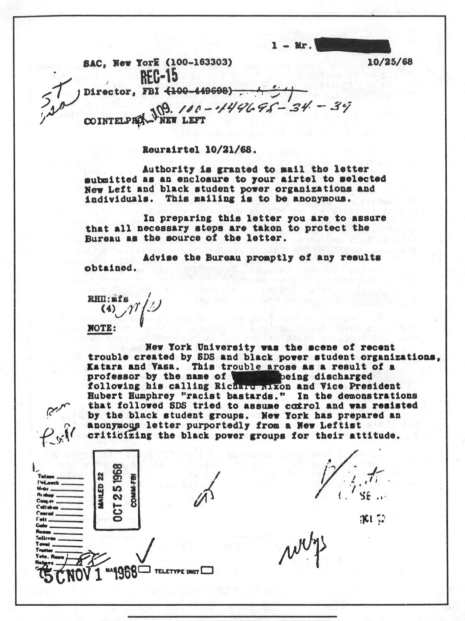

1 - Mr. ▆▆▆▆▆

SAC, New York (100-163303)   10/25/68

REC-15

Director, FBI (100-449698)

COINTELPRO - NEW LEFT

Reurairtel 10/21/68.

        Authority is granted to mail the letter
submitted as an enclosure to your airtel to selected
New Left and black student power organizations and
individuals. This mailing is to be anonymous.

        In preparing this letter you are to assure
that all necessary steps are taken to protect the
Bureau as the source of the letter.

        Advise the Bureau promptly of any results
obtained.

RHII:mfs
     (4)

NOTE:

        New York University was the scene of recent
trouble created by SDS and black power student organizations,
Katara and Vasa. This trouble arose as a result of a
professor by the name of ▆▆▆▆▆ being discharged
following his calling Richard Nixon and Vice President
Hubert Humphrey "racist bastards." In the demonstrations
that followed SDS tried to assume control and was resisted
by the black student groups. New York has prepared an
anonymous letter purportedly from a New Leftist
criticizing the black power groups for their attitude.

MAILED 22 OCT 25 1968 COMM-FBI

Letter approving NYU COINTELPRO.

not so much sinister as they were weird. A classic example may be found in the
proposal lodged in the accompanying November 21, 1968 memo from the SAC,
Philadelphia, to J. Edgar Hoover. Seriously garbling the realities pertaining to
hippies, Yippies!, and SDSers, the SAC apparently genuinely believed that periodic

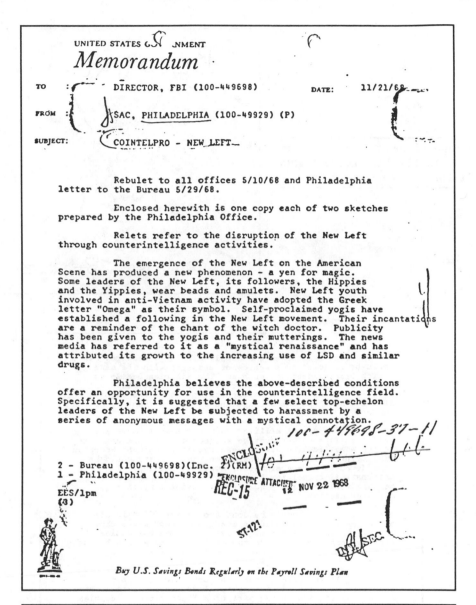

UNITED STATES GOVERNMENT

Memorandum

TO : DIRECTOR, FBI (100-449698)   DATE: 11/21/68

FROM : SAC, PHILADELPHIA (100-49929) (P)

SUBJECT: COINTELPRO - NEW LEFT

Rebulet to all offices 5/10/68 and Philadelphia letter to the Bureau 5/29/68.

Enclosed herewith is one copy each of two sketches prepared by the Philadelphia Office.

Relets refer to the disruption of the New Left through counterintelligence activities.

The emergence of the New Left on the American Scene has produced a new phenomenon - a yen for magic. Some leaders of the New Left, its followers, the Hippies and the Yippies, wear beads and amulets. New Left youth involved in anti-Vietnam activity have adopted the Greek letter "Omega" as their symbol. Self-proclaimed yogis have established a following in the New Left movement. Their incantations are a reminder of the chant of the witch doctor. Publicity has been given to the yogis and their mutterings. The news media has referred to it as a "mystical renaissance" and has attributed its growth to the increasing use of LSD and similar drugs.

Philadelphia believes the above-described conditions offer an opportunity for use in the counterintelligence field. Specifically, it is suggested that a few select top-echelon leaders of the New Left be subjected to harassment by a series of anonymous messages with a mystical connotation.

2 - Bureau (100-449698)(Enc. 2)(RM)
1 - Philadelphia (100-49929)
EES/lpm
(3)

Buy U.S. Savings Bonds Regularly on the Payroll Savings Plan

Memo detailing plan to use occult mysticism as a mechanism to sow "suspicion, distrust, and disruption" within new left circles at Temple University. Contrary to appearances, this seems *not* to have been a joke. Text and sample cartoon continue on following pages.

---

receipt of such nonsense, mailed anonymously, would cause "concern and mental anguish" on the part of "hand-picked" targets, and that "suspicion, distrust, and

Sample of the cartoons utilized in the COINTELPRO at Temple (right). Text of memo continues below.

The enclosed sketches are a sample of such a message. This could be followed by a series of messages with the same sketch bearing captions such as "The Siberian Beetle is Black" or "The Siberian Beetle Can Talk." The recipient is left to make his own interpretation as to the significance of the symbol and the message and as to the identity of the sender.

The symbol utilized does not have to have any real significance but must be subject to interpretation as having a mystical, sinister meaning. "The Chinese Scorpion," "The Egyptian Cobra," or some such similar name would be considered to have a sinister, mystical meaning. The mathematical symbol for "infinity" with an appropriate message would certainly qualify as having a mystical, sinister meaning.

Mailing could be done from a specified location or the mailing site could be changed on each subsequent message. Consideration might even be given to sending the first message from outside the United States with subsequent messages emanating from various cities in the United States.

It is believed that the periodic receipt of anonymous messages, as described above, could cause concern and mental anguish on the part of a "hand-picked" recipient or recipients. Suspicion, distrust, and disruption could follow.

The proposed action, suggested above, is basically a harassment technique. Its ultimate aim is to cause disruption of the New Left by attacking an apparent weakness of some of its leaders. It is felt there is a reasonable chance for success. The cost of such an operation to the Bureau is minimal. The Bureau's interest can be protected with the usual precautions taken in such matters.

SAC, Philadelphia (100-49929)   12/4/68

Director, FBI (100-449698) ~~bob~~   1 - Mr ████████
        REC-122 ///-449698-37-11   ~~█~~

COINTELPRO - NEW LEFT

Reurlet 11/21/68.

The observations of your office with regard to the captioned Program are appreciated and it is felt that with the proper selectivity of subjects the approach suggested in relet could be fruitful.

In choosing a subject for such an approach, a thorough knowledge of his background and activities is necessary. In this regard, the subject or subjects chosen should be individuals with whom we have close contact through live informant coverage. Through these informants, we might be able to enhance the effect of the mailings by planning "appropriate" interpretations of the symbols.

The significance of the symbols should be slanted so as to be interpreted as relating to something that is currently going on in the New Left. In this regard, the factional disputes within SDS and the dispute between SMC and the Radical Organizing Committee readily come to mind.

Prior to instituting such a Program and with the above comments in mind, submit your recommendations as to the appropriate subject to be included in such a Program along with the symbolisms to be used and the desired interpretations to be expected.

Take no steps to carry out this phase of the Program without prior Bureau approval.

MAILED ■
DEC 3 - 1968
COMM ██

RHH:jes
(4)

NOTE:
        By relet, PH took note of the fact that some leaders of the New Left, particularly the hippies and the Yippies, follow mysticism and various cults. PH believes that this propensity for symbolism can be used in the above Program by selecting a few top-echelon leaders as targets for a series of anonymous messages with mystical connotations. According to PH, the recipient of such a message would be left to make his own interpretation as to the significance of the symbol, as well as to the identity of the sender. PH pointed out that it might be possible to subject these individuals to a certain amount of mental anguish, suspicion, distrust, and disruption through these means.

J. Edgar Hoover approves the Temple COINTELPRO.

disruption" within the new left would follow. As may be seen in the accompanying December 4 letter of response from Hoover, the director quickly approved the idea, and a raft of "Siberian Beetle" cartoons were duly mailed. There is no record of the results.

In a far more serious vein, the IRS collaborated with the FBI in what amounted to a counterintelligence campaign. During the period 1968-74:

[T]he IRS gave to the FBI confidential tax information on 120 leaders of the anti-war and militant black movements, as part of the FBI's COINTELPRO activity. According to a February, 1969, FBI memo, the Bureau also succeeded in getting the IRS to inquire into many of these cases, anticipating that the inquiry "will cause these individuals considerable consternation, possibly jail sentences eventually" and would help the FBI achieve its objective of obtaining "prosecution of any kind" in order to "remove them from the movement." The IRS also furnished the FBI with a list of contributors to SDS developed in connection with an IRS audit of SDS. The IRS also passed the list on to the White House.[122]

Additionally, at the Bureau's behest, the IRS established a Special Services Staff (SSS) unit devoted to coordinating "activities in all Compliance Divisions involving ideological, militant, subversive, radical, and similar type organizations." This purview was shortly broadened to include all persons who traveled to Cuba, Algeria or North Vietnam, and those who "organize and attend rock festivals."[123] The program of punitive (and thus illegal) tax audits and other investigations which followed was "justified" because of a need to "help control an insidious threat to the internal security of this country". and because such "enforcement" might "have some salutary effect in this overall battle against persons bent upon destruction of this government," to wit: dealing a decisive "blow to dissident elements" within the U.S.[124] Altogether, SSS established files on 2,873 organizations including SDS and the BPP, of course, but also others such as the ACLU, American Library Association, American Jewish Congress, Common Cause, National Education Association, *New York Review of Books* and *Rolling Stone*. In addition, SSS files were opened on 8,585 individuals including such redoubtable "revolutionaries" as liberal New York Mayor John Lindsay, U.S. Senators Charles Goodell and Ernest Gruening, newspaper columnist Joseph Alsop, singers James Brown and Joan Baez, and actress Shirley MacLaine.[125]

War at Home

By 1969, the new left was developing a conscious emphasis on anti-imperialist analysis, combining its support to the black liberation movement (and Third World liberation movements more generally), its opposition to the war in Vietnam, and its belief that it must endeavor to reorganize its own society in a fundamentally different way than that mandated by the *status quo*. A central preoccupation of the movement focused on how to translate such analysis into action.[126] One of the ways in which this was approached was to begin to incorporate more "systematic" marxian appreciations of politics into the more-or-less theoretically inchoate new left vision. A second was to attempt to solidify alliances with black liberation formations such as the BPP. The FBI, of course, upped its COINTELPRO ante in an effort to prevent either initiative from materializing.

On the first count, as can be discerned in the accompanying November 3, 1969 letter from Hoover to the SAC, San Francisco, the Bureau utilized standard counter-

SAC, San Francisco   11/3/69

Director, FBI (62-111181)

DEMNOV   O COINTELPRO - NEW LEFT

ReLAairtel 10/23/69.

Referenced airtel states that the New
Mobilization Committee (NMC) has decided to purge the
Socialist Workers Party (SWP) and the Young Socialist
Alliance (YSA) from the antiwar demonstration to be held
in San Francisco on 11/15/69 and that all affiliation
with the SWP and the YSA is to be dissolved.

This situation seems to afford an excellent
opportunity to drive a wedge between the SWP and the
peace groups in the Los Angeles area.

Consistent with the security of your sources,
you should prepare an anonymous communication criticizing
the action taken by NMC in freezing the SWP and YSA out of
the forthcoming demonstration.

Forward a copy of this communication to the
Bureau along with your recommendations as to the groups
and individuals who should receive it. In addition, you
should consider furnishing this information to appropriate
cooperative news representatives. Take no action in this
respect without first obtaining Bureau authority.
1 - 100-449698
1 - Los Angeles (100-74253)   100-441614.

RHH:bjp/mef   ACT RECORDED
(6)   1st NOV 3 1969

NOTE:

        The New Mobilization Committee to end war in
Vietnam (NMC) is sponsoring a massive demonstration in
San Francisco on 11/15/69. Los Angeles has advised that
the leadership of NMC has decided to exclude the Socialist
Workers Party and its youth group, the Young Socialist
Alliance, from these demonstrations. This would seem to
offer an excellent opportunity to cause confusion in the
organizing for this mass demonstration by causing dissent
amongst its sponsors.

COINTELPRO targeting the Mobe and SWP.

intelligence techniques to "drive a wedge" between the new leftist New Mobilization Committee to End the War in Vietnam (called "Mobe," like the National Mobilization Committee which preceded it) and the old left SWP (this is the other side of
a COINTELPRO simultaneously aimed at the SWP; see Chapter 3). At the same time,
the Bureau was even more serious about wrecking the emergence of any meaningful
alliance between SDS and the BPP, and other non-white liberation organizations. As
is brought out clearly in the accompanying June 19, 1969 memo from Chicago SAC
Marlin Johnson to Hoover – and Hoover's response to Johnson in the accompanying

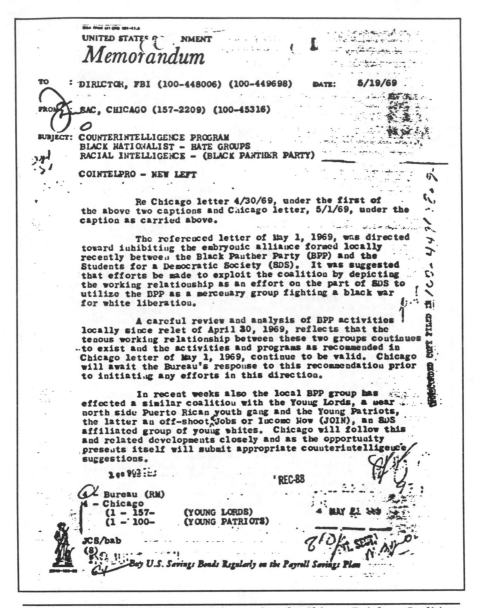

Memo proposing COINTELPRO action against the Chicago Rainbow Coalition.

June 21 letter – the FBI was quite active in sabotaging the establishment of a "Rainbow Coalition" between SDS, the BPP, the *Puertorriqueño* Young Lords Organization and a politicized white youth gang called the Young Patriots (this is another dimension of a COINTELPRO simultaneously aimed at the BPP; see Chapter 5).

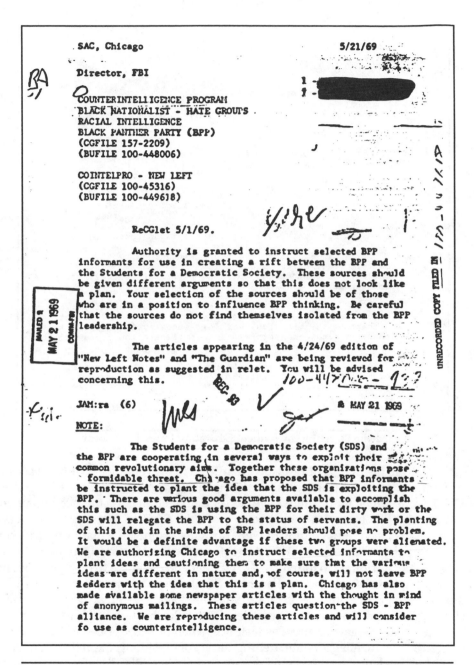

SAC, Chicago   5/21/69

Director, FBI

COUNTERINTELLIGENCE PROGRAM
BLACK NATIONALIST - HATE GROUPS
RACIAL INTELLIGENCE
BLACK PANTHER PARTY (BPP)
(CGFILE 157-2209)
(BUFILE 100-448006)

COINTELPRO - NEW LEFT
(CGFILE 100-45316)
(BUFILE 100-449618)

ReCGlet 5/1/69.

    Authority is granted to instruct selected BPP
informants for use in creating a rift between the BPP and
the Students for a Democratic Society. These sources should
be given different arguments so that this does not look like
a plan. Your selection of the sources should be of those
who are in a position to influence BPP thinking. Be careful
that the sources do not find themselves isolated from the BPP
leadership.

    The articles appearing in the 4/24/69 edition of
"New Left Notes" and "The Guardian" are being reviewed for
reproduction as suggested in relet. You will be advised
concerning this.

JAM:ra (6)

NOTE:

    The Students for a Democratic Society (SDS) and
the BPP are cooperating in several ways to exploit their
common revolutionary aims. Together these organizations pose
a formidable threat. Chicago has proposed that BPP informants
be instructed to plant the idea that the SDS is exploiting the
BPP. There are various good arguments available to accomplish
this such as the SDS is using the BPP for their dirty work or the
SDS will relegate the BPP to the status of servants. The planting
of this idea in the minds of BPP leaders should pose no problem.
It would be a definite advantage if these two groups were alienated.
We are authorizing Chicago to instruct selected informants to
plant ideas and cautioning them to make sure that the various
ideas are different in nature and, of course, will not leave BPP
leaders with the idea that this is a plan. Chicago has also
made available some newspaper articles with the thought in mind
of anonymous mailings. These articles question the SDS - BPP
alliance. We are reproducing these articles and will consider
fo use as counterintelligence.

The anti-Rainbow Coalition COINTELPRO is approved. Once again, note the
blatant utilization of racism as a means to separate political organizations, a
strategy which could not fail to have profound effects in the society at large.

```
    UNITED STATES G  ..  .. ..

    Memorandum          .  ..

TO   : Director, FBI (105-174254)              DATE:   10/13/7.
         Attention:  Counterintelligence and Special
                     Operations (Research Section)
FROM : SAC, Detroit (100-35108)    (P)

SUBJECT: COUNTERINTELLIGENCE PROGRAM
         IS - DISRUPTION OF NEW LEFT

                    Detroit is proposing the disruption of the
         physical plant of the Radical Education Project (REP), 3908
         Michigan Avenue, Detroit, Michigan.  REP is a full time
         publishing outfit of the New Left through whose auspices
         numerous virulent revolutionary treatises reach the Left.

                    In addition, the Black Panther Party (BPP) in
         Detroit receives BPP publications from San Francisco.
         Detroit has easy access to these papers after they arrive
         in Detroit.

                    The Bureau is requested to prepare and furnish
         to Detroit in liquid form a solution capable of duplicating
         a scent of the most foul smelling feces available.  In this
         case, it might be appropriate to duplicate the feces of the
         specie sus scrofa.

                    A quart supply, along with a dispenser capable
         of squirting a narrow stream for a distance of approximately
         three feet would satisfy the needs of this proposed technique.
```

Memo targeting the Radical Education Project in Detroit.

In Detroit, the COINTELPRO tactics utilized in preventing a coalition between the Panthers and SDS (through the latter's subsidiary Radical Education Project [REP]) were rather more innovative, as is demonstrated in the accompanying October 13, 1970 memo to the director from the SAC in that city. In Newark, however, the techniques employed were far more orthodox, a matter indicated in the accompanying October 16, 1970 Airtel from the local SAC to Hoover, detailing a bogus letter attributed to the city's SDS chapter and designed to instigate hostility between the new leftists and the Panthers. Similar methods were employed, albeit usually through "friendly press representatives," against individuals – especially celebrities – endeavoring to forge new left/BPP links through fundraising for such things as Panther legal defense. For instance, when BPP leader David Hilliard was arrested in 1970 for allegedly threatening the life of President Nixon during a public speech, actress Jane Fonda engaged in such activity in Hilliard's behalf. As a result, Richard Wallace Held, head of the local COINTELPRO section, tendered the accompanying June 17, 1970 Airtel outlining the sending of a bogus letter to *Hollywood Daily Variety* gossip columnist Army Archerd, expressly intended to

Date: 10/16/70

Transmit the following in _____
                                    (Type in plaintext or code)
   AIRTEL
Via _____
                                         (Priority)
- -

TO: DIRECTOR, FBI (100-449698)

FROM: SAC, NEWARK (100-50166) (P)

          COINTELPRO - NEW LEFT

     Re Newark letter, 9/28/70.

          In the 10/10/70 issue of, "The Black Panther", there
are cartoons on pages 3, 4, and 5, depicting a woman holding
a gun, a boy holding a gun and a "molotov cocktail" and an
elderly man holding a gun.

          It is suggested the following letter, handwritten
on "5 ¢ 10" store-type paper, be sent to the BPP at 93 Summit
Ave., Jersey City, NJ, BPP Headquarters:

     "Dear Pussycats:

          "I just read the 10/10/70 issue of your paper,
     particularly pages 3, 4 and 5 and was much im-
     pressed with the people's Army. A woman, a boy
     and an old man. Man, you sure are tough. You're
     a joke man. You're some vanguard of the oppressed
     black.

          "With your leaders fleeing the country and
     "Huey the Homo" afraid to raise his voice for fear
     he'll get busted again, I guess all you got left
     are the women, kids and old men. The rest are
     so dumb they can't be trusted with a weapon
     because they keep forgetting which end the bullet
     comes out of.

          "So go ahead, get high on wine and dream
     your alcoholic dreams of conquest. About the
     only successful conquest you can accomplish is
     over your modest and proper (what a joke)
     mattress back ladies auxiliary.

          "If you'd have joined us last year you'd have
     been a lot better off. You'd have had some
     brainpower behind you, but now? Big Zero,
     with a revolving door leadership.

                         Newark SDS"

          Full precaution will be taken to protect the Bureau
as the source of the letter, which will be written by a Special
Agent and mailed in Newark, NJ.

Airtel outlining plan to set SDS and the BPP at odds with one another in the
Newark area. Note the blatant appeal not only to racism, but to sexism and
homophobia in the bogus letter proposed. Unlike similar missives employed to
inflame relations between US and the BPP during the same period (see Chapter
V), this COINTELPRO engendered no lethal results, an outcome attributable
more to the restraint of the Panthers than of the FBI.

```
                                    Date:   6/17/70

nsmit the following in ─────────────────────────────────────────────
                                  (Type in plaintext or code)

    AIRTEL        AIR MAIL - REGISTERED
                                  (Priority)
─────────────────────────────────────────────────


    TO:       DIRECTOR, FBI

    FROM:     SAC, LOS ANGELES              (P)

    RE:       COUNTERINTELLIGENCE PROGRAM
              BLACK NATIONALIST-HATE GROUPS
              RACIAL INTELLIGENCE
              BLACK PANTHER PARTY (BPP)

          Re Los Angeles telotype to Bureau, 6/15/70,
    entitled "COMMITTEE UNITED FOR POLITICAL PRISONERS (CUPP),
    IS-MISCELLANEOUS, THREAT AGAINST PRESIDENT NIXON".

              Bureau authority is requested in sending the following
    letter from a fictitious person to ARMY ARCHERD, Hollywood
    "gossip" columnist for the "Daily Variety", who noted in his
    6/11/70 column that JANE FONDA, noted film actress, was to be
    present at the 6/13/70 Black Panther Party fund raising
    function sponsored by CUPP in Los Angeles.  It is felt that
    knowledge of FONDA's involvement would cause her embarrassment
    and detract from her status with the general public.

       "Dear Army,

          I saw your article about Jane Fonda in 'Daily
       Variety' last Thursday and happened to be present
       for Vadim's 'Joan of Arc's" performance for the
       Black Panthers Saturday night.  I hadn't been
       confronted with this Panther phenomena before but
       we were searched upon entering Embassy Auditorium,
       encouraged in revival-like fashion to contribute to
       defend jailed Panther leaders and buy guns for
       'the coming revolution', and led by Jane and one of

    ②- Bureau (RM)              REC 16
    2 - San Francisco (RM)
    2 - Los Angeles                          JUN 19 1970
    ────────────────────────    LA-110
      (6)
    pproved: _____  Sent _____ M   Per _____
             Special Agent in charge              • U. S. GOVERNMENT PRINTING OFFICE
```

Airtel targeting actress Jane Fonda.

cause Fonda "embarrassment and detract from her status with the general public."

Held appears to have specialized in such things. Only two months previously, he had launched a similar operation (and for similar reasons, albeit compounded by a sexual twist) against the actress Jean Seberg:

```
LA 157-4054

     the Panther chaps in a 'we will kill Richard
     Nixon, and any other M-----F----- who stands
     in our way' refrain (which was shocking to say
     the least!). I think Jane has gotten in over
     her head as the whole atmosphere had the 1930's
     Munich beer-hall aura.

     "I also think my curiosity about the Panthers
     has been satisfied.

                              "Regards

                              /s/ "Morris"

     If approved, appropriate precautions will be taken
to preclude the identity of the Bureau as the source of this
operation.
```

In April 1970, when Seberg was in her fourth month of pregnancy, the Bureau sought a way to make her an object lesson to any other parlor pinks who might be thinking of supporting the Panthers. According to one former FBI agent [M. Wesley Swearingen] who worked in Los Angeles at the time, a culture of racism had so permeated the Bureau and its field offices that the agents seethed with hatred toward the Panthers and the white women who associated with them. "In the view of the Bureau," [Swearingen] reported, "Jean was giving aid and comfort to the enemy, the BPP...The giving of her white body to a black man was an unbearable thought for many of the white agents. An agent [allegedly Held] was overheard to say, a few days after I arrived in Los Angeles from New York, 'I wonder how she'd like to gobble my dick while I shove my .38 up that black bastard's ass [a reference to BPP theorist Raymond "Masai" Hewitt, with whom Seberg was reputedly having an affair].'"[127]

On May 27, 1970, Held sent the accompanying Airtel to headquarters requesting approval to plant a story with Hollywood gossip columnists to the effect that Seberg was pregnant, not by her husband, Romaine Gary, but by a Panther. As indicated in the accompanying May 6 response by letter from Hoover, Held's idea was approved, although implementation was postponed "approximately two additional months," to protect the secrecy of a wiretap the Bureau had installed in the LA and San Francisco BPP headquarters, and until the victim's "pregnancy would be more visible to everyone." The director also took the time to stipulate that Seberg deserved to be "neutralized" simply because she'd been a "financial supporter" of the Black Panther Party. The schedule was apparently accelerated, because on June 6, Held sent Hoover the accompanying letter and attached newspaper clipping demonstrating the "success" of his COINTELPRO action: a column by Joyce Haber laying out the Bureau fiction, which had run in the *Los Angeles Times* on May 19. Known by the FBI to have been emotionally unstable and in the care of a psychiatrist before the operation began, Seberg responded to the "disclosure" by attempting suicide with an overdose of sleeping pills. This in turn precipitated the premature delivery of her

Date: 4/27/70

Transmit the following in _____

(Type in plaihtext or code)

Via _____ AIRTEL. _____   REGISTERED MAIL

(Priority)

TO: DIRECTOR, FBI (100-448006)

FROM: SAC, LOS ANGELES (157-4054) (P)

SUBJECT: COUNTERINTELLIGENCE PROGRAM
           BLACK NATIONALIST HATE GROUPS
           RACIAL INTELLIGENCE - BLACK PANTHER PARTY

    Re San Francisco airtel to the Bureau dated 4/23/70, entitled, "BLACK PANTHER PARTY (BPP), LOS ANGELES DIVISION, RM-BPP."

    Bureau permission is requested to publicize the pregnancy of JEAN SEBERG, well-known movie actress, by ████████████ Black Panther Party (BPP) ████████ by advising Hollywood "Gossip-Columnists" in the Los Angeles area of the situation. It is felt that the possible publication of SEBERG's plight could cause her embarrassment and serve to cheapen her image with the general public.

    It is proposed that the following letter from a fictitious person be sent to local columnists:

        "I was just thinking about you and remembered I still owe you a favor. So---------I was in Paris last week and ran into Jean Seberg, who was heavy with baby. I thought she and Romaine had gotten

  2 - Bureau (RM)
  2 - San Francisco (Info) (RM) REC-52   100 - 448066 - 1766
  2 - Los Angeles

RWH/fs   17 MAY 1 1970
(6)

                                            RACIAL INT. SECT.

Approved: _____ Sent _____ M Per _____
          Special Agent in Charge   U. S. GOVERNMENT PRINTING OFFICE : 1968 O - 345-088 (11)

Airtel initiating COINTELPRO against Jean Seberg.

fetus; it died two days later. Henceforth, a shattered Jean Seberg was to regularly attempt suicide on or near the anniversary of her child's death. In 1979, she was successful. Romaine Gary, her ex-husband (who all along maintained he was the father of the child) followed suit shortly thereafter.[128] There is no indication Richard Wallace Held ever considered this to be anything other than an extremely successful COINTELPRO operation.

```
LA 157-4054

          together again, but she confided the child
          belonged to              of the Black
          Panthers, one            The dear girl
          is getting around!

              "Anyway, I thought you might get a scoop
          on the others.  Be good and I'll see you soon.

                          "Love,

                              Sol"


              Usual precautions would be taken by the Los
          Angeles Division to preclude identification of the Bureau
          as the source of the letter if approval is granted.
```

Meanwhile, the Bureau continued to undertake COINTELPRO-New Left operations through various municipal police departments, inculcating its view of the opposition – and preferred modes of combatting it – among rank-and-file cops not only via its already pronounced interlocks with local red squads, but through a more broadly-focused program of publications such as *Anti-Terrorist Digest*, seminars, briefings and training sequences.[129] One outcome, according to a government commission assembled in 1969, was that grassroots police – never tolerant of or friendly toward "deviants" of any sort – rapidly and increasingly came to view "students, other anti-war protestors and blacks as a danger to our political system, [and] themselves as the political force by which radicalism, student demonstrations and black power [could] be blocked." They reported that the corresponding "police response to mass protest [had] resulted in steady escalation of conflict, hostility and violence" within U.S. society as a whole.[130]

Tangible examples of this trend were legion. In March 1968, for example, police suddenly and without warning attacked a Yippie! demonstration being conducted inside New York's Grand Central Station, frenetically clubbing demonstrators and bystanders alike.[131] A month later, in April, New York's finest followed up with a comparable attack against peaceful anti-war demonstrators assembled at Washington Square (and with the already-mentioned assault upon the students at Columbia).[132] The same month, as a prelude to the massive police violence directed against demonstrators during the Democratic convention, the Chicago police tac squad brutally assaulted an anti-war rally in the Loop.[133]

In June, police attacked a peaceful crowd assembled in Berkeley to hear speeches supporting the then-ongoing student uprising in France; there followed a week-long reign of terror during which police tear-gassed private residences, indiscriminately beat members of a crowd leaving a movie theater, gassed at least two first aid stations, broke into and vandalized a church, smashed the cameras of newspaper photographers, and sent at least 37 people to the hospital.[134] An official

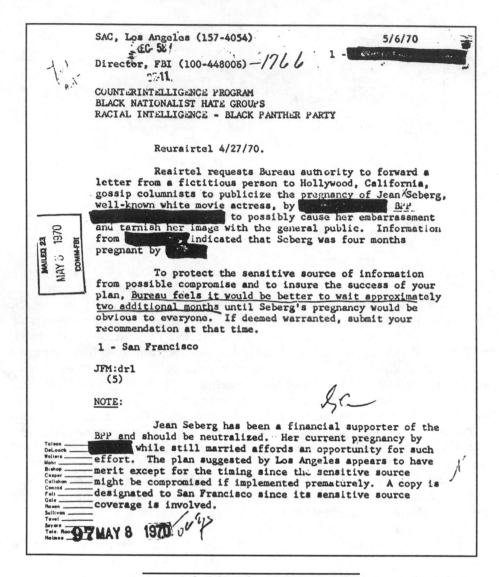

SAC, Los Angeles (157-4054)   5/6/70
   REC 58

Director, FBI (100-448006)—1766   1 -
   11.

COUNTERINTELLIGENCE PROGRAM
BLACK NATIONALIST HATE GROUPS
RACIAL INTELLIGENCE - BLACK PANTHER PARTY

        Reurairtel 4/27/70.

        Reairtel requests Bureau authority to forward a
letter from a fictitious person to Hollywood, California,
gossip columnists to publicize the pregnancy of Jean Seberg,
well-known white movie actress, by ▨▨▨▨▨▨▨ BPP
▨▨▨▨▨▨▨▨▨ to possibly cause her embarrassment
and tarnish her image with the general public. Information
from ▨▨▨▨▨ indicated that Seberg was four months
pregnant by ▨▨

        To protect the sensitive source of information
from possible compromise and to insure the success of your
plan, Bureau feels it would be better to wait approximately
two additional months until Seberg's pregnancy would be
obvious to everyone. If deemed warranted, submit your
recommendation at that time.

        1 - San Francisco

        JFM:drl
          (5)

        NOTE:

                Jean Seberg has been a financial supporter of the
        BPP and should be neutralized. Her current pregnancy by
        ▨▨▨▨▨▨ while still married affords an opportunity for such
        effort. The plan suggested by Los Angeles appears to have
        merit except for the timing since the sensitive source
        might be compromised if implemented prematurely. A copy is
        designated to San Francisco since its sensitive source
        coverage is involved.

MAILED 23 MAY 6 1970   COMM-FBI

Tolson
DeLoach
Walters
Mohr
Bishop
Casper
Callahan
Conrad
Felt
Gale
Rosen
Sullivan
Tavel
Soyars
Tele. Room
Holmes

97 MAY 8 1970

Approval of the Seberg COINTELPRO.

investigation revealed that "the most common [civilian] observation was that the
police appeared to have 'gone berserk" or 'lost their cool' or otherwise acted in a non-
rational way."[135] During the August convention in Chicago, the violence was even
more gratuitous. Over a thousand persons – including more than 65 of the approximately 300 media personnel assigned to cover street demonstrations – suffered
significant injuries at the hands of the police during convention week. As the Walker
Commission later put it:

JOYCE HABER

Miss A Rates as Expectant Mother

Let us call her Miss A, because she's the current "A" topic of chatter among the "ins" of international show business circles. She is beautiful and she is blonde.

Miss A came to Hollywood some years ago with the tantalizing flavor of a basket of fresh-picked berries. The critics picked at her acting debut, and in time, a handsome European picked her for his wife. After they married, Miss A lived in semi-retirement from the U.S. movie scene. But recently she burst forth as the star of a multimillion dollar musical.

Meanwhile, the outgoing Miss A was pursuing a number of free-spirited causes, among them the black revolution. She lived what she believed which raised a few Establishment eyebrows: Not because her escorts were often blacks, but because they were black nationalists.

Joyce Haber

And now, according to all those really "in" international sources, Topic A is the baby Miss A is expecting, and its father. Papa's said to be a rather prominent Black Panther.

Item by *Los Angeles Times* gossip columnist Joyce Haber (right) which caused Jean Seberg to miscarry and ultimately commit suicide. Excerpt from SA Richard Wallace Held's letter (below) taking credit for the column as a "successful" COINTELPRO.

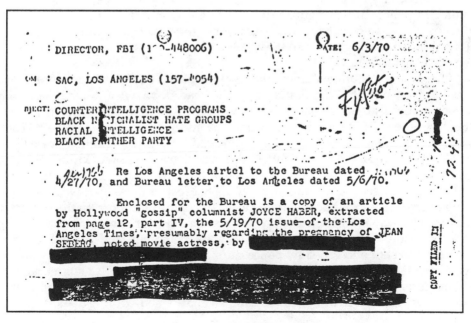

DIRECTOR, FBI (1 ⁊-448006)   DATE: 6/3/70

OM : SAC, LOS ANGELES (157-4054)

SUBJECT: COUNTERINTELLIGENCE PROGRAMS
BLACK NATIONALIST HATE GROUPS
RACIAL INTELLIGENCE -
BLACK PANTHER PARTY

Re Los Angeles airtel to the Bureau dated 4/27/70, and Bureau letter to Los Angeles dated 5/6/70.

Enclosed for the Bureau is a copy of an article by Hollywood "gossip" columnist JOYCE HABER, extracted from page 12, part IV, the 5/19/70 issue of the Los Angeles Times, presumably regarding the pregnancy of JEAN SEBERG, noted movie actress, by

The violence was made all the more shocking by the fact that it was often inflicted upon persons who had broken no law, disobeyed no order, made no threat. These included peaceful demonstrators, onlookers, and large numbers of residents who were simply passing through, or happened to live in, the areas where confrontations were occurring.[136]

In December 1969, the New York police once again attacked a peaceful demonstration, this time on the occasion of an appearance at a local hotel by President Nixon. Among other things, the cops yanked six people from a passing van, beat them with riot batons and trundled them into paddy wagons, apparently for the sole reason that they'd made a gesture indicating "peace" while driving by, and one had shouted from the window of the vehicle: "This is what Richard Nixon's fascist police are going to be like, and don't you forget it."[137]

May 1969 saw the so-called "People's Park" confrontation in Berkeley when students and community people attempted to prevent an area owned by the University of California, formerly devoted to low-cost housing, from being converted into a parking lot. When activists began to create a community park on the lot construction site, police attacked in a fashion which prompted even so establishmentarian a publication as Newsweek to observe that they "had gone riot, displaying a lawless brutality equal to that of Chicago, along with weapons and techniques that even the authorities in Chicago did not dare employ; the firing of buckshot at fleeing crowds and unarmed bystanders and the gassing – at times for no reason at all – of entire streets and portions of [the] college campus."[138] During the week of this wave of repression in Berkeley, even peaceful marches and demonstrations were arbitrarily banned, tear-gas was sprayed from helicopters, some 200 persons were badly injured by police clubs and gunfire (including one who was permanently blinded), and one man – James Rector – was killed.[139] During the week, California Governor Ronald Reagan strongly backed these police atrocities, asserting that, "If it's blood they want, let it be now."[140]

The deaths of student demonstrators at the hands of FBI-prepped local police was hardly a novelty. The first such fatality had occurred in May 1967 during demonstrations at Jackson State College (Jackson, Mississippi) when cops fired shotguns into an unarmed crowd, killing one and wounding two others.[141] Three students – Samuel Hammond, Delano Middleton and Henry Smith – were killed and 28 others wounded when South Carolina state troopers fired without warning on another group of peaceful demonstrators, this time from South Carolina State College in Orangeburg during February 1968. Most of those shot were hit while lying prone on the ground, attempting to get out of the line of fire (in the aftermath, the nine highway patrolmen identified as having done the shooting were "cleared of wrongdoing" and promoted).[142] In May 1969, another student, Willie Ernest Grimes, was shot and killed by police during demonstrations at North Carolina Agricultural and Mechanical College.[143] During February 1970, a student named Kevin Moran was killed and two others wounded by police gunfire – and several more otherwise injured by police and national guardsmen – during demonstrations which ultimately resulted in the burning of a Bank of America branch facility.[144] In March of the same year, 12 students were shot and 57 others injured by police during demonstrations at SUNY, Buffalo.[145]

Probably the most notorious incident involving the shooting of student demonstrators occurred at Kent State University in Ohio on May 4, 1970, when national guardsmen opened fire on a crowd protesting the U.S. invasion of Cambodia, killing four – Allison Krause, Jeffrey Miller, Sandra Scheuer and William Schroeder – and wounding nine (several of the dead and wounded were bystanders rather than demonstrators; one – Schroeder – was even a member of the campus ROTC unit).[146] Only days before, however, the Ohio guard had fired on a similar group at Ohio State University, wounding 20.[147] This was followed, on May 14, by Mississippi highway patrolmen actually firing into a dormitory at Jackson State (again), killing two – Phillip Gibbs and James Earl Green – and wounding twelve.[148] During July, two students – Rick Dowdell and Harry Rice – were killed by police at the University of Kansas in Lawrence,[149] another – Randy Anderson – shot to death on the campus of the University of Wisconsin in Milwaukee,[150] and black organizer Carl Hampton was gunned down in Houston, Texas.[151] Even as late as November 1972, police were still shooting student activists; two died as the result of a volley fired by deputy sheriffs at Southern University in New Orleans.[152]

In the last incident, a special commission created by the Louisiana state attorney general quickly determined there had been "no justification for the shootings," but the deputies went free.[153] It was by then an old story. In May 1971, a government commission investigating the murders at Kent State concluded – after a county grand jury had absolved local guardsmen of any wrongdoing – that the actions of the Ohio guard had been "unnecessary, unwarranted and inexcusable."[154] Ohio officials nonetheless refused to bring charges against those implicated, and U.S. Attorney General John Mitchell declined to convene a federal grand jury to follow up.[155] Ohio, in the meantime, had indicted 25 Kent State students, ex-students and faculty on felony charges such as "inciting to riot."[156] A county grand jury activated after the fatalities at Jackson State perhaps summed up the official attitude most succinctly when it not only found police killings of unarmed demonstrators to be "justified," but declared that protestors "must expect to be injured or killed when law enforcement officers are required to reestablish order."[157]

With the active assistance of the FBI, local police and national guard units consistently "explained" such conduct as being necessitated by the violent behavior of the victims themselves. It steadily came out, however, that much or most of the alleged new left violence was either fabricated or actually the result of Bureau/police tactics designed to rationalize the virulence of the repression before the public. At Kent State, for example, "during the ten days following the shootings, while the campus was closed, police ransacked every room among [the university's] thirty-one dormitories, without warrants, in search of weapons; they found a total of two hunting weapons [one of which was inoperable], sixty knives, three slingshots, several BB guns and a yellow button which stated, 'Dare to struggle, dare to win.'"[158] Still, the state – with active connivance by the FBI – pursued attempts to blame students in court for the actions of the Ohio National Guard, a matter which eventually led to Student Body President Craig Morgan and two others winning $5,000 judgments in malicious prosecution suits.[159]

At Ohio State, the official story was that activists closing and chaining the gates to the campus – allegedly preventing "crowd control" – had "forced" the guard to fire on demonstrators. It was later revealed that those who had committed the act in question were in reality members of the Ohio State Highway Patrol, deliberately attired in such a way as to impersonate demonstrators before the news media.[160] The use of such *provocateurs* to create the appearance of "justification" for even the worst forms of repression was consistent. Aside from such earlier-mentioned FBI infiltrators of the new left as William Divale, Phillip Abbott Luce, and *provocateurs* such as William Lemmer, Boyd Douglass and Howard Berry Godfrey:

> Probably the most-well known *agent provocateur* was Thomas Tongyai, known as Tommy the Traveler. Tongyai, who was paid by both the FBI and local police, spent over two years travelling among colleges in western New York state urging students to kill police, make bombs and blow up buildings. He supplied students with radical speakers, literature and films, tried to organize an SDS chapter at Hobart College, organized SDS conferences in Rochester and urged students to participate in the Weatherman "Days of Rage" in Chicago in October, 1969. Tongyai constantly talked violence, carried a grenade in his car, showed students how to use an M-1 rifle and offered advice on how to carry out bombings. After some students at Hobart College apparently took his advice and bombed the Hobart ROTC building, and Tongyai's cover was exposed, the local sheriff commented, "There's a lot of difference between showing how to build a bomb and building one." As a result of disturbances connected with Tongyai's activities on the Hobart campus, nine students and faculty faced criminal charges, but Tongyai was cleared by a local grand jury and went on to become a policeman in Pennsylvania.[161]

Similarly, "Horace L. Packer, an FBI informer who was the chief government witness in the Seattle Eight conspiracy case, testified he was under FBI instructions to 'do anything to protect my credibility.' He testified that while infiltrating SDS and Weatherman at the University of Washington he supplied campus radicals with drugs, weapons and materials used for preparing molotov cocktails. Packer even admitted he supplied and the FBI paid for paint used to spray the Federal courthouse in Seattle during a demonstration in February, 1970 – a key element in the charge of conspiracy to damage federal property which was one of the major charges of the case. Packer also testified that he used drugs, including 'acid, speed, mescaline' and cocaine while acting as a [provocateur], that he 'smoked dope all the time,' that he was arrested several times during campus demonstrations, and that he had violated the conditions of a suspended sentence he had received for participating in a Weatherman assault on ROTC facilities at the University of Washington."[162] Also in Seattle:

Probably the most incredible provocation incident involved an FBI and Seattle police informer, Alfred Burnett, who lured Larry Eugene Ward into planting a bomb at a Seattle real estate office on the morning of May 15, 1970, by paying Ward $75, providing him with the bomb and giving him transportation to the bombing scene. Ward, a twenty-two year old veteran who had been twice wounded and decorated three times for service in Vietnam, was shot and killed by waiting Seattle police as he allegedly fled after the bombing attempt, although he was unarmed, on foot and boxed in by police cars.[163]

Burnett, the key player in this Cerro Maravilla-like ambush (see Chapter 4), was "a twice-convicted felon who had been released from jail as the result of FBI statements that he could provide valuable information...Burnett said later, 'The police wanted a bomber and I got one for them. I didn't know Larry Ward would be killed.' Seattle Police Intelligence Chief John Williams blamed the FBI, stating, 'As far as I can tell Ward was a relatively decent kid. Somebody set this whole thing up. It wasn't the police department.' Subsequently, Seattle's mayor publicly advocated killing convicted bombers before a Senate committee, and citing the Ward case, noted the incidence of bombings in Seattle had declined since the slaying. He added, 'I suspect killing a person involved in a bombing...might be somewhat of a deterrent.'"[164]

In the so-called "Camden Twenty-Eight" case, the defendants were acquitted of all charges accruing from their breaking into a New Jersey Selective Service office and attempting to destroy the draft files therein after the trial judge instructed the jury to return verdicts of "not guilty" if it felt the government had gone to "intolerable lengths"and otherwise conducted itself in a manner "offensive to the basic standards of decency and shocking to the universal standards of justice" in setting up the "crime." The prosecution's star witness, Robert W. Hardy, had admitted on the stand that he had – upon instructions of the Bureau – infiltrated the group, proposed the action, provided "90 percent" of the burglary tools utilized, and offered his "expertise at breaking and entering" to allow the plot to go forward.[165] Elsewhere, "Another campus *agent provocateur* was Charles Grimm, who functioned as a local police and FBI informant on the campus of the University of Alabama at Tuscaloosa. Among his activities were the burning of Dressler Hall on the campus on May 7, 1970 (at the direction of the FBI, he said), the throwing of three molotov cocktails into a street on May 14, 1970 and the throwing of objects at police officers on the campus on May 18, 1970."[166]

Among those indicted by a federal grand jury in Detroit on March 6, 1970 for conspiracy to bomb police and military installations was Larry G. Grathwohl – reputedly one of "the most militant members" of the SDS Weatherman faction – an FBI infiltrator, known as a demolitions expert, who gave bomb-making lessons to the group, regularly brandished both a .357 magnum revolver and a straight razor, and admitted to the *New York Times* having personally participated in the bombing of a public school near Cincinnati in 1969.[167] Charges were dropped against Grathwohl (but not against his alleged co-conspirators who, by then, had gone underground), and he "retired" into the Bureau's witness protection program, eventually writing a sensationally self-serving account of his exploits entitled *Bringing Down America: An FBI Informer with the Weathermen.*[168]

Meanwhile, William Lemmer was hardly the only infiltrator/*provocateur* attempting to make the VVAW appear "violence prone." For instance, Reinhold Mohr, a secret member of the Kent State University police force, was arrested in April of 1972 by local cops while carrying in his car a rocket launcher and submachinegun he'd been trying to peddle to the campus chapter of the veterans' organization as a means – as he put it to the intended buyers – of "furthering the armed struggle against imperialism." Perhaps ironically, it was Kent State VVAW which tipped the city police that "there's a nut running around out there with a bunch of automatic weapons." Although Mohr was clearly in violation of a number of state and federal statutes, he was quickly released without charges when the chief of campus security and local FBI agents confirmed he'd "only followed orders" in attempting to foment violence.[169]

Another individual who, by his own account, expended a considerable amount of time and energy working to subvert VVAW was Joe Burton, a *provocateur* active in the Tampa, Florida area from 1972 to '74 (*i.e.: after* COINTELPRO had supposedly ceased to exist in 1971). Describing his assignment as being the "disruption of radical groups" from both the U.S. and Canada, Burton explained how the Bureau had dispatched counterintelligence specialists from headquarters to assist him in forging various documents and to establish a bogus radical organization dubbed the "Red Star Cadre." This front was used as a prop upon which Burton could "argue from the left" that various *bona fide* groups such as VVAW, the United Electrical Workers Union (UE), the American Federation of State, County and Municipal Employees (AFSCME), and the United Farm Workers (UFW) were "not militant enough" and to attempt to lure their members into violence and other illegal activities.[170] A comparable – if less effective – operation was run by a husband and wife team, Jill and Harry E. ("Gi") Shafer, III, through a bogus entity called the Red Star Collective in New Orleans. The Shafers were later used to infiltrate the support apparatus of the American Indian Movement (see next chapter), boasting afterwards that they'd managed to "divert" substantial funds raised for legal defense.[171]

In much the same fashion, Howard Berry Godfrey, the Bureau's operative within the right-wing Secret Army Organization in southern California hardly contented himself with participation in the attempted assassination of Peter Bohmer. To the contrary, as Godfrey later testified, he had served as a conduit during 1971 and '72 through which the FBI had pumped more than $60,000 worth of weapons and explosives into the terrorist group. Further, he admitted to having provided not only the explosive device, but also the demolitions training utilized by the SAO in its June 19, 1972 bombing of the left-leaning Guild Theater in San Diego.[172] As he himself subsequently acknowledged, by the time Godfrey's cover was blown he had participated in the burglaries of several southern California new left organizational offices, infiltrated the staff of the radical Message Information Center in Los

Angeles, and was working with SAO gunmen to compile a comprehensive list of left-wing activists to be "liquidated" over coming months. He was, of course, never prosecuted for even his most plainly criminal activities.[173]

On other fronts, an agent for the South Carolina Law Enforcement Division managed to work his way into a position as co-chair of the SDS chapter of the city of Columbia,[174] while a Texas state police infiltrator became chair of the University of Texas chapter.[175] In Chicago, a member of the red squad successfully infiltrated the SDS chapter at Northwestern University, led a sit-in action in 1968, and then participated in a 1969 Weatherman action involving the throwing of the college president off a stage which caused him to be expelled from the campus.[176] Yet another Chicago undercover operative admitted having provided explosives to the Weatherman group, while another – also posing as a Weatherman – acknowledged having led an assault upon a uniformed police sergeant during a demonstration widely publicized as "proving the violence" of the new left.[177] Another Chicago cop who infiltrated new left organizations admitted before a grand jury that he used the high position he attained in one group to advocate the shooting of police, and that he had "demonstrated the most strategic placement of snipers in downtown Chicago which would make possible the highest number of [police] casualties."[178] The list of examples goes on and on.

As former infiltrators/*provocateurs* such as Godfrey and Louis Tackwood (see Chapter 5) exposed the emergence of a systematic interlock between the FBI and state/local police units in southern California (particularly in Los Angeles), so too did a blue ribbon grand jury discover a similar development in Chicago. According to the grand jury report, released in November of 1975, beginning in early 1969 the CPD had "launched a massive intelligence campaign," filled with "unwarranted, unsupported and erroneous characterizations, assumptions and conclusions" – all of which it shared as a matter of course with the Bureau and other federal agencies – against a wide array of new left and other community groups, none of which exhibited any history of criminal activity. The entire operation "assaulted the fundamental freedoms of speech, association, press and religion, as well as the constitutional right to privacy of hundreds of persons," in the grand jury's view.[179]

The grand jury also noted the existence of a strong COINTELPRO-style dimension to the whole thing, not only by virtue of the activities of the police infiltrators mentioned in the preceding paragraph, but because the police and federal entities such as the FBI and Army Intelligence had cooperated in financing and directing a right-wing terrorist organization against new left activists throughout the Chicago area. Called the "Legion of Justice," this SAO-type group had for years beaten up police-selected targets, broken into movement offices and vandalized their property. Several Chicago red squad members testified to the effect that they considered it a "patriotic duty" to use Legion thugs to "disrupt the activities of [new left] organizations by destroying mailing lists, lists of financial contributors, office equipment and even stealing money," as well as to administer summary corporal punishment to those deemed politically objectionable by the Chicago *status quo.* The grand jury report also specifically noted that both the CPD and federal agencies (the 113th Military Intelligence Group, based in the Chicago suburb of Evanston, was mentioned by name), had destroyed evidence and generally refused to cooperate with the investigation.[180]

Within this panorama of infiltration, provocation, officially-sponsored vigilantism and extreme police brutality, the Bureau was able to pursue all manner of specific COINTELPRO actions designed to intimidate new left activists into political paralysis. For example, the accompanying postcard – attributed to the "Minutemen," a right-wing group well-known to have carried out a number of violent actions during the '60s – was sent to author Churchill during a period when he was serving as the Peoria, Illinois at-large organizer for SDS.[181] The card, also deployed against the staff of *The Black Panther* (see Chapter 5), was sent to a number of SDS members – usually those operating in locations remote from the urban hubs of new left activities – during the fall of 1970.

Such things were part of a generalized COINTELPRO strategy intended to "enhance the paranoia endemic to [new left] circles," and "get the point across that there is an FBI agent behind every mailbox."[182] Hence, in Chicago during the June 1969 SDS national convention, the Bureau and local red squad combined to assign over five hundred men to 'undercover' work. Most of them clustered outside the convention site – in full view of the SDS delegates – taking pictures of everyone in the area.[183] In another Chicago incident, in May of 1969:

> Chicago police and firemen appeared at the [SDS national headquarters, 1608 W. Madison], in response, they declared, to reports of a shooting and a fire in the office. When SDS [National Secretary Mike Klonsky] told them there was no shooting or fire, an agreement was reached to the effect that the fire chief alone could inspect the premises. However, a group of firemen attempted to enter the office, and when SDS staff members resisted, police joined the fray. Five SDS staffers were arrested and held on $1,000 bail on charges of "battery on an officer," "interfering with a fireman," and "inciting mob action."[184]

Under the circumstances, Brian Glick's description of what was happening as constituting a "war at home" seems entirely apt.[185] However, it also appears that participation in the hostilities was not entirely two-sided. To the contrary, it is quite likely that the widely-publicized "resort to violence" by the new left of the late 1960s and early '70s was largely the creation of the national police establishment rather than of the radicals themselves. Certainly, of the 862 bombings and attempted bombings which supposedly occurred between January 1969 and April 15, 1970, a decided majority entailed the direct involvement of FBI and local police *provocateurs*.[186] A good case can be made that the same rule pertains to many of the other more spectacular acts of physical confrontation attributed to the new left in the "friendly news media."[187]

Perhaps even more to the point, such COINTELPRO maneuvering established the context in which such new left violence as was not directly police-produced

Our nation can still be saved.
History will remember those who
help to save it. We will remember
those who don't.

"Minutemen"

Post Card

TRAITORS BEWARE

See the old man at the corner where you buy your papers? He may have a silencer equipped pistol under his coat. That extra fountain pen in the pocket of the insurance salesman who calls on you might be a cyanide gas gun. What about your milk man? Arsenic works slow but sure. Your auto mechanic may stay up nights studying booby traps. These patriots are not going to let you take their freedom away from them. They have learned the silent knife, the strangler's cord, the target rifle that hits sparrows at 200 yards. Traitors beware. Even now the cross hairs are on the back of your necks.

MINUTEMEN

Mr. Ward Churchill
Box 1368
Peoria, Illinois
61601

"Minutemen" death threat card utilized in COINTELPRO-New Left in the Midwest.

might occur: a combination of frustration at official repression of entirely legitimate dissident activities *vis à vis* institutionalized domestic racism and poverty, and an international pattern of imperialism signified by the government's patently criminal prosecution of an undeclared war in Indochina; rage at the violently physical form assumed by the repression (beatings, shootings, gassings), coupled to a consistent official policy of lying, victim-blaming and other misrepresentation in the media; and an increasing belief – often fostered by *agents provocateurs* – that some form of violence might in itself serve to rectify the situation. Arguably, even those few new left groups such as Weatherman SDS, which eventually placed their primary reliance upon armed struggle, did so largely for such reasons.[188]

Demise of the New Left

By the end of 1972, the mass movement which had comprised the new left had generally disintegrated, for a number of reasons, but notably because of COIN-TELPRO and its related forms of police pressure. There were, to be sure, some spectacular incidents of generalized repression during the finalé, as when the Washington, D.C. Metropolitan Police Force, supplemented by army and national guard troops – working in direct collaboration with FBI and Justice Department officials – conspired to suspend the constitutional rights of the 50,000 people assembled in the nation's capital to participate in the "Mayday" anti-war demonstrations held May 3-5, 1971.

> On May 3, seventy-two hundred persons were arrested, the largest total in American history, with the possible exception of the Palmer Raids. In the course of making the arrests, police abandoned all normal arrest procedures, including recording the names and alleged misdeeds of the arrestees. Hundreds of innocent bystanders, including journalists and government employees on their way to work, were scooped up in the police dragnet, and then held in overcrowded jail cells or in a hastily erected outdoor stockade. In subsequent days, another sixty-two hundred persons were arrested, including twelve hundred arrested while peacefully listening to a speech on the Capitol steps on May 5. President Nixon subsequently praised Washington police for a "magnificent job" and Attorney General John Mitchell urged local police [elsewhere] to follow the example. Deputy Attorney General Richard Kleindienst announced that police procedures had been justified under the doctrine of "qualified martial law," a constitutional doctrine which was previously unknown, but which had the virtue, as the Washington ACLU branch pointed out, of imposing "the conditions of martial law in fact" while avoiding a "formal proclamation with its legal requirements."[189]

In the wake of Mayday, literally thousands of "cases" were dropped by federal prosecutors or summarily dismissed by the courts, clarifying the fact that the arrests themselves had been intended as punishment (for purely political reasons, and without so much as a pretense of due process). Of the total of approximately 13,400 individuals arrested during the demonstrations, only 122 were convicted of minor offenses. Another 625 pled guilty or *nolo contendere* on uniformly petty charges, a matter which was followed up in 1974 by a federal district judge ordering – on the grounds of police coercion – that all such pleas be nullified and corresponding arrest records destroyed. In January of 1975, another federal court awarded the victims of the Mayday repression a total of $12,000,000 in "punitive damages," but in the meantime, the government had established quite clearly that mass demonstrations would not be an effective means of bringing about an alteration in U.S. Indochina policy.[190]

Also employed by the Nixon administration as a means of neutralizing the new left, undoubtedly as an adjunct to other such "legal" expedients as mass false arrests and bogus conspiracy trials, was an extraordinary series of federal grand jury "investigations."

> Beginning in 1970, federal grand juries throughout the country were convened for what clearly were general "fishing expeditions," coordinated by the Internal Security Division of the Justice Department, into the activities of radical and anti-war groups...Between 1970 and January, 1973, over one hundred grand juries in thirty-six states and eighty-four cities looked into dissident activities, and over one thousand persons were subpoenaed to appear before such bodies...Witnesses appearing before these grand juries were forced to testify in secret and without presence of legal counsel in the grand jury room, and under threat of contempt or jail sentences...Witnesses were asked detailed questions about their personal beliefs and associations and about their general [rather than criminal] knowledge of radical and anti-war activities...In several cases, grand juries interrogated witnesses with regard to alleged crimes in which indictments had already been handed down, indicating that one of the purposes of the investigations was to bolster indictments which did not have enough evidence behind them to sustain convictions.[191]

None of the normal safeguards of due process pertain to grand jury procedures; in the 1974 case, *U.S. v. Calandra*, the Supreme Court even ruled that a grand jury witness could be compelled to testify concerning evidence derived from illegal searches and seizures (such as FBI black bag jobs).[192] Refusal of subpoenaed radicals to cooperate in such inquisitional processes resulted in imprisonment without trial on charges of contempt, with the duration of incarceration left to the discretion of the presiding judge (but usually running for the duration of the period in which the grand jury was empaneled, as long as 18 months). The alternative, cooperation, left witnesses politically suspect, at best, in the eyes of their peers. Even when witnesses refused to cooperate with these secret proceedings, the FBI – which served as the primary investigative resource of the grand juries – sometimes opted to utilize COINTELPRO techniques to make it appear otherwise, neatly bad-jacketing them as informers. Hence, the grand jury became "an effective means by which the government [could] jail politically suspect persons [more-or-less at its discretion]" or destroy their political credibility.[193]

According to the Church Committee, the FBI engaged in 290 separate COIN-TELPRO actions between the formal start-up of its program against the new left in mid-1968 and the program's official termination in April 1971. Of these, some 40% were designed to keeping targeted activists from speaking, teaching, writing or publishing.[194] When one considers the far broader forms of legalistic and physical repression deliberately provoked by the Bureau as adjuncts and enhancements to its anti-new left COINTELPRO campaign, it is rather easy to see how and why the movement disintegrated when and as it did.

This is not to argue that the new left was free of defects, both in outlook and in practice, which might ultimately have led to its undoing. But, as even so staid a publication as the *Los Angeles Times* was willing to admit, such things "might not have destroyed the movement." However, the new left's internal confusions, disagreements and problems were "exploited [and] exaggerated by the government's planned program of sabotage and disruption," making solutions virtually impossible. This, in combination with the increasing viciousness with which Bureau-coached local police assaulted demonstrators, the steady string of gratuitous killings of activists on and off campus, the systematic infiltration and provocation, the relentless series of grand juries and conspiracy trials, as well as consistent media disinformation all served to sap "the movement's leadership, funds and morale," precipitating its collapse.[195] With it went by far the greatest potential for consolidation of a socially positive Euroamerican mass movement since the New Reconstruction period during and immediately following World War I (see Chapter 2).

By the mid-'70s, some former new left leaders had abandoned the struggle for social justice in favor of the very values they'd most vociferously opposed.[196] Others, such as Yippie! leader Abbie Hoffman had been driven underground when faced with lengthy prison sentences on extremely dubious charges.[197] Entire organizations, such as the Weatherman SDS faction, had transformed themselves into a series of clandestine cells with little hope of obtaining appreciable above-ground support.[198] What had been the broad-based and quite inclusive new left was reduced for all practical purposes to a gender-defined liberal feminism on the one hand, and a scattering of male-dominated, tiny and rabidly sectarian organizations such as the Communist Workers Party, Progressive Labor Party and Revolutionary Communist Party, USA on the other. Such emergent politics as these can only be viewed as being as fundamentally irrelevant to the flow of events in the United States as those of the old left SWP and CP,USA.[199] From the FBI perspective, COINTELPRO-New Left could have been assessed as little other than a tremendous success.

Chapter 7

COINTELPRO – AIM

> They [the Indians] are a conquered nation, and when you are conquered,
> the people you are conquered by dictate your future. This is a basic
> philosophy of mine. If I'm part of a conquered nation, I've got to yield to
> authority... [The FBI must function as] a colonial police force.
>
> – Norman Zigrossi –
> ASAC Rapid City
> 1977

In this brief statement, Assistant Special Agent in Charge Zigrossi summarized over two centuries of U.S. jurisdiction and "law enforcement" in Indian Country. From the country's founding through the present, U.S. Indian policy has consistently followed a program to subordinate American Indian nations and expropriate their land and resources. In much the same fashion as Puerto Rico (see Chapter 4), indigenous nations within the United States have been forced to exist – even by federal definition – as outright colonies.[1] When constitutional law and precedent stood in the way of such policy, the executive and judicial branches, in their turn, formulated excuses for ignoring them. A product of convenience and practicality for the federal government, U.S. jurisdiction, especially within reserved Indian territories ("reservations"), "presents a complex and sometimes conflicting morass of treaties, statutes and regulation."[2]

The FBI in Indian Country

The entrance of the FBI in law enforcement into Indian Country began in the 1940s – under clear congressional provisos that it should be neither primary nor permanent – as wartime funding cuts rendered staffing levels for Bureau of Indian Affairs (BIA) Special Officers inadequate.[3] Initially, the Bureau offered mere "investigative assistance" to the BIA, but over time all federal offenses came to be investigated by the FBI. By 1953:

> ...apparently because of FBI leadership, most U.S. Attorneys, and U.S. District Judges, recognized the FBI as having primary investigative jurisdiction for Federal law violations committed in Indian country, notwithstanding the wording of Congres-

231

sional appropriation acts since FY-1939 and Opinion M. 29669 dated August 1, 1938, issued by the Solicitor, U.S. Department of the Interior [indicating that such responsibilities were included in the duties of BIA Special Officers].[4]

The current situation is that:

> The BIA has trained criminal investigators on most reservations. These special officers conduct the initial investigation for the majority of serious crimes which occur on Indian reservations. Most U.S. Attorneys however, will not normally accept the findings of a BIA special officer as a basis for making a decision on whether to prosecute. Instead, most U.S. Attorneys require that the FBI conduct an independent investigation, often duplicative of the BIA investigation, prior to authorizing prosecution....[5]

All law enforcement on American Indian reservations has been made to revolve around the actions (and inactions) of the FBI. It is undoubtedly significant that while the typical BIA police officer is Indian, FBI agents and U.S. Attorneys are overwhelmingly white.[6]

Far from enhancing law enforcement, the FBI impedes it by slow response and insistence upon repeating the investigative work of BIA, often well after the fact. Until this process is completed, no arrests can be made and suspects remain at large.[7] Once an offender has been apprehended and charged, there is little chance they will be tried: "Precise statistics are not maintained by Federal law enforcement agencies, but it appears that in excess of 80 percent of major crimes cases, on the average, presented to the United States attorneys are declined for prosecution."[8] Unlike crimes committed off-reservation, there is no other jurisdiction under which the defendant can be tried if the U.S. Attorney declines to prosecute. The effect on many reservations has been that defendants have a better chance of going to jail for a traffic violation – tried in the tribal courts – than for rape or first degree murder. Indian/Indian crimes or crimes perpetrated by non-Indians against Indians – ranging from fraud to extreme violence – have received only minimal (if any) attention from police and prosecutors. Only those allegedly criminal acts undertaken by Indians against whites have tended to receive attention, filling the country's prisons with a disproportionately high number of Indians.[9] In this sense, it is entirely appropriate to observe that federal police functions in Indian Country are not devoted to law enforcement *per se*, but rather to maintenance of the *status quo* represented by Euroamerican domination and profiteering at the expense of American Indian people. The message has been that only those who rock the politico-economic boat risk criminal punishment.

With the passage of PL-280 in 1953, state and local agencies – also almost entirely white – assumed responsibility for on reservation law enforcement in many instances.[10] The overall effect of these policies has been that the quality of law enforcement in Indian Country has been egregious when measured by the standard of providing for the safety and security of the communities. Law enforcement concerning the most serious crimes is the responsibility of individuals who do not reside in the community and whose attitudes toward Indian people and their customs range from ignorance to hostility and contempt, *à la* Norman Zigrossi.In the case of state and local jurisdiction under PL-280, law enforcement is provided by reservation-adjacent communities with a reputation for vehement racism aptly summarized by an Itasca County, Minnesota, deputy sheriff: "[I]f all those Indians would just kill each other off, we wouldn't have to go up there [to the reservation]."[11] Slow to respond to complaints lodged by Indians, the police are viewed – justifiably – with suspicion by the community.[12]

Rise of the American Indian Movement

The late 1960s saw a resurgence of militant Indian activism focused on resistance to further depredation of Indian lands and resources, recovery of illegally expropriated land, preservation of cultural identity and opposition to racist attacks on Indian people and their culture. During the mid-'60s, a Cherokee college student named Clyde Warrior founded the militant National Indian Youth Council (NIYC) and began publishing a political broadside entitled *Americans Before Columbus*.[13] Even the typically staid National Congress of American Indians (NCAI) adopted an increasingly forceful tone under the leadership of Lakota law student Vine Deloria, Jr., who before the end of the decade was to write the seminal *Custer Died for Your Sins* and *We Talk, You Listen*.[14] It was in this atmosphere that the American Indian Movement (AIM) was founded in Minneapolis in 1968 by Dennis Banks and George Mitchell (both Anishinabés [Chippewas]). Patterning itself after the Black Panther Party, AIM initially focused itself on urban issues such as combating police harassment of Indian people. During the next two years members such as Clyde Bellecourt (Anishinabé), Russell Means (Oglala Lakota), Herb Powless (Oneida), John Trudell (Santee Dakota) and Joe Locust (Cherokee) changed its emphasis from a local to a national focus and from specifically urban issues to issues of treaty rights and the preservation of traditional Indian culture.[15]

In November 1969, national attention was suddenly focused on Indian issues when a coalition of Indian organizations, headed first by Richard Oaks (Mohawk) and later Trudell, and calling itself Indians of All Tribes (IAT), occupied Alcatraz Island. Citing an 1882 federal statute (22 *Stat.* 181) which provided for the establishment of Indian schools in abandoned federal facilities, the protestors demanded the establishment of a Center for Native American Studies and other cultural facilities on the abandoned island. The occupation ended after 19 months with an assault by a task force of U.S. marshals and the arrest of the occupiers. A prior agreement by the Department of Interior to convert Alcatraz to a national park featuring Indian themes never materialized. However, the massive media attention and resultant public support garnered by the Alcatraz occupation demonstrated its tactical effectiveness.[16] During the next two years, Indians occupied other abandoned military facilities across the country and Pacific Gas and Electric sites on Indian land in northern California.[17] AIM also engaged in a series of high-profile demonstrations – including the occupation of the *Mayflower II* on Thanksgiving Day 1970 and of Mt. Rushmore on July 4, 1971 – which continued to keep Indian issues in the public eye.[18]

In January 1972 an Oglala man named Raymond Yellow Thunder was tortured and murdered by two white men, Melvin and Leslie Hare, in the reservation-adjacent town of Gordon, Nebraska. When it became clear that local law enforcement agencies intended to take no action against Yellow Thunder's murderers, a force of over 1,000 Indians – mostly from the nearby Pine Ridge and Rosebud Reservations – headed by AIM leaders Dennis Banks and Russell Means, occupied Gordon for three days.[19] The result of the occupation was that Yellow Thunder's assailants were charged and jailed, a police officer suspended, and Gordon's authorities forced to take a stand against discrimination toward Indians. The effect of this action was described by historian Alvin Josephy, Jr.: "Although discrimination continued, AIM's reputation soared among reservation Indians. What tribal leaders had dared not to do to protect their people, AIM had done."[20] According to those FBI documents assembled by the Bureau in its reading room, it was at this juncture that agents were first assigned to keep close tabs on "AIM and related militant Indian nationalist organizations."

In the light of growing public and reservation support, the AIM leadership met at the home of Brûlé Lakota spiritual leader Leonard Crow Dog's home – called Crow Dog's Paradise – on the Rosebud Reservation in July of 1972 to plan their next action. From this meeting emerged the concept for The Trail of Broken Treaties. Caravans from reservations across the country would travel to Washington, D.C., arriving immediately before the November presidential elections. AIM hoped that given the timing and attendant press coverage, the Nixon administration might be willing to enter into negotiations to resolve Indian grievances.[21] The Trail began in San Francisco and Seattle in October and gathered support from reservations along its route as it moved eastward. A list of proposed federal actions for redressing grievances and restructuring the relationship between Indian nations and the U.S. – known as the "Twenty Points" – was formulated during a stopover in St. Paul, Minnesota.[22] When the caravan reached Washington, D.C. on November 3, a series of events rapidly led to the Indians seizing the national BIA headquarters and occupying it until November 5.[23] The unplanned confrontation ended when the administration – embarrassed by sensational news reporting – formally agreed to review and respond to the Twenty Points, as well as to non-prosecution of the occupiers and provision of $66,650 in travel expenses for caravan participants to return home.[24]

When the government recovered the BIA building, they discovered that a large number of "confidential" documents – primarily concerned with the low-yield leasing of reservation land – had been removed by the occupiers. One of the Trail's leaders, Hank Adams (Assiniboin/Lakota), volunteered to recover the documents and return them in batches, as they were copied and provided to the Indians to whom they pertained. After returning two loads of material, he was set up by an FBI *provocateur* named Johnny Arellano and arrested by the FBI in the process of return-ing another.[25] While the government made much in the media of the damage allegedly done to the building by caravan participants:

> Later events would indicate that the federal government had a substantial number of agents among the protesters, and some were so militant and destructive that they were awarded special Indian names for their involvement in the protest. It became apparent why the government had been so willing to agree not to prosecute the Indians: The presence of agent-provocateurs and the intensity of their work would have made it extremely difficult for the government to have proven an intent by the real Indian activists to destroy the building.[26]

It was thus during and immediately following the Trail of Broken Treaties that evidence emerges of the initiation of a counterintelligence program to neutralize AIM and its perceived leadership. An FBI document released to journalist Richard LaCourse under the FOIA reveals a program which closely parallels that directed against RAM in Philadelphia (see Chapter 5). It recommends that "local police put [AIM] leaders under close scrutiny, and arrest them on every possible charge until they could no longer make bail."[27] This tactic was immediately implemented against activists returning home from Washington, D.C. For instance, on November 22, 1972, Trail security coordinator Leonard Peltier was attacked in a Milwaukee restaurant by two off-duty policemen; he was beaten severely and then arrested and charged with the attempted murder of one of his assailants. Peltier was eventually acquitted when trial testimony revealed that one of the cops had shown his girlfriend a picture of Peltier and boasted of "help[ing] the FBI get a big one."[28] At about the same time, in South Dakota:

> As Russell Means led the Oglala Sioux remnants of the Trail of Broken Treaties through the town of Pine Ridge, the seat of government of the Oglala reservation, he may have noticed a stir of activity around police headquarters. Unknown to Means, tribal president Richard Wilson had secured a court order from the Oglala Sioux tribal court prohibiting Means or any other AIM member from speaking or attending any public meeting...Since the Oglala Sioux Landowners Association was meeting in Pine Ridge, Means, a member of this group, decided to attend and report what had actually happened in Washington. Before he had a chance to speak his mind, he was arrested by BIA special officer Delmar Eastman for violating this court order...The arrest was a blatant violation of the First Amendment, for it denied Means freedom of speech on the reservation where he was born and was an enrolled member.[29]

Documents released through the FOIA, such as the accompanying January 12, 1973 report from the Denver field office, show that the Bureau was compiling detailed profiles of AIM members and leaders as part of an "Extremist Matters" investigation. As is demonstrated in the accompanying January 10 teletype, almost entirely deleted under a national security classification, the Bureau was (for reasons

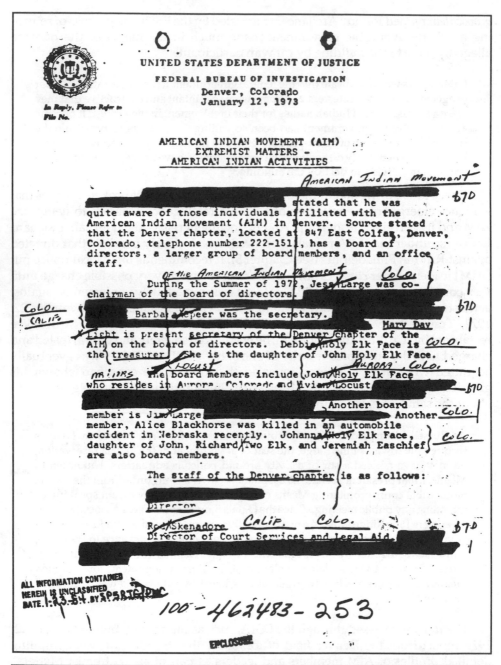

Early report showing intensive surveillance of Denver AIM chapter. The "100" coding prefix at bottom of page indicates an "Extremist Matters" investigation.

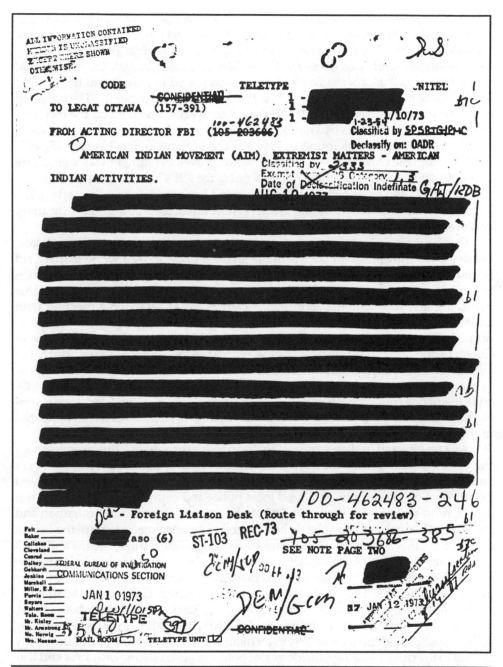

Early teletype demonstrating distribution of intelligence information on AIM within the international arena. Heavy deletion results from "National Security" classification.

which have never been specified) keeping the U.S. embassy in Ottawa apprised of AIM activities. On January 14, Russell Means and several other AIM members were arrested on fabricated charges in Scottsbluff, Nebraska while participating in a Chicano-Indian Unity Conference with the Denver-based Crusade for Justice. That night, Means' cell door was unlocked, a gun was placed in his cell and he was told by the police to "make a break for it." As the AIM leader later put it, "They wanted to off me during an escape attempt." When a complaint was filed on the incident, police claimed that Means had not been "properly searched" when he was booked and that the weapon was found in his cell. The accompanying January 15, 1973 teletype from the Omaha ASAC to the director proves the Bureau was well aware of the situation, but – in a manner reminiscent of the FBI's handling of police abuses against SNCC and other civil rights activists in Mississippi during the early '60s – local agents did absolutely nothing to intervene. Bureau records also show the unity conference was heavily surveilled and infiltrated.[30]

During the meeting in Scottsbluff, AIM received word that a 20-year-old Oglala, Wesley Bad Heart Bull, had been brutally stabbed to death by a white man, Darld Schmitz, in the reservation-adjacent town of Buffalo Gap, South Dakota. When Schmitz was charged with only the relatively minor offense of second degree manslaughter, AIM national coordinator Dennis Banks arranged a meeting with Custer County state's attorney Hobart Gates to discuss upgrading the charge to murder. Banks issued a call for Indians to assemble at the county courthouse in Custer to demonstrate support during the February 6 meeting. Two days prior to the event, however, a mysterious caller – believed to have have been an agent assigned to the Rapid City (South Dakota) resident agency – engaged in a COINTELPRO-style telephone conversation with *Rapid City Journal* reporter Lyn Gladstone claiming the action had been "canceled due to bad weather," an untruth which appeared in the paper on February 5.[31]

As a result – and in sharp contrast to the massive turnout in Gordon concerning the Yellow Thunder case only a few months before – only about 200 AIM members and supporters turned out to caravan to Custer.[32] Once there, they were confronted by an equal number of riot-equipped local police and county deputies, a state riot squad, representatives of the South Dakota Division of Criminal Investigation and the FBI.[33] Although county officials had agreed to an open meeting with the Indian community, they now insisted they would meet with only Banks, Means and Utah AIM leader Dave Hill (Choctaw); although the courthouse was a public building, the remainder of the group was not allowed inside, and was forced to remain outdoors in a heavy blizzard. The AIM leaders found prosecutor Gates to be adamantly against upgrading the charges. After insisting that justice was already being done, he declared the meeting at an end and told the AIM delegation to leave. When they refused, police attempted to forcibly evict them and a melee broke out which quickly spread to the crowd waiting outside as riot police attacked them with clubs and tear gas. The courthouse and nearby chamber of commerce building were set ablaze by teargas cannisters and 27 Indians were arrested on charges such as "incitement to

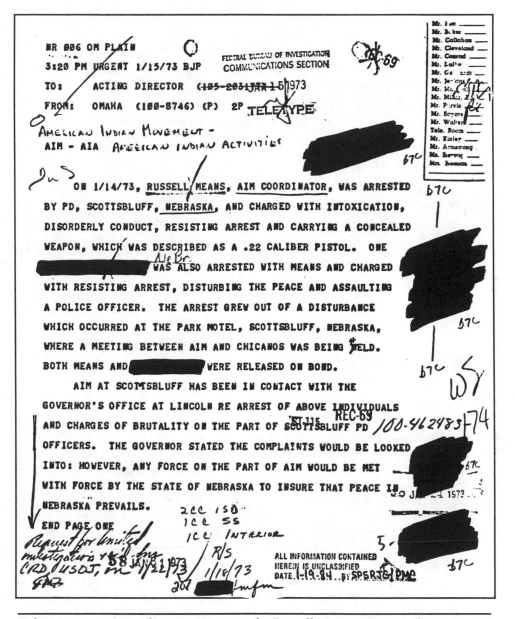

Teletype concerning police attempt to murder Russell Means. (Cont. on the next page.)

riot." Among those beaten by police and arrested was Sarah Bad Heart Bull, the victim's mother. She ultimately served five months in jail on charges resulting from the Custer police assault, while her son's murderer never served a day.[34]

```
OM 100-8746
PAGE TWO
      AFTER BEING LODGED IN THE SCOTTSBLUFF COUNTY JAIL, MEANS
CHARGED THAT A POLICE OFFICER PLACED A GUN IN HIS CELL AND
TAUNTED HIM TO TRY AND ESCAPE BUT HE REFUSED.  POLICE
OFFICIALS STATE MEANS WAS NOT SEARCHED PROPERLY WHEN BOOKED
AND THE GUN WAS NOT LOCATED ON HIM UNTIL HE WAS SEARCHED
AGAIN IN THE CELL.
      ON INSTANT DATE MEANS AND OTHER AIM LEADERS AT
SCOTTSBLUFF REQUESTED A MEETING WITH THE COUNTY COMMISSIONER.
THEY WERE ADVISED THAT THE COMMISSIONER WAS CURRENTLY IN
SESSION AND COUNCIL MEETINGS ARE OPEN TO THE PUBLIC.
ACCORDING TO SCOTTSBLUFF COUNTY OFFICIALS, MEANS AND OTHER
AIM LEADERS WANT A MEETING WITH COUNTY COMMISSION OFFICIALS
TO DISCUSS DISCRIMINATION OF INDIANS IN THAT AREA.
ADMINISTRATIVE:
      SOURCE OF ABOVE INFORMATION IS ██████████████████████
████████████                                           b7ø
   LHM FOLLOWS.
```

The violence and perversion of justice directed at the AIM group in Custer did not result from happenstance or mere "overreaction" on the part of local officials. As shown in the accompanying excerpt from a January 31, 1973 teletype sent to FBI headquarters by Minneapolis SAC Joseph Trimbach, the Rapid City office was by this point actively coordinating the activities of state and local police, state's attorneys in western South Dakota, and agents of the Bureau of Alcohol, Tobacco and Firearms (BATF), with regard to "AIM activities." The excerpted teletype also demonstrates that local police – with full knowledge of the FBI – had stonewalled U.S. Justice Department Community Relations Service representatives who were attempting to defuse the situation because the latter "appeared to favor AIM's cause." By early 1973 the Bureau had, with the enthusiastic cooperation of area police, set out to effect the physical repression of AIM while deliberately squelching attempts – from both governmental and dissident quarters – to achieve peaceful resolution of the racial/political conflicts around Pine Ridge, and elsewhere in Indian Country.

Wounded Knee

The smoke and tear gas had barely cleared from the streets of Custer when the

ON 1-29-73, ERNIE PEPIN, SHERIFF, CUSTER, ADVISED THAT
HE SPOKE TO CHIEF OF POLICE (COP), SCOTTSBLUFF, NEBRASKA,
WHO TOLD HIM THAT FIFTY TO SIXTY HARD-CORE AIM MEMBERS LEFT
SCOTTSBLUFF ON 1-27-73 AND HEADED NORTH TOWARD SOUTH DAKOTA.
COP, SCOTTSBLUFF, FURTHER ADVISED THAT AIM MEMBERS, WHILE
IN SCOTTSBLUFF, COLLABORATED WITH A CHICANO NAMED RAMON
PEREZ AND REPORTEDLY MADE A DEAL FOR APPROXIMATELY SIXTY
AUTOMATIC WEAPONS WHICH RESEMBLE THE THOMPSON SUBMACHINE GUN
OF MEXICAN MANUFACTURE. SCOTTSBLUFF COP ADVISED PEPIN THAT
HIS DEPARTMENT CONFISCATED THREE OF THESE GUNS AND THAT AIM
MEMBERS WERE CARRYING SUBSTANTIAL AMOUNTS OF MEXICAN MANUFACTURED
AMMUNITION. HE ALSO ADVISED THAT SOME AIM MEMBERS WERE OPENLY
CARRYING WEAPONS, WHICH THEY DID NOT EMPLOY. HE FURTHER
REPORTED THAT MANY AIM MEMBERS WERE HIGH ON "POT" DURING THEIR
OCCUPATION OF THE SCOTTSBLUFF AREA.

PEPIN ADVISED THAT SCOTTSBLUFF COP RECEIVED CALLS LAST
WEEK FROM MESSRS. TORREZ AND MARQUIS (PHONETIC) WHO CLAIMED
TO BE FROM JUSTICE DEPARTMENT, FROM CHICAGO AND WERE IN
SCOTTSBLUFF BECAUSE OF THE INDIAN SITUATION. HE ADVISED THAT
THEY APPEARED TO FAVOR AIM'S CAUSE AND IN ASKING MANY
QUESTIONS, CAUSED THE LOCAL AUTHORITIES MANY PROBLEMS. PEPIN
ADVISED THEY DID KNOW IF POSITIVE IDENTIFICATION OF
THESE INDIVIDUALS WAS MADE.

PEPIN CONTINUING, ADVISED THAT HE RECEIVED CALL LAST
WEEK FROM JESSE TAIL (PHONETIC) WHO CLAIMED TO BE A REPRESENTATIVE
OF "COMMUNITIVE SERVICES", U. S. JUSTICE DEPARTMENT, INQUIRING ABOUT
WESLEY BAD HEART BULL INCIDENT. TAIL APPEARED TO SYMPATHIZE
WITH INDIANS AND PEPIN GAVE HIM NO MORE INFORMATION THAN
WHAT WAS ALREADY PUBLIC KNOWLEDGE.

PEPIN ADVISED THAT ON 1-27-73, A 1970 FORD, HAULING
A U-HAUL TRAILER, WITH RHODE ISLAND PLATES ON THE TRAILER

Excerpt from a January 31, 1973 teletype falsely suggesting AIM was equipping itself with automatic weapons and delineating FBI collaboration with South Dakota police in preparing for AIM's arrival in Custer (continued on next page).

```
AFTER A SHORT PERIOD, DEPARTED AND HEADED NORTH.  PEPIN ADVISED
THAT THE COP, SCOTTSBLUFF, TOLD HIM THERE WERE MANY SOUTH
DAKOTA AND MONTANA INDIANS PRESENT AND THAT THE FOLLOWING
NUMBER OF CARS, BEARING AIM PARTICIPANTS FROM OUT-OF-STATE
WERE NOTED:  TEXAS, 4; SOUTH DAKOTA, 12; COLORADO, 13;
WYOMING, 4; KANSAS, 1; OKLAHOMA, 2; MINNESOTA, 2; WISCONSIN, 1.
     ON 1-29-73, IN PREPARATION FOR AIM'S ANTICIPATED ARRIVAL AT
RAPID CITY, STURGIS CO. SHERIFF AND REPRESENTATIVES FROM
SOUTH DAKOTA HIGHWAY PATROL, LOCAL POLICE, STATES ATTORNEY'S
         BUREAU OF
OFFICE, FEDERAL ALCOHOL, TAX AND FIREARMS AGENTS, AND AGENTS
OF FBI, HELD A STRATEGY SESSION AND DISCUSSED HOW TO PREVENT
VIOLENT CONFRONTATION FROM DEVELOPING, WHILE AT THE SAME TIME,
MAINTAINING LAW AND ORDER.
```

next round of confrontation between AIM and the federal government began. This time the locus of activity centered on Pine Ridge itself, and concerned a struggle between the "progressive" administration of the Oglala Sioux tribal president, Dick Wilson – who had already imposed an illegal ban on AIM members speaking or participating in meetings within what he apparently considered to be his private domain – and grassroots Indians on the reservation. Wilson, who had already held an office and been accused of having used the position to embezzle tribal funds, had been ushered into office with substantial government support in 1972.[35] Almost immediately, he had been bestowed with a $62,000 BIA grant for purposes of establishing a "tribal ranger group" – essentially his own private army – an entity which designated itself as "Guardians of the Oglala Nation" (GOONs or GOON Squad).[36] The Indian bureau also allowed him to hire his relatives into the limited number of jobs available through the tribal government, as well as to divert the virtual entirety of the tribal budget into support for his immediate followers rather than the Oglala Lakota people as a whole.[37] When traditionalist Oglalas complained, Wilson dispatched his GOONs. When victims attempted to seek the protection of the BIA police, they quickly discovered that perhaps a third of its roster – including its head, Delmar Eastman (Crow), and his second-in-command, Duane Brewer (Oglala) – were doubling as GOON leaders or members.[38] For their part, BIA officials – who had set the whole thing up – consistently turned aside requests for assistance from the traditionals as being "purely internal tribal matters," beyond the scope of BIA authority.

By mid-year, the *quid pro quo* attending federal support to the regime emerged.

In exchange for being allowed to run Pine Ridge as a personal fiefdom, Wilson was to sign over title to the northwestern one-eighth of the reservation – an area known as the Sheep Mountain Gunnery Range – to the National Park Service (which, like the BIA, is part of the Department of Interior).[39] Thus faced not only with Wilson's continued financial malfeasance and outright terrorizing of opponents, but with a significant loss of their already truncated landbase as well, the traditionals attempted to avail themselves of their legal right to impeach the corrupt official. The BIA responded by naming Wilson to serve as chair of his own impeachment proceedings, and the Justice Department dispatched a 65-member U.S. Marshals Special Operations Group (SOG) to Pine Ridge, to "maintain order."[40] Under such circumstances, Wilson was able to maintain his position when he finally allowed the impeachment vote to be taken on the afternoon of February 23, 1973. The same evening, he proclaimed a reservation-wide ban on any further political meetings.[41]

On February 24, more than 200 people – including most of the traditional Oglala chiefs – defied the meeting ban to assemble at the Calico Hall (north of Pine Ridge village). They vowed to continue meeting until "something was done about Dickie Wilson." At their request, Russell Means traveled from Rapid City to meet with the Calico Hall group; he then attempted to meet with Dick Wilson to discuss the traditionals' grievances.[42] The meeting was aborted when Means was attacked in the parking lot outside tribal headquarters by several of Wilson's GOONs.[43] When Justice Department Community Relations official John Terronez (incorrectly referred to in the excerpted January 31 teletype as Torrez) attempted to go through the marshals to arrange a parlay between the traditionals and Wilson, the head of the SOG unit, Reese Kash, instructed his subordinates to "inform Mr. Terronez that CP [Command Post] was unable to contact me."[44]

Attempts at negotiation having failed, the Calico Hall group decided on the evening of February 27 to join forces with AIM and caravan to the hamlet of Wounded Knee, about 15 miles east of Pine Ridge village. They intended to remain overnight in a local church and hold a press conference at this symbolic location the following morning.[45] They had agreed to release a statement demanding congressional hearings on the actions of the Wilson government, as well as treaty rights and BIA abuses generally. Ted Means and other AIM representatives were assigned to notify the media and coordinate transportation of reporters from Rapid City to the press conference site. However, at dawn on the 28th, those assembled at Wounded Knee found the roads to the hamlet blockaded by GOONs later reinforced by marshals service SOG teams and FBI personnel.[46] By 10 p.m., Minneapolis SAC Joseph Trimbach had flown in to assume personal command of the GOONs/BIA police, while Wayne Colburn, director of the U.S. Marshals Service, had arrived to assume control over his now reinforced SOG unit. Colonel Volney Warner of the 82nd Airborne Division and 6th Army Colonel Jack Potter – operating directly under General Alexander Haig, military liaison in the Nixon White House – had also been dispatched from the Pentagon as "advisors" coordinating an illegal (under provisions of the Posse Comitatus Act; 18 USCS § 1385) flow of military personnel, weapons and equipment to those besieging Wounded Knee.[47] As Rex Weyler has noted:

Documents later subpoenaed from the Pentagon revealed that Colonel Potter directed the employment of 17 APCs [armored personnel carriers], 130,000 rounds of M-16 ammunition, 41,000 rounds of M-40 high explosive, as well as helicopters, Phantom jets, and personnel. Military officers, supply sergeants, maintenance technicians, chemical officers, and medical teams remained on duty throughout the 71 day siege, all working in civilian clothes [to conceal their unconstitutional involvement in this "civil disorder"].[48]

By 3 a.m. on March 1, the colonels were meeting secretly with Trimbach and Colburn, as well as Colonel Vic Jackson of the California-based Civil Disorder Management School (CDMS), at nearby Ellsworth Air Force Base.[49] Jackson, a specialist in irregular warfare, seems likely to have been brought in to implement of one of two "domestic counterinsurgency scenarios" code-named "Garden Plot" and "Cable Splicer," which CDMS had been created to perfect.[50] By March 3, F-4 Phantom jets were making regular low-level reconnaissance runs over the hamlet, and the outright military nature of the federal buildup had otherwise become obvious. AIM proposed a mutual withdrawal of forces and negotiations, but the government, expressing a clear intent to settle the confrontation by force, declined this offer.[51] On March 5, Dick Wilson – with federal officials present – held a press conference to declare "open season" on AIM members on Pine Ridge, declaring "AIM will die at Wounded Knee."[52] For their part, those inside the hamlet announced their intention to remain where they were until such time as Wilson was removed from office, the GOONs disbanded, and the massive federal presence withdrawn.

Attempts at negotiation during the next few days were consistently rebuffed by government hardliners and, on March 8, AIM was warned that women and children should leave the defensive perimeter.[53] That evening an APC fired on an AIM patrol, wounding two men.[54] This was followed by a firefight on March 9 during which thousands of rounds of automatic weapons fire were poured into the hamlet by federal forces. AIM responded by firing a single magazine of ammunition from their only automatic weapon, a Chinese AK-47 brought home by a returning Vietnam veteran. This led to the circulation of disinformation in the media by FBI "public relations specialists" that the defenders were firing on federal positions with an M-60 machinegun.[55]

On the morning of March 11, the government temporarily lifted the siege (over protests by the FBI), apparently hoping its show of force had intimidated AIM into surrendering. Instead, more than 100 supporters streamed into Wounded Knee, bringing with them supplies and weapons.[56] The traditionals also utilized the opportunity to proclaim themselves an "Independent Oglala Nation" (ION), with rights specifically defined within the 1868 Fort Laramie Treaty, entirely separate from the IRA government headed by Dick Wilson. SAC Trimbach, along with several of his men disguised as "postal inspectors," then attempted to enter the hamlet to survey its defenses; detained at the perimeter by AIM security personnel, they were told to leave or be arrested by the ION.[57] His ploy to end the cease fire with a provocation successfully completed, Trimbach immediately used this incident as a basis for reestablishing his portion of the siege lines; faced with a *fait accompli*, the marshals shortly followed suit.⁵⁸ The Minneapolis SAC was reinforced in this course of action by veteran COINTELPRO specialist Richard G. Held, who had been sent to Pine Ridge from his position as SAC in Chicago (where he was even then orchestrating the cover up of the Bureau's role in the Hampton-Clark assassinations; see Chapter 5) to "consult" on the sorts of operations the FBI should undertake against AIM.⁵⁹ Trimbach's move was entirely consistent with a string of "reports" Held was at the time sending to headquarters asserting that other law enforcement agencies were not sufficiently tough in dealing with the "insurgents" – a bit of outright counterinsurgency vernacular which stuck, as is evidenced in the accompanying October 31, 1973 predication for investigation – stressing that all police personnel on the reservation should have been placed under direct Bureau control from the outset, and protesting a Justice Department prohibition on "shoot-to-kill" techniques on the siege line.⁶⁰ Given that the BIA police (and, by extension, the GOONs) had all along come under command of the FBI, these remarks could only have been directed at the U.S. Marshals Service.

Probably the most immediate result of Held's and Trimbach's renewed siege was the precipitation of a firefight on the afternoon of March 12, in which SA Curtis Fitzpatrick was wounded slightly, in the wrist. Bureau propagandists seized the opportunity to engage in an incredible bit of theatrics, arranging for Fitzpatrick to be "med-evacked" by military helicopter to Ellsworth Air Force Base, where a full complement of media personnel had been assembled to see him arrive with his head swathed in bandages.⁶¹ Simultaneously, an active campaign to "develop informants" and infiltrate *provocateurs* within Wounded Knee was under way. Among the former was Leroy Little Ghost, (Hunkpapa Lakota) from the Fort Totten Reservation in North Dakota, who was recruited with the guarantee of $2,000-20,000 (depending on how well he did) in cash for his services.⁶² Among the latter were Gi and Jill Shafer, withdrawn by the Bureau from running the bogus "Red Star Collective" in the South to serve as volunteer "medics" within the besieged hamlet.⁶³ Another *provocateur* sent into Wounded Knee by the FBI during this period was Douglass Durham – a former CIA operative, police officer, affiliate of organized crime in the Midwest and suspected murderer – who posed as a "part-Minneconjou Lakota" (at other times "part-Chippewa") and reporter for the radical Iowa periodical *Pax Today*.⁶⁴ The Bureau was also, as the accompanying excerpt from a teletype concerning KIXI radio reporter Clarence McDaniels makes clear, using media personnel as intelligence agents, both with and without their knowledge.

Meanwhile, the policy conflict between the FBI (and its BIA police/GOON surrogates) on one side and the U.S. Marshals Service and military on the other was sharpening. As the FBI's role in the siege increased under Richard Held's tutelage, so did the intensity of firefights and GOON depredations. Beginning on March 13, federal forces directed fire from heavy .50 caliber machineguns into the AIM positions, greatly increasing the probability of lethal injury to those inside. The

UNITED STATES DEPARTMENT OF JUSTICE

FEDERAL BUREAU OF INVESTIGATION

Albuquerque, New Mexico
October 31, 1973

(b7C)

EXTREMIST MATTER -
AMERICAN INDIAN MOVEMENT

b2-1   This investigation is based on information which
indicates that ██████████████ is engaged in activities
which could involve a violation of Title 18, U. S. Code,
Section 2383 (Rebellion or Insurrection) or 2384 (Seditious
Conspiracy), as indicated hereinafter.

██████ has been identified as being actively
involved in militant activities of the American Indian
Movement (AIM). Since January, 1973, AIM has been actively
involved in demonstrations and violent confrontations with
local authorities in Scottsbluff, Nebraska, and the Rapid
City and Custer areas of South Dakota. From February 27
through May 8, 1973, AIM leaders and members and their
supporters occupied the community of Wounded Knee, South
Dakota, by force of arms, taking a number of the community's
residents as hostages. Before surrendering to Federal
authorities, they engaged in numerous violent and destructive
acts; and gunfire was exchanged with Federal authorities
resulting in the death of two of the insurgents.

(b7C)

advised that during the course of AIM rioting in Custer,
South Dakota, on February 6, 1973, an old white Dodge panel
truck was parked near the curb on the west side of the
Custer County Courthouse. This truck bore Utah License
PN7007. ██████ stated that the individuals in this truck
were in the rioting with the AIM group and had criticized law
enforcement officers who were attempting to prevent any further
destruction and burning of buildings in Custer. ██████
stated that as the riots subsided he noticed that this group
returned to the truck, so he proceeded to the truck in an
attempt to identify these individuals. ██████ continued that

Predication for an investigation of the American Indian Movement. Note adoption of the vernacular of counterinsurgency warfare.

following month was characterized by alternating periods of negotiation, favored by the army and the marshals – which the FBI and GOONs did their best to subvert – and raging gun battles when the latter held sway. Several defenders were severely wounded in a firefight on March 17, and on March 23 some 20,000 more rounds were fired into Wounded Knee in a 24-hour period.[65] During the latter, the government

```
REPORTER, CLARENCE MC DANIELS, HAD RETURNED TO SEATTLE FROM
WOUNDED KNEE (WK), SOUTH DAKOTA, BUT AT THE REQUEST OF UPI,
NEW YORK, HAD AGREED TO RETURN TO WK. ACCORDING TO UPI, NEW
YORK, WK INDIANS WILL NOT TALK TO THEIR CORRESPONDENT; HOWEVER,
THEY HAVE IMPLICIT TRUST IN MC DANIELS AND WILL TALK TO HIM.
MC DANIELS LEFT SEATTLE 3-13-73 EN ROUTE WK, WAS LAST HEARD
FROM 160 MILES FROM WK STUCK IN SNOW STORM, HAD NOT REACHED WK
AS OF 10:00 AM, 3-16-73. MC DANIELS IS EXPECTED TO CONTINUE
FURNISHING COMPLETE COVERAGE OF ACTIVITIES AT WK TO KIXI BY
PHONE AND TAPES. HE WILL BE REQUESTED TO DO SPECIAL STORY
ON SEATTLE AREA PARTICIPANTS. HE IS UNAWARE THAT HIS STORIES
ARE NOT BEING PUBLICIZED IN FULL OR THAT THE INTELLIGENCE
INFORMATION AND HIS TAPES ARE BEING FURNISHED THE FBI. KIXI
OFFICIALS REQUEST HE NOT BE CONTACTED AT WK; HOWEVER, IF ANY
SPECIFIC INFORMATION IS NEEDED BY FBI, KIXI WILLING TO PASS
ON REQUEST AS NORMAL DUTY ASSIGNMENT WITH NO REFERENCE TO FBI.
MC DANIELS WILL BE MADE AVAILABLE TO FBI, SEATTLE, FOR FULL
INTERVIEW UPON RETURN TO SEATTLE AT WHICH TIME IT IS HOPED
ALL OF THE SEATTLE AREA PARTICIPANTS WILL BE IDENTIFIED WITH
```

Excerpt from teletype describing manipulation of news content and use of suppressed stories of reporter Clarence McDaniels as intelligence source, apparently without his knowledge.

forces suffered their only serious casualty when a marshal, Lloyd Grimm, was struck in the torso by a .30 caliber slug (probably fired by a GOON) and paralyzed.[66] Apparently with the intent of denying even biased first-hand coverage of the events, and in anticipation of another escalation in hostilities, the FBI banned further media access to the Wounded Knee area; on the day Grimm was hit, the Bureau announced that reporters who continued to report from inside the AIM/ION perimeter would face federal indictments when the siege ended.[67] At about the same time, the Bureau announced that anyone found attempting to bring supplies into Wounded Knee would be arrested on charges such as "conspiracy to abet a riot in progress."[68]

On April 6, AIM, ION and government moderates mustered another serious attempt to avoid further bloodshed, reaching a cease-fire agreement and the basis for a negotiated settlement.[69] The agreement was, however, violated by the government within 72 hours of its signing and the siege continued.[70] Consequently, on April 17, the government fired more than 4,000 rounds into the village, much of it .50 caliber armor-piercing munitions. Frank Clearwater (Apache) from North

Carolina, was fatally wounded in the back of the head by one of these heavy slugs as he lay sleeping in the hamlet church; he died on April 25. Five other AIM members were wounded less seriously.[71]

The FBI's "turf battle" with the "soft" elements of the federal government rapidly came to a head. On April 23, Chief U.S. Marshal Colburn and federal negotiator Kent Frizzell (a solicitor general in the Justice Department) were detained at a GOON roadblock and a gun pointed at Frizzell's head. By his own account, Frizzell was saved only after Colburn leveled a weapon at the GOON and said, "Go ahead and shoot Frizzell, but when you do, you're dead."[72] The pair were then released. Later the same day, a furious Colburn returned with several of his men, disarmed and arrested eleven GOONs, and dismantled the roadblock. However, "that same night... more of Wilson's people put it up again. The FBI, still supporting the vigilantes, had [obtained the release of those arrested and] supplied them with automatic weapons."[73] The GOONs were being armed by the FBI with fully automatic M-16 assault rifles, apparently limitless quantities of ammunition, and state-of-the-art radio communications gear. When Colburn again attempted to dismantle the roadblock:

FBI [operations consultant] Richard [G.] Held arrived by helicopter to inform the marshals that word had come from a high Washington source to let the roadblock stand...As a result, the marshals were forced to allow several of Wilson's people to be stationed at the roadblock, and to participate in...patrols around the village.[74]

On the evening of April 26, the marshals reported that they were taking automatic weapons fire from behind their position, undoubtedly from GOON patrols. The same "party or parties unknown" was also pumping bullets into the AIM/ION positions in front of the marshals, a matter which caused return fire from AIM security. The marshals were thus caught in a crossfire.[75] At dawn on the 27th, the marshals, unnerved from being fired on all night from both sides, fired tear gas cannisters from M-79 grenade launchers into the AIM/ION bunkers. They followed up with some 20,000 rounds of small arms ammunition. AIM member Buddy Lamont (Oglala), driven from a bunker by the gas, was hit by automatic weapons fire and bled to death before medics, pinned down by the barrage, could reach him.[76]

When the siege finally ended through a negotiated settlement on May 7, 1973, the AIM casualty count stood at two dead and fourteen seriously wounded. An additional eight-to-twelve individuals had been "disappeared" by the GOONs. They were in all likelihood murdered and – like an untold number of black civil rights workers in swamps of Mississippi and Louisiana – their bodies secretly buried somewhere in the remote vastness of the reservation.[77]

Wounded Knee marked the beginning rather than culmination of the FBI's campaign against AIM and its allies on Pine Ridge. As the military advisers and Colburn's marshals were withdrawn the FBI was now free of their scrutiny. The Bureau beefed up its Rapid City resident agency (within which area of responsibility the reservation falls) to fill in behind them. Although Richard G. Held returned to his post in Chicago, the tactical groundwork he had laid during the siege – a matter partially illuminated in the accompanying report, "The Use of Special Agents in Paramilitary Law Enforcement Operations in the Indian Country," which he wrote at the time but which was not generally disseminated until April 24, 1975 (under the signature of J.E. O'Connell) – supported counterinsurgency war on Pine Ridge over the next three years.

COINTELPRO–AIM

During the 36 months roughly beginning with the end of Wounded Knee and continuing through the first of May 1976, more thansixty AIM members and supporters died violently on or in locations immediately adjacent to the Pine Ridge Reservation. A minimum of 342 others suffered violent physical assaults.[78] As Roberto Maestas and Bruce Johansen have observed:

> Using only these documented political deaths, the yearly murder rate on Pine Ridge Reservation between March 1, 1973, and March 1, 1976, was 170 per 100,000. By comparison, Detroit, the reputed "murder capital of the United States," had a rate of 20.2 in 1974. The U.S. average was 9.7 per 100,000, with the range for large cities as follows: Detroit, 20.2; Chicago, 15.9; New York City, 16.3; Washington, D.C., 13.4; Los Angeles, 12.9; Seattle, 5.6; and Boston, 5.6. An estimated 20,000 persons were murdered in the United States in 1974. In a nation of 200 million persons, a murder rate comparable to that of Pine Ridge between 1973 and 1976 would have left 340,000 persons dead for political reasons in one year; 1.32 million in three. A similar rate for a city of 500,000 would have produced 850 political murders in a year, 2,550 in three. For a metropolis of 5 million, the figures would have been 8,500 in one year and 25,500 in three...The political murder rate at Pine Ridge between March 1, 1973, and March 1, 1976, was almost equivalent to that in Chile during the three years after the military coup supported by the United States deposed and killed President Salvador Allende...Based on Chile's population of 10 million, the estimated fifty thousand persons killed in three years of political repression in Chile at the same time (1973-1976) roughly paralleled the murder rate at Pine Ridge.[79]

Of these 60-plus murders occurring in an area in which the FBI held "preeminent jurisdiction," not one was solved by the Bureau. In most instances, no active investigation was ever opened. The same is true for the nearly 350 physical assaults, despite eye-witness identification the killers and assailants, who in each instance were known members of the Wilson GOON Squad. When confronted with the magnitude of his office's failure to come to grips with the systematic slaughter which was going on within its area of operations, Rapid City ASAC George O'Clock pleaded "lack of manpower" as a cause.[80] Yet O'Clock's office, which was customarily staffed with three agents before Wounded Knee, grew by nearly 300% – to eleven agents – during the first six months of 1973.[81] In March of that year, this force was itself augmented by a ten-member FBI SWAT unit to the tiny village of Pine Ridge, on the reservation itself.[82] This aggregate force of 21 was maintained for more

Memorandum

TO : Mr. Gebhardt

FROM : J. E. O'Connell

SUBJECT: THE USE OF SPECIAL AGENTS
OF THE FBI IN A PARAMILITARY
LAW ENFORCEMENT OPERATION IN
THE INDIAN COUNTRY

DATE: 4/24/75

1 – Mr. Gebhardt
1 – Mr. Bates
1 – Mr. O'Connell
1 – Mr. Gordon
1 – Mr. Wannall
1 – Mr. Mosher
1 – Mr. Gallagher
1 – Mr. Mintz
1 – Mr. Mooney
1 – Mr. McDermott

Asst. Dir.
Admin.
Comp. Syst.
Ext. Affairs
Files & Com.
Gen. Inv.
Ident.
Inspection
Intell.
Laboratory
Plan. & Eval.
Spec. Inv.
Training
Legal Coun.
Telephone Rm.
Director Sec'y

PURPOSE: This position paper was prepared for use of the
Director of the FBI to brief the Attorney General and the
Deputy Attorney General (DAG) on the role of the FBI
in the event of a major confrontation in ·Indian country
(Federal jurisdiction) where (1) the President decides
against the use of troops; and (2) the FBI is ordered
by the President and/or the Attorney General to deploy
FBI Special Agents in ·a paramilitary law' enforcement
situation, in lieu of the use of troops.

There is attached for ready reference a document
captioned "Background Paper on the American Indian and the
Takeover of Wounded Knee by the American Indian Movement (AIM)."
This study outlines early history of the American Indian,
jurisdiction of the FBI to investigate within the Indian
country, background on AIM and their record for violence,
history and background concerning the Pine Ridge Indian
Reservation of the Oglala Sioux Tribe in South Dakota,
a prelude to the occupation of Wounded Knee, the occupation
of Wounded Knee by AIM and the use of FBI, U. S. Marshals
and Bureau of Indian Affairs (BIA) Police at Wounded
Knee, South Dakota, during the period February 27 – May 8, 1973,
in a paramilitary law enforcement situation.

Enclosure : *100-462183* CONTINUED – OVER

NOT RECORDED

JCG:mcl/rlf (11)   46 AUG 11 1975 SEE ADDENDUM PAGE 6 1975

*What is the status of this situation
at this point. In a conference with AG
Saxbe we had a tentative agreement as
to our position. Was it handled?*

1975 expanded version of COINTELPRO specialist Richard G. Held's 1973 field notes
taken at Wounded Knee insisting that thenceforth the FBI would assume immediate and
absolute control over "paramilitary operations in Indian Country." Note strenuous
objection raised concerning official "shoot to wound" orders (continued on next 4 pages).

FBI INVOLVEME( ): The FBI was instructed ( ) the Department
of Justice (DOJ) in the latter part of 1972 to conduct
extremist and criminal investigations pertaining to AIM.
During the afternoon of February 27, 1973, approximately
200 members and supporters of AIM, carrying weapons, left
Calico Hall, Pine Ridge, South Dakota, in a car caravan and
were under surveillance by a few FBI Special Agents. Under
the leadership of Dennis James Banks and Russell Charles Means,
the caravan moved into Wounded Knee, South Dakota, on the
Pine Ridge Indian Reservation where they took eleven hostages
and burglarized the Wounded Knee trading post in violation of
Federal statutes involving crime on an Indian reservation. A
decision was made by SAC Joseph H. Trimbach, Minneapolis
Division, to set up roadblocks to contain the militants,
which roadblocks were manned by FBI Agents, U. S. Marshals,
and BIA Police. This is how the FBI first became involved
in the Wounded Knee armed standoff against the U. S. Government.

ROLE OF THE WHITE HOUSE, JUSTICE DEPARTMENT AND OTHER AGENCIES:
Decisions were made by the AG after regular and continuous
consultation with responsible officials representing the
White House, namely Mr. John D. Ehrlichman, Assistant to the
President for Domestic Affairs, Mr. Leonard Garment, Special
Consultant to the President, and his assistant, Bradley Patterson,
and officials in the U. S. Department of the Interior. On
February 28, 1973, the situation at Wounded Knee was evaluated
in a series of meetings between former AG Richard G. Kleindienst,
former DAG Joseph T. Sneed, former Associate DAG Charles D.
Ablard, and others. These three officials were responsible for
the decision making of the DOJ. Department of the Interior
officials and the BIA were involved as these agencies administer
Indian reservations under Federal jurisdiction.

PROBLEMS CONFRONTING THE FBI: The various other Federal
agencies involved in the Wounded Knee takeover were the U. S.
Marshals Service (USMS), BIA Police, DOJ Attorneys, public
information officers and Community Relations Service, the U. S.
Attorneys (USAs), Department of Defense, and the U. S. Army.
The DOJ sent Ralph Erickson, Special Assistant to the AG, to
Wounded Knee as the senior U. S. Government representative on
the scene. He was subsequently followed by 4 other DOJ
and/or Department of the Interior officials who assumed this
role during the 71-day siege from February 28 – May 8, 1973.

Throughout the operation there was a definite lack of
continuity as each senior representative replaced another.
Colonel Volney Warner (now General), Chief of Staff, 82nd
Airborne Division, was dispatched to Wounded Knee at the
outset to assess the situation and to recommend whether or
not troops should be utilized. The AG issued instructions
there was to be no confrontation and negotiations with the
militants by representatives of the DOJ were to be entered
into to resolve the matter and have the hostages released.

There was a divided authority among the many
agencies present at Wounded Knee, including church and
social groups. The senior Government representative,
Departmental Attorneys, and members of the USA's Staff
issued conflicting instructions. Each representative
present on the scene took instructions for the most part
from superiors of his own agency. For example, on
March 4, 1973, after consulting with Colonel Warner,
Ralph Erickson issued orders that the use of deadly force
by the law enforcement officers on the scene could only
be used in self-defense to avoid death or serious bodily

harm. In the application of force the officers, including
FBI Agents, were to aim to wound rather than kill. This was
in direct conflict with the policy of the Bureau that an
Agent is not to shoot any person except when necessary in
self-defense, that is, when he reasonably believes that he
or another is in danger of death or grievous bodily harm.
Special Agents are not trained to shoot to wound. Special
Agents are trained to shoot in self-defense to neutralize the
deadly force. The SACs on the scene and officials at FBIHQ
strenuously objected to orders such as this which had
previously been approved by the AG without consultation with
any FBI official.

On a number of occasions the Acting Director and
officials of the FBI requested the Administration and the
Department to consider the use of troops at Wounded Knee. In
Washington, D. C., DOJ officials in conjunction with other
Governmental agencies explored the possibility of using
troops. Colonel Warner on the scene recommended to the Chief
of Staff of the Army against the use of troops. The Government
concluded that such use would be undesirable because (1) it
would substantially increase the risk of loss of life, (2) the
full prestige of the U. S. Government would be committed to
what was primarily a dispute between rival tribal factions
and (3) the use of Army troops against these Indians might
be misinterpreted by the press and some citizens.

The FBI encountered extreme problems, both in the
field and at FBIHQ, in adapting to a paramilitary role.
The FBI was not equipped logistically to operate
in a paramilitary situation in open terrain which
ultimately ended in a 71-day siege. The FBI and USMS had
to be equipped with military equipment, including Armored
Personnel Carriers (APCs), M-16s, automatic infantry weapons,
chemical weapons, steel helmets, gas masks, body armor,
illuminating flares, military clothing and rations. Authority
had to be obtained from both the AG (and/or his representative)
and from the General Counsel, Department of Defense, prior to
requesting the military logistics adviser, Colonel Jack Potter,
to obtain the weapons and material through the Directorate
of Military Support (DOMS). This clearance was often not
forthcoming when clearance had to be obtained during the
night hours. This phase of the operation required the FBI
to maintain a constant 24 hour vigilance so as to equip
our Special Agents and the other law enforcement officers with
the weapons and material needed for a defensive operation.

OPINIONS OF THE SACS WHO WERE ON THE SCENE: SACs Richard G.
Held, Chicago; Herbert E. Hoxie, Milwaukee; Wilburn K. DeBruler
Atlanta; and Joseph H. Trimbach, Minneapolis, furnished their
observations regarding the Wounded Knee Special. In essence,
they advised complete confusion existed as there were a number
of DOJ representatives on the scene, each issuing conflicting
orders. There was no coordination between the agencies other
than that provided by the FBI, nor was there any advance
planning done. For example, DOJ officials and Director Wayne
Colburn, USMS, would fly back to Washington, D. C., presumably
for conferences and would return with new policy of which
FBIHQ was not aware. The military did not realize in many
cases that they were there to assist and not direct the FBI.
SAC Held at the time advised FBIHQ to have any success at
Wounded Knee it would be necessary to withdraw the "political
types" and make it an FBI operation under FBI direction and
leadership. SAC Hoxie stated at Wounded Knee there was a

constant vacillation of instructions and policy which was
devastating. SAC DeBruler believed the ill-advised
instructions given prolonged the incident at Wounded Knee
and in some measure resulted in unnecessary risk to law
enforcement personnel and others at the scene. All SACs
recommended should we in the future become involved in
another situation similar to Wounded Knee where Special
Agent personnel are deployed that the entire operation
be under the direction of FBI officials and when law
enforcement personnel from other agencies are involved
it should be clearly understood the FBI is in the
decision making role.

OPINIONS OF FBIHQ PERSONNEL: FBIHQ supervisory personnel
Were confronted with the major task of coordinating all
phases of the Wounded Knee paramilitary law enforcement
operation with the Department and other interested agencies,
including USMS, the Department of the Interior, and the
BIA. Many of the officials from the other agencies, including
the staff in the DAG's Office, were not trained law enforcement
personnel. It was necessary to constantly explain matters
and give advice from a law enforcement standpoint. As the
FBI was utilizing approximately 3 SACs and 150 Agents per
day at Wounded Knee in a defensive perimeter along with other
Federal officers which were receiving hostile fire, it was
necessary to insure that nothing was done in a decision
making role at the White House or DOJ which might result in
Federal law enforcement officers taking heavy casualties.
It was reported in the initial phase of Wounded Knee that the
militants were in possession of an M-60 machine gun and
AK-47s (Communist automatic assault rifles), which could
result in heavy casualties. It was necessary to convince
the decision makers that APCs were necessary for the protection
of the Special Agents and U. S. Marshals. When the APCs
came under hostile fire they could not be moved to a more
secure position without authority from the AG. It is the
consensus of opinion among the headquarters supervisors that
no Government official who is not a trained law enforcement
officer be permitted to direct a law enforcement operation the
magnitude of Wounded Knee.

RECOMMENDATION: The Director meet with the AG and DAG to
brief them on the Wounded Knee incident so that they fully
understand if such an incident occurs in the future or an
incident similar to Wounded Knee and the FBI is involved,
the FBI will insist upon taking charge from the outset and

than two years, until it was tripled during June and July of 1975, affording the Rapid
City office with the heaviest concentration of agents to citizens in the history of the
Bureau.[83]

While claiming to lack the resources to the literal death squad activity occurring
beneath his nose, O'Clock managed to find the wherewithal to compile more than
316,000 separate investigative file classifications on AIM members with regard to
the siege of Wounded Knee alone.[84] His agents also found the time and energy to
arrest 562 AIM members and supporters for participation in the siege, while another
600 individuals across the nation were charged for supporting the defenders.[85]
These 562 arrests resulted in the indictments of 185 persons, many on multiple
charges (none involving a capital crime). In the two years of trials which followed,

will not countenance any interference on an operational basis
with respect to our actions. They should understand the
FBI due to its long years of experience and training is able
to make law enforcement decisions without over-reacting
to protect the general public, its Special Agent personnel,
and the violators of the law. The AG and DAG should be
advised it is our broad policy in such instances as this to
"get in and get out as quickly as possible" with complete
regard for the safety of all concerned. · The FBI furthermore
would seize control quickly and take a definite, aggressive
stand where necessary. It should be clearly stated that the
FBI does not desire to become involved in any political
situations and definitely not participate in any discussion
where it is obviously political in nature.

ADDENDUM: J. B. ADAMS:ams   5/19/75

     We should hold up any action in contacting the Deputy Attorney
General and Attorney General as we are presently engaged in attempting to
clarify the respective roles of the Marshals, FBI, BIA and tribal police in
confrontations such as the recent Yankton incident. Appropriate recommendations in this latter area are forthcoming.

there were a total of fifteen convictions – mostly on minor charges – an extraordinarily low rate for federal prosecutions.[86] As Colonel Volney Warner later put it, "AIM's
most militant leaders are under indictment, in jail or warrants are out for their
arrest...the government can win, even if no one goes to jail."[87]

Although the Wounded Knee Legal Defense/Offense Committee (WKLDOC)
– a largely non-Indian coalition of attorneys established by National Lawyers Guild
activist Ken Tilsen to represent AIM in criminal proceedings undertaken against its
members and leadership – formally challenged U.S. jurisdiction over the Pine Ridge
Reservation, the government forged ahead with the prosecution of those it considered "key AIM leaders."[88] Indicative of the quality of justice involved in these

"Wounded Knee Leadership Trials" was that of Russell Means and Dennis Banks before District Judge Fred Nichol during 1974. Based on an FBI "investigation," the defendants were charged with 13 offenses each, including burglary, arson, possession of illegal weapons, theft, interfering with federal officers and criminal conspiracy; cumulatively, each faced more than 150 years in prison as a result.[89] The crux of the case was the "eyewitness" testimony of a young Oglala named Louis Moves Camp—whom Banks had earlier expelled from AIM due to his persistent misconduct—concerning the AIM leaders' actions inside Wounded Knee. The case collapsed when the defense established that Moves Camp was testifying about events allegedly occurring in South Dakota at a time when he had been on the west coast.[90]

But that was hardly all that was wrong with the federal case. Moves Camp had been recruited as a witness by David Price and Ronald Williams, two agents recently assigned to the Rapid City FBI office.[91] His participation as a prosecution witness was apparently obtained in exchange for a "deal" concerning charges of robbery, assault with a deadly weapon (two counts) and assault causing bodily harm (two counts)—adding up to a possible 20-year sentence—facing him in South Dakota.[92] He was also paid by the Bureau for his services.[93] Further, while staying at a resort in Wisconsin with SAs Price and Williams, awaiting his turn to testify against Means and Banks, Moves Camp appears to have raped a teenaged girl in nearby River Falls; after meeting for several hours with local police, Agent Price was able to fix this charge as well.[94] Minneapolis SAC Joseph Trimbach refused to allow prosecutor R.D. Hurd to administer a polygraph examination to Moves Camp prior to putting him on the stand;[95] Hurd lied to the court, asserting that the River Falls situation was "only a minor matter," such as "public intoxication."[96] Then it came out that the FBI and prosecution had—despite the filing of proper discovery motions by the defense—deliberately suppressed at least 131 pieces of exculpatory evidence which might have served to exonerate the defendants.[97] With this magnitude of government misconduct on the record, Judge Nichol responded by dismissing all charges against Means and Banks. In his decision, the judge observed that it was difficult for him to accept that "the FBI [he had] revered so long, [had] stooped so low," and:

> Although it hurts me deeply, I am forced to the conclusion that the prosecution in this trial had something other than attaining justice foremost in its mind... The fact that the incidents of misconduct formed a pattern throughout the course of the trial leads me to the belief that this case was not prosecuted in good faith or in the spirit of justice. The waters of justice have been polluted, and dismissal, I believe, is the appropriate cure for the pollution in this case.[98]

The dismissal of charges occurred before it became known that, contrary to Hurd's and Trimbach's sworn testimony, the FBI had infiltrated Banks' and Means' defense team.[99] The operative used for this purpose was Douglass Durham, then AIM's national security director and Dennis Banks' personal bodyguard. In this capacity, Durham attended all the defense team's meetings (enabling him to report their strategy to the FBI, thence to prosecutors), and exerted near-total control over the defendants' office ("Nobody saw Banks or Means without going through me. Period.").[100]

He also maintained free access to defense funds, from which he is suspected of having embezzled more than $100,000 during the course of the trial.[101] Far from the Bureau's having been unaware of the "problem," FBI records reveal that Durham met with his handlers, SAs Ray Williams and Robert Taubert, "regularly" and was given a raise because of the quality of his services during the trial.[102]

Such behavior on the part of the prosecution and the FBI might be considered anomalous were it true that Hurd was brought up on ethics charges before the American Bar Association (as Judge Nichol clearly desired), Louis Moves Camp charged with perjury, Trimbach removed from his position as SAC and the involved agents at least reprimanded, and Durham's undercover operation suspended. It was Nichol, however, who was removed from trying any further AIM-related cases.[103] Nothing at all was done to Moves Camp.[104] Far from being disbarred, R.D. Hurd was promoted and received an award for his performance, and was assigned a lead role in seeking convictions against other AIM leaders, such as Stan Holder, Carter Camp and Leonard Crow Dog.[105] Trimbach and his agents continued in their positions with no official censure, while spearheading the Bureau's anti-AIM campaign on Pine Ridge.[106] For his part, Douglass Durham remained in his capacity as a *provocateur* within AIM until the organization itself discovered his true identity.[107] Before this occurred, he played a leading role in the perversion of justice attending the notorious Skyhorse/Mohawk case in southern California.[108] After his exposure, he is thought to have been involved in the violent elimination of at least one of the witnesses to his grossly illegal "investigative techniques,"[109] and – still on the FBI payroll – served as the sole witness before the Senate Subcommittee on Internal Security, "establishing" that AIM was a "violent revolutionary organization."[110]

These results are consistent with a Bureau thrust, revealed in the accompanying May 4, 1973 teletype from the Los Angeles field office to Acting Director L. Patrick Gray, even before the Wounded Knee siege had ended, in which agents were busily concocting all manner of allegations concerning AIM's acquisition of "automatic weapons, bazookas, rocket launchers, hand grenades, land mines, and mortars" (none of which ever materialized). As the document makes clear, the compilation of such "information" was intended as a means of securing Gray's authorization to undertake to divide AIM from major funders such as Sammy Davis, Jr. It is instructive that in the same document there is an attempt to link AIM directly to the LA chapter of the Black Panther Party, against which similar methods and rationales had long been utilized as part of COINTELPRO-BPP (see Chapter 5). Such techniques couple nicely to the accompanying May 4, 1973 Airtel from Gray to his SAC, Albany, which recommends employment of typical counterintelligence measures against AIM and inclusion of AIM leaders in the Bureau's Administrative Index as "Key Extremists."

Far more explicit was a November 26, 1973 teletype from SA Richard Wallace Held's counterintelligence group in Los Angeles – which had handled the lethal repression visited upon the LA-BPP – to Gray, suggesting that "Los Angeles and Minneapolis consider possible COINTELPRO measures to further disrupt AIM

Excerpts from May 1973 teletype itemizing never-substantiated arms acquisitions by AIM and detailing COINTELPRO-type operation to deny the organization funding from Sammy Davis, Jr. (continued on next two pages).

leadership."[111] This leaves little doubt that counterintelligence specialists such as the younger Held continued to view their job assignments *vis à vis* AIM in precisely the same terms as they had with regard to organizations such as the BPP two years earlier, even if headquarters had in the meantime forbidden use of the customary vernacular. In a superficial exercise in "plausible deniability" the acting director replied in a December 4 teletype:

IN PAST, ADVISED THAT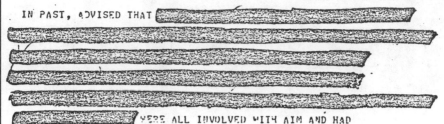

WERE ALL INVOLVED WITH AIM AND HAD
APPROXIMATELY $60,000 RECEIVED FROM SAMMY DAVIS, JR., AND
ANOTHER $140,000 FROM VARIOUS ROCK MUSIC GROUPS IN LOS ANGELES.
THIS MONEY ACCORDING ░░░░░░░░░░░░░ IS TO BE USED
TO BUY AUTOMATIC WEAPONS AND OTHER WEAPONRY FOR USE AT WOUNDED
KNEE, SOUTH DAKOTA.

SOURCE ALSO ADVISED THAT H̶X̶X̶X̶ THE GROUP INDICATED UPRISINGS
WERE TO OCCUR IN OKLAHOMA FOLLOWING WOUNDED KNEE.

THIRD SOURCE, WHO HAS PROVIDED RELIABLE INFORMATION
IN PAST ADVISED THAT ░░░░░░░░░░░ ACTIVIST IN CLEAVER
FACTION OF BLACK PANTHER PARY IN LOS ANGELES, INDICATED DESIRE
TO LOCATE SOME AUTOMATIC WEAPONS AS HE HAD BEEN APPROACHED BY SOME
INDIANS WHO WERE INTERESTED IN PURCHASING WEAPONS.

SOURCE UNABLE TO ASCERTAIN IDENTIFY OF INDIANS.

BUREAU REQUESTED TO ADVISE LAS VEGAS AS TO DESIRABILITY
OF CONTACTING SAMMY DAVIS, JR., TO (A) DETERMINE IF
DONATION MADE, (B) IF SO, TO CONSIDER ADVISING HIM AS TO WHAT
FUNDS ARE BEING USED FOR.

IT IS FELT DISCLOSURE OF THIS INFORMATION TO DAVIS WOULD
NOT JEOPARDIZE SOURCES.

IN REFERENCE TO BUTEL CALL MAY 4, 1973, CONCERNING
PURCHASE OF CLAYMORE MINES ░░░░░░░░░░░ AND SUBSEQUENT
DELIVERY TO WOUNDED KNEE, CONTACT WITH ALCOHOL, TOBACCO AND
FIREARMS, LOS ANGELES, REFLECTS THEY HAVE NO KNOWLEDGE OF SUCH
INFORMATION. IT SHOULD BE NOTED THAT INFORMATION FROM SOURCE ░░░░░
INDICATED THAT AIM WOULD BE IN POSITION TO PURCHASE
AUTOMATIC WEAPONS, BAZOOKAS, ROCKET LAUNCHERS, HAND GRENADES

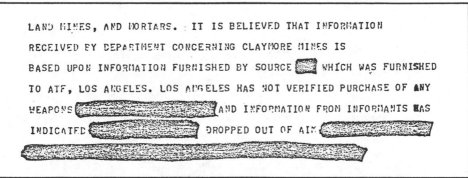

LAND MINES, AND MORTARS. IT IS BELIEVED THAT INFORMATION
RECEIVED BY DEPARTMENT CONCERNING CLAYMORE MINES IS
BASED UPON INFORMATION FURNISHED BY SOURCE ▓▓ WHICH WAS FURNISHED
TO ATF, LOS ANGELES. LOS ANGELES HAS NOT VERIFIED PURCHASE OF ANY
WEAPONS ▓▓▓▓▓▓▓▓▓▓ AND INFORMATION FROM INFORMANTS HAS
INDICATED ▓▓▓▓▓▓ DROPPED OUT OF AIM ▓▓▓▓

Los Angeles suggested that there appears to be a split between Means and Banks based on [deleted's] dismissal from AIM and suggested possible counterintelligence measures be taken to further disrupt AIM leadership...Your attention is directed to Bureau airtel to All Offices, dated 4/28/71, captioned "Counterintelligence Programs; IS - RM," setting forth that effective immediately all counterintelligence programs operated by the Bureau were being discontinued.[112]

What seems to have been at issue was Held's telltale use of terminology rather than the sort of tactics he was recommending. Indeed, as Bureau conduct in its use of Douglass Durham and the nature of its other involvement in the Banks/Means trial readily indicate, there is every indication that the FBI had already adopted the methods Held advocated for use against AIM.

As was noted above, a far more striking example of this than the utilization of agents *provocateurs*, disinformation and legal fabrications to neutralize AIM was the Bureau's reliance upon Wilson's GOON Squad to decimate the ranks of organizational members and supporters on Pine Ridge. Deployed in much the same fashion as appears to have been intended for the SAO by Held's LA COINTELPRO Section during 1971 and '72 (see Chapter 6), the GOONs functioned essentially as a reservation death squad. Among their first victims was Pedro Bissonette, the young head of the grassroots Oglala Sioux Civil Rights Organization (OSCRO), who had emerged as an ION leader at Wounded Knee. In the aftermath of the siege, the FBI had offered Bissonette a "deal" wherein all charges would be dropped against him in exchange for his testifying against the AIM leadership.[113] He refused, and countered that it was his intention to testify instead to the specifics of the graft and corruption permeating the Wilson administration, and the role of the government in perpetuating the situation. Subsequently, he was accosted by a GOON named Cliff Richards in the reservation-adjacent hamlet of White Clay, Nebraska on the afternoon of October 17, 1973. In the ensuing scuffle, Bissonette knocked his attacker to the ground, then got in his car and drove away.[114]

Although White Clay is outside BIA police jurisdiction, Pine Ridge police/GOON head Delmar Eastman immediately mobilized his entire force – assisted by several FBI spotter planes – in a reservation-wide manhunt for the "fugitive."[115] At

To: SAC, Albany

5/4/73

From: Acting Director, FBI

1 - R. E. Gebhardt
1 - G. C. Moore

AMERICAN INDIAN MOVEMENT (AIM)
EXTREMIST MATTERS

ReBuairtels 12/6/72 and 1/16/73 captioned "American Indian Activities, Extremist Matters."

Offices conducting preliminary inquiries relative to individual AIM chapters, if not already done, immediately submit results of investigation conducted to date in form suitable for dissemination under caption of individual chapter with recommendation relative to additional investigation. Where evidence of extremist activity or involvement by a chapter is determined or suspected, institute full and continuing investigation thereof to determine its activities, leaders, membership, and finances. Develop informants or sources in or close to each chapter. Also, institute individual investigations of members of such chapters to develop background and determine their activities and propensity for militancy or violence. Submit results thereof in form suitable for dissemination under individual's caption with your recommendation relative to further investigation.

Institute similar individual investigations of all AIM members and unaffiliated Indians arrested or involved in takeover of Wounded Knee, South Dakota, or similar confrontations or disorders elsewhere. Submit results under individual's caption in a form suitable for dissemination. If warranted, consider subject for inclusion in Administrative Index and _____ and for designation as a Key Extremist. EX-III REC-49 100-462483-57

2 - All Offices (Except Honolulu and San Juan)

MAILED 21
MAY - 7 1973
FBI

CAM:aso (117)

SEE NOTE PAGE TWO

**May 1973 teletype initiating a nation-wide, "forceful and penetrative interview program"
of all individual AIM activists with an eye toward their designation as "Key Extremists."
Note similarity to earlier COINTELPRO practice of convincing new left activists there was
"an agent behind every mailbox" (continued on next page).**

A forceful and penetrative interview program of individual activists should be instituted. Conduct interviews in accordance with existing instructions under SAC authority if facts necessitating Bureau approval are not present. Such a program should present excellent opportunity for developing extremist informants among Indian activists dedicated to violence and confrontations best exemplified by the Wounded Knee situation.

NOTE:

        Initial instructions to the field requested preliminary inquiries regarding individual AIM chapters. In view of recent militant and violent activities culminated by Wounded Knee on the part of AIM, its members, unaffiliated Indians as well as some confusion by the field as to when investigation should be instituted, further instructions are necessary to insure full and continuing investigations are instituted where appropriate. Minneapolis and Omaha are fully identifying individual Indians involved in and arrested during violent confrontations within their respective divisions and offices covering residences of such individuals are being advised and designated office of origin.

some point between 9 and 9:50 p.m. the same evening, Bissonette was stopped at a roadblock near Pine Ridge village and shot in the chest by a BIA police officer (and known GOON) named Joe Clifford. In Clifford's official report, he had been forced to shoot the victim, who had resisted arrest, jumping from his car brandishing a weapon. He recorded that he'd used a 12-gauge shotgun and that the shooting occurred at 9:48 p.m. Bissonette was pronounced dead on arrival at the Pine Ridge hospital at 10:10 p.m.[116] No weapon attributable to Pedro Bissonette was ever produced by the police. Several witnesses who drove by the scene, however, later submitted affidavits that a pool of blood indicating that Bissonette had already been shot was evident at shortly after 9 p.m., suggesting that the GOONs had delayed the victim's transport by ambulance to the nearby hospital (and medical attention) for approximately an hour, until he bled to death.[117]

Moreover, when WKLDOC attorney Mark Lane viewed the corpse in the hospital morgue at around midnight, he discovered that rather than having suffered a shotgun blast, Bissonette appeared to have been shot seven times with an "approximately .38 calibre handgun" in the chest. The shots, "any one of which might have killed him," were placed in a very tight cluster, Lane insisted, as if they'd been fired at point-blank range.[118] The attorney also recounted that it appeared Bissonette had been beaten prior to being shot.[119] He therefore quickly called Gladys Bissonette, the dead man's grandmother, and convinced her to demand an independent autopsy be performed. She agreed. Lane then phoned Assistant U.S. Attorney Bill Clayton in Rapid City, to notify him of the family's intent to pursue its legal right to commission such an autopsy. Clayton appears to have immediately called Delmar Eastman and instructed him to remove the body from the morgue –

at 3 a.m. – and have it transported, not only off the reservation, but out of the *state*, to Scottsbluff, Nebraska.[120] There, W.O. Brown, a government-contracted coroner, dissected the body, turned over whatever slugs he recovered to the FBI, and reached a conclusion corroborating Clifford's version of events. There was little left of the corpse for an independent pathologist to examine.[121] Despite the controversy swirling around Bissonette's death, and the existence of witness accounts contradicting the police story, the Bureau pursued no further investigation of the matter. OSCRO collapsed as a viable organization as a direct result of its leader's elimination.

Two years later, with the number of unsolved murders of AIM members and supporters on Pine Ridge having reached epic proportions,[122] and despite Wilson's loss in his third bid for the tribal presidency, the GOONs and their FBI cohorts were still pursuing the same lethal tactics. For instance, in the early evening of January 30, 1976, three cars containing 15 members of the GOON Squad pulled into the tiny hamlet of Wanblee (located in the northeastern sector of the reservation), a strong bastion of anti-Wilsonism. Spotting the car of Byron DeSersa, a young Oglala tribal attorney and AIM supporter who had announced his intention to bring criminal charges against a number of Wilsonites once the regime was disbanded, they gave chase, firing as they went. About four miles out of town, a bullet passed through the driver's-side door of DeSersa's car, catching him in the upper left thigh, nearly amputating his leg. DeSersa pulled over and dragged himself into a ditch, screaming at several friends who had been his passengers to run for their lives. He bled to death alongside the road as the GOONs chased the others through adjoining fields.[123]

The GOONs then returned to Wanblee, where they apparently passed a pleasant evening shooting up the homes of those who had opposed Wilson. The following morning, they firebombed several buildings and continued to drive around town taking random potshots. As the Commission on Civil Rights later determined, that afternoon – with the smoke still billowing from the GOONs' incendiary attacks – a pair of FBI agents arrived in Wanblee and were quickly informed by residents as to what had transpired. George Bettelyoun (Oglala), a passenger in DeSersa's car, provided precise identification of the killers, who included Dick Wilson's son Billy and son-in-law, a GOON leader named Chuck Richards.[124] The agents declined to make arrests, stating that they were there in a "purely investigative" capacity. They nonetheless managed to arrest Guy Dull Knife, an elderly Cheyenne who lived in Wanblee; Dull Knife, the agents declared, had disturbed the "peace" by protesting their inaction against the GOONs too loudly.[125] The citizens of Wanblee finally formed a vigilance committee on January 31, giving the marauders until sundown to be gone from their community or suffer the consequences. Delmar Eastman then dispatched a group of BIA police to escort the GOON contingent safely back to Pine Ridge village; again, no arrests were made. The Bureau, as usual, conducted no further investigation into either the DeSersa murder or the firebombings and other aspects of the GOONs' two-day terrorization of the hamlet.[126]

Later, while sparring with a congressional committee critical of the Bureau's performance on Pine Ridge during the mid-'70s, FBI Director William Webster was to cast his agents' role there as having been that of "peacekeepers." "Frankly [the Bureau] took...a little bit of a beating during those days in Wounded Knee period and afterwards," Webster asserted, "[but] our role should be an investigator's role, not a peacekeeper's role."[127] The director's use of the word "peacekeepers" in such a context is illuminating, insofar as this is the standard term in military and police parlance applied to counterinsurgency operatives.[128] The real meaning imbedded in the director's semantics is further revealed in the fact that FBI documents throughout the period in question – such as the accompanying February 6, 1976 memorandum from SAC, Portland to Director – openly and consistently refer to dissident Indians as "insurgents." Official protestations to the contrary notwithstanding, the FBI not only undertook a full-fledged COINTELPRO against AIM, it escalated its conceptual and tactical approach to include outright counterinsurgency warfare techniques. Only within this framework can the events discussed above be rendered comprehensible.

"RESMURS"

By early 1975, it had become clear to the opposition of Pine Ridge that its attempts to achieve resolution of its grievances through due process – whether by impeachment of Dick Wilson, electing another individual into his office, or the filing of formal civil rights complaints – were being systematically aborted by the very government which was supposed to guarantee them.[129] The FBI and BIA police structures were reinforcing rather than interfering with the pervasive GOON violence. Reservation conditions were being officially described by the U.S. Commission on Civil Rights as a "reign of terror."[130] The message was unequivocal: the dissidents could either give in and subordinate themselves to Wilson's feudal order, allowing the final erosion of Lakota rights and landbase, or they would have to physically defend themselves and their political activities. Hence Oglala traditionals requested that AIM establish centers for armed self-defense at various points on the reservation.

During the spring of 1975, the Northwest AIM Group – including Leonard Peltier, Frank Black Horse (adopted Oglala), Bob and Jim Robideau (both Anishinabés), and Darelle "Dino" Butler (Tuni) – set up a defensive encampment at the request of elders Harry and Cecilia Jumping Bull. The camp, was situated in a strongly pro-AIM area, on a property known as the Jumping Bull Compound, near the village of Oglala. It was referred to as "Tent City" in FBI communications, and became an immediate preoccupation of the Bureau and its GOON surrogates.[131] As was noted in a June 6, 1975 memorandum captioned "Law Enforcement on the Pine Ridge Indian Reservation:"

There are pockets of Indian population which consist almost exclusively of American Indian Movement (AIM) members and their supporters on the Reservation. It

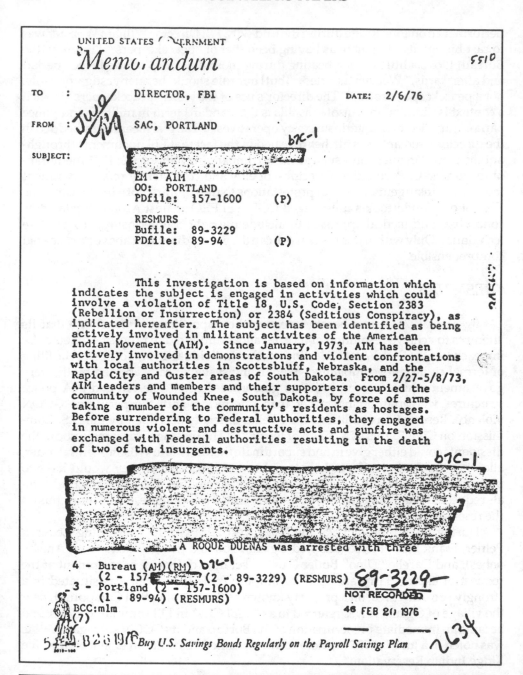

UNITED STATES GOVERNMENT

Memorandum   5510

TO   :   DIRECTOR, FBI   DATE: 2/6/76

FROM   :   SAC, PORTLAND

SUBJECT: b7C-1

                   EM - AIM
                   OO: PORTLAND
                   PDfile: 157-1600   (P)

                   RESMURS
                   Bufile: 89-3229
                   PDfile: 89-94   (P)

          This investigation is based on information which
indicates the subject is engaged in activities which could
involve a violation of Title 18, U.S. Code, Section 2383
(Rebellion or Insurrection) or 2384 (Seditious Conspiracy), as
indicated hereafter. The subject has been identified as being
actively involved in militant activites of the American
Indian Movement (AIM). Since January, 1973, AIM has been
actively involved in demonstrations and violent confrontations
with local authorities in Scottsbluff, Nebraska, and the
Rapid City and Custer areas of South Dakota. From 2/27-5/8/73,
AIM leaders and members and their supporters occupied the
community of Wounded Knee, South Dakota, by force of arms
taking a number of the community's residents as hostages.
Before surrendering to Federal authorities, they engaged
in numerous violent and destructive acts and gunfire was
exchanged with Federal authorities resulting in the death
of two of the insurgents.

                                                         b7C-1

          A ROQUE DUENAS was arrested with three

4 - Bureau (AIM)(RM) b7C-1
    (2 - 157   (2 - 89-3229) (RESMURS) 89-3229
3 - Portland (2 - 157-1600)
    (1 - 89-94) (RESMURS)   NOT RECORDED
BCC:mlm   46 FEB 20 1976
(7)

                                                          2634
Buy U.S. Savings Bonds Regularly on the Payroll Savings Plan

COINTELPRO as counterinsurgency. By 1976 the FBI's misrepresentation of AIM activities was down pat, and its characterization of AIM members as insurgents was standard.

is significant that in some of these AIM centers the residents have built bunkers which would literally require military assault forces if it were necessary to overcome resistance emanating from the bunkers.[132]

A later memorandum continued, "To successfully overcome automatic or semiautomatic weapons fire from such 'bunkers' it appears as though heavy equipment such as an armored personnel carrier would be required."[133] Whether or not the FBI actually believed this to be true, the fact is that no such bunkers ever existed. The alleged fortifications were later disclosed to have been abandoned root cellars and broken-down corrals. However, by then the Bureau had utilized such flights of fancy (or cynicism) as the rationale by which to justify provocation of a major "incident" and then a massive escalation of force by which it intended to destroy AIM and its Pine Ridge support base once and for all.

On the afternoon of June 25, 1975, SAs Ronald Williams and Jack Coler, accompanied by BIA police officers (both Oglalas and known GOONs) Robert Ecoffey and Glenn Little Bird, entered the Jumping Bull Compound, ostensibly searching for a 19-year-old Oglala AIM member, Jimmy Eagle, on what they said were charges of "kidnapping, aggravated assault, and aggravated robbery."[134] When they were told Eagle wasn't there and hadn't been seen in weeks, they left, but shortly picked up three Diné (Navajo) teenagers from the AIM camp – Norman Charles, Wilfred "Wish" Draper and Mike "Baby AIM" Anderson – hitchhiking along Highway 18, which runs between Oglala to Pine Ridge village. Williams and Coler questioned the three, not about Eagle, but about who *else* was residing in Tent City. The three were then released and returned to camp.[135]

Before mid-morning, June 26, local residents knew that something ominous was in the offing. Indians in and around the village of Oglala noted large numbers of paramilitary personnel – GOONs, BIA police, state troopers, U.S. Marshals, and FBI SWAT teams – massing in the area.[136] Around 11:30 a.m. SAs Coler and Williams returned to the Jumping Bull property. They were allegedly sent to serve an arrest warrant on Jimmy Eagle. However, it is clear they'd already ascertained he was not there and, in any event, the warrant for his arrest was not issued till July 7.[137] The agents drove past the buildings of the compound proper and directly toward the AIM camp. They stopped their cars, got out, and began firing their weapons. Members of the camp, believing themselves to be under attack from GOONs, returned fire.[138] This was apparently the cue for the prepositioned reinforcements to arrive; radio transmission logs from SA Williams indicate that he and his partner expected reinforcements to be immediate and massive once the firefight had been initiated.[139] Unfortunately for them, three teenagers who had been breakfasting in the compound quickly positioned themselves to cover the route intended by the relief force.[140] Using .22 caliber squirrel rifles, the youngsters shot out the tires of the first two backup cars – driven by SA J. Gary Adams and Fred Two Bulls, a BIA policeman and known GOON. Confronted with these meager potshots, Adams and Two Bulls promptly retreated, abandoning Coler and Williams.[141] Not until 6 p.m., when federal forces had swelled to over 250 men, including a SWAT unit airlifted in from the Bureau's training facility at Quantico, Virginia, and a vigilante force headed by South Dakota Attorney General William Janklow,[142] did the FBI finally mount an assault.[143] By this point, Williams and Coler were long since dead, and the Indians who had been in the AIM camp that morning had – other than a Coeur D'Alene named Joe Stuntz Killsright who had been killed, ostensibly by a long range shot fired by BIA police officer Gerald Hill[144] – made their escape.

Although the deaths of Coler and Williams were probably an unintended consequence, the provocation of the firefight achieved its intended objective: the public justification for a truly massive paramilitary assault on AIM and the Pine Ridge traditionals. As is shown in the accompanying memo from R.E. Gebhardt to J.E. O'Connell, dated June 27, 1975, the FBI's top COINTELPRO specialist, Richard G. Held – assigned as the Bureau's Chicago SAC, but already prepositioned in Minneapolis – immediately assumed control over the RESMURS ("Reservation Murders") investigation. Among those accompanying Held to South Dakota was "public information specialist" Tom Coll who immediately undertook a series of sensational press conferences in which he pronounced that the agents had been "lured into an ambush" by AIM and attacked from a "sophisticated bunker complex" where they were wounded and "dragged from their cars" before being "riddled" by "15-20 rounds each" from "automatic weapons." In Coll's accounts, Williams and Coler died while disabled and "begging for their lives." Both agents were "stripped," as part of their "executions," according to Coll.[145] Although literally none of this was true – a matter well known to Bureau investigators at least a day before the first press conference presided over by Tom Coll – such stories produced the lurid headlines necessary to condition public sentiment to accept virtually anything the FBI wished to impose upon AIM.[146] An additional advantage of Coll's media ploy was that it caused a senate select committee planning to investigate those FBI operations already directed against AIM to be indefinitely postponed, "under the circumstances."[147] It was a week before FBI Director Clarence Kelley quietly "corrected" this welter of disinformation, offered in the finest COINTELPRO style.[148]

Another star performer the Chicago SAC brought along was Norman Zigrossi, a young counterintelligence protégé whose mission it was to replace ASAC George O'Clock in Rapid City for the duration of the anti-AIM campaign.[149] The elder Held's son, Los Angeles COINTELPRO section head Richard W., was also involved in RESMURS from the outset, as is evidenced in the accompanying June 27, 1975 memo from O'Connell to Gebhardt. As is revealed in the accompanying July 26 memo, he had by that date joined his father at Pine Ridge, a locale in which the experience he had acquired while heading the Bureau's counterintelligence campaign against the LA-BPP (see Chapter 5) could be deployed against AIM, and his background overseeing SAO attacks against the left in southern California (see Chapter 6) might be used in connection with the GOONs. Actually, the younger Held probably arrived in South Dakota earlier, as is evidenced by the fact that RESMURS com-

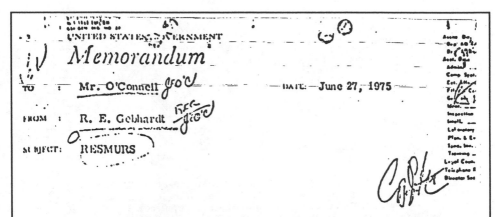

UNITED STATES GOVERNMENT

Memorandum

TO : Mr. O'Connell   DATE: June 27, 1975

FROM : R. E. Gebhardt

SUBJECT: RESMURS

Set forth below is a chronological recitation of information received and instructions given by Associate Director Callahan and Assistant Director Gebhardt regarding this matter.

At approximately 10:50 p.m., 6/26/75, we talked to Director Kelley. We brought him up to date as best we could at that time, namely, that two Agents were apparently attempting to execute an arrest warrant for an Indian charged with Assault with a Deadly Weapon and robbery when the shooting took place. There were four warrants in all on four individuals. Preliminary reports indicate one of the Agents said on the radio that they had been hit. Agents on the reservation responded. They came under fire but they were able to verify the two Agents had been killed. At that time the Agents who were brought into the area under the command of SAC Trimbach were moving into the area of the shooting on a gradual basis. They were approximately 1/2 mile on a perimeter. The area was described as a "group of houses" surrounded by "trees and foliage." At that time there were approximately 42 Agents present with 60 to 75 law enforcement officers and the firing being received was rifle-type fire. A quick check determined that the firing had ceased and that the area was secured but apparently there was some question as to whether some Indians were still in the houses. After a discussion with the field Director it was decided SAC Held should be ordered in to head up the investigation with Joe Trimbach as his No. 1 Man. The press release as read by Mr. Callahan was approved.

REC-26   89-3229

At 12:30 a.m. SAC Held was contacted in Minneapolis and approval was given to him to charter a plane to get him there.

JUL 10 1975

REG:mcw

CONTINUED - OVER

32

Memo assigning COINTELPRO specialist Richard G. Held, at the time Chicago SAC, to head up the RESMURS investigation. He had been prepositioned in Minneapolis.

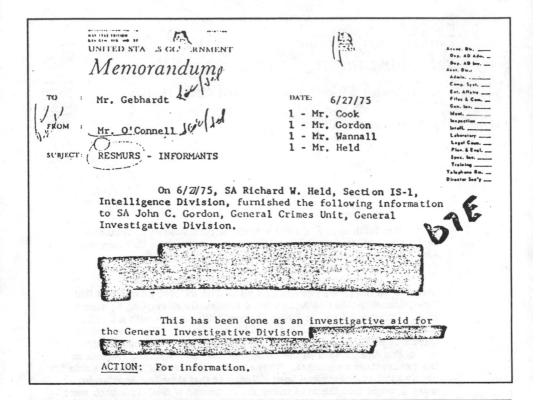

"All in the family." Memo showing participation of COINTELPRO specialist Richard W. Held, son of Richard G. Held, in the RESMURS investigation from its earliest moments.

munications – such as the accompanying June 30, 1975 memo from B.H. Cook to Gebhardt – suddenly adopted the practice of referring to Richard G. Held as "Dick" in order to distinguish him from his namesake.

The sorts of operations this stable of COINTELPRO aces had in mind had become apparent as early as June 27, when a task force of at least 180 SWAT-trained agents, supported by significant numbers of GOONs/BIA police and a scattering of federal marshals, began running military-style sweeps across Pine Ridge.[150] Outfitted in Vietnam-issue jungle fatigues, and equipped with the full panoply of counterinsurgency weaponry – M-16 assault rifles, M-14 sniper rifles, M-79 grenade launchers, plastic explosives, Bell UH-1B "Huey" helicopters, fixed-wing "Bird Dog" spotter planes, jeeps, armored personnel carriers, army-supplied communications gear and tracking dogs – this huge force spent nearly three months breaking into homes and conducting warrantless searches.[151] Their activities included outright air assaults upon the property of AIM member Sylvester "Selo" Black Crow near Wanblee (on July 8), and Crow Dog's Paradise (on September 5).[152] On July 12, an elderly resident of Oglala, James Brings Yellow, was frightened into a fatal heart

UNITED STATES GOVERNMENT

Memorandum

TO : DIRECTOR, FBI (89-3229)
ATTN: ASSISTANT DIRECTOR RAYMOND W.
WANNALL, INTELLIGENCE DIVISION   DATE: 7/26/75

FROM : SAC, PINE RIDGE (70-10239) (P)

SUBJECT: RESMURS

RE: SUPERVISOR RICHARD WALLACE HELD,
INTELLIGENCE DIVISION

    Supervisor HELD arrived at Pine Ridge, South
Dakota, Indian Reservation Command Post on 6/29/75, to
assist in RESMURS investigation. He was assigned three
important phases of this investigation; namely, the
correlation of Bureau-wide informants into the investigation;
the establishment of the confidential fund; and the
coordination of all intelligence information as it relates
to the American Indian Movement (AIM) and the RESMURS
investigation.

    Supervisor HELD's presence was especially
necessary during the initial stages of this investigation,
and his background in the intelligence and informant fields
proved most beneficial. He handled all of his assignments
in an outstanding manner, including the evaluation of all
intelligence information developed throughout the country
and on the Pine Ridge Indian Reservation.

    FBIHQ should continue to consider utilization of
supervisors of Supervisor HELD's caliber to afford on-the-spot
supervision in cases of this magnitude.

Memo showing Richard W. Held's presence on Pine Ridge as a supervisor at the peak of the RESMURS-related repression. The younger Held's "caliber" in such a capacity was no doubt proven by his earlier leadership of COINTELPRO-BPP in Los Angeles.

attack when a group of agents led by J. Gary Adams suddenly kicked in his door for no apparent reason.[153] With that, virtually the entire Oglala community – AIM and non-AIM alike – launched a petition drive demanding the FBI withdraw from Pine Ridge, and even the typically prostrate Sioux tribal councils endorsed the position.[154] The Bureau's July performance on Pine Ridge was such that the chairman of the U.S. Civil Rights Commission, Arthur J. Flemming, characterized what was happening as "an over-reaction which takes on aspects of a vendetta...a full-scale military type invasion." He went on to say:

> [The presence of such a a massive force] has created a deep resentment on the part of many reservation residents who feel that such a procedure would not be tolerated in any non-Indian community in the United States. They point out that little has been

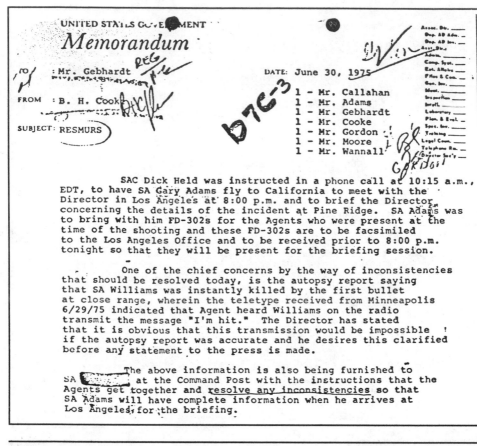

UNITED STATES GOVERNMENT

Memorandum

TO : Mr. Gebhardt   DATE: June 30, 1975

FROM : B. H. Cook

SUBJECT: RESMURS

1 - Mr. Callahan
1 - Mr. Adams
1 - Mr. Gebhardt
1 - Mr. Cooke
1 - Mr. Gordon
1 - Mr. Moore
1 - Mr. Wannall

SAC Dick Held was instructed in a phone call at 10:15 a.m.,
EDT, to have SA Gary Adams fly to California to meet with the
Director in Los Angeles at 8:00 p.m. and to brief the Director
concerning the details of the incident at Pine Ridge. SA Adams was
to bring with him FD-302s for the Agents who were present at the
time of the shooting and these FD-302s are to be facsimiled
to the Los Angeles Office and to be received prior to 8:00 p.m.
tonight so that they will be present for the briefing session.

One of the chief concerns by the way of inconsistencies
that should be resolved today, is the autopsy report saying
that SA Williams was instantly killed by the first bullet
at close range, wherein the teletype received from Minneapolis
6/29/75 indicated that Agent heard Williams on the radio
transmit the message "I'm hit." The Director has stated
that it is obvious that this transmission would be impossible
if the autopsy report was accurate and he desires this clarified
before any statement to the press is made.

The above information is also being furnished to
SA ▮▮▮▮ at the Command Post with the instructions that the
Agents get together and resolve any inconsistencies so that
SA Adams will have complete information when he arrives at
Los Angeles for the briefing.

Memo referring to Richard G. Held as "Dick" to distinguish him from his son during their joint participation in RESMURS. Note also the Bureau's belated concern with getting its story straight, "before any statement to the press."

---

done to solve numerous murders on the reservation, but when two white men are killed, "troops" are brought in from all over the country at a cost of hundreds of millions of dollars.[155]

Undeterred, SAC Held not only continued his sweeping operations, by which he sought to finally cow the traditionals, but requested a series of special grand juries be convened in Rapid City.[156] This last was an expedient by which he might exercise broad subpoena powers to compel testimony of Indian against Indian – thus undercutting the cohesion of the Pine Ridge resistance – and/or bring about the indefinite incarceration (for "contempt") of those who were perceived alternatively as "weak links" or as "hard cases" who refused to go on the stand.[157] By mid-July a strategy was emerging to at last divide the local reservation community from "outside agitators" such as the Northwest AIM group. Only in giving up their allies, so the reasoning went, would the Oglalas be able to save their own from what was being inflicted upon them. Cannily, Held seemed to realize that once the AIM/traditional solidarity which had been so painstakingly solidified over the previous four years was to some extent eroded in this fashion, it would be unlikely that it could ever be completely reconstituted. Hence, although by this point the FBI already had the names of some 20 Oglalas it thought had participated in the firefight which left the agents dead, the RESMURS investigation was geared almost exclusively toward obtaining a basis for prosecuting *only* non-Oglalas.[158] As is demonstrated in the accompanying July 17, 1975 teletype from Held to Director Kelley and "all offices via Washington," a high priority was already being placed on developing "information to lock [Northwest AIM member] Leonard Peltier into this case." The same document, of course, also points out that Held really had no clear idea at all as to "the actual events of the afternoon of June 26, 1975." Identification/apprehension of whoever truly shot Coler and Williams was playing a clear second fiddle to satisfaction of the Bureau's political agenda on the reservation.

Correspondingly, on November 25, 1975, federal indictments were returned against four individuals on two counts each of first degree murder and two more of "aiding and abetting" in the murders of SAs Ronald A. Williams and Jack R. Coler. Three of those targeted – Leonard Peltier, Dino Butler and Bob Robideau – were considered by the Bureau to be key leaders of the "outsider" Northwest AIM group. The other, Jimmy Eagle, appears to have been temporarily included merely to justify the presence of the agents on the Jumping Bull property in the first place. Eagle had turned himself in to the U.S. Marshals Service in Rapid City on July 9.[159] Butler was arrested on September 5, during the air assault on Crow Dog's Paradise.[160] For his part, Robideau was arrested near Wichita, Kansas on September 10, when the car he was driving caught fire and exploded on the Kansas Turnpike.[161] Thus, by October 16 – as is shown in the accompanying teletype of the same date – SAC Held considered his plan far enough along that he might return to his post in Chicago (where "urgent matters" attending the Hampton-Clark cover-up claimed his attention) despite the fact that Leonard Peltier was still at large, having in the meantime fled to Canada.[162]

In actuality Held's departure hardly marked the conclusion of his RESMURS involvement. To the contrary, as is evidenced in the accompanying January 29, 1976 memo written by R.J. Gallagher at FBI headquarters, he remained a guiding force at least until Peltier was arrested by Royal Canadian Mounted Police (RCMP) Inspector Edward W.J. Mitchell and a corporal, Dale Parlane, at the camp of traditional Cree leader Robert Smallboy (near Hinton, Alberta) on February 6.[163] Despite the fact that he was already well beyond normal retirement age, and undoubtedly as a result of the quality of the counterintelligence services he had rendered over the years, Held was promoted to serve as FBI associate director on July 20, 1976.[164] In this capacity as the Bureau's second in command, he was able to bring his unique talents to bear on the culmination of the RESMURS operation in particularly effective ways.

RESMURS

DAILY SUMMARY TELETYPE

RE RAPID CITY DAILY SUMMARY TELETYPE TO BUREAU AND OTHER
OFFICES DATED JULY 16, 1975.   IST-103

OSCAR BEAR RUNNER   18 JUL 23 1975

BEAR RUNNER APPEARED AT THE FEDERAL BUILDING IN RAPID CITY ON
JULY 16, 1975, AND PUBLICLY TORE UP THE COPY OF THE SUBPOENA WHICH
HAD BEEN ISSUED FOR HIM. HE STATED THE SUBPOENA WAS NOT VALID AS IT
HAD BEEN SERVED ON HIS FATHER. HE WAS SERVED WITH ANOTHER SUBPOENA
BUT MADE THE STATEMENT THAT HE WOULD NOT HONOR IT AS HE HAD NOT
APPEARED AT THAT LOCATION VOLUNTARILY.

    THE INVESTIGATION OF THIS CASE IS BEING DIRECTED TOWARDS:

    1) COMPLETELY IDENTIFYING ALL OF THE SUSPECTS, ADDING NEW ONES
OR ELIMINATING THEM AS APPROPRIATE;

    2) ESTABLISHING THE WHEREABOUTS OF THE SUSPECTS DURING THE
PERTINENT PERIOD;

    3) IDENTIFY AND LOCATE ALL OF THE RESIDENTS OF "TENT CITY" WHO
WERE THERE DURING ANY PERIOD OF ITS EXISTENCE AND/OR WHOSE FINGER-
PRINTS HAVE BEEN FOUND ON MATERIAL TAKEN FROM "TENT CITY;"

    4) EXAMINING THE EVIDENCE AND CONNECTING IT TO THE SUSPECTS;

    5) DEVELOP INFORMATION TO LOCK PELTIER AND BLACK HORSE INTO
THIS CASE;

    6) DEVELOP ADDITIONAL CONFIDENTIAL INFORMANTS AND SOURCES;

    7) COORDINATE WITH AUXILIARY OFFICES IN ORDER TO FULLY DEVELOP
BACKGROUND AND ACTIVITIES OF SUSPECTS WHO EITHER LIVE IN THEIR AREA
OR HAVE ASSOCIATES THERE;

    8) ATTEMPTING TO DEVELOP WITNESSES AND SOURCES WHO CAN AND WILL
TESTIFY AS TO THE ACTUAL EVENTS OF THE AFTERNOON OF JUNE 26, 1975.

    AS THE BUREAU IS AWARE, THE GRAND JURY IS BEING USED IN AN
EFFORT TO FACILITATE THIS LATTER ASPECT WHERE WITNESSES ARE
RELUCTANT TO FURNISH INFORMATION.

Teletype showing the FBI's use of a grand jury to coerce "reluctant witnesses" to "lock
Peltier...into" the RESMURS case.

```
                              OCT 16 1975
                                TELETYPE
RR 002  RC  CODE
1:10PM  URGENT  OCTOBER 16, 1975  AMJ
TO:   DIRECTOR, FBI
FROM:  RAPID CITY (70-10239)
ATTENTION: NICHOLAS P. CALLAHAN, ASSOCIATE DIRECTOR; JAMES B.
ADAMS, DEPUTY ASSOCIATE DIRECTOR; AND J. GALLAGHER, ASSISTANT
DIRECTOR.
RESMURS.

      SAC, CHICAGO HAS BEEN ON THE SCENE IN CHARGE OF CAPTIONED
SPECIAL SINCE THE EARLY MORNING HOURS OF FRIDAY, JUNE 27, 1975.
THE CURRENT STATUS OF THE INVESTIGATION IS SUCH THAT ALL BUT
TWO OF THE OUT-OF-DIVISION AGENTS HAVE BEEN RETURNED TO THEIR
OFFICE OF ASSIGNMENT.  THE CASE IS IN THE FINAL STAGES OF BEING
PREPARED FOR PROSECUTION BY MINNEAPOLIS PERSONNEL ASSIGNED TO
THIS DIVISION.  IN VIEW OF THIS AND IMPORTANT MATTERS REQUIRING
MY PERSONAL ATTENTION IN CHICAGO, IT IS MY INTENTION TO
RETURN TO CHICAGO ON SATURDAY, OCTOBER 18, 1975, UACB.

      THE PROSECUTION STAFF AND USDC JUDGE ANDREW W. BOGUE FOR
THE WESTERN DISTRICT OF SOUTH DAKOTA HAVE REQUESTED THAT SAC,
CHICAGO BE AVAILABLE FOR CONSULTATION, CASE PREPARATION AND
                                          REC-50  89-3229-1806
TESTIMONY IF NEEDED.  IT SHOULD BE NOTED THAT JUDGE BOGUE IN
ADDITION TO HEARING CASES, IS COORDINATING THE ACTIVITIES
```

Teletype noting the departure of Richard G. Held from the Pine Ridge area. The Chicago SAC returned to his home office where he continued his orchestration of the cover-up masking FBI involvement in the 1969 Hampton-Clark assassinations.

The RESMURS Trials

The murder trial of Dino Butler and Bob Robideau was conducted in Cedar Rapids, Iowa during June of 1976. Although Jimmy Eagle had been in custody even longer than they, and had supposedly confessed to participation in the killing of Coler and Williams, he was not docketed as a defendant. The trial was marked by a concerted effort on the part of the FBI and federal prosecutors to shape local opinion – especially that of the jury – against Butler and Robideau by casting AIM

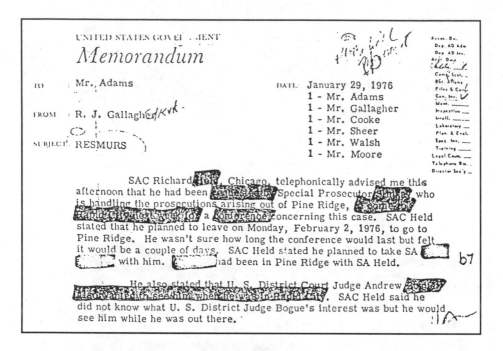

UNITED STATES GOVERNMENT

Memorandum

TO   : Mr. Adams

FROM   : R. J. Gallagher/KvK

SUBJECT: RESMURS

DATE: January 29, 1976

1 - Mr. Adams
1 - Mr. Gallagher
1 - Mr. Cooke
1 - Mr. Sheer
1 - Mr. Walsh
1 - Mr. Moore

SAC Richard ▓▓▓, Chicago, telephonically advised me this afternoon that he had been ▓▓▓▓▓▓▓ Special Prosecutor ▓▓▓▓▓, who is handling the prosecutions arising out of Pine Ridge, ▓▓▓▓▓▓ ▓▓▓▓▓▓▓▓▓▓▓▓▓▓ for a conference concerning this case. SAC Held stated that he planned to leave on Monday, February 2, 1976, to go to Pine Ridge. He wasn't sure how long the conference would last but felt it would be a couple of days. SAC Held stated he planned to take SA ▓▓▓ ▓▓▓▓ with him. ▓▓▓▓▓ had been in Pine Ridge with SA Held.

He also stated that U. S. District Court Judge Andrew ▓▓▓▓ ▓▓▓▓▓▓▓▓▓▓▓▓▓▓▓▓▓▓▓▓▓▓▓▓▓▓▓▓▓▓. SAC Held said he did not know what U. S. District Judge Bogue's interest was but he would see him while he was out there.

b7

Memo showing Richard G. Held's continuing involvement in RESMURS after his departure. Note Held's intention of meeting with Judge Andrew Bogue who, in the preceding document, appears to have been coordinating the prosecution's case.

as a "terrorist" organization. Despite the fact that, during the course of scores of trials, AIM had never attempted to free any of its members through armed action, the FBI launched a pretrial campaign to convince the citizenry and local law enforcement that they should expect "shooting incidents and hostage situations" to occur during the proceedings.[165] Then, on May 28, just before the trial began, the FBI began circulating a series of teletypes within the federal intelligence community alleging that AIM "Dog Soldiers" were planning to commit terrorist acts throughout the midwest. This was followed up on June 18 by the accompanying entry on AIM in the FBI's widely-circulated *Domestic Terrorist Digest*.

On June 21, the Bureau leaked one of its "Dog Soldier Teletypes" to local law enforcement and, not coincidentally, the media. It contended that, "Rudolfo 'Corky' Gonzales, a leader of the Brown Berets [sic: Gonzales was a leader of the Denver-based Crusade for Justice] reportedly [had] a rocket launcher and rockets either in his possession or available to him along with explosives, hand grenades and ten to fifteen M-16 rifles with banana clips." Gonzales' organization, the teletype went on, was on the verge of joining with AIM's supposed Dog Soldiers and the long-defunct SDS to use this array of weaponry "to kill a cop a day," using "various ruses" to "lure law enforcement officers into an ambush." On June 22, the accompanying follow-up

FBI EXHIBIT KKK
DOMESTIC TERRORIST DIGEST

Vol. VII, No. 3   June 18, 1976

BICENTENNIAL OVERVIEW

Indicators of violence have increased in connection with Bicentennial celebrations scheduled for July 4, 1976. In addition to previously reported statements from the American Indian Movement threatening to "blow out the candles" on America's birthday cake and from the Weather Underground to "bring the fireworks," the possibility of Puerto Rican independence groups engaging in terrorist activity exists.

While Bicentennial activities are set for virtually every city and town in the country; national attention is expected for celebrations in Washington, D. C., Philadelphia, and New York City. Large-scale counterdemonstrations are being organized for Washington and Philadelphia and a large number of foreign diplomats are expected to participate in "Operation Sail" (the arrival of sailing ships from many nations) in New York.

PUERTO RICAN INDEPENDENCE

The slogan "Independence for Puerto Rico—A Bicentennial Without Colonies" has been adopted by organizers of a planned, massive July 4 demonstration in Philadelphia. The Prairie Fire Organizing Committee (PFOC), the above-ground support arm of the Weather Underground, appears to be the driving force behind this demonstration, along with the Socialist Party of Puerto Rico (PSP), a Marxist-Leninist group which advocates independence for Puerto Rico.

Five members of the PSP were arrested in Puerto Rico on March 29, 1976, in possession of automatic weapons and 1,350 pounds of stolen iremite explosives. Reportedly, some of these explosives were earmarked for use in the U. S. during the Bicentennial and more than 1,000 pounds of the explosives remain in the hands of the PSP. All five of these individuals are reported to have traveled to Cuba in the past two years.

In addition, Puerto Rican independence has been one of the demands of the Armed Forces of Puerto Rican Liberation (FALN). This group most recently claimed ten simultaneous bombings in New York City, Washington, D. C., and Chicago in October, 1975. The FALN took responsibility for simultaneous bombings the year before in New York and the Fraunces Tavern bombing in January, 1975, which killed four and injured over 50 persons.

WEATHER UNDERGROUND

The Weather Underground (WU), which has taken credit for over 25 bombing since 1970, has repeatedly suggested in its magazine *Osawotomie* that revolutionaries should "bring the fireworks" to the Bicentennial. The latest issue also adopted the theme of Puerto Rican independence.

Jennifer Dohrn, a national leader of the PFOC, the WU support arm, urged a mass mobilization for July 4 in Philadelphia at the Hard Times Conference held in Chicago the first of this year. PFOC organized that conference, as well as the National Conference for a Peoples July 4th held in New York the end of March.

AMERICAN INDIAN MOVEMENT (AIM)

Support for American Indian protests was also a theme of the National Conference for a Peoples July 4th. An AIM spokesman told this conference that the candles on America's birthday cake would definitely be blown out. Indian militants have scheduled a caravan to arrive at Little Big Horn River, Montana, on June 26, the 100th Anniversary of General Custer's defeat there Further, a shoot-out last November between Indian militants and an Oregon State Police officer revealed Indian interest in Bicentennial activities, and their possession of a large amount of explosives and weapons.

AIM's inclusion in the FBI's *Domestic Terrorist Digest*.

leak was made, asserting that 2,000 Dog Soldiers, trained for guerrilla warfare in the "Northwest Territory," were to meet at the residence of AIM supporter Renee Howell in Rapid City, and begin an incredible campaign of "terrorist acts." Although Butler-Robideau defense attorney William Kunstler put FBI Director Clarence Kelley on the stand and forced him to admit the Bureau had "not one shred" of evidence to support these allegations, the disinformation continued to generate headlines through the remainder of the trial.[166] And, as the accompanying June 28, 1976 memo from J.G. Deegan to T.W. Leavitt makes plain, this was by conscious design of the FBI rather than through the story's having simply acquired "a life of its own."

Application of such time-honored COINTELPRO expedients was hardly the only step undertaken by the FBI in seeking to undercut the judicial process at Cedar Rapids. The Bureau also managed to get trumped-up allegations of an attempted jail break by Butler and Robideau into the trial record,[167] brought in a demonstrably bogus witness named James Harper to claim that both defendants had confessed to him in their cell,[168] and – if their subsequent testimony during the trial of Leonard Peltier is any indication – allowed agents such as J. Gary Adams to perjure themselves.[169] It was also established in court that Adams, Olen Victor Harvey and other agents improperly coerced false testimony from several key witnesses.[170] Still, presiding judge Edward McManus – "Speedie Eddie," certainly no friend of AIM – allowed the defense to base its case in an argument for self-defense, contingent upon examination of the context of anti-AIM violence fostered on Pine Ridge by the FBI

```
65113 ELVEG

        12

94210 R 8-21-81-024106

TTU2YJY RUEHFBAR693 1431845-UUUU--RUE VEG.

NR UUUUU ZZH

2817952 MAY 76

M DIRECTOR, FBI

O RUEBYJA/DEPUTY ATTORNEY GENERAL

    ATTN: ANALYSIS AND EVALUATION UNIT

JEBYJA/ASSISTANT ATTORNEY GENERAL, CRIMINAL DIVISION

    TN: INTERNAL SECURITY SECTION

    ATTN: GENERAL CRIMES SECTION

JEBYJA/U.S. MARSHAL'S SERVICE

JEHSE/U.S. SECRET SERVICE (PID)

JEBHGA/DEPARTMENT OF THE INTERIOR

T

NCLAS

MERICAN INDIAN MOVEMENT

    A SOURCE, WITH WHOM INSUFFICIENT CONTACT HAS BEEN MADE TO

TERMINE RELIABILITY BUT WHO IS IN A POSITION TO FURNISH

LIABLE INFORMATION, ADVISED AS FOLLOWS ON MAY 21, 1976.
```

The second of the so-called "Dog Soldier Teletypes" (continued on next 3 pages).

and its GOON cohorts from 1972 onwards. Butler and Robideau were thus able to call expert witnesses such as Idaho Senator Frank Church, who had headed up a major investigation of COINTELPRO and who testified that what the defendants were contending was quite in line with known FBI counterintelligence practices.[171] Similarly, U.S. Civil Rights Commission investigator William Muldrow went on the stand to testify that the Bureau had implemented a "reign of terror" at Pine Ridge.[172] Butler and Robideau never claimed not to have fired on Williams and Coler; they claimed instead that, under the circumstances the FBI itself had created on the reservation, they were justified in doing so. On July 16, 1976 the jury agreed, returning verdicts on "not guilty by reason of self-defense" upon both men.[173]

Confronted by this unexpected defeat in court, the government was placed in

DOG SOLDIERS," WHO ARE PRO-AMERICAN INDIAN MOVEMENT (AIM) MEMBERS

WHO WILL KILL FOR THE ADVANCEMENT OF AIM OBJECTIVES, HAVE BEEN

TRAINING SINCE THE WOUNDED KNEE, SOUTH DAKOTA, INCIDENT IN 1973.

THESE DOG SOLDIERS, APPROXIMATELY 2800 IN NUMBER, HAVE BEEN TRAINING

IN "THE NORTHWEST TERRITORY" (NOT FURTHER DESCRIBED) AND ALSO AN

UNKNOWN NUMBER HAVE BEEN TRAINING IN THE DESERT OF ARIZONA.

THESE DOG SOLDIERS ALLEGEDLY ARE UNDERGOING GUERRILLA WARFARE

TRAINING EXPERIENCES (NOT FURTHER DETERMINED).

THE DOG SOLDIERS ARE TO ARRIVE AT THE YANKTON SIOUX

RESERVATION, SOUTH DAKOTA (WAGNER, SOUTH DAKOTA) IN ORDER TO

ATTEND THE TRADITIONAL SIOUX SUN DANCE AND INTERNATIONAL TREATY

CONFERENCE. THE SUN DANCE AND THE CONFERENCE ARE TO OCCUR ON THE

YANKTON RESERVATION IN EARLY JUNE OF 1976 AND THIS SUN DANCE AND

CONFERENCE ARE TO SERVE AS A COVER FOR THE INFLUX OF DOG SOLDIERS

(THE SECOND BIENNIAL INTERNATIONAL INDIAN TREATY CONFERENCE IS

SCHEDULED FOR MAY 28-JUNE 6, 1976, YANKTON RESERVATION).

AT THE CONCLUSION OF THE ACTIVITIES ON THE SIOUX RESERVATION

THE DOG SOLDIERS ARE TO MEET ON JUNE 29, 1976, OR IMMEDIATELY THERE-

AFTER, AT 20 NORTH STREET, RAPID CITY, SOUTH DAKOTA, THE RESIDENCE

OF RENEE HOWELL. AT THIS MEETING FINAL ASSIGNMENTS WILL BE GIVEN

TO THE DOG SOLDIERS FOR TARGETS THROUGHOUT THE STATE ON THE FOURTH

OF JULY WEEKEND. CURRENTLY SOME DOG SOLDIERS FROM THE "NORTHWEST

TERRITORY" ARE IN THE STATE OF SOUTH DAKOTA WATCHING THE MOVEMENTS OF

PUBLIC EMPLOYEES AT PUBLIC BUILDINGS. THE DOG SOLDIERS

ASSIGNMENTS ARE TO BE CARRIED OUT BETWEEN JULY 1 AND JULY 5, 1976.

ALLEGED TARGETS ARE AS FOLLOWS: 1. THE CHARLES MIX COUNTY COURT

HOUSE, LAKE ANDES, SOUTH DAKOTA WHERE VALVES ON THE HEATING SYSTEMS

BOILER ARE TO BE SET (INCLUDING THE SAFETY VALVE) IN SUCH A WAY

THAT THE BOILER WILL BLOW UP. 2. STATE CAPITOL, PIERRE, SOUTH

DAKOTA, (NO FURTHER DETAIL). 3. FT. RANDALL DAM, PICKSTOWN,

SOUTH DAKOTA, WOULD HAVE TURBINES BLOWN UP. SHORT CIRCUITING
POWER. 4. THE DOG SOLDIERS WERE "ON THE LINE" TO ASSASSINATE
THE GOVERNOR OF SOUTH DAKOTA. 5. SNIPING OF TOURISTS ON INTERSTATE
HIGHWAYS IN SOUTH DAKOTA. 6. TAKING ACTION TO MT. RUSHMORE.
7. TO "BURN FARMERS" AND SHOOTING EQUIPMENT IN THE WAGNER,
SOUTH DAKOTA, AREA. 8. TO ASSAULT THE STATE PENITENTIARY IN
SIOUX FALLS, SOUTH DAKOTA, TO ASSASSINATE AN INMATE. 9. TO BLOW
UP BUREAU OF INDIAN AFFAIRS (BIA BUILDINGS IN THE WAGNER, SOUTH
DAKOTA, AREA).

THE DOG SOLDIERS ARE ALLEGEDLY TO BE ARMED WITH M-16'S AND
NES WHICH ARE HIDDEN IN PORCUPINE, SOUTH DAKOTA, AREA, ON
ROSEBUD INDIAN RESERVATION.
SAM MOVES CAMP, AN ACTING AIM MEMBER, PINE RIDGE, SOUTH DAKOTA,
EDLY TRANSPORTS THE ABOVE WEAPONS FROM REDMAN STREET
ER UNKNOWN), OMAHA, NEBRASKA, TO THE RESIDENCE OF CHARLIE
EZK, PORCUPINE, SOUTH DAKOTA. ABOUREZK, WHO IS INVOLVED
THE DOG SOLDIERS IS THE SON OF A UNITED STATES SENATOR, JAMES
REZK, SOUTH DAKOTA. ADDITIONALLY, SAM MOVES CAMP ALLEGEDLY
S A 1966 OLDSMOBILE, FOUR-DOOR, BLACK OVER BROWN, AND RESIDES
VISTA, NEBRASKA (BELIEVED TO BE A SUBURB OF OMAHA, NEBRASKA).
SOURCE LEARNED THAT DYNAMITE WAS STORED AT THE HOME OF TONY
R. GREENWOOD, SOUTH DAKOTA, IN SEPTEMBER, 1975, AND DYNAMITE
ALSO STORED AT THE HOME OF GREGORY FRANCIS ZEPHIER, SR., ALSO
AS GREG, WAGNER, SOUTH DAKOTA, IN FEBRUARY, 1975.
SOURCE HAS HEARD THAT WILBURT PROVOST, ALSO KNOWN AS WILLIE,
E OF RUSSELL MEANS' "HIT MEN" AND THAT WALLACE LITTLE, JR.,
KNOWN AS JUNE LITTLE, WHO IS EXPERT WITH EXPLOSIVES HAS ONCE
CHER OF THE DOG SOLDIERS IN THE "NORTHWEST TERRITORY"
GREG ZEPHIER, WAGNER, SOUTH DAKOTA, IS LISTED AS THE DIRECTOR
E AIM, SOUTH DAKOTA, ACCORDING TO JANICE STARK, CLERK.

```
NCORPORATION RECORDS, SOUTH DAKOTA SECRETARY OF STATE, AS OF
 LY 18, 1975.

    A SECOND SOURCE ADVISED THAT RUSSELL MEANS HOLDS NO NATIONAL
 FICE IN AIM, HOWEVER, HE IS MEMBER OF THE AIM CENTRAL COMMITTEE, TH

ECISION-MAKING BODY OF AIM.

    THE AMERICAN INDIAN MOVEMENT (AIM) WAS FOUNDED IN MINNESOTA
1968, DEDICATED TO IMPROVING CONDITIONS FOR THE AMERICAN
 NDIAN, AIM LED AND PARTICIPATED IN CONFRONTATIONS WITH LOCAL
 UTHORITIES IN SCOTTSBLUFF, NEBRASKA, AND THE RAPID CITY-CUSTER
 EAS OF SOUTH DAKOTA, AIM LED THE TAKEOVER AND OCCUPATION OF
 OUNDED KNEE, SOUTH DAKOTA, IN FEBRUARY - MAY, 1973.
```

something of a quandary as to what to do next. By July 20, 1976, as is shown in the accompanying teletype sent by ASAC Norman Zigrossi to Director Kelley and his associate, Richard G. Held, the Bureau had begun to analyze "what went wrong" during the Cedar Rapids prosecution. Zigrossi's conclusions – such as the defense being "allowed freedom of questioning of witnesses" and the allowing of testimony "concerning past activities of the FBI relating to COINTEL PRO [sic]" – had been accepted by the Bureau leadership. As is evidenced in the accompanying August 10 memo from B.H. Cooke to Richard J. Gallagher, a meeting was convened between Kelley and Held, along with FBI officials James B. Adams, Gallagher, John C. Gordon, and Herbert H. Hawkins, Sr., on the one hand and U.S. Attorney Evan Hultman, along with his director, William B. Gray, on the other. At the meeting, it was decided to pursue Held's strategy of prosecuting only non-Oglalas by dropping charges against Jimmy Eagle "so that the full prosecutive weight of the Federal Government could be directed against Leonard Peltier."

The next step was to do a bit of shopping for a judge. Just as McManus was used to replace Judge Fred Nichol after the latter reached conclusions unfavorable to the prosecution during the Banks-Means trial of 1974, so too was McManus arbitrarily replaced after allowing a semblance of due process during the first RESMUR trial. He was replaced by Judge Paul Benson, a former AUSA from North Dakota and Nixon appointee who had made considerable personal investment in Indian lands. After a series of meetings conducted in Rapid City with ASAC Zigrossi and his FBI colleagues, as well as prosecutor Hultman (defense attorneys were neither invited nor informed) – ostensibly held, in contradiction of every tangible shred of evidence concerning the organization's conduct during the many trials of its members, to

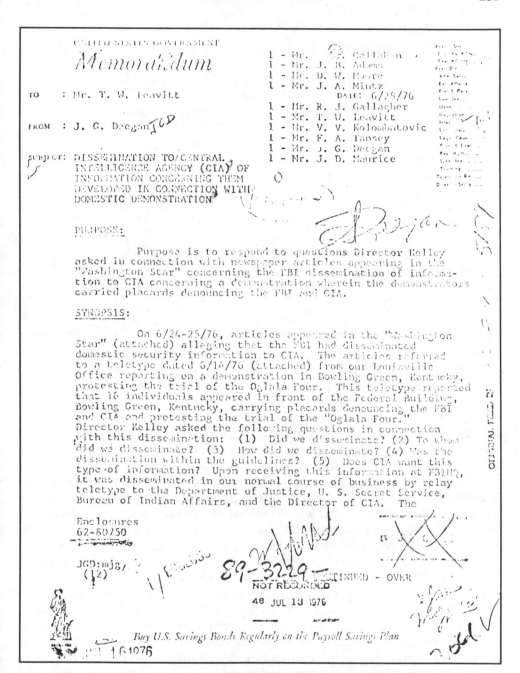

UNITED STATES GOVERNMENT

Memorandum

TO : Mr. T. W. Leavitt

FROM : J. G. Deegan

SUBJECT: DISSEMINATION TO CENTRAL
INTELLIGENCE AGENCY (CIA) OF
INFORMATION CONCERNING THEM
DEVELOPED IN CONNECTION WITH
DOMESTIC DEMONSTRATION

1 - Mr. C. Callahan
1 - Mr. J. B. Adams
1 - Mr. D. W. Moore
1 - Mr. J. A. Mintz
DATE: 6/28/76
1 - Mr. R. J. Gallagher
1 - Mr. T. W. Leavitt
1 - Mr. V. V. Kolombatovic
1 - Mr. F. A. Tansey
1 - Mr. J. G. Deegan
1 - Mr. J. D. Maurice

PURPOSE:

Purpose is to respond to questions Director Kelley asked in connection with newspaper articles appearing in the "Washington Star" concerning the FBI dissemination of information to CIA concerning a demonstration wherein the demonstrators carried placards denouncing the FBI and CIA.

SYNOPSIS:

On 6/24-25/76, articles appeared in the "Washington Star" (attached) alleging that the FBI had disseminated domestic security information to CIA. The articles referred to a teletype dated 6/16/76 (attached) from our Louisville Office reporting on a demonstration in Bowling Green, Kentucky, protesting the trial of the Oglala Four. This teletype reported that 16 individuals appeared in front of the Federal Building, Bowling Green, Kentucky, carrying placards denouncing the FBI and CIA and protesting the trial of the "Oglala Four." Director Kelley asked the following questions in connection with this dissemination: (1) Did we disseminate? (2) To whom did we disseminate? (3) How did we disseminate? (4) Was the dissemination within the guidelines? (5) Does CIA want this type of information? Upon receiving this information at FBIHQ, it was disseminated in our normal course of business by relay teletype to the Department of Justice, U. S. Secret Service, Bureau of Indian Affairs, and the Director of CIA. The

Enclosures
62-80750

JGD:mjs
(12)

89-3229
NOT RECORDED
48 JUL 13 1976

CONTINUED - OVER

Memo discussing sharing of RESMURS information with the CIA (continued on next page).

dissemination was made to CIA on the basis of the fact that
that agency was being denounced during the course of the
demonstration reported on and this is in accordance with the
Attorney General (AG) guidelines for dissemination matters in that
we are authorized to collect and disseminate this type of
information.   In response to press inquiries to the CIA, a
representative of the CIA advised the press that this
dissemination should not have been made to CIA.   However, it
is now developed that the CIA representative making this
statement to the press was unaware at the time that the disseminated document contained information regarding the protest
against the CIA.   Liaison Officer ascertained that the Director
of Security of CIA asked that the FBI meet with him on Monday,
6/28/76, for further discussions concerning this matter.

RECOMMENDATION:

          For information. Results of conference with CIA on
6/28/76, will be furnished along with appropriate recommendations
concerning the handling of matters described above.

APPROVED: _____   Ext. Affairs ....   Laboratory ....
Assoc. Dir. _____   Fin. & Pers. ......   Legal Coun. _____
Dep. AD Adm. ....   Gen. Inv. ....   Plan. & Eval. ....
Dep. AD Inv. _____   Ident. ....   Rec. Mgmt. ....
Asst. Dir.: ,   Inspection _____   Spec. Inv. ....
Adm. Serv. ....   Intell. _____   Training ....

develop security plans countering "expected AIM terrorism" – Benson staged a
pretrial hearing on January 14, 1977.[174] During the proceeding, he announced the
trial of Leonard Peltier would be moved from its scheduled location in Cedar
Rapids, where AIM had developed strong support, to the far more conservative
Fargo, North Dakota. He also began a sequence of evidentiary rulings which
precluded Peltier's attorneys from developing the sort of self-defense case – center-
ing on the FBI's COINTELPRO operations against AIM and other dissident groups
– which had proven successful in the Butler-Robideau trial.[175]

Meanwhile, the U.S. was engaged in fraudulently extraditing Peltier from
Canada. This was done on the basis of a single piece of substantive evidence, an
affidavit sworn to by an Oglala woman named Myrtle Poor Bear, who was supposedly an eyewitness to the deaths of Williams and Coler. As it turned out, Poor Bear
had a history of deep psychological disorder, for which she had undergone extensive treatment. This seems to have been a matter well known to FBI agents David
Price and William Wood when they essentially abducted her – she was charged
with, and apparently suspected of, no particular crime – and held her incommuni-
cado in motels in Gordon, Nebraska and Sturgis, South Dakota for approximately
one month.[176] During this period, the agents prepared, and Poor Bear signed, not one
but three mutually contradictory affidavits concerning Peltier's "guilt" in the
RESMURS matter.[177] In the documents (which accompany this text), Poor Bear
variously claimed to have witnessed and not to have witnessed the shootings, and
to have been a "girl friend" of Peltier, to whom he "confessed" his deeds. At more
or less the same time, Poor Bear was also signing affidavits prepared by Price and

NR005 RC PLAIN

7:28PM URGENT JULY 20, 1976 DCW

TO: DIRECTOR, FBI

F   CHICAGO

FROM: ASAC, RAPID CITY (70-L0239) (P)

ATTENTION: GENERAL INVESTIGATIVE DIVISION; GENERAL CRIMES

UNIT.

RESMURS, RE ANALYSIS OF ROBIDEAU AND BUTLER TRIAL.

RE BUREAU TELEPHONE CALL JULY L9, L976 REQUESTING

INFORMATION AS TO POSSIBLE REASONS WHY JURY FOUND DEFENDANTS

ROBIDEAU AND BUTLER NOT GUILTY ON JULY L6, L976.

IT IS FELT THAT SUFFICIENT TESTIMONY FOR CONVICTION

OF DEFENDANTS WAS PRESENTED TO THE JURY. FOR EXAMPLE,

AN EYE WITNESS, I/M NORMAN BROWN TESTIFIED THAT HE OB-

SERVED BOTH DEFENDANTS FIRING SHOULDER WEAPONS AT SA'S

WILLIAMS AND COLER. ANOTHER EYE WITNESS, I/M, WILFRED

DRAPER, OBSERVED ROBIDEAU LEAVE CRIME SCENE CARRYING

SHOTGUN WITH "FBI DENVER" ON STOCK AND ALSO PLACED WEAPONS

IN THE HANDS OF THE DEFENDANTS WHICH WERE LINKED TO THE

CRIME SCENE THROUGH SHELL CASINGS LOCATED AT THE CRIME

SCENE. IN ADDITION, DRAPER TESTIFIED TO A CONVERSATION   22 JUL ·· 1976

HE OVERHEARD BETWEEN PELTIER, ROBIDEAU AND BUTLER WHEREBY

PELTIER STATED HE MOVED THE AGENTS AROUND THE CAR SO THAT

June 1976 teletype analyzing the recently concluded Cedar Rapids trial of Dino Butler and Bob Robideau. The purpose of the document is to determine "what went wrong" with the case against the first two RESMURS defendants, with an eye towards rigging the rules of the upcoming Peltier trial in order to obtain a conviction (continued on next 3 pages).

ROBIDEAU AND BUTLER COULD FINISH THEM OFF.

A CELLMATE OF BUTLER'S TESTIFIED REGARDING DETAILED
ADMISSIONS BY BUTLER RE KILLINGS OF AGENTS.

PHYSICAL EVIDENCE WAS PRESENTED LINKING DEFENDANTS
TO CRIME SCENE INCLUDING ROBIDEAU'S FINGERPRINT FOUND INSIDE
THE DOOR HANDLE OF WILLIAMS' CAR. ADDITIONAL TESTIMONY
REVEALED THAT COLER'S .308 CARBINE WAS FOUND IN
ROBIDEAU'S CAR AT WICHITA, KANSAS, WITH ONE OTHER
WEAPON LINKED TO THE CRIME SCENE.

THE ABOVE ARE ONLY SOME EXAMPLES OF KEY EVIDENCE
PRESENTED BY THE GOVERNMENT DURING THE TRIAL.

ACCORDING TO NEWS ACCOUNTS SETTING FORTH RESULTS
OF INTERVIEW OF CERTAIN JURORS, THE JURY APPARENTLY WANTED
THE GOVERNMENT TO SHOW THAT ROBIDEAU AND BUTLER ACTUALLY
PULLED THE TRIGGER AT CLOSE RANGE. EVIDENTLY, DRAPER'S
STATEMENT SET OUT ABOVE DID NOT ACCOMPLISH THIS.

SET FORTH BELOW ARE SOME OF THE REASONS POSSIBLY LEADING
TO ACQUITTAL.

L. DURING COURSE OF TRIAL, THE COURT, APPLYING
"COLLATERAL ESTOPPEL", PROHIBITED GOVERNMENT FROM
ENTERING INTO EVIDENCE CERTAIN KEY EXHIBITS; SIX CASINGS
FIRED FROM SA COLER'S REVOLVER, SIX CASINGS FIRED FROM
SA WILLIAMS' REVOLVER. THESE ITEMS LOCATED IN ONE-ROOM
CABIN WHERE DEFENDANT BUTLER WAS ARRESTED SEPTEMBER 5, L975.
IN ADDITION, AN M-L RIFLE LINKED TO CRIME SCENE BY SHELL
CASINGS, LOCATED IN SAME CABIN WHERE BUTLER WAS ARRESTED
WAS NOT ALLOWED TO BE CONNECTED WITH DEFENDANT BUTLER UNDER
THIS RULING. THE JUDGE'S RULING IN THIS MATTER
IS INCONSISTANT WITH PREVIOUS JUDICIAL RULINGS.

2. OVER STRONG OBJECTIONS BY GOVERNMENT, THE
DEFENSE WAS ALLOWED FREEDOM OF QUESTIONING OF WITNESSES
RAISING INNUENDO WITH IRRELEVANT, IMMATERIAL AND
HERESAY TESTIMONY.

3. THE COURT ALLOWED TESTIMONY CONCERNING PAST
ACTIVITIES OF THE FBI RELATING TO THE COINTEL PRO AND SUB-
SEQUENTLY ALLOWED THE CHURCH REPORT INTO EVIDENCE.

4. THE COURT RULINGS RELATING TO BRADY AND
JENCKS MATERIAL FORCED THE GOVERNMENT TO FURNISH THE
DEFENSE WITH ALL FD-302'S PREPARED BY SPECIAL AGENTS
WHO TESTIFIED FOR THE GOVERNMENT. THIS AGAIN
IS INCONSISTENT WITH PREVIOUS INTERPRETATIONS OF THE JENCKS
RULE.

5. THE JUDGE RECESSED TRIAL FOR TEN DAYS FOLLOWING
PRESENTATION OF GOVERNMENT'S CASE TO ATTEND A JUDICIAL
CONFERENCE. THIS ALLOWED THE DEFENSE ADDITIONAL TIME TO
REBUT GOVERNMENT'S CASE AND CAUSED A GREATER TIME SPAN
FROM THE GOVERNMENT'S PRESENTATION TO TIME OF DELIBERATION
BY THE JURY.

6. THE COURT CONTINUALLY OVERRULED GOVERNMENT
OBJECTIONS AND ALLOWED IRRELEVANT EVIDENCE; FOR EXAMPLE,
INTRODUCTION OF SEVEN BUREAU DOCUMENTS (SIX TELETYPES AND
ONE TERRORIST DIGEST) WHICH WERE DISSEMINATED AT HEADQUARTERS
LEVEL TO OTHER LAW ENFORCEMENT AGENCIES. AS A RESULT,
THE DEFENSE INFERRED THE FBI CREATED A CLIMATE OF FEAR ON
THE RESERVATION WHICH PRECIPITATED THE MURDERS. THE
DEFENSE, THROUGH THE INTRODUCTION OF THESE DOCUMENTS,
ATTEMPTED TO REDUCE THE CREDIBILITY OF SPECIAL AGENT
TESTIMONY.

7. THE DEFENSE WAS UNCONTROLLED IN ITS DEALINGS WITH
THE NEWS MEDIA DUE TO LACK OF "GAG" RULE, HOWEVER, THE
PROSECUTION WAS UNABLE TO COMMENT TO THE NEWS MEDIA.

8. THE JURY WAS NOT SEQUESTERED, THEREFORE, IT HAD
AVAILABLE NUMEROUS HEADLINES ADVERSE TO THE GOVERNMENT
AND THE RESULTS OF DAILY CONFERENCES WITH NEWS MEDIA
BY DEFENSE COUNSEL. DURING TRIAL NUMEROUS PRESS REPORTS
DETRIMENTAL TO THE FBI IN UNRELATED MATTERS APPEARED IN

LOCAL NEWSPAPER.

9. IT APPEARED THAT THE JURY HAD A DIFFICULT TIME
PUTTING THE CASE TOGETHER BECAUSE OF THE NUMEROUS SIDEBARS
WHICH DETRACTED FROM THE PRESENTATION AND FLOW OF THE
CASE TO THE JURY, NOTING THAT THIS CASE IS MOST COMPLI-
CATED.

ON JULY L7, L976, THE CEDAR RAPIDS "GAZETTE" CARRIED
A NEWS ARTICLE RECORDING THE RESULTS OF AN INTERVIEW WITH
JURY FOREMAN. THE FOREMAN IN THIS ARTICLE STATED IT WAS
THE CONCENSUS OF THE L2 INDIVIDUALS THAT "THE GOVERNMENT
JUST DID NOT PRODUCE SUFFICIENT EVIDENCE OF GUILT". HE
STATED THAT IN THE END ANALYSIS THOSE JURORS WHO ARGUED
FOR CONVICTION ADMITTED THAT REASONABLE DOUBT DID EXIST.
THE JURY FOREMAN STATED ALL AGREED THAT EXCESSIVE FORCE
WAS USED ON JUNE 26, L975, BUT THAT THE GOVERNMENT DID NOT
SHOW THAT EITHER OF THE DEFENDANTS DID IT. THE ARTICLE
FURTHER RELATED "AND WHILE IT WAS SHOWN THAT THE DEFENDANTS
WERE FIRING GUNS IN THE DIRECTION OF THE AGENTS, IT WAS HELD
BY THE JURORS THAT THIS WAS NOT EXCESSIVE IN THE HEAT OF
PASSION. HE SAID AN IMPORTANT FACET WAS THE DEFENSE'S
CONTENTION THAT AN ATMOSPHERE OF FEAR AND VIOLENCE EXISTED
ON THE RESERVATION AND THAT THE DEFENDANTS ARGUABLY COULD
HAVE BEEN SHOOTING IN SELF-DEFENSE. THE AIDING AND ABETTING
THEORY WAS, IN THE END, DISMISSED BECAUSE THE JURORS WERE
NOT CONVINCED THE DEFENDANTS KNEW THE AGENTS WERE TO BE
KILLED AND THEREFORE, ACCORDING TO THE LAW, COULD NOT BE
HELD RESPONSIBLE".

THIS NEWS ARTICLE, ALONG WITH OTHERS APPEARING IN THE
"GAZETTE" BEING FORWARDED TO THE BUREAU FOR ITS REVIEW.

IT IS NOTED THE DEFENSE UTILIZED DURING THIS TRIAL
THE SERVICES OF NINE ATTORNEYS, MANY OF WHICH WERE VASTLY
EXPERIENCED IN CRIMINAL DEFENSE.

CHICAGO BEING FURNISHED COPY FOR SAC INFORMATION.

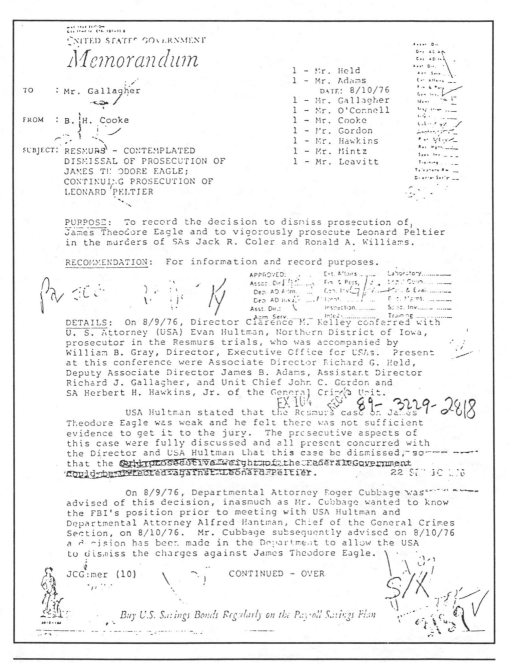

UNITED STATES GOVERNMENT

Memorandum

TO : Mr. Gallagher

FROM : B. H. Cooke

SUBJECT: RESMURS - CONTEMPLATED
DISMISSAL OF PROSECUTION OF
JAMES THEODORE EAGLE;
CONTINUING PROSECUTION OF
LEONARD PELTIER

DATE: 8/10/76

1 - Mr. Held
1 - Mr. Adams
1 - Mr. Gallagher
1 - Mr. O'Connell
1 - Mr. Cooke
1 - Mr. Gordon
1 - Mr. Hawkins
1 - Mr. Mintz
1 - Mr. Leavitt

PURPOSE: To record the decision to dismiss prosecution of
James Theodore Eagle and to vigorously prosecute Leonard Peltier
in the murders of SAs Jack R. Coler and Ronald A. Williams.

RECOMMENDATION: For information and record purposes.

DETAILS: On 8/9/76, Director Clarence M. Kelley conferred with
U. S. Attorney (USA) Evan Hultman, Northern District of Iowa,
prosecutor in the Resmurs trials, who was accompanied by
William B. Gray, Director, Executive Office for USAs. Present
at this conference were Associate Director Richard G. Held,
Deputy Associate Director James B. Adams, Assistant Director
Richard J. Gallagher, and Unit Chief John C. Gordon and
SA Herbert H. Hawkins, Jr. of the General Crime Unit.

USA Hultman stated that the Resmurs case on James
Theodore Eagle was weak and he felt there was not sufficient
evidence to get it to the jury. The prosecutive aspects of
this case were fully discussed and all present concurred with
the Director and USA Hultman that this case be dismissed, so
that the full prosecutive weight of the Federal Government
could be directed against Leonard Peltier.

On 8/9/76, Departmental Attorney Roger Cubbage was
advised of this decision, inasmuch as Mr. Cubbage wanted to know
the FBI's position prior to meeting with USA Hultman and
Departmental Attorney Alfred Hantman, Chief of the General Crimes
Section, on 8/10/76. Mr. Cubbage subsequently advised on 8/10/76
a decision has been made in the Department to allow the USA
to dismiss the charges against James Theodore Eagle.

JCG:mer (10)   CONTINUED - OVER

Buy U.S. Savings Bonds Regularly on the Payroll Savings Plan

August 1976 memo capsulizing the decision to drop RESMURS charges against Jimmy
Eagle in order to place "full prosecutive weight of the Federal Government" upon Leonard
Peltier It should be noted the FBI earlier alleged that Eagle had "confessed."

Affidavit

Myrtle Poor Bear, being first duly sworn, deposes and states:

1. I am an American Indian born February 20, 1952, and reside at Allen, South Dakota, one of the United States of America.

2. I first met Leonard Peltier in Bismarck, North Dakota, during 1971. During March, 1975, I again met Leonard Peltier at St. Francis, South Dakota, United States of America. During April, 1975, I went to North Dakota to see him as a girl friend of his. About the last week of May during 1975 I and Leonard Peltier went to the Jumping Bull Hall near Oglala, South Dakota, United States of America. There were several houses and about four or five tents. When Leonard Peltier arrived, he gave orders on what was to be done. I was his girl friend at this time. About a week after we arrived, about the second week of June, 1975, Leonard Peltier and several others began planning how to kill either Bureau of Indian Affairs Department, United States Government police or Federal Bureau of Investigation, United States Government, agents who might come into the area. Leonard Peltier was mostly in charge of the planning. All persons involved in the planning had special assignments. There was also a detailed escape route planned over the hills near the Jumping Bull Hall area. I was present during this planning. Leonard Peltier always had a rifle and usually had a pistol near him. The pistol was usually under a car seat. About one day before the Special Agents of the Federal Bureau of Investigation were killed, Leonard Peltier said he knew the Federal Bureau of Investigation or the Bureau of Indian Affairs were coming to serve an arrest warrant on Jimmy Eagle. Leonard Peltier told people to get ready to kill them and he told me to get my car filled with gas to be ready for an escape. I left Jumping Bull Hall at this point and did not return. During August, 1975, I met Leonard Peltier again at Crow Dog's Paradise on the Rosebud Indian Reservation, South Dakota, United States of America. We talked about the killing of the two Federal Bureau of Investigation agents near Jumping Bull Hall. Leonard said it makes him sick when he thinks about it. He said that one of the agents surrendered, but he kept shooting. He said it was like a movie he was watching but it was real, he was acting right in it. He said he lost his mind and just started shooting. He said he shot them and just kept pulling the trigger and couldn't stop.

Subscribed and sworn to before me this 19th day of February, 1976.

/s/
Deputy Clerk
United States District Court
District of South Dakota

/s/
Myrtle Poor Bear

Affidavit 1, in which SAs David Price and William Wood have Myrtle Poor Bear recounting how it was she who overheard the planning of the Northwest AIM group to lure SAs Coler and Williams to their deaths in an ambush. Note that there is no claim Poor Bear witnessed the firefight, but that she heard Leonard Peltier order the agents killed beforehand, and that he later "confessed to her."

Affidavit 2, in which SAs Price and Wood not only have Poor Bear, as Peltier's "girl friend," overhear RESMURS planning, but witness Peltier killing both agents. Note details on escape route designed to explain away the Bureau's embarrassing inability to apprehend suspects at the scene of the firefight. Also note how the method of killing corresponds to the FBI's contrived "execution" scenario.

Affidavit

Myrtle Poor Bear, being first duly sworn, deposes and states:

1. I am an American Indian born February 20, 1952, and reside at Allen, South Dakota, one of the United States of America.

2. I first met Leonard Peltier in Bismarck, North Dakota, during 1971. During March, 1975, I again met Leonard Peltier at St. Francis, South Dakota, United States of America. During April, 1975, I went to North Dakota to see him as a girl friend of his. About the last week of May during 1975 I and Leonard Peltier went to the Jumping Bull Hall near Oglala, South Dakota, United States of America. There were several houses and about four or five tents. When Leonard Peltier arrived, he gave orders on what was to be done. I was his girl friend at this time. About a week after we arrived, about the second week of June, 1975, Leonard Peltier and several others began planning how to kill either Bureau of Indian Affairs Department, United States Government police or Federal Bureau of Investigation, United States Government, agents who might come into the area. Leonard Peltier was mostly in charge of the planning. All persons involved in the planning had special assignments. There was also a detailed escape route planned over the hills near the Jumping Bull Hall area. I was present during this planning. Leonard Peltier always had a rifle and usually had a pistol near him. The pistol was usually under a car seat. About one day before the Special Agents of the Federal Bureau of Investigation were killed, Leonard Peltier said he knew the Federal Bureau of Investigation or the Bureau of Indian Affairs were coming to serve an arrest warrant on Jimmy Eagle. Leonard Peltier told people to get ready to kill them and he told me to get my car filled with gas to be ready for an escape, which I did. I was present the day the Special Agents of the Federal Bureau of Investigation were killed. I saw Leonard Peltier shoot the FBI agents. During August, 1975, I met Leonard Peltier again at Crow Dog's Paradise on the Rosebud Indian Reservation, South Dakota, United States of America. We talked about the killing of the two Federal Bureau of Investigation agents near Jumping Bull Hall. Leonard said it makes him sick when he thinks about it. He said that one of the agents surrendered, but he kept shooting. He said it was like a movie he was watching but it was real, he was acting right in it. He said he lost his mind and just started shooting. He said he shot them and just kept pulling the trigger and couldn't stop.

Subscribed and sworn to before me this 23rd day of February, 1976.

/s/
Deputy Clerk
United States District Court
District of South Dakota

/s/
Myrtle Poor Bear

UNITED STATES OF AMERICA
STATE OF SOUTH DAKOTA
COUNTY OF PENNINGTON

IN THE MATTER OF THE EXTRADITION ACT. R.S.C. 1970 CHAP.
E-21 AND IN THE MATTER OF LEONARD PELTIER, ALSO
KNOWN AS LEONARD LITTLE SHELL, LEONARD WILLIAMS,
JOHN YELLOW ROBE, ERWIN YELLOW ROBE, LEONARD
JOHN PELTIER

Affidavit

Myrtle Poor Bear, being first duly sworn, deposes and states:

1. That I am the Myrtle Poor Bear, of Allen, South Dakota, United States of America, who was the deponent in an affidavit sworn the 23rd day of February, 1976. This affidavit is sworn by me to give further information.

2. Attached hereto and marked Exhibit "A" to this, my Affidavit, is a photograph marked February 12, 1976, and I testify and depose that the person shown on the said photograph is a person known to me as Leonard Peltier and is the person I spoke of in my deposition of February 23, 1976, and the person referred to herein as Leonard Peltier.

3. I recall the events of June 26, 1975, which occurred at the area of Jumping Bull Hall near Oglala on the Pine Ridge Indian Reservation in the State of South Dakota, United States of America.

4. Sometime during the early part of that day, at approximately 12:00 Noon, Leonard Peltier came into the residence of Harry Jumping Bull which is located in the area of Jumping Bull Hall and said, "They're coming." I understood this to mean that police or agents of the Federal Bureau of Investigation were in the immediate area. A short time later, I saw a car which I recognized to be a government car near Harry Jumping Bull's house. I went down to the creek bottom a couple of hundred yards from the house. I heard shooting. I left the creek bottom area and walked approximately 50 yards to where I saw two cars, both of which I recognized to be government cars, because of the large radio antennaes mounted on the rear of these cars and I had previously seen many cars of a similar type driven by government agents in the same area. When I got to the car, Leonard Peltier was facing a man which I believed to be a special agent of the Federal Bureau of Investigation. This man was tall with dark hair. This man threw a handgun to the side and said something to the effect that he was surrendering. Leonard Peltier was pointing a rifle in the direction of this man. The man was holding his arm as if he was wounded and was leaning against the car previously mentioned. There was another man who I believed to be a special agent of the Federal Bureau of Investigation lying face down on the ground and there was blood underneath him. I started to leave and was grabbed by the hair by another person and could not

Affidavit 3, actually submitted to the Canadian courts, in which the agents totally abandon the notion of Poor Bear's having overheard planning for an ambush. Instead they have their victim provide considerable additional detail as an "eyewitness." Note also the absence of any alleged confession on the part of Leonard Peltier.

Wood to the effect that she was the girl friend of another AIM leader, Richard Marshall, to whom he had confessed the murder of an Oglala named Martin Montileaux. The Poor Bear "information" was the decisive factor in Marshall's first degree murder conviction and receipt of a life sentence on April 6, 1976.[178] It was also the key ingredient in Canadian Justice W.A. Schultz's determination that Leonard Peltier should be extradited to the U.S., reached on June 18, 1976, and Minister of Justice Ron Basford's order that the extradition be executed on December 16, 1976.[179]

Poor Bear later recanted all

get away. I turned again and saw Leonard Peltier shoot the man who was standing against the car. I heard a shot come from the rifle that Leonard Peltier was holding and I saw that rifle jump up still in his hands. I saw that man's body jump into the air and fall to the ground. The man fell face down on the ground. This happened in an instant. I freed myself from the person that was holding me and ran up to Leonard Peltier just as he was aiming his rifle at the man who had just fallen to the ground. I pounded Leonard Peltier on the back. He yelled something at me which I cannot recall. I turned, ran and left the area. As I was running away, I heard several more shots from the area from which I had just fled.

Subscribed and sworn to before me this 31st day of March, 1976.

/s/
Deputy Clerk
United States District Court
District of South Dakota

/s/
Myrtle Poor Bear

"evidence" she'd offered – both by affidavit and through direct testimony – against Peltier and Marshall, contending that she had been grossly coerced by the FBI into providing false information (e.g.: she'd witnessed nothing, and knew neither man in any way at all).[180] Among the methods used to achieve these results, aside from her virtual kidnapping by Price and Wood, appear to have been the use of morgue photos of the body of AIM member Anna Mae Aquash, who had earlier reported being threatened with death by Price unless she cooperated in the RESMURS investigation.[181] Having been hustled back to South Dakota from Oregon by SA J. Gary Adams on February 10, after being arrested in the Brando motor home, Aquash had promptly disappeared. Her body – dead for several days –was discovered in a ravine near the village of Wanblee by Oglala rancher Roger Amiotte on February 24, 1976. Price was among a number of lawmen who atypically gathered to view the corpse in situ at this remote location, but claimed not to recognize the victim.[182] He and his partner, William Wood, then followed the ambulance carrying the body all the way to the Pine Ridge Hospital morgue (some 115 miles) where an autopsy was performed by the faithful coroner, W.O. Brown. Brown pronounced death to have been caused by "exposure," and ordered burial in a common grave at the nearby Red Cloud Cemetery. Prior to burial, Wood caused "Jane Doe's" hands to be severed and shipped – as is shown in the accompanying February 26, 1976 airtel from the Minneapolis SAC to Kelley – to the FBI crime lab in Washington, D.C., for "identification purposes."[183]

The hands were identified as belonging to Anna Mae Pictou Aquash on March 3 (see accompanying Identification Division report, dated March 10, 1976) and the

```
                            2/26/76


RTEL



        DIRECTOR, FBI (ATTN. LATENT FINGERPRINT SECTION)
OM:     SAC, MINNEAPOLIS (70-NEW) (P)
BJECT:  UNSUB; UNKNOWN VICTIM-DECEASED
        INDIAN FEMALE LOCATED AT
        WANBLEE, SOUTH DAKOTA
        2/24/76
        CIR - POSSIBLE MANSLAUGHTER
        OO: MINNEAPOLIS

        Re:  Rapid City nitel dated 2/24/76.

        Enclosed herewith is one pair of hands taken from
sub at the time of autopsy on 2/25/76.  Unsub located by
A officers on the Pine Ridge Indian Reservation, 2/24/76.
aliminary autopsy failed to determine cause of death,
wever, pathologist determined unsub to be Indian female,
-25 years of age, 5'2" tall, weighing 110 pounds, having
dergone gall blader surgery and childbirth.

        The Laboratory is requested to conduct appropriate
amination in an effort to obtain and identify fingerprints.





- Bureau
  1 - Package (RM)(in a man.l)
- Minneapolis
```

"Enclosed...one pair of hands." Airtel sent as cover with the box containing
Anna Mae Aquash's body parts to the FBI crime lab. It should be noted that
had the Bureau followed usual procedures in attempting identification by
dental x-ray, the bullet lodged in the victim's skull would have been revealed.

victim's family in Nova Scotia, suspecting foul play, requested that WKLDOC
attorney Bruce Ellison file for exhumation of the body and an independent autopsy.[184]
This was conducted by Minneapolis pathologist Garry Peterson on March 11. In less
than five minutes, Peterson concluded that death was caused, not by exposure, but
by a lead slug "consistent with being of either .32 or .38 caliber" having been fired
point blank into the base of the skull.[185] In Rapid City, ASAC Zigrossi thereupon
announced a homicide investigation was being opened into the matter (it is
apparently still ongoing, nearly 14 years later).[186] But by then, according to subse-

```
:: ::: FEDERAL BUREAU OF INVES. GATION
                Washington, D. C. 20535
                   REPORT
                   of the
           IDENTIFICATION  DIVISION
           LATENT FINGERPRINT SECTION

: FILE NO.                      March 10, 1976
  H.F NO.
  NT CASE NO. B-26932

SAC, Minneapolis




  INSUB.;
  UNKNOWN VICTIM - DECEASED
  INDIAN FEMALE LOCATED AT
  WANBLEE, SOUTH DAKOTA
  2/24/76
  CIR - POSSIBLE MANSLAUGHTER


  RENCE:   Airtel 2/26/76
  INATION REQUESTED BY:    Minneapolis
  MENS:           One set of hands


          This report confirms and supplements Butel of
  /3/76.  This report also confirms and supplements Bucal
  o Rapid City, RA on 3/3/76.

          See attached page for result of comparison of
  inger impression obtained from submitted hands with
  ingerprints of Annie Mae Aquash, FBI #275229P1.

          Specimens being returned under separate
  over.
```

Lab report confirming positive identification of "Jane Doe," dead on Pine Ridge of alleged exposure, as Anna Mae Aquash, who in reality had been shot, execution-style, in the back of the head. Note return of "specimens" to Rapid City.

quent testimony, agents Price and Wood had already – long since – taken to showing the morgue photos to Myrtle Poor Bear, identifying the "unidentified" corpse as being that of Aquash, and explaining to their captive that she'd end up "the same way" unless she did exactly what they wanted. Poor Bear quoted Wood as informing her, in specific reference to Aquash, that "they [Price and Wood] could get away with killing because they were agents."[187]

In any event, with Peltier illegally but securely in custody, and with the defense's hands tied by Judge Benson's odd assortment of evidentiary rulings, the

FBI set about fabricating a "factual" basis upon which prosecutor Hultman could obtain a conviction. First, Bureau ballistics experts "established" – on the basis of no tangible evidence whatsoever – that Williams and Coler had been killed by shots fired from a .223 caliber AR-15 rifle.[188] A highly circumstantial case that an AR-15 had been fired into the agents at close range was made through introduction of a single shell casing allegedly found in the trunk of Coler's car (which had been open during the fighting),supposedly discovered, not during the FBI's initial examination of the car, but at some point well after the fact.[189] Then, the head of the Bureau's Firearms and Tool Marks Unit, Evan Hodge, falsely cast the impression – the FBI already having (and hiding) conclusive evidence to the contrary – that only one AR-15 was used by the Indians during the Oglala firefight.[190] From there, Hodge, went on to testify that he had been able to link the cartridge casing purportedly recovered from Coler's trunk to a weapon used by the Northwest AIM group and found in Bob Robideau's burned out car on the Kansas Turnpike. However, as is shown in the accompanying October 2, 1975 teletype from Hodge to Clarence Kelley, these ballistics tests had produced the exact opposite results.[191] But once the ballistics chief's assertions on the stand were accepted by the jury, it followed that whoever among the Northwest AIM group could be shown to have carried an AR-15 during the firefight would be viewed, *ipso facto*, as the "murderer."

Then came the *pièce de résistance*. SA Fred Coward was then put on the stand to testify – as he had *not* been at Cedar Rapids – that in the midst of the firefight he had been peering through a meager 2x7 rifle scope. At a distance of "approximately 800 meters" (about one-half mile), through severe atmospheric heat shimmers, he claimed to have recognized Leonard Peltier, whom he admitted he had never seen before that moment. Peltier, Coward claimed, was running away from the location of the dead agents' cars – at an oblique angle to Coward's position, so that the identification had necessarily to be made in profile – carrying an AR-15 rifle.[192] With that, AUSA Lynn Crooks, who at Cedar Rapids had vociferously contended that Coler and Williams had died at the hands of a "gang of ruthless ambushers,"reversed himself before the Fargo jury arguing that Peltier had been a "lone gunman":

Apparently Special Agent Williams was killed first. He was shot in the face and hand by a bullet...probably begging for his life, and he was shot. The back of his head was blown off by a high powered rifle...Leonard Peltier then turned, as the evidence indicates, to Jack Coler lying on the ground helpless. He shoots him in the top of the head. Apparently feeling he hadn't done a good enough job, he shoots him again through the jaw, and his face explodes. No shell even comes out, just explodes. The whole bottom of his chin is blown out by the force of the concussion. Blood splattered against the side of the car.[193]

Under the weight of such cynical and deliberately sensational closing argumentation, unhampered by a number of exculpatory documents the FBI had illegally withheld despite defense discovery motions, the jury found Peltier guilty on two counts of first degree murder on April 18, 1977. Judge Benson then again did his part, passing life sentences on each count, to run consecutively. Contrary to stated U.S. Bureau of Prisons (BoP) policy – which held at the time that the facility was reserved for "incorrigible" repeat offenders (Peltier had no prior convictions) and those who have created major problems within other facilities of the federal prison system – the defendant was taken directly to the super-maximum security federal prison at Marion, Illinois.

An appeal of Peltier's conviction was immediately filed with the U.S. Eighth Circuit Court of Appeals, based more-or-less equally on Judge Benson's evidentiary rulings and documented FBI misconduct both in and out of court. The appeals case was compelling, as is reflected in the observation of one of the judges on the three member panel, Donald Ross, in connection with the Poor Bear affidavits:

> But can't you see...that what happened, happened in such a way that it gives some credence to the claim of the...Indian people that the United States is willing to resort to any tactic in order to bring somebody back to the United States from Canada. *And if they are willing to do that, they must be willing to fabricate other evidence as well*[emphasis added].[194]

In the end, however, while noting serious problems with the FBI's handling of "certain matters," and consequently expressing considerable "discomfort" with their decision, the court opted to allow the judgment against Peltier to stand on February 14, 1978.[195] An explanation of this strange performance may perhaps be found in the fact that shortly thereafter, William Webster – Chief Judge of the Eighth Circuit Court, and initial chair of the panel which considered Peltier's appeal – left the court for a new job: he had been named *Director of the FBI*, a matter of which he was aware well before the Peltier decision was tendered.[196] On February 11, 1979, the U.S. Supreme Court refused, without explanation, to review the lower court's decision.[197]

In 1981, as a result of an FOIA suit filed by Peltier's attorneys, some 12,000 pages of previously classified FBI documents relating to the Peltier case were released (another 6,000-odd pages were withheld under the aegis of "national security" in this purely domestic matter).[198] Based upon precedents that the withholding of exculpatory evidence – such as the accompanying October 2, 1975 ballistics teletype – by the prosecution was grounds for retrial, an appeals team filed a motion in this regard with Judge Paul Benson in April of 1982. Since certain documents obtained through the FOIA also revealed what appear to have been improper pretrial meetings between the prosecution, the FBI and Benson, the judge was simultaneously asked to remove himself from further involvement in the proceedings.[199] This was essentially *pro forma*; given his previous record in the Peltier case, few were surprised when Benson rejected both of these motions on December 30, 1982.

A new appeal was then filed with the Eighth Circuit Court and, on April 4, 1984, the appeals court reversed Benson's decision. Citing the apparent contradiction

PLAINTEXT   TELETYPE   URGENT

1-Mr. Callahan
1-Mr. Gordon
1-Mr. E. Hodge
COMMUNICATIONS SECTION

TO SAC, RAPID CITY (70-10239)

FROM DIRECTOR FBI (89-3229)

RESMURS

OCT 0 2 1975
1207pam
TELETYPE

REFERENCE YOUR TELETYPE 9/12/75 AND LABORATORY REPORT
PC-N0133 NM, 8/5/75.

THE .308 WINCHESTER CALIBER REMINGTON MODEL 760, CARBINE,
SERIAL NUMBER OBLITERATED, OBTAINED FROM SPECIAL AGENT MIKE
GAMMAGE, BUREAU ALCOHOL, TOBACCO AND FIREARMS, (BATF) U.S.
TREASURY DEPARTMENT, WAS IDENTIFIED AS HAVING FIRED .308
WINCHESTER CALIBER CARTRIDGE CASE, Q336 IN REFERENCED LABORATORY
REPORT, RECOVERED AT RESMURS SCENE FROM DENVER BUCAR.

TRAINING DIVISION, QUANTICO, ADVISES THAT NO FIRED
SPECIMENS FROM THE .308 WINCHESTER CALIBER REMINGTON, MODEL
760, CARBINE, SERIAL NUMBER 6967042 ON FILE.

EFFORTS CONTINUING AT REMINGTON ARMS COMPANY TO SUPPLY
BUREAU WITH SERIAL NUMBERS OF ALL MODEL 760 CARBINES IN .308
WINCHESTER CALIBER PRODUCED AND SHIPPED TO CUSTOMERS FROM JULY
TO DECEMBER, 1969, IN ATTEMPT TO PROVE IDENTITY OF RECOVERED
CARBINE BY PROCESS OF ELIMINATION METHOD AS IT IS BELIEVED
MAJORITY OF THESE WEAPONS WERE PRODUCED FOR AND RECEIVED BY
THE BUREAU.

REC-61 89-3229 1675

RECOVERED .223 CALIBER COLT RIFLE RECEIVED FROM SA
BATF, CONTAINS DIFFERENT FIRING PIN THAN THAT IN RIFLE USED
AT RESMURS SCENE

b7C

EXAMINATIONS CONTINUING.

REPORT FOLLOWS.

This teletype, among the exculpatory documents withheld by the FBI during the trial of Leonard Peltier, shows that Bureau ballistics tests conclusively determined that the rifle attributed to the defendant had *not* fired the cartridge casing allegedly recovered from the trunk of SA Coler's car. FBI firearms expert Evan Hodge testified to the opposite at trial.

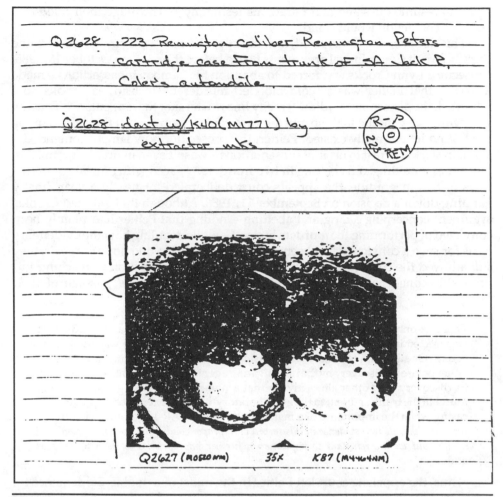

Q2628 .223 Remington caliber Remington-Peters cartridge case from trunk of SA Jack R. Coler's automobile.

Q2628 ident w/K40(M1771) by extractor mks

R-P
O
.223 REM

Q2627 (MOB20 NM)   35X   K87 (M4464NM)

FBI lab notes detailing firing pin test performed with the "Wichita AR-15," showing that it did not match the crucial casing recovered at RESMURS scene. At trial, Evan Hodge testified that the test was "inconclusive."

implied by the October 2, 1975 teletype, and the critical nature of the .223 casing to the government's case, the court ordered an evidentiary hearing on the ballistics evidence.[200] The hearing was held in Paul Benson's regular courtroom in Bismarck, North Dakota at the end of October 1984. There, a very nervous Evan Hodge explained that the conflict between his trial testimony and the documentary record arose from a "misinterpretation."[201] Although Hodge steadily dug the hole deeper and was eventually caught by William Kunstler committing what would for "civilians" be described as constituting perjury, Benson allowed the distraught agent to resume the stand and retract his testimony.[202] The judge then ruled that Peltier's conviction would stand.

This decision was anticipated, and the appeals team went straight back to the Eighth Circuit Court. In oral arguments heard before the court on October 15, 1985, prosecutor Lynn Crooks was forced to abandon his flamboyant assertions – made at trial – that Peltier was a "cold blooded murderer." Instead, as Crooks now admitted, the government "[didn't] really know who shot those agents."[203] Thus, he was willing to concede that the murder case conjured up against the defendant by the FBI no longer really existed. Peltier, the prosecutor now lamely contended – again in stark contrast to his trial presentations – wasn't even in prison for murder, but rather for aiding and abetting in two murders.[204] Faced with official contradictions of this magnitude, the appeals court deliberated for nearly a year, finally handing down a decision on September 11, 1986. Although they rejected Crooks' argument concerning aiding and abetting – noting that Peltier had plainly been convicted of performing the murders himself – while detailing how the evidentiary basis for such a conviction had been eroded, probably beyond hope of repair, they *still* allowed the conviction to stand. Their collective motivation in reaching this untenable conclusion was put straightforwardly in one brief passage of their opinion:

> There are only two alternatives...to the government's contention that the .223 casing was ejected into the trunk of Coler's car when the Wichita AR-15 was fired at the agents. One alternative is that the .223 casing was planted in the trunk of Coler's car either before its discovery by the investigating agents or by the agents who reported its discovery. The other alternative is that a non-matching casing was originally found in the trunk and sent to the FBI laboratory, only to be replaced by a matching casing when the importance of a match to the Wichita AR-15 became evident...*We recognize that there is evidence in this record of improper conduct on the part of some FBI agents, but we are reluctant to impute even further improprieties to them* [emphasis added].[205]

Thus, the appellate court left Peltier in the midst of a double-life sentence for "crimes" both it and the trial prosecutor acknowledged had never been proven rather than delve more deeply into the illegal FBI activities attending his case. The defense immediately petitioned for reconsideration by the full Eighth Circuit Court rather than the three member panel – composed of Judges Gerald Heaney, Donald Ross and John Gibson – which had rendered the decision.[206] The *en banc* hearing was denied several months later, a development which left the appeals team with no alternative but to once again petition the Supreme Court.[207] On October 5, 1987, the high court refused, for the second time and again without explanation, to review the case of Leonard Peltier.[208] Judge Heaney later described the decision as the most difficult of his legal career because, in his view, "the FBI was at least as responsible for what happened as Leonard Peltier."[209] The judge failed to explain why, if this is the case, only Peltier is sitting in prison – without legal recourse – while the FBI agents involved have been allowed to simply go on about their business.

Implications of COINTELPRO–AIM

In many ways, the stark unwillingness of the federal government to accord Leonard Peltier even a modicum of elementary justice is symbolic of the entire AIM experience during the 1970s and, more broadly posed, of the U.S. relationship to American Indians since the first moment of the republic. The message embedded, not only in Peltier's imprisonment, but in the scores of murders, hundreds of shootings and beatings, endless show trials and all the rest of the systematic terrorization marking the FBI's anti-AIM campaign on Pine Ridge, was that the Bureau could and would make it cost-prohibitive for Indians to seriously challenge the lot assigned them by policy-makers and economic planners in Washington, D.C. The internal colonization of Native America is intended to be absolute and un-equivocal.

Thus it was that AIM, arguably the most hopeful vehicle for some meaningful degree of indigenous pride and self-determination in the U.S. during the late 20th century was destroyed as a viable national political organization. In the end, as Dennis Banks has observed:

> The FBI's tactics eventually proved successful in a peculiar sort of way. It's remarkable under the circumstances – and a real testament to the inner strength of the traditional Oglalas – that the feds were never really able to divide them from us, to have the traditionals denouncing us and working against us. But, in the end, the sort of pressure the FBI put on people on the reservation, particularly the old people, it just wore 'em down. A kind of fatigue set in. With the firefight at Oglala, and all the things that happened after that, it was easy to see we weren't going to win by direct confrontation. So the traditionals asked us to disengage, to try and take some of the heaviest pressure off. And, out of respect, we had no choice but to honor those wishes. And that was the end of AIM, at least in the way it had been known up till then. The resistance is still there, of course, and the struggle goes on, but the movement itself kind of disappeared.[210]

At another level, the nature of the FBI's assault against AIM during the mid-1970s demonstrated the willingness and ability of the Bureau to continue COIN-TELPRO-style operations even at the moment such methods were being roundly condemned by the Senate Select Committee on Intelligence Activities, and FBI officials at the highest levels were solemnly swearing before congress that all such "techniques" had been abandoned, long since. Indeed, as has been shown in this chapter, there is ample evidence that – at least in terms of sheer intensity and lethal results – the counterintelligence program directed at AIM represented a marked escalation over what had been done when such things had been designated by the formal COINTELPRO acronym. As Russell Means has put it, "COINTELPRO is COINTELPRO, no matter what they choose to call it."[211]

Further, getting away with COINTELPRO-AIM at the precise instant it was supposedly being chastised and "reformed" due to earlier COINTELPRO "ex-

> The government's right to continue full investigation of AIM and certain affiliated organizations may create relevant danger to a few citizen's privacy and free expression, but this danger must be weighed against society's right to protect itself against current domestic threats.
>
> The Supreme Court has observed that "unless the government safeguards its own capacity to function and to preserve the security of its people, society itself could become so disorderly that all rights and liberties would be endangered." United States v. United States District Court, 407 U. S. 297, 312 (1972).
>
> 2. Scope of Investigation
>
> Investigative Techniques
>
> The key to the successful investigation of AIM is substantial, live, quality informant coverage of its leaders and activities. In the past, this technique proved to be highly effective. ▓▓▓▓▓▓▓▓▓▓▓▓ As a result of certain disclosures regarding informants, AIM leaders have dispersed, have become extremely security conscious and literally suspect everyone. This paranoia works both for and against the movement and recent events support this observation. ▓▓▓▓
>
> When necessary, coverage is supplemented by certain techniques which would be sanctioned in preliminary and limited investigations.
>
> Physical surveillance is another useful technique and should be utilized when deemed appropriate.
>
> No mail covers or electronic surveillance have been used to investigate AIM and none is anticipated at this time. ▓▓▓▓

The logic of COINTELPRO, as evidenced in this excerpt from a 1976 document concerning the basis for an "investigation" of AIM and its supporters. Note the mention of the deliberate fostering of "paranoia" among AIM leaders through the use of informers, and insistence on the right of government to suppress dissent outweighs the rights of citizens to "privacy and free expression" (continued on next 2 pages).

cesses" appears to have inculcated within the Bureau hierarchy a truly overweening sense of arrogance.[212] They were quite prepared to openly defend the rationale of COINTELPRO, even while pretending to disavow it, a matter readily evidenced in the accompanying excerpt from the FBI's June 1976 "Predication for Investigation of Members and Supporters of AIM," a position paper drafted by Richard G. Held and delineating the thinking underlying what was being done to the organization. The right of the government to "defend itself" from dissent, in this official Bureau view, clearly outweighs the rights of citizens to "privacy and free expression."

In 1953, just prior to the passage of PL-280, Felix Cohen, one of the foremost scholars of Indian law compared the role of the Indians in America to that of the Jews

Review of existing publications dealing with AIM is, of course, a useful investigative tool.

It is noted, the Senate Select Committee on Intelligence, at the conclusion of its recent investigation concerning United States Intelligence agencies, recommended among other restraints, that court orders would be required for almost all "intrusive techniques including wiretaps, electronic bugs, mail covers, and etc., but not secret informants." Interestingly, the committee found that electronic surveillance had been used in only about 5% of all domestic investigations; whereas informants have played a role in 80%.

Dissemination

Reports are disseminated when appropriate, to interested agencies, including the Department of Justice, CIA, Secret Service, DIA, and Military Intelligence. In view of foreign travel by AIM leaders and interest in AIM abroad, periodic reports from and to foreign agencies, for information relative to above activities, as well as an interchange of information between the FBI and the CIA, is necessitated.

Due to the AIM's violence potential, which is frequently directed toward local and state governments and police officers, timely dissemination of specific intelligence information affecting their agencies, is of utmost importance.

Reporting

Reports concerning AIM will continue to be submitted semi-annually. Initial reports on leaders and members are evaluated to determine the need for future investigation and thereafter additional reports will be submitted annually or to meet dissemination requirements.

Because AIM is engaged in activities which involve the use of force or violence and the violation of Federal laws, it is recommended a full investigation be conducted of the movement and its national leaders. Full investigation of local AIM chapters its leaders, and members, should be recommended on an individual basis where information is confirmed after conducting a preliminary or limited investigation that the chapter or individual member is engaged in activities as set forth above.

If above recommendation is approved, additional investigation of individuals should be initiated based on allegations of involvement with this organization and involvement in activities indicating the possible use of force or violence and the violation of Federal laws. The purpose of such an investigation should be to fully identify the individual and determine the nature and extent of his activities. This investigation would normally be completed at the preliminary level, unless it is determined that the individual is in a position of leadership.

Any full investigation involves a degree of privacy invasion and that of a person's right to free expression. Informant coverage is the least intrusive investigative technique capable of producing the desired results. Thus, because of specific factors surrounding

this case, it is recommended that a full investigation
be conducted.

It is necessary that the federal government
do what is reasonable to protect itself. Many Americans
tend to overlook the fact that the United States has
constitutionally guaranteed rights which are just as
inviolate as those of the individual. To accept at face
value, an AIM argument, that it is being set upon by the
Central Intelligence Agency (CIA), FBI, and Bureau of
Indian Affairs (BIA), as part of a government conspiracy
to destroy the movement, and as a result, back off, would
result in the eventual abdication of this governmental
responsibility.

The government's right to investigate such
groups should be recognized and maintained.

The highest court in this country has ruled on
numerous occasions that the United States has the right
and duty to protect iself from anarchy and safeguard
itself from violence.

The Supreme Court has also stated, "We recognize
that domestic security surveillance may involve different
policy and practical considerations from the surveillance
of an 'ordinary crime.' The gathering of security intelligence
is often long — range and involves the interrelation of
various sources and types of information.

The exact targets of such surveillance may be
more difficult to identify than in surveillance operations
against many types of crimes in Title III. Often, too,
the emphasis of domestic intelligence gathering is on
the prevention of unlawful activity or the enhancement
of the government's preparedness of some possible future
crises or emergencies. Thus, the focus of domestic
surveillance may be less precise than that directed
against more conventional types of crime." United States v.
United States District Court, 407 U. S. 297, 312 (1972).

The outcome of future AIM agitation is unclear,
particularly in light of the possibility of two of its
main leaders being temporarily removed from society and
sent to prison in the near future. Although a number
of AIM lieutenants are "waiting in the wings," they
appear to lack charisma and backing the original leaders
enjoy.

in modern Germany. He noted that, "Like the miner's canary, the Indian marks the shift from fresh air to poison air in our political atmosphere...our treatment of Indians, even more than our treatment of other minorities, reflects the rise and fall of our democratic faith."[213] Given that all that happened on and around Pine Ridge occurred long after COINTELPRO allegedly became no more than a "regrettable historical anomaly,"[214] Cohen's insight holds particular significance for all Americans. In essence, if we may ascertain that COINTELPRO remained alive and well years after it was supposed to have died, we may assume it lives on today. And that, to be sure, is a danger to the lives and liberties of everyone.

Chapter 8

Conclusion
COINTELPRO Lives On

I tremble for my country when I reflect that God is just.

– Thomas Jefferson –

According to the official histories, COINTELPRO existed from late 1956 through mid-1971. During this period, the FBI admits to having engaged in a total of 2,218 separate COINTELPRO actions, many of them coupled directly with other sorts of systematic illegality such as the deployment of warrantless phone taps (a total of 2,305 admitted) and bugs (697 admitted) against domestic political targets, and receipt of correspondence secretly intercepted by the CIA (57,846 separate instances admitted). The chart on the following page illustrates the sweep of such activities during the COINTELPRO era proper.[1]

This however, is dramatically insufficient to afford an accurate impression of the scope, scale and duration of the Bureau's domestic counterinsurgency function. None of the FBI's vast proliferation of politically repressive operations conducted between 1918 and 1956, covered to some extent in the preceding chapters, are included in the figures. Similarly, it will be noted that certain years within the formal COINTELPRO period itself have been left unreported. Further, it should be noted that *none* of the Bureau's host of counterintelligence operations against the Puerto Rican *independentistas* during the years supposedly covered were included in the count. The same can be said with regard to COINTELPRO aimed at the Chicano movement from at least as early as 1967.[2]

Even in areas, such as its campaign against the Black Panther Party, where the FBI disclosed relatively large segments of its COINTELPRO profile, the record was left far from complete. During the various congressional committee investigations, the Bureau carefully hid the facts of its involvement in the 1969 Hampton-Clark assassinations.[3] Simultaneously, it was covering up its criminal withholding of exculpatory evidence in the murder trial of LA Panther leader Geronimo Pratt.[4] Recently, it has also come to light that the FBI denied information to congress concerning entirely similar withholding of exculpatory evidence in the murder trial of New York Panther leader Richard Dhoruba Moore.[5] How many comparable coverups are at issue with regard to the anti-Panther COINTELPRO alone remains a mystery. Given the Bureau's track record, on this score, however, it is abundantly clear that much of the worst of the FBI's performance against the Panthers remains "off record."

Admitted FBI Illegalities During the COINTELPRO Era				
Year	COINTELPROs	Taps	Bugs	Mail Openings
1956	N/A	N/A	N/A	N/A
1957	35	N/A	N/A	N/A
1958	51	N/A	N/A	666
1959	65	N/A	N/A	1964
1960	115	114	74	2342
1961	184	140	85	3520
1962	147	198	100	3017
1963	128	244	83	4167
1964	230	260	106	5396
1965	220	233	67	4503
1966	240	174	10	5984
1967	180	113	0	5863
1968	123	82	9	5322
1969	280	123	14	5384
1970	180	102	19	4975
1971	40	101	16	2701
1972	N/A	108	32	1400
1973	N/A	123	40	642
1974	N/A	190	42	N/A

Then there is the matter of the Bureau's continuation of domestic political counterintelligence operations after 1971 despite well-publicized governmental claims that the program ceased, and the FBI's abandonment of the acronym COIN-TELPRO itself. One indication of this is revealed in the accompanying chart. During the three years (1972-74) following the point at which COINTELPRO was supposedly terminated, the frequency with which the Bureau engaged in warrantless bugging and wiretapping increased dramatically (bugging from 16 instances in 1971 to 42 in 1974; wiretaps from 101 instances in 1971 to 190 in 1974). The relationship between these ELSUR activities and the fact that the FBI maintained an ongoing involvement in *de facto* COINTELPRO is brought out clearly in the accompanying July 29, 1975 teletype from Director Clarence Kelley to all SACs inquiring as to the proportion of "warrantless electronic surveillance" then being devoted to "counterintelligence purposes" associated with "domestic security investigations."[6]

The reality of COINTELPRO's continuation was masked not only behind the dropping of the descriptive title, but a retooling of the terminology utilized to define its targets as well. During the 1950s and early 1960s, the Bureau typically followed the McCarthyesque practice of defining those subject to "neutralization" as being

```
                                          1 - Mr. N. P. Callahan
                                          1 - Mr. T. J. Jenkins
                                          1 - Mr. J. B. Adams
        CODE              TELETYPE               NITEL
                                          1 - Each Assistant Director
   TO ALL SACS                                JULY 29, 1975
     ALL LEGATS
                                      (1) - Mr. A. B. Fulton
   FROM DIRECTOR, FBI                     PERSONAL ATTENTION
                                          1 - Mr. T. J. Deakin
```

ATTORNEY GENERAL'S REQUEST RE SENSITIVE INVESTIGATIVE
TECHNIQUES.

THE ATTORNEY GENERAL, NOTING THE DEPARTMENT IS REVIEWING
ACTIVITIES CONDUCTED UNDER PRESIDENTIAL AUTHORITY FOR
USE OF WARRANTLESS ELECTRONIC SURVEILLANCE FOR FOREIGN
INTELLIGENCE, INCLUDING COUNTERINTELLIGENCE PURPOSES, REQUESTED
A REVIEW OF ALL OTHER ACTIVITIES WHICH ARE OR CAN BE CONDUCTED
BY THE BUREAU INVOLVING NONCONSENSUAL, WARRANTLESS INTRUSION
UPON REAL OR PERSONAL PROPERTY; NONELECTRONIC EAVESDROPPING
UPON CONVERSATIONS THOUGHT BY THE PARTICIPANTS TO BE PRIVATE;
INTERCEPTION OR OTHER RECEIPT NOT AUTHORIZED BY THE SENDER
OR RECEIVER OF THE CONTENTS OF WIRE, RADIO OR WRITTEN
COMMUNICATIONS; AND ALL OTHER ACTIVITIES, WHETHER OR NOT
INVOLVING ELECTRONIC SURVEILLANCE OR PHYSICAL INTRUSION, THAT
MIGHT BE CALLED INTO QUESTION OR SHOULD BE REVIEWED.

THE ATTORNEY GENERAL REQUESTED A DESCRIPTION OF THE TYPES
OF SUCH ACTIVITIES NOW BEING CONDUCTED BY THE BUREAU, AND ALSO
ANY ADDITIONAL TYPES WHICH THE BUREAU CONSIDERS ITSELF
AUTHORIZED TO CONDUCT. IN ADDITION, A REPORT ON ANY SUCH
PAST ACTIVITIES WAS ALSO REQUESTED BY THE ATTORNEY GENERAL.

CANVASS YOUR PERSONNEL FOR ANY SUCH TYPES OF ACTIVITIES
CONDUCTED IN YOUR OFFICE AND NOTE WHETHER USED IN ORGANIZED
CRIME, GENERAL CRIMINAL, FOREIGN INTELLIGENCE, OR DOMESTIC
SECURITY INVESTIGATIONS.

Teletype directly linking warrantless ELSURs with counterintelligence and domestic security operations, four years after COINTELPRO had supposedly been terminated.

"subversives." By the second half of the latter decade, however, such vernacular was archaic and discredited. Hence, COINTELPRO specialists shifted to habitual use of the phrase "political extremist" in defining their quarry; the organizations and individuals focused upon during this peak period of COINTELPRO might also be described as "violent" or "violence prone," but they were acknowledged as being politically so nonetheless.

After 1971, with the FBI increasingly exposed before the public as having conducted itself as an outright political police, the Bureau sought to revise its image, ultimately promising never to engage in COINTELPRO-type activities again. In this context, it became urgently necessary – if counterintelligence operations were to continue – for any hint of overt orientation to subjects' politics to be driven from agents' vocabularies, preferably in favor of a term which would "inspire public support and confidence" in the Bureau's covert political mission. This pertained as much to internal documents as to public pronouncements, insofar as the possibility of FOIA disclosure of the former was emerging as a significant "menace."

The Advent of "Terrorism"

This was accomplished in the immediate aftermath of COINTELPRO's alleged demise, as is shown in the accompanying April 12, 1972 Airtel from Director L. Patrick Gray to the SAC, Albany. The word selected was "terrorist," applied here to members of the Black Panther Party *cum* Black Liberation Army who had only months earlier still been designated as "agitators" and "key extremists."[7] Such a word-choice allowed the deployment of a raft of associated terms such as "guerrillas" and – in the case of the American Indian Movement – "insurgents." The public, which experience had shown would balk at the idea of the FBI acting to curtail political diversity *as such*, could be counted on to rally to the notion that the Bureau was now acting only to protect them against "terror." Thus, the Bureau secured a terminological license by which to pursue precisely the same goals, objectives and tactics attending COINTELPRO, but in an even more vicious, concerted and sophisticated fashion.

The results of such linguistic subterfuge were, as was noted in the introduction to this book, readily evidenced during the 1980s when it was revealed that the FBI had employed the rubric of a "terrorist investigation" to rationalize the undertaking of a multi-year "probe" of the nonviolent CISPES organization – extended to encompass at least 215 other groups, including Clergy and Laity Concerned, the Maryknoll Sisters, Amnesty International, the Chicago Interreligious Task Force, the U.S. Catholic Conference, and the Virginia Education Association – opposed to U.S. policy in Central America.[8] Needless to say, the CISPES operation was attended by systematic resort to such time-honored COINTELPRO tactics as the use of infiltrators/*provocateurs*,[9] disinformation,[10] black bag jobs,[11] telephone intercepts,[12] conspicuous surveillance (to make targets believe "there's an agent behind every mail box"),[13] and so on.

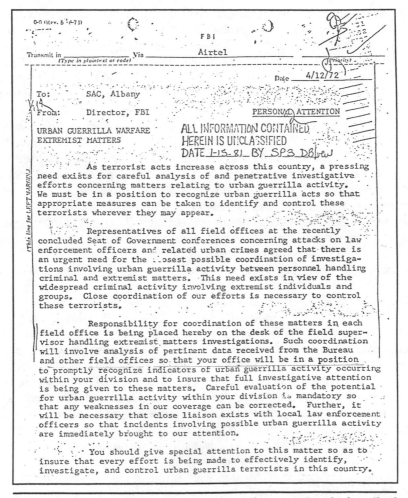

Early Airtel applying the term "terrorist" to those previously described as "activists," "radicals," "agitators" or "political extremists."

The same veneer of "counter-terrorism" has also been applied to operations conducted against the devoutly pacifist Silo Plowshares organization – committed to anti-nuclearism/anti-militarism – a situation so ludicrous as to provoke COIN-TELPRO veteran John Ryan to refuse to participate. Ryan, who had two commendations to his credit during a 21-year career, and who was less than two years short of retirement at the time, was fired as a result of his stand.[14] Meanwhile, Plowshares "terrorists" such as Katya Komisaruk, Jerry Ebner, Helen Woodson, Lin Romano, Joe Gump, Ann and Jim Albertini, George Ostensen, Richard Miller and Father Carl Kabat were being ushered into long prison sentences for such things as "conspiring" to trespass at U.S. nuclear facilities.[15]

Even in instances involving actual armed struggle on the part of liberation movements – leaving aside the probability that earlier applications of COIN-TELPRO tactics had done much to convince adherents that no other route to effect positive social change lay open to them – the Bureau had been duplicitous in its approach. One need only examine the case of Assata Shakur (s/n: Joanne Chesimard) to get the picture. Publicly and sensationally accused by the FBI of being the "revolutionary mother hen" of a BLA cell conducting a "series of cold-blooded murders of New York City police officers," Shakur was made the subject of a nationwide manhunt in 1972.[16] On May 2, 1973, she, BLA founder Zayd Malik Shakur (her brother-in-law) and Sundiata Acoli (s/n: Clark Squire) were subjected to one of the random harassment stops of blacks on the New Jersey Turnpike for which the Jersey state troopers are so deservedly notorious. Apparently realizing who it was they'd pulled over, the two troopers – Werner Foerster and James Harper – opened fire, wounding Assata Shakur immediately. In the fight which followed, both Zayd Shakur and trooper Foerster were killed, trooper Harper and Sundiata Acoli wounded. Both surviving BLA members were captured.[17]

Assata was, however, charged with *none* of the killings which had ostensibly earned her such celebrated status as a "terrorist." Instead, the government contended she had participated in bank robberies, and the state of New York accused her of involvement in the killing of a heroin dealer in Brooklyn and the failed ambush of two cops in Queens on January 23, 1973.[18] She was acquitted of every single charge in a series of trials lasting into 1977. Meanwhile, she was held without bond, in isolation and in especially miserable local jail facilities.[19] Finally, having exhausted all other possibilities of obtaining a conviction, the authorities took her to trial in New Jersey in the death of trooper Foerster. Despite the fact that Sundiata Acoli had long-since been convicted of having fired the fatal bullets – and medical testimony indicating her wounds had incapacitated her prior to the firefight itself – Assata Shakur was convicted of first degree murder by an all-white jury on March 25, 1977. She was sentenced to life imprisonment.

The travesty imbedded in all this was unmistakable, and Shakur's circumstances remained the topic of much discussion and debate. This became all the more true on the night of November 2, 1979, when a combat unit of the BLA set the prisoner free from the maximum security building of the Clinton Women's Prison in New Jersey.[20] It is instructive that this organization of what the police and the FBI were busily portraying as "mad dog killers" appear to have gone considerably out of their way to insure that *no one*, including the guards, was hurt during the prison break. For her part, Assata Shakur – now hyped by the Bureau as "the nation's number one terrorist fugitive" despite the state's failure to link her to any concrete "act of terrorism"[21] – was quietly provided sanctuary in Cuba where she remains today.

Meanwhile, the FBI was utilizing the spectacle of the BLA cases – in combination, it claimed, with threats created by the *Puertorriqueño* FALN and two right-wing clandestine groups, the Cuban exile Omega 7 and the "Serbo-Croatian Liberation

Front"[22] – as a rationale to establish the sort of instrument of political repression which had been only embryonic during the COINTELPRO era proper. What emerged in 1980 was a formal amalgamation of FBI COINTELPRO specialists and New York City red squad detectives known as the Joint Terrorist Task Force (JTTF), consolidating the more *ad hoc* models of such an apparatus which had materialized in cities like Chicago and Los Angeles during the late '60s.[23]

In many ways, the JTTF and the way it has been able to project the image of organizations and individuals engaged in armed struggle, has been the defining characteristic of domestic political repression during the 1980s. We will examine three cases which demonstrate this point.

The Revolutionary Armed Task Force

The Revolutionary Armed Task Force (RATF) evolved from a multi-organizational community service project in the South Bronx known as the Lincoln Detox Center, dedicated to combatting the plague of heroin addiction afflicting black inner cities during the mid-70s. Nominally headed by an acupuncturist and RNA member named Mutulu Shakur (s/n: Jeral Wayne Williams), Lincoln Detox proved highly successful in applying the cures to heroin addiction pioneered by Malcolm X during the early '60s. Working from an increasing base of activists and ex-addicts, it pursued the Black Panther Party's agenda of developing programs leading to increased community self-control and self-sufficiency. It was perhaps because of the project's very success that government funding was withdrawn and police used to evict staffers on November 29, 1978.[24]

After Lincoln Detox was forcibly returned to the orbit of conventional (and typically unsuccessful) heroin treatment programs, Mutulu Shakur acted to establish a private entity dubbed the Black Acupuncture Advisory Association of North America (BAAANA) to continue the work. The organization established a heroin treatment facility in Harlem. According to the JTTF, a subset of BAAANA was the BLA-led RATF, formed in 1978 to provide a funding base for the heroin clinic by robbing banks and armored trucks.[25] On October 20, 1981, the BAAANA/BLA/RATF ensemble came unwrapped as the result of a failed armored truck robbery in West Nyack, New York, in which two guards were killed and several RATF members captured.[26] Mutulu Shakur and several others escaped, but were forced underground; BAAANA rapidly dissolved thereafter.[27]

In the aftermath, the JTTF rapidly captured a number of other RATF members, killing one (Mtyari Sundiata; s/n: Samuel Lee Smith) on October 23.[28] In the trials which followed, the defendants were tried under "RICO" (Racketeer Influenced and Corrupt Organizations Act; 18 USCS § 1961-1968) charges – anti-racketeering statutes, seldom utilized against organized crime – and sentenced to long stretches in prison.[29] Relatedly, after RATF supporter Susan Rosenberg and an associate, Tim Blunk (a neurology researcher), were captured at a cache of explosives in Cherry Hill, New Jersey on November 29, 1984, they received utterly unprecedented 58 year sentences for *possession*. This is compared to the seven year sentence received by Dennis Malvesi, a right-wing fanatic convicted of actually using explosives to blow up abortion clinics during the early 1980s.[30]

Far more instructive with regard to the JTTF's (and, more broadly, the FBI's) handling of the "Brinks Case" than the way in which it dealt with the RATF *per se*, is the way it utilized the matter as a pretext by which to conduct operations against other elements of the left. For instance, in the wake of the West Nyack incident, U.S. Attorney John S. Martin, Jr. convened (at the request of the Bureau) a federal grand jury in New York, casting an extremely wide net across east coast dissidents in what one attorney described as "not so much an effort to gather evidence in the Brinks case itself, as to compel testimony which provides comprehensive general intelligence on personal and organizational relationships within the left as a whole."[31] Thirteen key activists were jailed for as long as eighteen months because of their "contempt" in refusing to cooperate with this fishing expedition.[32]

The New York grand jury gambit proved so successful that by late 1983 the FBI had requested a second be convened in Chicago, ostensibly to explore links discovered between the RATF and Puerto Rican *independentista* formations such as the FALN. This led in due course to the imprisonment of five key members of the *Movimiento de Liberación National* (MLN) – Ricardo Romero, María Cueto, Steven Guerra, Julio Rosado and Andrés Rosado – for up to three years for the "criminal contempt" of refusing to cooperate.[33] Yet a third such grand jury was set in place during 1984, this one assigned to probe the John Brown Anti-Klan Committee (JBAKC), an organization said to have "fraternal relations" with the RATF, the FALN, and other "terrorist" entities. Another six key activists went to jail for refusal to collaborate.[34]

Symptomatic of the sort of "hard information" generated by the grand juries and other JTTF investigative activities related to the RATF are the following "proofs" that the May 19th Communist Organization was part of a "terrorist network" (a characterization extended by the Bureau in the *New York Post* as early as October 1981):

- A 1985 Profile in Terrorism lists as a "terrorist incident," the arrest of nine "May 19th Communist Organization members" for trespassing during a sit-in at the ticket office of South African Airways in New York City.

- Other May 19th Organization activities posited by the Bureau as "evidence of terrorism" include attending peaceful demonstrations sponsored by CISPES, conducting an educational forum at Boston University, holding a nonviolent public rally in New York, publicly advocating solidarity with the Southwest African Peoples' Organization (SWAPO), and having inter-organizational contact with CISPES.

- Advocacy of the right of oppressed peoples to engage in armed struggle and specifically endorsement of the escape of Assata Shakur are listed as "terrorist activities" undertaken by the "May 19th Communist Coalition [sic; Organization]."

- FBI Director William Webster offered as "links" between the May 19th Communist Organization and the FALN the fact that May 19th members were known to have attended "rallies and functions" supportive of Puerto Rican independence. Similarly, Webster claimed to have uncovered links between May 19th and the RATF based on the facts that the organization openly engaged in "support of New Afrikan Freedom Fighters" and "one person [Silvia Baraldini] associated with May 19th was arrested in the Nyack incident [emphasis added]."[35]

Being thus gratuitously (or maliciously) cast by the FBI as a terrorist group is not a laughing matter as the experience of a black Harlem study group headed by Coltrane Chimarenga (s/n: Randolph Simms) bears out. Infiltrated by a JTTF *provocateur* named Howard Bonds in 1984, the membership was shortly arrested *en masse* on criminal conspiracy charges and publicly branded "Son of Brinks."[36] They were accused of planning at least two bank robberies and to free RATF members Sekou Odinga and Kuwasi Balagoon. Despite the prosecutor's introduction of some 450 pages of affidavits – including lengthy excerpts from wiretap logs – and testimony of Bonds, the jury appears to have ended up believing that most or all of the "conspiracy" was a product of the infiltrator's own actions and/or imagination. They voted for acquittal on all substantive charges, convicting seven of the eight defendants only on charges of possession of restricted weapons and phoney IDs.[37] Afterwards, several jurors publicly commented that the JTTF tactics revealed at trial had constituted a "clear violation of the civil rights and liberties of the accused," and that the conduct of the "counter-terrorists" themselves represented "a far greater threat to freedom" than anything Chimarenga's group might have contemplated.[38]

The defendants in the "Son of Brinks" case ultimately went free, even though they had spent nearly a year bound up in legal proceedings – and were thus thoroughly neutralized in terms of their political organizing – in what turned out to be, at best, an utterly frivolous case on the part of the government. Less lucky was Dr. Alan Berkman, a founder of JBAKC whose long history of activism included a stint as a medic at Wounded Knee, several years working at Lincoln Detox, and staunch support of the black liberation and *independentista* movements. Indicted in 1983 for having rendered medical assistance to Marilyn Buck, an RATF member allegedly wounded in the leg at Nyack, Berkman successfully went underground before being captured in Philadelphia in mid-1985. He was then held without bond for two years, until a 1987 trial which resulted in his conviction as an "accessory" in the Brinks case. He was the first individual since Dr. Mudd, the man accused of rendering medical aid to John Wilkes Booth after the Abraham Lincoln assassination, to be so charged. Berkman was sentenced to twelve years imprisonment for his "involvement in terrorism."[39]

Organizations as such also suffered direct physical consequences from the JTTF's RATF-related "investigation." For instance, on January 31, 1983, "the FBI carried out a massive raid on the Madame Binh Graphics Collective in Brooklyn, New York. The May 19th Communist Organization used this studio for its First Amendment protected organizing activities. The warrant to search the graphics studio falsely stated it was the home of Donna Borup [a May 19th activist]. In the course of the search the FBI destroyed printing equipment and seized large quantities of political literature and art work."[40] No charges were ever brought against Borup, the ostensible focus of the raid, a matter which has prompted many people to conclude her pursuit was merely a pretext by which the Bureau accomplished its real objective of disrupting the Madame Binh Collective's ability to function.

Ironically, many supposedly progressive groups and individuals have joined the chorus supporting the FBI's "campaign against terrorism" on the left, arguing that the "menace" posed by armed struggle somehow "justifies" virtually any politically repressive activity in which the Bureau might care to engage, and that those who engage in or support "terrorism" deserve whatever fate the state wished to accord them, no matter how cruel, unusual or "anomalous."[41] Such victim-blaming attitudes are precisely what the FBI requires as a basis for its conduct of the broadest forms of ideological warfare, a matter the CISPES investigation should have proven beyond any reasonable doubt.

To underscore the matter even further, it is only fair to observe that the Bureau has shown no inclination to cast such broad nets over the radical right. This holds true even when the FBI has investigated such unabashed terrorist organizations as the neo-nazi "Bruder Schweigen" – or "Silent Brotherhood," otherwise known as "The Order" – a group which admittedly performed the cold-blooded murder of Alan Berg (a Jewish talk show host in Denver), killed a Missouri state trooper, "executed" a third individual and conducted a series of armored car and bank robberies netting several times the amount attributed to the RATF.[42] The group was also heavily involved in counterfeiting.

The Resistance Conspiracy Case

Stemming to some extent from the FBI's anti-RATF operation, the "Resistance Conspiracy Case" (*U.S. v. Whitehorn, et al.*, CR 88-145-05) concerns seven long-term white activists accused of planning and involvement in the execution of "a terrorist bombing campaign" during the early '80s. Among the more notable actions they are alleged to have carried out were the placing of explosives at the National War College and U.S. Capitol Building in 1983 as protests against the U.S. invasion of Grenada. One of the seven accused, Betty Ann Duke, has evaded capture to date. Five of the six in custody – Marilyn Buck, Susan Rosenberg, Tim Blunk, Linda Evans and Dr. Alan Berkman – are already serving lengthy prison sentences on RATF-related matters.[43] The sixth, Laura Whitehorn, has been held in "preventive detention," without bond or trial for more than four years.[44] The defendants face 40 years apiece in prison if convicted.

There are certain glaring defects in the government's approach to the case. All the defendants except Whitehorn have already been convicted of the specific acts they are accused of having conspired to commit. This blatant exercise in double jeopardy has been challenged in a motion to dismiss, addressed recently by a federal court decision that – while the case could go forward – prosecutors would be required to demonstrate additional actions on the part of the defendants in order for the matter to be bound over to a jury.[45] For its part, the Justice Department has expressed strong displeasure at not being allowed to simply try the same case over and over, under a variety of billings, stacking up virtually limitless penalties against those it wishes to persecute.

In some ways even more problematic, FBI and prosecutors have already been caught trying to withhold exculpatory evidence from the defense. Contrary to the seeming federal certainty embodied in the indictment handed down on May 11, 1988 that these particular individuals were guilty as charged, it has become increasingly evident the Bureau really has no idea who was involved in the bombings. For instance,

> ...in a *Washington Post* newspaper article run several days after the capitol bombing, the FBI apparently had evidence tending to show similarities between the 8 to 11 bombings in the New York and Washington, D.C. areas and the capitol bombing. On the basis of facts unknown to the defendants, they suspected (1) the Farabundo Marti Liberation Front (FMLN), (2) the United Freedom Front (UFF), (3) the Palestine Liberation Organization (PLO), (4) the Democratic Revolutionary Front (FDR), or (5) the Committee in Solidarity with the People of El Salvador (CISPES) of the bombing... Suspicions of involvement in the bombing by groups 1 through 4 were voiced by the FBI Director William H. Webster and Special Agent Theodore M. Gardner to the *Washington Post* in an article printed November 13, 1983.[46]

Subsequently, in a *Post* article run on March 15, 1984, an FBI spokesperson announced that the Armed Resistance Unit (ARU) – the organization to which the six present defendants all belonged – was *not* involved in the bombings. Further:

> While testifying before the Senate Committee on the Judiciary's Subcommittee on Security and Terrorism in 1985, Mr. Webster stated that the FBI believed the UFF to have been responsible for the bombing(s). He testified...categorically that "the progress we have made with the group called the United Freedom Front will reflect itself in diminished activity by the group that claims credit for the Capitol bombing."[47]

As is pointed out by the defense, "information generated and possessed by the FBI's National Bomb Data Center must have aided the FBI, and others, [in] casting its suspicions over groups and persons other than the Revolutionary Fighting Group (RFG) [ARU], and the Red Guerilla Resistance (RGR)."[48] Susan Rosenberg also points out that she and several other defendants were in prison at the time several of the bombings were carried out.[49] Despite *bona fide* discovery motions, the government has refused to divulge the documents relevant to how it arrived at its various conclusions that entities other than those now accused are responsible for the actions at issue.

As Mary O'Melveny, a defense attorney, put it: "The defendants' direct guilt or innocence...appears immaterial to the government, which has constructed an indictment to convict the six on charges of aiding and abetting and of 'conspiracy to influence, change and protest practices of the United States...through the use of violent and illegal means.'"[50] In this instance, "aiding and abetting" can be construed to mean ideological solidarity. "Influence, change and protest" can mean statements of advocacy or support of the bombers. No concrete action, or demonstrable interaction with those engaged in the action, is technically necessary for the defendants to be "guilty." This affords an interesting perspective upon U.S. Attorney Jay Stephens' assertion at the time of the indictment: "Let this be a warning to those who seek to influence the policies of the U.S. through violence and terrorism that we will seek unrelentingly to bring them to justice."[51]

The Resistance Conspiracy group is thus to stand as a symbol of the government's ability to define dissidents as terrorists at its own discretion and regardless of the facts. Under such circumstances it follows that dissent *per se* can be made punishable by long prison terms, a matter which, as O'Melveny puts it, makes a point "which says to people, 'Shut up. And don't even consider stepping out of very narrow bounds of protest.' That's what I think this case is all about."[52] Certainly, such an objective is well within the spirit of COINTELPRO, and would represent a major "accomplishment" in terms of political repression, if achieved.

The question nonetheless arises as to why this particular group of people has been selected to serve as the example. On the one hand, an answer of sorts may lie in the fact that they are convenient, already in custody and found guilty of "terrorist involvements." On the other hand, as O'Melveny points out, there is little to be gained by adding 40 years more to the 70 year sentence now carried by Marilyn Buck, the 58 year sentences carried by Susan Rosenberg and Tim Blunk, or the 45 years Linda Evans is now serving. Tactically at least, it would make far more sense for the FBI to try to neutralize a whole new group of activists.

The truth of the matter may well lie in something as simple as pique and vindictiveness on the part of certain Bureau officials. Evans, Buck and Whitehorn are former members of SDS aligned with the Weatherman faction who made the transition to the clandestine Weather Underground Organization in 1970. Berkman also had an affinity to the latter through its aboveground support entity, the Prairie Fire Organizing Committee (PFOC). Rosenberg and Blunk, who are younger, appear to have more-or-less cut their activist teeth on Weather politics. Collectively, they participated in a process of greatly embarrassing the FBI in its spectacular inability to apprehend WEATHERFUGS (**Weatherman Fugitives**) throughout the 1970s.

Worse for the Bureau, the very methods employed in trying to break the Weather Underground's political apparatus came back to haunt individual FBI officials in court, perhaps the only time this has ever happened. In 1978, former FBI

Director L. Patrick Gray, former acting Associate Director W. Mark Felt, former Assistant Director for the Domestic Intelligence Division Edward S. Miller, and former supervisor of the New York field office's Squad 47 (the COINTELPRO section) John Kearney were indicted for having conspired to "injure and oppress citizens of the United States" in their anti-Weatherman operations. After a lengthy 1980 trial, Felt and Miller were found guilty by a jury, the only FBI personnel ever tried and convicted of COINTELPRO-related offenses. They were freed on appeal bond, but were apparently losing, given Ronald Reagan's April 1981 intervention to pardon them rather than see two such "loyal public servants" go to prison for their misdeeds.[53] Several of the resistance conspiracy defendants were extremely active during the course of the officials' trial, utilizing its precedent value to increase public consciousness concerning the FBI's true nature. Their organizing seems to have been deeply humiliating to FBI officials, especially after their colleagues were convicted.

This humiliation undoubtedly increased dramatically when, shortly after Reagan bestowed his pardons, former WEATHERFUGS Judy Clark and Dana Biberman entered a lawsuit (*Clark v. U.S.*, 78 Civ. 2244 (MEL)) against the FBI, seeking $100 million in damages on behalf of those victimized by the anti-Weatherman operations and injunctive relief to insure the Bureau never utilized such tactics again:

> Several of the defendants in [the Resistance Conspiracy] case were active participants in the *Clark v. United States* civil lawsuit against the FBI. They assisted in legal research, built public support for the case, conducted community organizing, received discovery and were, along with the plaintiffs, subject to continuing acts of government harassment.[54]

There being no presidential remedy available to fix this particular problem, the Bureau was forced to reach "a monetary settlement favorable to the plaintiffs."[55] In the end, then, the Resistance Conspiracy case may have nothing at all to do with bullets and bombs. To the contrary, it seems likely – notwithstanding the undeniable chilling effect it is intended to impart across the entire spectrum of left politics in the U.S. – it is designed to salve the wounded egos of the Bureau's COINTELPRO specialists. It is, as Susan Rosenberg would say, "pay-back time."

The Ohio 7

The cases of the Ohio 7 concern a group of white activists who formed the United Freedom Front (UFF) – otherwise known as the Sam Melville-Jonathan Jackson Brigade (SMJJ)[56] – and are accused of engaging in a series of bombings during the early 1980s. Among the many such actions they are alleged to have undertaken was detonating an explosive charge at a South African Airways office on December 16, 1982, as a protest against ongoing cordial relations between the U.S. government and South Africa's apartheid regime. The same day, they are said to have bombed an office facility of the IBM Corporation because of the computer giant's provision of sophisticated computer systems to the South African military and police. On

March 19, 1984, according to the state, they bombed a second IBM office complex, this time in commemoration of the 1960 Sharpeville Massacre in which South African police murdered seventy unarmed black men, women and children. In September of 1984, they are charged with having carried out one of two bombings of offices belonging to the Union Carbide Corporation because of its economic activity in South Africa.[57] As was the case with the bombings attributed to the Resistance Conspiracy defendants, warning phone calls prevented anyone from being killed or injured by those associated with the Ohio 7.*

The seven – Jaan Laaman, Barbara Curzi-Laaman, Richard Williams, Carol and Tom Manning, Pat Gros Levasseur and Ray Luc Levasseur – were the focus of the most intensive and wide-ranging JTTF campaign to date, at least so far as is known. This assumed the form of BOSLUC (an acronym derived from combining the first three letters of Boston, the city in which the operation was headquartered, and Ray Luc Levasseur's middle name), an effort initiated in 1982 and eventually drawing not only the FBI and New York police establishments, but the BATF and police representation from Massachusetts, Maine, Vermont, New Hampshire, Ohio, Pennsylvania and New Jersey as well.[58]

BOSLUC initially concentrated its energies in the Boston area, largely due to an incident in 1982 in which black community activist Kazi Touré (s/n: Christopher King) was stopped by state police on Route 95, near Attleboro, Massachusetts. A sharp exchange of gunfire followed, leaving two troopers wounded and Touré in custody, a passenger in the latter's car having escaped.[59] The fugitive was identified as UFF member Jaan Laaman. The Attleboro firefight closely followed a similar event on Route 80 in rural New Jersey when state trooper Philip Lamonaco stopped a car driven by Tom Manning and, apparently recognizing the occupant, opened fire. Lamonaco ended up dead. Police subsequently contended Richard Williams had been with Manning at the time of the shooting.[60]

By early 1984, frustrated at coming up dry in Massachusetts, the JTTF expanded the scope of BOSLUC to encompass all of New England in what was dubbed "Western Sweep":

Agents of the task force seized many citizens resembling the Ohio 7 and subjected them to public humiliation and physical abuse prior to any positive identification. A family was surrounded by police after leaving a diner, and the father was beaten and searched in front of his [wife and children] in the parking lot. Another family was pulled over on the highway and forced at gunpoint to lie face-down in the rain on the pavement. Another man's teeth were broken with the barrel of a gun. In Pennsylvania, a paramilitary team landed in a field, surrounded a family in their home and held them hostage for six hours. These people had the simple misfortune [of looking] like members of the Ohio 7.[61]

No expense was spared, as "surveillance by electronic means, paid informants

---

* Some Ohio 7 members have been accused of a 1976 courthouse bombing in Suffolk County, Massachusetts, in which people were injured. No credible evidence of this has, however, been produced (See Note 72, this chapter).

and photographic methods yielded 500,000 pages of material from investigations of the Ohio 7. In designated areas, numerous pen registers [electronic devices which, when installed on a phone, reveal the number of any phone calling it] were obtained, then hundreds of BOSLUC agents would conduct an intelligence sweep; the idea was that the increased police activity would generate more phone calls [from UFF members] to sympathizers and all [such] calls would be subject to FBI investigation. A casual mention by a distant relative of Tom Manning of the name 'Tommy' in a telephone conversation brought a small army of agents into the bedroom of a stranger in less than an hour."[62]

> The newly minted agents of Western Sweep went out, knocked on doors, stopped cars, set up roadblocks and saturated the area with wanted posters [including photos of the children of the accused]. They contacted schools, day-care centers and medical facilities with photos and medical and dental records. Many activists were repeatedly interviewed, followed and harassed. The women's community in western Massachusetts was contacted by FBI agents offering assistance after a rash of telephone threats. The FBI assistance turned out to hinge on cooperation with Western Sweep. In the estimation of the government, one out of every three residents of [Massachusetts, Connecticut, Vermont and New Hampshire] was contacted during Western Sweep.[63]

Ultimately, such heavy-handedness was for naught. BOSLUC was finally able to home in on the first of the SMJJ group through use of a mainframe computer donated by the Grumman Corporation. Utilizing a sophisticated database and name-matching program, agents were able to trace Patricia Gros Levasseur through a series of aliases to a post office box in Columbus, Ohio.[64] They then staked out the postal facility and, when she showed up for her mail on November 3, 1984, they followed her home to a house in nearby Deerfield. Ray Luc and Pat Gros Levasseur, along with their three daughters, were captured the following morning.[65] At about the same time, some 75 FBI SWAT-team members, armed with a warrant for Richard Williams and an armored personnel carrier known as "Mother," had surrounded a house at 4248 West 22nd Street in Cleveland; Williams, Jaan and Barbara Curzi-Laaman, and the Laaman's three children were captured.[66] The Mannings initially evaded the roundup, but were eventually traced via the serial numbers on a gun seized in the raid on the Cleveland address and captured, along with their children, on April 24, 1985.[67]

Federal treatment of the children of the captured Ohio 7 members is instructive. Upon the arrest of their parents, the three Levasseur girls were whisked away for a solid five hours of interrogation by the FBI and representatives of the New Jersey State Police. Afterwards, they were turned over to welfare department officials despite the fact that a number of relatives – none accused of any crime, and all gainfully employed – lived in the area and expressed their willingness to take them in. Later, Carmen Levasseur, the eldest daughter at age eight, recounted how, when she expressed that she'd grown hungry during the initial interrogation, an agent had offered her a pizza and $20 to provide incriminating information against her mother and father, as well as the whereabouts of Tom and Carol Manning.[68] The three Laaman children underwent much the same experience.[69] As for the Manning children – Jeremy (aged 11), Tamara (aged five) and Jonathan (aged three) – they were repeatedly interrogated and arbitrarily placed in a foster home despite repeated attempts by Tom Manning's sister Mary, and her husband, Cameron Bishop, to obtain custody.[70] The Mannings were finally compelled to began a hunger strike in prison in order to force authorities to release their children into the custody of Carol's sister.[71]

In the series of trials which followed the capture of the Ohio 7, the government relied heavily upon the testimony of an informant named Joseph Aceto (aka: Joseph Balino), a former member of Statewide Correctional Alliance for Reform (SCAR), a prisoners-rights organization founded in Portland, Maine during the early 1970s by Tom Manning and Ray Luc Levasseur.[72] Aceto offered considerable "evidence" concerning the original formation of the SMJJ, its evolution into UFF, and supposedly first-hand recollections of the defendants' having described their bombing and bank-robbing exploits to him. Only later did it emerge conclusively that the government's star witness had consistently lied under oath, passing off third-hand gossip and utter fabrications as conversations in which he himself had participated.[73] It also came out that Aceto had been diagnosed as psychotic and administered heavy doses of the tranquilizer Mellaril - to "increase his veracity" – prior to testimony.[74] To top things off, it was revealed that, in exchange for such testimony, the FBI had arranged for him to be released from prison where he was serving a life sentence for a brutal stabbing murder and placed on the federal witness protection program (a package with an $800 per month stipend).[75] All this information had been withheld from the defense – and consequently from the jury – at trial.

As the prosecutorial smoke cleared in 1987, Ray Luc Levasseur had been convicted of six bombing charges and had been sentenced to 45 years imprisonment. Tom Manning had also been convicted of six bombing charges and sentenced to 53 years, as well as murder in the death of New Jersey state trooper Lamonaco (a life sentence to run consecutively to the bombing sentence). Richard Williams had been convicted on six bombing charges and sentenced to 45 years; he was not convicted in the Lamonaco killing, but is to be retried. Jaan Laaman was convicted on six bombing charges and sentenced to 53 years. Carol Manning and Barbara Curzi-Laaman were convicted of lesser accessory charges and sentenced to 15 years apiece. Pat Gros Levasseur was convicted of harboring a fugitive (her husband), and sentenced to five years.[76]

Apparently unsatisfied with the virtually permanent incarceration meted out to each of the male "principles" in the Ohio 7 case, hoping to secure heavier sentences against the women, and generally seeking to set a more spectacular "example," the government next resorted to the same double-jeopardy ploy being utilized in the Resistance Conspiracy case. All seven defendants were charged – on the basis of actions for which they had *already* been convicted – of "seditious conspiracy" and violation of the RICO statute. The holes in the case became almost immediately apparent as charges were dropped against both Tom Manning and Jaan Laaman, in order to "simplify proceedings," according to prosecutors.[77] Next, Barbara Curzi-Laaman was severed from the trial after the court (finally) ruled that the FBI's 1984 SWAT raid on her home, which resulted in her capture, had been illegal.[78] The government then began offering reduced sentence deals to any defendant who would enter a guilty plea; Carol Manning accepted the offer.[79]

In the end, after a trial lasting ten months (February-November 1989), costing more than $10 million, and in which nearly 250 witnesses took the stand, the jury acquitted the three remaining defendants – Ray Luc and Pat Gros Levasseur, and Richard Williams – of both charges on November 27, 1989.[80] Pat Gros Levasseur was released from custody on a "time served" basis, while her husband was returned to the federal prison at Marion, Illinois to continue serving his existing sentence. Williams was transferred to the custody of New Jersey authorities, pending a retrial in the death of state trooper Lamonaco.

The Most Imprisoned People on Earth?

The verdicts reached in the final Ohio 7 trial represent something of a victory for political liberty and common sense in the U.S. They demonstrate that a jury of average citizens will, when exposed to a reasonable amount of factual information and given adequate time to think through the issues, reject as implausible govern-ment contentions that any small group of radicals – no matter how "secretive and violent" – are capable of seriously plotting to "overthrow the government by force of arms." So much for the notion of seditious conspiracy. Similarly, the verdicts show clearly that, under appropriate conditions, the same jury will conclude that political formations which engage in bank expropriations and similar activities – while they may have engaged in criminal behavior under the law – are no more guilty of "racketeering"than were the founding fathers at the Boston Tea Party.

Other recent verdicts also offer glimmers of hope, as when on August 26, 1989 a jury acquitted *Puertorriqueño independentista* leader Filiberto Ojeda Ríos of at-tempted murder of a federal agent and seven other charges stemming from Richard W. Held's island-wide ride in 1985.[81] As was the case in the 1976 Cedar Rapids trial of Bob Robideau and Dino Butler, the outcome of Ojeda Ríos' ordeal proves that an ordinary jury – once again assuming it is presented with a sufficient range of facts – will arrive at the conclusion that armed self-defense is an entirely legitimate response to the sorts of tactics employed by the FBI against political dissidents.

Other examples are more grim. Leonard Peltier, Geronimo Pratt, the New York 3 and many other victims of earlier COINTELPRO operations remain in prison despite overwhelming evidence that they were railroaded into their respective cells.[82] And additional casualties continue to accrue. For instance, there is Mumia Abu-Jamal, a former BPP member in Philadelphia, convicted and sentenced to death on July 3, 1982, ostensibly for having killed a cop, despite eyewitnesses having identified an entirely different individual as the assailant. On March 6, 1989, the Pennsylvania Supreme Court denied Abu-Jamal's last possible appeal prior to the electric chair even while acknowledging that "genuine doubt" exists as to the killer's identity.[83]

Indeed, use of the prison system for purposes of political neutralization appears to have become the preferred mode for the FBI and associated police agencies by the end of the 1980s. At present, the U.S. enjoys the dubious distinction of having a greater proportion of its population incarcerated than any western industrialized country. Its imprisonment just of its Euroamerican citizens is tied – at 114 per 100,000 – with Austria for first place. Its rate of imprisonment of African-Americans – 713 per 100,000 – is, however much higher: 25 times the Netherlands' 28 per 100,00 rate of incarcerating its citizenry.[84] The proportion of the black population presently imprisoned in the U.S. is almost exactly double that in South Africa.[85] More, both federal and state policymakers have lately made no secret of their intention to double the number of available prison beds during the coming decade, "privatize" an additional large number of penal facilities, and to develop extensive application of "electronic incarceration techniques" which will require the building of no new physical structures. Following these projections, even the most conservative arithmetic makes it plain the U.S. elite is fully prepared to triple or even quadruple the already burgeoning North American prison population. At the point such plans are consummated, the U.S. citizenry will have become – barring unforeseen eventualities elsewhere – the most imprisoned people on the face of the earth.[86]

While such a trend represents an exercise in social engineering going well beyond any conceivable definition of "counterintelligence" *per se*, it obviously affords modern COINTELPRO operatives a perfect cover under which to conduct their business; hence, the increasing emphasis upon criminalizing political dissidents as "terrorists" and "racketeers" throughout the 1980s. Of late, this process of criminalization has been accelerated considerably under the rubric of a national "war on drugs," headed up by such veteran COINTELPRO specialists as Richard W. Held in San Francisco. Little is said about the fact that the "black street gangs" now decried by the FBI as sources of "drugs and violence in our cities" are exactly the same entities secretly supported by the Bureau in its COINTELPROs against such anti-drug political formations as the Black Panther Party twenty years ago.[87] Even less is mentioned of the CIA's role in establishing these gang-based drug distribution mechanisms during the same period (for the dual purposes of narcotizing political unrest at home and generating revenues with which to fund covert "off the shelf" operations abroad).[88] SAC Held has, however, proven quite vocal in extending utterly unsubstantiated assertions that contemporary political organizations such as the Black Guerrilla Family are important components of the drug scene.[89] Meanwhile, the "drug wars" veneer may well already be in use as a screen behind which the selective assassination of key political activists may be carried out. A notable example of this last was the execution-style murder of Panther founder Huey P. Newton in Oakland, on August 22, 1989.[90]

In some ways more to the point of what is occurring is the nature of the prison facilities the federal system has begun to spawn. Based generally on the "Stammheim Model" perfected by West Germany during the early 1970s, these include the Marion "super-max" prison for men in southern Illinois, and the Marianna prison's high security unit (HSU) for women in northern Florida.[91] The Marianna facility was piloted at the federal women's prison at Lexington, Kentucky during the 1980s. Its purpose was unabashedly political as is demonstrated in the U.S. Bureau of Prison's official criteria for incarceration:

> [A] prisoner's past or present affiliation, association or membership in an organization which has been demonstrated as being involved in acts of violence, attempts to disrupt or overthrow the government of the U.S. or whose published ideology include advocating law violations in order to "free" prisoners...[92]

Constructed some thirty feet underground in total isolation from the outside world, painted entirely white to induce sensory deprivation, with naked florescent lights burning 24 hours per day and featuring rules severely restricting diet, correspondence, reading material and visits, the HSU was deliberately designed to psychologically debilitate those imprisoned there. This was coupled to a program of intentional degradation in which the incarcerated women were strip searched, often by male guards, and observed by male guards while showering and using the toilets. Perhaps worst of all, the Bureau of Prisons (BoP) refused to set any formal criteria by which the women might work their way back out of the HSU once they were confined there. The objective was to invoke in them a sense of being totally at the mercy of and dependent upon their keepers.[93] In the polite language of the John Howard Association:

> Through a year or more of sensory and psychological deprivation, prisoners are stripped of their individual identities in order that compliant behavior patterns can be implanted, a process of mortification and depersonalization.[94]

The techniques involved have been described by Amnesty International in the accompanying chart. As early as 1962, Dr. Edgar Schein described the methodology at issue rather more straightforwardly in an address to all federal maximum security prison wardens in Washington, D.C.:

> In order to produce marked changes in behavior, it is necessary to weaken, undermine, or remove supports for old attitudes. I would like you to think of *brainwashing* not in terms of... ethics and morals, but in terms of the deliberate changing of human behavior by a group of men who have relatively complete control over the environment in which the captives live... [These changes can be induced by] isolation, sensory deprivation, segregation of leaders, spying, tricking men into signing written statements which are then shown to others, placing individuals whose will power has been severely weakened into a living situation

with others more advanced in *thought reform,* character invalidation, humiliations, sleeplessness, rewarding subservience, and fear [emphasis added].[95]

Dr. Richard Korn, in a 1987 report on Lexington commissioned by the ACLU, framed the matter even more clearly. In Korn's estimation, the purpose of an HSU-style facility is to:

...reduce prisoners to a state of submission essential for their ideological conversion. That failing, the next objective is to reduce them to a state of psychological incompetence sufficient to neutralize them as efficient, self-directing antagonists. That failing, the only alternative is to destroy them, preferably by making them desperate enough to destroy themselves.[96]

Of the three political women incarcerated in the Lexington HSU – Susan Rosenberg and Silvia Baraldini of the RATF case and *independentista* Alejandrina Torres – all had ceased menstruating, were afflicted with insomnia and suffered chronic hallucinations before the facility was ordered closed in 1988.[97] By then, the HSU had been condemned as a violation of elemental human rights by organizations ranging from Amnesty International to the ACLU.[98] The BoP response was that it was "satisfied" with its Lexington experiment, and would replicate the HSU's essential features at its Marianna facility, designed to hold several hundred women rather than a mere handful.[99]

Marion is even more entrenched. Established in 1963 as a replacement for the infamous Alcatraz super-maximum prison, which had grown cost-prohibitive to maintain, it contains the first (created in 1972) of the federal government's formal Stammheim-style behavior modification "control units."[100] The ideological function intended for control units was made apparent virtually from the outset when *independentista* Raphael Cancel Miranda was sent there to undergo "thought reform" after having served more than fifteen years in confinement.[101] By 1983, the control unit model was deemed so successful by BoP authorities that the occasion of an "inmate riot" was used as a pretext by which to convert the entire prison into a huge behavior modification center.[102] Since that year, all of Marion has been on "lock down" status, with prisoners confined to their cells, in isolation 23 hours per day, often chained spread-eagled – for "disciplinary reasons" – to their concrete slab "bunks." Strip searches are routine, prisoners are shackled upon leaving their cells for any reason, all contact visits are forbidden and reading material is tightly restricted. As was the case at Lexington, no clear criteria for getting out of Marion have ever been posited by the BoP; the length and extent of prisoners' torment is left entirely to the discretion of prison officials.[103]

Also as was the situation in the Lexington HSU, a significant number of those incarcerated at Marion are political prisoners or Prisoners of War. At present, these include *independentista* Oscar Lopez-Rivera; black liberationists Richard Thompson-El, and Kojo Bomani Sababu; Virgin Islands Five activist Hanif Shabazz Bey; Euroamerican Prisoners of War Bill Dunne and Ray Luc Levasseur; and Plowshares activist Larry Morlan. Scores of others have spent varying lengths of time there. In

Biderman's Chart on Penal Coercion

Source: *Amnesty International Report on Torture, 1983.*

General Method	Effects (Purposes)	Variants
1. Isolation	Deprives victim of all social supports of his ability to resist. Develops an intense concern with self. Makes victim dependent upon interrogator.	Complete solitary confinement, complete isolation, semi-isolation, group isolation.
2. Monopolization of perception.	Fixes attention upon immediate predicament; fosters introspection. Eliminates stimuli competing with those controlled by captor. Frustrates all actions not consistent with compliance.	Physical isolation, darkness or bright light, barren environment, restricted movement, monotonous food.
3. Induced debility; exhaustion.	Weakens mental and physical ability to resist.	Semi-starvation, exposure, exploitation of wounds, induced illness, sleep deprivation, prolonged constraint, prolonged interrogation, forced writing, overexertion.
4. Threats	Cultivates anxiety and despair	Threats of death, threats of non-return, threats of endless interrogation and isolation, threats against family, vague threats, mysterious changes of treatment.
5. Occasional indulgences.	Provides positive motivation for compliance. Hinders adjustment to deprivation.	Occasional favors, fluctuations of interrogation attitudes, promises, rewards for partial compliance, tantalizing.
6. Demonstrating "omnipotence."	Suggests futility of resistance.	Confrontation, pretending cooperation taken for granted, demonstrating complete control over victim's fate.
7. Degradation	Makes cost of resistance appear more damaging to self-esteem than capitulation. Reduces prisoners to "animal level" concerns.	Personal hygeine prevented. Filthy, infested surroundings, demeaning punishments, insults and taunts, denial of privacy.
8. Enforcing trivial demands.	Develops habit of compliance.	Forced writing, enforcement of minute rules.

another parallel with Lexington, Marion has been repeatedly condemned by a broad range of organizations, including Amnesty International, as systematically violating United Nations proscriptions against torture and other minimum standards required by international law with regard to the maintenance of prison populations.[104] Rather than favorably altering the situation inside Marion, the BoP has indicated that it considers the lockdown permanent, and has begun to clone off comparable environments – such as the N-2 "death unit" at Terre Haute (Indiana) federal prison – in other maximum security facilities for men.

Although U.S. District Judge Barrington Parker ordered the Lexington HSU closed on August 15, 1988 – on the specific basis of its use as a political prison – his decision was overturned by a federal appeals court on September 8, 1989.[105] As Susan Rosenberg has put it: "The appeals court held that the government is free to use the political beliefs and association of prisoners as basis for treating us more harshly and placing us in maximum security conditions. Further, the appeals court ruling means that no court can question or dispute the prison's decision even if those decisions involve the prisoner's politics or political identity...This legal decision gives official sanction to the BoP to place political prisoners into control units."[106] The rulers of Orwell's totalitarian empires could not have put it better than the judiciary of the United States.

The Shape of Things to Come

This may well be the shape of things to come, and in a frighteningly generalized way. A pattern is emerging in which the "attitude adjustment" represented by police and prison becomes a normative rather than exceptional experience of power in the U.S. If the present dynamics of spiraling police power and state sanctioned secrecy, proliferating penal facilities and judicial abandonment of basic constitutional principles is allowed to continue unabated, it is easily predictable that upwards of 20% of the next generation of Americans will spend appreciable time behind bars in prison environments making present day Sing Sing and San Quentin seem benign by comparison. Another not inconsiderable percentage of the population may be expected to undergo some form of "electronic incarceration," either in their homes or at some government-designated "private" facility. The technologies for this last have been developed over the past twenty years, are even now being "field tested" (*i.e.*: used on real prisoners), and will undoubtedly be perfected during the coming decade.[107]

In such a context, the classic role of domestic counterintelligence operations will logically be diminished; any hint of politically "deviant" behavior will likely be met with more-or-less immediate arrest, packaging as a "criminal" by the FBI and its interactive counterparts in the state and local police, processing through the courts and delivery to one or another prison for an appropriate measure of behavior modification. The social message – "don't even *think* about rocking the boat, under *any* circumstances" – is both undeniable and overwhelming. At this point, it will be necessary to assess the legacy of COINTELPRO not only as having perpetuated, but of having quite literally transcended itself. It will have moved from covert and relatively selective or "surgical" repression of dissent to the overt and uniform suppression of political diversity *per se*, from a secretive safeguarding of the parameters of "acceptable" political expression to the open imposition of orthodoxy, from somewhat constrained service to to socio-economic *status quo* to outright social pacification and maintenance of a rigid social order.

It is perhaps ironic that it is at precisely the moment the police state apparatus inherent to the Soviet Union and its various eastern European satellites appears to be crumbling that the U.S. police state shows every indication of consolidating itself at a new and unparalleled level of intensity and sophistication. But it should certainly come as no surprise. The entire 70 year history of the FBI has given fair warning. The COINTELPRO era provided a detailed preview of what was to come. And, not only the continuation, but the systematic legitimation of all that was worst about COINTELPRO during the 1970s and '80s has been sufficiently blatant to set alarm bells ringing loudly in the mind of anyone wishing to consider the matter. The sad fact is, however, that other than during certain peak periods of repression – notably the Palmer Raids, the McCarthy period, and at the very end of the COIN-TELPRO era – such things have received only scant attention from the left. Instead, concern with questions of police power and the function of prisons has been consigned mainly to lawyers and a scattering of researcher-activists whose work has been typically viewed as "marginal," "esoteric" and even "paranoid," and thus of little utility to the "positive" and "more important" agendas of progressives.

A dismal – but entirely plausible – prospect is that such circumstances have long since foreclosed on our collective ability to do much about the danger in which we are now engulfed. U.S. progressivism presently seems to stand *vis à vis* the "law enforcement" establishment like a person who has walked to the middle of a railway bridge and suddenly faces a locomotive bearing down on him or her at miles per hour. There is no way to outrun the engine of destruction, and no place to turn for safety. Worse, the posture of far too many people on the left suggests they are continuing to amble along with their backs to the train, *still* remaining unaware that they are just about to be run over. This last is readily borne out by the number of progressives who have rallied nationally to the cause of removing assault rifles and other semi-automatic weapons from the hands of the populace, while doing nothing to confront the rampant proliferation of SWAT capabilities among police forces throughout the country.[108] Another choice indicator may be apprehended in the range of ostensibly progressive individuals and groups which have lately queued up to "take *back*...streets" they never had in the first place, righteously endorsing a government-sponsored "war on drugs" entailing unprecedented police prerogatives to engage in no-knock entry, warrantless search and seizure, the routine "interdiction" of people of color driving along the nation's highways, uncompensated impoundment of personal property, massive applications of physical and electronic surveillance, the use of preventive detention on a wholesale basis, and myriad other abridgements of civil rights and liberties which would have remained unthinkable just five years ago.[109]

Grounds for Hope, Program for Action

A cynic might argue, and with considerable justification, that a people which follows such a course will eventually get exactly what it deserves: fascism (and, Bertram Gross' phrase notwithstanding, the form is hardly "friendly"[110]). Demonstrably, we are at or very near this point. Yet, despite all, we remain very far from a social consensus on either the acceptability or inevitability of such an outcome. As the very existence of the RATF, Resistance Conspiracy, Ohio 7, *Los Macheteros* and the FALN, and a range of other entities makes abundantly clear, there are still many who are prepared to struggle with every fiber of their beings to prevent the culmination of fascist reality in the U.S. And, as the jurors who acquitted Filiberto Ojeda Ríos, the "Son of Brinks" group, and those of the Ohio 7 tried for seditious conspiracy and RICO violations have shown beyond any real question, there remain numerous "plain, ordinary, apolitical folk" who can and will respond favorably to such a stance when afforded a tangible opportunity to do so. These people, activists and jurors alike, regardless of the issues and perspectives which may divide them, are nonetheless bound together in what the German theoretician Rudi Dutschke once defined as the "anti-authoritarian impulse."[111] Herein lies the hope – perhaps the only hope – of an alternative to the specter described herein.

To be sure, mere hope is no solution to anything. It represents a point of departure, no more. The development of viable options to avert consummation of a full-fledged police state in North America will require a deep rethinking, among many who purport to oppose it, of priorities and philosophical positions, including the near hegemony of pacifism and nonviolence on the left. The emphasis accorded confrontation with the police and penal systems will have to increase rapidly and dramatically within virtually all groups pursuing progressive social agendas, from environmentalism to abortion rights. The fates of prisoners, *particularly* those incarcerated for having been accused of engaging in armed struggle against the state, must thus be made a central concern – and primary focus of activism – in every politically conscious sector of the U.S. population. Understandings must be achieved that what is currently being done to political prisoners and prisoners of war, in "exemplary" fashion, is ultimately designed for application to far wider groups than is now the case; that the facilities in which such things are done to them are intended to eventually house us all; that the enforcement apparatus which has been created to combat their "terrorism" simultaneously holds the capacity to crush all that we hold dear or seek to achieve, soon and perhaps irrevocably. In sum, if we do not move – and quickly – to overcome our tactical differences to the extent that we can collectively and effectively confront the emergent structure of "law enforcement" in this country, all the rest of our lofty and constructive social preoccupations will shortly be rendered meaningless by the very forces we have all too frequently elected to ignore.

There are many points of attack open to us, places where important victories can and must be attained. These include renewed and concerted efforts to extend real community control over local police forces, the dismantling of localized police SWAT capabilities, the curtailment or elimination of national computer net participation by state and local police forces, the abolition of police "intelligence" units, and deep cuts in the resources (both monetary and in terms of personnel) already allocated to the police establishment. The judicial system, too, must become an increasing focus of broad-based progressive attention; not only is substantial support work vitally necessary with regard to activists brought to court on serious charges, but every judicial ruling – whether or not it is rendered in an overtly political trial – which serves to undercut citizen rights while legitimating increased police intervention in the political process must be met with massive, national expressions of outrage and rejection. It is incumbent upon us to infuse new force and meaning into "the court of public opinion," using every method at our disposal. By the same token, maximal energy must be devoted to heading off the planned expansion of penal facilities across the U.S. and securing the abolition of "control units" within every existing prison in the country. The BoP and state "adult authorities" must also be placed, finally, under effective citizens' control, and the incipient "privatization" of large portions of the "prison industry" must be blocked at all costs. Plainly, this represents a tremendously ambitious bill of fare for any social movement.

Coming to grips with the FBI is of major importance. The Bureau has long since made itself an absolutely central ingredient in the process of repression in America, not only extending its own operations in this regard, but providing doctrine, training and equipment to state and local police, organizing the special "joint task forces" which have sprouted in every major city since 1970, creating the computer nets which tie the police together nationally, and providing the main themes of propaganda by which the rapid build-up in police power has been accomplished in the U.S. Similarly, the FBI provides both doctrinal and practical training to prison personnel – especially in connection with those who supervise POWs and political prisoners – which is crucial in the shaping of the policies pursued within the penal system as a whole. Hence, so long as the FBI is able to retain the outlook which defined COINTELPRO, and to translate that outlook into "real world" endeavors, it is reasonable to assume that both the police and prison "communities" will follow right along. Conversely, should the FBI ever be truly leashed, with the COINTELPRO mentality at last rooted out once and for all, it may be anticipated that the emergent U.S. police state apparatus will undergo substantial unraveling.

In the concluding chapter of *Agents of Repression*, we offered both tactical and strategic sketches of how the task of bringing the Bureau to heel might be approached. In his book, *War at Home*, Brian Glick extends these ideas in certain directions. At the same time, both we and Glick indicated that our recommendations should be considered anything but definitive, and that readers should rely upon their own experience and imaginations in devising ways and means of getting the job done. Since publication of those books, a number of people have contacted us to expand upon our ideas and to enter new ones. Although the specifics vary in each case, there are two consistent themes underlying such contributions. These are first that is it is imperative more and more people take the step of translating their consciousness into active resistance and, second, that this resistance must be truly multifaceted and flexible in form. We heartily agree.

Hence, we would would like to close with what seems to us the only appropriate observation, paraphrasing Malcolm X and Huey P. Newton: We are confronted with the necessity of a battle which must be continued until it has been won. That choice has already been made for us, and we have no option to simply wish it away. To lose is to bring about the unthinkable, and there is no place to run and hide. Under the circumstances, the FBI and its allies must be combatted by all means available, and *by any means necessary*.

Organizational Contacts

The following are organizations currently involved in the sorts of work described in the conclusion to this book. People wishing to become involved in the sorts of struggles thus represented should contact one or more of them for further information.

Emergency Committee for
Political Prisoners
P.O. Box 28191
Washington, D.C. 20038

Committee to End the Marion
Lockdown
343 S. Dearborn, Suite 1607
Chicago, IL 60604

Center for Constitutional
Rights/Movement Support
666 Broadway, 7th Floor
New York, NY 10012

National Committee to Free
Puerto Rican Prisoners
P.O. Box 476698
Chicago, IL 60647

National Committee Against
Repressive Legislation
501 C Street, NE
Washington, DC 20002

New Afrikan People's
Organization
P.O. Box 11464
Atlanta, GA 30310

Justice for Geronimo
Campaign
214 Duboce Avenue
San Francisco, CA 94103

National Alliance Against
Racist/Political Repression
126 W. 119th Street
New York, NY 10026

National Emergency Civil
Rights Committee
175 Fifth Avenue
New York 10010

The National Prison Project
1616 P Street, NW
Washington, DC 20035

Comm. to Fight Repression
Box 1435, Cathedral Station
New York, NY 10025

Peltier Defense Committee
P.O. Box 583
Lawrence, KS 66044

Saxifrage Group
1484 Wicklow
Boulder, CO 80303

Anti-Repression Resources
P.O. Box 122,
Jackson, MS 39205

National Lawyers Guild
55 Ave. of the Americas
New York, NY 10013

Nuclear Resister
P.O. Box 43383
Tucson, AZ 85733

People's Law Office
633 S. Dearborn, No. 1614
Chicago, IL 60604

The Real Dragon
P.O. Box 3294
Berkeley, CA 94703-9901

Political Rights Defense
Fund
P.O. Box 649, Cooper Station
New York, NY 1000

Partisan Defense Committee
c/o R. Wolkensten, Esq.
P.O. Box 99, Canal St. Station
New York, NY 10013

Free Puerto Rico Committee
P.O. Box 022512
Cadman Plaza, Brooklyn
New York, NY 11202

End Papers

I say it has gone too far. We are dividing into the hunted and the hunters. There is loose in the United States today the same evil that once split Salem Village between the bewitched and the accused and stole men's reason quite away. We are informers to the secret police. Honest men are spying on their neighbors for patriotism's sake. We may be sure that for every honest man two dishonest ones are spying for personal advancement today and ten will be spying for pay next year.

– Bernard De Voto –
1949

Notes

Preface

1. Churchill, Ward, and Jim Vander Wall, *Agents of Repression: The FBI's Secret War Against the Black Panther Party and the American Indian Movement*, South End Press, Boston, 1988.

2. Glick, Brian, *War at Home: Covert Action Against U.S. Activists and What We Can Do About It*, South End Press, Boston, 1989.

3. Taylor, Flint, and Margaret Vanhouten (eds.), *Counterintelligence: A Documentary Look at America's Secret Police*, National Lawyer's Guild, Chicago, 1982.

4. U.S. Senate, Select Committee on Intelligence, *The FBI and CISPES*, 101st Congress, 1st Session, Rep. No. 101-46, U.S. Government Printing Office, Washington, D.C., 1989.

5. U.S. House of Representatives, Committee on the Judiciary, Subcommittee on Civil and Constitutional Rights, *Break-Ins at Sanctuary Churches and Organizations Opposed to Administration Policy in Central America*, Serial No. 42, 100th Congress, 1st Session, Government Printing Office, Washington, D.C., 1988, Hearing of February 19-20, 1987, pp. 432 ff. Also see Harlan, Christi, "The Informant Left Out in the Cold," *Dallas Morning News*, April 6, 1986; Gelbspan, Ross, "Documents show Moon group aided FBI," *Boston Globe*, Apri l 18, 1988; and Ridgeway, James, "Spooking the Left," *Village Voice*, March 3, 1987. For more on Varelli's role and the FBI's attempt to scapegoat him, see Gelbspan, Ross, "COINTELPRO in the '80s: The 'New' FBI," *Covert Action Information Bulletin*, No. 31 (Winter 1989), pp. 14-16.

6. See, for example, the FBI teletype on p. 18. Also see Buitrago, *Report on CISPES Files Maintained by FBI Headquarters and Released Under the Freedom of Information Act*, Fund for Open Information and Accountability, Inc., New York, 1988; *Groups Included in the CISPES Files Obtained from FBI Headquarters*, Center for Constitutional Rights, 1988; Ridgeway, James, "Abroad at Home: The FBI's Dirty War," *Village Voice*, February 9, 1988.

7. U.S. House of Representatives, Committee on the Judiciary, Subcommittee on Civil and Constitutional Rights, *CISPES and FBI Counter-Terrorism Investigations*, Serial No. 122, 100th Congress, 2nd Session, U.S. Government Printing Office, Washington, D.C., 1989, Hearing of September 16, 1988, pp. 116-27. The changing public positions taken by Webster and Sessions concerning the FBI's CISPES operations are well traced in Buitrago, Ann Mari, "Sessions' Confessions," *Covert Action Information Bulletin*, No. 31 (Winter 1989), pp. 17-19.

8. Zinn, Howard, *A People's History of the United States*, Harper and Row Publishers, New York, 1980, p. 543. Also see Johnson, Loch, *A Season of Inquiry: The Senate Intelligence Investigation*, University of Kentucky Press, Lexington, 1985, pp. 221, 271; and Hersh, Seymour, *The Price of Power*, Simon and Schuster, New York, 1983, p. 295.

9. The campaigns against Church and Bayh are documented in the files of Political Research Associates, Cambridge, Mass. On Wright, see Barry, John M., *The Ambition and the Power: The Fall of Jim Wright, A True Story of Washington*, Viking, New York, 1989.

10. *The FBI and CISPES, op. cit.*, p.15.

11. *Break-Ins at Sanctuary Churches and Organizations Opposed to Administration Policy in Central America, op. cit.*, pp. 515-6.

12. *The FBI and CISPES, op. cit.*, p.1.

13. Tolan, Sandy, "Tough Guys Don't Dance: How the FBI Infiltrated Earth First," *Village Voice*, July 25, 1989, p. 19; Ridgeway, James and Bill Gifford, "The Gritz Gets His," *Village Voice*, July 25, 1989, pp. 18; Kuipers, Dean, "Raising Arizona," *Spin*, September 1989, p. 32.

14. "U.S. Targets NLG Attorney in Grand Jury Contempt," *National Lawyers Guild Notes*, May-June 1990, pp. 11-2.

15. *A Report from the City of Birmingham, Alabama to the United States Senate Judiciary Committee on the Harassment of African-American Birmingham City Officials by Offices of the United States Attorney, The Federal Bureau of Investigation, and the Internal Revenue Service (Criminal Division)*, reprinted in *Congressional Record*, Vol. 136, No. 23, March 9, 1990. "Harassment of African American Elected Officials," Resolution of the National Council of Churches, November 16, 1989; Sawyer, Mary R., *Harassment of Black Elected*

Officials: Ten Years Later, Voter Education and Registration Action Inc., Washington, D.C., 1987.

16. Gitlin, Todd, *The Sixties: Years of Hope, Days of Rage*, Bantam Books, 1987, pp. 363-4. The discovery of the covert operation is described in *War at Home, op. cit.*, p. 47.

16. "Quoted from *"Racial Matters:" The FBI's Secret File on Black America, 1960-1972*, was published by The Free Press, New York, 1989, pp. 297, 293-4, 322-3, 295, 316.

Introduction

1. U.S. Senate Select Committee to Study Government Operations with Respect to Intelligence Operations, *Intelligence Activities and the Rights of Americans, Book II*, 94th Congress, 2d Session, U.S. Government Printing Office, Washington, D.C., 1976.

2. Theoharis, Athan, "Building a File: The Case Against the FBI," *Washington Post*, October 30, 1988.

3. Theoharis' credentials in being cast as an expert in this regard are rather impressive on their face, and include several books on or related to the topic. These include *The Yalta Myths: An Issue in U.S. Politics, 1945-1955* (University of Missouri Press, Columbia, 1970), *The Seeds of Repression: Harry S. Truman and the Origins of McCarthyism* (Quadrangle Books, Chicago, 1971), *Spying on Americans: Political Surveillance from Hoover to the Huston Plan* (Temple University Press, Philadelphia, 1978), *The Truman Presidency: The Origins of the Imperial Presidency and the National Security State* (E.M. Coleman Enterprises, New York, 1979), *Beyond the Hiss Case: The FBI, Congress, and the Cold War* (Temple University Press, Philadelphia, 1982), and, with John Stuart Cox, *The Boss: J. Edgar Hoover and the Great American Inquisition* (Temple University Press, Philadelphia, 1988). He has also co-edited, with Robert Griffith, *The Specter: Original Essays on the Cold War and the Origins of McCarthyism* (New View Points, New York, 1974). Hence, he had ample reason to know better than most of the things he claimed to believe in his review. One explanation of why he said them anyway is that we failed to cite any of his proliferate material in *Agents*. His ego appears to have suffered mightily as a result.

4. It's a bit surprising Theoharis elected to challenge our contention that COINTELPRO was continued after the FBI claimed it was ended. In his own *Spying on Americans (op. cit.*, p. 150), he observes, "The decision to terminate COINTELPRO was not then a decision to terminate COINTELPRO-type activities...In April 1971, [J. Edgar] Hoover had simply ordered discontinuance of a formal, and for that reason vulnerable, program. In the future such activities could still be instituted *ad hoc*." Nor is this mere theorizing on the author's part, a matter he makes quite clear on the following page: "The Senate Select Committee on Intelligence Activities investigation of COINTELPRO [to which Theoharis served as a consultant], moreover, uncovered at least three COINTELPRO-type operations conducted after Hoover's April 28, 1971, termination order." We will be forgiven for observing that this is *exactly* the thesis in *Agents* Theoharis chose to attack most vociferously.

5. It should be noted that the reviewer's reasoning here runs directly counter to that which he himself expressed (*ibid.*, p. 151) when he quoted staff counsel to the Senate Select Committee Barbara Banoff in 1975: "The Committee has not been able to determine with any [great] precision the extent to which COINTELPRO may be continuing. Any proposals to initiate COINTELPRO-type actions [or reports on such actions] would be filed under the individual case caption. The Bureau has over 500,000 case files, and each one would have to be searched." Certainly, this rule applies to AIM and its members as much as to any other organization or individuals. For the record, Banoff refers to five previously undisclosed COINTELPROs rather than the three Theoharis acknowledges having been ongoing after 1971 (see note 3, above).

6. For starters, it should be mentioned that thousands of documents and the testimony of scores of witnesses went into preparation of the Select Committee's report on the COINTELPRO waged against the Black Panther Party (*The FBI's Covert Program to Destroy the Black Panther Party*, U.S. Government Printing Office, Washington, D.C., 1976). By contrast, when the Senate Subcommittee on Internal Security prepared its report on AIM during the same year (*Revolutionary Activities in the United States: The American Indian Movement*, U.S. Government Printing Office, 1976), *no* official documents and only *one* witness – FBI infiltrator/*provocateur* Douglass Durham – were utilized as a basis.

7. This led directly to one of the three post-1971 "COINTELPRO-type" operations Theoharis acknowledges: "The leaking of derogatory information about Daniel Ellsberg's lawyer to Ray McHugh, chief of the Copley News Service." (*Spying on Americans, op. cit.*, p. 151).

8. The break-in at the Media resident agency, which occurred on the night of March 8, 1971, compromised the secrecy of COINTELPRO and thereby set in motion a process of high level "re-

evaluation" of the program's viability. This led to an April 28 memorandum from Charles D. Brennan, number two man in the COINTELPRO administrative hierarchy, to his boss, FBI Assistant Director William C. Sullivan. Brennan recommended the acronym be dropped, but that the activities at issue be continued under a new mantle "with tight procedures to insure absolute secrecy." Hoover's famous "COINTELPRO termination" memo of the following day was merely a toned-down paraphrase of the Brennan missive. In another connection, it should be noted that publication of the COINTELPRO documents taken from the Media office was not in itself sufficient to cause the FBI to admit either the long-term existence or the dimension of its domestic counterintelligence activities. Instead, this required a suit brought by NBC correspondent Carl Stern after the reporter had requested that Attorney General Richard Kleindienst provide him with a copy of any Bureau document which "(i) authorized the establishment of Cointelpro – New Left, (ii) terminated such program, and (iii) ordered or authorized any change in the purpose, scope or nature of such program" on March 20, 1972. Kleindienst stalled until January 13, 1973 before denying Stern's request. Stern then went to court under provision of the 1966 version of the FOIA, with the Justice Department counter-arguing that the judiciary itself "lacks jurisdiction over the subject matter of the complaint." Finally, on July 16, 1973 U.S. District Judge Barrington Parker ordered the documents delivered to his chambers for *in camera* review and, on September 25, ordered their release to Stern. The Justice Department attempted to appeal this decision on October 20, but abandoned the effort on December 6. On the latter date, Acting Attorney General Robert Bork released the first two documents to Stern, an action followed on March 7, 1974 by the release of seven more. By this point, there was no way to put the genie back in the bottle, and the Senate Select Committee as well as a number of private attorneys began to force wholesale disclosures of COINTELPRO papers.

9. The classic articulation of how this was rationalized came in the 1974 Justice Department report on COINTELPRO produced by an "investigating committee" headed by Assistant Attorney General Henry Peterson. After reviewing *no* raw files (innocuously worded FBI "summary reports" were accepted instead), but still having to admit that many aspects of COINTELPRO violated the law, the Peterson committee nonetheless recommended against prosecuting *any* of the Bureau personnel involved: "Any decision as to whether prosecution should be undertaken must also take into account several other important factors which bear on the events in question. These factors are: first, the historical context in which the programs were conceived and executed by the Bureau in response to public and even Congressional demands for action to neutralize the self-proclaimed revolutionary aims and violence prone activities of extremist groups which posed a threat to the peace and tranquility of our cities in the mid and late sixties; second, the fact that each of the COINTELPRO programs were personally approved and supported by the late Director of the FBI; and third, the fact that the interference with First Amendment rights resulting from individual implemented program actions were insubstantial." The Senate Select Committee and other bodies went rather further in their research and used much harsher language in describing what had happened under COINTELPRO auspices, but the net result in terms of consequences to the Bureau and its personnel were precisely the same: none.

10. Examples abound. Early instances come with Jimmy Carter's Executive Order 12036, signed on January 24, 1978, which moved important areas of intelligence/counterintelligence activity under the umbrella of "executive restraint" rather than effective oversight, and the electronic surveillance loopholes imbedded in S. 1566, a draft bill allegedly intended to protect citizens' rights from such police invasion of privacy, which passed the senate by a vote of 99-1 on April 20, 1978. This was followed on December 4, 1981 by Ronald Reagan's Executive Order 12333, expanding the range of activities in which U.S. intelligence agencies might "legally" engage. Then there was the Intelligence Identities Protection Act of 1982 which made it a "crime" to disclose the identities of FBI informants, infiltrators and *provocateurs* working inside domestic political organizations. And, in 1983, Reagan followed up with Executive Order 12356, essentially allowing agencies such as the FBI to void the Freedom of Information Act by withholding documents on virtually any grounds they choose. Arguably, things are getting worse, not better.

11. For an in-depth analysis of the disinformation campaign at issue, see Weisman, Joel D., "About that 'Ambush' at Wounded Knee,"*Columbia Journalism Review*, September-October 1975.

12. To the contrary, as Theoharis quotes Barbara Banoff in *Spying on Americans, op. cit.*, p. 151, "a search of all investigative files" rather than merely those the FBI consents to release in any given instance stands to reveal hidden COINTELPRO activity.

13. U.S. Commission on Civil Rights, *Report of Investigation: Oglala Sioux Tribe, General Election, 1974*, U.S. Government Printing Office, Washington, D.C., 1974.

14. U.S. Commission on Civil Rights, *Monitoring of Events Related to the Shootings of Two FBI Agents on the Pine Ridge Reservation*, Mountain States Regional Office, Denver, CO, July 9, 1975.

15. The statement comes from the trial transcript of *U.S. v. Dennis Banks and Russell Means*, (383 F.Supp. 368, August 20, 1974) as quoted in the *New York Times*, September 17, 1974. For further information, see *Dennis Banks and Russell Means v. United States* (374 F.Supp. 321, April 30, 1974).

16. Public summary of jury foreman Robert Bolin, quoted in the *Cedar Rapids* (Iowa) *Gazette*, July 17, 1976.

17. In fact, the Senate Select Committee for which Theoharis worked reached exactly the opposite conclusion: "While the FBI considered federal prosecution the 'logical' result, it should be noted that key activists [such as the Panther leadership] were chosen not because they were suspected of having committed or planning to commit any specific federal crime." (U.S. Congress, Senate Select Committee on Government Operations with Respect to Intelligence Activities, *Final Report: Supplementary Detailed Staff Reports on Intelligence Activities and the Rights of Americans, Book III*, 94th Congress, 2d Session, U.S. Government Printing Office, 1976).

18. See Ji Jaga (Pratt), Geronimo, *Report on the Prison Suit Pratt v. Rees*, Geronimo Pratt Defense Committee, San Francisco, 1982. For a fuller elaboration of the overall case, see Churchill, Ward, and Jim Vander Wall, "COINTELPRO Against the Black Panthers: The Case of Geronimo Pratt," *Covert Action Information Bulletin*, No. 31, January 1989, pp. 35-9.

19. Means finally served a year in the South Dakota State Prison at Sioux Falls, but not for any charge among the original forty. Rather, he was sentenced for his "contempt" of South Dakota Judge Richard Braithwaite, signified by refusing to stand when the judge entered the courtroom, and by defending himself when the judge ordered armed deputies to physically assault him as a consequence. At the time of his release from prison, Means was on the Amnesty International list of persons to be adopted as a prisoner of conscience; see *Proposal for a commission of inquiry into the effect of domestic intelligence activities on criminal trials in the United States of America*, Amnesty International, New York, 1980.

20. The Moves Camp affair is covered exceedingly well in Matthiessen, Peter, *In the Spirit of Crazy Horse*, Viking Press, New York, 1984, pp. 93-8.

21. *Ibid.*, pp. 113-6.

22. This was admitted by the government before the U.S. Eighth Circuit Court of Appeals on April 12, 1978 (*United States v. Leonard Peltier*, C77-3003).

23. See Matthiessen, *op. cit.*, pp. 345-6.

24. For a synthesis of this sort of material documented in *Agents*, see Churchill, Ward, "Renegades, Terrorists, and Revolutionaries: The Government's Propaganda War Against the American Indian Movement," *Propaganda Review*, No. 4, April 1989.

25. Note once again that both the Senate Select Committee and Theoharis himself long ago reached the conclusion that the FBI had simply abandoned tell-tale headings like "COINTELPRO" while continuing political counterintelligence operations hidden under individual file captions. Such conclusions correspond very well with statements made under oath by former agents such as M. Wesley Swearingen that, "The program had been 'officially' discontinued in April, 1971, but agents...continued to carry out the program's objectives." (Swearingen Deposition, Honolulu, Hawaii, October 1980, p. 2).

26. See, for example, *Harassment Update: Chronological List of FBI and Other Harassment Incidents*, Movement Support Network and Center for Constitutional Rights/National Lawyers Guild Anti-Repression Project, New York, January 1987 (Sixth Edition).

27. For a solid examination of the government conspiracy to "get" Garvey by whatever means it could conjure up, see Hill, Robert A., "The Foremost Radical of His Race: Marcus Garvey and the Black Scare, 1918-1920," *Prologue*, No. 16, Winter 1984. A broader view of the man and his accomplishments is offered in Vincent, Ted, *Black Power and the Garvey Movement*, Nzinga Publishing House, Oakland, CA, 1987. Also see Cronon, E. Davis, *Black Moses: The Story of Marcus Garvey and the United Negro Improvement Association*, University of Wisconsin Press, Madison, 1955.

28. A massive collection of documents on the Hiss case is available in book form, edited by Edith Tiger under the title *In Re Alger Hiss* (Hill and Wang Publishers, New York, 1979). There are also a number of good books available on the subject. A particularly interesting early example is Cook, Fred J., *The Unfinished Story of Alger Hiss*, William Morrow Company, New York, 1958. Also see Chabot Smith, John, *Alger Hiss: The True Story*, Holt, Rinehart and Winston Publishers, New York, 1976. Perhaps the

definitive treatment of the matter may be found in Weinstein, Allen, *Perjury: The Hiss-Chambers Case*, Alfred A. Knopf Publisher, New York, 1978.

29. For further information on the FBI's anti-CISPES operations, see Buitrago, Ann Mari, *Report on CISPES Files Maintained by the FBI and Released under the Freedom of Information Act*, FOIA, Inc., New York, January 1988.

30. There was another ostensible COINTELPRO conducted during the 1960s with which we do not deal (the FBI itself lists a total of twelve in its reading room catalogue, but several of these were directed against the same general target, *e.g.*: COINTELPRO-CP,USA and Operation Hoodwink). This was the so-called Counterintelligence Program – White Hate Groups, directed primarily at the ku klux klan, undertaken by COINTELPRO head William C. Sullivan during the period of the most significant civil rights activism in the South, and continued for several years. Although writers such as Athan Theoharis (see *Spying on Americans, op. cit.*) and Don Whitehead (see his *Attack on Terror: The FBI Against the Ku Klux Klan in Mississippi*, Funk and Wagnall's Publishers, New York, 1970) have made much of this undertaking, we have elected not to include it along with our analyses of operations directed against progressive organizations because it seems to have been altogether different in intent.While we recognize that there was (and probably is) a genuine counterintelligence dimension to the Bureau's dealings with the klan, its purpose seems all along to have been not so much to destroy the klan and related groups as to gain control of them in order to use them as surrogate forces against the left. As Glick (*op. cit.*) observes at pages 12-3, "This unique 'program' functioned largely as a component of the FBI's operations against the progressive activists who were COINTELPRO's main targets. Under the cover of being even-handed and going after violent right-wing groups, the FBI actually gave covert aid to the Ku Klux Klan, Minutemen, Nazis, and other racist vigilantes. These groups received substantial funds, information and protection – and suffered only token FBI harassment – so long as they directed their violence against COINTELPRO targets. They were not subjected to serious disruption unless they breached this tacit understanding and attacked established business and political leaders."

Chapter 1: Understanding Deletions in FBI Documents

1. Buitrago, Ann Mari, and Leon Andrew Immerman, *Are You Now or Have You Ever Been in the FBI Files?* Grove Press, New York, 1981, p. 53.

2. This, in the vernacular, is called an "XGDS [Exempt from General Declassification Schedule]," defined in E.O. 11652, Section 5 (A), 5 (B), and is a Bureau favorite.

3. Buitrago and Immerman, *op. cit.*, p. 61.

4. There was an earlier Reagan executive order, E.O. 12333, signed on December 4, 1981, which paved the way for this. See Editors, "The Executive Order," *Covert Action Information Bulletin*, No. 16, March 1982.

5. Buitrago and Immerman, *op. cit.*, p. 72.

6. See "Former Agent [M. Wesley Swearingen] Challenges Claims on Withholding Files in SWP Case," *Access Reports 5*, January 23, 1979, pp. 8-9. The former agent's understanding of the situation is corroborated by no less an authority on the subject than J. Edgar Hoover, who, in a 1968 memorandum to the attorney general, conceded that: "...as a general rule, all of our security informants are available for interview by Department attorneys and for testimony if needed"; cited in "ACLU Plaintiff's Memorandum in Opposition to Federal Defendants' Motion to Reconsider June 7, 1977 Order Relating to Informer's Privilege," *American Civil Liberties Union v. City of Chicago* (N.D. Ill. No. 75 C 3295, 1978), p. 14.

7. Buitrago and Immerman, *op. cit.*, p. 69.

8. See the U.S. House of Representatives report on operational definitions under the 1966 version of the Freedom of Information Act reproduced in Marwick, Christine M. (ed.), *Litigation Under the Amended Freedom of Information Act*, Center for National Security Studies, Washington, D.C., (Fourth Edition) 1978, p. 15.

9. *Department of the Air Force v. Rose*, 45 U.S. 352, 369-70 (1976).

10. *Access Reports*, Access Reference File, 14.05.

11. Buitrago and Immerman, *op. cit.*, p. 78.

12. The Pratt FOIA documents are stored by the law offices of Jonathan Lubell, New York.

13. The Hampton-Clark FOIA documents are stored by the People's Law Office, Chicago.

Chapter 2: COINTELPRO–CP,USA

1. U.S. Senate, Select Committee to Study Government Operations with Respect to Intelligence Activities, *Intelligence Activities and the Rights of Americans, Book II*, 94th Congress, 2d Session, U.S. Government Printing Office, Washington, D.C., 1976, pp. 14 (esp. n. 82), 66, 211.

2. Quoted in U.S. Senate, Select Committee to Study Government Operations with Respect to Intelligence Activities, *Hearings on Intelligence Activities, Vol. 6: The Federal Bureau of Investigation*, 94th Congress, 1st Session, U.S. Government Printing Office, Washington, D.C., 1975, pp. 372-6.

3. Quoted in *Intelligence Activities and the Rights of Americans, Book II, op. cit.*, pp. 66-7.

4. Actually, there were two left factions which broke off from the SPA in September 1919: the CP and the Communist Labor Party (CLP), headed by John Reed, Benjamin Gitlow and Alfred Wagenknecht. The differences between the CP and the CLP were both sectarian and miniscule, and they were ordered merged by the Comintern in 1921. See Draper, Theodore, *The Roots of American Communism*, Viking Press, New York, 1963, pp. 50-79. Also see Rosenstone, Robert A., *Romantic Revolutionary: A Biography of John Reed*, Vintage Books, New York, 1981, pp. 354-5.

5. See Goldstein, Robert Justin, *Political Repression in Modern America, 1870 to the Present*, Schenkman Publishing Co./Two Continents Publishing Group, Ltd., Cambridge/London, 1978, p. 141. Also see Noggel, Earl, *Into the Twenties: The United States from Armistice to Normalcy*, University of Illinois Press, Urbana, 1974, pp. 31-45; and Murray, Robert K., *Red Scare: A Study in National Hysteria*, McGraw-Hill Publishers, New York, 1964, pp. 7-9.

6. Quoted in Coben, Stanley, *A. Mitchell Palmer: Politician*, Columbia University Press, New York, 1963, p. 209.

7. Goldstein, *op. cit.*, pp. 149-50. Also see Murray, *op. cit.*, pp. 193-4; Jensen, Vernon H., *The Price of Vigilance*, Rand-McNally Publishers, Chicago, 1968, p. 275; and Lowenthal, Max, *The Federal Bureau of Investigation*, Harcourt-Brace Publishers, New York, 1950, pp. 83-143.

8. See Jaffe, Julian K., *Crusade Against Radicalism: New York During the Red Scare*, Kennikat Publishers, Port Washington, NY, 1972, pp. 179-81. Also see Warth, Robert, "The Palmer Raids," *South Atlantic Quarterly*, No. 48, January 1949, pp. 1-23; Murray, *op. cit.*, pp. 196-7; and Coben, *op. cit.*, pp. 219-21.

9. See Chafee, Zechariah, *Free Speech in the United States*, Atheneum Publishers, New York, 1969, pp. 247-60. Also see Murray, *op. cit.*, p. 198; Coben *op. cit.*, pp. 221-2; and Warth, *op. cit.*, p. 7. It should be noted that J. Edgar Hoover went personally to the dock to watch the *Buford* depart.

10. Goldstein, *op. cit.*, p. 156. Also see Preston, William Jr., *Aliens and Dissenters*, Harper and Row Publishers, New York, 1966, pp. 217-21; Murray, *op. cit.*, pp. 210-7; Coben, *op. cit.*, pp. 222-9; and Chafee, *op. cit.*, pp. 204-5.

11. Goldstein, *op. cit.*, p. 157. Also see Howe, Irving, and Lewis Coser, *The American Communist Party*, Praeger Publishers, New York, 1962, p. 51.

12. Goldstein, *op. cit.* Also see Muzik, Edward J., "Victor L. Berger: Congress and the Red Scare," *Wisconsin Magazine of History*, No. 47, Summer 1964.

13. Goldstein, *op. cit.* Also see Warth, *op. cit.*, pp. 16-17 and Coben, *op. cit.*, p. 241.

14. Curiously, Secretary Wilson was to decide in May of the same year that membership in the CLP was *not* sufficient grounds for denaturalization and deportation.

15. Quoted in Johnson, Donald, *The Challenge of American Freedoms*, University of Kentucky Press, Lexington, 1963, p. 163. The judge also noted that GID infiltration of the CP and CLP had been so great by January 2, 1919 that J. Edgar Hoover had actually been in a position to instruct his operatives to convene party meetings to fit the schedules desired by his raiders.

16. Goldstein, *op. cit.*, p. 101. Although the mass pressure subsided, such was not the case with targeted leaders. CP head Charles E. Ruthenburg, to name a prominent example, never spent a day free of trials and/or appeals from 1919 until his death in 1927; see Howe and Coser, *op. cit.*, pp. 52-64 and Draper, *op. cit.*, pp. 197-395. On the Non-Partisan League, see Morlan, Robert L., *Political Prairie Fire: The Non-Partisan League, 1915-1922*, University of Minnesota Press, Minneapolis, 1955.

17. See Shannon, David, *The Socialist Party of America*, Quadrangle Books, Chicago, 1967, p. 163. Also see Draper, *op. cit.*, pp. 158, 190, and 206-7.

18. On Passaic, see Johnpole, Bernard K., *Pacifist's Progress: Norman Thomas and the Decline of American Socialism*, Quadrangle Books, Chicago, 1970, p. 48. On New Bedford, see Bernstein, Irving, *The*

Lean Years, Penguin Books, Baltimore, 1966, p. 203. On Gastonia, see Howe and Coser, *op. cit.*, pp. 243-5. All three strikes were accompanied by extreme police violence and other gross violations of constitutional rights without so much as a hint of interference from the federal government.

19. On the Unemployed Movement, see Schlesinger, Arthur M., *The Crisis of the Old Order*, Houghton-Mifflin Publishers, Boston, 1966, pp. 219-20. On the Bonus Army, see Lisio, Donald J., *The President and Protest: Hoover, Conspiracy and the Bonus Riot*, University of Missouri Press, Columbia, 1974. A sample of the methods used comes in the form of a May 1932 incident in Melrose Park, Illinois in which police lined movement protestors up against a wall and hosed them down with submachineguns, wounding eight; see Bernard, Edgar, *et. al.*, *Pursuit of Freedom: Civil Liberty in Illinois*, Chicago Civil Liberties Union, 1942, p. 163.

20. Examples of this abound. CP National Secretary Dennis was arrested five separate times in Los Angeles between November 1929 and March 1930 on charges such as "speaking without a license." Such treatment was typical; in 1948, he was among the first U.S. citizens actually convicted under the Smith Act (see *Digest of the Public Record of Communism in the United States*, Fund for the Republic, New York, 1955, pp. 31-6). Barton, Secretary of the Alabama branch of the party, was arrested in the town of Bessemer during the summer of 1936 and charged under a local "seditious literature law" with possessing copies of *The Nation* and *The New Republic*; a magistrate informed him that, "It's all communist stuff and you cannot have it in Bessemer," before sentencing him to 180 days at hard labor and a $100 fine (see Auerbach, Jerold S., *Labor and Liberty: The LaFollette Committee and the New Deal*, Bobbs-Merrill Publishers, Indianapolis, 1966, pp. 94-6; also see Kreuger, Thomas A., *And Promises to Keep: The Southern Conference on Human Welfare*, Vanderbilt University Press, Nashville, TN, 1967, pp. 1-10). At the specific request of Franklin D. Roosevelt, San Francisco CP branch leader Sam Darcy and Harry Bridges, president of the International Longshoremen's and Warehousemen's Union, were unsuccessfully targeted for deportation in the aftermath of the 1934 San Francisco general strike. From there, Bridges' saga is all but unbelievable. Roosevelt persisted and, in 1940, the House of Representatives voted 330-42 to proceed with deportation even without a legal basis. The victim appealed and showed evidence that he had severed all connection with the CP in early 1937. Roosevelt nonetheless instituted executive deportation proceedings in February 1941. In September of that year, a "special examiner" appointed by the president determined that the labor leader was indeed "subversive" and warranted deportation. Bridges appealed to the Board of Immigration, which ruled in his favor. Acting Attorney General Francis Biddle then overruled the board and ordered that deportation should occur in May 1942. Bridges filed an emergency appeal with the Supreme Court, which issued a stay until it had time to review the matter more thoroughly. This did not occur until after Roosevelt's death in 1945, at which time the high court ruled in Bridges' favor. But all was not over. In May 1949, congress indicted Bridges, ostensibly for having perjured himself when he claimed in a deposition entered before the Supreme Court that he was not a communist in 1945. He was convicted, but appealed and the Supreme Court upheld him in 1953 (meanwhile, two committees formed to assist in his legal defense were placed on the attorney general's list of subversive organizations solely because of their affiliation with his case). Finally, in 1956, the Eisenhower administration tried unsuccessfully to have Bridges deported under provision of the Taft-Hartley Act (Labor-Management Relations Act, 61 *Stat.* 136 [1947]). Hence, for more than twenty years, the government pursued an unrelenting quest to banish Harry Bridges, apparently for no reason other than objections to his ideological perspective (see Larrowe, Charles P., *Harry Bridges: The Rise and Fall of Radical Labor*, Lawrence Hill Publisher, New York, 1972).

21. On Imperial Valley, see Jamieson, Stuart, *Labor Unionism in American Agriculture*, U.S. Government Printing Office, Washington, D.C., 1954, pp. 80-6; also see McWilliams, Carey, *Factories in the Fields*, Peregrine Press, Santa Barbara, CA, 1971, pp. 212-5. On Harlan County, see Bubka, Tony, "The Harlan County Coal Strike of 1931," *Labor History*, No. 11, Winter 1970, pp. 41-57; also see Tindall, George B., *The Emergence of the New South*, Louisiana State University Press, Baton Rouge, 1967, pp. 383-6.

22. The estimate is extrapolated from Goldstein, *op. cit.*, pp. 228-9: "The American Communist Party had made major gains during the war. CP membership...doubled during the war years, reaching about seventy-five thousand to eighty-five thousand by May, 1945." These figures accord well with the post-war estimate of 80,000 CP members advanced by FBI Assistant Director William C. Sullivan in his letter of resignation to J. Edgar Hoover on October 6, 1971 (the letter is reproduced verbatim as Appendix C in Sullivan, William C., with Bill Brown, *The Bureau: My Thirty Years in Hoover's FBI*, W.W. Norton Co., New York, 1975). Hence, we have simply divided the 80,000 figure in half to arrive at a rough estimate of party membership during the late 1930s.

23. On formation of HUAC (also called the "Dies Committee" in its early days, after its founder), see Patterson, James T., *Congressional Conservatism and the New Deal*, University of Kentucky Press, Lexington, 1967; also see Ogden, August R., *The Dies Committee*, Catholic University Press, Washington, D.C., 1945. On the effect of the Non-Aggression Pact upon U.S. domestic politics, see Bell, Leland V., *In Hitler's Shadow: The Anatomy of American Nazism*, Kennikat Publishers, Port Washington, NY, 1973; also see Smith, Geoffrey S., *To Save a Nation: American Countersubversives, the New Deal and the Coming of World War II*, Basic Books, New York, 1973. This context, of course, led to legislation, and not only the Smith Act of 1940. In March of 1938, congress approved a measure which called for the deportation of any alien who advocated *"any* changes in the American form of government [emphasis added]" (see Swisher, Carl, "Civil Liberties in Our Time," *Political Science Quarterly*, No. 55, September 1940, p. 340). This was followed, on October 14, 1940, by passage of the Nationality Act (54 *Stat.* 1137) which provided for deportation of communists, and exclusion of anyone who, during the decade prior to applying to immigrate, had been affiliated with communist parties or ideologies. On October 17 of the same year, the Voorhis "Anti-Propaganda" Act (54 *Stat.* 1201) was passed, requiring the registration of all organizations "advocating the overthrow of *any* government [emphasis added]." Ironically, about all this last statute accomplished was to bring about the registration of five anti-nazi organizations which listed their purpose as the pursuit of overthrowing the Hitler government in Germany. For its part, the CP simply severed all formal ties with the Soviet Comintern, and thus avoided the whole thing. See Nissen, D.R., *Federal Anti-Communist Legislation, 1931-41*, unpublished M.A. Thesis, University of Illinois, Urbana, 1955, pp. 24, 65-9. Also see Chafee, *op. cit.*, p. 461.

24. The full text of Roosevelt's 1939 directive is reproduced in U.S. House of Representatives, Committee on Internal Security, *Hearings on Domestic Intelligence Operations for Internal Security Purposes*, *Part I*, 93d Congress, 2d Session, U.S. Government Printing Office, Washington, D.C., 1974, pp. 3336-7.

25. Sullivan and Brown, *op. cit.*, p. 128.

26. *Ibid.*, p. 21. The Bureau was also engaged in a considerable amount of wiretapping of the CP during this period, in direct violation of the Federal Communications Act of 1934 (48 *Stat.* 1064; Section 605), which reads in part, "No person not being authorized *by the sender* shall intercept any communication and divulge or publish the existence, contents, substance, purport, effect, or meaning of such intercepted communication to any person [emphasis added]." In the 1937 case *U.S. v. Nardone* (58 S.Ct. 275, 302 U.S. 379, 82 L.Ed. 314), the Supreme Court clearly determined that the prohibition against wiretapping applied equally to federal agencies as to private citizens; Attorney General Robert H. Jackson therefore issued Order No. 3343 (March 15, 1940) forbidding all FBI wiretapping. On May 21, however, Franklin D. Roosevelt secretly invoked "executive privilege" to reverse the high court position, informing Jackson: "You are authorized and directed in such cases as you may approve...to authorize investigating agents that they are at liberty to secure information by listening devices direct to the conversation or other communications of persons suspected of subversive activities against the Government of the United States, including suspected spies." Jackson proceeded to allow Hoover to exercise his own "best judgment" concerning when, where and whom to tap. It is dubious that Roosevelt's directive was ever of legal standing, given that both other branches of the federal government had specifically expressed the opposite view. Roosevelt's directive might have provided the FBI a form of legitimation for its wiretapping activities had director Hoover not chosen to ignore the president's qualifying language in the same document – *"You are requested to limit [wiretapping and bugging] to a minimum and to limit them insofar as is possible to aliens* [emphasis added]." – when engaging in anti-CP operations. That this was intentional distortion rather than an "error" on the part of the Bureau was plainly revealed when Hoover convinced Attorney General Tom Clark to persuade Harry Truman to "reaffirm" the Roosevelt directive in 1946 providing a text which avoided the qualification altogether, thereby *finally* establishing a presidential directive for what the FBI had been doing all along. Truman duly complied with what was requested, but stipulated (at the suggestion of Assistant Attorney General Payton Ford) that the directive be kept secret. Hence, on July 8, 1949, Hoover issued Bureau Bulletin No. 34, instructing his agents to protect the FBI (and the administration) from the embarrassment which might accrue if the extent of electronic surveillance (and the illegal entries of various premises which usually went with the task of installing bugs) became known. This, he said, should be done by the simple expedient of not including "sensitive" information in their memoranda and reports to FBI headquarters: "[Hereafter], facts and information which are considered of a nature not expedient to disseminate or would cause embarrassment to the Bureau, if distributed" should be omitted from

everything but the "administrative pages" of Bureau documents. This allowed both Clark and Hoover (and, by extension, Truman) to simply deny what had become official policy.

27. The full text of the 1943 directive is contained in *Hearings on Domestic Intelligence Operations for Internal Security Purposes, Part 1, op. cit.,* p. 3337.

28. Quoted in U.S. Senate, Select Committee to Study Government Operations with Respect to Intelligence Activities, *Final Report: Supplementary Detailed Staff Reports on Intelligence Activities and the Rights of Americans, Book III,* 94th Congress, 2d Session, U.S. Government Printing Office, Washington, D.C., 1976, p. 16.

29. See *Intelligence Activities and the Rights of Americans, Book II, op. cit.,* pp. 66, 211 (n. 1). Also see Caute, David, *The Great Fear: The Anti-Communist Purge Under Truman and Eisenhower,* Simon and Schuster, New York, 1978. Cronin, it should be noted, was provided FBI files from which to prepare a 1945 report on "American Communism" for the American Catholic archbishops, and a 1946 sequel which went to the U.S. Chamber of Commerce.

30. Memorandum, Attorney General Tom Clark to President Harry S. Truman, August 17, 1948; Truman draft statement undated. Both documents are lodged in the Harry S. Truman Library.

31. Truman Papers, PPF 1-F, January-July 1950; Harry S. Truman Library.

32. Goldstein, *op. cit.,* p. 319. For embedded quote, see Carr, Robert K., *The House Committee on Un-American Activities,* Cornell University Press, Ithaca, NY, 1952, p. 169.

33. *Spying on Americans, op. cit.,* p. 134; Theoharis goes on to note that "FBI investigative reports...served to popularize the conclusion of bureau officials that radicals were subversive, to sensitize the American public to the internal security threat, and concomitantly to discredit individuals and/or organizations active in radical politics." The Subversive Activities Control Board was established by the McCarran Act and bore responsibility for implementing the law's "communist registration" provisions. The loyalty and security programs came into formal existence on June 20, 1940 with the U.S. Civil Service Commission's issuance of Circular No. 222, ostensibly banning all members of "the Communist Party, the German Bund, or any Communist, Nazi or Fascist organizations" from government employment. To create an enforcement mechanism, the U.S. House of Representatives passed House Resolution 66 on January 8, 1941, authorizing the FBI to "make such investigation as it might deem proper with respect to employee loyalty and employment policies and practices in the Government." H.R. 66 and corresponding FBI investigations were used in turn as the basis for a demand by the House, tendered on July 25, 1946, that the federal executive establish "a complete and unified program that will give adequate protection to our Government against individuals whose primary loyalty is to governments other than our own" (U.S. House of Representatives, Committee on the Civil Service, *Report of Investigation with Respect to Employee Loyalty and Employment Policies and Practices in the Government of the United States,* in A. Devitt Venech Papers, Harry S. Truman Library). On March 22, 1947, President Truman effected Executive Order 9835, creating a full-blown "loyalty program" and assigning the FBI a prominent role therein. The matter of the "twelve Communist party leaders...indicted under the Smith Act of 1940" refers to the so-called Dennis Case [*U.S. v. Dennis, et. al.,* 183 F.2d 201 (2nd Cir. 1950)]. As Sanford J. Ungar puts it in his *FBI: An Uncensored Look Behind the Walls* (Little, Brown and Company, Boston, 1976, p. 131): "[T]he Justice Department used the Smith Act and enormous legal resources in an effort to destroy the American Communist party. In the Dennis Case, which took nine months to try in 1949, the government prosecuted Eugene Dennis and ten other top leaders of the [CP,USA]; the case resulted in a Supreme Court declaration in 1950 [*Dennis v. U.S.,* 71 S. Ct. 857, 341 U.S. 494, 95 L. Ed. 1137, reh'g. denied, 72 S. Ct. 20, 342 U.S. 842, 96 L. Ed. 636 and 78 S. Ct. 409, 355 U.S. 936, 92 L. Ed. 419] that the Smith Act was a constitutional means for a society to protect itself. Even if the people and organizations prosecuted had little actual prospect of successfully overthrowing the government, the majority ruled, a conspiracy to try and do so could be punished." The nature of the high court's logic in this is taken up in Chapter 3. Ultimately, in addition to the twelve defendants in the Dennis case, 68 "second string" CP members were prosecuted under the Smith Act during 1951 and 1952; Goldstein, *op. cit.,* p. 332.

34. Hoover is quoted from Mollan, Robert, "Smith Act Prosecutions: The Effects of the *Dennis* and *Yates* Cases," *University of Pittsburgh Law Review,* No. 1126, June 1965, pp. 707-10. The director also appears to have claimed that the Bureau "knew every Communist in the United States" during May of 1950. Nonetheless, the numbers proved exceedingly slippery. For instance, in his 1953 report to congress, Hoover claimed – probably to influence the newly-installed Eisenhower administration – that

CP membership was more than double his 1950 estimate, 24,796, despite a further three years of unrelenting anti-communist activity having passed. See Cook, Fred J., *The FBI Nobody Knows*, Pyramid Press, New York, 1965, p. 44.

35. Quoted in Theoharis, *Seeds of Repression, op. cit.*, p. 137.

36. The pertinent portion of Eisenhower's statement reads, "On September 6, 1939, January 8, 1943, and July 24, 1950, Presidential Directives were issued requesting all law enforcement officers, both Federal and State, to promptly report all information relating to espionage, sabotage, subversive activities and related matters to the nearest field office of the [FBI];" the statement is reproduced in *Hearings on Domestic Intelligence Operations for Internal Security Purposes, Part 1, op. cit.*, pp. 3337-8.

37. *Intelligence Activities and the Rights of Americans, Book II, op. cit.*, pp. 46-7. It should be noted that the FBI always maintained that COMINFIL was an intelligence rather than counterintelligence program (as it has maintained that its anti-CP activities during World War II and the McCarthy period consisted of intelligence operations). In fact, the distinction between such terms is, in Bureau vernacular, murky-to-nonexistent. Counterintelligence requires an "intelligence" basis – infiltrators and informers, (often illegal) surveillance and "black bag jobs" (burglaries and other illegal entries of premises) – in order to be actualized. On the other hand, FBI Associate Director (and COINTELPRO specialist) William C. Sullivan tended to refer to the "counterintelligence measures necessary" to conduct adequate intelligence operations. For him – and he had operational control of such things for a decade – the terms were virtually synonymous. At one point in his memoirs, while describing what was clearly a *counter*intelligence program against the new left, he actually says, "We used the same investigative techniques against the New Left that we used successfully against the Communist party: wiretapping, informants, hidden microphones – the lot" (Sullivan and Brown, *op. cit.*, p. 149). The chances are that COMINFIL included an ample measure of counterintelligence activity, just as COINTELPRO included intelligence-gathering characteristics.

38. *Spying on Americans, op. cit.*, p. 133; on page 136, the author notes that "Hoover's 1956 decision [to launch COINTELPRO-CP,USA] was unique not because the bureau began to 'disrupt' radical organizations – the FBI had been doing that at least since 1941 – but [only] because it initiated a formal program based on written directives and responsive to direct supervisory control of the FBI director." Such "uniqueness" is, to say the least, not particularly important at all. The issue is, plainly, the nature of the Bureau's domestic counterintelligence activities, not its reporting channels. Verbal directives obviously serve the same purpose as written ones, albeit they are harder to confirm, so long as they are carried out by agents in the field (as it is clear they were, both before 1956, and after 1971).

39. *Ibid.*, p. 136; "By August 1956 bureau officials no longer considered the Communist party an actual espionage or sabotage threat [if, indeed, they ever did]."

40. *Ibid.*, p. 135; the high court rulings were *Communist Party v. Subversive Activities Control Board*, 35 U.S. 115 (1956); *Pennsylvania v. Nelson*, 350 U.S. 497 (1956); *Peters v. Hobby*, 349 U.S. 331 (1955); *Service v. Dulles*, 354 U.S. 363 (1957); *Cole v. Young*, 351 U.S. 536 (1956); *Watkins v. United States*, 354 U.S. 178 (1957); *Yates v. United States*, 354 U.S. 298 (1957); and *Jencks v. United States*, 353 U.S. 657 (1957). It is worth noting, in connection with this quote, that many FBI infiltrators achieved high rank in the CP, and thus helped set the very policy for which the party was ostensibly being persecuted. Others – three of whom testified to this effect during the Dennis trial – recruited actively for the CP, one even admitting he had done so among his "friends and relatives" in order to be "convincing" (!); see Lowenthal, *op. cit.* Such activities hardly ended when Eisenhower came into office. According to the Department of Justice, in a statement issued in August 1955, the FBI had paid a total 47 infiltrators a sum of $43,000 to operate within the CP during the period July 1953 through April 1955;see Emerson, Thomas I.,David Haber and Norman Dorsen, *Political and Civil Rights in the United States*, Little, Brown Publishers, Boston, 1967, p. 392.

41. Quoted in *Intelligence Activities and the Rights of Americans, Book II, op. cit.*, p. 281.

42. "Minutes of Cabinet Meeting, November 6, 1958;" lodged in the Dwight David Eisenhower Library, Abilene, Kansas; partially reproduced in *Intelligence Activities and the Rights of Americans, Book III, op. cit.*, pp. 69-70.

43. Goldstein, *op. cit.*, p. 407.

44. The letter is quoted in *Hearings on Intelligence Activities, Vol. 6, op. cit.*, pp. 821-6. Hoover also sent a letter outlining "internal security investigations" to the White House on July 25, 1961 at the explicit request of John F. Kennedy. Although the FBI director again failed to detail some of the more extreme activities involved in COINTELPRO-CP,USA, he revealed more than enough – as he had on several

earlier occasions – to cause anyone even vaguely concerned with fundamental political freedom to become alarmed. John Kennedy, as with Eisenhower and Truman, made no move to intervene.

45. *Hearings on Intelligence Activities, Vol. 6., op. cit.,* p. 601.

46. Goldstein, *op. cit.,* pp. 447-8. Also see Donner, Frank J., "Let Him Wear a Wolf's Head: What the FBI Did to William Albertson," *Civil Liberties Review,* No. 3, April/May 1978, pp. 12-22; Berman, Jerry J., and Morton H. Halperin (eds.), *The Abuses of the Intelligence Agencies,* Center for National Security Studies, Washington, D.C., 1975, p. 28; *Intelligence Activities and the Rights of Americans, Book II, op. cit.,* pp. 214, 240-8; *Intelligence Activities and the Rights of Americans, Book III, op. cit.,* pp. 46, 59, 72 ; and *Hearings on Intelligence Activities, Vol. 6, op. cit.,* pp. 18-9, 763-5.

47. On the number of COINTELPRO actions undertaken against the CP, see Goldstein, *op. cit.,* p. 407. On estimates of CP membership in 1946 and 1941, see Sullivan resignation letter in Sullivan and Brown, *op. cit.,* pp. 265-77. The information on the average age of CP members comes from the text of the latter book, at p. 148.

48. *Ibid.,* pp. 148-9.

49. *Ibid.,* p. 149; the plan was never consummated because the Soviets never shipped the horses.

50. Sullivan letter to Hoover, *op. cit.*

51. See Ungar, *op. cit.,* p. 306. Sullivan's talk was delivered to the United Press International Editors and Publishers Conference in Williamsburg, Virginia.

52. Letter from J. Edgar Hoover to William C. Sullivan, dated September 11, 1971, reproduced in full in Sullivan and Brown, *op. cit.,* p. 264.

Chapter 3: COINTELPRO–SWP

1. Ungar, *op. cit.,* p. 131; the other case was brought against a tiny pro-nazi group. In the SWP case, the defendants – which included top party leaders such as James Cannon and Farrell Dobbs – appealed, unsuccessfully, upon conviction in December 1941; see *Dunne v. United States,* 138 F.2d 137 (8th Cir. 1943), *cert. denied,* 320 U.S. 790 (1944). The FBI's actions against the SWP were also supposedly predicated on the party's possible violation of the 1938 Foreign Agents Registration Act (22 U.S.C. § 611 *et. seq.*), a matter which never resulted in the filing of charges. Concerning the SWP's formation in 1938, it occurred as a result of Leon Trotsky's loss of a power struggle with Josef Stalin in the USSR, resulting in the former's expulsion from the Bolshevik Party in 1927 and deportation from the Soviet Union in 1929. Meanwhile, in 1928, the Comintern had ordered the CP, USA to expel all followers of Trotsky within the U.S., which it did. The outcasts immediately reformed themselves as the Communist League (CL), began publishing a weekly newspaper titled *The Militant,* and merged themselves in 1934 with the American Workers Party (AWP), forming the Workers Party (WP). In 1936, the WP itself merged briefly with the SPA. When this arrangement did not work out, allegedly due to the SPA's "reformist tendencies" (the SPA version is that the WP was expelled for being "disruptive"), the former WP membership broke off, establishing itself this time as the SWP; the group joined Leon Trotsky's newly created Fourth International – which had emerged from Trotsky's International Left Opposition organization, to which the CL/WP/SWP group had belonged all along – the same year. The party's youth arm, the Young Socialist Alliance (YSA), was not formed until 1957.

2. Zinn, *op cit.,* p. 411. An interesting sidebar to the SWP Smith Act case is that it may well have been used to propel racketeer Teamster leader Jimmy Hoffa into power. As Goldstein (*op. cit.*) puts it at pp. 252-3: "[T]he SWP bastion among Minneapolis truckers was an increasing threat to conservative Teamsters leadership under Dan Tobin and Jimmy Hoffa, who were political allies of the Roosevelt administration. By 1938, the SWP faction of the Teamsters Union had organized two hundred fifty thousand men in eleven states in the northwest...In June, 1941, the SWP Teamsters withdrew from the AFL and joined the CIO. Tobin complained to Roosevelt on June 13 about the switch and referred to his own support to Roosevelt in 1940 and the 'radical Trotskyite' nature of the CIO teamsters. He asked Roosevelt to move against 'those disturbers who believe in the policies of foreign radical governments.' The White House press secretary shortly afterwards told the press that Roosevelt condemned the CIO for chartering the SWP group and had asked that the 'government departments and agencies interested in this,' be immediately notified. The June 28 [FBI] raid followed, resulting in indictments of twenty-nine members of the SWP, including the top union leadership in Minneapolis, under the Smith Act. Acting Attorney General Francis Biddle publicly termed the arrests the beginning of a nationwide drive against

dangerous radicals and communists. Despite the fact that no evidence was ever presented indicating any 'actual danger to either our government or our democratic way of life' eighteen SWP leaders were convicted and sent to jail for twelve to sixteen months. The trial succeeded in destroying the SWP in Minneapolis, and in the long run helped bring about the rise of Jimmy Hoffa instead of Trotskyites in the leadership of the Teamsters Union." On the Tobin/Roosevelt meeting, see Bernstein, Irving, *The Turbulent Years*, Houghton Mifflin Company, Boston, 1970, p. 781. On the Biddle statement, raid and trial, see Pahl, Thomas L., "The Dilemma of a Civil Libertarian: Francis Biddle and the Smith Act," (*Journal of the Minnesota Academy of Science*, No. 34, 1967, pp. 161-3), and "The G-String Conspiracy, Political Reprisal or Armed Revolt? The Minnesota Trotskyite Trial" (*Labor History*, No. 8, Winter 1967, pp. 30-52).

3. The Jackson opinion, and brilliant analysis of it, appear in Davis, David Bryan, *The Fear of Conspiracy*, Cornell University Press, Ithaca, NY, 1971. It should be noted that the Supreme Court's interpretation of the constitutional reality in this instance, could it have been retroactively applied, would have led to the immediate imprisonment of Thomas Jefferson, who felt it was the moral "duty" of the citizenry to forcibly overthrow the federal government approximately once every ten years. It was perhaps for this reason that Jefferson's were among the books banned from government libraries during the period in which Jackson's opinion was rendered (Zinn, *op. cit.*, p. 422).

4. Wilkinson, Frank, *The Era of Libertarian Repression – 1948 to 1973: from Congressman to President, with Substantial Support from the Liberal Establishment*, University of Akron Press, Akron, Ohio, 1974.

5. *96 Congressional Record*, 1950, pp. 15520-1.

6. Ungar, *op. cit.*, p. 132.

7. Concerning the level of FBI activity against the SWP during this period, the government's own record of the matter "enumerates 20,000 days of wiretaps and 12,000 days of listening 'bugs' between 1943 and 1963. It documents 208 FBI burglaries of offices and homes of the SWP and its members, resulting in the theft or photographing of 9,864 private documents"; Jayko, Margaret (ed.), *FBI on Trial: The Victory in the Socialist Workers Party Suit Against Government Spying*, Pathfinder Press, New York, 1988, p. 6.

8. The document appears in *Hearings on Intelligence Activities*, Vol. 6, *op. cit.*, p. 377.

9. The defendants were Robert Williams, Mae Mallory (his assistant), local Monroe residents Richard Crowder and Harold Reade, and Robert Lowry, a white Freedom Rider from New York. The group was charged with kidnapping as the result of an incident occurring on the evening of August 27, 1961. Williams managed to get out of the country, remaining exiled in Cuba, China and elsewhere for more than a decade. See Williams, Robert, *Negroes with Guns*, Third World Press, Chicago, 1973. Also see Williams' "1957: The Swimming Pool Showdown," *Southern Exposure*, No. 8, Summer 1980, pp. 22-4.

10. Perkus, Cathy (ed.), *COINTELPRO: The FBI's Secret War on Political Freedom*, Monad Press, New York, 1975, p. 93. Jayko, *op. cit.*, also details at p. 62 how: "In 1962 the FBI sent an anonymous letter to Berta Green, an SWP member and leader of the CAMD, accusing a black group involved in CAMD of misusing funds. The FBI also placed an anonymous telephone call about this accusation to one of the defendants. These communications were designed to cause strife between CAMD and the black group...In 1962 the FBI learned from an informant that CAMD was receiving financial support from the NAACP. The New York FBI office sent an anonymous letter to the NAACP stating that the CAMD was dominated and controlled by 'the Trotskyist branch of the communist movement.' The FBI believed the anonymous letter stopped the NAACP aid to CAMD...In 1962 Mayor Leo Carlin of Newark designated a certain day as CAMD Day in Newark. The Newark FBI office sent a memorandum to a newspaper contact, describing the SWP as 'a militantly revolutionary group.' The letter stated that the function of the CAMD was to instigate militant action and demonstrations. Mayor Carlin sharply curtailed the intended ceremonies...In 1964 the FBI sought to use an incident relating to CAMD in an effort to discredit the SWP in the civil rights field. There was a theft of CAMD funds from the home of a Monroe, North Carolina civil rights leader, whom an SWP member, George Weissman, was visiting at the time. The FBI sent an anonymous communication to various persons, including the black author James Baldwin and a *New York Times* reporter. The communication contained a sardonic poem, which in effect charged that Weissman had stolen the money."

11. Jayko, *op. cit.*, pp. 93-4.

12. Ungar, *op. cit.*, pp. 127-8; Paton ultimately had to go to court to force the FBI to destroy the file it had opened on her as a result. Such cases were hardly unusual during the late 1960s.

13. *Ibid.*, p. 411; the case at issue was *Socialist Workers Party, et al. v. Attorney General of the United States, et al.*, No. 73 Civ. 3160 (463 F.Supp. 515 [1978]).

14. As Perkus, *op. cit.*, points out at pp. 164-5, "Three thousand students and over 250 professors signed petitions supporting Starsky's right to academic freedom... But the regents refused to renew his contract and he lost his job in June 1970... Since ASU he has lost two other teaching jobs in California for political reasons." Nor was Starsky alone among SWP members, both inside and outside academe, in being targeted in this fashion. For instance, as Judge Greisa observes (Jayko, *op. cit.*, p. 65): "In 1964 the Newark FBI office sent an anonymous letter to Murray Zuckoff's employer. Zuckoff was an organizer of the SWP Newark branch and an alternate member of the SWP National Committee. The employer then told Zuckoff that he must discontinue his SWP activities if he wanted to retain his job." Relatedly, the judge recounts (at p. 66) how an "SWP member named [Will] Reissner testified..that he was informed by his supervisor at work that the FBI questioned the supervisor every six months over a period of three years. The FBI also questioned the minister who married Reissner and his wife. Finally, Reissner testified that when he re-applied for an apartment in New York City, after having left the city and returned, the landlord refused to rent to him again, and said that during his earlier tenancy, the FBI had come to the landlord's office 'constantly' and had questioned the landlord and his secretary about Reissner. The landlord did not want 'to go through that again.'"

15. Chomsky, Noam, "Introduction," in Perkus, *op. cit.*, pp. 9-10. He goes on to note that, "There is a fundamental difference between Watergate and Detroit. In the case of the events surrounding Watergate, the victims were men of power who expected to share in the ruling of society and the formation of ideology. In Detroit, the victims were outsiders, fair game for political repression of a sort that is quite normal. Thus, it is true, in a sense, that the punishment of Nixon and his cohorts was a vindication of our system, as this system actually operates in practice. The Nixon gang had broken the rules, directing against the political center a minor variant of the techniques of repression that are commonly applied to radical dissent."

16. Perkus, *op. cit.*, p. 40-1.

17. The document is reproduced in *ibid.*, pp. 58-9; the anti-Halstead endeavor was markedly harsher than those aimed at other major SWP candidates such as John Clarence Franklin (1960-61) and Clifton DeBerry (1964). See *ibid.* for documents. Judge Greisa, in his 1986 decision, reproduced in Jayko, *op. cit.*, pp. 23-133, makes note of similar sorts of COINTELPRO operations aimed at the SWP's black mayoral candidate in San Francisco, Sam Jordan, in 1963 (p. 61); Paul Boutelle, the SWP's black candidate for vice president in 1968 and mayor of New York in 1969 (pp. 61-2); and black SWP senatorial candidate Larry Stewart from New Jersey in 1964 (p. 65).

18. Quoted in Perkus, *op. cit..*, p. 63.

19. Quoted in *ibid.*, p. 102.

20. See Judge Greisa's 1986 decision, quoted in Jayko, *op. cit.*, pp. 63-5.

21. *Intelligence Activities and the Rights of Americans, Book III, op. cit.*, p. 73. The case at issue is *Stern v. Richardson*, 367 F.Supp. 1316 (D.D.C. 1973).

22. Lobash, Arnold H., "316 Used by FBI in Informer Role," *New York Times*, September 5, 1976, p. 24; the author indicates these activities had been continued without interruption from the point of COINTELPRO-SWP's initiation in 1961 through the point of his report in 1976 (*i.e.*: five years after the COINTELPRO supposedly ended, and a full decade after the Bureau claimed to have ended its practice of burglarizing its targets for other reasons). Judge Greisa, in Jayko (*op. cit.*), concludes among other things that: "During the period 1960-76 there were a total of about 300 member informants and about 1,000 non-member informants used by the FBI in the SWP investigation" (p. 48), that the total percentage of SWP membership ran at about 10% throughout the '60s and still stood at least as high as 3% in 1976 (pp. 51-2), that many of these individuals consistently fit the role of *provocateurs* (pp. 53-4), "[a]bout 55 FBI informants held offices or committee positions in SWP and YSA between 1960 and 1976 [while] approximately 51 informants served on executive committees or executive boards (pp. 54-5), and that during the period in question these infiltrators "supplied the FBI with about 12,600 SWP and YSA documents, about 7,000 of which were intended to be available only within the organizations. These private documents included membership lists, financial records, financial budgets and projections, minutes of meetings, mailing lists, and correspondence. The member informants generally obtained the documents from SWP and YSA offices, although at least one member informant obtained confidential documents from the residence of another member...Many of the member informants served over

lengthy periods of time. This provided the FBI with a steady and voluminous flow of detailed information. [O]ne unidentified informant worked in a local SWP office over a ten-year period opening all mail and regularly furnishing the FBI with [information] not publicly available" (p. 55). Greisa also identifies two of the more effective infiltrators of the SWP/YSA during this period as having been Edward Heisler in Chicago and Ralph DeSimone in Berkeley. "Those offices were also entered twice in 1947. By far the largest number of surreptitious entries took place in New York City between 1958 and 1966 and occurred at SWP and YSA offices. There were 193 such incidents...Other cities in which the FBI entered into SWP or YSA offices include Newark (in 1947 and 1957), Chicago (1949), Detroit (1954), Boston (1959), and Milwaukee (1965). In addition, the FBI entered the homes of SWP members in Detroit (1957), Newark (1951), Hamden, Connecticut (1960), and Los Angeles (1960)."

23.See Judge Greisa's decision, quoted in Jayko, *op. cit.*, pp. 56-7.

24. Goldstein, *op. cit.*, p. 420. Judge Greisa, in Jayko (*op. cit.*) at pp. 72-3, summarizes the matter as follows: "In toto the FBI made at least 204 surreptitious entries of SWP and YSA offices and at least four such entries of SWP members' homes. During these entries at least 9,864 documents were removed or photographed. The first such entry was of the SWP offices in Minneapolis in January 1945.

25. Chomsky in Perkus, *op. cit.*, pp. 34-5. He goes on to observe that, "As for the state instruments of repression, one can expect little change in coming years, at least until the rise of mass-based popular organizations devoted to social change and an end of oppression and injustice."

26. Ungar, *op. cit.*, p. 128. It should be noted that only three of the 1,388 separate COINTELPRO actions admittedly carried out by the FBI against the CP-USA directly impacted upon the SWP; see Greisa in Jayko, *op. cit.*, at p. 59.

27. The case is the same as that cited in Note 13 (above). The Political Rights Defense Fund is a coalition consisting of six members of congress, the NAACP and several other black rights organizations, the American Federation of State, County and Municipal Employees and other union formations, the CP, USA, SWP and Democratic Socialists of America.

28. For examples of the federal motions, see *In re United States*, 556 F.2d 19 (2d Cir 1977), *cert. denied*, 436 U.S. 962 (1978), and *In re Attorney General*, 596 F.2d 58 (2d Cir.) *cert. denied*, 444 U.S. 903 (1979).For SWP discovery motions, see *Socialist Workers Party v. Attorney General*, 458 F.Supp. 895 (S.D.N.Y. 1978) and *Socialist Workers Party v. Attorney General*, 458 F. Supp. 923 (S.D.N.Y. 1978).

29. The SWP was awarded $42,500 with regard to damages suffered from COINTELPRO disruption activities, $96,500 related to FBI surreptitious entries, and $125,000 because of what was done by informants and infiltrators. The damages were charged against the federal government, listing not only the FBI Director, but the Attorney General of the United States, Secretary of the Treasury, Secretary of Defense, Postmaster General, Secretary of the Army, Director of Central Intelligence, Director of the Secret Service, Director of the Defense Intelligence Agency, Civil Service Commissioners, President of the United States, Commissioner of Immigration and Naturalization Service, Secretary of State and United States as a whole as being culpable insofar as each party had cooperated in or known of at least some of the actions undertaken under COINTELPRO-SWP, had reason to know these actions were wrong or illegal, but had done nothing to stop them.

30. In response to Greisa's broad injunction, several of the agencies designated by the judge as being culpable in the suit – including the FBI, Justice Department, INS and Department of Defense – filed affidavits with the court attempting to show cause why they should be able to maintain access to the illegal files: "The Justice department...argued that if an injunction was issued, federal police agencies must have the right to use the information in the sealed files in self-proclaimed 'emergency' situations, either by obtaining an exemption from any federal judge anywhere in the country, or, in cases of extreme urgency, by simply using the information and notifying the court later. Flatly rejecting this demand, Greisa ruled that on the 'very rare' occasion that any government agency should ever want access to any information covered in the injunction, it must apply to him and inform the SWP and YSA that it is doing so to afford them the opportunity to respond...The court also rebutted the attempt of the Secret Service to use the specter of potential violence against public officials to justify continued use of the files.'As far as the evidence shows,' wrote Greisa, 'the materials involved have little or no information bearing on national security, and no information about actual or planned violence against public officials, but rather a mass of information about peaceful political activities and the private lives of individuals.' The Secret Service, 'like the other agencies, should be bound to perform their tasks on the basis of *lawfully* obtained information [emphasis in the original].'"See Jayko, *op. cit.*, p. 11.

31. Boudin, Leonard, "Foreword," in *ibid*, pp. 1-4.

Chapter 4: COINTELPRO–Puerto Rican Independence Movement

1. See *Intelligence Activities and the Rights of Americans, Book II, op. cit.*, p. 422. Ladd mentions that there were 10,763 Security Index cards on members of the two groups in question as of 1946. The index was continued and, in a July 25, 1961 report to President John F. Kennedy, presidential adviser McGeorge Bundy explained its use as being "the list of individuals to be considered for apprehension and detention...in a period of emergency" (*ibid.*, pp. 465-6).

2. Fernandez, Ronald, *Los Macheteros: The Wells Fargo Robbery and the Violent Struggle for Puerto Rican Independence*, Prentice-Hall Publishers, New York, 1987, p. 133; the Pacific islands of Guam and the Philippines were also extracted as territorial concessions from Spain. It should also be noted that the appropriation of Puerto Rico was not simply a result of the war, as is commonly argued. Rather, the island was an object of North American desire well before hostilities commenced. Consider, for example, a passage from a letter from Senator Henry Cabot Lodge to Colonel Theodore Roosevelt, even as the opening guns were being fired: "Puerto Rico is *not forgotten*, and *we mean to have it* [emphasis added]." Or, again, contemplate Secretary of State William Day's assurance to Lodge, offered in June of 1898, that, "There is no question on Puerto Rico, everyone is agreed on that." Both quotations, and several in the same vein by Roosevelt himself, appear in *Selections from the Correspondence of Theodore Roosevelt and Henry Cabot Lodge, Vol. 1*, New York, n.d., p. 267.

3. Carr, Raymond, *Puerto Rico: A Colonial Experiment*, Vintage Books, New York, 1984, pp. 36-9. The "Insular Cases" are *Downes v. Bidwell* (21 S.Ct. 770, 182 U.S. 244, 45 L.Ed. 1088, 1901) and *De Lima v. Bidwell* (21 S.Ct. 743, 182 U.S. 1, 45 L.Ed. 1041, 1901); they were reaffirmed in *Balzac v. Puerto Rico* (42 S.Ct. 343, 258 U.S. 298, 66 L.Ed. 627, 1922). Representative Richardson's statement appears in the *Congressional Record*, 56th Congress, 1st Session, U.S. Government Printing Office, Washington, D.C., 1900, p. 2266. The best overall view of the processes in question may be found in Berbusse, Edward J., *The United States in Puerto Rico, 1898-1900*, University of North Carolina Press, Chapel Hill, 1966.

4. Carr, *op. cit.*, p. 36.

5. *Ibid.*, pp. 37-8. The initial *Puertorriqueño* counter-arguments were often less than distinguished, as is witnessed by the complaint that "a people with 400 years of civilization in back of them [would be forced by U.S. colonialism] to conditions below those freely granted to the Zuñi Indians and the lower and more barbaric inhabitants of the Southwest Territories;" see U.S. Senate, *Hearings Before the Committee on Pacific Islands and Puerto Rico* (Senate Document 147), 56th Congress, 1st Session, U.S. Government Printing Office, Washington, D.C., 1900, p. 249.

6. Pagán, Bolívar, *Historia de los Partidos Políticos Puertorriqueños, 1898-1956, Tomo I*, San Juan, Puerto Rico, 1972, pp. 176, 184. The Jones Act ultimately superceded the Foraker Act in 1928, allowing Puerto Rico at least nominally to elect its own parliament. It should be noted, however, that this was not done until well after U.S. economic penetration of the island had been completed, citizenship/conscription had been imposed, and the general grip on the island's polity otherwise consolidated. As the *independentistas* argue, the "liberalization" was thus more illusory than real. A good overview of the arguments may be found in Blaut, James, "Are Puerto Ricans a National Minority?" *Monthly Review*, Vol. 29, No. 5, May 1977.

7. Vardaman, Senator James K., in the *Congressional Record*, 64th Congress, 2d Session, U.S. Government Printing Office, Washington, D.C., 1917, p. 7474.

8. Carr, *op. cit.*, p. 164. The author explains that Albizu was educated at Harvard where he formed close relationships with supporters of the Irish Republican Army (IRA). He seems to have incorporated what he learned of the Irish armed struggle with his own sense of the *Puertorriqueño* tradition of nationalism, forging a revolutionary perspective which remains potent on the island to this day.

9. Quoted in *El Mundo*, San Juan, Puerto Rico, June 28, 1933. Also see Torres, J. Benjamin, *Pedro Albizu Campos Obras Escogodes*, 3 Volumes, Editorial Jelofe, San Juan, Puerto Rico, 1975.

10. See Ungar, *op. cit.*, pp. xvii-xviii. No estimate of actual FBI manpower on the island during the 1930s is available.

11. Riggs is quoted from *El Mundo* in Ribes Tovar, Federico, *Albizu Campos*, Plus Ultra Press, New York, 1971, p. 61.

12. Carr, *op. cit.*, p. 62.

13. Riggs was shot to death on February 23, 1936 by two *independentistas*, Hiram Rosado and Elias Beauchamp. As Fernandez, *op. cit.*, observes at p. 144, "Taken into custody, [Rosado and Beauchamp] were first beaten and then, within an hour of their capture, murdered by the police."

14. *Ibid.*

15. *Ibid.*, p. 145. The author notes that, "Even the composition of the first jury was suspect because Puerto Rico had two million native residents and five thousand American residents." Further, federal prosecutor Cecil Snyder is known to have named the individual members of the second jury at a cocktail party held at the residence of Blanton Winship, the island's governor, before the first trial had even concluded; see Kent, Rockwell, *It's Me O Lord*, Dodd-Mead Publishers, New York, 1955, p. 504. The appeal history may be found in *Albizou* [*sic*] *v. U.S.*, 88 F. 2d 138 (1st Cir. 1937), *cert. denied*, 301 U.S. 707, 57 S. Ct. 940, 81 L. Ed. 1361 (1937).

16. Cecil Snyder is quoted in Matthews, Thomas, *Puerto Rican Political Parties and the New Deal*, University of Florida Press, Gainesville, 1960, pp. 268-9.

17. Gautier, Carmen, María Teresa Blanco and María del Pilar Arguellas, *Persecution of the Puerto Rican Independence Movements and Their Leaders by the Counterintelligence Program (COINTELPRO) of the United States Federal Bureau of Investigation (FBI)*, 1960-1971, unpublished study provided by the authors (copy on file), 1979, p. 10. The paper was produced as an intervention to the United Nations Special Commission on Puerto Rico (of the Commission on Decolonization) in 1980. Also see Editors, "COINTELPRO En Puerto Rico," *Pensamiento Critico*, Summer 1979.

18. *Ibid.* The authors indicate that in a discussion with Corretjer in 1978, Representative Vito Marcantonio of New York pointed out "that this case was both the first time that a judge imposed such a brutal sentence in Grand Jury proceedings, and [that it] served as a precedent for similar actions against American Communists after the [Second World] War." They refer readers, for further information, to Clark, Larry D., *The Grand Jury: The Use and Abuse of Political Power*, Quadrangle Books, Chicago, 1975, pp. 23-5. Also see Neufield, Russell, "COINTELPRO in Puerto Rico," *Quash: Newsletter of the National Lawyers Guild Grand Jury Project*, August/September 1982.

19. Fernandez, *op. cit.*, p. 145.

20. Hays, Arthur Garfield (Chair), "Report of the Commission of Inquiry on Civil Rights in Puerto Rico," reprinted in José Lopez (ed.), *Puerto Rican Nationalism: A Reader*, Editorial Coqui, Chicago, 1971, p. 89. There remains some confusion as to who exactly fired the first shot; see Johnson, R.A., *Puerto Rico: Commonwealth or Colony?* Praeger Publishers, New York, 1980, pp. 24, 36-8.

21. Fernandez, *op. cit.*, p. 146.

22. See the testimony of the chair of the *Comité unitario contra la represión y por la defensa de los presos políticos* before the United Nations Commission on Decolonization, 1980; UN A/A 109/PV 1175, p. 37.

23. See Anderson, Robert W., *Party Politics in Puerto Rico*, Stanford University Press, Palo Alto, CA, 1965, p. 104. For a broad "liberal imperialist" overview of the context, see Wells, Henry, *The Modernization of Puerto Rico: A Political Study of Changing Values and Institutions*, Harvard University Press, Cambridge, MA, 1969.

24. See Morales Carrión, Arturo, *Puerto Rico: A Political and Social History*, W.W. Norton Publishers, New York, 1983, pp. 203-4. For contextual information on the Nationalist-PIP link during this period, see Zavala, Iris, and Rafael Rodríguez (eds.), *The Intellectual Roots of Independence: An Anthology of Puerto Rican Political Essays*, Monthly Review Press, New York, 1972.

25. "I am going to ask the people of the United States, if the people of Puerto Rico allow it with their votes, to establish this high precedent: to finish in the world the liquidation of the colonial system which began to be liquidated on the Fourth of July, 1776." The more militant segment of the PIP termed Muñoz' strategy "treason." See U.S. House of Representatives, Committee on Public Lands, *Hearings Before the Committee on Public Lands: Puerto Rico Constitution*, 81st Congress, 1st Session, U.S. Government Printing Office, Washington, D.C., 1950, pp. 94-5.

26. Fernandez, *op. cit.*; Muñoz' testimony may be found in *Hearings Before the Committee on Public Lands: Puerto Rico Constitution*, *op. cit.*

27. For example, the following appeared in *El Imparcial*, a thoroughly "responsible" San Juan daily, on May 12, 1950: "We do not want intermediate solutions...The constitution [offered by congress] is only a colonial modality. The people do not want a little liberty. They want full liberty."

28. The full text of this speech appears in Ribes Tovar, *op. cit.*

29. Fernandez, *op. cit.*, p. 149.

30. *Ibid.* Three of these individuals – Lolita Lebrón, Irwin Flores, and Rafael Cancel Miranda – along with the surviving Truman assailant, Oscar Collazo, became the "longest held political prisoners in the Western Hemisphere;" see Gautier, Blanco and Arguellas, *op. cit.*, p. 11. Lebrón was finally released on the order of Jimmy Carter in 1979.

31. On the relative disarray of the *independentistas* during the late 1950s, see Matthews, *op. cit.* Also see Figueroa, Loida, *History of Puerto Rico*, Anaya Books, New York, 1974.

32. Memorandum from Director, FBI, to the SAC, San Juan, December 15, 1967; it is reproduced *en toto* in Gautier, Blanco and Arguellas, *op. cit.*, p. 28.

33. Memorandum from the Director, FBI, to the SAC, San Juan, dated June 1, 1962; reproduced *en toto* in Gautier, Blanco and Arguellas, *op. cit.*, p. 68.

34. *Ibid.*, pp. 61-5. The authors cite the April 26, 1961 memo from the San Juan SAC to the Director (reproduced herein) with regard to *El Mundo*; a March 31, 1966 memo from Hoover to the SAC, San Juan, with regard to the *San Juan Star*; a memo from the San Juan SAC to Hoover on January 3, 1969 with regard to *El Imparcial*; and a memo from the SAC, San Juan, to COINTELPRO head William C. Sullivan on February 8, 1962 with regard to *El Vigía*. It is interesting to note that while Sullivan was in charge of the COINTELPRO in Puerto Rico throughout the duration of its formal existence, he never so much as mentions it – nor even the island – in his "frank" and "candid" memoirs (Sullivan and Brown, *op. cit.*). On the other hand he refers continuously to counterintelligence activities against the CP, discusses them in the context of the new left, repeatedly mentions operations against the black liberation movement, and devotes several pages to his exploits against the ku klux klan. One doubts this was an oversight. But, before judging Sullivan too harshly in this connection, one would do well to note that former Church Committee consultant Athan Theoharis, in his exploration of COINTELPRO (*Spying on Americans, op. cit.*), repeats exactly the same pattern, albeit Theoharis devotes rather more emphasis to how the Bureau supposedly deprived the klan of its civil rights (Theoharis devotes 4 pages to COINTELPRO – CP,USA, less than half a page to COINTELPRO – SWP, 6 pages to "COINTELPRO – White Hate Groups," 2 pages to the COINTELPROs against the black liberation movement overall, and 2 pages to COINTELPRO – New Left, most of it devoted to the break-in at the Media, Pennsylvania resident agency which disclosed the fact that COINTELPRO existed at all). There are obviously aspects of what has gone on in North America's Caribbean colony that *no* "responsible" commentator wants brought up. Such are the mechanics of apology and distortion.

35. The FCC appears to have cooperated in this; Memorandum from the SAC, San Juan, to the FBI Director, January 28, 1963.

36. Memorandum from the SAC, San Juan, to the Director, FBI, dated May 29, 1963.

37. Gautier, Blanco and Arguellas, *op. cit.*, pp. 69-72. The authors point out that while there is presently no documentation available from the FBI itself linking the Bureau to the bombings, the blatant pattern of non-arrest/non-prosecution of perpetrators fits well within the mold of COINTELPRO "pseudo-gang" operations (documented in the COINTELPRO-Black Liberation Movement chapter of this book).

38. *Ibid.*, p. 74.

39. Memorandum, SAC, San Juan to Director, FBI, November 13, 1967.

40. Memorandum, (name deleted), San Juan to William C. Sullivan, dated May 31, 1966.

41. A memorandum discussing this, from W.R. Wannall to William C. Sullivan is dated May 31, 1966.

42. Editorial, "The Puerto Rican Revolution," *Soulbook*, Vol. I, No. 3, Fall 1965.

43. Memorandum from the SAC, New York to the Director, FBI, November 30, 1965. Also see the return memo from Hoover to the New York SAC on December 9, in which the mailing was approved.

44. Memorandum, SAC, New York to Director, FBI, October 23, 1967; the reason specified as "justifying " this action was that "[name deleted], an MPIPR leader" had spoken at an anti-Vietnam war rally in New York on August 6, 1967.

45. Memorandum from (name deleted) to William C. Sullivan, dated April 26, 1966.

46. The cartoon was proposed in a memo from COINTELPRO specialist J.F. Bland (in San Juan) to William C. Sullivan (no date; FBI file number 005-93125). Sullivan evidently approved, as a memo dated August 29, 1966 from the San Juan SAC to the director indicates it had been "successful" and that the MPIPR believed "the cartoon originated with either the CIA or the police of Puerto Rico."

47. Memorandum from the SAC, New York to the Director, FBI, October 10, 1961; the SAC seems to have felt it would be a good idea to spread disinformation that Doña Laura was Juarbe's mistress although he acknowledged there was no substance to the idea. Such deliberate sexual smears appear to have been considered an especially effective COINTELPRO tactic.

48. Memorandum, (name deleted), to C.D. Brennan, February 12, 1971; memorandum, SAC, San Juan to Director, FBI, January 29, 1971.

49. Mari Bras, Juan, speech before the United Nations Commission on Decolonization, September 24, 1977. The matter of his son's assassination has never been resolved despite the "best efforts" of the FBI and island police.

50. Quoted in López, Alfredo, *Doña Licha's Island: Modern Colonialism in Puerto Rico*, South End Press, Boston, 1988, p. 145.

51. *Ibid.*, p. 146.

52. The information derives from the sworn deposition of Gloria Teresa Caldas de Blanco, a former secretary in the San Juan field office, taken by attorney Ludmilia Rivera Burgos at Hartford, Connecticut, December 25, 1984.

53. López, *op. cit.*, p. 146; the PIP offices were bombed three times during the 1970s, the PSP office once.

54. Blanco deposition, *op. cit.*

55. Gautier, Blanco and Arguellas, *op. cit.*, p. 111.

56. *Ibid.*, p. 67.

57. López, *op. cit.*, pp. 147-8.

58. According to López (*ibid.*, p. 147), "Randall had been legal counsel to the National Labor Relations Board during the period when that board outlawed the militant National Union Construction Firm... As legal counsel to some of the top [U.S.] firms operating in Puerto Rico – firms specializing in using the law to obstruct worker organizing – Randall was the epitome of the corporate militant."

59. *Ibid.*, pp. 147-59; jury foreman Antonio Fuentes later remarked that, "It was an easy decision [to acquit]. There was really a lot of talk and evidence, but absolutely nothing showing the defendants guilty."

60. Quoted in *ibid.*, p. 149.

61. Carr, *op. cit.*, p. 372; López, *op. cit.*, p. 149.

62. See Nelson, Anne, *Murder Under Two Flags: The U.S., Puerto Rico and the Cerro Maravilla Cover-Up*, Ticknor and Fields Publishers, New York, 1986. Also see Berkam, Judy, "The Crime of Cerro Maravilla," *Puerto Rico Libre*, May/June 1979; and Suarez, Manuel, "Ex-Puerto Rican Police Agent Guilty in Slaying of Two Radicals," *New York Times*, March 9, 1988.

63. Fernandez, *op. cit.*, p. 113.

64. The police were charged with a total of 46 counts of perjury and obstruction of justice, and convicted of 45 of them. Sentenced were Angel Perez Casilla, commander of the Puerto Rican police intelligence division (20 years), intelligence division agent Rafael Moreno (30 years), intelligence division agent Rafael Torres Marrero (20 years), special arrests squad agent Luis Reverón Martínez (25 years), intelligence division sergeant Nelson González Pérez (24 years), intelligence division agent Juan Bruno González (16 years), special arrests squad agent José Ríos Polanco (10 years), intelligence division lieutenant Jaime Quiles (12 years), intelligence division agent William Colón Berríos (12 years), and intelligence division sergeant Nazario Mateo Espada (6 years). See Suarez, Manuel, *Requiem on Cerro Maravilla: Police Murders in Puerto Rico and the U.S. Government Coverup*, Waterfront Press, Maplewood, NJ, 1987, p. 300.

65. *Ibid.*, p. 328. This correction of González Molavé's behavior has been attributed to the *independentista* clandestine armed formation *Los Macheteros*.

66. *Ibid.*, p. 361. This "resolution" of the Cerro Maravilla assassinations is entirely similar to that which pertained *vis à vis* the 1969 assassinations of Illinois Black Panther leaders Mark Clark and Fred Hampton (see next chapter).

67. Jaimes, M. Annette, and Ward Churchill, "Behind the Rhetoric: English-Only as Counterinsurgency Warfare," *Issues in Radical Therapy: New Studies on the Left*, Vol. XIII, Nos. 1-2, Winter-Spring 1988, p. 46. Also see "Secret Counter-Insurgency Conference Held in Puerto Rico," *SI Research Papers*, October 1982, p. 1. It should be noted that Louis O. Giuffrida has been a favorite government consultant on matters of political repression since at least the late 1960s. At the outset, he was active mainly in California, where he helped devise the consortium of federal, state and local police units used against the black liberation movement in that state (see next chapter). His advice was subsequently sought by the White House with regard to putting down the American Indian Movement on Pine Ridge during the mid-1970s (see Chapter 7). And, shortly after the San Juan conference, he became the Reagan administration's head of the Federal Emergency Management Agency, the entity charged with authority to round up "political undesirables" for "preventive detention" in concentration camps during periods of "national emergency." For further information, see Conclusion, Note 23.

68. Jaimes and Churchill, *op. cit.* Also see Butler, R.E. "Rusty," *On Creating a Hispanic America: A Nation Within a Nation?* Center for Inter-American Security, Washington, D.C., 1985.

69. A good example of this was the raid upon the home of *San Juan Star* reporter Coqui Santaliz' residence in which the manuscripts to a novel she was writing and a book of poetry she had finished were seized, along with assorted notebooks and tapes of interviews and music. Santaliz was arrested, detained, and interrogated for more than twelve hours before being released without ever having been charged with a crime. Much of her property was never returned. Meanwhile, as "the events at Ms. Santaliz's house were taking place, other commandos were doing the same things at the houses and offices of some thirty-seven other people. As military helicopters hovered in support, the agents held people in their homes for as long as eighteen hours, sometimes physically abusing them...They took reams of notes, tapes, film, mountains of books from several lawyers, writers, and scholars. They wrecked dozens of original celigraphs of the renowned painter Antonio Martorell. And they ransacked the offices of *Pensamiento Crítico*, a respected journal of critical thought, confiscating notes, tapes, film, typesetting equipment, and the rollers of the printing press...the FBI had trained for this type of action in Puerto Rico...their raids were skillfully conducted and coordinated;" López, *op. cit.*, pp. 140-1. Also see Fernandez, *op. cit*, pp. xi-xiv.

70. Ojeda Ríos and several of his co-defendants have been held in isolation, without bond, on non-capital indictments for several years. For further information on such "preventive detention" measures, accruing under the so-called "Bail Reform Act of 1984," see Chapter 8. Also see Churchill, Ward, "The Third World at Home: Political Prisoners in the United States," *Zeta*, June 1990.

71. Both quotations accrue from Edwin Meese's stint on *Meet the Press* during September 1985. It should be remembered that the Wells Fargo expropriation, which is what the FBI claimed the raid was all about, involved no deaths or even injury to anyone. So much for "bloody acts of terrorism." For a broad analysis of the use of similar rhetoric in the context of U.S. policy, see Herman, Edward S., *The Real Terror Network: Terrorism in Fact and Propaganda*, South End Press, Boston, 1982.

72. The quotation comes from a press conference given by Berríos in San Juan, September 9, 1985.

73. The government was specifically outraged that the FBI hadn't bothered to inform it of the incipient action, as required under the island's constitution, and that the Bureau had engaged in wholesale wiretapping, which is expressly prohibited. See Fernandez, *op. cit.*, p. xii.

74. On *Grupo pro-Uso Voto del MPI*, see memorandum from SAC, New York to Director, FBI, dated May 4, 1967; as is shown in a memo from the San Juan SAC to Hoover on December 21, 1963, the *Grupo* had first been created in that year to subvert the Puerto Rican elections; it was resurrected in 1967 specifically to undercut the U.N. process. Concerning the formation of the Committee Against Foreign Domination, see memorandum from the FBI Director to the San Juan SAC, September 2, 1966. On Committee disinformation activities, see memorandum from (name deleted) to William C. Sullivan, September 28, 1966, and a memo from Hoover to the SAC, San Juan, October 20, 1966.

75. Memorandum, Director, FBI to SAC, San Juan, May 2, 1967.

76. Carr, *op. cit*, p. 353. Perhaps the best articulation of the meaning of this finding, albeit from a reverse perspective, comes in the testimony of PIP head Rubén Berríos Martínez before the Decolonization Committee in 1981 (A/AC 109/L 1344 Add. 1, p. 11).

77. See, for example, the press release of the U.S. Mission to the United Nations, 68(79), August 15, 1979.

78. Carr, *op. cit.*, p. 363. The U.N. measure in question was an Omnibus Resolution (A/36/L20). The question of Puerto Rican independence was to be on the agenda prepared by the U.N. Secretariat for 1982.

Chapter 5: COINTELPRO–Black Liberation Movement

1. Hill, "Foremost Radical of His Race," *op. cit.*, p. 215. On St. Louis and Houston, see Pinkney, Alphonso, *The American Way of Violence*, Vintage Books, New York, 1972. For what may be the best assessment of the meanings of Garvey and Garveyism in light of subsequent black nationalist developments, see Pinkney, Alphonso, *Red, Black, and Green: Black Nationalism in the United States*, Cambridge University Press, New York, 1976.

2. For further information on the ugly status occupied by blacks at this juncture, see Woodward,

C. Vann, *The Strange Career of Jim Crow*, Oxford University Press, New York, (Third Revised Edition) 1974. Another very useful exposition may be found in DuBois, W.E.B., *The Autobiography of W.E.B. DuBois: A Soliloquy on Viewing My Life From the Last Decade of Its First Century*, International Publishers, New York, 1968.

3. Hill, *op. cit.* Among those considered as representative of "New Negro" leadership were A. Philip Randolph, Chandler Owen, Cyril V. Briggs, William Bridges, W.A. Domingo, Hubert H. Harrison and Marcus Garvey. They are contrasted by Hill to an "old guard" composed of individuals such as Robert Russa Moton, Emmett Scott, Kelly Miller, W.E.B. DuBois and William Monroe Trotter.

4. *Ibid.*, pp. 215-6. For further general information, see Levin, Murray, *Hysteria in America: The Democratic Capacity for Repression*, Basic Books, New York, 1971. On the wave of lynching in 1919, see Chadbourn, James H., *Lynching and the Law*, Unversity of North Carolina Press, Chapel Hill, 1933. Also see White, Walter, *Rope and Faggot: A Biography of Judge Lynch*, Arno Press, New York, 1969; and Roper, Arthur S., *The Tragedy of Lynching*, University of North Carolina Press, Chapel Hill, 1932.

5. Vincent, *op. cit.*, p. 202. Also see Garvey, Amy Jacques (ed.), *Philosophy and Opinion of Marcus Garvey, or Africa for the Africans*, Frank Cass and Co., London, 1967, p. 148. Garvey was indicted on February 15, 1923 on technical charges of conspiracy and mail fraud as a result of his fundraising activities intended to capitalize autonomous black business enterprises within the U.S. He was arrested on February 20. His trial began on March 18, 1923, and lasted about a month. Convicted on one count of fraud, he was sentenced to five years in federal prison, plus a $1,000 fine. He appealed the verdict and lost, serving some two and one-half years in Atlanta before President Calvin Coolidge commuted his sentence on November 18, 1927. Coolidge's action was designed to allow Garvey's deportation as an "undesirable alien" to his native Jamaica. As Otto Kirchheimer has observed in his *Political Justice: The Use of Legal Procedure for Political Ends* (Princeton University Press, Princeton, NJ, 1969), Garvey's was the "classic case."

6. Vincent, *op. cit.*, p. 203.

7. See Harris, William H., *Keeping the Faith: A. Philip Randolph, Milton P. Webster, and the Brotherhood of Sleeping Car Porters*, University of Illinois Press, Urbana, 1977. Also see Marable, Manning, "A. Philip Randolph: A Political Assessment," in his *From the Grassroots: Social and Political Essays Towards Afro-American Liberation*, South End Press, Boston, 1980, pp. 59-88; Bontemps, Arna, "Most Dangerous Negro in America," *Negro Digest*, September 1961; and Murphy, Paul L., "Sources and Nature of Intolerance in the Twenties," *Journal of American History*, No. 51, June 1964.

8. Johnson, *op. cit.*, p. 165. The documented inception of FBI surveillance of the NAACP occurred in 1924. Actually, government scrutiny of the organization probably began in 1910, when it was founded by W.E.B. DuBois in the wake of a lethal race riot in Springfield, Illinois. See Zinn, *op. cit.*, p. 340.

9. Hoover's memorandum is reproduced and attendant analysis offered in *Intelligence Activities and the Rights of Americans, Book III, op. cit.*, pp. 412-44.

10. Goldstein, *op. cit.*, pp. 253-4.

11. See *Intelligence Activities and the Rights of Americans, Book II, op. cit.*, pp. 319, 450-4.

12. See Emerson, Thomas I., *The System of Freedom of Expression*, Vintage Books, New York, 1970.

13. The more important cases include *NAACP v. Alabama ex. rel. Patterson* (1958), *Louisiana ex. rel. Gremillion v. NAACP* (1961), *Gibson v. Florida State Investigating Committee* (1963), and *Dombrowski v. Pfister* (1965). Also, as Howard Zinn points out in his *SNCC: The New Abolitionists* (Beacon Press, Boston, 1964, pp. 17-74, 183), an important related decision was reached in 1962 when four civil rights workers were charged with "inciting to insurrection" under a Georgia statute. A three-judge Supreme Court panel reviewed the matter, determined the law (which carried the death penalty) was unconstitutional, and ordered the prisoners' release.

14. Garrow, David J., *The FBI and Dr. Martin Luther King, Jr.*, Penguin Books, New York, 1981, p. 22.

15. Kelly's memorandum is reproduced in U.S. Department of Justice, *Report of the Justice Department Task Force to Review FBI Martin Luther King, Jr., Security and Assassination Investigations*, Washington, D.C., January 11, 1977.

16. Cross is mentioned in a memorandum from Atlanta agent Robert A. Murphy to J. Stanley Pottinger, at FBI headquarters, in July 1958. Interestingly, Murphy suggests the "SWP connection" is *not* a sufficient basis from which to undertake a COMINFIL investigation. Pottinger apparently did not agree; see Pottinger, J. Stanley, "Martin Luther King Report" (to U.S. Attorney General Edward H. Levi), U.S. Department of Justice, Washington, D.C., April 9, 1976.

17. The King file was opened by the New York rather than Atlanta field office. It should be noted that although the Bureau has always maintained that there was no COMINFIL activity directed at King and the SCLC during the 1950s, the code prefixed to the files on both was "100," indicating they were viewed as "internal security" or "subversive" matters. The numerical file prefix for material accruing from what was considered an investigation of civil rights activities *per se* would have been "44."

18. See U.S. Senate, Committee on the Judiciary, *FBI Statutory Charter – Appendix to Hearings Before the Subcommittee on Administrative Practice and Procedure, Part 3,* 95th Congress, 2d Session, U.S. Government Printing Office, Washington, D.C., 1979, pp. 33-73.

19. Concerning King, see *Lee v. Kelly,* Civil Action No. 76-1185, U.S. District Court for the District of Columbia, "Memorandum Opinion and Order" (by U.S. District Judge John Lewis Smith, Jr.), January 31, 1977. Certain of the information on both King and Walker was attributed by FBI Associate Director Cartha D. DeLoach to NAACP head Roy Wilkens (see report on the SCLC from Atlanta agent Robert R. Nichols to DeLoach, dated July 1961). Wilkens later vehemently denied any such interaction between himself and the Bureau; see Lardner, George Jr., "Wilkens Denies Any Link to FBI Plot to Discredit King," *Washington Post,* May 31, 1978.

20. Levison's CP membership was never established although it was demonstrable that he maintained close relations with party members from roughly 1949 through '54. The speech attributed to Wofsy was actually drafted by Levison and can be found in *Proceedings of the Fourth Constitutional Convention of the AFL-CIO, Vol. I,* American Federation of Labor – Congress of Industrial Organizations, Washington, D.C., 1962, pp. 282-9. Levison also had much to do with the preparation of the manuscript for King's first book, *Stride Toward Freedom* (Harper and Brothers Publishers, New York, 1958); see King, Coretta Scott, *My Life With Martin Luther King, Jr.,* Holt, Rinehart and Winston Publishers, New York, 1969.

21. Such Bureau activities with regard to Levison were nothing new and seem to have stemmed largely from reports coming from "Solo," two brothers – Jack and Morris (Chilofsky) Childs – who served from as early as 1951 as highly placed FBI informants within the CP,USA. It was they who appear to have originally "linked" Levison to the party even though they could never attest to his actual membership and essentially stopped referring to him by early 1954. J. Edgar Hoover's predictable (and quite unsubstantiated) response was to declare Levison a "secret" CP member; see Garrow, *op. cit.,* pp. 21-77.

22. Memorandum, SAC, New York, to Director, FBI, captioned "Martin Luther King, Jr., SM-C," and dated June 21, 1962. Shortly thereafter, the New York field office began to openly affix a COMINFIL caption to correspondence concerning King and the SCLC. The Atlanta field office followed suit on October 23. The designation was officially approved by FBI headquarters supervisor R.J. Rampton in identical letters to the SACs on the latter date.

23. Targeting the SCLC under COINTELPRO-CP,USA was first proposed by the SAC, New York in a memorandum to Hoover dated September 28, 1962. The operation was approved by memo in an exchange between Assistant Director William C. Sullivan and one of his aides, Fred J. Baumgardner, on October 8. The initial five newspapers selected for purposes of surfacing the anti-King propaganda were the *Long Island Star-Journal, Augusta* (GA) *Chronicle, Birmingham* (AL) *News, New Orleans Times–Picayune,* and the *St. Louis Globe Democrat* (where the reporter utilized in spreading the lies was Patrick J. Buchanan, later part of the White House press corps under Presidents Nixon and Reagan, as well as a current host on the Cable News Network *Crossfire* program).

24. King's index placement was accomplished through a series of memoranda, culminating in one sent by Hoover via T.W. Kitchens to Kenneth O'Donnell on May 4, 1962. On the implications of being placed on the Reserve Index, see Goldstein, Robert Justin, "The FBI's Forty Year Plot," *The Nation* (No. 227, July 1, 1978) and "An American Gulag? Summary Arrest and Emergency Detention of Political Dissidents in the United States," *Columbia Human Rights Law Review* (No. 10, 1978).

25. The ELSURS authorization was signed by Kennedy on October 10, 1963 and provided to FBI liaison Courtney A. Evans. The attorney general's main concern, detailed in the minutes of his meeting with Evans, seems to have been not that the bugging and tapping of King and the SCLC for purely political purposes was wrong, but that it might be found out. Once Evans convinced him that this was genuinely improbable, "the Attorney General said he felt [the FBI] should go ahead with the technical coverage of King on a trial basis, and to continue if productive results were forthcoming." See Denniston, Lyle, "FBI Says Kennedy OKed King Wiretap," *Washington Evening Star,* June 18, 1969. Also see O'Leary,

Jeremiah, "King Wiretap Called RFK's Idea," *Washington Evening Star*, June 19, 1969. Concerning continuation of the taps after the "trial period" had concluded, see Rowan, Carl, "FBI Won't Talk about Additional Wiretappings," *Washington Evening Star*, June 20, 1969.

26. The New York SAC reported in a memorandum to Hoover, dated November 1, 1963, and captioned "Martin Luther King, Jr., SM-C; CIRM (*JUNE*)," that his agents had tapped all three SCLC office lines in his area of operations, with coverage on two lines beginning October 24. He also recommended installation of a tap on the residence line of civil rights leader Bayard Rustin; the tap was approved and installed in early January 1964. On November 27, 1963, the Atlanta SAC informed Hoover by a memo captioned "COMINFIL, RM; Martin Luther King, Jr., SM-C (*JUNE*)," that Atlanta operatives had tapped King's home phone and all four organizational SCLC lines in that city as of November 8.

27. The document was entitled "Communism and the Negro Movement – A Current Analysis." It was completed on October 15, 1963 and submitted to Assistant Director Sullivan, who passed along a copy to headquarters supervisor Alan H. Belmont. From there, it was "distributed through the government-wide intelligence community" and "the various military services" despite the fact that Belmont concluded it lacked substance and might be seen as little more than "a personal attack upon Martin Luther King." See Garrow, *op. cit.*, pp. 73-5.

28. Memorandum, William C. Sullivan to Alan H. Belmont, August 30, 1963, captioned "Communist Party, USA, Negro Question, IS-C." The document is quoted in full in U.S. Congress, Joint Committee on Assassinations, *Hearings on the Investigation of the Assassination of Martin Luther King, Jr.*, *Vol. 6*, 95th Congress, 2d Session, U.S. Government Printing Office, Washington, D.C., 1978, pp. 143-4. For interesting insights in this connection, see Jacobs, James, "An Overview of National Political Intelligence," *University of Detroit Journal of Urban Law*, No. 55, 1978, pp. 854-6.

29. For its disinformation campaign, the Bureau made ample use of "friendly media contacts" such as the nationally-syndicated columnist Joseph Alsop, who proved quite willing to smear King in print on the basis of FBI "tips" lacking so much as a shred of supporting evidence. Concerning the IRS, as Garrow (*op. cit.*) notes at p. 114, "In mid-March [1964] the Internal Revenue Service reported that despite careful scrutiny it had been unable to discover any violations in either King's or SCLC's tax returns. Director Hoover scrawled 'what a farce' on the margin when the disappointing memo reached his desk."

30. The instructions by Sullivan to Whitson and others are summarized in a memorandum from a member of the Internal Security Section named Jones to FBI Associate Director Cartha D. DeLoach on December 1, 1964, captioned simply "Martin Luther King, Jr." For further information, see Lardner, George, Jr., "FBI Bugging and Blackmail of King Bared, *Washington Post*, November 19, 1975. Also see Horrock, Nicholas M., "Ex-Officials Say FBI Harassed Dr. King to Stop His Criticism," *New York Times* (March 9, 1978), and Kunstler, William, "Writers of the Purple Page," *The Nation* (No. 227, December 30, 1978).

31. Garrow, *op. cit.*, p. 127. It appears DeLoach had to content himself with the "contributions" of right-wing hacks like Victor Riesel. However, Bureau efforts to place the "story" in more respectable quarters are known to have included overtures to – at the very least – reporters John Herbers of the *New York Times*, James McCartney of the *Chicago Daily News*, David Kraslow of the *Los Angeles Times*, Eugene Patterson of the *Atlanta Constitution*, Lou Harris of the *Augusta Chronicle*, and syndicated columnist Mike Royko. Herbers appears to have passed word of what was happening to civil rights leader James Farmer, who confronted DeLoach with the matter during an appointment on December 2, 1964.

32. Memorandum, William C. Sullivan (via R.F. Bates) to Cartha D. DeLoach, dated January 21, 1966 and captioned "Martin Luther King, Jr., SM-C (*JUNE*)." Also see a memo from Fred J. Baumgardner (via Bates) to Sullivan, dated January 14, 1966 and captioned COMINFIL SCLC, IS-C (*JUNE*).

33. In his memoirs, Sullivan makes much of the "wrongness" of Hoover's largely cosmetic attempt to bring certain of the FBI's political operations within some sort of bounds of legality. The former assistant director is unequivocal that he believes this to have been a weakness in the director's character, and that the Bureau should have been allowed to operate free of *any* legal or moral constraints when "fighting subversives." See Sullivan and Brown, *op. cit.*, especially p. 205, for this interesting commentary on a top COINTELPRO official's perspective on "law enforcement."

34. There are serious questions concerning the possibility that the FBI might have been involved in the assassination of Martin Luther King. See, for example, Lane, Mark, and Dick Gregory, *Code Name "Zorro:" The Assassination of Martin Luther King, Jr.*, Prentice-Hall Publishers, Englewood Cliffs, NJ, 1977. Also see Lawson, James, "And the Character Assassination That Followed," *Civil Liberties Review*, No.

5, July-August 1978. Of further interest, see Lewis, David L., *King: A Biography*, University of Illinois Press, Urbana, 1979, especially pp. 399-403.

35. Gid Powers, Richard, *Secrecy and Power: The Life of J. Edgar Hoover*, The Free Press, New York, 1987, p. 458.

36. Marable, Manning, *Race, Reform and Rebellion: The Second Reconstruction in Black America, 1945-1982*, University of Mississippi Press, Jackson, 1984, p. 124.

37. Garrow, *op. cit.*, p. 154. Also see a memorandum from Hoover to Attorney General Herbert Brownell (who approved the initial taps on "national security" grounds), dated December 31, 1956 and captioned ELIJA MOHAMMED [*sic*], INTERNAL SECURITY – MUSLIM CULT OF ISLAM; memo from Fred J. Baumgardner to William C. Sullivan, September 8, 1961, captioned NATION OF ISLAM – IS-NOI; memo from SAC, Phoenix to FBI Headquarters, June 30, 1965, captioned NATION OF ISLAM – IS-NOI; and a memo from Hoover to Attorney General Nicholas Katzenbach dated July 1, 1966 and captioned NATION OF ISLAM – IS-NOI.

38. Garrow, *op. cit.*, p. 281. The file classification prefix code pertaining to the Nation of Islam and its leaders was "105," indicating they were viewed collectively as an internal security matter.

39. For additional information and reproduction of documents relevant to the killing of Malcolm X, see Breitman, George, Herman Porter and Baxter Smith (eds.), *The Assassination of Malcolm X*, Pathfinder Press, New York, 1976. It should be noted that, during the last year of his life, Malcolm X adopted the Islamic name, El Hajj Malik El Shabazz; see Breitman, George, *The Last Year of Malcolm X: The Evolution of a Revolutionary*, Schocken Publishers, New York, 1968.

40. See Carmichael, Stokely, and Charles V. Hamilton, *Black Power: The Politics of Liberation in America*, Vintage Books, New York, 1967; and Lester, Julius, *Look Out, Whitey! Black Power's Gon' Get Your Momma*, Grove Press, New York, 1969. Also see Carmichael's "What We Want," in Mitchell Cohen and Dennis Hale (eds.), *The New Student Left: An Anthology*, Beacon Press, Boston (Revised and Expanded Edition), 1967, pp. 109-19; Kilson, Martin, "Black Power: The Anatomy of a Paradox," *Harvard Journal of Negro Affairs*, No. 2, 1968, pp. 30-4; Franklin, Raymond S., "The Political Economy of Black Power," *Social Problems*, No. 16, Winter 1969, pp. 286-301; and Ofari, Earl, "W.E.B. DuBois and Black Power," *Black World*, No. 19, August 1970, pp. 26-8. For a succinct overview of the transformation in SNCC politics during this period, see Roberts, Gene, "The Story of Snick: From 'Freedom Rides' to 'Black Power'," *New York Times Magazine*, September 25, 1966. More developed views of the predicates for the shift may be found in Morris, Alden D., *The Origins of the Civil Rights Movement: Black Communities Organizing for Social Change*, The Free Press, New York, 1984.

41. See Brown, H. (Hubert) Rap, *Die Nigger Die!*, The Dial Press, Inc., New York, 1969. Also see Barbour, E.D. (ed.), *The Black Power Revolt*, The Sargent Press, Boston, 1968; and Forman, James, *The Making of Black Revolutionaries*, Macmillan Publishers, New York, 1972. Of further interest, see Leonard, Edward A., "Ninety-Four Years on Non-Violence," *New South*, No. 20, April 1965, pp. 4-7; Wilkens, Roy, "Whither Black Power?" *Crisis*, August-September 1966, p. 354; and Rustin, Bayard, "'Black Power' and Coalition Politics," *Commentary*, No. 42, September 1966, pp. 35-40.

42. Marable, *Race, Reform and Rebellion, op. cit.*, pp. 102-3. For more on the Detroit rebellion, see Hersey, John, *The Algiers Motel Incident*, Alfred A. Knopf Publishers, New York, 1968. Of related interest, see Hayden, Tom, *Rebellion in Newark: Official Violence and Ghetto Response*, Vintage Books, New York, 1967; and Gilbert, Ben W., *et. al.*, *Ten Blocks From the White House: Anatomy of the Washington Riots of 1968*, Frederick A. Praeger Publishers, New York, 1968. For an overall appraisal of the motivations underlying the urban rebellions from the perspective of a former CORE field secretary, see Wright, Nathan Jr., *Black Power and Urban Unrest: Creative Possibilities*, Hawthorn Books, Inc., New York, 1967. In general, see Boesel, David, and Peter H. Rossi (eds.), *Cities Under Siege: An Anatomy of the Ghetto Riots, 1964-1968*, Basic Books, New York, 1971.

43. "Project Build" was an apprenticeship program funded through the Department of Labor which would supposedly bring large numbers of blacks into the construction crafts (from which they had historically been almost totally excluded) as highly paid skilled workers. The government, however, conscientiously failed to utilize its power to force exclusionary unions to comply with the law by hiring the blacks thus trained. Thus, in Philadelphia, the Operating Engineers Union was allowed to accept federal funds to run a training program while simultaneously excluding blacks (by definition) from full union membership and corresponding employment. In Boston, Sheet Metal Workers' Union head James Kelly, who also accepted training funds, became at the same time an open member of a white

paramilitary organization which systematically terrorized the families of the union's own black trainees. Needless to say, under such conditions very few blacks ever actually benefited from Project Build. Indeed, after a full decade of existence and millions of dollars spent, barely 25 percent of all black apprentices accepted into the program had completed it, and those who had were almost universally unemployed or dramatically under-employed. See Marable, *Race, Reform and Rebellion, op. cit.,* pp. 132-3.

44. The sheer cynicism embodied in the passage of such legislation is glaringly revealed in the fact that the amendments to the Civil Rights Act, passed in 1968, contained a "conspiracy" provision – popularly known as "The Rap Brown Law" – which made it a federal crime to cross state lines "with intent to incite riot." In practical terms, the provision meant that it would henceforth be considered illegal to agitate for social change. On the 1965 Voting Rights Act, see Thernstrom, Abigail M., "The odd evolution of the Voting Rights Act," *Public Interest,* No. 55, Spring 1979, pp. 49-76.

45. Much of the thinking here centered itself in the revolutionary theoretical work of Frantz Fanon during the Algerian war of liberation during the 1950s; see Adam, Hussein A., "Frantz Fanon: His 'Understanding'," *Black World,* No. 21, December 1971, pp. 4-14. For early articulations running in this vein, see Meier, August, "The Revolution Against the NAACP," *Journal of Negro Education,* No. 32, Spring 1963, pp. 146-52, and "The Dilemmas of Negro Protest Strategy," *New South,* No. 21, Spring 1966, pp. 1-18; Gregor, A. James, "Black Nationalism: A Preliminary Analysis of Negro Radicalism," *Science and Society,* No. 26, Fall 1963, pp. 415-32; and Williams, Robert F., "USA: The Potential of a Minority Revolution," *The Crusader Monthly Newsletter,* No. 5, May-June 1964, pp. 1-7. More developed, but still seminal views may be found in Zangrando, Robert L., "From Civil Rights to Black Liberation: The Unsettled 1960s," *Current History,* No. 62, pp. 281-99; Allen, Robert L., "Black Liberation and the Presidential Race," *Black Scholar,* No. 4, September 1972, pp. 2-6; Cleaver, Eldridge, "On Lumpen Ideology," *Black Scholar,* No. 4, November-December 1972, pp. 2-10; Antarah, Obi, "A Blueprint for Black Liberation," *Black World,* No. 22, October 1973, pp. 60-6; and Ofari, Earl, "Black Labor: Powerful Force for Liberation," *Black World,* No. 22, October 1973, pp. 43-7. For a broader view, see Marable, Manning, *Blackwater: Historical Studies in Race, Class Consciousness, and Revolution,* Black Praxis Press, Dayton, OH, 1981.

46. Quoted in Goldstein, *Political Repression in Modern America, op. cit.,* p. 450.

47. Clark's memorandum is reproduced *en toto* in *Intelligence Activities and the Rights of Americans, Book II, op. cit.,* pp. 491-3.

48. *Ibid.* On the Congress of Racial Equality, see Meier, August, and Elliott Rudwick, *CORE: A Study in the Civil Rights Movement,* Oxford University Press, New York, 1973. Also see Bell, Inge Powell, *CORE and the Strategy of Nonviolence,* Random House Publishers, New York, 1968; and Farmer, James, *Lay Bare the Heart,* Alfred A. Knopf Publishers, New York, 1985.

49. Memorandum, Hoover to the SAC, Albany, August 25, 1967; reproduced in full in *Hearings on Intelligence Activities,* Vol. 6, *op. cit.,* p. 383.

50. *Intelligence Activities and the Rights of Americans, Book III, op. cit.,* pp. 492-3. TOPLEV and BLACPRO functioned more or less along the lines of COMINFIL. One of the more notable successes of the latter was to secure the services of James A. Harrison, comptroller of the SCLC, as an informant. By the fall of 1967, every FBI field office was assigned at least one, and in some cases as many as four, agents devoted exclusively to development of "quality non-organizational sources...for the purpose of expeditiously infiltrating militant black nationalist organizations." The Ghetto Informant Program, also called "Ghetto Listening Post," was launched at this time and, by the summer of 1968, employed some 3,248 snitches, in addition to an "unknown number" of such "assets" already in place under TOPLEV and BLACPRO. Hoover described this small army of contract spies as being "inadequate," and demanded a major expansion of its ranks during the fall of 1968. See also, New York Field Office Inspection Report (no date; *circa* May 1968); New York Field Office Inspection Report, October 27, 1968; and memorandum from George C. Moore to William C. Sullivan, September 3, 1968.

51. Marable, *Race, Reform and Rebellion, op. cit.,* pp. 124-5. On pp. 106-7, he notes that Sellers' indictment stemmed from his February 7, 1968 organization of a black student demonstration at South Carolina State College which"later culminated in a white police riot, leaving 3 students killed and 33 wounded." Sellers himself was among those shot, but that did not prevent his being held in a tiny death row cell on both a pending federal draft resistance charge and the new state "incitement to riot" count. He was convicted of the Selective Service charge seven weeks after what was by then called the

"Orangeburg Massacre," and ultimately of incitement as well (nearly two years later). This last was solely on the basis of a speech he'd given *two nights before* the fatal outbreak, a matter which led columnist Tom Wicker to muse in the pages of the *New York Times* on September 29, 1970 that the whole affair showed, "how casual is this country's sense of justice for black people, how careless it is of its own humanity." Meanwhile, Stokely Carmichael experienced a near-Garveyite fate: "When a Carmichael appearance at Vanderbilt University [during the fall of 1967] accidentally coincided with an urban rebellion [in Nashville, four days later] in which 94 persons were jailed, Tennessee legislators demanded that Carmichael be deported from the US [presumably to his native Trinidad]." For further information see Sellers, Cleveland, and Robert Terrell, *The River of No Return: The Autobiography of a Black Militant and the Life and Death of SNCC*, William Morrow and Company, New York, 1973.

52. O'Reilly, Kenneth, *"Racial Matters:" The FBI's Secret File on Black America, 1960-1972*, The Free Press, New York, 1989, pp. 275-6. Also see *Intelligence Activities and the Rights of Americans, Book III, op. cit.*, pp. 491-2. By the time the Ghetto Informant and Rabble Rousers Index projects got under way, "the main listing [of the Security Index, from which alleged rabble rousers were drawn] included the names of Martin Luther King and 1,497 other black Americans. The FBI added the names of an additional 400 blacks during the Kennedy and Johnson years. The largest category listed 673 Black Muslims, followed by 476 communists (or former communists or suspected fellow travelers), 66 SNCC activists, 60 Revolutionary Action Movement members, and 222 persons in the general black nationalists' category...The percentage of communists listed in the Security Index declined steadily throughout the [1960s] – from 83.8 percent in 1961, to 55.9 percent by the time LBJ left the White House."

53. Powers, *op. cit.*, p. 425.

54. The text of the report on the anti-RAM operation, from the SAC, Philadelphia to Hoover on August 30, 1967 (*i.e.*, it had been executed in large part *before* COINTELPRO-Black Liberation Movement had ostensibly begun) appears in Churchill and Vander Wall, *Agents of Repression, op. cit.*, pp. 45-7. It leaves no doubt as to Hoover's intent in recommending replication of the tactic elsewhere.

55. O'Reilly, *op. cit.*, pp. 281-2.

56. *Ibid.*, pp. 330-1.

57. Memorandum, SAC, Boston, to FBI Director, May 4, 1973. As O'Reilly observes (*op. cit.*, p. 276), "In March 1968 the Rabble Rouser Index received a new name, the Agitator Index, and headquarters directed the field to submit 'visual material relating to violence by black extremists.' Division Five [Sullivan's COINTELPRO Section] wanted 'clear, 8" by 10" photographs.' Sullivan's men also requested a photograph of each of the one hundred or so persons listed on the Agitator Index. Upon receiving and pasting the photos in the Black Nationalist Photograph Album, Division Five sent copies of this mug book to the field, along with a Racial Calendar highlighting 'the dates of...racial events.' To make sure that his agents could track any 'militant black nationalist' who might 'turn up' in another country, Hoover approved distribution of the Black Nationalist Photograph Album to the CIA and Royal Canadian Mounted Police." Photo album subjects such as Hakim Jamal were thus obviously high-priority targets for COINTELPRO "neutralization." Also see *Intelligence Activities and the Rights of Americans, op. cit.*, pp. 510-2, 517-8.

58. Quoted in Hinds, Lennox S,, *Illusions of Justice: Human Rights Violations in the United States*, Iowa School of Social Work, University of Iowa, Iowa City, 1978, p. 121.

59. For further information on the case, see Obadele, Imari Abubakari, *Free the Land! The True Story of the Trials of the RNA 11 in Mississippi*, House of Songhay, Washington, D.C., 1984. Aside from Obadele, the other members of the RNA 11 were Karim Njabafudi (s/n: Larry Jackson), RNA Vice President Hekima Ana, Offoga Quddud (s/n: Wayne Maurice James), Addis Ababa (s/n: Denis Shillingford), Chumaimari Askardi (s/n: Charles Stalling), Tamu Sana (s/n: Ann Lockhart), Njeri Quddus (s/n: Toni Rene Austin), Spade de Mau Mau (S.L. Alexander), Aisha Salim (s/n: Brenda Blount), and Tawwab Nkruma. It should be noted that three weeks after the raid in Jackson, some 65 Detroit police raided RNA national headquarters in that city at the behest of the head of the local FBI COINTELPRO section. Nine key RNA cadres were arrested on charges such as "spitting" and "talking back to a police officer." Concerning the RNA political agenda, see Obadele's *Foundations of the Black Nation: A Textbook of Ideas Behind the New Black Nationalism and the Struggle for Land in America*, House of Songhay, Detroit, 1975.

60. See Lumumba, Chokwe, "Short History of the U.S. War on the R.N.A.," *Black Scholar*, No. 12, January-February 1981, pp. 72-81. Several defendants were convicted on the automatic weapons charge despite the fact that they contended that it was actually a perfectly legal semi-automatic rifle, and a

federal firearms expert at trial – in a live-fire demonstration – could not show that the weapon was capable of delivering automatic fire.

61. See Marine, Gene, *The Black Panthers*, New American Library, New York, 1969, pp. 7-27. Also see Schanche, Don A., *The Panther Paradox: A Liberal's Dilemma*, David McKay Publishers, New York, 1970. Hoover's remark is quoted from the *New York Times* (September 8, 1968) in *Intelligence Activities and the Rights of Americans, Book III, op. cit.*, p. 187. It also appeared in memo form and in letters to private individuals.

62. The 10-Point Program of the Black Panther Party tends to speak for itself: "1) We Want freedom. We want power to determine the destiny of our black community. 2) We want full employment for our people. 3) We want an end to the robbery by the white man of our black community. 4) We want decent housing, fit shelter for human beings. 5) We want education for our people that exposes the true nature of this decadent American society. We want education that teaches us our true history and our role in the present day society. 6) We want all black men to be exempt from military service. 7) We want an immediate end to *police brutality* and the *murder* of black people. 8) We want freedom for black men held in federal, state, county, and city prisons and jails. 9) We want all black people when brought to trial to be tried in court by a jury of their peer group or people from their black communities, as defined by the Constitution of the United States. 10) We want land, bread, housing, education, clothing, justice and peace [emphasis in the original]."

63. This exercise of constitutional rights by the Panthers in California caused those same rights to be suspended in that state. Debate on the "Panther Law," which was to prohibit the carrying of *any* weapon by citizens without the express permission of the state, led to a group headed by party chairman Bobby Seale taking weapons into the California State Assembly itself on May 2, 1967. Although the action itself was a perfectly legal symbolic gesture under then-prevailing California law, Seale himself entered through the wrong door and ended up – shotgun in hand – on the floor of the assembly rather than in the spectator's gallery. Since carrying a weapon onto the assembly floor was technically illegal, the error cost Seale a year in jail and was quickly latched onto by anti-Panther propagandists as evidence of party "violence." See Seale, Bobby, *Seize the Time: The True Story of the Black Panther Party and Huey P. Newton*, Vintage Books, New York, 1970, pp. 153-71.

64. The mainstay of FBI and police contentions that Panther policy equalled "violence" concerned the shooting death of Oakland, California police officer John Frey (and the wounding of officer Herbert Heanes) on the night of October 28, 1967. Panther leader Newton, who received severe gunshot wounds to the abdomen during the altercation, was acquitted of murder but found guilty of manslaughter in the matter on September 8, 1968. He was sentenced to serve fiftenn years. Even this conviction was, however, overturned (on evidentiary grounds) by the California Supreme Court less than two years later, and sent back to trial. When it became clear to the jury that officers Frey and Heanes had stopped Newton's car for no particular reason on the fatal night (as part of a deliberate harassment campaign ordered by Oakland "Panther Squad" head Ray Brown), that there were other non-police parties involved in the confrontation, that police shots had probably been fired first, that there was no evidence that Newton had fired a weapon at all and that he was probably the first party wounded, the state was unable to obtain a conviction on any charge. See Keating, Edward M., *Free Huey! The True Story of the Trial of Huey P. Newton for Murder*, Ramparts Press, Berkeley, CA, 1971.

65. Marable, *Race, Reform and Rebellion, op. cit.*, p. 122. The party also consciously based much of its public posture on the pronouncements of Thomas Jefferson (despite the fact that Jefferson had been a slave owner). See, as but one of myriad examples of this, Newton, Huey P., "What We Want Now! What We Believe," in John J. Bracey, Jr., August Meier and Elliott Rudwick (eds.), *Black Nationalism in America*, Bobbs-Merrill Publishers, Indianapolis, 1970, pp. 526-33. The prevailing federal view of the evolution of the BPP during its first five years of existence may be found in U.S.House of Representatives, Committee on Internal Security, *Gun Barrel Politics: The Black Panther Party, 1966-1971* (92d Congress, 1st Session, U.S. Government Printing Office, Washington, D.C., 1971) and *The Black Panther Party: Its Origins and Development as Reflected in Its Official Weekly Newspaper, The Black Panther-Community News Service* (92d Congress, 1st Session, U.S. Government Printing Office, Washington, D.C., 1971).

66. For the 5,000 figure see Marable, *Race, Reform and Rebellion, op. cit.*, p. 123. Gid Powers (*op. cit.*, at p. 458) estimates party membership at 3,000. Goldstein (*Political Repression in Modern America, op. cit.*, p. 524) accommodates both numbers: "By October, 1968, 'healthy and functioning size' chapters were in operation in New York, Chicago, Los Angeles, Denver, and Omaha, as well as the San Francisco Bay

area. In New York City, nearly eight hundred members were recruited in June, 1968 alone. In the fall of 1968, the Panthers had a membership of over two thousand, and claimed a readership of over one hundred thousand for their weekly newspaper [*The Black Panther*]...At its peak in 1969, before repression began to decimate the party, the Panthers had an estimated membership of five thousand." Also see Major, Reginald, *A Panther is a Black Cat: A Study In Depth of the Black Panther Party – Its Origins, Its Goals, Its Struggle for Survival*, William Morrow and Company, New York, 1971.

67. See Newton, Huey P., *Revolutionary Suicide*, Harcourt Brace Jovanovich, Inc., New York, 1973, especially Chapter 11 ("The Brothers on the Block"), pp. 73-7. Also see Cleaver, *op. cit.*

68. See Newton, Huey P., "Huey Newton Speaks to the Movement About the Black Panther Party, Cultural Nationalism, SNCC, Liberals and White Revolutionaries," in Philip S. Foner (ed.), *The Black Panthers Speak*, J. B. Lippincott Company, Philadelphia/New York, 1970, pp. 50-66.

69. Seale, *op. cit.*, pp. 211-22. The event not only cemented the alliance between the BPP and SNCC, it raised more than $10,000 in defense funds for party founder Huey P. Newton, at the time appealing his conviction in the Frey killing (see Note 63 above).

70. Marable, *Race, Reform and Rebellion, op. cit.*, p. 124. Also see Brown, *Die Nigger Die! op. cit.*

71. At p. 133, COINTELPRO head William C. Sullivan (Sullivan and Brown, *op. cit.*) describes Cardoza as a "tough customer." While what Sullivan meant by this is left unclear, the infiltrator is suspected of involvement in the earlier-mentioned March 9, 1970 car bomb assassinations of SNCC activists Ralph Featherstone and Ché Payne.

72. The Bureau was also busy trying to split up the SNCC leadership during this period. In *Agents, op. cit.*, at p. 50, we reproduce a document proposing a bogus letter designed to achieve this effect *vis à vis* H. Rap Brown, Stokely Carmichael and James Forman.

73. See Newton, Huey P., *To Die for the People*, Vintage Books, New York, 1972, p. 191.

74. Memorandum, SAC, New York, to Director, FBI, September 5, 1978.

75. Seale (*op. cit.*, p. 207) places the date of the BPP decision to work with the Peace and Freedom Party as being "three weeks after I got out of jail" (December 8, 1967) on the earlier-mentioned Sacramento weapons charge (see Note 62 above). The decision was thus taken on roughly December 29 or 30. He also notes Bay Area SDS members Bob Avakian and Rick Hyland as being primary white radical initiators of the alliance.

76. Cleaver, Eldridge, *Soul on Ice*, Delta Books, New York, 1968. Cleaver had written the book while in California's Soledad and San Quentin prisons while serving nine years of an indeterminate sentence for rape. His 1967 parole to work for *Ramparts* and subsequent induction into the BPP went far toward solidifying the party's desired links with "the lumpen behind the walls."

77. Seale, *op. cit.*, pp. 207-11. Some 25,000 votes were actually cast for Newton, despite his manslaughter conviction, in California's Seventh Congressional District.

78. Scheer, Robert, "Introduction," in Eldridge Cleaver, *Post-Prison Writings and Speeches*, Ramparts/Vintage Books, New York, 1969, p. xix. The article in question appeared in the *Ramparts* May 1968 issue.

79. Scheer, *op. cit.*, pp. xix-xxi. While this may appear on its face to have been a purely local police action, it is a matter of record that Ray Brown maintained close liaison with the San Francisco FBI office on matters relating to the BPP during the whole period. What happened thus appears to have happened with at least FBI foreknowledge, if not outright complicity.

80. Judge Sherwin's decision is quoted in *ibid.*, p. xx.

81. *Ibid.*, pp. xx-xxi.

82. *Ibid.*, p. xxi. Cleaver made maximal use of the appeal period, continuing his Peace and Freedom Party appearances, and engaging in a vociferous first amendment campaign against California Governor Ronald Reagan and the Regents of the University of California for their actions in blocking his teaching of an invited course at Berkeley. The attendant publicity – and support Cleaver's position attracted – no doubt further unnerved the political and police establishments, increasing their collective desires to get him out of the picture.

83. On Cleaver's periods in Cuba and Algeria, see Lockwood, Lee, *Conversation with Eldridge Cleaver, Algiers*, Delta Books, New York, 1970. On Algeria and France, see Cleaver, Eldridge, *Soul on Fire*, World Books, Waco, TX, 1978. It becomes readily apparent in the latter book that Cleaver had lost his mind. The role of the various COINTELPRO operations which were aimed at him in producing this result is unclear, but must be assessed as having been significant.

84. Freed, Donald, *Agony in New Haven: The Trial of Bobby Seale, Ericka Huggins and the Black Panther Party*, Simon and Schuster Publishers, New York, 1973, p. 65. The estimate of police numbers is taken from the trial testimony of LA Panther leader Elaine Brown, quoted at p. 279.

85. Memorandum, SAC, San Diego, to Director, FBI, February 20, 1969.

86. Memorandum, Newark SAC to FBI Director, August 25, 1969; memorandum, Director, FBI to SAC, Newark, September 16, 1969.

87. Baraka, Amiri, *The Autobiography of LeRoi Jones*, Freundlich Books, New York, 1984, pp. 250-84. Also see Karenga, Maulana (Ron), *Roots of the US/Panther Conflict* (Kawaida Publications, San Diego, 1976, p. 7): "[The FBI] interjected violence into...[the] normal rivalries of two groups struggling for leadership of the black movement...We're still recovering and rebuilding from that. We knew it wasn't going to be a tea party, but we didn't anticipate how violent the U.S. government would get."

88. O'Reilly, *op. cit.*, p. 317.

89. Years later, SAC Johnson denied under oath in a federal court that his intent had been to incite violence in this matter. A "hit," he claimed to have believed, the explicit language of his own memoranda to the contrary notwithstanding, was "something nonviolent in nature." See Greene, Bob, "Laundered Box Score? No hits, no guns, no terror," *Chicago Sun-Times*, February 12, 1976.

90. The Mau Mau letter is covered in a memorandum from SAC Johnson to Hoover dated December 30, 1968, and a reply to Johnson from Hoover on January 30, 1969. The operations *vis à vis* other organizations are detailed in the evidentiary display incorporated into *Iberia Hampton, et. al., Plaintiffs-Appellants v. Edward V. Hanrahan, et. al., Defendants-Appellees*, Civ. Nos. 77-1968, 77-1210, and 77-1370, U.S. Eighth Circuit Court of Appeals, 1979 (hereinafter referred to as *Appeal*), Exhibit PL#26.

91. See *Appeal*, PL#412 (Dep. pp. 307-8 and 310) and 413 (Dep. pp. 234 and 305-7). For more on O'Neal, see McClory, Robert, "Agent Provocateur," *Chicago Magazine*, February 1979, pp. 78-85. Reportedly, there were three FBI infiltrators within the Chicago BPP chapter.

92. The police raiding team was composed of Groth, Joseph Gorman, William Corbett, Raymond Broderick, Lynwood Harris, George Jones, John Ciszewski, Edward Carmody, Phillip Joseph "Gloves" Davis, John Marisuch, Fred Howard, and William Kelly.

93. Davis, a black cop notorious in Chicago for his brutality, appears to have administered the first (relatively minor) wound to the unconscious Hampton, using an M-1 carbine, and to have earlier killed Clark with a point-blank shot to the chest from the same weapon. As concerns the fatal wounds to Hampton, an exchange between police was overheard by Panther survivors after the BPP leader had been shot once: "(Voice) That's Fred Hampton. (Second Voice) Is he dead? Bring him out [of his bedroom]. (First Voice) He's barely alive; he'll make it. (Two shots ring out and a third voice, believed to be Carmody's states) He's good and dead now." The information on Hampton having been drugged prior to the raid accrues from a thin-layer chromatography examination performed on a sample of the victim's blood by Cook County Chief Toxicologist Eleanor Berman. For further details, see *Agents, op. cit.*, pp. 68-76.

94. *Appeal* (Transcript) at 3462-3. Satchell was hit four times, Anderson twice, and Brewer twice. No police officer was injured in any way. See Gottlieb, Jeff, and Jeff Cohen, "Was Fred Hampton Executed?" *The Nation*, No. 223 December 25, 1976. Also see Anonymous, "FBI Harassment of Black Americans," *Bilalian News*, January 1980.

95. Arlen, Michael J., *An American Verdict*, Doubleday, Inc., Garden City, NJ, 1974, p. 59. On the overall raid, see Commission of Inquiry into the Black Panthers and the Police, *Search and Destroy*, Metropolitan Applied Research Center, New York, 1973. Also see Moore, Gilbert, *A Special Rage*, Harper and Row Publishers, New York, 1972. Of further interest, see the 1970 Newsreel film, *The Murder of Fred Hampton*, produced in Chicago by an anonymous crew. The forensic conclusions concerning who fired first, how many rounds were fired by each side, and how this was determined by Herbert MacDonell, an independent expert in criminalistics, may be found in Lewis, Alfred Allen, and Herbert Leon MacDonell, *The Evidence Never Lies: The Casebook of a Modern Sherlock Holmes*, Holt, Rinehart and Winston, New York, 1984 (see Chapter 3, "The Black Panther Shoot-out/in").

96. See "Panther Trial," *New York Times*, February 18, 1977: "FBI documents in evidence show that O'Neal was rewarded for his efforts with $300 bonus." The article also notes that in "1969-70, O'Neal earned $30,000 as a paid FBI informant." *Appeal*, PL#94, is a Bureau memo, dated December 17, 1969, authorizing payment of the bonus. O'Neal was paid on December 23.

97. Goldstein, *Political Repression in Modern America, op. cit.*, pp. 528-9; Ungar, *op. cit.*, pp. 465-6. Also

see Anonymous, "A Collective Dedication: Ten Years After the Murder of Fred Hampton," *Keep Strong,* December 1979/January 1980.

98. See Levin, S.K., "Black Panthers get bittersweet revenge," *The Colorado Daily,* November 10, 1982. Also see O'Reilly, *op. cit.,* p. 315, where he quotes People's Law Office attorney Flint Taylor as observing the settlement constituted an "admission of the conspiracy that existed between the F.B.I. and Hanrahan's men to murder Fred Hampton." For more on Richard G. Held, see Churchill, Ward, "COINTELPRO as a Family Business," *Zeta Magazine,* March 1989, pp. 97-101. *Provocateur* William O'Neal apparently committed suicide in late February 1990 via the messy expedient of running down an embankment onto Chicago's Stevenson Expressway and being hit by an oncoming taxi.

99. Pratt's sleeping habits derived from a spinal injury suffered while serving in Vietnam as a member of the Army's elite 82nd Airborne Division during 1967. The much decorated combat veteran – he was awarded some 18 medals for valor while in Southeast Asia – was placed in the FBI's Key Black Extremist portfolio within a year of his discharge, apparently because of his obvious military skills and because he'd succeeded the murdered Bunchy Carter as head of the LA-BPP chapter. The personal information on Pratt accrues from a summary of his case, entitled *G's Life and Times, 1967-72,* prepared by Brian Glick for the Geronimo Pratt Defense Committee in 1979. It is available through the Jonathan Lubell law offices in New York City.

100. See Durden-Smith, Jo, *Who Killed George Jackson? Fantasies, Paranoia and the Revolution,* Alfred A. Knopf, Publishers, New York, 1976, pp. 134-5. Interestingly, infiltrator Cotton Smith seems to have been trapped inside, along with the *bona fide* Panthers, when the firing broke out. By all accounts, he acquitted himself well in the defense.

101. *Ibid.,* p. 134. As in Chicago, the police later claimed the raid was necessitated by reports that illegal weapons were being kept in the Panther facility. In Chicago, O'Neal had informed SA Mitchell days before the event, however, that he'd checked and all weapons in Fred Hampton's apartment were "clean." In LA, the "hook" was that a Panther named George Young, who was also a member of the Marine Corps, was known to have been at Camp Pendleton, California, on the night a batch of M-14 rifles was stolen from the armory there. This, according to LAPD Criminal Conspiracy Section Detective Ray Callahan, was sufficient basis for the police to have "reason to suspect" the weapons were being kept at the LA party headquarters. What the detective neglected to mention was that he and his colleagues also knew that Young had been *serving time in the stockade* at the Marine base on the night in question, and had thus been in no position to steal anything. When queried about this odd circumstance by LA Municipal Judge Antonio Chavez during the subsequent trial of the Panther defenders, Callahan responded, "I didn't think it was important."

102. As CCS infiltrator of the BPP Louis Tackwood later put it in a book he prepared in conjunction with the Citizens Research and Investigation Committee (*The Glass House Tapes: The Story of an Agent Provocateur and the New Police-Intelligence Complex,* Avon Books, New York, 1973, pp. 237-8): "[T]he FBI works hand in hand with [CCS]...Los Angeles has more power as a Police Department goes, because of the proximity of working with CII [the Criminal Intelligence and Investigation unit of the California State Police] and also the FBI." At pp. 213-4, he observes that, "There ain't nowhere they can't go. CCS, they're like federally sponsored. Like J. Edgar Hoover says, 'They're my boys, they're my boys.'" Also see the interview with former FBI infiltrator Cotton Smith (currently serving a life sentence for murder in Kentucky) which appeared under the title "Ex-FBI Agent Exposes Use of Informants to Destroy the BPP," in *Freedom Magazine,* Vol. 18, No. 5, January 1985, pp. 28-40.

103. See "63 Verdicts End Panther Trial," *Los Angeles Tribune,* December 24, 1971.

104. See memorandum from (deleted), Los Angeles, to (deleted), Intelligence Division, captioned "Elmer Gerard Pratt," February 9, 1970.

105. Quoted in Elliff, John T., *Crime, Dissent and the Attorney General,* Sage Publications, Beverly Hills, CA, 1971, p. 140.

106. Goldstein, *Political Repression in Modern America, op. cit.,* pp. 526-7. For further information on the killing of Panthers by law enforcement personnel, see Epstein, Edward J., "The Panthers and the Police," *New Yorker,* February 13, 1971, pp. 45-77. For further information on the gratuitous arrests of party members, see Donner, Frank, "Hoover's Legacy," *The Nation,* June 1, 1974, p. 613.

107. Marable, *Race, Reform and Rebellion, op. cit.,* p. 143. For further information on Rice and Poindexter, see Hinds, *op. cit.,* pp. 119-22.

108. Garry, Charles R., "The Persecution of the Black Panther Party," in Foner, *op. cit.,* pp. 257-8.

109. Quoted in Harris, Richard, *Justice*, Avon Books, New York, 1970, p. 239.

110. O'Reilly, *op. cit.*, pp. 302-3. SA Charles Gain is quoted in Bergman, Lowell, and David Weir, "Revolution on Ice: How the Black Panthers Lost the FBI's War of Dirty Tricks" (*Rolling Stone*, September 9, 1976, at p. 49), as saying the San Francisco office performed as it did because, "There was a tremendous fear of Hoover out there. It was almost all they talked about. They were afraid of being sent to some awful post in Montana." If this is indeed some sort of honest explanation of agent motivations, Gain's persistent use of the word "they" is peculiar at best, since *he* was a prime mover in the office's anti-Panther COINTELPRO operations.

111. Goldstein, *Political Repression in Modern America, op. cit.*, p. 529.

112. The case in question was *U.S. v. David T. Dellinger, et. al.*, No. 69-180, 1969. Perhaps the best handling of Seale's part in the legal proceedings may be found in Schultz, John, *Motion Will Be Denied: A New Report on the Chicago Conspiracy Trial*, William Morrow and Company, New York, 1970, pp. 37-84. For literal transcript material, see Clavir, Judy, and John Spitzer (eds.), *The Conspiracy Trial*, Bobbs-Merrill Company, Indianapolis, 1970.

113. Aside from Seale, the defendants in the Rackley murder case were Warren Kimbro, Lonnie McLucas, George Sams, Ericka Huggins, Frances Carter, George Edwards, Margaret Hudgins, Loretta Luckes, Rose Smith, Landon Williams and Rory Hithe.

114. The FBI has never admitted that George Sams was an infiltrator, but there are telltale clues. First, Sams was the only first-hand prosecution witness ever called to the stand with regard to the Rackley case, even when the state was losing. One may assume he was thus the only such witness they had. And the state's predication for charges held the basis as being material provided by "a trusted *ten year informant* [emphasis added]." Meanwhile, as Freed (*op. cit.*) recounts at p. 25, during the summer of 1969, before Sams had been apprehended and supposedly "turned state's evidence," as the supposedly vagrant fugitive "traveled around the country, spending large sums of money, certain things began to happen to the Panthers. Each city he visited [Washington, Denver, Indianapolis, Salt Lake City, Des Moines, Detroit, San Diego and Chicago among them] was thereafter subjected to predawn raids by combinations of city, state and federal police. But Sams was never caught; he always managed to leave before the raids were made." In fact, the "harboring" of this alleged "fugitive" was the basis for many of the neutralizing arrests of local BPP chapter members during this period. Although virtually none of these charges were ever taken to court, the cumulative bail involved both financially strapped the party and, once it was broke, left many of its cadres in jail for extended periods without having been convicted of anything at all. Such is the stuff of COINTELPRO, not of coincidence.

115. See "8 Panthers Held in Murder Plot," *New Haven Register*, May 22, 1969; "Second 'Victim' Sought in Panther Case," *New Haven Journal-Courier*, May 23, 1969; and "8 Suspects in Killing to Face High Court," *New Haven Register*, May 23, 1969.

116. Kimbro entered his plea on January 16, 1970, a few days after receiving a visit from his older brother, a police officer. It is doubtful that either he or his brother expected the life sentence handed down on June 23, 1971.

117. McLucas was convicted of conspiracy to murder and sentenced in August 1970; charges of murder, kidnapping, conspiracy to kidnap, and binding with intent to commit a crime were dismissed.

118. Sams was convicted on all counts and sentenced to life imprisonment on June 23, 1971. It seems likely that he'd crossed the line of exposure beyond which the FBI could no longer protect him and the Bureau simply gave him up, much as it did another of its star performers, Gregory Dewey Clifford, convicted of the 1987 dismemberment murder of a woman named Gerri Patton in Denver. See Hogan, Frank, "Witness for the Prosecution: Accused murderer Gregory Clifford doesn't have any friends – except in the FBI," *Westword*, Vol. 11, No. 20, January 13-19, 1988.

119. Associated Press Wire Service, "Ex-Chief Says New Haven Police Had No Evidence Against Seale," April 4, 1972. Chief Ahern stated that he had been "astonished" when prosecutor Arnold Markle had decided to try Seale for the Rackley murder. The only pretense of a link between Seale and the crime turned out to be the fact that the BPP leader had had a speaking engagement at Yale University in New Haven on April 19, 1969, two days before Rackley was killed. It was this circumstance which caused Yale President Kingman Brewster to make his much publicized 1971 remark doubting whether a black revolutionary "could get a fair trial anywhere in the United States." For further information on Panther activities in New Haven during the Seale/Huggins trial, see Burstein, Robert, *Revolution as Theater: Notes on the New Radical Style*, Liveright Publishers, New York, 1971; also see Erikson, Erik H., and Huey P. Newton, *In Search of Common Ground*, W.W. Norton and Company, New York, 1973.

120. Goldstein, *Political Repression in Modern America, op. cit.*, p. 529. The case at issue is *State of Connecticut v. Bobby G. Seale*, Superior Court of New Haven (Connecticut), No. 15844, 1971.

121. For Seale's own assessment of the impact of what was done to him in the name of "due process," see his *A Lonely Rage*, Times Books, New York, 1978.

122. Goldstein, *Political Repression in Modern America, op. cit.*, p. 527. Also see Chevigny, Paul, *Cops and Rebels*, Pantheon Press, New York, 1972. Thomas, like all police infiltrators of the New York BPP, was a member of the NYPD's Special Services Department, an entity that worked hand-in-glove with the local FBI COINTELPRO section in exactly the same fashion as CCS in Los Angeles, Ray Brown's Oakland Panther Squad, and the State's Attorney's Police did in Chicago. During the late 1970s, the Special Services Department was utilized as the basis for the NYPD to become a participant in a formal federal/local political police combine called the Joint Terrorist Task Force (see Chapter 8).

123. O'Reilly, *op. cit.*, p. 299. The author points out on the same page that a certain amount of such activity was constrained by the FBI's concern that its massive electronic surveillance of the BPP would be disclosed in court. For example, Hoover ultimately quashed the planned 1970 prosecution of Panther Chief of Staff David Hilliard for having "threatened the life" of President Richard M. Nixon during a speech, precisely because defense discovery motions were homing in on Bureau taps of the defendant's home and several BPP offices. However, as Garry (*op. cit.*, p. 259) points out, before charges were dropped Hilliard was forced to ante a $30,000 bail secured from a bondsman with 190% collateral in order not to spend several months in jail without trial.

124. Goldstein, *Political Repression in Modern America, op. cit.*, p. 527. The 21 defendants were Lumumba Shakur (s/n: Anthony Coston), Afeni Shakur (s/n: Alice Williams), Analye Dhoruba (s/n: Richard Moore), Kwando Kinshasa (s/n: William King), Cetewayo (s/n: Michael Tabor), Ali Bey Hassan (s/n: John J. Casson), Abayama Katara (s/n: Alex McKeiver), Sundiata Acoli (s/n: Clark Squire), Curtis Powell, Robert Collier (a former RAM member, convicted of a conspiracy to blow up the Statue of Liberty in 1965), Baba Odinga (s/n: Walter Johnson), Shaba Om (s/n: Lee Roper), Joan Bird, Jamal (s/n: Eddie Joseph), Lonnie Epps, Lee Barry, Mshina (s/n: Thomas Berry), Sekou Odinga (s/n: Nathaniel Burns), Larry Mack, Kuwasi Balagoon (s/n: Donald Weems) and Richard Harris. A 22nd defendant, Fred Richardson, was added in November 1969. Of these, only thirteen actually went to trial. Two defendants, Balagoon and Harris, were incarcerated in New Jersey awaiting trial on charges of robbery and attempted murder (of which they were acquitted) when the case went to court. Two others, Jamal and Epps, being under age, were separated for trial in juvenile court. One, Lee Barry, an epileptic, had been rendered too ill by the conditions of his confinement to stand trial at all. And four others, Sekou Odinga, Larry Mack, Mshina and Richardson, escaped to join Eldridge Cleaver in Algeria. Acquittal of the first thirteen on all counts, however, caused the cases to evaporate against the remaining nine (see Kempton, Murray, *The Briar Patch: The People of the State of New York v. Lumumba Shakur, et. al.*, E.P. Dutton Company, New York, 1973). The state hardly lost interest in the defendants, even after the resounding "not guilty" verdicts. As of this writing, all but a handful are either dead or serving lengthy sentences in maximum security institutions. The biographies of several appear in Committee to End the Marion Lockdown, *Can't Jail the Spirit: Political Prisoners in the U.S.*, Chicago, 1989.

125. At least five police infiltrators – Eugene Roberts, Ralph White, Carlos Ashwood, Roland Hayes and Wilbert Thomas – had moved into the New York BPP from almost the moment it was established by SNCC organizer Joudon Ford in April 1968. Three of the five were called to testify at trial. Even with this ground-level coverage, however, the police could produce no physical evidence of the alleged conspiracy – or the Panthers' "military" propensity in general – other than the fact that Kwando Kinshasa had authored a "training manual" entitled *Urban Guerrilla Warfare*, and Collier had been in possession of some short lengths of brass pipe and enough black powder to fill a small talcum box. With this, the jury and public were meant to believe, the defendants were going to blow up five department stores and several police stations. Infiltrator Ralph White (a police detective) was revealed in open court to be a drunkard, womanizer and habitual law violator (despite having a pristine personnel file) who could ultimately testify only that he had heard Afeni Shakur "say some rough things" (a sample of her dismantling his assertions on cross examination may be found in Kempton, *op. cit.*, at pp. 234–40), and that he "knew" Lumumba Shakur and Kwando Kinshasa had been keeping blasting caps (which were not found by police raiders on the day of the arrests) in the Harlem Panther headquarters. Patrolman Ashwood, the second infiltrator, was also forced to admit that he'd never really seen anyone do anything, although he'd "heard some things" (an excerpt from Afeni Shakur's cross examination of

Ashwood may be found in *ibid.*, at p. 245). Eugene Roberts, who had worked "undercover" since joining the New York police in 1964 and had infiltrated Malcolm X's break-away organization to become one of the Muslim leader's bodyguards – Roberts was the man who attempted to revive Malcolm by mouth-to-mouth resuscitation on the night of the assassination – could do no better than produce tapes of conversations between various of the defendants. See Zimroth, Peter L., *Perversions of Justice: The Prosecution and Acquittal of the Panther 21*, Viking Press, New York, 1974.

126. O'Reilly, *op. cit.*, p. 318. No charges were dismissed. The 13 defendants who actually went to trial were found innocent of all 156 counts filed against them.

127. For a juror's-eye view of the government's case, see Kennebeck, Edwin, *Juror Number Four: The Trial of Thirteen Black Panthers as Seen From the Jury Box*, W.W. Norton and Company, New York, 1973. For the defendants' perspectives, see *Look For Me In the Whirlwind*, Revolutionary People's Communication Network, New York, 1971.

128. Goldstein, *Political Repression in Modern America, op. cit.*, pp. 529-30. The Senate document referred to is *Final Report: Supplementary Detailed Staff Reports on Intelligence Activities and the Rights of Americans, Book III, op. cit.*, p. 200. The basic disagreement within the BPP, upon which the Bureau was able to build this particular COINTELPRO, was entirely induced by FBI and police actions over the preceding two years. This issue distilled to what proportion of the party's dwindling legal defense resources should be apportioned to the needs of the "old guard" such as Newton (on appeal), Seale (fighting the Rackley murder charge) and David Hilliard (charged with "threatening the life of the President of the United States") *vis à vis* the needs of relative newcomers such as the Panther 21. As O'Reilly (*op. cit.*) observes at p. 318: "The Cleaver faction revolved around [defense of] the so-called Panther 21."

129. Kempton, *op. cit.*, p. 189. Again, such outcomes can hardly be said to have been the furthest thing from COINTELPRO specialists' minds. In a January 28, 1971 Airtel to his SACs in Boston, Los Angeles, New York and San Francisco, J. Edgar Hoover pointedly observed that "Newton responds *violently* to any question of his actions or policies or reluctance to do his bidding. He obviously responds hastily without getting all the facts or consulting with others...[Therefore] recipients must maintain the present high level of counterintelligence activity...It appears Newton may be on the brink of mental collapse and we must [thus] intensify our counterintelligence [emphasis added]." Cleaver adherent Weaver was killed shortly thereafter, and Newtonite Napier appears to have been killed as a retaliation. In 1972, four New York BPP members, including Panther 21 defendants Jamal and Dhoruba Moore, were tried for murder in the Napier slaying; the jury hung ten to two for acquittal. Rather than undergo retrial on the murder charge, all four entered subsequent guilty pleas to second degree manslaughter and were sentenced to less than four years each.

130. An FBI infiltrator named Thomas E. Mosher later testified before congress that Bennett had been killed by Jimmy Carr as a result of a "successful" bad-jacketing operation, and that he had assisted Carr in cremating Bennett's remains. He contended that he had informed the FBI of what had happened, guided agents to the cremation site in the Santa Cruz Mountains, and had helped them gather bone fragments and other remains; Mosher was extremely upset because the Bureau had taken no action as a result of the murder. Instead (as is shown in the document accompanying the text) the murder was utilized to up the ante in exacerbating the Newton-Cleaver split. An FBI reporting document dated January 14, 1972, and captioned BLACK PANTHER PARTY, LOS ANGELES DIVISION, EXTREMIST MATTER, reveals that Sandra Lane Pratt had been shot five times at close range, stuffed into a sleeping bag, and dumped alongside an LA freeway. Concerning the assassination of Carr, see Carr, Betsy, "Afterword," in *Bad: The Autobiography of James Carr*, Herman Graf Associates, New York, 1975, pp. 207-35. The Bennett murder is also mentioned as part of the FBI's fomenting the "Newton-Cleaver Split" in Newton, Huey P., *War Against the Panthers: A Study of Repression in America*, (dissertation), University of California at Santa Cruz, 1980.

131. See "Let Us Hold High the Banner of Intercommunalism and the Invincible Thought of Huey P. Newton," *The Black Panther*, Center Section, January 23, 1971. Pratt's wife, "Red," and other LA-BPP members, including Will Stafford, Wilfred Holiday and George Lloyd were also expelled in the same statement. The piece was apparently proposed and prepared by Elaine Brown, widely suspected among former party members of having been a police agent.

132. The victim was a 28-year-old white school teacher named Caroline Olsen. Her husband, Kenneth – who was playing tennis with her at the time of the assault – was wounded but survived. He

testified at trial that one of the two black assailants who first robbed and then shot him and his wife was Geronimo Pratt. Immediately after the murder (on December 24, 1968), however, he had positively identified another black man, Ronald Perkins (who looked nothing like Pratt), as having been the culprit. His story on this changed only after having been extensively "coached" by LAPD detectives utilizing "photo spreads" to believe Pratt was actually the man he'd seen.

133. Julio Butler testified at trial that Pratt had "bragged" to him of having killed Caroline Olsen. Butler also testified that he had severed all ties with the LA County Sheriff's Department, by which he'd been employed prior to joining the BPP, and that he'd never worked for the FBI or CIA. He was, however, a paid "informant" of the FBI beginning at least as early as August of 1969, and continuing until at least as late as January 20, 1970. Although his pay records (if any) for the year have not been disclosed, he filed monthly informant reports with the LA FBI office throughout 1970. His "Racial Informant" file was not closed until May of 1972, immediately prior to his going on the stand in the Pratt trial. After he entered his perjured testimony against Pratt, he was given suspended sentences on four separate felony convictions, and received federal assistance in completing *law school*. See Glick, *G's Life and Times, op. cit.*

134. See Amnesty International, *Proposal for a commission of inquiry into the effect of domestic intelligence activities on criminal trials in the United States of America, op. cit.*, p. 29: "[The defense obtained] over 7,000 pages of FBI surveillance records dated after 2 January 1969. Elmer Pratt claimed earlier records would reveal that he was at a meeting in Oakland at the time of the murder on 18 December 1968 but the FBI's initial response to this was that there had been no surveillance before 1969. This was later shown to be untrue." Also see *Pratt v. Webster, et. al.*, 508 F.Supp. 751 (1981) and the dissenting remarks of Judge Dunn in *In Re Pratt*, 112 Cal. App. 3d 795 – *Cal. Rptr.* – (Crim. No. 37534. Second Dist., Div. One, 3 December 1980).

135. Pratt might have established his whereabouts on the night of the murder as having been Oakland rather than Santa Monica through the direct testimony of others who had attended. These individuals – including Bobby and John Seale, David and June Hilliard, Nathan Hare, Rosemary Gross and Brenda Presley – were all aligned with the Newton faction and therefore declined to speak in the defendant's behalf. Several movement attorneys have also indicated they refused to represent Pratt, based upon requests received from Newton or his delegates. Under such conditions, no local raising of defense funds was possible. The COINTELPRO also seems to have been quite effective with regard to the other side of the split. Of the Cleaver faction, only Kathleen (Neal) Cleaver appears to have made any serious attempt to assist the target. See Glick, *G's Life and Times, op. cit.*

136. It should be noted that by the time Pratt became eligible for parole, Ray Brown – former head of the Oakland Panther Squad – was chair of the state parole board. Despite the obvious implications, Brown refused to recuse himself in deliberations upon Panther paroles. When Pratt finally came up for review in 1987, LA Deputy District Attorney Diane Visani was allowed to object to his release after more than 15 years' incarceration on the basis that, "I think we still have a revolutionary man [here]. He *does* have a network out there. If he chooses to set up a revolutionary organization upon his release from prison, it would be easy for him to do so [emphasis in original]." (Visani's comments are recorded in a *60 Minutes* report on the Pratt case aired on November 29, 1987.) This, of course, has nothing at all to do with the Olsen murder; Geronimo Pratt's imprisonment is thus overtly political, in the words of the very office which prosecuted him.

137. O'Reilly, *op. cit.*, p. 321. As of this writing, new evidence has surfaced which makes it clear that Dhoruba Moore was tried as part of a COINTELPRO operation – jointly undertaken by the FBI and the NYPD Special Services Division – to neutralize him through "the judicial process." It appears his case will be ordered back to trial, and that he may very well be acquitted. But, in the interim, he has served 19 years in a maximum security prison. See Conclusion, Note 5 for further detail.

138. See Glick, Brian, *A Call for Justice: The Case of the N.Y. 3*, Committee to Support the New York Three, New York, 1983. Also see, "Petition for a Writ of Habeas Corpus," *Herman Bell, et. al. v. Thomas A. Coughlin, et. al.*, (89 Civ. 8408), United States District Court for the Southern District of New York, 1989.

139. The Jackson matter is extremely complicated, and is covered in more detail in *Agents, op. cit.*, pp. 94-9. A thumbnail sketch is that the victim was convicted of a $70 gas station stickup at age 18 and sentenced to serve one-year-to-life under California's indeterminate sentencing law. In 1970, he had already served ten years, when he was accused, along with two other black inmates – John Cluchette and Fleeta Drumgo, the three became known as the "Soledad Brothers" – in the killing of a prison guard, John V. Mills, in retaliation for the killing of three black prisoners (W.L. Nolen, Cleveland Edwards and Alvin

"Jug" Miller) by other guards (the best source on the Soledad Brothers case is probably Yee, Min S., *The Melancholy History of Soledad Prison: In Which a Utopian Scheme Turns Bedlam,* Harpers Magazine Press, New York, 1973). At about the same time, Jackson's *Soledad Brother* (Coward-McCann Publishers, New York, 1973) was released, with an introduction by Jean Genet, making him an international politico-literary figure; a second book, *Blood In My Eye* (Random House Publishers, New York, 1972) was published posthumously. There then began a frenzied period of slightly more than a year – captured very well in Armstrong, Gregory, *The Dragon Has Come: The Last Fourteen Months in the Life of George Jackson* (Harper and Row Publishers, New York, 1974) – in which the BPP inducted him to an honorary position within its leadership, a major defense effort was assembled in order to combat the murder charge against him (and to secure his release from prison), the authorities moved him to San Quentin, and a COINTELPRO was apparently launched through which to neutralize both Jackson and as many of his supporters as possible. This included an August 7, 1970 operation at the Marin County Civic Center, near the prison, in which Jackson's 17-year-old brother, Jonathan, was lured into attempting to liberate George by armed force from a courtroom in which he was supposed to appear at a hearing involving three other black prisoners, Ruchell McGee, William Christmas and James McClain. In the event, George Jackson was held at San Quentin on the fateful day, Jonathan walked into a police trap and, in the fusillade which ensued, was killed along with Marin County Judge Harold J. Haley, Christmas and McClain; Assistant District Attorney Gary Thomas was paralyzed for life by a police bullet, while McGee and a juror were badly wounded. Tellingly, the police action was commanded by CCS detectives Ray Callahan and Daniel Mahoney – more than 350 miles out of their LA jurisdiction – and backed up by FBI agents from southern California (see *The Glass House Tapes, op. cit.*) In the aftermath, the Bureau claimed that Soledad Brothers Defense Committee head Angela Y. Davis had coordinated the whole affair – although it turned out there was absolutely no evidence to support such a contention – President Richard M. Nixon proclaimed her to be "the country's number one terrorist fugitive," and she became the focus of a much-publicized nation-wide search. Captured in New York on the night of October 13, 1970, Davis was transported back to California without the legal protocol of extradition and confined for more than a year before being found innocent of all charges (see Davis, Angela Y., *et. al., If They Come In The Morning,* Signet Books, New York, 1971). Meanwhile, according to *provocateur* Louis Tackwood, the plot to assassinate Jackson himself – involving CCS, CII, the FBI and California penal officials – proceeded apace. It culminated on August 21, 1971, whenJackson was gunned down in a courtyard of San Quentin during an alleged escape attempt (see Tackwood, Louis E., "My Assignment was to Kill George Jackson," *The Black Panther,* April 21, 1980, pp. 4-6). Officials offered a bizarre "explanation" of what had happened, contending that Jackson had utilized a huge 9 mm. Astra-600 pistol provided by BPP Field Marshal Landon Williams to attempt an escape. Supposedly, the weapon had been smuggled into the prison by an attorney named Stephen J. Bingham and then concealed by Jackson under an Afro wig and used to take over the prison's "adjustment center" before the attempted breakout (on the utter implausibility of these and other aspects of the official version of events, see the *San Francisco Chronicle,* August 28, 1971). Four guards were killed during the adjustment center takeover. On October 1, 1971, a Marin County grand jury indicted seven persons, six prisoners – including Fleeta Drumgo and another prisoner named Johnny Spain, known collectively as the "San Quentin Six" – and attorney Bingham, on 45 counts of murder, conspiracy and assault concerning the events of August 21. The six went to trial in July of 1975, and three – including Drumgo –were acquitted on August 12, 1976.The remaining three – including Johnny Spain – were convicted and sentenced to multiple life terms of imprisonment. For his part, Stephen Bingham was forced underground for fifteen years, finally surfacing during the spring of 1986 and being acquitted of any wrongdoing in early '87. Meanwhile, Drumgo and Cluchette were also acquitted of the murder charge against them in the death of guard John Mills – the original Soledad Brothers case – and both were paroled. Fleeta Drumgo was mysteriously shotgunned to death on an Oakland street corner on November 24, 1979. In 1988, new evidence concerning police and FBI involvement in the death of George Jackson caused the case of Johnny Spain to be reopened; he is currently free, pending further developments.For further informa-tion on the aftermath of the Jackson assassination, see Clark, Howard, *American Saturday,* Richard Marek Publishers, New York, 1981, pp. 301-19.

140. For more information on the Bernstein/Panther connection, see Wolfe, Tom, *Radical Chic and Mau Mauing the Flak Catchers,* Farrar, Straus and Giroux, New York, 1970.

141. *Intelligence Activities and the Rights of Americans, Book III, op. cit.,* pp. 208-9.

142. Memorandum from Hoover to the SAC, San Francisco, dated March 5, 1970.
143. *Intelligence Activities and the Rights of Americans, Book III, op. cit.*, p. 210.
144. *Ibid.*, pp. 210-1.
145. Memorandum from FBI Headquarters to Chicago and seven other field offices, dated May 15, 1970.
146. *Intelligence Activities and the Rights of Americans, Book III, op. cit..*, pp. 214-5. A memorandum from the New York field office to Hoover, dated October 11, 1969, also describes contacts made by agents with officials of United Airlines in an effort to cause an air freight rate increase *vis à vis* the Panther newspaper in hopes that it will bankrupt the publication, or at least curtail its distribution.
147. Memorandum from the SAC, New York, to Hoover and the San Francisco field office, dated October 11, 1969.
148. Memorandum from the San Diego SAC to Hoover, dated May 20, 1970.
149. *Ibid.*
150. Memorandum from the SAC, New York to Hoover, dated August 19, 1970.
151. *Intelligence Activities and the Rights of Americans, Book III, op. cit.*, pp. 406-7. All 233 anti-Panther COINTELPRO operations acknowledged occurred between August 1968 and early 1971. It should be noted that there could well have been a number of additional actions aimed at the BPP during the critical period which were never acknowledged by the FBI. It is also apparent that a number of the admitted operations were continued after 1971, all FBI avowals and Senate Select Committee assurances to the contrary notwithstanding. During the latter period, it is highly probable that new (unadmitted) COINTELPROs were also launched. The Senate committee, after all, never really assumed physical control over the FBI's filing system, and was thus always dependent upon the Bureau's willingness to tell the truth when stating that all relevant records had been produced. This is a dubious proposition at best, as the Hampton-Clark suit and many other examples abundantly demonstrate. The 233 figure must therefore be considered as a conservative estimate rather than a hard fact.
152. There are no good historical accounts of the BLA. A rather biased sketch, from a bourgeois perspective, but containing at least some of the salient information, may be found in Castellucci, John, *The Big Dance: The Untold Story of Weatherman Kathy Boudin and the Terrorist Family That Committed the Brinks' Robbery Murders*, Dodd, Mead and Company, New York, 1986. A sectarian view from the left may be found in Tani, E., and Kaé Sera, *False Nationalism/False Internationalism: Class Contradictions in Armed Struggle*, Seeds Beneath the Snow Publications, Chicago, 1985. Additional information may be found in Shakur, Assata, *Assata: An Autobiography*, Lawrence Hill Publishers, Westport, CT, 1987.

Chapter 6: COINTELPRO–New Left

1. The earliest attempt to articulate the SDS vision in book format seems to have been Newfield, Jack, *A Prophetic Minority*, New American Library, New York, 1966. What is perhaps the best account of the origins and early evolution of SDS can be found in Miller, James, *"Democracy is in the Streets:" From Port Huron to the Siege of Chicago*, Simon and Schuster Publishers, New York, 1987. Several of the seminal documents of the organization are included in Albert, Judith Clavir, and Stewart Edward Albert (eds.), *The Sixties Papers: Documents of a Rebellious Decade*, Praeger Publishers, New York, 1984. Other critical documents may be found in older books, such as Cohen and Hales, *op. cit.*; Jacobs, Paul, and Saul Landau (eds.), *The New Radicals*, Random House Publishers, New York, 1966; Kenniston, Kenneth (ed.), *The Young Radicals*, Harcourt, Brace and World Publishers, New York, 1968; Teodori, Massimo (ed.), *The New Left: A Documentary History*, Bobbs-Merrill Company, Indianapolis, 1969; and Long, Priscilla (ed.), *The New Left*, Porter Sargent Publishers, Boston, 1969.
2. The most comprehensive account of the evolution of the new left through time, issues and actions may be found in Sale, Kirkpatrick, *SDS*, Random House Publishers, New York, 1973. Less exhaustive, but in some ways more interesting accounts may be found in Calvert, Greg, and Carol Neiman, *A Disrupted History: The New Left and the New Capitalism*, Random House Publishers, New York, 1971; and Potter, Paul, *A Name for Ourselves*, Little, Brown and Company, New York, 1971. For more on the concept of participatory democracy, see Lynd, Staughton, "The New Radicalism and Participatory Democracy," *Dissent*, Summer 1965.
3. Sullivan and Brown, *op. cit.*, p. 147. For information on the Columbia student uprising, see Grant, Joanne, *Confrontation on Campus*, Signet Books, New York, 1969.

4. Sullivan and Brown, *op. cit.*, p. 147.

5. Goldstein, *op. cit.*, p. 443. Although the Bureau allegedly discontinued its wholesale use of unwarranted bugs and wiretaps on June 1, 1965 as a result of a ban imposed upon such practices by Lyndon Johnson, it is obvious that this imposed no real curtailment of FBI ELSURS activities. Johnson's order banning unwarranted wiretaps and bugs was drafted by Attorney General Katzenbach on April 10, 1965. Hoover wrote to Katzenbach assuring discontinuance on September 14 of the same year. The director also issued an order purporting to ban further surreptitious entries on July 19, 1966. For further information, see U.S. Department of Justice, "Wiretaps," in *Administrative History, Vol. III*, lodged in the Lyndon B. Johnson Presidential Library, Austin, Texas. Also see "Unwarranted FBI Electronic Surveillance," in *Intelligence Activities and the Rights of Americans, Book III, op. cit.*, pp. 271-351.

6. See Divale, William Tulio, with Joseph James, *I Lived Inside the Campus Revolution*, Cowels Book Company, Los Angeles, 1973. Divale claimed, with corroboration from the FBI, that he infiltrated "the student left" at UCLA in early 1965 and, among other things, organized an SDS chapter at Pasadena City College. He proudly admitted to having served as a *provocateur* within the southern California movement – "I was a leader, not a follower" for at least three years before he surfaced in 1969. He was paid more than $15,000 by the FBI for his "services." Another individual who is known to have acted in such a capacity is Phillip Abbott Luce, who infiltrated the Progressive Labor Party (PLP) and its affiliate, the May 2 Movement (M2M; also associated with SDS) in 1962. In 1965, he surfaced to offer a sensational article to the *Saturday Evening Post* entitled "Why I Quit the Extreme Left" (it was run on May 8, 1965). Later the same year, he was called to testify before the House Un-American Activities Committee to "prove" the new left was "communist controlled,"and went on to author a book on the subject (with ample help from the HUAC staff) entitled *The New Left*, David McKay, Inc., New York, 1966.

7. *Intelligence Activities and the Rights of Americans, Book II, op. cit.*, pp. 105, 110; *Intelligence Activities and the Rights of Americans, Book III, op. cit.*, pp. 146-54.

8. *Ibid.*, pp. 146-54, 301. The FBI officially discontinued its own mail cover program in 1964, largely because it was duplicating that of the CIA, from which it had been receiving information accruing from the Agency's illegal reading of U.S. radicals' letters since at least as early as 1958. Consequently, during the period 1958-1973, the Bureau received a total of 57,846 pieces of mail illegally intercepted by the CIA, with the greatest quantities coming during the late 1960s: 5,984 pieces in 1966, 5,863 in 1967, 5,322 in 1968, and 5,384 in 1969. Only 666 pieces had been received in 1968, and 642 in 1973, allegedly the final year of the arrangement (*ibid.*, p. 632). Also see U.S. Senate, Select Committee to Study Governmental Operations with Respect to Intelligence Activities, *Hearings Before the Senate Select Committee to Study Governmental Operations with Respect to Intelligence Activities, Volume IV: Mail Opening*, 94th Congress, 1st Session, U.S. Government Printing Office, Washington, D.C., 1975.

9. Quoted in Finman, Ted, and Stewart MacCaulay, "Freedom to Dissent: The Vietnam Protests and the Words of Public Officials," *Wisconsin Law Review*, Summer 1966, pp. 676-7.

10. The Freedom Rides were conceived and organized by SNCC activist James Forman, utilizing two Supreme Court rulings, *Morgan v. Virginia* and *Boynton v. Virginia*, prohibiting racial discrimination in interstate transportation and terminal accommodations as a basis to try to force federal intervention in the South. Many embryonic new leftists participated.

11. O'Reilly, *op. cit.*, p. 84. The fate of the first bus is described as follows at pp. 83-4: "When the Greyhound parked for its scheduled fifteen-minute rest stop, an angry mob surrounded it and began smashing windows and slashing tires. Police officers diverted the mob and the bus pulled out, but Ku Kluxers pursued in cars, catching up to the bus six miles out of town, when the tires either went flat from the earlier slashing or were shot out. A homemade bomb came through one of the windows. The bus quickly filled with smoke. The passengers tried to flee, but the mob held the door shut. The realization that the bus might explode finally forced them to back up, and they beat the riders as they left the bus." The FBI had been present through the whole affair, but had done absolutely nothing to intervene.

12. *Ibid.*, p. 86. At p. 87, the author continues, "Sergeant Cook exercised little restraint when forwarding material to the Klan. Gary Rowe [an FBI informant whom Cook believed to be a *bona fide* klansman], described his access to police files as complete. Cook once opened two file drawers in his office [concerning civil rights activists] and told Rowe to help himself, 'for the use of the KLAN, in general.' Material leaked to Rowe and other Klansmen, [Birmingham SAC Thomas] Jenkins advised headquarters, included 'information concerning potential violence given [Cook] by the Birmingham

FBI office.' The Klan, in turn, supplied ad hoc personnel for the police department's surveillance squad. Klansmen covered black churches and movement meetings, jotting down license plate numbers, and sometimes rode around on patrol in squad cars." At p. 86, O'Reilly notes that local FBI agents "suspected" close ties between the Klan and the Birmingham police since at least as early as September 1960. Yet the flow of civil rights movement-related material to the police continued unabated. See additionally, memoranda, SAC, Birmingham, to Director, FBI, September 30, 1960; May 5, 1961; April 19, 1961; April 24, 1961; April 25, 1961; and April 26, 1961.

13. Stone is quoted in Overstreet, Harry, and Bonaro Overstreet, *The FBI in Our Open Society*, W.W. Norton Publishers, New York, 1969, pp. 167-8.

14. FBI jurisdiction – for enforcement as well as investigation – clearly accrued from the Civil Rights Act of 1866 (Title 18 U.S.C. § 241, § 242). The former section made it a felony punishable by ten years in prison and a $5,000 fine for two or more persons to conspire to deprive "any citizen" of his or her civil rights. The latter section, describing a misdemeanor, composed what is popularly referred to as the "color-of-law statute," making it illegal under federal law for any local official (including police officers) to use his or her office to deny any citizen his or her civil rights.

15. The "FBI had a consistent history of avoiding civil rights work." See U.S. Commission on Civil Rights (report by Arnold Trebach to Attorney General Robert F. Kennedy), *Report – Book 5, Justice*, U.S. Government Printing Office, Washington, D.C., 1961. Also see U.S. Commission on Civil Rights, *Law Enforcement: A Report on Equal Protection in the South*, U.S. Government Printing Office, Washington, D.C., 1965. None of this is intended to indicate that the brunt of anti-civil rights violence was not borne by black activists. Consider, as just a few examples of what was going on in this regard, the matter of SNCC leader Bob Moses, beaten bloody on August 22, 1961 by Billy Gaston, cousin of the local sheriff, while attempting to register blacks to vote in Amite County, Mississippi; SNCC organizer Travis Britt, beaten senseless by a white mob while trying to register voters in the same location on September 5; SNCC organizer John Hardy, pistol-whipped by registrar of voters John Q. Woods for trying to register blacks in Tylertown, Mississippi on September 7; SNCC supporter Herbert Lee, shot and killed by Mississippi state legislator Eugene H. Hurst on September 25; Louis Allen, a black witness to the Lee murder, shot to death by local police in order to prevent his testimony against State Congressman Hurst in 1962; the handcuffing and shooting (three times, in the back of the neck) of activist Charley Ware (whose pregnant wife was also pistol-whipped) by Baker County (Georgia) Sheriff L. Warren "Gator" Johnson; SNCC members Moses, and Randolph T. Blackwell beaten, and Jimmy Travis shot in the head while the three were doing voter registration work near Greenwood, Mississippi in 1963; the gratuitous beating of SNCC activist Marion King, seven months pregnant, by sheriff's deputies at the Mitchell County (Georgia) Jail when she attempted to take food to her husband, Slater, and other SNCC activists incarcerated there (she suffered a stillbirth as a result); the beating (with a cane) of C.B. King, Slater's brother, by Dougherty County (Georgia) Sheriff Cull Campbell, also in 1963. The list could be extended through hundreds of such incidents. For additional information, see Carson, Claybourne, *In Struggle: SNCC and the Black Awakening of the 1960s*, Harvard University Press, Cambridge, MA, 1981.

16. O'Reilly, *op. cit.*, p. 80. Also see Elliff, John T., "Aspects of Federal Civil Rights Enforcement: The Justice Department and the FBI," *Perspectives in American History*, No. 5, 1971, pp. 605-73. An interesting participant account of this period may be found in Peck, James, *Freedom Ride*, Simon and Schuster Publishers, New York, 1962.

17. See *Intelligence Activities and the Rights of Americans, Book III, op. cit.*, p. 456. Also see memorandum, (deleted) to Alex Rosen (FBI General Intelligence Division head), February 26, 1960.

18. O'Reilly, *op. cit.*, p. 103. The author quotes former head of the FBI's Inspection Division, W. Mark Felt, as observing that the Kennedys tended to view the Bureau as their "own private police force" with regard to surveillance of civil rights activists. A nice summary of some portions of this may be found in a memorandum from James F. Bland to William C. Sullivan, dated April 10, 1962. Also see Horne, Gerald, *Communist Front? The Civil Rights Congress, 1946-1956*, Fairleigh Dickinson University Press, Rutherford, NJ, 1988.

19. See Cagin, Seth, and Philip Dray, *We Are Not Afraid: The Story of Goodman, Schwerner, and Chaney, and the Civil Rights Campaign in Mississippi*, Macmillan Publishers, New York, 1988. Also see U.S. Department of Justice, "Prosecutive Summary," No. 1613, Washington, D.C., December 19, 1964. It should be noted that Chaney, Schwerner and Goodman worked for CORE rather than SNCC. The Mississippi Freedom Summer Project was an initiative of COFO, the Council of Federated Organiza-

tions, consisting of SNCC, CORE, SCLC and the NAACP. Also see Belfrage, Sally, *Freedom Summer*, Viking Press, New York, 1965. Of further interest, see Woodley, Richard, "It Will Be a Hot Summer in Mississippi," *The Reporter*, May 21, 1964.

20. Bowers is quoted in a report on the "racial situation in Mississippi" tendered by the Atlanta field office of the FBI, dated September 28, 1964, with reference to the comment having been reported by the Bureau's Klan infiltrators in "early 1963." For further contextual information, see Rothschild, Mary Aikin, *A Case of Black and White: Northern Volunteers and the Southern Freedom Summers, 1964-1965*, Greenwood Press, Westport, CT, 1982.

21. This conservative count accrues from Bureau monograph number 1386 (author unknown), entitled *Student Nonviolent Coordinating Committee* (FBI File No. 100-43190), completed in August 1967. The document draws upon information available to agents *at the time*. Also see Spain, David M., "Mississippi Autopsy," *Ramparts* (Special Edition), 1964.

22. On SA Helgeson's response, or lack of it, see King, Mary, *Freedom Song*, William Morrow and Company, New York, 1987, pp. 378-85. The agent interacted similarly, not only with Sherwin Kaplan, a Friend of SNCC volunteer who reported Chaney, Schwerner and Goodman missing at about 10 p.m. on the fatal evening (*i.e.*: as they were being released, when an FBI inquiry with the Neshoba County Sheriff's Office might actually have done some good), but with another white activist, Robert Weil, and the author, a SNCC activist, as well as Justice Department Attorney Frank Schwelb, all around 11 p.m. When SNCC activist Aaron Henry called again a bit later, Helgeson "took the information curtly and did not allow a chance for further conversation."

23. O'Reilly, *op. cit.*, p. 165.

24. *Ibid.*; the Jackson FBI office, meanwhile, was still sandbagging with a vengeance, telling SNCC activist Bill Light in response to a question as to whether the Bureau would attempt to find the missing men that SNCC should direct all such "inquiries...to the Justice Department." Also see Holt, Len, *The Summer That Didn't End*, Morrow Publishers, New York, 1965.

25. Moses put his message out in the form of a letter to the parents of all Mississippi Freedom Summer volunteers, circa June 22, 1964. This is noted in a memorandum from FBI official Alex Rosen to Alan H. Belmont on July 8, 1964. The FBI's concern with the actions of Mrs. Schwerner and Mrs. Chaney may be discerned in a memorandum (names deleted) concerning the wiretap log of a phone call from Rita Schwerner to the White House on June 25, 1964, and another call to May King on the same date (WATS Reports, Box 37). Cronkite's comment is recorded in the transcript of the CBS News Report, June 25, 1964. Also see Huie, William Bradford, *Three Lives for Mississippi*, WCC Books, New York, 1965; and McCord, William, *Mississippi: The Long Hot Summer*, W.W. Norton Publishers, New York, 1965.

26. On the FBI buildup and its causes, see Von Hoffman, Nicholas, *Mississippi Notebook*, David White Publishers, New York, 1964, p. 38. Also see Sutherland, Elizabeth (ed.), *Letters From Mississippi*, McGraw-Hill Publishers, New York, 1965, p. 118. Corroboration accrues in a letter from J. Edgar Hoover to Walter Johnson, dated July 13, 1964.

27. On the director's visit to Mississippi, see Welch, Neil J., and David W. Marston, *Inside Hoover's FBI*, Doubleday Publishers, Garden City, NY, 1984, pp. 102, 106-7. Also see Navasky, Victor, *Kennedy Justice*, Atheneum Publishers, New York, 1971, p. 107.

28. See Doar, John, and Dorothy Landsberg, "The Performance of the FBI in Investigating Violations of Federal Laws Protecting the Right to Vote, 1960-1967," in U.S. Senate, Committee on the Judiciary, Subcommittee on Constitutional Rights, *Hearings on FBI Counterintelligence Programs*, 93d Congress, 2d Session, U.S. Government Printing Office, Washington, D.C., 1974, pp. 936-7.

29. O'Reilly, *op. cit.*, p. 173. The t-shirt clad torso was never identified, as was the case with several other black bodies found in Mississippi swamps during the search for Chaney, Schwerner and Goodman. Two other torsos discovered in the Old River near Tallulah, Louisiana were correlated with names. They were Charlie Eddie Moore and Henry H. Dee, both non-activist black 19-year-olds, apparently murdered by the klan in the Homochitto National Forest because of the mistaken notion that they were part of a nonexistent "Black Muslim gun-running plot." No particular effort seems to have been made to solve any of these apparent homicides, or even to identify the bodies, which undoubtedly were among the more than 450 separate incidents of racist violence SNCC chronicled as having occurred in Mississippi during Freedom Summer (June 15 - September 15, 1964); see Minnis, Jack, *Mississippi – A Chronology of Violence and Intimidation Since 1961*, Student Nonviolent Coordinating Committee (internal document), Atlanta, 1963. Also see Moody, Anne, *Coming of Age in Mississippi*, Dial Press, New York, 1968, p. 338.

30. Memorandum, Attorney General Nicholas Katzenbach to President Lyndon B. Johnson, September 4, 1964. Also see U.S. Department of Justice, "Prosecution Summary," No. 1613, *op. cit.*, and "Supplemental Summary," No. 1822, March 5, 1965.

31. Quoted in Cagin and Dray, *op. cit.*, p. 452. Sentencing is covered at p. 435. Also see *United States v. Cecil Ray Price, et. al.*, Crim. No. 5291, Federal District Court of Southern Mississippi, October 11-21, 1967. Of further interest, see Woodley, Richard, "A Recollection of Michael Schwerner," *The Reporter*, July 16, 1964; and Goodman, Carolyn, as told to Bernard Asbell, "My Son Didn't Die in Vain!" *Good Housekeeping*, May 1965.

32. Sullivan and Brown, *op. cit.*, pp. 129-30.

33. The Bureau's claimed "coverage" of the klan derives from a letter from Hoover to Attorney General Katzenbach, dated September 2, 1965.

34. Hoffman, Abbie, *Soon to be a Major Motion Picture*, G.P. Putnam's Sons, Publishers, New York, 1980, p. 69.

35. As O'Reilly, *op. cit.*, puts it at p. 217, Rowe was actively suspected of "involvement in the firebombing of the home of a wealthy black Birmingham resident, A.G. Gaston, the detonating of shrapnel bombs in black neighborhoods, and the murder of a black man in the 1963 demonstrations," and there was speculation the FBI had covered for him on each of these matters. The author also notes that Rowe had appeared to inform on a plot to kill a civil rights activist, the Reverend Fred Shuttlesworth, but that the supposed assassin, John Wesley Hall, also turned out to be an FBI infiltrator. As to the 16th Street church bombing which left four children dead (they were Carole Robertson, Denise McNair, Addie Mae Collins and Cynthia Wesley, ages four through fourteen), the Bureau opened what it dubbed the BAPBOMB (for "Baptist Bombing") investigation. As O'Reilly observes on p. 112, "Another informant, John Wesley Hall, named Rowe as a member of a three-man klan security committee that held veto power over all proposed acts of violence; this raised the possibility that Rowe might have been involved in the Baptist Church bombing. In fact, the Birmingham police considered Rowe a prime suspect. But the FBI did not investigate. Hall, who went by the nickname of "Nigger," went on the Bureau payroll two months *after* the explosion despite a polygraph test that convinced FBI agents in Alabama that he had been involved in the crime. Hall also admitted having moved some dynamite for the principle BAPBOMB suspect, Robert E. ("Dynamite Bob") Chambliss, a fifty-nine-year-old truck driver for an auto parts company who had joined the Ku Klux Klan in 1924. Two weeks after the bomb exploded on Sixteenth Street, the Birmingham Recorder's Court sentenced Chambliss, Hall, and another suspect, Charles Arnie Cagle, on a misdemeanor charge – possession of an explosive without a permit." Despite this wealth of readily available information, the FBI was for some reason never able to "crack the case." So much for BAPBOMB. Also see Raines, Howell, "The Birmingham Bombing Twenty Years Later: The Case That Won't Close," *New York Times Magazine*, July 24, 1983.

36. See Rowe, Gary Thomas Jr., *My Undercover Years with the Ku Klux Klan*, Bantam Books, New York, 1976. Also see Sullivan and Brown, *op. cit.*, pp. 131-3, and O'Reilly, *op. cit.*, pp. 217-23. At p. 221, the latter notes that in the fall of 1978, a Lowndes County, Alabama grand jury finally acted against Rowe, indicting him as the man who had in fact pulled the trigger in the Liuzzo murder.

37. The defendants appealed and were freed on appeal bond until the circuit court upheld their conviction on April 27, 1967. Thomas and Wilkins were then ordered to federal prison, where neither served more than five years of his ten-year sentence. Eaton, meanwhile, had died of a heart attack while awaiting the appeals decision and never served any time at all.

38. The case is *Muhammad Kenyatta v. Roy Moore, et. al.*, No. 377-0298 (R) (N.D. Miss., 1985). The book in question is Whitehead, Don, *Attack on Terror, op. cit.* Other examples of the genre include Sentner, David, *How the FBI Gets Its Man*, Avon Books, New York, 1965, and Tully, Andrew, *The FBI's Most Famous Cases*, William Morrow and Company, New York, 1965. In 1975, when the television movie of the Whitehead potboiler was aired, Michael Schwerner's father was provoked into attempting to refute at least the more obvious lies involved; see Schwerner, Nat, "Mississippi: Whitewashing the FBI," *Rights*, April-May, 1975.

39. See memorandum, E.T. Turner to W.A. Branigan, dated August 23, 1964. Also see Wise, *op. cit.*, pp. 288-91.

40. An interesting summary of the Bureau's Atlantic City operation may be found in Lasky, Victor, *It Didn't Start With Watergate*, Dell Books, New York, 1978, pp. 178-85. The author notes that DeLoach utilized the services of Atlantic City SAC Leo Clark, pledging Clark to secrecy even where the Secret Service was concerned. Also see Miller, Mike, "The MFDP," *The Movement*, May 1965.

41. Miller, *op. cit.*, pp. 184-217. Also see Lynd, Staughton, "Toward an Interracial Movement of the Poor," *Liberation*, July 1969. For participant accounts of ERAP efforts in specific cities, see Gitlin, Todd, and Nanci Hollander, *Uptown: Poor Whites in Chicago*, Harper and Row Publishers, New York, 1970 (this concerns the "Jobs Or Income Now" – JOIN – project; and Hayden, *op. cit.* (concerning the Newark Community Union Project, NCUP). Also see Sale, *op. cit.*, pp. 131-50.

42. Sale, *op. cit.*, pp. 162-3. Weinberg was the individual who coined the absurd phrase, quickly popularized by the mass media, "Never trust anyone over thirty."

43. For a fairly comprehensive elaboration of the thinking involved, see Lipset, Seymour M., and Sheldon S. Wolin (eds.), *The Berkeley Student Revolt*, Doubleday Publishers, Garden City, NY, 1965. Also see Wolin, Sheldon S., and John H. Schaar (eds.), *The Berkeley Rebellion and Beyond*, New York Review of Books, New York, 1970. Another thoughtful and succinct articulation may be found in Davidson, Carl, *The New Radicals and the Multiversity*, Students for a Democratic Society (pamphlet), Chicago, 1968. Davidson was SDS Interorganizational Secretary, 1967-68.

44. The initial commitment of U.S. ground troops (other than "advisors") on March 8, 1965 was only 3,500 men. Within nine weeks, however, the number had grown to more than 90,000 as units such as the elite 1st Air Cavalry and 101st Airborne Divisions were committed. On July 28, President Lyndon Johnson publicly announced that he had already slated 125,000 U.S. troops for combat duty, and that the number might go as high as 200,000 by the end of the year. (See MacLear, Michael, *The Ten Thousand Day War: Vietnam, 1945-1975*, St. Martin's Press, New York, 1981, pp. 128-50.) The attention of student radicals – virtually all of whom were of draft age – was riveted by these developments.

45. The text of Potter's speech is included in Albert and Albert, *op. cit.*, at pp. 218-25.

46. For the best account of the trip, see Lynd, Staughton, and Thomas Hayden, *The Other Side*, New American Library, New York, 1966.

47. On the practical outcome of the debate within SDS concerning the emphasis (or lack of same) to be placed on anti-war organizing, see the text of a speech delivered in Washington, D.C., during an October 27, 1965 demonstration against the war, by SDS president Carl Oglesby (who replaced Potter in this position during the summer of that year); included in Teodori, *op. cit.*, at pp. 182-8.

48. Goodman, Mitchell (ed.), *The Movement Toward a New America: The Beginnings of a Long Revolution*, Knopf/Pilgrim Press, New York/Philadelphia, 1970, p. xi. An interesting participant perspective on one of the core aspects of new left opposition to the Vietnam war may be found in Ferber, Michael, and Staughton Lynd, *The Resistance*, Beacon Press, Boston, 1971; a good view on other dimensions of the anti-war effort may be obtained in Foster, Julian, and Durward Long, *Protest! Student Activism in America*, William Morrow and Company, New York, 1970.

49. *Intelligence Activities and the Rights of Americans, Book III, op. cit.*, pp. 249, 487-90.

50 See Student National Coordinating Committee, "The Basis of Black Power," *New York Times*, August 5, 1966.

51. See Carmichael, Stokely, "What We Want," *New York Review of Books*, September 26, 1966. By February 17, 1968 – at the point of the merger between SNCC and the BPP – Carmichael's position had hardened to the point where he delivered "A Declaration of War" as a speech, the text of which was printed in the *San Francisco Express Times* on February 22.

52. For an excellent reading on "new class theory" in its formulation during this period, see Hayden, Tom, "The Politics of the Movement," *Dissent*, January/February 1966. Also see Calvert, Gregory, "In White America: Radical Consciousness and Social Change," *The National Guardian*, March 1967; as well as Rowntree, John, and Margaret Rowntree, "Youth as Class," *Midpeninsula Observer*, August 12, 1968. A more contemporary tracing of the theory's evolution may be found in Walker, Pat (ed.), *Between Labor and Capital: The Professional-Managerial Class*, South End Press, Boston, 1979.

53. Probably the best example of this is Editors of *U.S. News and World Report, Communism and the New Left: What They're Up to Now*, Collier/Macmillan Company, London, 1969, in which the anonymous authors (thought to include several FBI "public relations specialists") worry at great length about the nonexistent influence of Bettina Aptheker, head of the Berkeley DuBois Club and daughter of CP, USA historian Herbert Aptheker, on "the anti-war movement." Attention is also paid to the effects of participation by the YSA and PLP in "New Left affairs." Another, somewhat earlier but delightfully ridiculous treatment of the same subject matter – assembled with ample assistance of the Bureau – is Allen, Gary, *Communist Revolution in the Streets*, Western Islands Publishers, Boston and Los Angeles, 1967. Ironically, it was the largely sterile DuBois Clubs rather than the vibrant new left organizations

which suffered most from such misinformation. In March 1966, after FBI reports prompted inflammatory statements about them by Attorney General Nicholas Katzenbach, DuBois Club members were assaulted outside their Brooklyn headquarters by neighborhood toughs who had previously ignored them; a few hours later, a bomb blew up the group's national headquarters in San Francisco (see Cray, Ed, *The Enemy in the Streets*, Doubleday Publishers, Garden City, NY, 1972, p. 223). In 1967, J. Edgar Hoover described the tiny and rather impotent organization as being "the new blood of international communism" (quoted in Finman and MacAulay, *op. cit.*, at p. 633), with the result that it was quickly banned from campuses such as those of the University of Illinois and University of Indiana systems (see *Chicago Sun-Times*, February 16 and March 15, 1967).

54. Kirkpatrick Sale (*op. cit.*, p. 64) describes the formation of PLP as follows: "On July 1, 1962, some fifty people meeting at the Hotel Diplomat in New York City established a new political organization on the left. Its fourteen-member coordinating committee consisted entirely of people who had been members of the Communist Party and quit or were purged in late 1961 and early 1962 for being 'ultra-leftists' and 'agents of the Albanian party' – *i.e.*, 'Maoists.' Among them: Milton Rosen, who became chairman of the new group; Mortimer Scheer, vice chairman and head of West Coast operations; Fred Jerome, the editor of the group's five-month-old magazine; and Bill Epton, a black man. The name of the organization: the Progressive Labor Movement [changed to 'Party' on April 18, 1964]." On pp. 121-2, Sale describes the creation of M2M by PLP. At least some portion of the right-wing confusion as to who or what, exactly, comprised the new left may have been genuine, given SDS' staunch adherence to the principle of not excluding self-proclaimed communists; see Haber, Alan, *Nonexclusionism: The New Left and the Democratic Left*, Students for a Democratic Society (pamphlet), New York, 1965.

55. Sale, *op. cit.*, p. 351. The budget of the SDS national office was $87,000 – virtually all of it raised by the membership – for the year.

56. Teodori, *op. cit.*, p. 481.

57. *Ibid.*, p. 482.

58. MacLear, *op. cit.*, p. 169. The troop level at the time of Westmoreland's request was approximately 470,000. The U.S. absorbed more than 16,000 combat fatalities during 1967, more than three times the number sustained in 1965. By this point, perhaps 750,000 Vietnamese had died as a result of the U.S. intervention, with another 1.3 million rendered homeless.

59. Sale, *op. cit.*, pp. 369-74.

60. *Ibid.*, pp. 375-7. The confrontation led to the first "conspiracy to incite a riot" charge being levied against SDSers, the so-called "Oakland Seven": Frank Bardacke, Terry Cannon, Reese Erlich, Steve Hamilton, Bob Mandel, Mike Smith and Jeff Segal. They were later acquitted after Oakland policeman Robert Wheeler was forced to admit that he'd provided demonstration organizers with the hand-held walkie-talkies which allowed them to listen in on police communications, and the possession of which was used by the prosecution as evidence that a conspiracy had occurred. Another Oakland cop, Bruce Coleman, confessed on the stand that, acting in an "undercover [infiltrator/*provocateur*] capacity," he'd provided firecrackers for use in unnerving police during the demonstrations, and had explained the tactic to demonstrators at an SDS meeting before the event. See Rothschild, Emma, "Notes from a Political Trial," in Paul Lauter and Florence Howe (eds.), *Trials of the Resistance*, Vintage Books, New York, 1970, pp. 114-5.

61. An interesting participant account of the Pentagon demonstration may be found in Mailer, Norman, *The Armies of the Night: History as a Novel, The Novel as History*, New American Library, New York, 1968.

62. Sale, *op. cit.*, pp. 377-9. The Hilton confrontation resulted in the second "conspiracy to incite a riot" charge against SDS leaders, this time Ted Gold, Mark Rudd, and Ron Carver. The charges were later dropped. An excellent participant summary, not only of this action, but of the whole sweep of SDS anti-war activity in New York during this period may be found in Rader, Dotson, *I Ain't Marchin' Anymore*, Paperback Library, New York, 1969.

63. Anti-ROTC demonstrations occurred at Arizona, Brandeis, Howard, Louisiana State, Rutgers and San Francisco State Universities, among others. Anti-military recruitment protests were undertaken at Adelphi, Berkeley, U/Cal Irvine, University of Colorado, Harvard, Indiana, Iowa, Michigan State, Oberlin, Pratt Institute, Princeton, Stony Brook, Washington University and Yale. Anti-CIA recruitment actions were to be found at Brandeis, Brown, University of Colorado, Kentucky, Pennsylvania, and Tulane. Demonstrations against Dow recruiters were also conducted at Boston University,

Brandeis, California (Berkeley, Los Angeles State, San Jose, San Fernando Valley, and UCLA campuses), Chicago, CCNY, Connecticut, Harvard, Illinois, Indiana, Iowa, Minnesota, NYU, Pennsylvania, Rochester, Vanderbilt, and Wisconsin. The list is hardly complete.

64. A partial list of examples includes exposure of a $125,000-per-year contract between the CIA and Columbia's School of International Affairs which had been repeatedly denied by Dean Andrew Cordier; "Project Michigan," part of a $21.6 million contract with the Pentagon by which the University of Michigan was to perfect infrared sensing equipment for use in jungle warfare; uncovering of a multimillion dollar Penn State contract to run an ordnance laboratory and assist in the development of the U.S. nuclear submarine fleet; production of a 21-page report by SDS at MIT, detailing how the "private" institution was dependent on the government for 79% of its financing, a situation engendering substantial military research; other discoveries included the participation of fifty universities in the Pentagon's "Project Themis" and working in everything from a $30 million-per-year counterinsurgency research effort to developing chemical and biological warfare techniques. See New Left Notes, September 25, 1967.

65. The extent and systematic nature of government lying vis à vis its Indochina policy and prosecution of an undeclared war in that region was fully documented in secret reports, studies and memoranda. Although much remains hidden to this day, a sufficient quantity of such information was eventually "leaked" by Rand Corporation consultant Daniel Ellsberg to establish the case beyond any vestige of reasonable doubt. A selection of the pertinent documents were published as The Pentagon Papers: The Defense Department History of United States Decisionmaking on Vietnam (Senator Mike Gravel Edition, Four Volumes), Beacon Press, Boston, 1971.

66. Goldstein, Political Repression in Modern America, op. cit., pp. 440-1. Also see Mitford, Jessica, The Trial of Dr. Spock, The Reverend William Sloane Coffin, Jr., Michael Ferber, Mitchell Goodman, and Marcus Raskin, Vintage Books, New York, 1970. The case at issue was U.S. v. William Sloane Coffin, Jr., et.al., 50 U.S.C. App. 462 (a). The defendants were charged with such "misdeeds" as distributing a pamphlet entitled A Call to Resist Illegitimate Authority, produced by an anti-war organization, RESIST, nominally headed by Noam Chomsky and Dwight MacDonald. Ferber was specifically cited in the indictment for having delivered a speech entitled "A Time to Say No" at Boston's Arlington Street Church on October 16, 1967. Coffin and Spock were also cited for giving certain speeches. During the period encompassing the trial (December 1, 1967 through December 1, 1968), 537 students who had turned in their draft cards as an act of resistance lost their student deferments and were declared eligible for immediate conscription by Selective Service Director General Lewis Hershey. An SDS member at the University of Oklahoma in Norman was also reclassified for immediate induction into the army because his draft board (in its own words) "did not feel [his] activity as a member of SDS [was] to the best interest of the U.S. government." See Civil Liberties, June 1969. Also see Sale, op. cit., p. 407.

67. Finman and MacAulay, op. cit.

68. Intelligence Activities and the Rights of Americans, Book III, op. cit., pp. 510-2.

69. Department of Justice Press Release, November 18, 1974.

70. In March 1967, the Columbia Daily Spectator confirmed a report disseminated by a local SDS research committee headed by Ted Gold that the university was secretly affiliated with IDA, and had been since 1959. Student protest was immediately forthcoming, meeting with a promise from President Kirk to form a committee to "study" the question and recommend "guidelines" concerning the nature of such institutional relationships. A year later, in March 1968, when not much had resulted from the committee's work, SDS led a militant demonstration inside Columbia's Low Library, demanding the IDA connection be immediately broken. It was for this that SDS leaders were to be "disciplined" by the Kirk administration; Kirk also banned further demonstrations of any sort inside university buildings. See Avorn, Jerry, Andrew Crane, Mark Jaffe, Oren Root, Jr., Paul Starr, Michael Stern and Robert Stulberg, Up Against the Ivy Wall: A History of the Columbia Crisis, Atheneum Publishers, New York, 1969, pp. 15-21. Concerning the gym site and related issues, see Faculty Civil Rights Group of Columbia University, The Community and the Expansion of Columbia University, Columbia University, December 1967.

71. The action represented the first time that SDS and Columbia's Student Afro-American Society (SAS) had undertaken a joint effort. The first building occupied – by SDS – was Hamilton Hall; this subsequently became an exclusively SAS-occupied facility. Low Library, Mathematics, Avery and Fayerweather Halls were also occupied. See Kahn, Roger, The Battle for Morningside Heights, William Morrow and Company, New York, 1970.

72. The initial six demands of the Columbia demonstrators read as follows: 1) All disciplinary action now pending and probations already imposed upon six students (as a result of the earlier anti-IDA demonstration) be immediately terminated and a general amnesty be granted to those students participating in this demonstration. 2) President Kirk's ban on demonstrations inside University buildings be dropped. 3) Construction of the Columbia gymnasium in Morningside Park cease at once. 4) All future disciplinary action taken against University students be resolved through an open hearing before students and faculty which adheres to standards of due process. 5) Columbia disaffiliate, in fact and not merely on paper, from the Institute for Defense Analysis; and President Kirk and Trustee William A.M. Burden resign their positions on IDA's Board of Trustees and Executive Board. 6) Columbia University use its good offices to obtain dismissal of charges now pending against those participating in demonstrations at the gym construction site in the park. See Avorn, *et al., op. cit.*, pp. 52-3.

73. The police assault at Columbia, involving at least 1,000 men of the NYPD (the bulk of them members of the "Tactical Police Force," or riot police) came on the night of April 30, 1968. 712 students were arrested and at least 148 injured, some of them seriously. See Nevard, Jacques, *Interim report prepared by the First Deputy Commissioner of Police: Arrests Made on the Complaint of Columbia University Administration of Students Trespassing in School Buildings*, New York City Police Department, May 4, 1968. When the administration moved to expel SDS members Mark Rudd, Nick Freudenburg and Morris Grossner in the wake of this event, students reoccupied Hamilton Hall, declared a strike and did open battle with the police on May 21. In this exchange, 138 more students were arrested and an unknown number injured. 66 students were ultimately suspended. Meanwhile, Harlem community activists, supported by SDS, had seized a Columbia-owned tenement in Morningside Heights on May 17, and held it until the police moved in and arrested 117 persons (56 of whom were Columbia students). See Avorn, *et. al., op. cit.*, p. 301. For an SDS leader's perspective on these developments, see Rudd, Mark, "Notes on Columbia," *The Movement*, March 1969.

74. The memo is quoted at length in *Intelligence Activities and the Rights of Americans, Book III, op. cit.*, pp. 516-7. One of the reasons for the vociferousness of the FBI's response to new left actions at Columbia may well have been that student activists were very nearly bringing down the government of Charles DeGaulle in France at virtually the same time. See Priaulx, Allan, and Sanford J. Ungar, *The Almost Revolution: France – 1968*, Dell Books, New York, 1969; and Touraine, Alain, *The May Movement: Revolt and Reform*, Random House Books, New York, 1971. A participant account of the thinking which led to the French student revolt may be found in a book written by one of the movement's leaders: see Cohn-Bendit, Daniel, *Obsolete Communism: The Left-Wing Alternative*, McGraw-Hill Publishers, New York, 1968. A broader conceptual analysis is offered in Hirsh, Arthur, *The French New Left: An Intellectual History from Sartre to Gorz*, South End Press, Boston, 1981. A worldwide perspective on the evolution of the student movement during this crucial year may be found in Katsiaficas, George, *The Imagination of the New Left: A Global Analysis of 1968*, South End Press, Boston, 1987.

75. Project MERRIMAC, begun in February 1967, was a relatively small and localized (in Washington, D.C.) effort employing perhaps a dozen infiltrators which collected information on the general plans, associations, activities and funding of fifteen targeted area groups including Women's Strike for Peace and the Washington Urban League. Project RESISTANCE, initiated in December 1967, was a much larger effort to obtain information on dissident individuals and organizations, included production of weekly situation reports which were secretly distributed within the U.S. intelligence community, and amassed 600-700 files containing the names of between 12,000-16,000 people. The project was ostensibly terminated in June 1973. See Rockefeller, Nelson, *Report to the President by the Commission on CIA Activities Within the United States*, Manor Publishers, New York, 1975, pp. 151-9. Operation CHAOS, launched in August 1967, continued until March 1974, when it was supposedly abandoned. In 1976, a senate staff report noted that, "A major purpose of CHAOS activity in actual practice became its participation with the FBI in the Bureau's internal security work." See *Intelligence Activities and the Rights of Americans, Book III, op. cit.*, p. 716.

76. Goldstein, *Political Repression in Modern America, op. cit.*, p. 457.

77. *Intelligence Activities and the Rights of Americans, Book III, op. cit.*, pp. 749-50.

78. Goldstein, *Political Repression in Modern America, op. cit.*, p. 458. The author goes on to note that, "Among the stranger activities of Army intelligence agents were the monitoring of protests by welfare mothers in Milwaukee; infiltration of a coalition of church youth groups and young Democrats in

Colorado; attending a Halloween party for elementary school children in Washington, D.C. on the suspicion a local 'dissident' might be present; monitoring classes at New York University, where a prominent civil rights leader was teaching; attending a conference of priests in Washington, D.C., held to discuss birth control; and using government money to buy liquor and marijuana in order to infiltrate a commune in Washington, D.C. during a counter-inaugural demonstration in January, 1969. Information collected and/or sought for inclusion in Army files included information on the political, financial and sexual lives of individuals and information on the leaders, plans, purposes and funding of dissident organizations." Also see U.S. Senate, Committee on the Judiciary, Subcommittee on Constitutional Rights, *Army Surveillance and Civilians: A Documentary Analysis*, 92d Congress, 1st Session, U.S. Government Printing Office, Washington, D.C., 1971. Of further interest, see Pyle, Christopher, "CONUS Intelligence: The Army Watches Civilian Politics," in Charles Peters and Taylor Branch (eds.), *Blowing the Whistle*, Praeger Publishers, New York, 1972; and Pyle, Christopher, "Spies Without Masters: The Army Still Watches Civilian Politics," *Civil Liberties Review*, Summer 1974, pp. 38-49.

79. See Emerson, *op. cit.*, p. 145. Also see Sale, *op. cit.*, p. 443.

80. Quoted in *Intelligence Activities and the Rights of Americans, Book III, op. cit.*, pp. 515-6.

81. Excerpts from Hayden's testimony before both HUAC and the National Commission on the Causes and Prevention of Violence (to which he was also called as a witness) form a volume entitled *Rebellion and Repression*, World Publishing Company, Cleveland, OH, 1969. Among the others who were called before HUAC were Abbie Hoffman and former SDSer/Vietnam Day Committee organizer Jerry Rubin. An account of their experience may be found in Rubin, Jerry, *Do It!*, Simon and Schuster Publishers, New York, 1969.

82. Established policymakers in Washington, D.C. were experiencing something far different from a consensus on the matter by this point. After the Vietnamese Tet Offensive of January-February 1968 proved beyond question that General Westmoreland's "light at the end of the tunnel" to victory was a hoax – and the good general resultantly requested an additional 206,000 troops beyond the half-million he already had at his disposal, a move which would have necessitated calling up the reserves as well as raising the already huge numbers of men being conscripted – Secretary of Defense Clark Clifford (previously a firm supporter of the war) himself began to call upon Lyndon Johnson to begin as rapid as possible a U.S. withdrawal. The secretary was hardly alone in adopting this position. For his part, realizing his Vietnam policy was untenable, Johnson announced on March 31, 1968, that he would not seek reelection as president. Meanwhile, at least two major Democratic contenders for the presidential nomination – Senators Robert Kennedy of New York and Eugene McCarthy of Minnesota – had begun to explicitly orient their campaigns to promises of ending the war. Similarly, the Republican candidate, Richard M. Nixon, campaigned on the basis of having a "secret plan" to bring hostilities to a close. There is no evidence that the FBI launched COINTELPROs to neutralize these defeatists. See Joseph, Paul, *Cracks in the Empire: State Politics in the Vietnam War*, South End Press, Boston, 1981.

83. Quoted in *Hearings on the Federal Bureau of Investigation, op. cit.*, p. 534.

84. Rockefeller, *op. cit.*, pp. 117-21; *Intelligence Activities and the Rights of Americans, Book III, op. cit.*, pp. 495-505.

85. The commission report was published under the byline of its chair as Walker, Daniel, *Rights in Conflict, the Violent Confrontation of Chicago During the Week of the Democratic National Convention: A Report to the National Commission on the Causes and Prevention of Violence*, Bantam Books, New York, 1968. A number of useful participant insights are to be found in Hoffman, Abbie ("Free"), *Revolution for the Hell of It*, Dial Press, New York, 1968. An excellent overview of the "police riot" thesis offered by the Walker Commission, and one in which the idea is implicitly found to amount to a cover up of what actually happened (a police riot might accurately be said to have occurred had the police rank and file gotten out of control of their superiors; instead, the police simply followed orders tendered by higher-ups) may be found in Schultz, John, *No One Was Killed: Convention Week, Chicago – August 1968*, Big Table Publishing Company, Chicago, 1969.

86. Goldstein, *Political Repression in Modern America, op. cit.*, p. 487. For participant views on the meaning of this government strategy of repression to various tendencies within the new left, see Hoffman, Abbie, *Woodstock Nation*, Vintage Books, New York, 1969; and Hayden, Tom, *Trial*, Holt, Rinehart and Winston Publishers, New York, 1970.

87. *Ibid.*, pp. 487-8. This is the same case referred to in the preceding chapter. Also see Epstein, Jason, *The Great Conspiracy Trial: An Essay on Law, Liberty and the Constitution*, Random House Publishers, New

York, 1970; and Lukas, J. Anthony, *The Barnyard Epithet and Other Obscenities: Notes on the Chicago Conspiracy Trial*, Harper and Row Publishers, New York, 1970. Other excellent readings on the trial may be found in Levine, Mark, *et al.* (eds.), *The Tales of Hoffman*, Bantam Books, New York, 1970; and Meltsner, Michael, and Victor Navasky (eds.), *The "Trial" of Bobby Seale*, Priam Books, New York, 1970.

88. A good summary of the charges and the context in which they arose may be found in Weiner, Bernard, "What, Another Conspiracy?" *The Nation*, November 2, 1970. The Seattle Eight included seven SDSers: Joe Kelly, Roger Lippman, Michael Justesen, Susan Stern, Jeffrey Dowd, Chip Marshall and Michael Ables.

89. An assessment of the Seattle Eight contempt sentences and the effect of the trial upon the movement in the Washington region accrues in Weiner, Bernard, "The Orderly Perversion of Justice," *The Nation*, February 1, 1971. In March of 1973, seven of the defendants (the eighth had gone underground and missed the entire trial), apparently exhausted by the ongoing appeals process, entered *nolo contendere* pleas to the contempt charges and served sentences ranging from thirty days to five months (as opposed to the one-year-minimum sentences originally handed down by Judge Boldt). At that point, mission accomplished, the government dismissed all the substantive charges which had caused the trial in the first place.

90. See Donner, Frank, and Eugene Cerruti, "The Grand Jury Network," *The Nation*, January 3, 1972, pp. 11-2. The other conspiracy defendants named were Sister Elizabeth McAlister, the Reverend Joseph Wenderoth, the Reverend Neil McLaughlin, Anthony Scoblick (an ex-priest), and Eqbal Ahmad (a non-christian Pakistani). Although several were not Catholic, all were members of a "Catholic left" anti-war group called the East Coast Conspiracy to Save Lives. At the time of Hoover's statement and the subsequent conspiracy indictment, both Berrigans (leading members of a direct action organization called the Resistance, as well as the East Coast Conspiracy) were in jail, serving sentences resulting from their participation in the destruction of draft records at the Selective Service Office in Cantonsville, Maryland on May 17, 1968 (an act which led to the trial of the so-called "Cantonsville Nine:" both Berrigans, Thomas Lewis, George Mische, David Darst, Mary Moylan, Thomas and Mary Melville, and John Hogan). Phillip Berrigan was also serving a sentence for his participation in a similar destruction of draft records at the Selective Service Office in Baltimore on October 27, 1967 (bringing about the trial of the "Baltimore Four:" Berrigan, David Eberhart, Thomas Lewis and James Mengel).

91. The psychiatrist's report is quoted in Nelson, Jack, and Ronald J. Ostrow, *The FBI and the Berrigans: The Making of a Conspiracy*, Coward, McCann and Geoghegan, Inc., New York, 1972, pp. 476-7. Douglass' profile included desertion from the army, two attempts at suicide, and numerous arrests and conviction on such charges as passing bad checks, impersonating an army officer and assaulting an FBI agent. His own father testified in court that, "He has told me so many lies practically all his life that I can't believe nothing he tells me."

92. Goldstein, *Political Repression in Modern America, op. cit.*, p. 489.

93. *New York Times*, June 28, 1973. For further information, see Berrigan, Daniel, *America is Hard to Find: Notes from the Underground and Danbury Prison*, Doubleday Publishers, Garden City, NY, 1972.

94. Nelson and Ostrow, *op. cit.*, p. 197.

95. An indication of the evolution of Ellsberg's thinking on Vietnam – based upon his virtually unlimited access to classified documents and firsthand experience in the combat zone – can be found in his *Papers on the War*, Pocket Books, New York, 1972. The government attempted to block publication of the papers in the press, temporarily securing an injunction banning publication; this was overruled by the Supreme Court in *New York Times v. U.S.* An excellent synthesis of the material contained in the Pentagon Papers may be found in Stavins, Ralph, Richard J. Barnet and Marcus G. Raskin, *Washington Plans an Aggressive War*, Random House Publishers, New York, 1971.

96. *Civil Liberties*, January 1965. Also see Schrag, Peter, *Test of Loyalty*, Simon and Schuster Publishers, New York, 1974. As charged, Ellsberg faced 155 years in prison, Russo 25. A good overview of the case, both in and out of court, is to be found in Ungar, Sanford J., *The Papers and the Papers: An Account of the Legal and Political Battles Over the Pentagon Papers*, E.P. Dutton Publishers, New York, 1975.

97. See Wicker, Tom, "The Iron Curtain," *New York Times*, November 19, 1972. About all the papers showed was that "the American people had been systematically misled by their elected and appointed leaders." The prosecutor argued that there was no need to establish that the documents were actually "vitally important or that their disclosure would be injurious to the United States," only that they were officially classified. As to the "lawfulness" of the government's withholding information, no statutory authority existed at that time; the whole system of classification was predicated on executive orders.

98. Goldstein, *Political Repression in Modern America, op. cit.*, pp. 490-1. Also see Schrag, *op. cit.*, pp. 260-72. Concerning the attempt to discredit Ellsberg, see Editors, *The Senate Watergate Report*, Bantam Books, New York, 1975, pp. 64-71. Charles Colson pleaded guilty on June 3, 1974 to obstruction of justice for his masterminding of a scheme to obtain, prepare and disseminate derogatory information on Ellsberg prior to and during the course of the latter's trial. He was sentenced to a year in prison. On July 12, 1974 John Ehrlichman and plumbers G. Gordon Liddy, Bernard Barker and Eugenio Martinez were themselves convicted of conspiracy to violate Ellsberg's civil rights in connection with the burglary of Dr. Fielding's office. Ehrlichman was also convicted of three counts of perjury for having denied under oath his role in the "bag job." See Sussman, Barry, *The Great Cover-up: Nixon and the Scandal of Watergate*, Signet Books, New York, 1974.

99. See Cook, Fred, "Justice in Gainesville," *The Nation*, October 1, 1973.

100. See Donner, Frank J., and Richard I. Lavine, "Kangaroo Grand Juries," *The Nation*, November 29, 1973.

101. Cook, "Justice in Gainesville," *op. cit.* It should be noted that, at trial, Major Adam Klimkowski, commander of the Miami Police Special Investigation Unit (red squad) admitted that it was not the defendants, but one of his undercover agents, who proposed acquiring machineguns for use at the convention. The accused made no effort to take the infiltrator up on his offer to finance the purchase of such hardware. See the *New York Times*, August 9, 1973.

102. On the Sinclair case, see Goodell, Charles, *Political Prisoners in America*, Random House Publishers, New York, 1973, pp. 199-206. The only longer sentence on so trivial an "offense" went to SNCC organizer Lee Otis Johnson, sentenced in Texas to serve thirty years for having given a single joint to an undercover cop. Both men served over three years before their convictions were overturned on appeal.

103. One of the better known examples of this concerns the case of Martin Sostre, a black Buffalo, NY anarchist and head of a community anti-drug program convicted in 1967 of having dealt heroin from his radical book store. Sostre was sentenced to life as an "habitual felon," but finally paroled in February 1976 after the recantation of the chief witness against him, and the suspension and indictment on drug charges of the main police witness against him. He had by then served eight years for a crime it is more than dubious he ever committed. See Copeland, Vincent, *The Crime of Martin Sostre*, McGraw-Hill Publishers, New York, 1970. The case is also covered in Amnesty International, *Report on Torture*, Farrar, Straus and Giroux Publishers, New York, 1975, p. 193.

104. Donner, Frank, "Theory and Practice of American Political Intelligence," *New York Review of Books*, April 22, 1971.

105. *Civil Liberties*, May 1971. One of the earliest and most celebrated of the desecration cases occurred when Yippie! leader Abbie Hoffman attempted to honor his 1968 HUAC subpoena while wearing a shirt fashioned from a flag. Arrested by federal marshals and charged with violation of Title 18 U.S.C. – a statute purportedly "protecting" not only the flag, but the 4-H Club cloverleaf and Smokey the Bear from "defacing and defiling" – Hoffman was convicted and sentenced to thirty days in jail. The conviction was subsequently overturned on first amendment grounds. See *Soon to be a Major Motion Picture, op. cit.*, pp. 166-70.

106. *Civil Liberties*, September and October 1970; February 1971.

107. See Gunther, Gerald, and Noel T. Dowling, *Constitutional Law and Individual Rights, 1974 Supplement*, Foundation Press, New York, 1974, pp. 307-14. Also see Thomas, William R., *The Burger Court and Civil Liberties*, King's Court Press, Brunswick, OH, 1976, pp. 97-108.

108. See Burks, John, "The Underground Press," in Editors of *Rolling Stone, The Age of Paranoia*, Pocket Books, New York, 1972, pp. 21, 56-7.

109. See Leamer, Laurence, *The Paper Revolutionaries: The Rise of the Underground Press*, Simon and Schuster Publishers, New York, 1970, pp. 138-41.

110. The ban is covered in Glessing, Robert J., *The Underground Press in America*, Indiana University Press, Bloomington, 1971, p. 37.

111. Leamer, *op. cit.*, pp. 131-5. Also see *Time* , March 23, 1970.

112. See Rips, Geoffry, "The Campaign Against the Underground Press," (A Pen American Center Report), in *UnAmerican Activities*, City Lights Books, San Francisco, 1981, p. 112. Also see Leamer, *op. cit.*, pp. 141-6. Even such small, short-lived and erratic papers as *Spiro*, in Peoria, Illinois, came in for close FBI and local police scrutiny and harassment, as author Churchill's own FBI files readily attest.

113. Leamer, *op. cit.*, pp. 146-53. Also see Mackenzie, Angus, "Sabotaging the Dissident Press," *Columbia Journalism Review*, March 3, 1981.

114. *Civil Liberties*, October 1969. Also see, Armstrong, David, *A Trumpet to Arms: Alternative Media in America*, South End Press, Boston, 1981.

115. See, for example, Raymond, John, "Files Recently Released: FBI Spying on the Black Student Union Revealed," *Common Ground*, Vol. III, No. 7, April 18, 1978.

116. See the *New York Times*, July 18 and October 20, 1967; August 9, 1968. In some ways, Lynd got off easy. In 1974, a University of Arkansas professor was convicted of violating the state's criminal anarchy law as well as a statute forbidding communists from holding positions of employment funded by the state, apparently solely on the basis of his membership in the Progressive Labor Party. See Lyons, Gene, "Letter from the Land of Opportunity," *New York Review of Books*, May 30, 1974, pp. 33-6.

117. See *The Chronicle of Higher Education*, February 14, 1972 and *Champaign-Urbana Courier*, April 2, 1974. Parenti sued the trustees for $175,000 in damages; the trustees ultimately settled the matter out of court for an undisclosed sum.

118. See Manchester, William, *The Glory and the Dream*, Bantam Books, New York, 1975, pp. 1201-1205.

119. See McElvoy, James, and Abraham Miller, "The Crisis at San Francisco State," in Howard S. Becker (ed.), *Campus Power Struggles*, Aldine Publishers, Chicago, 1970. Also see Sale, *op. cit.*, pp. 518-9.

120. See the *San Diego Union*, May 9 and May 17, 1972.

121. See Zoccino, Nanda, "Ex-FBI Informer Describes Terrorist Role," *Los Angeles Times*, January 26, 1976; and Viorst, *op. cit.* Also see Parenti, Michael, *Democracy for the Few*, St. Martin's Press, New York, 1980, p. 24.

122. Goldstein, *Political Repression in Modern America*, *op. cit.*, pp. 481-2. Also see *Intelligence Activities and the Rights of Americans, Book III*, *op. cit.*, pp. 850-1.

123. Quoted in Berman and Halperin, *op. cit.*, p. 90.

124. The statements accrue from IRS internal memoranda quoted in *Intelligence Activities and the Rights of Americans, Book III*, *op. cit.*, pp. 881-2, 884-5.

125. Goldstein, *Political Repression in Modern America*, *op. cit.*, pp. 482-3.

126. Probably the clearest expressions of this may be found in "You Don't Need a Weatherman to Know Which Way the Wind Blows," a collective position paper introduced by Karen Ashley, Bill Ayers, Bernardine Dohrn, John Jacobs, Jeff Jones, Gerry Long, Howie Matchinger, Jim Mellen, Terry Robbins, Mark Rudd and Steve Tappis at the June 1969 SDS national convention in Chicago and published in *New Left Notes*, June 18, 1969. Another significant articulation of this trend came in a speech entitled "A Strategy to Win," delivered by SDS Education Secretary Bill Ayers at the Midwest National Action Conference held in Cleveland, August 29-September 1, 1969, and published in *New Left Notes*, September 12, 1969. Both items are reproduced in Jacobs, Harold (ed.), *Weatherman*, Ramparts Press, San Francisco, 1970 (at p. 51 and p. 183, respectively). This is not to argue that Weatherman was somehow *the* manifestation of anti-imperialist consciousness within the new left. To the contrary, as Sale (*op. cit.*) makes quite clear in his definitive study, the roots of conscious anti-imperialism within SDS reach back to at least as early as the 1965-66 period. Further, it seems fair to say that by 1969, virtually all new left formations had adopted the rhetoric and trappings of anti-imperialism in one form or another. For an alternative view of the locus of anti-imperialism within the white movement, one drawn from a Progressive Labor perspective, see Adelson, Alan, *SDS: A Profile*, Charles Scribners's Sons, Publishers, New York, 1972.

127. Gid Powers, *op. cit.*, p. 459. Also see deposition of former FBI agent M. Wesley Swearingen, taken in October 1980, Honolulu, Hawaii.

128. See Richards, David, *Played Out: The Jean Seberg Story*, Playboy Press, New York, 1981, especially pp. 237-8.

129. See Stark, Rodney, *Police Riots*, Wadsworth Publishers, Belmont, CA, 1972, pp. 110-3, 163-6.

130. Quoted in Skolnick, *op. cit.*, pp. 282, 289.

131. Stark, *op. cit.*, p. 6.

132. Skolnick, *op. cit.*, p. 347.

133. *Civil Liberties*, September 1968.

134. Stark, *op. cit.*, pp. 32-54.

135. Quoted in *ibid.*, pp. 53-4.

136. Walker, *op. cit.*, pp. 1, 5.

137. See Kerry, Peggy, "The Scene in the Streets," in Theodore Becker and Vernon G. Murray (eds.), *Government Lawlessness in America*, Oxford University Press, New York, 1971, pp. 59-68.

138. Quoted in Harris, *op. cit.*, p. 176.

139. See Lewis, Grover, "Prisoners of the War in Sunny California," in Becker and Murray, *op. cit.*, pp. 133-8. The sprayed gas saturated U/Cal classrooms (ironically affecting hundreds of "apolitical" and "reactionary" students, faculty and administrators, many of whom actively opposed the demonstrators), a Berkeley hospital, and a nearby swimming pool where neighborhood mothers and their children were attempting to escape the hostilities and the heat. Ten deputies and two ex-deputies were subsequently indicted under federal statutes for having fired their weapons at demonstrators and bystanders with intent to inflict summary punishment. Also see Wolin and Schaar, *op. cit.*, pp. 73-95.

140. Reagan is quoted from *Newsweek*, January 6, 1975.

141. Scranton, *op. cit.*, p. 338.

142. Pinkney, *op. cit.*, p. 178. Clark, *op. cit.*, p. 157.

143. Sale, *op. cit.*, p. 641.

144. *Ibid.*, p. 632. In December 1974, a federal judge ordered the arrest records of more than 600 people dragooned during the Santa Barbara police action expunged on the basis of systematic violation of even their most elementary civil rights. See the *Los Angeles Times*, December 10, 1974.

145. Sale, *op. cit.*, p. 632.

146. See Scranton, *op. cit.*, pp. 233-410, for the official version of the events at Kent State. Also see Davies, Peter, *The Truth About Kent State: Challenge for the American Conscience*, Farrar, Straus and Giroux Publishers, New York, 1973.

147. Sale, *op. cit.*, p. 632.

148. Scranton, *op. cit.*, pp. 411-65.

149. Sale, *op. cit.*, p. 641.

150. *Ibid.*

151. *Ibid.* Carl Hampton was engaged in building a city-wide Rainbow Coalition (called the People's Party II) similar to that attempted in Chicago a year earlier. SDSer Bartee Haile was seriously wounded in the police raid which left Hampton dead.

152. *Newsweek*, November 27, 1972.

153. *Champaign-Urbana Courier*, July 12, 1973.

154. Scranton, *op. cit.*, p. 289.

155. Mitchell's successor, Elliot Richardson, did convene a grand jury which indicted eight guardsmen – Leon Smith, Barry Morris, Matthew McManus, James McGee, Lawrence Shafer, Ralph Zoller, James Pierce, and William Perkins – for having conspired to deprive their victims of their civil rights. Federal District Judge Frank Battisti, however, took the killers off the hook in November of 1974 by ordering a *directed* verdict of acquittal rather than leaving the matter to the jury. See Kelner, Joseph, and James Munves, *The Kent State Coverup*, Harper and Row Publishers, New York, 1980.

156. The Portage County (Ohio) Grand Jury indicted 24 students and ex-students, as well as one professor, on October 16, 1970. On November 14, Judge William K. Thomas upheld the constitutionality of the state anti-riot statute under which the indictments were effected. The trial of the first five defendants began on November 22, 1971 in Ravenna, Ohio, resulting in the conviction of or entry of guilty pleas by three persons, all on minor rather than substantive charges. Two of the five were acquitted entirely on December 8, whereupon the state dropped all charges against the remaining twenty defendants. See the *Chicago Sun-Times*, December 26, 1971.

157. Quoted in Scranton, *op. cit.*, p. 458.

158. Goldstein, *Political Repression in Modern America, op. cit.*, p. 512.

159. See Stone, I.F., *The Killings at Kent State*, Vintage Books, New York, 1971. Also see *Civil Liberties*, April 1973.

160. See the *New York Times*, October 31, 1970.

161. Goldstein, *Political Repression in Modern America, op. cit.*, pp. 474-5. Also see Donner, Frank, "The *Agent Provocateur* as Folk Hero," *Civil Liberties*, September 1971.

162. Goldstein, *Political Repression in Modern America, op. cit.*, p. 475. Also see the *Seattle Times*, December 7, 1970. More generally, see Marx, Gary T., "Thoughts on a Neglected Category of Social

Movement Participant: The *Agent Provocateur* and Informant," *American Journal of Sociology*, No. 80, September 1974, pp. 402-42.

163. Goldstein, *Political Repression in Modern America*, *op. cit.*, p. 473.

164. *Ibid.*, pp. 473-4. For another discussion of the death of Larry Ward, see the *Chicago Sun-Times*, May 30, 1971. The mayor's statement is quoted in Donner, "Hoover's Legacy," *op. cit.*, p. 693.

165. *New York Times*, May 21 and August 9, 1973.

166. Goldstein, *Political Repression in Modern America*, *op. cit.*, p. 477. Also see Chevigny, *op. cit.*, pp. 251-2; and *Civil Liberties*, July 1973.

167. *New York Times*, May 20, 1973. Also see anonymous, "Unsettled Accounts," *Berkeley Tribe*, August 21, 1970, reprinted in Jacobs, *Weatherman*, *op. cit.*, pp. 464-70. Those named in the initial Detroit indictment included virtually the entire national leadership of the Weatherman SDS faction: Mark Rudd, Bill Ayers, Kathy Boudin, Bernardine Dohrn, Linda Evans, Bo Burlingham, Dianne Donghi, Ronald Fleigelman, Naomi Jaffe, Russ Neufield, Jane Spielman, and Cathy Wilkerson, as well as Grathwohl. A second indictment, replacing the first and handed down on December 7, 1972, deleted the names of Grathwohl and Spielman, but retained the remainder of the original list while adding John Fuerst, Leonard Handelsman, Mark Real and Roberta Smith. Although the government charged those named with specific acts involving the construction and transportation of explosive devices in Cleveland, San Francisco, Tucson and St. Louis – and with the firebombing of a police officer's home in Cleveland on March 2, 1970 – no one was ever taken to trial. Another federal indictment against the Weatherman leaders, handed down in Chicago on April 2, 1970, and charging that they'd crossed state lines with intent to incite riots in the Windy City during the Weatherman "Days of Rage" (October 8-11, 1969) netted precisely the same result although the combination of unsubstantiable charges was sufficient to propel the "Weather Fugs" – all of whom had gone underground prior to the indictments – into the FBI's "most wanted" category for several years. Named in the Chicago indictment were Rudd, Ayers, Boudin, Evans, Dohrn, Jeff Jones, Judy Clark, John Jacobs, Howie Matchinger, Terry Robbins, Mike Spiegel and Larry Weiss.

168. Grathwohl, Larry, as told to Frank Reagan, *Bringing Down America: An FBI Informer in the Weathermen*, Arlington House Publishers, New Rochelle, NY, 1976. Grathwohl's cover was blown on April 15, 1970, when he fingered Linda Evans and Dianne Donghi for arrest on the Weather indictments and federal fugitive charges. The supposed federal cases against both women were immediately dropped.

169. Stone, *op. cit.*, p. 124. Mohr, of course, was allowed to continue his career as a "public servant" in the police.

170. See Crewdson, John, "FBI Reportedly Harassed Radicals After Spy Program Ended," *New York Times*, March 23, 1975. Also see Glick, *War at Home*, *op. cit.*, pp. 27-8.

171. Weyler, *op. cit.*, pp. 169-70. Also see Lawrence, Ken, *The New State Repression*, International Network Against the New State Repression, Chicago, 1985, pp. 4-5.

172. *The Glass House Tapes*, *op. cit.*, pp. 161-4. Also see Zoccino, *op. cit.*

173. *San Diego Union*, January 11-18, 1976.

174. Sale, *op. cit.*, p. 408.

175. See Herbert, Barbara, "Jack Weatherford," in Cowan, Paul, Nick Egelson and Nat Hentoff, with Barbara Herbert and Robert Wall (eds.), *State Secrets: Police Surveillance in America*, Holt, Rinehart and Winston, Publishers, New York, 1974, p. 227.

176. See Donner, "Theory and Practice of American Political Intelligence," *op. cit.*. Also see Levine, *op. cit.*, pp. 60-1.

177. *San Diego Evening Tribune*, October 16, 1975.

178. See Cook County (Illinois) Grand Jury, "Improper Police Intelligence Activities: A Report of the Extended March, 1975, Cook County Grand Jury," *First Principles I*, January 1976, p. 9.

179. *Ibid.*, pp. 3-11.

180. *Ibid.*, inclusive. Also see the *Chicago Sun-Times*, April 13 and October 16, 1975. The grand jury report prompted a series of suits against the CPD and various federal intelligence agencies – including the FBI – by Chicago activist groups. These were largely scuttled by a court-imposed "settlement;" see *Alliance to End Repression v. City of Chicago*, 742 F.2d, 1984. For further information, see Editors, "The Red Squads Settlement Controversy," *The Nation*, July 11, 1981.

181. The card, which was a standard COINTELPRO item in such areas as down-state Illinois, was

mailed on September 29, 1970 from the small town of Lacon (near Peoria). It thus followed hard on the heels of a September 9 letter from the SAC, Springfield (Illinois) to Hoover, captioned SM – ANA (WEATHERMAN), in which it is stated that Churchill – at the time affiliated with the Weatherman faction of SDS – "in addition to being investigated in connection with New Left activities in the Peoria area, has been the subject of inquiry in connection with the report of SA [name deleted] Milwaukee 8/14/70, captioned UNSUB: Bombing of Telephone Exchange, Electric Substation and Water Reservoir, Camp McCoy, Wisconsin." The document concludes, after much further deletion, with the observation that "appropriate recommendations" will be "maintained for Cointelpro action, which may neutralize the activities of this individual." The person within the Peoria resident agency assigned "the Churchill case" from 1969-71 – and who was thus in all probability responsible for the COINTELPRO actions aimed against him – was SA Bill Williams. Churchill, of course, had nothing whatsoever to do with the August 1970 bombings at Camp McCoy.

182. The quote is taken from a document excerpted in *Intelligence Activities and the Rights of Americans, Book II, op. cit.*, p. 127, n. 635.

183. Sale, *op. cit.*, pp. 532-3.

184. Goldstein, *Political Repression in Modern America, op. cit.*, p. 517. Also see Sale, *op. cit.*, p. 348.

185. Glick, *War at Home, op. cit.* Also see Powers, Thomas, *The War at Home: Vietnam and the American People, 1964-1968*, Grossman Publishers, New York, 1973.

186. The estimated number of bombings comes from *Scanlon's Magazine*, January 1971.

187. An excellent study of the mainstream media handling of information on the new left may be found in Gitlin, Todd, *The Whole World Is Watching: Mass Media in the Making and Unmaking of the New Left*, University of California Press, Berkeley, 1980. Also see Porter, William E., *Assault on the Media: The Nixon Years*, University of Michigan Press, Ann Arbor, 1976; and Murdock, Graham, "Political Deviance: The Press Presentation of a Militant Mass Demonstration," in Cohen, Stanley, and Jock Young (eds.), *The Manufacture of the News*, Sage Publications, Beverly Hills, CA, 1973, pp. 156-75. Of further interest, see Winick, Charles (ed.), *Deviance and the Mass Media*, Sage Publications, Beverly Hills, CA, 1978.

188. On the thinking which went into Weatherman, see Jacobs, *Weatherman, op. cit.*; and Sale, *op. cit.* Also see Powers, Thomas, *Diana: The Making of a Terrorist*, Houghton-Mifflin Publishers, New York, 1971; and Daniels, Stuart, "The Weatherman," *Government and Opposition*, No. 9, Autumn 1974, pp. 430-59. On an "unaffiliated" group which followed more-or-less the same trajectory, see Melville, Samuel, *Letters From Attica*, William Morrow and Company, New York, 1972; and Alpert, Jane, *Growing Up Underground*, William Morrow and Company, New York, 1981. For an excellent topical counterargument to the "Weather" response to conditions in the U.S., see Albert, Michael, *What Is To Be Undone*, Porter Sargent Publishers, Boston, 1974.

189. Goldstein, *Political Repression in Modern America, op. cit.*, pp. 498-9. Also see Glasser, Ira, "The Constitution and the Courts," in Alan Gartner, Colin Greer and Frank Riesman (eds.), *What Nixon is Doing to Us*, Harper and Row Publishers, New York, 1973. The police response to Mayday was the result of "lessons learned" during the largest mass demonstration in U.S. history, the so-called "Moratorium" held in Washington, D.C. from November 13 through November 15, 1969. It should be noted that in the earlier event, the Nixon administration called out 40,000 troops and had machineguns set up on the steps of the capitol building. For its part, the FBI intensified its anti-new left counterintelligence operations by ordering up the bank records of persons who'd written checks to cover the cost of transportation of some groups of demonstrators, visiting bus companies to threaten the management with federal subpoenas if they rented vehicles to demonstration organizers, and so on. See *Civil Liberties*, July 1972. Also see Hoffman, Paul, *Moratorium: An American Protest*, Tower Books, New York, 1973.

190. See *Civil Liberties*, November 1975; *Los Angeles Times*, January 17, 1975; and Cray, *op. cit.*, p. 235.

191. Goldstein, *Political Repression in Modern America, op. cit.*, p. 493. Also see Cowan, Paul, "Inquisition in the Courtroom," in *State Secrets, op. cit.*

192. For example, a grand jury investigating the Pentagon Papers case jailed Harvard professor Samuel Poppin for refusing to reveal research sources to whom he'd promised confidentiality; see Donner and Lavine, *op. cit.*, pp. 522-4. In another instance, five new left activists were jailed for refusing to testify before a grand jury convened in Phoenix. They served five months before the term of the jury expired. Upon release, they were immediately served with subpoenas to a new grand jury proceeding, thus beginning the whole thing over again; see Donner and Cerrutti, *op. cit.*

193. See Mead, Judy, "Grand Juries," *First Principles II*, September 2, 1976. Also see Fine, David, "Federal Grand Jury Investigations of Political Dissidents," *Harvard Civil Rights-Civil Liberties Law Review*, No. 7, 1972, pp. 432-77; and Bendant, James R., "A Disturbing Shift in the Grand Jury's Role," *Los Angeles Times*, October 2, 1974. Of further interest, see Cowan, *op. cit.*; Donner and Lavine, *op. cit.*; and Goodell, *op. cit.*, pp. 233-54.

194. *Intelligence Activities and the Rights of Americans*, *op. cit.*, pp. 214-5.

195. *Los Angeles Times*, September 22, 1975.

196. Probably the worst example of this is former SDS, Vietnam Day Committee and Yippie! leader Jerry Rubin; see his *Growing Up at 37*, M. Evans Publishers, New York, 1976. Unfortunately, while Rubin may be most prominent in this regard, he is hardly alone.

197. Concerning Hoffman's period underground avoiding prosecution on spurious cocaine trafficking charges which could have resulted in mandatory life imprisonment, see Hoffman, Anita, and Abbie Hoffman, *To America With Love: Letters from the Underground*, Stone Hill Publishing Company, New York, 1976. Also see Hoffman, Abbie, *Square Dancing in the Ice Age*, South End Press, Boston, 1982; and *Soon to be a Major Motion Picture*, *op. cit.*

198. Probably the best articulation of the logic of the Weather Underground Organization (WUO) comes in the form of a 1975 film entitled *Underground* by Emile de Antonio, Mary Lampson and Haskell Wexler. Information on this score may also be obtained from the 1974 book, *Prairie Fire*, produced by the WUO and distributed by its above-ground link, the Prairie Fire Organizing Committee (PFOC). Also see the various issues of the WUO tabloid, *Osawatomie*, distributed by the PFOC during the second half of the '70s.

199. The essence of the drift into remote sectarianism may be discerned in Franklin, Bruce, *From the Movement Toward Revolution*, Van Nostrand Reinhold Publishing Company, New York, 1971. Franklin was, at the time, a professor of English at Stanford University and head of Venceremos, an entity which emerged as a "left tendency" from what had been called the Bay Area Radical Union (BAYRU). The "right tendency" of BAYRU, headed by Bob Avakian, became the Revolutionary Communist Party, USA. Both Franklin and Avakian had been associated with the Revolutionary Youth Movement II faction of SDS after it splintered off from the main Revolutionary Youth Movement (RYM) group which was by then (summer 1969) calling itself Weatherman. RYM itself had come into being as an expedient to expel the Progressive Labor Party which had invaded and was attempting to subvert SDS for its own purposes. Avakian's main claim to fame seems to have been his connection with the Oakland group of the BPP, for whom he served as Huey Newton's errand boy. Of such idiocy do movements collapse, with a squish rather than a crash. See Sale, *op. cit.*, pp. 557-657. An interesting analysis, dealing in part with this sort of dynamic, is to be found in Lasch, Christopher, *The Agony of the American Left*, Random House Publishers, New York, 1969.

Chapter 7: COINTELPRO–AIM

1. ASAC Zigrossi's observation, offered in his official capacity, would seem clear enough in this regard. The perspective – and use of the term "colony" to describe the status of American Indian nations – is hardly isolated; see, for example, U.S. Commission on Civil Rights, *The Navajo Nation: An American Colony*, U.S. Government Printing Office, Washington, D.C., September 1975.

2. Clinton, Robert N., "Development of Criminal Jurisdiction Over Indian Lands: The Historical Perspective," *Arizona Law Review*, Vol. 17, No. 4, 1975, p. 951. In this article Clinton offers a comprehensive summary of U.S. jurisdiction over Indian lands from 1776 to the end of the 19th century. Also see Price, Monroe, *Law and the American Indian: Readings, Notes and Cases*, Bobbs-Merrill Company, Indianapolis, 1973.

3. .See American Indian Policy Review Commission, *Final Report, Task Force 9: Law Consolidation, Revision and Codification* (hereinafter referred to as *Task Force 9 Report*), Vol. 2, U.S. Government Printing Office, Washington, D.C., 1977, pp. 173-4.

4. *Ibid.* The appropriation act and opinion mentioned make it clear that neither the congress nor the Interior Department intended the FBI role on Indian reservations to become prominent or entrenched.

5. *Ibid.*, P. 174.; see p. 176 for a profile of BIA Special Officers.

6. U.S. Commission on Civil Rights, *Indian Tribes: A Continuing Quest for Survival*, U.S. Government Printing Office, Washington, D.C., 1981 , p. 145. As late as 1982, the FBI Section Chief for Indian Matters

and Government Crimes, Allan Meyer, was forced to admit that the Bureau had a total of only "approximately 30" agents who were American Indians, and many of these were not assigned to deal with enforcement on reservations; see U.S. House of Representatives, Committee on the Judiciary, Subcommittee on Civil and Constitutional Rights, *Hearing on FBI Authorization on Indian Reservations*, (Serial No. 138), U.S. Government Printing Office, Washington, D.C., March 31 and June 17, 1982, p. 15.

7. *Ibid.*, p. 149.

8. *Ibid.*, pp. 154-5.

9. According to the 1970 census, American Indians comprised only about .5% of the aggregate U.S. population. Yet, according to the Bureau of Prisons, they comprised in excess of 3% of the federal prison population throughout the '70s. In states with proportionately high Indian populations, the situation in state prisons is much the same.

10. *Quest for Survival, op. cit.*, pp. 143-5. Using South Dakota as an example, local (state, county and municipal) law enforcement during the mid-'70s was composed of more than 95% white personnel; see Stevens, Don, and Jane Stevens, *South Dakota: The Mississippi of the North, or Stories Jack Anderson Never Told You*, Self-Published Pamphlet, Custer, SD, 1977. Surrounding states, such as Nebraska, Wyoming, Montana, Minnesota and North Dakota follow much the same pattern, as do other states with sizable Indian populations, like Oklahoma, New Mexico, Arizona, Oregon and Washington. On jurisdiction, see Goldberg, Carol E., "Public Law 280: The Limits of State Jurisdiction Over Reservation Indians," *UCLA Law Review*, No. 22, 1975.

11. Quoted in *Quest for Survival, op. cit.*, p. 143.

12. *Ibid..*, pp. 143-50.

13. The most accessible material on Clyde Warrior and the establishment of NIYC may be found in Steiner, Stan, *The New Indians*, Delta Books, New York, 1968.

14. Deloria, Vine Jr., *Custer Died for Your Sins: An Indian Manifesto* (Macmillan Publishers, New York, 1969) and *We Talk, You Listen: New Tribes, New Turf* (Macmillan Publishers, New York, 1970).

15. See Burnette, Robert, with John Koster, *The Road to Wounded Knee*, Bantam Books, New York, 1974, pp. 196-7.

16. See Blue Cloud, Peter (ed.), *Alcatraz is Not an Island*, Wingbow Press, Berkeley, CA, 1972. The author makes it clear that IAT was on firm legal footing in undertaking its occupation, relying not only upon the 1882 statute, but upon Title 25 U.S.C. 194 – "In all trials about the right of property in which an Indian may be a party on one side, and a white person on the other, the burden of proof shall rest upon the white person, whenever the Indian shall make out a presumption of title in himself upon the fact of previous possession or ownership" – in pressing their claim. On December 23, 1969, Joint Resolution 1042 (115 C.R. 215, H 12975) of congress concurred with the Indian position, and instructed the executive branch to negotiate an acceptable resolution to the IAT demands. Hence, the Interior Department agreement mentioned in the text. Despite the clearly illegal nature of its actions in doing so, however, the Nixon administration simply ignored its obligations to follow through once IAT was removed from the island. No subsequent administration has improved upon the Nixon record.

17. On the occupations of military facilities, see Blue Cloud, *op. cit.* pp. 86-96. Concerning the struggles over PG&E landholdings, see Jaimes, M. Annette, "The Pit River Indian Land Claim Dispute in Northern California," *Journal of Ethnic Studies*, Vol. 14, No. 4, Winter 1987, pp. 47-64.

18. Burnette and Koster, *op. cit.*, pp. 196-7.

19. Weyler, *op. cit.*, pp. 48-9. Russell Means has been quoted as informing the city fathers that, "AIM has come here today to put Gordon on the map. And if justice is not done in this case, we're coming back to take Gordon *off* the map."

20. See Josephy, Alvin Jr., *Now That the Buffalo's Gone: A Study of Today's American Indians*, Alfred A. Knopf Publishers, New York, 1982, p. 237. The significance of Yellow Thunder's murder, and AIM's response, should be assessed in the context of a veritable wave of such grotesque crimes against individual Indians sweeping across the country at that time. These included the gunning down of IAT leader Richard Oaks in California on September 20; his killer, a white man named Michael Morgan, was freed on the basis of "self-defense" even though it was established at trial that Oaks was unarmed at the time of his death. On July 1, a 19-year-old O'Otam (Papago) youth named Phillip Celay had been shot to death by Sheriff's Deputy David Bosman near Ajo, Arizona; this was ruled "justifiable homicide," although Celay was also unarmed when killed. In Philadelphia, Leroy Shenandoah, a highly decorated Onandaga Special Forces veteran of Vietnam, who had been selected to serve in the honor guard

attending the casket of John F. Kennedy, was also shot to death by police while unarmed; another "justifiable homicide." It was in this context that Means observed, "It seems Indian-killing is still the national pastime," and declared AIM had assumed responsibility for putting a stop to it.

21. See Burnette and Koster, *op. cit.*, pp. 197-9.

22. See Deloria, Vine Jr., *Behind the Trail of Broken Treaties: An Indian Declaration of Independence*, Delta Books, New York, 1974, pp. 47-8.

23. The confrontation and occupation arose because of Interior Department officials reneging on pledged support to the Trail (primarily food and housing) when it reached Washington. They then proceeded to deny requests by the Indians to hold ceremonies at the grave of Ira Hayes, a Pima who had helped in the famous flag raising above Mt. Suribachi during the battle for the island of Iwo Jima during World War II, in Arlington National Cemetery. With that, caravan members simply overpowered police at the BIA building, evicted employees, and established the facility as a shelter and headquarters for themselves. See Editors, *BIA, I'm Not Your Indian Anymore: Trail of Broken Treaties*, Akwesasne Notes, Mohawk Nation via Rooseveltown, New York, 1973, pp. 8-13.

24. Weyler, Rex, *Blood of the Land: The U.S. Government and Corporate War Against the American Indian Movement.*, Vintage Books, New York, pp. 53-4 describes how the travel expenses were delivered by the Nixon administration: "The administration, unable to cut such a a deal officially without rocking the boat at the Department of Interior, executed the agreement in fine Nixon-era, Watergate style...The negotiators shuffled off to the White House. An hour later, Means saw a large black limousine pull up in the rear of the BIA building. Out of the car stepped black-trenchcoated Presidential Counsel John Dean and Chief of Staff H.R. Haldeman. Dean carried a briefcase. Inside the building the two man opened the briefcase, exposing fresh, crisp hundred-dollar bills – travel expenses in cash." Then White House aides Leonard Garment and Frank Carlucci (more lately Ronald Reagan's chief of the National Security Council and Secretary of Defense) are also reported to have delivered several brown paper bags full of old bills coming from the Committee to Re-Elect the President (CREEP); see *BIA, I'm Not Your Indian Anymore, op. cit.*, p. 16.

25. *Behind the Trail of Broken Treaties*, pp. 58-60. Arellano's services seem to have been shared by the Bureau and the Washington, D.C. metropolitan police force during this period; he was noted as being among the "most militant AIM members," continuously "pushing for physical confrontation," during the BIA building occupation itself.

26. Deloria, *op. cit.*, p. 57. Among the other government media ploys utilized to attempt to publicly discredit AIM during this period was to trot out National Tribal Chairman's Association (NTCA) head Webster Two Hawk (then president of the Rosebud Sioux tribe) to condemn the caravan participants as being composed of "irresponsible self-styled revolutionaries" before the media. NTCA was wholly government funded during this period, and Two Hawks' expenses related to this D.C. junket were underwritten by the White House. Two Hawk was promptly defeated for reelection on the Rosebud Reservation by Trail leader Robert Burnette after claiming that AIM lacked "a base of support among grassroots Indians."

27. *The Circle*, March 1979, p. 8.

28. Matthiessen, *op. cit.* , pp. 56-8. Others arrested at various points around the country while returning from the Trail included Alida and Andrea Quiroz (in Rialto, California), Myron C. Thomas (in Chicago), David Molino (in Redlands, California), Whitney Grey (on the Salt River Reservation, near Phoenix), and Steve Mesa and Cynthia J. deVaughn (in Los Angeles).

29. Burnette and Koster, *op. cit.*, 220. Burnett recounts having called the White House directly to obtain Means' release after this bogus arrest. Weyler (*op. cit.*, pp. 70-1) also notes that the Means brothers – Russell, Ted, Bill and Dale ("Dace") – owned a 190 acre land parcel they'd inherited on Pine Ridge. The land was held in trust and leased to a non-Indian rancher by the BIA; after they joined AIM, monies accruing from the lease were withheld. The same tactic appears to have been used consistently to "punish" others perceived as AIM members or supporters on the reservation as well.

30. For a description of the Scottsbluff meeting, see Burnette and Koster, *op. cit.*, p. 221. Also see Weyler, *op. cit.*, p. 68. "Unity conference of minorities held in Scottsbluff," *Rapid City Journal*, January 15, 1973, p. 3. Others arrested with Means in this instance included AIM members John "Two Birds" Arbuckle, Stan Holder, Carter Camp, and Leroy Casades (a suspected FBI infiltrator, then involved with the Chicano Crusade for Justice); see "Another AIM leader arrested in Scottsbluff," *Rapid City Journal*, January 16, 1973.

31. Gladstone, Lyn, "Custer Demonstration Canceled," *Rapid City Journal*, February 5, 1973.

32. The count of caravan participants accrues from Weyler, *op. cit.*, p. 68.

33. See Matthiessen (*op. cit.*, p. 64) for a description of the array of police and intelligence personnel on hand.

34. This description of the Custer events and Sarah Bad Heart Bull's incarceration derives from Burnette and Koster, *op. cit.*, pp. 221-3. It should be noted that most of those arrested were badly beaten with riot batons, as were a number of those who were not charged. No police were injured in this much-publicized incident of "AIM violence."

35. During the early 1960s, Wilson and his wife had fled Pine Ridge for Arizona ahead of conflict-of-interest charges in which she was director of and he a contract plumber for the Oglala Sioux Housing Authority. Upon his return, Wilson went to work for then tribal secretary Robert Mousseau until both were indicted on misappropriation charges. Wilson fled again, but his boss went to jail. See Burnette and Koster, *op. cit.*, p. 8. According to former tribal council member Severt Young Bear and numerous other sources, Wilson also managed a thriving bootlegging business on Pine Ridge during his periods of residence there.

36. The purpose of the GOON Squad was always frankly political. As Wilson himself put it in testimony before a committee headed by South Dakota Senator James Abourezk in 1974, "[They are] an auxiliary police force...we organized this force to handle people like Russell Means and other radicals"; this portion of Wilson's testimony is included in Saul Landau's film, *Voices From Wounded Knee* (Institute for Policy Studies, Washington, D.C., 1974). In addition to the $62,000 in BIA "seed money," Wilson is thought to have expended as much as $347,000 in federal highway improvement funds meeting his GOON payroll between mid-1972 and early-1976. A 1975 General Accounting Office report, however, makes it clear that since the Wilsonites essentially kept no books, it was impossible to determine exactly how large sums of money had been spent.

37. Wilson hired his brother, Jim, to head the tribal planning office at $25,500 (plus a reported annual take of $15,000 in "consulting fees"); *New York Times*, April 22, 1975. Another brother, George, was retained to help the tribe manage its affairs at a rate of approximately $20,000 annually, while his wife was named director of the reservation Head Start Program at a salary of $18,000. Wilson's son "Manny" (Richard Jr.) was put on the GOON payroll, as were several cousins and nephews. Wilson also raised his own salary from $5,500 to $15,500 (plus lucrative consultancies at tribal expense) within the first six months he was in office; Matthiessen, *op. cit.*, p. 62. At the time all this was happening, the annual *per capita* income among Pine Ridge residents was less than $1,000; McCall, Cheryl, "Life on Pine Ridge Bleak," *Colorado Daily*, May 16, 1975. When questioned about the propriety of such practices, Wilson responded, "There's no law against nepotism;" quoted in Editors, *Voices From Wounded Knee, 1973*, Akwesasne Notes, Mohawk Nation via Rooseveltown, NY, 1974, p. 34.

38. Weyler, *op. cit.*, p. 60. Matthiessen (*op. cit.*, p. 62) notes that both Eastman and Brewer were "notorious" on Pine Ridge in this regard.

39. The so-called Sheep Mountain Gunnery Range is an area "borrowed" from the Oglalas by the U.S. War Department in 1942 in order that Army Air Corps flyers could practice aerial bombardment there. It was supposed to be returned at the end of World War II, but wasn't. By the late 1960s, Pine Ridge traditionals were beginning to press for recovery of the land. The government might even have complied, but, in 1971, a National Uranium Research Evaluations (NURE) satellite orbited by NASA detected rich deposits of uranium in the area. While this was kept secret, the Wilson regime was installed and maintained on the reservation, apparently for the primary purposes of assigning clear title over the land to the U.S. Wilson did in fact sign a document on June 24, 1975 which purportedly transferred 76,200 acres of the Sheep Mountain area to the Badlands National Monument; this culminated on January 2, 1976 with the signing of the *Memorandum of Agreement Between the Oglala Sioux Tribe of South Dakota and the National Park Service of the Department of Interior to Facilitate Establishment, Development, Administration and Public Use of the Oglala Sioux Tribal Lands, Badlands National Monument.* Congress followed up by passing Public Law 90-468, stipulating that while the Oglalas could recover the surface area at such time as they indicated a desire to do so by referendum – an interesting inversion of the 1868 Fort Laramie Treaty provision requiring express consent from three-fourths of all adult Lakotas in order to legitimize any Lakota land *cession* – but *not* the mineral rights. The National Park Service then incorporated the added territory into its *Master Plan: Badlands National Monument* (Rocky Mountain Regional Office, Denver, 1978). For information on the precise disposition and quality of the Sheep Mountain uranium deposits, see Gries, J.P., *Status of Mineral Resource Information on the Pine Ridge Reservation*, BIA Report No. 12, U.S. Department of Interior, Washington, D.C., 1976.

40. On the impeachment initiative, see "Pine Ridge Conspiracy Charge Made," *Rapid City Journal,* February 17, 1973. Concerning the buildup of marshals, see Weyler, *op. cit.,* pp. 71-2.

41. See "Impeachment Charges Against Wilson Dropped," *Rapid City Journal,* February 23, 1973. Although there were nineteen members of the Oglala Sioux Tribal Council at the time, the vote to retain Wilson was 4-0; fifteen members of the council actively boycotted the proceedings rather than run the gauntlet of GOONs, marshals and BIA police, only to have Wilson rule them out of order. See *Voices From Wounded Knee, 1973, op. cit.,* pp. 17-26.

42. Regarding AIM's community relations effort, see "Police, AIM to keep things cool," "Coalition to work on race issues," and Harold Higgins' "Hot Springs meeting 'productive,'" all in the *Rapid City Journal,* February 16, 1973.

43. The "meeting...ended when five of Wilson's supporters [GOONs] cornered the AIM leader in a parking lot and tried to beat him up. Means broke through the cordon and escaped;" Burnette and Koster, *op. cit.,* p. 74.

44. *Voices From Wounded Knee, 1973, op. cit.,* p. 75.

45. As traditional Lakota elder Ellen Moves Camp (quoted in Matthiessen, *op. cit.,* p. 68) puts it: "We didn't know we were going to be crowded in there by a bunch of guns and stuff, military and FBI and marshals and GOONs. We didn't talk about going there and taking over Wounded Knee. That was the furthest thing from our minds. But what choice did the government give us?" Every other Wounded Knee veteran the authors have spoken with – more than thirty – agree with Moves Camp on this point.

46. Weyler, *op. cit.,* pp. 76-9.

47. Trimbach was operating in fine fashion: When, at about 11 a.m. on the first day of the siege, Justice Department community relations representative Terronez phoned him to attempt to arrange for the Bureau to allow AIM to hold its press conference and for both sides to then stand down, Trimbach threatened to have him arrested for "interfering with federal officers"; see *Voices From Wounded Knee, 1973, op. cit.,* p. 23. Colburn, for his part, had already brought an additional fifty SOG personnel into the area, as is evidenced in a memo sent by him to Reese Kash at Pine Ridge on February 20. This made the total number of U.S. marshals participating in the siege of Wounded Knee at least 135, at the outset.

48. *Ibid.,* p. 81. Warner and Potter were specifically ordered to wear civilian clothes, in order to hide the fact of direct military participation at Wounded Knee. They arranged for supply sergeants, maintenance personnel and medical teams to be present on the federal perimeter throughout the 71-day siege, all similarly attired in civilian garb. Further, the colonels placed a special army assault unit to be placed on 24-hour-a-day alert at Ft. Carson, Colorado for the duration of the siege. See *The Nation,* November 9, 1974. Also see *University Review,* the same month.

49. The meeting was first reported in *Akwesasne Notes,* Early Summer 1974.

50. CDMS is a subpart of the California Specialized Training Institute (CSTI), founded at government request during the late 1960s by Louis O. Giuffrida, an exponent of the theories of British counterinsurgency specialists Frank Kitson and Robin Evelegh. The purpose of the whole operation is to develop a coherent doctrine for the physical repression of political dissent, and to train personnel in its application. Garden Plot and Cable Splicer were officially (if secretly) commissioned plans to utilize the entire apparatus of state repression – the military, national guard, police and intelligence forces, as well as "private" organizations – in a coordinated manner to put down "civil disorders" within the U.S. See Lawrence, *op. cit.,* and Butz, Tim, "Garden Plot: Flowers of Evil," *Akwesasne Notes,* Vol. 7, No. 5, Early Winter 1975. Also see *The Glass House Tapes, op. cit.,* and Jaimes and Churchill, *op. cit.* For the thinking of Evelegh, see his *Peace-Keeping in a Democratic Society: The Lessons of Northern Ireland,* C. Hurst and Company, London, 1978. Regarding Kitson, see his *Low Intensity Operations: Subversion, Insurgency and Peace-Keeping,* Stackpole Books, Harrisburg, PA, 1971. Another good reading is Butz, Tim, "Garden Plot and Swat: US Police as New Action Enemy," *Counterspy,* Fall 1974.

51. The government instead offered to allow the defenders to leave through the roadblocks without being immediately arrested. They would, however, have been subject to later arrest and prosecution. See *Voices from Wounded Knee, op. cit.,* p. 45.

52. *Ibid.,* pp. 46-7.

53. Those attempting to negotiate a cease fire now included not only Justice Department community relations officials such as Terronez, but clergymen like the Methodist minister, Reverend John Adams. Reportedly, Adams was threatened with death on March 9, 1973, by a federal marshal, unless he ceased his attempts to mediate. The individual who delivered the ultimatum concerning women and children was Ralph Erikson, Justice Department liaison to the FBI; *ibid.,* pp. 51-2.

54. Burnette and Koster, *op. cit.*, p.234.

55. See *Voices from Wounded Knee, op. cit.*, pp. 50-2. On the report of the M-60, see *ibid.*, p. 41. Also see Weyler, *op. cit.*, p. 82. It should be noted – as any Vietnam combat veteran can readily attest – that the AK-47 assault rifle and the M-60 machinegun sound nothing alike when fired. Given the number of such veterans among the federal forces manning the siege lines, it seems highly unlikely that the FBI's false reporting in this instance was born of genuine error or confusion.

56. See Ciccione, F. Richard, "New peace talks set with Indians," and "Tentative agreement reached," *Rapid City Journal*, March 7, 1973; also see "Abernathy visits Wounded Knee; Kunstler, Berrigan plan to come," *Rapid City Journal*, March 8, 1973. Of further interest, see Ciccione, F. Richard, "Indians seek removal of lawmen at Wounded Knee," *Rapid City Journal*, March 10, 1973.

57. Burnette and Koster, *op. cit.*, p. 58. Burnette also suggests (at p. 238) that a female U.S. marshal was successfully infiltrated into Wounded Knee on the same afternoon (March 11), disguised as a reporter. Trimbach's gambit paid a perhaps unexpected dividend in addition to providing an immediate rationale to reopen hostilities: the detention of the six "postal inspectors" provided a basis for three of the very few successful prosecutions the government was able to achieve as a result of Wounded Knee. In June of 1975 – as part of the "Wounded Knee Leadership Trials" – AIM leaders Leonard Crow Dog, Stan Holder and Carter Camp were found guilty of "interference with federal officers in performance of their lawful duty" in this regard.

58. See *Voices from Wounded Knee, op. cit.*, pp. 54-8. Also see Ciccione, F. Richard, "Federal authorities re-establish barriers around Wounded Knee," *Rapid City Journal*, March 13, 1973. Of further interest, see Gladstone, Lyn, "Tension grows on reservation," *Rapid City Journal*, March 9, 1973.

59. On Held's presence and function, see Matthiessen, *op. cit.*, p. 109.

60. On the contents of Held's reports, see *ibid.*, p. 134.

61. The firefight had been initiated by Fitzpatrick and another agent attempting to chase an AIM vehicle through the defense perimeter, into Wounded Knee. FBI spokespersons subsequently claimed they thought the vehicle – a rented van – was "either overdue at a rental agency [!?!] or stolen." It was neither. See Ciccione, F. Richard, "FBI agent shot, 'sovereign state' proclaimed: Wounded Knee circumstances jury topic," *Rapid City Journal*, March 12, 1973. Also see Burnette and Koster, *op. cit.*, pp. 237-8. The issue of when the FBI had decided it was appropriate to use lethal force to recover cars "overdue at rental agencies" seems never to have been raised by "responsible media representatives."

62. Other than initial expense money, Little Ghost never collected. Shortly after arriving at Wounded Knee, he "defected" to AIM and told his story to Tom Cook, a reporter from the Indian quarterly tabloid, *Akwesasne Notes*. See *Voices From Wounded Knee*, 1973, *op. cit.*, p. 123.

63. Weyler, *op. cit.*, pp. 169-70. The Shafers managed little damage, as they were shortly detected. Also see Lawrence, *op. cit.*, pp. 4-5.

64. Between 1959 and 1961, Durham worked in Guatemala in the CIA operation to support the Bay of Pigs invasion of Cuba. In late 1961, he was hired by the Des Moines, Iowa police force. On July 5, 1964, his wife died as the result of a beating administered by him. Examined by a police psychiatrist, he was diagnosed as a "violent schizoid...unfit for office involving public trust." The psychiatrist who performed the examination recommended immediate institutionalization. The Des Moines police, apparently more concerned with avoiding further scandal than anything else, arranged simply for his resignation and a promise that he would seek out patient therapy. With charges dropped, he opted to ignore the latter aspect of the agreement, moving instead into an active association with organized crime. Over the next several years, he made his living – by his own account – running a prostitution operation out of a Des Moines bar, as well as by brokering drug deals and serving as a fence for stolen goods ("everything from cars to toasters"). He was apparently recruited as a clandestine operative by the FBI in 1971, in exchange for non-prosecution on a number of charges stemming from his activities. See Giese, Paula, "Profile of an Informer," *Covert Action Information Bulletin*, No. 24, Summer 1985, pp. 18-9.

65. Three persons were shot inside Wounded Knee during this exchange, including a Chicano medic from southern Colorado named Rocky Madrid, who was hit in the abdomen. See the account by *Los Angeles Free Press* reporter Ron Ridenour, who witnessed the whole thing, contained in Weyler, *op. cit.*, p. 83.

66. Burnette and Koster, *op. cit.*, p. 243; *Voices From Wounded Knee*, 1973, *op. cit.*, p. 128. The several Wounded Knee veterans with whom the authors have discussed this matter uniformly suggest that Grimm was probably struck by a GOON round fired from behind his position.

67. The ban was actually imposed on March 21, that is, before the heavy firefight which wounded Rocky Madrid. When it became clear that direct reporting was still going on, the threat of prosecution was added on March 23. Virtually all mainstream media representatives bowed to such intimidation – apparently with little protest – and subsequently reported as "news" the contents of packaged "press briefings" offered by the FBI each afternoon in Pine Ridge village (miles from the scene). The only holdouts against this domestic replication of the Vietnam "five o'clock follies" syndrome were alternative press representatives such as Tom Cook and Betsy Dudley, who opted to remain inside the AIM/ION perimeter for the duration of the siege. Both were arrested by the FBI on May 7, 1973 and their notes impounded. Charges were later dropped. See *Voices From Wounded Knee, 1973, op. cit.*, pp. 118-23.

68. *Ibid.*, pp. 124-5. This national effort was begun on March 20, 1973. On that, often utilizing information derived from infiltrators of organizations which had expressed support for AIM's actions at Wounded Knee, the Bureau began alerting state and local police concerning activist-driven vehicles leaving for South Dakota. These would then be stopped on "routine warrant checks" or other spurious excuses. If they were discovered to contain supplies of food, medicine or winter clothing, they would be impounded and the occupants turned over to the FBI for federal charges. In such cases, the Bureau falsely and habitually informed the media that the confiscated cargo included "weapons" and "ammunition." Minnesota attorney Karen Northcott has estimated that "several hundred" arrests took place across the country in this connection; almost all such charges were dropped prior to trial, but the AIM supply network was seriously undercut as a result (see "Negotiations halted by storm; Indians low on supplies," *Rapid City Journal*, March 15, 1973). By mid-April, the situation inside the hamlet was so serious that a Boston-based support group organized an air drop to provide at least some food and medication for the sick. Federal forces fired on the little planes when they made their parachute runs on April 17, and then fired on several children who attempted to run to one of the bundles which had landed outside the AIM/ION perimeter. While none of the children was hit, the federal action in shooting at them provoked a heavy – and this time lethal – firefight. As usual, the FBI utilized the direct presence of media representatives to announce that what had been parachuted into Wounded Knee had been "arms and ammunition" – the flight manifest listed nothing but food, soap and cigarette tobacco – and filed charges against the participants accordingly. These were later dropped. See Zimmerman, Bill, *Airlift to Wounded Knee*, The Swallow Press, Chicago, 1976.

69. There were five principle points to the agreement: 1) Both sides would cease fire to allow while settlement negotiations were undertaken, and federal forces would withdraw to at least 400 yards distance from the AIM/ION position. 2) Russell Means would leave Wounded Knee and submit to arrest. He would then be allowed to go to Washington, D.C. to negotiate directly with the Nixon administration concerning points 3 and 4. 3) A federal investigation into the abuses of the Wilson regime would be followed by legal action to remedy the situation on Pine Ridge. 4) A presidential commission would review the status of the 1868 Fort Laramie Treaty. 5) There would be a sixty-day moratorium on further arrests pending grand jury indictments, if any.

70. When Means arrived at the White House, along with AIM spiritual leader Leonard Crow Dog, he discovered that – contrary to the terms of the cease-fire – the administration position had shifted to one of refusing to talk further until everyone inside Wounded Knee surrendered. Means then proceeded to Los Angeles to raise funds through a speaking engagement at UCLA. While he was there, news arrived of Clearwater's killing. In a rage, Means announced he was returning to "the combat zone" immediately. The FBI then moved in and, after a wild automobile chase, captured him. He was held on a whopping $125,000 bond although accused of no violent crime. See Burnette and Koster, *op. cit.*, pp. 244-5.

71. Frank Clearwater and his wife Morning Star, a North Carolina Cherokee, had only arrived at Wounded Knee in the small hours of the morning. SAC Trimbach delayed his emergency medical evacuation for some 45 minutes. Although the Marshals Service granted Morning Star a safe conduct pass, she was promptly arrested by the FBI when she attempted to accompany her husband to the hospital, and held at the Pine Ridge jail until after his death. Dick Wilson then denied permission for the victim to be buried at Wounded Knee, as his widow requested, on the false grounds that "only Oglalas can be buried on this reservation." The Bureau went Wilson one better, falsely informing the media that Clearwater had not been an Indian at all, but was instead a "white man impersonating an Indian." See *Voices from Wounded Knee, op. cit.*, pp. 176-9. Also see Zimmerman, *op. cit.*, pp. 277-8.

72. Frizzell, Kent, personal interview with National Public Radio reporter Scott Schlagle, 1989 (tape on file).

73. *Voices from Wounded Knee, op. cit.*, p. 190.

74. *Ibid.*, p. 193. Also see Butz, Tim, "Bringing Vietnam Home," *Akwesasne Notes*, Early Winter 1975.

75. The situation caused a rather interesting radio dialogue – recorded in Butz, *ibid.* at 213 – between the marshals and AIM security inside Wounded Knee in which the government Red Arrow command post stated that it had honored a cease-fire agreement, but was taking automatic weapons fire. When AIM security replied that it too was taking fire, and had thought it was coming from the marshals, Red Arrow responded: "Ten-four. A couple of our RBs (Road Blocks) have reported firing and they don't know who is in those positions. They report that it is being fired *into* Wounded Knee." AIM security then queried, "You're pretty sure we've got a third party out there firing on us with automatic weapons?" Red Arrow replied, "That's what it sounds like."

76. *Ibid.*, p. 202-22. Unlike the Clearwater case, Wilson was unable to block Lamont's burial at Wounded Knee insofar as the victim was an enrolled Oglala. His grave now stands beside the mass burial site containing the remains of the more than 300 of his ancestors slaughtered by the 7th Cavalry in the same location in 1890.

77. On the night of April 23, 1973 the U.S. Marshals Service and AIM security at Wounded Knee monitored a GOON radio communication stating that eight of their number, armed with M-16s, had captured "a dozen hippies" trying to backpack supplies into the AIM/ION positions. The marshals dispatched a BIA police unit (which had been brought in from another reservation) to take charge of the prisoners, but the GOONs fired upon this patrol when it approached them. None of the captives was ever seen or heard from again. The Justice Department apparently considered the possibility that they'd been murdered and disposed of *en masse* by the GOONs quite credible; shortly after the siege ended, the department requested Rosebud Tribal President Robert Burnette accompany Solicitor General Kent Frizzell and two FBI agents in a search for the bodies of at least eight unknown individuals thought to have been murdered and secretly buried "by white vigilantes or Wilson's men." See Burnette and Koster, *op. cit.*, p. 248. Also see *Voices From Wounded Knee, 1973, op. cit.*, p. 193.

78. The number of those murdered accrues from a list, including names and dates – and in some cases locations of the homicides – in 61 cases compiled by Candy Hamilton, a legal researcher for the Wounded Knee Legal Defense/Offense Committee during 1975 and '76 (copy on file). Hamilton has stated to the authors that she believes her compilation is incomplete, and should include at least "eight or nine" more individuals, the details on whom she was unable to pin down.

79. Johansen, Bruce, and Roberto Maestas, *Wasíchu: The Continuing Indian Wars.*, Monthly Review Press, New York, 1979, pp. 83-4. The authors rely on the *FBI Uniform Crime Report* for 1975 in obtaining much of their data.

80. Johansen and Maestas, *op. cit.*, p. 88.

81. *Ibid.* These figures apply only to regularly assigned agents, and say nothing of the extraordinarily high volume of agent "through traffic" – personnel sent to perform a particular task and who depart upon its completion – in the Rapid City office during the same period.

82. Matthiessen, *op. cit.*, p. 173. These agents lived off-reservation, largely at the Hacienda Motel in Gordon, Nebraska. They made the commute, approximately forty miles each way, every working day.

83. For details on the super-saturation of agents on Pine Ridge during 1975, see U.S. Department of Justice, *Report of the Task Force on Indian Matters*, Washington, D.C., 1975, pp. 42-3. The data is exclusive of the nearly 250 agents sent to perform special duty on Pine Ridge during July and August of 1975.

84. U.S. Senate, Committee on the Judiciary, Subcommittee on Internal Security, *Revolutionary Activities Within the United States: The American Indian Movement*, U.S. Government Printing Office, Washington, D.C., August 1976; p. 61.

85. Wounded Knee Legal Defense/Offense Committee, "Letter to Contributors," Minneapolis, February 1976, p. 1.

86. See U.S. House of Representatives, *Hearings Before the Subcommittee on Civil and Constitutional Rights, 97th Congress, 1st Session on FBI Authorization, March 19, 24, 25; April 2, 8, 1981*, U.S. Government Printing Office, Washington, D.C., 1981.

87. Quoted in Garbus, Martin, "General Haig of Wounded Knee," *The Nation*, November 9, 1974.

88. The jurisdictional hearing was held as a part of *U.S. v. Consolidated Wounded Knee Cases*, CR. 73-5019, and was heard in the federal court in Lincoln, Nebraska by District Judge Warren K. Urbom, beginning December 16, 1974. On January 17, 1975, Urbom rendered a decision which said that although the Lakota were indeed "once a fully sovereign nation," both time and continuous violation of the principles of that status had rendered them otherwise. Hence, despite the still-binding nature of the 1868

Fort Laramie Treaty, the judge held that the government did have jurisdiction to try the defendants even though their alleged crimes had occurred exclusively within Indian territory. As Vine Deloria, Jr. subsequently pointed out, if his reasoning was applied to statutes such as those pertaining to murder, it would mean they too are now invalid, given that they are "old, and have been constantly violated over the years." Perhaps due to the glaringly tenuous nature of the government's logic in asserting jurisdiction against the Wounded Knee defendants, a compromise agreement was reached in which charges were dismissed against all rank and file AIM members/supporters while prosecution went forward against only a handful of selected leaders. Much of the testimony entered during the "Sioux Sovereignty Hearing" may be found in Dunbar Ortiz, Roxanne, *The Great Sioux Nation: Sitting in Judgement on America*, International Indian Treaty Council/Moon Books, New York/San Francisco, 1977. Also see Tilsen, Ken, "Fair and Equal Justice," *Quare*, September 1976.

89. The case in question is *U.S. v. Banks and Means*, Nos. Cr. 73-5034, Cr. 73-5062, Cr. 73-5035, and Cr. 73-5063, (374 F.Supp. 321 [1974]).

90. "Judge Nichol expressed astonishment that the FBI, which had been 'developing' this witness for six weeks, had not verified a story that the defense had shot to pieces overnight"; Matthiessen, *op. cit.*, p. 94. Records of a Monterey, California cable television company showed clearly that Moves Camp had been appearing – live – on its local origination channel at some of the very moments he was supposedly witnessing Banks and Means engaging in illegal acts at Wounded Knee. It was also established that he had been active on the San Jose State College campus throughout the month of April 1973. In other words, he'd spent most of the entirety of the Wounded Knee siege in northern California (Weyler, *op. cit.*, p. 119). Banks had expelled Moves Camp from AIM due to his persistent abuse of drugs and alcohol, and general disruptive behavior.

91. Price and Williams conducted secure and secret meetings with Moves Camp at Ellsworth Air Force Base, near Rapid City, during the period August 5 through August 10, 1974. It appears they drew up a series of false affidavits for the "witness" to sign in the course of these meetings. It would also have been at this time that the *quid pro quo* for Moves Camp's testimony was arranged.

92. On the charges against Moves Camp, see Matthiessen, *op. cit.*, p. 94. The witness was also a suspect in several Rapid City area rapes at the time.

93. Federal records, disclosed at trial, showed Moves Camp had been paid $2,074.50 in "expenses" – although he had been housed, fed and transported by the FBI since the moment he became a witness – and "*fees.*"

94. As defense attorney Larry Leaventhal summarized the testimony presented on the matter at trial: "At the time of the alleged rape incident Louis Moves Camp was spending a few days in the presence of FBI agents Williams and Price [at the J&R Dude Ranch, just across the Minnesota line, in Wisconsin]...[who] by their own testimony consumed great amounts of alcohol in the presence of Moves Camp. Moves Camp thereafter left their company. The following morning a young [River Falls, Wisconsin] woman attempted to press rape charges against Louis Moves Camp, with the county attorney's office. Her complaint was initially processed, and then following contact between the FBI agents and the county attorney the complaint was sidetracked."Quoted in Weyler, *op. cit.*, p. 119.

95. As the matter is put in *First Session on FBI Authorization (1981)*, *op. cit.*, p. 282: "[Prosecutor] Hurd himself met with the witness [Moves Camp] three times before putting him on the stand, and apparently he had some doubts about his truthfulness, since he requested a lie detector test that [SAC] Trimbach refused." Also see Adams, J.P., "AIM and the FBI," *Christian Century*, No. 92, April 2, 1975.

96. When confronted with the River Falls incident at trial, Hurd attempted to stonewall, insisting that Moves Camp had been charged only with "public intoxication," and that his witness could not be impeached on such basis. The real situation was then brought out by defense attorneys, who demonstrated that Hurd was aware of it prior to making his false assertions to the court (he had been informed by Minneapolis ASAC Philip Enloe at least a week earlier). Judge Nichol thereupon called the attorneys into his chambers and informed Hurd that "the whole sordid [River Falls] situation is going to come out," and the prosecutor apparently broke down and cried. Nichol formally censored Hurd for his performance: "Mr. Hurd deceived the Court up here at the bench in connection with the Moves Camp incident in Wisconsin. It hurts me deeply. It's going to take me a long time to forget it...to that extent, I think the prosecutor in this case was guilty of misconduct; it was certainly not in accordance with the highest standards we ought to expect from those officers that represent what I used to think was the majesty of the United States Government. I guess its been a bad year for justice, a bad year for justice." Transcript, quoted in Weyler, *op. cit.*, p. 121.

97. As Judge Nichol put it: "It is my feeling that the prosecution's offering testimony that was directly contradicted by a document [FBI affidavits signed by another discredited witness, Alexander Richards] that was in its possession is inexcusable and possibly a violation of American Bar Association Standards on the Prosecutive Function...if [this] was not deliberate deception, it was grossly negligent conduct...131 discoverable or arguably discoverable pieces of [exculpatory] evidence which weren't turned over [to the defense]...The defendants have expressed a profound distrust of the FBI...The expression of distrust is understandable...The FBI was negligent at best." Quoted in Weyler, *op. cit.*, pp. 116-7.

98. Trial transcript quoted in *New York Times*, September 17, 1974.

99. Prosecutor Hurd tendered an affidavit to Judge Nichol on April 3, 1974, in response to a defense motion for disclosure of any federal infiltration of the defense team, stating categorically that no such infiltration had occurred. This was a lie. Hurd later admitted that SAC Trimbach – who also professed to the court that he was "unaware" of any such infiltration – had earlier informed him that the FBI had an informant "very close to one of the defendants."

100. As WKLDOC coordinator Ken Tilsen summed up the situation, "There was no person other than the defense counsel and the defendants themselves who knew more about the total plans, and stratagems of the defense than Douglass Durham." Ironically, one of the tasks assigned to Durham in his role as security director was to insure that no government infiltrators penetrated the defense organization. This allowed him to isolate Banks in particular from many *bona fide* AIM members. Tilsen is quoted in Brand, Johanna, *The Life and Death of Anna Mae Aquash*, James Lorimer Publishers, Toronto, 1978, p. 99. As Durham himself put it in *Revolutionary Activities Within the United States: The American Indian Movement* (*op. cit.*, p. 61), "I was the one who issued the passes for the defense attorneys to get into their own rooms. I cleared the defense attorneys...I controlled security all around them [the defendants]." Also see Tilsen, Kenneth, "The FBI, Wounded Knee and Politics," *The Iowa Journal of Social Work*, Fall 1976.

101. The $100,000 figure is raised in Brand, *op. cit.*, pp. 98-9. At p. 123, Matthiessen, *op. cit.*, quotes AIM member Nilak Butler as concurring with the figure, and observing that the money was being diverted into "a second account under the name of Douglass Durham." Although this was ultimately reported to the FBI, no investigation is known to have occurred.

102. Durham's Bureau compensation was raised from $900 to $1,000 per month midway through the trial. Brand (*op. cit.*, p. 99) quotes SAC Trimbach as admitting to having known that just one of Durham's two handlers had met with the infiltrator "nearly 50 times" during the eight-month proceeding. This hardly squares with the SAC's pretense that he "had no knowledge" of Durham's infiltration of the defense team.

103. Nichol was replaced by U.S. District Judge Edward McManus, nicknamed "Speedie Eddie" by AIM defendants, for the rapidity with which he processed them through to conviction and sentencing. See Deloria, Vine Jr., "Who Knows What Violence We Can Expect?" (*Los Angeles Times*, August 17, 1975) for background.

104. To the contrary, the FBI appears to have arranged suspension of the perjurer's prosecution on the pending charges in both South Dakota and Wisconsin. In April of 1975, Moves Camp was critically wounded by a rifle bullet in the hamlet of Wanblee (on Pine Ridge) after having been accused of raping a local woman. See Matthiessen, *op. cit.*, p. 100.

105. Hurd's commendation was bestowed shortly after charges were dismissed because of his consistent misconduct during the Banks/Means trial. He was then named as chief prosecutor against Crow Dog, Camp and Holder in their "leadership trial" in Cedar Rapids, Iowa during June 1975 on charges stemming from the Wounded Knee siege. The trial judge was Edward McManus. In these changed circumstances, Hurd was able to obtain convictions, but no prison time against the defendants. He was then assigned to prosecute Crow Dog in two consecutive cases in Rapid City involving alleged assaults against suspected FBI operatives who had invaded his home on the Rosebud Reservation. In the first instance – in which even William McCloskey, one of the supposed victims, ultimately stated under oath that the Brûlé spiritual leader had not done what he was accused of doing – Hurd was able to win a conviction from an all-white jury. U.S. District Judge Robert Merhige (who had been sent on special assignment to South Dakota from his bench in Virginia expressly to "clear the docket of AIM cases by Thanksgiving") imposed a maximum five-year sentence on November 28, 1975 under the stated logic that, even if Crow Dog was not guilty as charged, he should have used his "religious

position" to "avert violence." In the second case, in which Crow Dog had to be returned to Rapid City from his prison cell in the federal facility at Lewisburg, Pennsylvania to stand trial, Hurd was again successful despite the fact that numerous witnesses testified that it had been Crow Dog's alleged victims who had attacked *him* and his wife, Mary, rather than the other way around. Merhige again cooperated by imposing a second five-year sentence, to run consecutive with the first, making the defendant subject to a total of ten years imprisonment. Crow Dog ultimately served 27 months before his sentence was commuted on March 21, 1977, after Amnesty International indicated its intention of adopting him as a "prisoner of conscience," and the National Council of Churches, World Council of Churches and U.S. Commission on Civil Rights all began investigating the circumstances of his convictions. No doubt as a result of all this good work, R.D. Hurd was named to a judgeship in South Dakota in 1981. See *Proposal for a commission of inquiry into the effect of domestic intelligence activities on criminal trials in the United States of America, op. cit.* Also see Erdoes, Richard, "Crow Dog's Third Trial," *Akwesasne Notes*, Vol. 8, No. 1, Early Spring 1976; and Weyler, *op. cit.*, pp. 187-9.

106. Trimbach remained SAC in Minneapolis, in overall charge of the Bureau's focal anti-AIM operations, until June 27, 1975, when he was temporarily replaced by COINTELPRO expert Richard G. Held, sent in to manage the FBI's "final assault" against AIM on Pine Ridge. Price and Williams were both assigned to work directly on the reservation against AIM.

107. Durham's true identity was discovered on March 7, 1975, when WKLDOC attorneys discovered an informant report signed by him among papers released pursuant to a discovery motion in one of the Wounded Knee cases. When confronted with the document by WKLDOC director Ken Tilsen and others, he admitted his relationship to the FBI. Tilsen's recollections on Durham's confession are contained in Weyler, *op. cit.*, p. 169.

108. The Skyhorse/Mohawk case involved the brutal stabbing murder of Los Angeles cab driver George Aird on October 10, 1974. His body was found at what was called "AIM Camp 13," in Box Canyon (in Ventura County), near the location of the former Manson "family" headquarters at the Spahn Movie Ranch. The facility had some months earlier been ordered closed by Dennis Banks because it was attracting a "rabble of dopers and crazies." Douglass Durham, in his capacity as AIM national director of security and apparently using funds funnelled to him by Virginia "Blue Dove" DeLuse, an actress and FBI infiltrator of LA-AIM, quietly kept the camp open, even going so far as to install a new sign announcing its "AIM sponsorship." In the wake of the discovery of Aird's body, the Ventura County Sheriff's department apprehended three individuals – Marvin Redshirt (an Oglala, non-AIM member), Holly Broussard (Redshirt's non-Indian girlfriend), and Marcella "Makes Noise Eaglestaff" McNoise (another non-Indian) – in possession of the murder weapon. It was quickly established that Aird was last seen alive with the three in the back seat of his cab, shortly before his death. Redshirt admitted having committed the crime. The case seemed rather open and shut. However, the Ventura County Sheriff was shortly visited by agents from the LA FBI office who explained that they had information from a "confidential source" (never disclosed, but thought to have been Durham) that the real killers of Aird were two LA-AIM leaders named Paul "Skyhorse" Durant (Anishinabé) and Richard "Mohawk" Billings (Mohawk). In a strange chain of events which has never been adequately explained by Ventura County prosecutors, charges were then dropped against Redshirt, Broussard and McNoise (against whom there was considerable evidence), and levied against Skyhorse and Mohawk. The three culprits were then deployed as "eyewitnesses" of what the accused had done to Aird. Press coverage of the charges – prominently featuring photos of Durham's sign – was sensational. Durham utilized his position within AIM to convince Banks and others that Skyhorse and Mohawk were "probably guilty" of the sordid act, thereby depriving them of organizational legal support until well after Durham's own exposure as an FBI infiltrator. The defendants ultimately received AIM support and were freed after a mistrial, but not before they had served 31 months apiece without bond. This last was in no small part due to the fact that after his exposure, in February 1976, Durham had gone into court disguised as a "psychologist from the University of Iowa" to offer "expert testimony" that the accused were "psychotic" and would represent a "danger to society" if granted bail. Redshirt finally went to prison, but not for the Aird slaying. Instead, he was convicted and sentenced for having stabbed Holly Broussard during a 1978 dispute in Hot Springs, South Dakota; at the time of the incident, both were still receiving federal support for their services in what had ostensibly been a local California case. More detailed background is provided in Matthiessen, *op. cit.*, 114-6. Also see "FBI Pins Brutal Slayings on AIM," *The Guardian*, December 1, 1974; and Blackburn, D., "Skyhorse and Mohawk: More Than a Murder Trial,"

The Nation, December 24, 1977.Of further interest, see Anonymous, "Wounded Knee Trials Go On – The Invisible Man in Phoenix and an FBI Behind Every Mail Box" (*Akwesasne Notes*, Early Spring 1975), and "Anatomy of an Informer" (*Akwesasne Notes*, Early Summer 1975).

109. The victim was a young Brûlé Lakota woman named Jancita Eagle Deer, whose battered body turned up alongside a lonely Nebraska blacktop, just south of the Rosebud Reservation, on April 4, 1975. The official cause of death was listed by Aurora, Nebraska coroner Donald J. Larson as being "hit and run," although no autopsy was performed. The coroner also noted Eagle Deer also appeared to have been beaten prior to having been run over. She had been the "companion" of Douglass Durham for more than a year, since he had brought her from Iowa to testify in tribal court that a virulently anti-AIM candidate for South Dakota attorney general, William Janklow, had raped her on January 14, 1967, when he had been attorney for the Rosebud Sioux Tribe and she had been his fifteen-year-old babysitter. Durham then arranged for her charges to be trumpeted as AIM accusations in the area press, knowing full well that the results of a 1967 FBI investigation of the charge would be withheld and that Janklow would simply refuse to appear before the tribal bench. Thus left with no evidentiary basis other than Eagle Deer's testimony to support the allegations, AIM would be made to appear to have gratuitously smeared the candidate, a matter virtually guaranteed to garner him a large sympathy vote. This is precisely what happened, as Janklow rode in on a last-minute landslide while promising to "put AIM leaders either in jail, or under it." He was true to his promise, a situation which afforded an obvious boon to the FBI's anti-AIM campaign. After this rather sophisticated electoral ploy, Durham seldom allowed Eagle Deer out of his sight. "She knew too much," as WKLDOC researcher Candy Hamilton later put it. For her part, Eagle Deer seems to have become psychologically dependent upon her "benefactor." In any event, she remained with him even after he was unmasked as a *provocateur*. The victim was last seen leaving the home of her brother, Alfred, on the Rosebud, at about 1 p.m. on April 4 in the company of a man matching Durham's description, driving a car matching the description of one belonging to the infiltrator's father. No FBI investigation was ever undertaken in the matter. Much of this reconstruction accrues from direct interviews with Hamilton and AIM member Nilak Butler. It is also worth noting that surviving member of the Des Moines, Iowa AIM chapter leadership, Aaron Two Elk (Oglala), believes that Durham was "probably" the party who tampered with the brake lines of an automobile belonging to chapter head Harvey Major, causing Major's death in a 1974 car crash. Major had, at the time of his death, become convinced that Durham was a *provocateur*. No investigation into the causes of the fatal "accident" was ever undertaken. For further information, see Kantner, Elliott, "The FBI Takes Aim at AIM," *Seven Days*, April 11, 1977. Also see Giese, Paula, "Secret Agent Douglass Durham and the Death of Jancita Eagle deer," *North Country Anvil*, March-April 1976. For more on Janklow, see Churchill, Ward, "The Strange Case of 'Wild Bill' Janklow," *Covert Action Information Bulletin*, No. 24, Summer 1985.

110. Durham's testimony may be found, *en toto*, in *Revolutionary Activities Within the United States: The American Indian Movement*, *op. cit.* It should be noted that immediately after his stint before the subcommittee, Durham – while *still* on the FBI payroll – undertook a speaking tour throughout the midwest on behalf of the John Birch Society, whipping up anti-AIM sentiment in the region. For further information, see Adams, J.P., "AIM, the Church, and the FBI: The Douglass Durham Case," *Christian Century*, No. 92, May 14, 1975. Also see Paula Giese's pamphlet, *Anatomy of an Informer* (American Indian Movement, White Earth, MN, 1976).

111. Quoted in *First Session on FBI Authorization (1981)*, *op. cit.*, p. 294. Original documents have never been released.

112. *Ibid.*

113. Details of the deal may be found in Matthiessen, *op. cit.*, p. 100.

114. See Oglala Sioux Civil Rights Organization, *The Murder of Pedro Bissonette*, circular released from Manderson, SD, October 18, 1973.

115. The BIA police logs at Pine Ridge for October 17, 1973 bear out that despite his lack of jurisdiction in the matter (which, even if it could have been established that Bissonette started the fracas, would have amounted to no more than a simple assault charge), Eastman ordered a full mobilization and reservation-wide manhunt for Bissonette. At least five roadblocks were set up for this purpose. Several spotter aircraft were used in the search and, since the BIA were not thus equipped, it has been presumed by researchers and reservation residents alike that at least some of these were provided by the FBI.

116. Clifford's report also states clearly that Bissonette was shot almost immediately after exiting his

vehicle, which is to say at a location very close to it. Non-police witnesses, however, consistently place the blood pool marking the body's location as having been at least 45 feet from the nearest vehicle. See Churchill, Ward, and Jim Vander Wall, "Strange War on the Lakota: The Case for a Congressional Investigation of FBI Activity on Pine Ridge Reservation, 1972-1976," *Rolling Stock*, No. 14, 1987.

117. The witness affidavits were collected by WKLDOC attorneys and researchers during the week following Bissonette's death. Copies were provided to ASAC George O'Clock at the Rapid City resident agency. The originals were lodged in the WKLDOC files, turned over by Ken Tilsen to the Minnesota Historical Society during the early 1980s.

118. In an unpublished report prepared for WKLDOC and submitted on October 20, 1973, Lane indicated that the cluster of seven holes centered on Bissonette's breastbone in a "very tight group, approximately three by five inches." According to Lane's observations, there was no evidence of burning or blast such as would have resulted had the victim been hit by a shotgun at a range close enough to have made such a pattern; he therefore deduced that a weapon on the order of a ".38 calibre police revolver" had been used to inflict the wounds from a somewhat longer range (at least ten feet distance). Lane also noted that the corpse had three bullet holes in a tight pattern in the right hand, indicating the victim had not been holding a weapon when shot, but had instead had been vainly attempting to ward off the fatal shots; a grazing wound to the right side of the neck was also observed. Finally, in addition to bruises on the body's face and rib cage, suggesting that a beating had been administered prior to the shooting, Lane detected irritation of the skin in numerous places, suggesting burns "by teargas or some other caustic substance" prior to death. None of this, of course, remotely squares with the police version, either of what happened, or of the wounds inflicted. Hence, Lane's desire for an autopsy conducted by an independent pathologist.

119. In an interview conducted by WKLDOC researcher Candy Hamilton in 1974 (copy on file), Gladys Bissonette indicated that she'd already decided to demand such an autopsy. Lane's call, by her account, simply confirmed her decision and accelerated the timing of her notification to federal authorities (she'd planned to do this several hours later on the morning of October 18).

120. According to Lane, U.S. Attorney Clayton assured him during the early-morning call verbally that the body would not be removed from the morgue at Pine Ridge hospital, "or otherwise tampered with," until an independent pathologist could be brought in to perform the autopsy, "either alone, or in conjunction with a pathologist retained by the federal government." They agreed that this shouldn't take "more than 24 hours, 48 at most." According to Pine Ridge BIA police head Delmar Eastman, however, Clayton phoned him only minutes after the recorded time of Lane's call demanding an independent pathologist, and ordered that the body be removed to Scottsbluff "immediately." When queried by reporters on the matter, Eastman responded that he'd acted "under direct orders from Bill Clayton;" see the *Rapid City Journal*, October 19, 1973.

121. Although Brown had facilities to store the body in Scottsbluff until arrival of an independent pathologist, he appears to have performed his autopsy hurriedly and alone, destroying much of the physical evidence Lane and Gladys Bissonette wished to have examined. His conclusion corroborating the police version of events should hardly be considered conclusive; W.O. Brown is the same coroner who determined that AIM activist Anna Mae Aquash – killed by a bullet to the base of the skull – died "of natural causes" in 1976 (see below). In the entirety of his career as a federal contract coroner, Brown never once found cause to contradict an official version of a death, no matter how outlandish. For further information, see Anonymous, "Pine Ridge After Wounded Knee: The Terror Goes On," *Akwesasne Notes*, Early Summer 1975.

122. An incomplete list of AIM members and supporters killed on or near Pine Ridge from March 1973 through March 1976 would read as follows: Frank Clearwater (4/17/73), between eight and twelve individuals packing supplies into Wounded Knee (4/73), Buddy Lamont (4/27/73), Clarence Cross (6/19/73), Priscilla White Plume (7/14/73), Julius Bad Heart Bull (7/30/73), Donald He Crow (8/7/73), Philip Black Elk (9/21/73), Melvin Spider (9/22/73), Aloysius Long Soldier (10/5/73), Philip Little Crow (10/10/73), Pedro Bissonette (10/17/73), Allison Fast Horse (11/20/73), Edward Means, Jr. (2/18/73), Edward Standing Soldier (2/18/74), Lorinda Red Paint (2/27/74), Roxeine Roark (4/19/74), Dennis LaComte (9/7/74), Jackson Washington Cutt (9/11/74), Robert Reddy (9/16/74), Delphine Crow Dog (11/9/74), Elaine Wagner (11/30/74), Floyd S. Binias (11/30/74), Yvette Lorraine Lone Hill (12/28/74), Leon L. Swift Bird (1/5/75), Stacy Cottier (3/20/75), Edith Eagle Hawk and her two children (3/21/75), Jeanette Bissonette (3/27/75), Richard Eagle (3/30/75), Hilda R. Good Buffalo (4/

4/75), Jancita Eagle Deer (4/4/75), Ben Sitting Up (5/20/75), Kenneth Little (6/1/75), Leah Spotted Eagle (6/15/75), Joseph Stuntz Killsright (6/26/75), James Brings Yellow (7/12/75), Andrew Paul Stewart (7/25/75), Randy Hunter (8/25/75), Howard Blue Bird (9/9/75), Jim Little (9/10/75), Olivia Binias (10/26/75), Janice Black Bear (10/26/75), Michelle Tobacco (10/27/75), Carl Plenty Arrows, Sr. (12/6/75), Frank LaPointe (12/6/75), Lydia Cut Grass (1/5/76), Byron DeSersa (1/30/76), Lena R. Slow Bear (2/6/76), Anna Mae Pictou Aquash (approximately 2/14/76), Hobart Horse (3/1/76), Cleveland Reddest (3/26/76). This tally, which totals 60-64 individuals – depending upon whether one counts eight or twelve dead among those missing along the Wounded Knee perimeter – results from combining a list entitled "The Murder of AIM Members and Supporters on Pine Ridge to Date," compiled by WKLDOC researcher Candy Hamilton in September 1976, and another published as "The Deaths at Pine Ridge in the Reign of Terror, 1973-1976," in *Akwesasne Notes*, Vol. 8, No. 5, Midwinter 1976-77. Both sources stipulate their itemization is far from complete. Nor does the count include individuals murdered after March 1976, including Betty Jo Dubray (4/28/76), Marvin Two Two (5/6/76), Julia Pretty Hips (5/9/76), Sam Afraid of Bear (5/24/76), Kevin Hill (6/4/76), Betty Means (7/3/76), and Sandra Wounded Foot (7/19/76).

123. See U.S. Commission on Civil Rights, *Events Surrounding Recent Murders on the Pine Ridge Reservation in South Dakota*, Rocky Mountain Regional Office, Denver, March 31, 1976, pp. 1-2. It should be noted that Byron DeSersa was the nephew of Aaron DeSersa, the vociferously anti-Wilson editor of a Manderson, South Dakota newspaper titled the *Shannon County News*. Aaron's home had been firebombed by GOONs on the night of March 1, 1973 and his wife, Betty, badly burned. See Burnette and Koster, *op. cit.*, p. 228.

124. "The FBI was notified, but the Bureau...did nothing but drive around the area," see U.S. Commission on Civil Rights, *Hearing Held Before the U.S. Commission on Civil Rights: American Indian Issues in South Dakota*, Hearing Held in Rapid City, South Dakota, July 27-28, 1978, U.S. Government Printing Office, Washington, D.C., 1978, p. 33. It is worth noting that Chuck Richards was a member of a GOON clan so brutal that it was commonly referred to as the "Manson Family" on Pine Ridge. He himself was known, of course, as "Charlie Manson."

125. On the arrest of Guy Dull Knife – as well as the overall context of the DeSersa murder – see Matthiessen, *op. cit.*, pp. 258-9.

126. There was a breakthrough, of sorts, in the DeSersa murder case on the night of January 31, 1976. Apparently unapprised of the FBI/BIA police policy of non-arrests in the matter, local police in the off-reservation town of Martin, South Dakota, apprehended one of the GOONs, Charles David Winters. Winters seems to have made statements implicating several of his colleagues, including Chuck Richards and Billy Wilson, before being released on a paltry $5,000 bond (a sum which should be compared to the $125,000 bonds routinely set for the release of Russell Means and other AIM leaders on Wounded Knee charges involving no physical violence). As the legal situation threatened to unravel, a deal was arranged wherein Richards and Wilson were acquitted on the basis of "self-defense," although it was amply demonstrated that DeSersa and his passengers had been unarmed and fleeing at the time of the killing. In exchange, Winters and a GOON leader named Dale Janis accepted plea bargained convictions on charges of second-degree manslaughter. They ultimately served less than two years apiece for what had clearly been a cold-blooded murder. See Matthiessen, *op. cit.*, p. 259.

127. *1st Hearing on FBI Authorization*, *op. cit.*, p. 896. Webster's argument essentially reduces to the suggestion that if congress would not look too deeply into what the Bureau had already done on Pine Ridge, he would promise to insure it wouldn't happen again. This is, of course, a time-honored FBI subterfuge – perfected by J. Edgar Hoover – designed to avoid both scrutiny and accountability while continuing business as usual.

128. See, for example, Evelegh, *op. cit.*, and Kitson, *op. cit.* Also see Klare, Michael T., and Peter Kornbluh (eds.), *Low Intensity Warfare: Counterinsurgency, Proinsurgency and Antiterrorism in the Eighties*, Pantheon Publishers, New York, 1988. The official military view of the matter may be found in U.S. Army Training and Doctrine Command, *US Army Operational Concept for Low Intensity Conflict*, TRADOC Pamphlet No. 525-44, Ft. Monroe, VA, 1986.

129. Some 150 official civil rights complaints were filed against the Wilsonites were filed during the Wounded Knee negotiations alone. The FBI investigated none of them. Dennis Ickes of the Justice Department "pursued" 42 on the basis of other "departmental resources," and determined that two looked "very good" in terms of prosecuting members of the GOON Squad. They were never submitted

to a grand jury, however; consequently, no indictments were returned or arrests made. The same situation prevailed through the end of 1976. See Weyler, *op. cit.*, p. 95.

130. *Events Surrounding Recent Murders on the Pine Ridge Reservation in South Dakota, op. cit.* Civil Rights Commission investigator William Muldrow, from the Rocky Mountain Regional Office, would later apply the same description on the witness stand when he testified as an expert in behalf of Dino Butler and Bob Robideau, defendants charged with murdering two FBI agents and who argued their innocence on the basis of having acted in self-defense.

131. See Matthiessen, *op. cit.*, pp. 139-51, for an account of the establishment of the camp at the Jumping Bull Compound.

132. The document is quoted in a July 8, 1975, memorandum titled "RESMURS Press Coverage Clarification." It has never been released in full.

133. *Ibid.*

134.The charges stemmed from a brawl involving Eagle and several other teenagers who had been drinking together. During the altercation, Eagle and his friends had taken a pair of well-worn cowboy boots from one of the other youths who later filed a complaint. There had been no kidnapping or allegations that such an act had occurred. So, with scores of homicides uninvestigated due to a professed lack of FBI manpower on Pine Ridge, *two* agents were assigned to pursue a teenager accused of the theft of a pair of used cowboy boots. Such a prioritization of Bureau resources, is questionable, to say the least. Additionally, the warrant Williams and Coler claimed to be trying to serve on June 25 and 26, 1975 did not exist. The only warrant issued for Eagle (or anyone else) with regard to the "Cowboy Boot Caper," was dated July 7 – well *after* the FBI had publicly announced its service was the reason for Coler's and Williams' repeated forays into the Jumping Bull Compound – and was for misdemeanor robbery. He was ultimately acquitted of even this.

135. Concerning the questioning of Draper, Charles and Anderson, see Matthiessen, *op. cit.*, p. 156. They appear to have more-or-less willingly revealed that, as things stood, only eight males of fighting age might be expected to be in the AIM camp: themselves, Leonard Peltier, Bob Robideau, Dino Butler, Norman Brown and an Oglala named Dusty Nelson (aka John Star Yellow Wood).

136. *Ibid.*, p. 194. Matthiessen quotes Oglala traditional (and AIM supporter) Edgar Bear Runner to the effect that at least 150 such personnel were hovering in the immediate Oglala area before Williams and Coler went onto the Jumping Bull compound. This is substantially corroborated by a *New York Times* account published on June 27, 1975 which also notes that at least 100 more FBI SWAT personnel appear to have been on alert at the Bureau's training facility at Quantico, Virginia, awaiting word to move to South Dakota; at least they were mobilized, outfitted, shipped halfway across the country, and placed on line at Pine Ridge within five hours of the first shot being fired. Another strong clue that the Oglala firefight was preplanned by the FBI rests in the fact that Chicago SAC – and leading COINTELPRO specialist – Richard G. Held, who would head up the Bureau's Pine Ridge operations in the wake of the shooting, had *already* been detached from his position and prepositioned in Minneapolis two days before the fact; Minneapolis SAC Joseph Trimbach, who was subordinated to Held, left for Pine Ridge less than an hour after the first shot was fired (well before it was known that any agents had been killed). Held himself arrived on the reservation at about the same time as the Quantico SWAT personnel, bringing with him a counterintelligence protégé named Norman Zigrossi, already selected to replace ASAC George O'Clock in Rapid City.

137. A copy of the warrant is on file.

138. The authors have received this information directly from AIM members who were there: Nilak and Dino Butler, Bob Robideau, as well as several individuals who prefer to remain anonymous. All accounts – which were obtained individually – concur that the Indians did not initially realize they were exchanging shots with FBI agents. They responded simply to the fact that they were being fired on "by party or parties unknown," as Nilak Butler puts it.

139. Linda Price, a stenographer at the Rapid City resident agency (and wife of SA David Price) who monitored and logged Williams' radio transmissions at the outset of the firefight, was interviewed concerning what she'd heard by ASAC George O'Clock a short while later. According to Ms. Price, Williams had urgently and repeatedly called upon "somebody" to "get to the high ground" near his and Coler's position to cover their line of retreat. At one point, he radioed that if such cover were provided, he and his partner could "still get out of here." A bit later, just before he ceased transmitting altogether, he urged: "Come on guys! Come on guys!" During the subsequent trial of Bob Robideau and Dino Butler

in Cedar Rapids, Iowa, for the deaths of Williams and Coler (*U.S. v. Butler and Robideau*, CR76-11 N.D. Ia., 1976), other agents such as J. Gary Adams, Dean Hughes, and Edward Skelly also testified to having received such transmissions. This, of course, raises the obvious question of who the trapped agents expected to come rapidly to their assistance in a remote area of the reservation other than the 150-odd SWAT personnel prepositioned in the immediate area, a matter lending considerable weight to the idea that the firefight was preplanned by the FBI. Further enhancing this concept are the facts that the complete Bureau radio logs of Williams' transmissions on June 26, 1975 have been classified as secret. Similarly, tapes of these transmissions inadvertently made by the South Dakota State Police on the morning in question were withheld as being "confidential," at the specific request of the FBI, according to then South Dakota Attorney General William Janklow (see the *Washington Post*, July 9, 1975).

140. The three teenagers were Mike Anderson, Norman Charles and Norman Brown (Navajos, each 15-to-16-years-old), all members of the "core eight" the Bureau expected to encounter on the Jumping Bull property. Other Indian men the FBI subsequently identified – rightly or wrongly – as having been "shooters" during the firefight were David Sky (Oglala), Sam Loud Hawk (Oglala), Kenny Loud Hawk (Oglala), June Little (Oglala), Bruce "Beau" Little (Oglala), Jerry Mousseau (Oglala), Hobart Horse (Oglala), Cris Westerman (Sisseton-Wahpeton Dakota), Richard Little (Oglala), Frank Black Horse (aka Frank DeLuca, an Italian from Cleveland adopted by a Pine Ridge family), Leon Eagle (Oglala), Herman Thunder Hawk (Oglala), Jimmy Eagle (Oglala), Melvin Lee Houston (Oglala/Anishinabé), Dave Hill (Choctaw), and Joe Stuntz Killsright (Coeur D'Alene).

141. Adams, who was on-site and seems to have been the FBI agent in charge during at least the early phase of the firefight, spent a considerable period of time hiding in a ditch once his tire had been shot out. It appears to have been largely his decision to withhold the approximately 150 reinforcements to Coler and Williams he had at his immediate disposal until even more "help" arrived. By that point, of course, the two agents were dead. In light of this performance, it is probable that Williams' and Coler's interrogation of Draper, Anderson and Charles the evening before had led the FBI to the conclusion that only eight potential combatants would be encountered in the AIM camp on June 26, and that these could be quickly overwhelmed by the more than 15 to 1 odds which had been deployed. In the event, the interrogation itself alerted the Indians that something was up, a matter causing as many as 25 local men to assemble, "just in case." Hence, when the firefight began, Williams and Coler confronted perhaps 30 rather than the anticipated eight fighters. By all appearances, when they discovered the odds to be "only" 5 to 1 in their favor, Adams and his colleagues simply turned tail and ran for cover, refusing to move in for several hours. It was perhaps a personal sense of guilt over his own conduct on the morning Williams and Coler died which motivated Adams to behave with brutality during his subsequent interrogations of the AIM teenagers mentioned above, as well as Norman Brown, another 16-year-old.

142. The arrival of Janklow's vigilantes on the scene is yet another evidence that the firefight was preplanned. By his own account, Janklow had received a phone call that fighting was occurring at Oglala "around noon" on June 26. At the time, he was at his office in Pierre, South Dakota, virtually dead-center in the state. He notified his assistant, William Delaney, and the pair went to their respective homes to arm themselves. They then went to the local airport where an aircraft and pilot just happened to be ready and waiting, and were flown to the town of Hot Springs, in the far southwestern portion of the state. At Hot Springs, they rounded up "about 20" well-armed men whom they later described as "deputies" (none were law enforcement personnel), and then drove the sixty-odd miles to Oglala. After all this, they still arrived in time to participate in the FBI's massive "assault" on the Jumping Bull Compound. Such a sequence of events is clearly improbable, unless Janklow had advance warning and had placed Delaney, the pilot, and the Hot Springs crew on standby prior to the event. An AIM participant's recounting of the arrival of the Janklow group may be found in a letter from Bob Robideau to attorney Jack Schwartz, dated June 11, 1976.

143. Although it was reasonably obvious that the defenders had departed prior to the assault, the Bureau and its associates – undoubtedly enraged by the deaths of Williams and Coler –utilized the opportunity to devastate the structures in the Jumping Bull Compound with rifle and automatic weapons fire, render them uninhabitable with large amounts of teargas, and then engage in the apparently deliberate shooting-up of personal items such as family photos. A good survey of this gratuitous property damage may be found in the film *Annie Mae: A Brave-Hearted Woman*, produced and directed by Lan Brookes Ritz (Brown Bird Productions, Los Angeles, 1979). An official account may be found in a report by U.S. Civil Rights Commission investigator William Muldrow to Regional Director

Shirley Hill Witt, titled *Monitoring of Events Related to the Shooting of Two FBI Agents on the Pine Ridge Indian Reservation* (Rocky Mountain Regional Office, Denver, July 9, 1975).

144. According to the 302 Report of SA Gerard Waring for June 26, 1975, Joe Stuntz Killsright was killed by a single long-range shot to the forehead fired by BIA policeman Gerald Hill, with whom Waring had taken up a position. Hill, however, was unequipped with a scoped weapon capable of delivering an aimed shot at the range in question (approximately 800 meters, or one-half mile). Waring, on the other hand, was carrying a .30-06 rifle with a sniper-scope. Hence, it is widely believed that if there is any truth at all that Killsright was hit–fatally or otherwise–by a long-range shot, Waring fired it. There are serious questions about how Killsright died. In a June 28, 1975 press statement, South Dakota Assistant Attorney General William Delaney, who was on the scene, noted that the body appeared to him to have been struck by a "burst across the back" (implying automatic weapons fire at close range). NPR reporter Kevin McKiernan, whom the FBI unintentionally allowed onto the scene as well, corroborated Delaney's observation of torso wounds – "blood was leaking from the jacket sleeve" – and added that the corpse was wearing an FBI field jacket (suggesting the possibility that agents had covered up their handy work by adding the jacket after the fact). McKiernan also stated repeatedly (including in direct conversations with author Churchill) that he observed no blood indicating a head wound; this is corroborated by side-view and full-face photos of Killsright after death, in the possession of former WKLDOC attorney Bruce Ellison, which reveal no wound to the forehead. It would be almost impossible to resolve the controversy insofar as the body was immediately delivered by the FBI to its ubiquitous Nebraska contract coroner, W.O. Brown; Brown's autopsy, as always, "confirmed" the already officially reported cause of death. See Crewdson, John, "Two FBI Men Die, Indian Slain ," *New York Times*, June 27, 1975.

145. The UPI wire report on June 27, 1975 is typical of what was reported as a result of the first Coll-orchestrated press conference: "Two FBI agents were ambushed and killed with repeated blasts of gunfire Thursday in an outbreak of bloodshed appearing to stem from the 1973 occupation of Wounded Knee...the agents, on the Oglala Sioux Reservation to serve a warrant, were sucked into an ambush, dragged from their cars, and shot up to 15 to 20 times with automatic weapons...An agent said: 'This is a regular coup de gras [sic] by the Indians.' The agents were taken from their cars, stripped to their waists, then shot repeatedly in their heads." In actuality, as Coll well knew, the agents had been dispatched to the Jumping Bull property rather than having been "lured," there were – as has been noted – *no* "bunkers" or other defensive emplacements, the evidence indicated both agents had left their cars of their own accord rather than being "dragged," neither agent had been hit more than three times, neither agent had been "stripped," and there was no evidence of automatic weapons having been employed by the Indians. For analysis of Coll's systematic disinformation, see Weisman, *op. cit.* The U.S. Commission on Civil Rights (Muldrow, *op. cit.*) described his releases, *in toto*, as being "either false, unsubstantiated, or directly misleading." For further information, see Clavir, Judy Gumbo, and Stew Albert, "Open Fire! or the FBI's History Lesson," *Crawdaddy*, November 1976.

146. The "RESMURS Story" received saturation coverage in the national media for the initial week after the firefight. During this period, only the *Minneapolis Tribune* – for which Kevin McKiernan served as a correspondent – appears to have seriously questioned the FBI's fabricated version of events. The *Tribune* was also the only major paper to mention in its headlines the fact that an Indian, as well as two agents, had been killed during the firefight.

147. The letter, announcing this "success" to Richard G. Held, was sent by FBIHQ on July 3, 1975. It reads in part: "Attached is a letter from the Senate Select Committee (SSC), dated 6-23-75, addressed to [Attorney General] Edward S. Levi. The letter announces SSC's intent to conduct interviews relating to Douglass Durham, a Bureau informant. The request obviously relates to our investigation at 'Wounded Knee' and our investigation of the American Indian Movement. This request was received 6-27-75, by Legal Division...On 6-27-75 [the day of Coll's press extravaganza], Patrick Shae, staff member of the SSC, requested we hold in abeyance any action on the request in view of the Agents at Pine Ridge Reservation, South Dakota."

148. Kelley opted to offer his disclosure that virtually all the information heretofore provided by the Bureau on the subject of the agents' deaths was "inaccurate" during a press conference conducted at the Century Plaza Hotel in Los Angeles on July 1, 1975. He was in LA to attend the funerals of Williams and Coler, both of whom were buried there, and could thus rest assured that the implications of his "corrections" would be appropriately lost amidst a wave of national sympathy for the two men's

families. It is noteworthy that Kelley took care that Richard G. Held was on hand during the press conference to back him up. For further information, see Bates, Tom, "The Government's Secret War on the Indian," *Oregon Times* February-March 1976.

149. Zigrossi, who had been well down in the ranks of Bureau hopefuls prior to accompanying Held to Pine Ridge, was amply rewarded for the nature of his services in directly supervising what the FBI did on the reservation in 1975 and '76. By 1979, he had been promoted to serve as SAC, San Diego, cutting nearly a decade off the time normally required for even the most promising agent to assume so exalted a position. For further information, see Johansen, Bruce, "The Reservation Offensive," *The Nation*, February 25, 1978.

150. See Worster, Terry, "FBI combing Pine Ridge," *Rapid City Journal*, June 28, 1975.

151. See Muldrow, *op. cit.*, for official confirmation of equipment and tactics. Author Churchill also witnessed portions of what is described, first-hand.

152. The air assault on Selo Black Crow's property was led by SA David Price. The agents possessed no warrant and didn't so much attempt to search Black Crow's home and outbuildings "for fugitives" allegedly sought in the RESMURS investigation, as destroy the structures while he and his wife were held at gunpoint. Black Crow appears to have earned Price's personal animus a few months earlier when he refused to talk with the agent, or allow Price on his land without a proper warrant (see "Wanblee man charges FBI with searching without a warrant," *Rapid City Journal*, July 5, 1975). Price was also involved in the 100 agent assault on Crow Dog's Paradise – supposedly provoked by reports of two teenagers having had a fist fight there – during which the Brûlé spiritual leader was deliberately humiliated by being separated from the male captives and forced to squat naked among a throng of women and children who were also being detained. Crow Dog's life was also apparently threatened by an agent – allegedly J. Gary Adams – during the ensuing transport of the arrestee to Pierre, South Dakota (see Crow Dog's interview in Ritz, *op. cit.*).

153. On the death of James Brings Yellow, see Matthiessen, *op. cit.*, p. 211.

154. The petition was initially reported in the *New York Times*, June 30, 1975. Also see "Injunction to be filed for FBI removal," *Rapid City Journal*, July 9, 1975. Concerning the tribal council endorsement, see "Lakota council approves resolution asking FBI removal," *Rapid City Journal*, July 14, 1975.

155. Letter from Arthur J. Flemming, Chairman, U.S. Commission on Civil Rights to U.S. Attorney Edward S. Levi dated July 22, 1975.

156. The first such grand jury was convened on July 14, 1975. Held had been able to rely upon the services of AUSA Bill Clayton – who had earlier assisted the Bureau by ordering the nocturnal removal of Pedro Bissonette's body from the Pine Ridge morgue – in facilitating jury formation. Seeking the jury had been one of Held's first acts upon arriving in South Dakota (see Kroese, Ron, "Material witnesses to testify on killings," *Rapid City Journal*, July 2, 1975). A second jury was impaneled in late August, and ultimately – in November – returned the RESMURS four indictments requested by the FBI.

157. A "hard case" was Joanna LeDeaux, a WKLDOC legal assistant who refused to testify. U.S. District Judge Andrew Bogue, who informed her that the "keys to your cell are in your mouth," sent her to the federal women's facility at San Pedro, California for eight months as a result. Pregnant at the time of her incarceration, she was forced to deliver her baby behind bars. A "weak link" was Angie Long Visitor, a young (and apolitical) Oglala mother of three, whose main offense seems to have been that she was married to one of the Jumping Bull sons, and lived in the compound on the family property. All evidence indicates that she, her husband, and their children ran for safety – away from the firefight – the moment the shooting started on June 26, 1975. They were hardly in a position to witness much of anything. Long Visitor did testify and appears to have told prosecutors what little she knew. She did not, however, tell them what the FBI wanted to *hear*. Hence, she was jailed for three months for "withholding information." Upon release, she was immediately served with another *five* subpoenas, and the performance was repeated. The tactic, pursued by both Norman Zigrossi and Bill Clayton, seems to have been to cause such pain for both the mother and her children that some other member of the Jumping Bull clan might offer more substantial testimony in exchange for her freedom. Ultimately, the bewildered young woman was forced to take the stand against Leonard Peltier during his 1977 Fargo trial, where she could ultimately offer no testimony useful to the prosecution. Instead, she spent most of her time weeping uncontrollably. Thus shattered, she was finally released after nearly two years of unrelenting federal pressure. See, among other items, "Affidavit for Detention of Angie Long Visitor as a Material Witness in the Matter of *United States v. Leonard Peltier*, CR-75-5106-1 (signed by ASAC, Rapid

City, Norman Zigrossi and submitted by AUSA William Clayton to U.S. District Judge Andrew Bogue on January 17, 1977), and "Motion to Review Conditions of Release and Petition for Extraordinary Remedies in the Matter of Angie Long Visitor, Material Witness," (No. 77-1080, submitted to the United States Eighth Circuit Court of Appeals by Quick, Tilsen and Quick, Attorneys for the Plaintiff, January 27, 1977).

158. A review of the entire 12,000 pages of RESMURS investigative documents released under provision of the FOIA to Peltier defense attorney Bruce Ellison in 1981 reveals that although given agents developed what they felt to be the beginnings of strong cases against several area residents, these were consistently abandoned – under SAC Held's handling – in favor of "developing" the suspects for deployment in court against the Northwest AIM leadership. On balance, it is abundantly clear from the record that Held and his immediate assistants had a predetermined outcome in mind, and shaped the RESMURS effort accordingly.

159. Eagle was wanted with regard to the May 17, 1975 assault on an Oglala named James Catches at the point he turned himself in. He was immediately charged with theft in the "Cowboy Boot Caper" – other, more serious, charges supposedly levied against him in this matter having by this point mysteriously evaporated– and held on $25,000 bond. On July 28, he was charged with murdering Williams and Coler, ostensibly on the basis of a jailhouse "confession" he made to an FBI informant named Gregory Dewey Clifford, which just happened to dovetail perfectly with a later discarded Bureau contention that a .45 caliber Thompson submachinegun had been used by Northwest AIM during the firefight. His bail was immediately raised to $250,000. On October 12, he was convicted of the assault upon Catches and sentenced to six years (he was paroled in mid-1977). As has been noted, he was acquitted in the cowboy boot matter. The RESMURS charges were simply dropped for reasons which will be discussed below.

160. According to Butler, he was taken from Crow Dog's to the federal building in Pierre, South Dakota, where he was interrogated for six solid hours by SAs Olen Victor Harvey and Charles Kempf. The agents offered him money and a "new identity" if he would turn on the other members of his group. The alternative, they explained, was that the accused would be murdered by the FBI if he didn't spend the rest of his life in prison. One agent, thought to have been Harvey, promised to "personally blow [Butler's] fucking head off" (see Matthiessen, *op. cit.*, p. 233). Butler ultimately served a two-year prison term for having been a "felon in possession of a weapon" at the time of his apprehension at Crow Dog's.

161. Robideau was heading a group composed of Kamook Banks (aka Darlene Nichols, an Oglala), her baby, and her sister, Bernardine Nichols, Keith DeMaris, and Jean Bordeaux (all Oglalas), as well as Mike Anderson and Norman Charles (both Navajo) which was attempting to evade the FBI net on Pine Ridge and Rosebud. Near Wichita, on the Kansas Turnpike, a defective muffler set their 1964 Mercury station wagon ablaze, ultimately detonating a store of ammunition they were carrying in the back. Robideau, who had crawled beneath the car to attempt to extinguish the blaze, was partially blinded by the explosion, a matter which led to the group's immediate capture." Nichols and Bordeaux were not charged, essentially on the basis that they were "uninvolved minors." Anderson was charged, but not prosecuted, for reasons which have never been explained. Norman Charles, Keith DeMaris and Kamook Banks were all convicted of weapons violations and received probation. On the same charges, Robideau was convicted and sentenced to ten years in Leavenworth, allegedly due to his having had prior felony convictions as a youth (Bob Robideau, various interviews with the authors).

162. The FBI contended that Peltier had traveled to Oregon in a motor home belonging to Marlon Brando, the actor, and driven by Dennis Banks, by then a fugitive from a July 26, 1975 conviction stemming from his participation in the 1973 Custer County Courthouse confrontation. Banks had gone underground rather than submit to the custody of South Dakota Attorney General William Janklow, who had campaigned with a promise to "put the AIM leadership either in jail or under it," and who had publicly stated that "the way to deal with AIM leaders is with a bullet between the eyes." On the night of February 14, 1976, Oregon state troopers – acting on a tip provided by the Portland FBI office – stopped the motor home and a lead car near the small town of Ontario, along the Oregon-Idaho border. They took into custody Kenny Loudhawk and Russ Redner, AIM security members who had been in the lead car. From the motor home, they arrested Kamook Banks and Anna Mae Aquash. According to the police, who produced no evidence to substantiate their story other than Banks' thumbprint from a pickle jar inside the motor home, Peltier and Dennis Banks escaped across an open field, firing as they went. Also according to police – although no evidence of this was ever produced either – a quantity of dynamite

was found in the motor home. Redner and Loudhawk were promptly charged with carrying concealed weapons – Buck knives, common in most rural areas – and held on $50,000 bond apiece. Kamook Banks, eight months pregnant, was held on $100,000 bond until authorities could revoke her probation on the earlier Kansas conviction (see note 198, above); she was eventually released when it was established that the government was engaging in vindictive prosecution against her, but not before her baby – christened "Iron Door Woman" in acknowledgement of her surroundings – was born. Anna Mae Aquash was whisked back to South Dakota, where she was shortly murdered (see below) by the FBI. Dennis Banks turned up in San Francisco, where he was successfully able to petition – on the basis of Janklow's death threats – California Governor Jerry Brown not to honor South Dakota's attempts to extradite him (this situation continued until Brown left office, at which time Banks successfully relocated to the tiny Onandaga Reservation in upstate New York, placing himself under protection of the traditional chiefs; he finally negotiated a deal with South Dakota in 1984 which allowed him to serve fourteen months in prison under a guarantee of physical safety and finally retire the Custer matter). Meanwhile, charges stemming from the motor home incident were dropped against Peltier. U.S. District Judge Frank Belloni, citing a complete lack of evidence, also dismissed all charges in the matter against the Bankses, Loudhawk and Redner on May 12, 1976. However, AUSA Sidney Lezak appealed Belloni's decision and was able to get charges reinstated against the four in March 1980. The case came before U.S. District Judge James Redden in May 1983, and was again dismissed, this time on the sixth amendment grounds that the defendants had been denied the due process of a speedy trial. AUSA Charles Turner, who had replaced Lezak, again appealed, and was turned down by the Ninth Circuit Court in mid-1984. Turner then appealed to the U.S. Supreme Court and was rewarded, on January 21, 1986, with an opinion declaring that since the defendants had bothered to enter a defense, they had thereby waived their sixth amendment rights. Under this strange interpretation of the constitution, the case was ordered back to trial in 1988, making it the longest-running criminal action in U.S. history. It was finally "resolved" by an offer extended by prosecutor Turner that if Banks would enter a guilty plea on reduced charges, he would be given probation and all charges would be dropped against his wife, Redner and Loudhawk. Having long since retired from political activism, the former AIM leader opted to cut his losses and accept the deal. For further information, see Churchill, Ward, "Due Process Be Damned: The Case of the Portland Four," *Zeta*, January 1988. Also see Johansen, Bruce, "Peltier and the Posse," *The Nation*, October 1, 1977.

163. According to the reports of Sergeant Mitchell and Corporal Parlane, submitted on February 7, 1976, they were sent to Smallboy's camp on the basis of an "informant's tip" provided to Canadian authorities by "U.S. police officials" (the FBI). Parlance notes that at the time Peltier was arrested, he was in possession of two loaded revolvers, an M-1 rifle and a .30-.30 caliber carbine, but offered no resistance. With Peltier at the time were Ronald Blackman (aka: Ron Janvier), a *Métis* AIM member from Canada, and Frank Black Horse. Black Horse was supposedly a prime suspect in the RESMURS investigation at the time, and was also arrested. Unlike Peltier, however, U.S. authorities made no subsequent effort to extradite Black Horse, who remained in Canada and has subsequently dropped from sight.

164. Richard G. Held was 71 at the time of his retirement in 1980. Hence, he had reached "mandatory" retirement age by 1976, the time of his promotion to associate director. The entire period of his stint as second in command of the Bureau was spent on a special "waiver" status similar to that held earlier by J. Edgar Hoover himself. During 1985 and '86, he refused repeated attempts by author Churchill to interview him either by phone or at his suburban Chicago residence.

165. Bureau personnel held several press conferences – at which it was announced, among other things, that federal snipers would be posted on the courthouse roof throughout the trial, as a "security measure" – and private meetings with local law enforcement personnel in Cedar Rapids during May 1976 to stress such points. This was reinforced, on May 11, by the U.S. Attorney's Office sending marshals to visit with every employee in the federal building to prep them on what actions to take in the event of a "terrorist incident." On May 24, ASAC Norman Zigrossi tipped Pennington County Sheriff Mel Larson, in Rapid City, that AIM had a "huge arms cache" in a vacant lot in that city, which was intended for "use in the near future." Accordingly, Larson undertook a spectacular "emergency excavation" of the lot, attempting to thwart "AIM terrorism" in the full glare of national publicity. The fact that Sheriff Larson recovered only three spent shotgun shells for his efforts was largely outweighed in the media by the sensational nature of why his men were digging in the first place.

166. In the Butler-Robideau trial transcript (Appendix A, p. 3), Kelley responded to Kunstler's

question of whether the Bureau had "one shred of evidence" to back up the accusations of AIM terrorism it was spreading, Kelley replied, "I know of none. I cannot tell you." Under oath, the director also stated that, despite the teletypes and AIM's then-current listing in the FBI's *Domestic Terrorist Digest*, "It is my very definite knowledge that the American Indian Movement is a movement which has fine goals, has many fine people, and has as its general consideration of what needs to be done, something that is worthwhile; and it is not tabbed by us as an un-American, subversive, or otherwise objectionable organization." Meanwhile, in Rapid City, Sheriff Mel Larson – apparently not chagrined over the fiasco of his search for an "AIM arms cache" (see note 202, above) – issued a widely publicized announcement, openly based on the FBI's teletypes, that he was canceling all leaves for his men and placing law enforcement in Pennington County on "full alert and mobilization" in anticipation of an outbreak of AIM terrorism in western South Dakota over the 4th of July holiday. The whole absurd scenario was thus kept before the public until the virtual moment of the Cedar Rapids verdict. South Dakota Senator James Abourezk, whose son Charlie had been named as a Dog Soldier participant for no apparent reason other than FBI retaliation for the senator's outspoken criticism of the Bureau's operations in his state, went on record describing the matter as a "smear campaign" which "smacks of a total setup that these unfounded, unverified reports are given such widespread distribution" (quoted in Matthiessen, *op. cit.*, pp. 288-9).

167. The attempted jailbreak charges stemmed from an April 19, 1976 incident at the Pennington County Jail in Rapid City, where Bob Robideau and Dino Butler were being held pending their RESMURS trial, when Sheriff Mel Larson "invited" SAs J. Gary Adams, William Wood, Dean Hughes, Fred Coward and David Price to participate in a search of the facility. Supposedly, they found a set of hacksaw blades in one of the two cells, housing sixteen men, which were examined. Although the blades, assuming their existence and that they were not planted, could have belonged to any of the prisoners, Robideau was immediately tabbed as the "owner." Shortly, agents Coward and Hughes advanced the charge that Robideau and Butler had conspired with two other AIM members being held in the jail, Kenny Kane and Alonzo Bush (both Oglalas), to break out, and contended that WKLDOC attorney Bruce Ellison had been the party who smuggled the blades in. Substantiation of these charges seems to have rested entirely upon the willingness of another prisoner, Marvin Bragg (aka: Ricky Lee Waters), a black man accused of ten brutal rapes of elderly women, to testify. Coward and Hughes appear to have offered Bragg assistance in beating the approximate eighty year sentence he was facing in exchange for his aid in this matter. Although much was made of the escape conspiracy claim during the Cedar Rapids trial, all charges against Butler and Robideau in this regard were dropped almost as soon as they were acquitted in the RESMURS case. As Robideau sums it up, "The whole thing was just a ploy to sway the jury against us at Cedar Rapids." As concerns Ellison, it turned out he had been meeting in St. Louis, Missouri, with U.S. Attorney Evan Hultman at the very moment his alleged offense occurred in Rapid City, a matter known to the FBI.

168. James Harper was at the time being held in jail at Cedar Rapids on a fugitive warrant from Texas and awaiting the outcome on extradition hearings concerning a desire by the State of Wisconsin to prosecute him for theft by fraud. Under cross-examination by defense attorney Kunstler, he readily admitted that he was used to "lying to law enforcement officials," and had lied "numerous times in [his] life" to get what he wanted. In this case, he appears to have wanted protection from prosecution in Texas and Wisconsin, a matter evidenced by the fact that he entered a suit against the U.S. Attorney's Office for breach of contract when he was later extradited despite the lies he'd extended under oath against Butler and Robideau. See Anonymous, "Who Are the Real Terrorists?" *Akwesasne Notes*, Late Fall 1976.

169. Any comparison of the testimony entered by Adams and several other agents against Butler and Robideau in Cedar Rapids with the testimony they entered concerning the same events against Leonard Peltier at Fargo raises the clear probability of perjury on their part in one or the other trial, or possibly in both. It was undoubtedly for this reason that Peltier trial judge Paul Benson ruled from the outset – in a very illuminating interpretation of the rules of evidence, not to mention conceptions of justice – that defense attorneys would not be allowed to use transcripts of the Cedar Rapids testimony to impeach testimony entered by the agents against Peltier.

170. Among these witnesses was sixteen-year-old Wish Draper, who had been "strapped to a chair" in the police station at Window Rock, Arizona (on the Navajo Reservation) while being "interrogated" by SAs Charles Stapleton and James Doyle. Unsurprisingly, he then agreed to "cooperate," albeit he admitted under oath that his testimony consisted of lies and that prosecutors had told him precisely

what "facts" he was to recount (Peltier Trial Transcript, pp. 1087-98). Then there was seventeen-year-old Norman Brown, who, during an interrogation conducted by SAs J. Gary Adams and Olen Victor Harvey on September 22, 1975, was told that unless he "cooperated," he would "never see [his] family again" and would "never walk the earth again." On the stand, Brown admitted that he had become "exceptionally frightened" by these death threats, and agreed to allow the FBI and prosecutors to script his testimony (Peltier Trial Transcript, pp. 4799-4804, 4842-3). Another such witness was fifteen-year-old Mike Anderson, who was arrested along with Bob Robideau after their car exploded on the Kansas Turnpike on September 10, 1975. That night, Anderson was "interrogated" in his cell by SAs Adams and Harvey, who offered both the carrot of assistance with pending criminal charges and the stick of "beating the living shit out of" him to obtain "cooperation." A second interview, conducted by agents Adams and Doyle on the Navajo Reservation on February 1, 1977, gained the desired result (Peltier Trial Transcript, pp. 840-42). Anderson, however, attempted to go on the stand in Peltier's behalf near the end of the Fargo trial, and – perhaps as a consequence – was killed in a mysterious automobile accident on the Navajo Reservation in 1979 (see Matthiessen, op. cit., p. 439).

171. Most of Church's examples were drawn from the record of COINTELPRO-BPP. The senator made it clear that the Bureau deliberately released false information in order not only to discredit targeted individuals and organizations, but also to see violence perpetrated against them in many instances. There is some indication in the record that Church considered what had been done to AIM to amount to a de facto COINTELPRO, regardless of what the FBI chose to call such things by 1976. For further information, see Churchill, Ward, and Jim Vander Wall, "The FBI Takes AIM: The FBI's Secret War Against the American Indian Movement," The Other Side, Vol. 23, No. 5, June 1987.

172. Muldrow testified that, "A great deal of tension and fear exist on the Reservation. Residents feel that life is cheap, that no one really cares about what happens to them...Acts of violence...are commonplace. Numerous complaints were lodged in my office about FBI activities" (quoted in Matthiessen, op. cit., p. 318).

173. To his great credit, McManus read the jury the full text of the law governing self-defense as part of his instruction before sending them into deliberations. As jury foreman Robert Bolin put it after the trial, "The jury agreed with the defense contention that an atmosphere of fear and violence exists on the reservation, and that the defendants arguably could have been acting in self-defense. While it was shown that the defendants were firing guns in the direction of the agents, it was held that this was not excessive in the heat of passion." Bolin also made it clear that the jury would have reached the same conclusion had it been shown – which it was not – that Robideau and Butler had actually fired the rounds which killed Williams and Coler. Finally, the jury foreman noted that, in certain segments of the prosecution case, the jury "didn't believe a word" uttered by the government's witnesses. (quoted in ibid.)

174. In 1982, Peltier's attorneys, arguing that this series of secret meetings constituted collaboration between the judge, prosecution and FBI, moved that Benson recuse himself from further involvement in the case. Benson refused, countering that – despite a total absence of evidence of AIM terrorism, in court or elsewhere – the meetings had been necessitated by the "likelihood" that Peltier's supporters would violently disrupt the trial and possibly attempt to free the defendant. No answer was provided as to why, if this was really the basis of the meetings, defense counsel – whom, one must assume, would have a bona fide concern with any real threat of terrorist acts in the courtroom – were deliberately excluded. See "Motion to Vacate Judgement and for a New Trial in the Matter of the United States v. Leonard Peltier, C77-303," U.S. District Court for the District of North Dakota, April 20, 1982; Benson's response, conveyed earlier by memorandum, is summarized in United States Court of Appeals for the Eighth Circuit, United States v. Leonard Peltier, 731 F. 2d 550, 555 (8th Cir. 1984).

175. As WKLDOC attorney Karen Northcott later summarized the matter: "Defense evidence which had convinced the jury of the innocence of Butler and Robideaux [sic] was ruled inadmissible at Peltier's trial. He was not allowed to present a case of self-defense." See Northcott's pamphlet, The FBI in Indian Communities, American Friends Service Committee, Minneapolis, 1979.

176. Motel receipts and other items show that Price and Wood held Poor Bear in motel rooms from early February through the night of February 23, 1976. On February 24, they appear to have turned her over to SA Edward Skelly, who then continued to hold her in a motel room in Belle Fourche, South Dakota. See Matthiessen, op. cit., p. 454.

177. The first two affidavits were signed on February 19 and 23, respectively. The third affidavit, which was utilized in obtaining Peltier's extradition, was signed on March 23, 1976.

178. Martin Montileaux was fatally wounded in the restroom of the Longhorn Bar – located in the hamlet of Scenic, South Dakota, just north of the Pine Ridge boundary – on the night of March 1, 1976. Pennington County sheriff's deputies shortly arrested Marshall and Russell Means, who'd been in the bar earlier in the evening on charges they'd participated in the shooting. Prior to his death from complications resulting from his wounds on March 15, Montileaux repeatedly and emphatically denied that either Montileaux or Means had been among his assailants. State Attorney General William Janklow nonetheless opted to charge both men with murder. Marshall was convicted on April 6, 1976, largely on the basis of the "first-hand" testimony of Myrtle Poor Bear, who had been provided as a surprise witness by agents Price and Wood. He was sentenced to life imprisonment. Means, in a separate trial in which Poor Bear did not appear, was acquitted on June 17, 1976. Marshall maintained his innocence, and became one of the three U.S. prisoners for whom Amnesty International demanded retrial on the basis of FBI counterintelligence activities directed against them (the other two were Geronimo Pratt and Leonard Peltier; see *Proposal for a commission of inquiry into the effect of domestic intelligence activities on criminal trials in the United States of America, op. cit.*). There was, of course, no official response to the Amnesty International position. In 1984, with all due process remedies foreclosed, Marshall accepted a deal with Janklow – by now governor of South Dakota, and eyeing a seat in the U.S. senate, but suffering certain national image problems as a result of his threats against Dennis Banks and other anti-AIM conduct – to get out of prison. The *quid pro quo* appears to have been that Marshall would "admit" having shot Montileaux, thus finally validating one of the governor's anti-AIM assertions, and Janklow would engineer an immediate parole. Marshall was correspondingly released from the South Dakota State Prison at Sioux Falls on December 20, 1984. In August of 1989, he was returned to Sioux Falls to resume his life sentence as a result of alleged drug transactions on the Pine Ridge Reservation. William Janklow, meanwhile, lost in his bid to become a senator and is finally out of public office.

179. Peltier defense attorneys used the Poor Bear affidavits to take up the matter of extradition treaty fraud (under the Extradition Act, R.S.C. 1970, Chap. E-21) in the Canadian courts, beginning in late 1977. Presented with the evidence, Canadian Minister of External Affairs Allen MacEachen called for an "urgent investigation" of FBI and Justice Department behavior in the matter. Upon review in 1978, Canadian Supreme Court Justice R.P. Anderson concluded that, "It seems clear that the conduct of the U.S. government involved misconduct from inception." Canadian Justice W.A. Schultz, whose name had been brought up as having possibly cooperated with U.S. authorities despite knowledge of the nature of the Poor Bear material, sued and won a retraction, on the basis of having been unaware of "any such fraud." By 1986, Canadian Member of Parliament Jim Fulton had formally stated on the floor of the House of Commons that, "[The nature of Peltier's extradition] constitutes treaty fraud between our nations." He and more than sixty other Canadian MPs have consequently demanded Peltier's return to Canada, and have explored the possibility of abrogating the Canada-U.S. extradition treaty unless the federal government complies. See "External Affairs: Canada-U.S. Extradition Treaty – Case of Leonard Peltier, Statement of Mr. James Fulton," in *House of Commons Debate, Canada*, Vol. 128, No. 129, 1st Session, 33rd Parliament, Official Report, Thursday, April 17, 1986.

180. Poor Bear's recantation regarding her Peltier "evidence" occurred on the stand during his Fargo trial, is contained in the trial transcript, and is a matter of appeal record. She also recanted, and was corroborated by her father in doing so, during Marshall's appeals process (quoted in *Win Magazine*, December 1, 1980). In 1977, she was called as a witness by the Minnesota Citizens Commission to Review the FBI (a federally-sponsored entity, convened in the same fashion as that charged with examining official conduct in Chicago in the wake of the 1969 Hampton-Clark assassinations); a videotape of this testimony was made by WKLDOC attorney Karen Northcott and is filed at the law offices of Kenneth Tilsen in Minneapolis. Poor Bear also told her story in a popular forum through *People Magazine*, April 20, 1981.

181. Poor Bear has repeatedly testified and otherwise asserted that this occurred. When queried under oath by the Minnesota Citizens Review Commission as to whether he'd used such photos to intimidate his captive, SA Price responded, "I don't recall" (transcript quoted in Matthiessen, *op. cit.*, p. 455). On Aquash's assertions that her life had been threatened by the FBI, and SA Price in particular, see McKiernan, Kevin, "Indian woman's death raises many troubling questions," *Minneapolis Tribune*, May 30, 1976. Also see Oppenheimer, Jerry, "The Strange Killing of a Wounded Knee Indian," (*The Washington Star*, May 24, 1976), and "Questions raised about FBI's handing of Aquash Case," (*Rapid City Journal*, May 25, 1976). Former WKLDOC researcher Candy Hamilton and AIM member Nilak Butler, both of

whom were personal friends of Aquash, each recount having been told by the victim that SA Price had threatened her life unless she "cooperated."

182. The matter is well covered in *First Session on FBI Authorization, (1981), op. cit.*, esp. pp. 267-76. Aquash's body, although somewhat decomposed, was quite recognizable; author Churchill, without having been informed as to the identity of the body at issue, and having never been personally acquainted with the victim, was able to identify Aquash from morgue photos shown him years later.

183. In the film *Annie Mae: A Brave Hearted Woman, (op. cit.)* AIM leader John Trudell points out (correctly) that in order for the FBI to have made a fingerprint identification of Aquash from the severed hands, someone with the Bureau's Rapid City office had to have sent along the suggestion that the hands were probably hers; the role of the crime lab in such cases being merely to confirm or disprove such speculations from the field. Trudell also points out that the usual manner in which such confirmations of identification are performed is through dental x-rays, but that coroner Brown failed to perform *any* x-rays of the body's skull. Trudell therefore concludes that the severing of Aquash's hands was an unnecessary mutilation of "enemy dead" by the FBI, and a by-product of Brown's attempted cover up of the real cause of death. The mutilation scenario is strongly reinforced in Trudell's recounting of how, when Aquash's hands were finally returned to be buried with the rest of her remains, SA William Wood smilingly "pitched the box" containing the body parts to WKLDOC attorney Bruce Ellison. For further information, see Brant, *op. cit.*

184. Ellison attempted to file his motion for exhumation with U.S. District Judge Andrew Bogue in Rapid City on March 8, 1976. Apparently having gotten wind of WKLDOC's intentions, and realizing that Bogue would have little option but to approve such a motion entered in behalf of the victim's family, SA William Wood appeared a short while before Ellison asking for exhumation on behalf of the Bureau. Bogue granted Wood's request.

185. According to Shirley Hill Witt, director of the Rocky Mountain Regional Office of the U.S. Commission on Civil Rights, and her assistant, William Muldrow, "On March 11 [1976] the body was exhumed in the presence of FBI agents and Dr. Garry Peterson, a pathologist from Minneapolis, Minnesota, who had been brought in by Aquash's family to examine the body. X-rays revealed a bullet of approximately .32 caliber in her head. Peterson's examination revealed a bullet wound in the back of the head surrounded by a 5x5 cm. area of subgaleal reddish discoloration" (see *Events Surrounding Recent Murders on the Pine Ridge Indian Reservation, op. cit.*, p. 3). In his own account, even before the x-rays, Peterson "noticed a bulge in the dead woman's left temple and dry blood in her hair" and that "the back of the head had been washed and powdered...a .32 caliber bullet accounting for the bulge in the temple. There were powder burns around the wound in the neck" (see Brand, *op. cit.*, p. 131). As Hill Witt and Muldrow further point out on p. 3, hospital personnel who had attended the initial autopsy professed not to be surprised by Peterson's findings insofar as they had observed blood leaking from the corpse's head during Brown's examination and had therefore all along doubted the finding that death had been caused by exposure.

186. The FBI, apparently proceeding on the belief that the bad-jacketing efforts undertaken against Aquash by certain of the Bureau's *provocateurs* (notably Douglass Durham and Darryl "Blue Legs" Stewart) may have caused her death, has consistently – and without success – attempted to build a case that AIM members executed her as a "suspected informer." As late as the summer of 1987, agents were interviewing former AIM members on Pine Ridge and in the Denver area in this vein. Meanwhile, there is no indication that the FBI has so much as deposed either Price or Wood – whose bizarre behavior in connection with the victim is very much on record – during this lengthy "homicide investigation." See Churchill, Ward, "Who Killed Anna Mae?" *Zeta*, December 1988, pp. 96-8.

187. Peltier trial transcript, quoted in Matthiessen, *op. cit.*, p. 350.

188. There was no primary evidence in the RESMURS case. No slugs were recovered from either Williams' or Coler's bodies, and only fragments of .22 caliber *series* projectiles – which could have been fired from any of a number of different types of small bore weapon – were recovered from the ground beneath the two agents. The Bureau crime lab could not even determine whether these fragments were from slugs fired on the day of the firefight. The FBI retained two different coroners – Robert Bloemendaal and Thomas Noguchi – in an attempt to corroborate its theories. Bloemendaal ascertained that Coler's first wound (rather than only the last, as the prosecution maintained at trial) had been mortal, and that it was caused by a very large bore .44 magnum slug, fired at long rather than short range, which had passed through the door of his car, splaying, before striking his left arm and nearly severing it (see Peltier

trial transcript at 591-3, 626, and 633-5). Bloemendaal also found that Williams had received a "potentially fatal" wound by a round – also .44 caliber and fired from some distance – which passed through his left arm and entered his body at the belt line (see a heavily deleted teletype from Zigrossi to Kelley, dated February 12, 1976, and captioned RESMURS INVESTIGATION; also see Peltier trial transcript at 587-8, 623-4, 589 and 593). Bloemendaal also found that both agents had been struck by different calibers of slugs, fired at various ranges. Such conclusions had been sufficient for the "group murder" case presented at Cedar Rapids, but contradicted the "lone gunman" case the prosecution intended to present against Peltier. Hence, Noguchi was retained to try again. He proceeded to engage in a rather interesting fishing expedition, firing assorted weapons (spanning the range from .22 to .45 caliber) at various ranges into "animal parts," then attempting to match the results to the wounds suffered by the dead agents. He obtained inconclusive results at best, finding that each man had been struck at least once by "a small, high-powered rifle fired at close range" (Peltier trial transcript at 589 and 593). Like the projectile fragments, this description could be applied to any of a number of weapons, including those of .22 magnum, .222 caliber, .223 caliber and possibly .30 caliber series. Certainly, the coroners found nothing demonstrating the "murder weapon" had been an AR-15. In the end, the most useful material for prosecutors accruing from the evidence provided by pathologists was not the result of autopsies, etc., but an array of gory color photos of Williams and Coler shortly after their deaths. While Judge McManus had restricted prosecutorial use of such emotional but largely irrelevant material at Cedar Rapids, so as not to unnecessarily taint the jury's view of the defendants, Judge Benson allowed dozens of the pictures to be introduced against Peltier (Peltier trial transcript at 544-6).

189. Coler's car had been gone over with a fine tooth comb by investigators working on site in the immediate aftermath of the firefight. No AR-15 "ammunition component" was found in Coler's open trunk. To the contrary, the Bureau's operant theory for more than a month after RESMURS began – an idea agents attempted to "confirm" when contriving Jimmy Eagle's supposed jailhouse confession, and in the initial statements prepared for Norman Brown, Wish Draper and Mike Anderson – was that the agents had been killed with a .45 caliber Thompson submachinegun. Concerning the AR-15 cartridge casing itself – described by the prosecution as "the most important piece of evidence" in the Peltier case – the Bureau could never quite seem to determine who found it, when, or what happened to it after it was found. The discovery was originally attributed to the chief of the FBI's Firearms and Toolmarks Division, Courtland Cunningham. At least that's what is maintained in a July 1, 1976 affidavit prepared at FBI headquarters and sent to Rapid City for Cunningham's signature (see Peltier trial transcript at 2113-4). On the stand during Peltier's trial, however, Cunningham denied having found the cartridge casing, and stipulated the affidavit he'd signed was "incorrect" (Peltier trial transcript at 2114-26). Instead, Cunningham contended that the casing had been found by a fingerprint specialist named Winthrop Lodge. Lodge then testified that he had discovered the item during an examination of Coler's car on June 29, 1975, and had then turned it over to Cunningham (Peltier trial transcript at 3012-3, and 3079-80). On cross examination, Lodge began to contradict himself, first claiming that he had not removed evidentiary material from Coler's car, then stating that "some" material had been removed, and then asserting that "all evidence had been inventoried and removed from the vehicle" (Peltier trial transcript at 3112-20). When pressed on what had happened to this material, including the cartridge casing he'd allegedly found, Lodge first insisted that he'd turned it all over to Cunningham, but had unaccountably failed to get the receipt required by Bureau evidentiary procedures designed to prevent false evidence from being gratuitously introduced somewhere along the line. He then switched stories, stating that "not all the evidence" gathered from Coler's car had been turned over to Cunningham. Some, he contended, "were carried back to Pine Ridge and turned over to the agent personally in charge of the evidence." Lodge couldn't say who this agent was, exactly what had been "carried back" to him, or why the unorthodox decision had been taken to turn certain unreceipted evidentiary items over to Cunningham and some to another agent (Peltier trial transcript at 3137-8 and 3162-3). In other words, there was never anything resembling a clear record of where the FBI's "most important piece of evidence" came from, when it was "found," where it was found, by whom it was found, or what happened to it between the time it was allegedly found and the time it was catalogued at the FBI crime lab in Washington, D.C. Such "contamination" of the evidentiary chain – allowing as it does for the introduction of false evidence – is typically sufficient to cause the material to be disallowed from introduction into any trial, never mind a capital case such as RESMURS.

190. On September 11, 1986, a three judge panel of the Eighth Circuit Court found, upon review of

documents released and hearings held subsequent to Peltier's conviction, that the "one AR-15" theory advanced by the prosecution in Fargo had been false, and that the FBI had *known* it was false. Indeed, the evidence indicated "several" AR-15s had been used by Indians during the Oglala firefight. See U.S. Court of Appeals for the Eighth Circuit, "Appeal from the United States District Court for the District of North Dakota, *United States v. Leonard Peltier*," No. 95-5193, St. Louis, Missouri, September 11, 1986.

191. At trial, Hodge testified that a firing pin test conducted with the Wichita AR-15 for purposes of making a comparison with the cartridge casing supposedly found in Coler's trunk was "inconclusive" because of "a lack of marks on the bolt face in the condition I received" the rifle (Peltier trial transcript at 3235 and 3247). Hodge's October 2, 1975 teletype shows this to have been untrue; the test conclusively proved the cartridge casing had *not* been fired through the AR-15 in question. Hodge then performed a much less (even by his own definition; see Peltier trial transcript at 3248) definitive extractor test and used this to advance a "link" between the weapon and the cartridge casing (Peltier trial transcript at 3247). Hodge also claimed on the stand not to have examined the crucial casing until "December or January" of 1975 or '76 (Peltier trial transcript at 3233-4 and 3388), a line of testimony designed to explain the slow evolution of the Bureau's "evidence" against Peltier. In actuality, as a raft of documents subsequently released under the FOIA reveal, the casing had been being "handled" in the lab since at least as early as the first week of August 1975. Under the circumstances, a much more likely explanation for the pace of the AR-15 investigation is that it simply did not fit in with the RESMURS script the Bureau was trying to follow during the early days; only later, as the scenario developed, did it become important. The evidence was then tailored accordingly.

192. Coward's testimony on this is to be found in the Peltier trial transcript at 1305. The defense then requested that Judge Benson and/or the jury attempt to duplicate such an identification. Benson refused either to do so himself, or to allow jury participation in such a "stunt" (Peltier trial transcript at 1797). As an alternative, the defense retained James R. Hall, the owner of a local sporting goods store and an individual well-versed in the use of rifle scopes, to conduct an appropriate test. Using a comparable 2x7 scope at the same distance Coward had specified, but under cool, clear atmospheric conditions (far superior to those the agent would have necessarily encountered at Oglala on June 26, 1975, a hot day following a heavy rain) Hall was consistently unable to identify a close friend standing still and facing the viewer. Benson allowed Hall – a well respected man in Fargo – to testify on the results of his tests, *but only with the jury absent* (see Peltier trial transcript at 3786-90). There is some indication that the FBI performed its own tests, with equally poor results. In sum, the "eyewitness" sighting sworn to by SA Coward was a virtual physical impossibility. Relatedly, BIA Police Officer/GOON Marvin Stoldt, who was partnered with Coward on June 26, and who shared his rifle scope from the same range, "positively identified" Jimmy Eagle as being among the Indians present on the Jumping Bull property. This is reflected in Coward's 302 Report for June 26. The problem here was that Eagle, by the government's own admission, had been nowhere near the firefight. Benson ruled that the 302 Report containing this misidentification – which would surely have cast appropriate doubt upon Coward's own supposed sighting of Peltier – would not be allowed as evidence (Peltier transcript at 1351).

193. Peltier trial transcript at 5011.

194, U.S. Circuit Court of Appeals for the Eighth District, "Motion to Vacate Judgement and for a New Trial in the Matter of the *United States v. Leonard Peltier*, Criminal No. C77-3003," transcript at 7327-28 (April 12, 1978).

195. U.S. Circuit Court of Appeals for the Eighth District, "Finding of the United States Eighth Circuit Court of Appeals in the Matter of the *United States v. Leonard Peltier*, C77-3003, Motion to Vacate Judgement and for a New Trial," St. Louis, Missouri, September 14, 1978.

196. It should be noted that Webster is known to hold strange views, not only on the nature of justice, but on race and gender relations as well. For instance, he is was a member of a "social club" called the "Mysterious Order of the Veiled Prophets," explicitly barring membership to blacks or women, during his tenure as an appeals court judge in St. Louis.

197. *United States v. Peltier*, 858 F.2d 314, 335 (8th Cir. 1978), *cert. denied*, 440 U.S. 945 (1979).

198. *Peltier v. Department of Justice*, CA. No. 79-2722 (D.D.C.).

199, See "Motion to Vacate Judgement and for a New Trial, *Peltier v. United States*, Crim. No. C77-3003" (D.N.D. filed April 20, 1982) and "Motion for Disqualification of Hon. Paul Benson, *Peltier v. United States*, Crim. No. C77-3003," (D.N.D. filed December 15, 1982).

200. United States Court of Appeals for the Eighth Circuit, *United States v. Leonard Peltier*, 731

F.2d., 550, 555 (8th Cir. 1984). At p. 4, the judges noted: "The importance of [the ballistics evidence] to the government's case against Peltier cannot be ignored. During the argument to the jury at the close of the trial, counsel for the government stated,'One shell casing is ejected into the trunk of the agent's car which was open, one shell casing, perhaps *the single most important piece of evidence in this case* [emphasis added]."

201. The October 2 teletype, Hodge asserted, referred to comparison of the AR-15 to other cartridges found at the scene of the firefight, not to the .223 cartridge from SA Coler's trunk. When questioned as to why he had not tested that cartridge against the Wichita AR-15 immediately, Hodge claimed he was not aware of the urgent need to do so. This proved to be, as the Eighth Circuit Court was later to put it, "inconsistent with...several teletypes from FBI officials, agents requesting [Hodge] to compare submitted AR-15 rifle with .223 casing found at the scene, and [Hodge's] response to these teletypes."

202. In trying to salvage something of the integrity of the Bureau's evidentiary chain regarding the key cartridge casing, Hodge swore that he – and he *alone* – had handled the item once it arrived at the ballistics lab. Kunstler then pointed out that a second person's handwriting appeared on the lab notes pertaining to the casing. After a bit of perplexity, Hodge altered his testimony that both he and a lab assistant named Joseph Twardowski had been involved with the item. Kunstler then queried Hodge whether he was absolutely certain he and Twardowski were the only individuals with access to the crucial evidence. Hodge replied emphatically in the affirmative. Kunstler then produced yet another lab report on the matter, with still another person's handwriting on it, demanding that an independent handwriting analyst be retained by the court "to determine the identity of the unknown party who is at issue here." Court was then recessed for the day. An hour later, counsel were called back to court by Judge Benson, who stated that "Mr. Hodge has something he wishes to say to you." Hodge then took the stand and explained that he had "mis-spoken" when he insisted for the record that he, and then he and Twardowski, had been the only individuals with access to the cartridge casing. When Kunstler asked how many people might actually have had such access, Hodge replied, "I really can't say." In other words, as Kunstler put it at a press conference shortly thereafter, "For all their pious assurances to the contrary, made repeatedly and under oath, the FBI cannot really say for certain that this is the same cartridge casing found in the trunk of agent Coler's car, if indeed any such casing was ever found. And the fact of the matter is that to the extent that given FBI agents have been saying otherwise is the extent to which they have been lying through their teeth."

203. *Peltier v. United States*, Transcript of Oral Arguments before the U.S. Court of Appeals for the Eighth District, October 14, 1985, p. 18. For further information, see Kunstler, William, "The Ordeal of Leonard Peltier," *Covert Action Information Bulletin*, No. 24, Summer 1985.

204. *Ibid.*, p. 19. Crooks' attempt to change the charge on which Peltier had been convicted from murder to aiding and abetting murder provoked the following exchange with a bewildered Judge Gerald Heaney: *Heaney*: Aiding and abetting Butler and Robideau [who had been acquitted]? *Crooks*: Aiding and abetting whoever did the final shooting. Perhaps aiding and abetting himself. And hopefully the jury would believe that in effect he did it all. But aiding and abetting, nevertheless."

205. United States Circuit Court of Appeals for the Eighth District, "Appeal from the United States Court for the District of North Dakota in the Matter of *United States v. Leonard Peltier*, Crim. No. 85-5192," St. Louis, Missouri, October 11, 1986, p. 16.

206. "Petition for Rehearing and Suggestion for Rehearing En Banc for Appellant Leonard Peltier, *United State v. Leonard Peltier*, Crim. No. C77-3003," United States Circuit Court of Appeal for the Eighth District (1986).

207. See "Petition for Reconsideration of the Denial of the Petition for Rehearing and Suggestion for Rehearing En Banc, *United States v. Leonard Peltier*," No. 85-5192, United States Circuit Court of Appeals for the Eighth District (1986).

208. The appeal to the Supreme Court was based in a need for the high court to clarify whether in its decision in the case *United States v. Bagley* (U.S. 105 S. Ct. 3375 [1985]) it had meant the new evidence must be sufficient to have "possibly" changed the outcome of original jury deliberations – or whether it is required that new evidence would "probably" have resulted in this outcome – for a retrial to be mandated. The Eighth Circuit opted for the latter interpretation in its Peltier decision, while the Ninth Circuit had already utilized the more lenient standard in another case. In refusing to hear the Peltier appeal, the Supreme Court chose to leave this important due process issue clouded; see "Court refuses

to hear Peltier appeal," *Rapid City Journal*, October 6, 1987. Also see Churchill, Ward, "Leonard Peltier: The Ordeal Continues," *Zeta*, March 1988.

209. Heaney, U.S. Circuit Judge Gerald, interview on the CBS television program *West 57th Street*, aired on September 14, 1989.

210. Banks, Dennis, conversation with Ward Churchill, Boulder, CO, March 14, 1987 (notes on file).

211. Means, Russell, conversation with Ward Churchill, Boulder, CO, September 12, 1989 (notes on file).

212. For analysis on this point, see Berman, Jerry J., "FBI Charter Legislation: The Case for Prohibiting Domestic Intelligence Investigations," *University of Detroit Journal of Urban Law*, No. 55, 1978, pp. 1041-77. Also see Beichman, Arnold, "Can Counterintelligence Come in from the Cold?" *Policy Review*, No. 15, Winter 1981, pp. 93-101. Of further interest, see Ungar, Sanford J., "An Agenda for Rebuilding the FBI," *Washington Post*, August 21, 1977.

213. Cohen, Felix S., "The Erosion of Indian Rights, 1950-53: A Case Study in Bureaucracy," *Yale Law Journal*, Vol. 62, 1953, p. 390.

214. Kelley, FBI Director Clarence, statement at press conference, Los Angeles, CA, July 5, 1975 (notes on file).

Chapter 8: Conclusion

1. The data concerning COINTELPRO actions accrues from *Hearings on the Federal Bureau of Investigation*, op. cit., p. 601; that concerning taps, bugs and mail openings comes from *Final Report of the Senate Select Committee to Study Government Operations with Respect to Intelligence Activities, Book III: Intelligence Activities and the Rights of Americans*, op. cit., pp. 301, 632.

2. See Martinez, Elizabeth, "The Perils of Pilar: What Happened to the Chicano Movement?," *Zeta*, April 1989.

3. It will be recalled that at the time of the Church Committee hearings in 1975, Chicago SAC Richard G. Held was still swearing in court that the FBI had no documents relevant to the Hampton-Clark matter, and was actively denying that a Bureau infiltration was involved.

4. At the time the "official record" of COINTELPRO was compiled, the FBI was still denying – as it had at trial – the existence of ELSURS logs which could have exonerated Geronimo Pratt. The Bureau also denied – on appeal – that Pratt was a specific COINTELPRO target, a contention which was revealed to be absolutely untrue by a massive release of documents pursuant to the victim's successful 1981 FOIA suit.

5. On March 17, 1989, writing for the Supreme Court of the State of New York, Justice Peter McQuillan concluded that FOIA documents obtained by Richard Dhoruba Moore's attorneys in 1985-86 demonstrated beyond any reasonable doubt that COINTELPRO collusion between the FBI and NYPD concerning the manipulation of witnesses "might well have" led to a verdict of "not guilty," had the jury during Moore's 1972 "trial" been aware of it. McQuillan further noted that, had these COINTELPRO activities been known at the time Moore's direct appeal was decided in 1976 (it had been argued at the same time the Church Committee hearings were occurring), the situation would have "compelled reversal" of Moore's conviction. But the FBI withheld *all* such information from both the courts and congress. In what may be the ultimate testimonial to the real quality of American justice, the New York high court decided, in the face of all this, to allow Moore's conviction to stand. The rationalization upon which this decision was based is simply that, once direct appeals have been exhausted, New York law does not *require* reversal of a conviction, no matter *what* evidence is subsequently introduced. Hence, Dhoruba Moore continued to serve a life sentence concerning "crimes" for which even the courts admit he was never fairly convicted, for more than a year after McQuillan's opinion was rendered. Finally, on March 22, 1990, after his attorneys introduced the fact that an earlier New York high court decision made reversal of convictions *mandatory* in cases where it could be proven that exculpatory evidence had been withheld by the government, he was grudgingly released. For further information, see Debo, Dan, "COINTELPRO Lives On: The Unending Ordeal of Dhoruba Moore," *New Studies on the Left*, Vol. XIV, Nos. 1-2, Spring-Summer 1989, pp. 136-7.

6. These are, of course, the descriptive phrases which had been used to define COINTELPRO. It will be noted that, in the teletype, Kelley claims "Presidential authority" as a cover for the ELSURS activities;

obviously, if such authority were being extended as a means of regulating Bureau behavior rather than as a blanket beneath which agents could do essentially whatever to whomever, whenever they wanted, the FBI director would not have had to ask who was doing what to whom (and for what purpose) at that time. Further, researchers such as Louis Wolf have determined COINTELPRO is being more formally continued "under two new FBI cryptonyms: COMTEL and TOPLEV, presumably for Communications Intelligence [or Communist Intelligence; the authors] and Top Level." See Wolf, Louis, "COINTELPRO Gets a New Name," *Covert Action Information Bulletin*, No. 31, Winter 1989, p. 57.

7. The document is drawn from those generated by the NEWKILL investigation, integral to the aforementioned case of Richard Dhoruba Moore.

8. For a complete list, see Press Release, "GROUPS INCLUDED IN THE CISPES FILES OBTAINED FROM FBI HEADQUARTERS," Center for Constitutional Rights, New York, January 27, 1988.

9. A classic example is that of Frank Varelli, a Salvadoran infiltrated by the FBI into the Dallas CISPES chapter in 1982, and who persistently both reported inaccurate information on chapter activities (which provided a rationale for continuing the Bureau's "investigation") and sought to persuade chapter members to engage in actual illegal activities. See King, Wayne, "F.B.I.'s Papers Portray Inquiry Fed by Informer," *New York Times*, February 13, 1988.

10. One need go no further than the application of the term "terrorist" to CISPES and other targeted organizations, even as a "suspicion," to apprehend disinformation being employed in a most forthright manner. Both former FBI Director William Webster and the present director, William Sessions, made such claims repeatedly in the media. See, for example, Sherron, Philip, "F.B.I.'s Chief Says Surveillance Was Justified," *New York Times*, February 3, 1988, and "Reagan Backs F.B.I. Surveillance: Accepts Bureau Report That There Was Solid Basis for Effort Aimed at Critics," *New York Times*, February 4, 1988. For valuable insights into how this works, see Donner, Frank, "The Terrorist as Scapegoat," *The Nation*, No. 226, May 20, 1978, pp. 590-4.

11. More than 200 incidents of burglaries of the homes and offices of Central America activists – in which political materials such as documents and computer disks were taken while valuables were left untouched – are chronicled as having occurred from the beginning of 1984 through the beginning of 1988. The list is undoubtedly incomplete. See *Harassment Update: Chronological List of FBI and Other Harassment Incidents*, Movement Support Network and Anti-Repression Project for the Center for Constitutional Rights, New York, January 1987; also see *Harassment Update*, Center for Constitutional Rights, New York, January 27, 1988.

12. *Ibid.* For example, "On July 29, 1986, a Center for Constitutional Rights staff person reported that when her travel agent telephoned, although she was home and her answering machine on, no message came over. Instead, a man answered who said: 'I'm her boyfriend and a policeman, I'll take the message.'"

13. *Ibid.* Also see Hirschorn, Michael W., "Newly Released Documents Provide Rare Look at How FBI Monitors Students and Professors," *Chronicle of Higher Education*, February 10, 1988.

14. See "Once a G-Man, Now a Pacifist: A costly conversion," *Newsweek*, November 23, 1987.

15. The FBI advanced the interesting concept during the Plowshares cases that any action which curtailed, or was intended to curtail, the state's ability to project violence – disabling a nuclear missile, for instance – should be considered "terrorism." It follows that planning or even discussing such an act would amount to "terrorist conspiracy."

16. Assata Shakur was supposedly sought for involvement in the "execution style murders" of New York police officers Joseph Piagenti and Waverly Jones on May 21, 1971, and Gregory Foster and Rocco Laurie on January 28, 1972. A good survey of the sensationalist, Bureau-provoked coverage of the charges may be found in Shakur, Assata, *Assata: An Autobiography*, Lawrence Hill and Company, Westport, Conn., 1987. For a police-eye view, see Steedman, Albert A., *Chief!*, Avon Books, New York, 1975.

17. After her arrest, Shakur penned an open letter to the black community apologizing for the "sloppiness" and "lax security" which led her and her colleagues to travel the turnpike despite knowledge that "racist police continually hassle black people" seen driving thereon. For further information, see Jaimes, M. Annette, "Self-Portrait of a Black Liberationist," *New Studies on the Left*, Vol. XIV, Nos. 1-2, Winter-Spring 1989.

18. Shakur was charged with robbing the Bankers Trust Branch in Queens of $7,697 on August 23, 1971 and the Manufacturers Hanover Trust in the Bronx of $3,700 on September 29, 1972. The killing of

the heroin dealers occurred in Brooklyn on January 3, 1973. As was revealed at trial, the government had essentially no case in any of these matters.

19. The saga of Shakur's trials, and the nature of the conditions for her incarceration are brought out in a series of articles published in the *New Brunswick Home News* during the period 1975-77.

20. Prior to Clinton, Assata Shakur was housed briefly at the New Jersey State Youth Reception and Correction center at Yardville, and at the Alderson (West Virginia) Federal Prison for Women. The combat unit was a "mixed group," composed o BLA members, and former members of the Weather Underground Organization.

21 It is worth noting that even had Shakur participated in the Jersey Turnpike firefight in the manner claimed by prosecutors – a matter which seems highly dubious, given medical evidence – she would demonstrably have been engaged in armed self-defense rather than "terrorism." The state's definition of "terrorism" is in this instance more than somewhat suspect.

22. It seems doubtful that the FBI was ever particularly concerned with the activities of Omega 7, a CIA-created organization of Batistite Cubans used as a hemispheric anti-communist terrorist apparatus specializing in assassinations during the 1960s and '70s. It wasn't until Omega 7 was shown to have been involved in the car bomb assassination of former Allende government official Orlando Letelier and researcher Ronni Moffit in Washington, D.C., on September 21, 1976 that the public became in any way concerned with the Cubans' activities. The Bureau was thus able to (cynically) list the government-supported operations of Omega 7 as a reason for increasing its emphasis on domestic "counter-terrorism" (see Dinges, John, and Saul Landau, *Assassination on Embassy Row*, Pantheon Publishers, New York, 1980). As to the Serbo-Croatian group, aside from claiming credit for a single flash-powder explosion at New York's John F. Kennedy International Airport in 1979, they seem to have accomplished so little as to have been virtually non-existent. It should be considered an active proposition that the whole thing was a police/FBI ruse designed to whip up public support for the emerging campaign of "anti-terrorism." In any event, it should be clear that the real weight of what was going on was all along placed upon the left in counterintelligence circles.

23. A development roughly corresponding with the emergence of the JTTF was the establishment of the Federal Emergency Management Agency (FEMA) through Jimmy Carter's E.O. 12148, in 1977. This was an extension from the Federal Emergency Preparedness Agency (FEPA), created in 1976, under Gerald Ford's E.O. 11921. In 1980, with the advent of the Reagan administration, FEMA was used as the vehicle for creation of a quasi-secret, centralized "national emergency" entity, headed by a federal "emergency czar." Appointed into the latter position was Louis O. Giuffrida, the former national guard general and counterinsurgency enthusiast who had built up the California Specialized Training Institute (CSTI) and contributed heavily to the Garden Plot and Cable Splicer plans of the late 1960s and early '70s, before going on to serve as a government consultant during the repression of AIM and during the 1979 "counterterrorism conference" held in Puerto Rico, among other things (see Chapters 4 and 7). While FEMA's charter called for planning and training activities concerning "natural disasters, nuclear war, the possibility of enemy attack on U.S. territory, and incidents involving domestic civil unrest," Giuffrida focused his agency's energy and resources entirely upon the last category. By January 1982, this emphasis had led to the preparation of a joint FEMA-Pentagon position paper, entitled "The Civil/Military Alliance in Emergency Management," which effectively voided provisions of the 1877 *Posse Comitatus* Act (prohibiting military intervention in domestic disturbances). The plan was considerably reinforced by Reagan's top secret National Security Decision Directive (NSDD 26) during the spring of 1982, a pronouncement which appears to have formally interlocked FEMA, not only with the military but with the National Security Council (NSC). By 1984, Giuffrida had installed his old friend General Frank S. Salcedo, another counterinsurgency expert, as head of the agency's "Civil Security Division" (CSD) and had established a "Civil Defense Training Center" – based on the CSTI model – near Emmitsville, Maryland. Here, more than 1,000 civilian police from around the country received what FEMA euphemistically referred to as "military police methods" for quelling domestic political unrest. Meanwhile, in cooperation with the Pentagon and various federal and local police agencies, CSD engaged in a series of national training exercises – "Proud Saber/Rex-82, "Pre-Nest," and "Rex-84/Night Train," etc. – in preparation for a suspension of the constitution in case of massive domestic political turmoil. The exercises envisioned "at least 100,000" U.S. citizens, identified as "national security threats" being rounded up and thrown into concentration camps for unspecified periods. Simultaneously, FEMA was opening files on the U.S. activists who would comprise those interned

whenever the exercise plans were put into "real world" practice. This last placed FEMA in direct conflict with the FBI, precipitating a power struggle in which Bureau Director William Sessions ultimately prevailed, compelling Giuffrida to turn over the more than 12,000 political dossiers his agency had already assembled. The contest had also brought Attorney General William French Smith into the fray, a matter which led the Justice Department to conclude that FEMA's activities were openly unconstitutional and "seek to establish new Federal Government management structures or otherwise task Cabinet departments and other federal agencies." The structural outcome of this dispute is unclear. However, the issue seems to have been resolved in immediate sense by the FBI – well aware of the personal venality often associated with those who make a fetish of enforcing political orthodoxy – opening an investigation into the possibility that Giuffrida had misappropriated government funds. The Bureau was quickly able to determine that the FEMA boss had engaged in *"de facto* nepotism" by placing only his cronies in key positions within his agency, and had mis-spent taxpayer monies by, among other things, lavishing $170,000 in furnishings upon an opulent bachelor pad for himself. In 1985, Giuffrida quietly resigned, taking most of his "crew" with him when he went. Since then, FEMA has been more-or-less back-burnered, its core political activities incorporated under the mantle of the FBI-dominated JTTF. For further information, see Reynolds, Diana, "FEMA and the NSC: The Rise of the National Security State," *Covert Action Information Bulletin*, No. 33, Winter 1990.

24. The state Addiction Services Agency had stopped funding Lincoln Detox five years earlier, in 1973, positing as its rationale the fact that heroin withdrawal at the center cost $261 per client (with a very low recidivism rate), as compared to $57 per client in methadone-based programs (showing nearly 100% recidivism). The activists sustained the Lincoln Detox effort even with funding thus constricted. More than 50 members of the NYPD were finally used to oust them after Mayor Ed Koch suspended *all* further funding in 1978.

25. According to the JTTF, the RATF was responsible for a $13,800 robbery from a Citibank branch in Manhattan on October 10, 1977; a $8,300 robbery from a Chase Manhattan branch on May 27, 1978; a $200,000 robbery of a Coin Deposit Corporation armored truck in Livingston, New Jersey on December 19, 1978; a $105,000 robbery of a Coin Deposit Corporation armored truck at the Garden State Plaza Mall (New Jersey) on September 11, 1979; the attempted robbery of an IBI armored truck in Greenberg, New York during December of 1979; the $529,000 robbery of a Purolator armored truck in Inwood, Long Island on April 22, 1980; the unsuccessful robbery of a Purolator armored truck in Danbury, Connecticut on March 23, 1981; a $292,000 robbery of a Brinks truck in the Bronx on June 2, 1981 in which one guard was killed and another wounded; and two unsuccessful attempts to rob a Brinks truck in Nanuet, New York in October, 1981. In addition, the group is credited with breaking Assata Shakur out of her New Jersey prison on November 2, 1979.

26. Captured were Kathy Boudin, David Gilbert and Judy Clark, all former members of the Weather Underground Organization, and Sam Brown, a black man only recently brought into the RATF.

27. Those who allegedly escaped from West Nyack, in addition to Mutulu Shakur, were Mtyari Sundiata (s/n: Samuel Lee Smith), Kuwasi Balagoon, Chui Ferguson, Edward Joseph, and Nehanda Obafemi (s/n: Cheryl Lavern Dalton), all former members of the BPP, BLA or RNA. Marilyn Buck and Susan Rosenberg, white members of RATF, were also accused of involvement; Buck was allegedly wounded in the leg at Nyack.

28. RATF members captured within six months of the West Nyack incident include Sekou Odinga, Anthony LaBorde, Kuwasi Balagoon, Chui Ferguson, and Edward Joseph, all former Panther 21 defendants. Also arrested in the same connection were James York, Silvia Baraldini, Bilal Sunni-Ali and Iliana Robinson.

29. Kuwasi Balagoon, Judy Clark and David Gilbert were found guilty of robbery and murder on September 15, 1985. Balagoon died in prison in 1987. Clark and Gilbert are serving 75-year-to-life sentences (in 1985, Clark was also convicted of "conspiring to escape" and received an unprecedented sentence of two years in solitary confinement). Kathy Boudin pleaded guilty to the same charges and is serving a 44 year sentence. Sekou Odinga and Silvia Baraldini were convicted of RICO charges on September 3, 1983 and sentenced to 40 and 43 years respectively (Odinga was also convicted of attempted murder and sentenced to 25-years-to-life, this sentence to run consecutive with the others). Edward Joseph and Chui Ferguson were convicted of being accessories to RICO conspiracy in the same trial as Odinga and Baraldini; they were sentenced to twenty years apiece. Bilal Sunni-Ali and Iliana Robinson were acquitted on the RICO charges. Marilyn Buck was not captured until May 11, 1985;

Mutulu Shakur more than a year later. They were tried together on RICO charges in 1987, convicted, and sentenced to fifty years each (Buck's sentence does not begin until she finishes serving a twenty year weapons and escape sentence, already in progress).

30. See "Defendants Motion to Dismiss the Indictment for Governmental Misconduct," *U.S. v. Laura Whitehorn, et al.*, CR. No 88-145-05 (HHG), United States Court for the District of Columbia, January 3, 1989, p. 56:

> The political nature of these grossly disproportionate sentences is evidenced by comparing punishments imposed on Ku Klux Klan members, abortion clinic bombers and other right-wing defendants whose offenses cause death and serious injuries, and are motivated by racist violence, greed and hatred. Ku Klux Klan organizer Don Black was convicted of possession of massive quantities of explosives and weapons in 1984, yet served only 24 months in prison and was released and permitted to engage in Klan recruitment. Edward Hefferman, a right-wing "survivalist" convicted of possession of 1,000 pounds of dynamite and 18 fully constructed pipe bombs was sentenced to six months to two years and served six months...Victor Vancier and other members of the Jewish Defense League pled guilty to firebombing and other acts of bombings, arsons, extortions and fraud, and received only 10 year sentences or less.

At p. 55, the motion also notes that,

> The 58-year sentences given to Blunk and Rosenberg exceeded the single *largest* sentences imposed in 1982 for violations of [the same laws under which they were convicted] by 33 years. They were 38 years longer than the longest sentence imposed on any defendant in 1982 or 1983 for violation of *any* section of the federal explosives act...The Blunk and Rosenberg sentences were two and one-half times the 1985 average of Kidnapping, three times the average for Second Degree Murder, four times the average for Bank Robbery, nine times the 1985 average for Felony Distribution of Narcotics, ten times the 1985 average for assault, and sixteen times the 1985 average for possession of firearms. Their sentence was longer than every person convicted in 1982 and 1983 of racketeering, conspiracy, fraud, theft, larceny, burglary, assault, escape, riot, sedition, perjury, bribery, and graft, and all but one of the 901 defendants sentenced for possession and distribution of heroin.

31. Statement by attorney Susan Tippograph, October 13, 1982.

32. Those jailed were Eve Rosahn, Fulani Sunni-Ali, Jerry Gaines, Yaasmyn Fula, Larry Mack, Richard Delaney, Asha Sundiata (s/n: Debra Buckman), Dr. Alan Berkman, Iliana Robinson, Shaheem Abdul Jabbar (s/n: John Crenshaw), Silvia Baraldini, and Bernardine Dohrn.

33. See Calhoun, Patricia, "Grand Slam," *Westword*, December 14, 1983.

34. The six imprisoned JBAKC activists were Christine Rico, Sandra Roland, Steven Burke, Bob Lederer, Terry Bisson and Julie Nalibor. They were held up to eight months.

35. The points are extracted from the aforementioned "Motion to Dismiss" in *Whitehorn, et al.*, at pp. 37-8. The motion relies upon written responses to interrogations entered by Webster on February 4, 1982, and the director's testimony before the Senate Subcommittee on Security and Terrorism on February 11. At pp. 32-3, the motion points out that "within a week of the Brinks incident, [New York SAC Kenneth] Walton and other FBI officials were claiming that the FBI had found links among the Weather Underground, the Black Liberation Army and the Black Panther Party, and that they were investigating possible connections with the [FALN]. FBI suggestions of possible Cuban Intelligence (DGI) involvement immediately arose as well, and on October 25, 1981, FBI chief spokesman Roger Young asserted that the Cuban Intelligence service 'has been supportive in the past of the Weather Underground.' The FBI claimed that the Brinks incident might be linked to domestic and foreign political groups was given wide play in the media." But as soon as public exposure on the matter had been accomplished, the Bureau promptly dropped the whole baseless assertion, never bringing it up during the several RATF trials which ensued.

36. The charges were filed by FBI agent David B. Mitchell, a member of the JTTF. The "Son of Brinks" label seems to have been dreamed up by New York ASAC (and JTTF commander) Lee F. Laster.

37. Those convicted on the ID and weapons charges were Coltrane Chimarenga, Omawale Clay, Ruth Carter, Yvette Kelly, Roger Wareham and Robert Taylor.

38. The jury views are quoted in Castellucci, *op. cit.*, pp. 293-4.

39. As with the Rosenberg and Blunk sentences, Berkman's is virtually unprecedented in its severity. The average federal sentence for a comparable "offense" is two years, making his punishment six times the norm. This harsh judgment was rendered despite his having been diagnosed as afflicted with a potentially fatal cancer, making it possible he'd not live out his sentence. Further, having been convicted of no violent act, or otherwise meeting any criteria for such placement, he was immediately sent to the federal "super-maximum" prison at Marion, where 23 1/2 hour per day "lock down" conditions prevail on a permanent basis.

40. See "Defendants' Reply to Government's Response to Defendants' Motion to Dismiss for Prosecutorial Misconduct," *U.S. v. Whitehorn, et al.*, CR. No. 88-0145 (HHG), United States District Court for the District of Columbia, February 10, 1988, p. 8.

41. For an excellent example of this sort of sanctimonious self-indulgence, see Frankfort, Ellen, *Kathy Boudin and the Dance of Death*, Stein and Day Publishers, New York, 1983.

42. The Order or *Bruder Schweigen* (Silent Brotherhood) was an organization founded by Robert Jay Mathews, a former member of the John Birch Society and Minutemen, in 1982. An associate of Richard Butler's "Aryan Nations" Church of Jesus Christ Christian in Idaho, Mathews – who was himself an Odinist – carefully recruited members who subscribed to the visions of genocide and racial purity propounded in *The Turner Diaries* (National Vanguard Books, Arlington, VA, 1978), a novel by William Pierce, a former aide to American Nazi Party leader George Lincoln Rockwell. In short order, he'd gathered together a cadre of Gary Lee Yarbrough, David Tate, Bruce Carrol Pierce, Denver Parmenter, Ken Loff, Randy Duey, James Dye and Robert and Sharon Merki. The group received "inspiration" from Robert Miles, pastor of an identity christian church in Michigan, and a leading figure in the U.S. racist movement. It then recruited armorer/trainers – Randall Rader, Richard Satari and Andrew Barnhill – from another batch of right-wing religious fanatics, The Covenant, Sword and Arm of the Lord (CSA), in Arkansas. Thus rostered and equipped with automatic weapons, the group set out on a process of sparking the race war outlined in *The Turner Diaries*. To finance their plan, they first tried counterfeiting (with mixed results) and then turned to banks and armored trucks. On December 17, 1983, they robbed the Citibank branch in Innis Arden, Washington of $25,952. On January 30, they robbed the Mutual Savings Bank in Spokane of $3,600. On March 16, they robbed a Continental armored truck of $43,345 in Seattle. On April 23, they took $531,713 from a Continental armored truck in Seattle; $301,334 was in checks, which they discarded, making their cash haul $230,379. On May 23, they "executed" Walter West, a fringe member of their group, with a hammer and a gunshot to the head; Mathews had become concerned West was compromising security by his loose talk in bars. On the evening of June 18, 1983, they undertook their first act of sparking the "race war" by machinegunning KOA radio talk show host Alan Berg, a Jew, in his Denver driveway; Berg was hit at least twelve times with .45 caliber bullets from a MAC-10 machine pistol fired at close range, dying instantly. On July 19, they robbed a Brinks armored truck of $3.8 *million* near Ukiah, California. After that, the FBI moved in, using an informant named Tom Martinez, "turned" after being apprehended in Philadelphia passing some of the gang's counterfeit money. Mathews himself was killed on December 8, 1983 on Whidbey Island (near Seattle), after an all-night siege of a house in which he was holed up. The other members of The Order were picked up at various points around the country over the next few months. One of them, David Tate, killed a Missouri state trooper with a MAC-10 machine pistol before giving himself up. Ultimately all the men directly involved in the organization went to prison, several on very long sentences. And it is true that the government applied the same RICO statutes in their case used against the RATF and other left-wing defendants. But conspicuously absent from the FBI's handling of the matter was the sort of movement-wide investigation of organizations on the right which marked the CISPES probe, the broad use of grand juries to neutralize key right-wing activists who had some loose association with The Order, or the public branding of anyone and everything sharing even remote ideological affiliation with Mathews group as being "terrorist." The sorts of "law enforcement" practices engaged in by the Bureau *vis à vis* the left are thus of an emphatically different sort than those pursued when some element of the radical right gets out of control. For further information, see Flynn, Kevin and Gary Gerhardt, *The Silent Brotherhood: Inside America's Racist Underground*, The Free Press, New York, 1989. Also see Coates, Jim, *Armed and Dangerous: The Rise of the Survivalist Right*, The Noonday Press, New York, 1987.

43. The sentences of Buck, Rosenberg, Blunk and Berkman have already been outlined. Linda Evans is serving a total of 45 years as a result of a conviction for having "harbored" RATF fugitive Marilyn Buck (they were arrested outside a Dobbs Ferry, New York diner on May 11, 1985), as well as being "a felon in possession of firearms," having rendered false statements to obtain four firearms, and having "caused false statements to appear in Bureau of Alcohol, Tobacco, and Firearms records." As with other RATF defendants, the severity of the sentence imposed in Evans' case shatters all conceivable standards of "equal justice before the law." The norm in harboring cases is five years. In felon/firearms cases not involving related convictions for use of the weapons, the usual sentence is 3-5 years. Typically, all sentences would run concurrently, rather than the consecutive sentencing Evans received. Even had the harboring sentence been set to run consecutive to a cluster of weapons sentences, the defendant's punishment would have added up to 8-10 years. The difference between that and 45 years speaks for itself.

44. This makes Whitehorn far and away the longest-held U.S. citizen under such circumstances in the country's history, with *Puertorriqueño* activist Filiberto Ojeda Ríos running a close second. Joe Doherty, a member of the Irish Republican Army accused by the British of "terrorist activity" in 1980 – but who escaped from jail before his 1981 trial – holds the record for such incarceration in a U.S. jail. Doherty was arrested in New York on June 18, 1983 as an "illegal alien." On December 12, 1984, Judge John E. Spizzo, ruled that Doherty could not be extradited to Northern Ireland insofar as his case falls under the "political exemption clause" of the U.S./Britain extradition treaty. The federal government has continuously appealed and otherwise maneuvered to get around the law ever since (meanwhile refusing to simply deport the prisoner to Ireland, out of British jurisdiction). Doherty remains in jail as of this writing.

45. See "Court Permits Prosecution of 3 in Bombings," *New York Times*, November 5, 1989.

46. "Motion to Dismiss," *op. cit.*, p. 74.

47. *Ibid.*

48. *Ibid.*, pp. 75-6. The RFG and RGR are organizations with which some of the defendants were associated, in addition to the ARU.

49. Quoted in Day, Susie, "Political Prisoners: Guilty Until Proven Innocent," *Sojourner: The Women's Forum*, February 1989, p. 18.

50. Quoted in *ibid.* For further information, see Day, Susie, "Resistance Conspiracy Trial," *Zeta*, September 1989.

51. Quoted in Whitehorn, Laura, "Counterinsurgency in the Courtroom: The 'Resistance Conspiracy Case,'" *Covert Action Information Bulletin*, No. 31, Winter 1989, p. 47.

52. Quoted in Day, *op. cit.*

53. Pell, *op. cit.*, pp. 193-4. Charges were dismissed against Kearney after he adopted the "Nuremburg Defense," claiming he was "only following orders." Gray, on the other hand, was allowed to walk because – incredibly – he was held to have been "too highly placed" to have been responsible for what went on in the field.

54. "Motion to Dismiss," *op. cit.*, p. 30.

55. *Ibid.*

56. Jonathan Jackson is covered in Chapter 5. Sam Melville was a white activist convicted of leading an anti-corporate bombing campaign in New York during the late '60s and killed during the bloody repression of the prisoner revolt at Attica Prison in 1971. See Melville, Samuel, *Letters from Attica*, William Morrow and Company, New York, 1972.

57. See Levasseur, Ray Luc, "Opening Statement to the Jury," published by the Sedition Committee, Boston, 1985. The Sharpeville Massacre occurred on April 21, 1960. The second Union Carbide bombing is attributed to the Red Guerrilla Resistance.

58. Smith, Maggie, and Valerie West, "BOS-LUC, Western Sweep and the Ohio Seven: A Case Study in Counterinsurgency," unpublished manuscript provided to the authors by Ray Luc Levasseur.

59. The UFF was known to have provided support and security to Touré during his organizing efforts concerning the busing of school children in Boston during 1980 and '81. The initial JTTF approach seems to have been to try and crack the UFF through relatively visible activists such as Touré, and hopefully neutralize the latter in the process. Taken to trial in 1985 on charges stemming from the 1982 Attleboro firefight (he'd been held without bail during the interim), Touré was acquitted of assault with intent to murder, but convicted of state and federal firearms violations. He is presently serving a six year

sentence in the federal prison at Lewisburg, Pennsylvania; upon release, he is to begin serving a five year sentence in a state prison for exactly the same "offenses," but under Massachusetts rather than federal law. Obviously, normal standards of double jeopardy do not apply to targets for political repression in the U.S. See Kahn, Ric, "Fed Excesses: Going too far to get the Ohio 7," *The Boston Phoenix*, July 8, 1988.

60. Tom Manning acknowledges having killed Lamonaco, but maintains it was a matter of self-defense, the trooper having started shooting first. Interestingly, the state contends Manning did *not* shoot Lamonaco, arguing that Richard Williams was in Manning's car, and that he fired the fatal shots. Williams rebuts that he was not there, and Manning confirms his story. In their 1987 trial in the matter, Manning was convicted of "felony murder" (that is, of being in commission of a completely different felony – flight to avoid prosecution – which led up to the killing, but not of pulling the trigger) and was sentenced to life imprisonment. Ironically, having simultaneously put Manning in prison for life while deciding he was not Lamonaco's killer, the jury then failed to convict Williams of anything at all. We thus have a man serving time for a death the jury determined he did not cause, and for which no killer has been identified. Williams is scheduled for retrial in 1990. See Bailey, Dennis, "Underground," *The Boston Globe Magazine*, March 26, 1989.

61. Smith and West, *op. cit.*

62. *Ibid.*

63. *Ibid.* In retrospect, it is widely believed by those victimized that the FBI itself arranged the campaign of telephone threats against individual western Massachusetts feminists and women's facilities in order to put itself in the position of offering "protection" in exchange for "cooperation" in breaking the Ohio 7 case. Whether or not Bureau personnel actually made or arranged for the calls, the idea of agents attempting to broker the fundamental services for which they are paid speaks for itself. If agents did orchestrate the threats, which seems entirely possible, it should be remarked that the whole ploy was also blatantly sexist, presuming as it does that "the weaker sex" would be inordinately susceptible to such terror tactics. That the whole thing sounds like a classic COINTELPRO-style operation goes without saying.

64. The sequence of events began when the owner of a storage facility in Binghamton, New York was clearing out a locker on which rent had not been paid in nearly two years. In the process, he discovered the pieces of a disassembled shotgun and, for some reason, decided to contact the FBI about it. The locker had been rented to "Salvadore Bella," an alias attributed to Tom Manning, so the Bureau dispatched a team of investigators. Among the locker's other contents, they found a mail order catalogue addressed to "Jack Horning," of Danbury, Connecticut. In Danbury, agents located a babysitter who had worked for "Jack and Paula Horning," and who recounted having been in the car when the latter was involved in a minor traffic accident some years previously. Going through old accident reports, the agents discovered that "Mrs. Horning" had produced a driver's licence in the name of "Judy Hymes," and that the car involved had been registered to "John Boulette," an alias attributed to Ray Luc Levasseur. Using the Grumman computer, the FBI then ascertained that "Mrs. Hymes" held a current post office box in Columbus, Ohio. They staked it out, identified the box holder as Pat Gros Levasseur when she showed up to collect her mail, and then followed her home to Deerfield. The Ohio 7 arrests began the following morning. See Bailey, *op. cit.*

65. *Ibid.*

66. Agents had followed Williams from the Levasseur residence the day before. On June 20, 1988, U.S. District Judge William G. Young determined that the SWAT operation in Cleveland which led to the arrests of Williams and the Laamans had been illegal, a violation of the Fourth Amendment rights of the latter couple. See Kahn, *op. cit.*

67. Utilizing the Grumman computer, agents were able to trace the gun to a dealer in Norfolk, Virginia. The buyer listed a local mail drop as an address, and after a month-long stakeout, the FBI was able to effect its capture of the Mannings. See Bailey, *op. cit.*

68. During the aforementioned June 20, 1988 pretrial hearing, Judge Young stipulated that, "if a law enforcement officer tried to bribe the child, that shocks my conscience and...no system of individual liberty worthy of the name should permit that of a minor child." The other two Levasseur children are Simone (then aged six) and Rosa (aged four).

69. The massive FBI SWAT raid which resulted in the capture of the Laamans and Richard Williams occurred in the midst of a birthday party for Ricky Laaman, the youngest child at age four. The Levasseurs were captured *en route* to the party.

70. Cameron Bishop was a member of the SDS chapter at Colorado State University (Ft. Collins) accused of dynamiting power lines near Denver in 1967. He subsequently spent eight years underground, most of it as one of the FBI's ten "most wanted" fugitives, before being captured in 1975 in East Greenwich, Rhode Island. At the time of his arrest, Bishop was accompanied by Ray Luc Levasseur. The experience seems to have been one of the factors which prompted Levasseur to go underground himself, only a few months later. Bishop was convicted of sabotage and sentenced to serve twenty years; the conviction was, however, overturned on appeal.

71. The Manning children were interrogated by FBI agents from five to ten times each, and may have suffered severe psychological trauma as a result. Jeremy, the eldest, refuses to discuss his ordeal and breaks down in tears at the mere mention of his experience at the hands of the Bureau. When questioned on the matter by the press, FBI media coordinator James Waldrop offered "no comment" on agent participation in the grilling of the children. A bit more candidly, Norfolk Deputy City Attorney Dan Hagemeister challenged whether the youngsters were even entitled to legal counsel during their repeated interrogations: "Do we really need a bunch of lawyers saying 'Don't answer that' to an 11-year-old?" he asked reporters. See Bisson, Terry, and Sally O'Brien, "Young Hostages," *The Nation*, August 5, 1985.

72. Manning and Levasseur went underground in 1975 after the murder of a local Portland activist named Stevie Poullen. Poullen, it turned out, had been targeted for elimination by a police "death squad" formed by a cop named Bertrand Surphes. Surphes was sentenced to prison for his organizing activities but, when it was disclosed that their names were on the police death list, the two future Ohio 7 members dropped out of sight. See Levasseur, Ray Luc, "My Name Is Ray Luc Levasseur: Statement to the Court, January 10, 1989," *New Studies on the Left*, Vol. XIV, Nos. 1-2, Spring-Summer 1989, p. 104.

73. For example, Aceto testified that Ray Luc Levasseur had told him the SMJJ planned to bomb the Suffolk County (Massachusetts) Courthouse prior to the April 1976 event. After the bombing, according to the version given by Aceto on the witness stand, Levasseur explained to him that the group had used "twelve sticks of dynamite" in accomplishing the job. Aceto later recanted these assertions – which were the only means by which the government could "link" any of the Ohio 7 to an offensive action in which people were injured – admitting that the first of the alleged conversations never took place, and that the "twelve sticks of dynamite" statement had been gleaned not from Levasseur, but from rumors circulated on the "movement grapevine." Tellingly, police explosives experts in Massachusetts determined only six sticks of dynamite had been used at Suffolk. See Kahn, *op. cit.*

74. Smith and West, *op. cit.*

75. Aceto had originally gone to prison on a breaking and entering conviction. While serving that sentence, he stabbed another inmate to death, pled guilty to the charge, and received a life sentence. Arguably, once he agreed to the FBI's deal to testify in exchange for a release from prison, he became utterly dependent upon the Bureau to keep him out, "snitches" having virtually zero life expectancy behind bars. He was, by all accounts, an extremely "cooperative" prosecution witness as a result. See Kahn, *op. cit.*

76. See Baily, *op. cit.* Ray Luc Levasseur was sent directly to the federal "super-max" prison at Marion, Illinois. Tom Manning was lodged in the super-max control unit at Trenton State Prison in New Jersey

77. How this move "simplified" anything is a bit of a mystery insofar as the case against all seven defendants was the same. A better explanation is perhaps that the government sought to appear "moderate" by virtue of dropping charges against the two men it calculated had already been neutralized for life. The dismissal of charges occurred on August 30, 1989. See "Ohio 7 Minus 2: On Trial for Seditious Conspiracy," *The Insurgent*, September 1989, p. 3.

78. The Justice Department initially contended it would try Curzi-Laaman separately. With the recent acquittal of her former codefendants on both counts, however, this seems quite unlikely.

79. Carol Manning's acceptance of the deal should not necessarily be construed as an actual admission of guilt. After the Aceto travesty, etc., she had little reason to extend much faith to the "due process" of the U.S. judicial system. She faced up to sixty years additional imprisonment if convicted of seditious conspiracy and RICO violations. The deal offered was for a sentence to run concurrently with her existing fifteen year incarceration. Her decision seems mostly predicated on an assessment of which route would lead to her earliest release from prison.

80. See "Three Cleared of Seditious Conspiracy," *New York Times*, November 28, 1989. Additional

analyses of the case may be found in Hoeffle, Paul, and Phil Garber, "Seduced and Abandoned," *Zeta*, February 1989; and Ogden, Don, "Ohio Seven: The Whole Truth Goes Untold," *The Guardian*, September 15, 1989. It should be noted that the acquittals occurred despite court rulings that many defense witnesses – such as the acclaimed historian Howard Zinn – would not be allowed to testify.

81. Ojeda Ríos was accused of shooting an agent in the face on August 30, 1985 when the FBI attempted to kick in the door of his San Juan home. The defendant did not deny firing the shot which struck the agent, but contended that given the agent's behavior, the history of the Bureau's anti-*independentista* COINTELPRO, and the fact that his family were in the apartment, he was justified in shooting. The jury agreed. Prior to his acquittal, Ojeda Ríos had been held without bond – despite having suffered a heart attack while in captivity – for four and a half years. See "Filiberto is Free!," *La Patria Radical*, Vol. 2, No. 2, September 1989.

82. See Churchill, Ward, "The Third Word at Home: Political Prisoners in the United States," *Zeta*, June 1990.

83. See Churchill, Ward, "Wages of COINTELPRO: The Case of Mumia Abu-Jamal," *New Studies on the Left*, Vol. XIV, Nos. 1-2, Spring-Summer 1989, pp. 96-9.

84. The figures are derived from Murphy, Jim, *A Question of Race*, Center for Justice Education, Albany, NY, 1988, Chart I.

85. *Ibid.*, p. 3.

86. For further information, see Austin, James, and Aaron McVey, *The NCCD Prison Population Forecast: The Growing Imprisonment of America*, National Council on Crime and Delinquency, San Francisco, 1988. Also see Nagel, William C., "On Behalf of a Moratorium on Prison Construction," *Crime and Delinquency*, Fall 1977, pp. 154-72.

87. A classic example of this is the FBI's recent assessment that the El Rukn organization is a "primary" instrument of drug commerce in Chicago's south side. Bureau reports conveniently neglect to mention that El Rukn is the current name of what was once known as the Black P. Stone Nation, the entity FBI COINTELPRO specialists used as a counter against the strongly anti-drug Black Panther chapter in that city. Once the Chicago Panthers were destroyed, the P. Stones *cum* Rukns predictably filled the vacuum thus created. For all its present posturing about "combatting drug traffic," the Bureau clearly decided drugs were preferable to social change in Chicago in 1969. The same general dynamic pertains to the notorious Crips and Bloods organizations in Los Angeles. For the latest Bureau propaganda line on the subject, see King, Patricia, "A Snitch's Tale: The Killer Gang (An informer tells about life as an 'El Rukn')," *Newsweek*, November 6, 1989, p. 45.

88. Concerning the CIA's role in establishing modern drug distribution in the United States, see McCoy, Alfred W., with Cathleen B. Read and Leonard P. Adams II, *The Politics of Heroin in Southeast Asia*, Harper Torchbooks, New York, 1972. Also see videotapes of various lectures presented by attorney Daniel Sheehan, *circa* 1984-87, available through the Christic Institute, Washington, D.C. CIA involvement in the more recent cocaine trafficking is also relatively well known; see Scott, Peter Dale, and Jonathon Marshall, *The Politics of Cocaine: Drugs, Contras, and the C.I.A.*, Black Rose Books, Montréal, Canada, 1989.

89. No evidence has ever been disclosed linking the Black Guerrilla Family to any facet of the drug trade. Nonetheless, see Held's assertions to the contrary in the *San Francisco Examiner*, August 25, 1989. This is but one example.

90. Newton's killer shot him in the forehead at pointblank range, then bent over to shoot him twice more in the temple, a very calm and professional execution. The day after the murder, the Oakland police announced it had "no clues" as to the killer's identity, but "suspected" (for unexplained reasons) that the matter was "drug related." On August 24, two days after the murder, the *San Francisco Examiner* ran a story stating that the police had arrested three men fleeing the scene immediately after the event. Oakland police lieutenant Mike Simms quickly convened a press conference to deny the whole thing but, when it turned out that the arrest had been videotaped and the tapes were aired by local TV stations, Simms was forced to admit the department had had "suspects" in custody all along. There were, Simms insisted – contrary to the visual evidence appearing on television – only *two* men apprehended. On the morning of August 25, the police suddenly announced that one of them, 25-year-old Tyrone Robinson was a member of the Black Guerrilla Family and that *therefore* it was almost certainly a drug-related killing. Then, curiously, the police offered the information that Robinson "appeared" to have acted in self-defense after Newton "pulled a gun" during an argument concerning a cocaine debt. The story is

currently being clung to – by police and accused alike – despite the facts that no witnesses overheard an argument (about cocaine or anything else) prior to the shooting, no weapon attributable to Newton was recovered from the scene, and, even if there had been, this would not explain the two shots fired as a *coup de grâce*. Further, no one has yet identified the third man taken into custody by police just after Newton's murder. All told, the death of Huey P. Newton bears every sign of having been a political assassination. For further information, see Saxifrage Group, "Huey P. Newton: Tribute to a Fallen Warrior," *New Studies on the Left*, Vol. XIV, Nos. 1-2, Spring-Summer 1989, pp. 129-35.

91. Concerning Stammheim and the horrors that occur therein, see Ryan, Mike, "The Stammheim Model: Judicial Counterinsurgency," *New Studies on the Left*, Vol. XIV, Nos. 1-2, Spring-Summer 1989, pp. 45-69.

92. Letter from U.S. Bureau of Prisons Director J. Michael Quinlan to Congressman Robert W. Kastenmeier (D., Wis.), September 20, 1987.

93. For more on the Lexington HSU, see O'Melveny, Mary, "U.S. Political Prison: Lexington Prison High Security Unit," *Covert Action Information Bulletin*, No. 31, Winter 1989. It should be mentioned that O'Melveny observes that one BoP official, Southeast Regional Director Gary R. McCune, has acknowledged having attended a special course given by the FBI on how to deal with "terrorists" in prison. McCune is responsible for the Lexington facility. Also see Reuben, William A., and Carlos Norman, "Brainwashing in America? The Women of Lexington Prison," *The Nation*, June 27, 1987, pp. 881-4; and Halsey, Peggy, "Undue Process," *Christianity in Crisis*, Vol. 48, No. 4, March 21, 1989, pp. 81-4.

94. *Report on the U.S. Penitentiary at Marion*, John Howard Association Report, October 1987, p. 1.

95. Quoted in National Committee to Support the Marion Brothers, *Breaking Men's Minds*, Chicago, 1987.

96. Korn, Dr. Richard, *Effects of Confinement in HSU*, study prepared for the ACLU Foundation National Prison Project, 1987; attached to major ACLU report (see note 97, below).

97. Presentation by attorney Jan Susler, University of Colorado at Boulder, March 13, 1988. Also see Rosenberg, Susan, "Reflections on Being Buried Alive," *Covert Action Information Bulletin*, No. 31, Winter 1989; and Silverstrim, Elaine, "The Ordeal of Alejandrina," *The Witness*, Vol. 71, No. 2, February, 1988.

98. See Amnesty International, *The High Security Unit, Lexington Federal Prison, Kentucky*, (AI Index: AMR 51/34/88), New York, 1988. For the ACLU position, see *Report on the High Security Unit for Women, Federal Correctional Institution, Lexington, Kentucky*, National Prison Project of the ACLU Foundation, New York, August 25, 1987.

99. See Baker, Scott, "Activists attack new women's control unit," *The Guardian*, March 23, 1988.

100. See Lyden, Jacki, and Paula Schiller, "The Prison That Defies Reform," *Student Lawyer*, May 1987, pp. 9-17.

101. Conversation with Raphael Cancel Miranda, Mayaguez, Puerto Rico, January 10, 1990.

102. Lyden and Schiller, *op. cit.* It is worth noting that the plan to turn Marion into an experimental "closed" facility was known to prisoners well before the fact. This was apparently a major contributing factor in the "riot" upon which the lock-down was supposedly predicated. Also see Dunne, Bill, "The U.S. Penitentiary at Marion Illinois: An Instrument of Oppression," *New Studies on the Left*, Vol. XIV, Nos. 1-2, Winter-Spring 1989, pp. 9-19.

103. Lyden, Jacki, "Marion Prison: Inside the Lockdown," *All Things Considered* broadcast, October 28, 1986, produced by Paula Schiller, National Public Radio. Transcript published by Committee to End the Marion Lockdown, Chicago, 1987. Also see Cunningham, Dennis, and Jan Susler (eds.), *Transcript of the People's Tribunal to Expose the Crimes of the Marion and Lexington Control Units*, Committee to End the Marion Lockdown, Chicago, October 24, 1987.

104. See Amnesty International, *Allegations of Inmate Treatment in Marion Prison, Illinois, USA*, (AI Index: AMR 51/26187), New York, May 1987. Also see Cunningham, Dennis, and Jan Susler, *A Public Report About a Violent Mass Assault Against Prisoners and Continuing Illegal Punishment and Torture of the Prison Population at the U.S. Penitentiary at Marion, Illinois*, Marion Prisoners Rights Project, Chicago, 1984. Relatedly, see Benjamin, Thomas B., and Kenneth Lux, "Solitary Confinement as Psychological Torture," *California Western Law Review*, 13(265), 1978, pp. 295-6.

105. Judge Parker's decision was rendered in *Baraldini v. Thornburgh*, C.A. 88-5275, 1988: "It is one thing to place persons under greater security because they have escape histories and pose special risks to our correctional institutions. But consigning anyone to a high security unit for past political associations they will never shed unless forced to renounce them is a dangerous mission for this

country's prison system to continue."

106. Rosenberg, Susan, "Growing repression of political prisoners," *Gay Community News*, November 5, 1989, p. 5.

107. Concerning the inception phase of this development program, see Cooper, Lyn, Elliot Curie, Jon Frappier, Tony Platt, Betty Ryan, Richard Schauffler, Joy Scruggs and Larry Trujillo, *The Iron Fist in the Velvet Glove: An Analysis of U.S. Police*, Center for Research on Criminal Justice, Berkeley, CA, 1975, pp. 38-48.

108. For a survey of the sorts of weapons and other technologies in common use by SWAT units, see Dewar, Michael, *Weapons and Equipment of Counter-Terrorism*, Arms and Armor Press, London, 1988. Also see, Churchill, Ward, "To 'Serve and Protect'?" *New Studies on the Left*, Vol. XIV, Nos. 1-2, Spring-Summer, 1989, pp. 205-9.

109. This should by no means be construed as an argument in favor of drugs and/or drug gangs. It is, however, very much an argument in favor of the sort of anti-drug activity undertaken by the OAAU and Black Panther Party in which participants endeavor to take "the streets" – for the first time – not only from the drug dealers but, more importantly, from the state as well. This is posed as a viable alternative to the Bush administration's present war on the black and Latino communities.

110. Gross, Bertram, *Friendly Fascism: The New Face of Power in America*, South End Press, Boston, 1982.

111. See Dutschke, Rudi, "On Anti-authoritarianism," in Carl Oglesby (ed.), *The New Left Reader*, Grove Press, New York, 1969, pp. 243-53.

Bibliography

Books

Albert, Michael, *What Is To Be Undone*, Porter Sargent Publishers, Boston, 1974.

Albert, Stewart, and Judith Clavir-Albert (eds.) *The Sixties Papers: Documents of a Rebellious Decade*, Praeger Publishers, New York, 1984.

Aldeson, Alan, *SDS: A Profile*, Charles Scribner's Sons, Publishers, New York, 1972.

Allen, Gary, *Communist Revolution in the Streets*, Western Islands Publishers, Boston and Los Angeles, 1967.

Alpert, Jane, *Growing Up Underground*, William Morrow and Company, New York, 1981.

Amnesty International, *Report on Torture*, Farrar, Straus and Giroux Publishers, New York, 1975.

_____, *Proposal for a commission of inquiry into the effect of domestic intelligence activities on criminal trials in the United States of America*, Amnesty International, New York, 1980.

Anderson, Robert W., *Party Politics in Puerto Rico*, Stanford University Press, Palo Alto, CA, 1965.

Arlen, Michael J., *An American Verdict*, Doubleday, Inc., Garden City, NJ, 1974.

Armstrong, David, *A Trumpet to Arms: Alternative Media in America*, South End Press, Boston, 1981.

Armstrong, Gregory, *The Dragon Has Come: The Last Fourteen Months in the Life of George Jackson*, Harper and Row Publishers, New York, 1974.

Avorn, Jerry, Andrew Crane, Mark Jaffe, Oren Root, Jr., Paul Starr, Michael Stern and Robert Stulberg, *Up Against the Ivy Wall: A History of the Columbia Crisis*, Atheneum Publishers, New York, 1969.

Auerbach, Jerold S., *Labor and Liberty: The LaFollette Committee and the New Deal*, Bobbs-Merrill Publishers, Indianapolis, 1966.

Austin, James, and Aaron McVey, *The NCCD Prison Population Forecast: The Growing Imprisonment of America*, National Council on Crime and Delinquency, San Francisco, 1988.

Baraka, Amiri, *The Autobiography of LeRoi Jones*, Freundrich Books, New York, 1984.

Barbour, E.D. (ed.), *The Black Power Revolt*, The Sargent Press, Boston, 1968.

Barry, John M., *The Ambition and the Power: The Fall of Jim Wright, A True Story*, Viking Press, New York, 1989.

Becker, Howard S. (ed.), *Campus Power Struggles*, Aldine Publishers, Chicago, 1970.

Becker, Theodore, and Vernon G. Murray (eds.), *Government Lawlessness in America*, Oxford University Press, New York, 1971.

Bell, Inge Powell, *CORE and the Strategy of Nonviolence*, Random House Publishers, New York, 1968.

Bell, Leland V., *In Hitler's Shadow: The Anatomy of American Nazism*, Kennikat Publishers, Port Washington, NY, 1973.

Berbusse, Edward J., *The United States in Puerto Rico, 1898-1900*, University of North Carolina Press, Chapel Hill, 1966.

Belfrage, Sally, *Freedom Summer*, Viking Press, New York, 1965.

Berman, Jerry J., and Morton Halperin (eds.), *The Abuses of Intelligence Agencies*, Center for National Security Studies, Washington, D.C., 1975.

Bernard, Edgar, *et al.*, *Pursuit of Freedom: Civil Liberty in Illinois*, Chicago Civil Liberties Union, 1942.

Bernstein, Irving, *The Lean Years*, Penguin Books, Baltimore, 1966.

_____, *The Turbulent Years*, Houghton-Mifflin Publishers, Boston, 1971.

Berrigan, Daniel, *America is Hard to Find: Notes from the Underground and Danbury Prison*, Doubleday Publishers, Garden City, NY, 1972.

Blackstock, Harry (ed.), *COINTELPRO: The FBI's Secret War on Political Freedom*, Monad Press, New York, 1987.

Blue Cloud, Peter (ed.), *Alcatraz Is Not an Island*, Wingbow Press, Berkeley, CA, 1972.

Boesel, David, and Peter H. Rossi (eds.), *Cities Under Siege: An Anatomy of the Ghetto Riots, 1964-1968*, Basic Books, New York, 1971.

Bracey, John J. Jr., August Meier and Elliott Rudwick (eds.), *Black Nationalism in America*, Bobbs-Merrill Publishers, Indianapolis, 1970.

Brand, Johanna, *The Life and Death of Anna Mae Aquash*, James Lorimer Publishers, Toronto, 1978.

Breitman, George, *The Last Year of Malcolm X: The Evolution of a Revolutionary*, Schocken Publishers, New York, 1968.

Breitman, George, Herman Porter and Baxter Smith (eds.), *The Assassination of Malcolm X*, Pathfinder Press, New York, 1976.

Brown, H. Rap, *Die Nigger Die!*, The Dial Press, Inc., New York, 1969.

Brustein, Robert, *Revolution as Theater: Notes on the New Radical Style*, Liveright Publishers, New York, 1971.

Buitrago, Ann Mari, and Leon Andrew Immerman, *Are You Now or Have You Ever Been in the FBI Files?* Grove Press, New York, 1981.

Burnette, Robert, and John Koster, *The Road to Wounded Knee*, Bantam Books, New York, 1974.

Cagin, Seth, and Philip Dray, *We Are Not Afraid: The Story of Goodman, Schwerner, and Chaney, and the Civil Rights Campaign in Mississippi*, Macmillan Publishers, New York, 1988.

Calvert, Greg, and Carol Neiman, *A Disrupted History: The New Left and the New Capitalism*, Random House Publishers, New York, 1971.

Carmichael, Stokely, and Charles V. Hamilton, *Black Power: The Politics of Liberation in America*, Vintage Books, New York, 1967.

Carson, Clayborne, *In Struggle: SNCC and the Black Awakening of the 1960s*, Harvard University Press, Cambridge, MA, 1981.

Carr, Jimmy, *Bad: The Autobiography of Jimmy Carr*, Herman Graf Associates, New York, 1975.

Carr, Raymond, *Puerto Rico: A Colonial Experiment*, Vintage Books, New York, 1984.

Carr, Robert K., *The House Committee on Un-American Activities*, Cornell University Press, Ithaca, NY, 1952.

Castellucci, John, *The Big Dance: The Untold Story of Weatherman Kathy Boudin and the Terrorist Family That Committed the Brink's Robbery Murders*, Dodd, Mead and Company, New York, 1986.

Caute, David, *The Great Fear: The Anti-Communist Purge Under Truman and Eisenhower*, Simon and Schuster Publishers, New York, 1978.

Chabot Smith, John, *Alger Hiss: The True Story*, Holt, Rinehart and Winston Publishers, New York, 1976.

Chadbourn, James H., *Lynching and the Law*, University of North Carolina Press, Chapel Hill, 1933.

Chafee, Zechariah, *Free Speech in the United States*, Atheneum Publishers, New York, 1969.

Chardwick, Christine M. (ed.), *Litigation Under the Amended Freedom of Information Act*, Center for National Security Studies, Washington, D.C., 1978.

Churchill, Ward (ed.), *Critical Issues in Native North America*, (Vol. I), International Work Group on Indigenous Affairs, Copenhagen, Denmark, 1989.

Churchill, Ward, and Jim Vander Wall, *Agents of Repression: The FBI's Secret Wars Against the Black Panther Party and the American Indian Movement*, South End Press, Boston, 1988.

Citizens Research and Investigation Committee and Louis E. Tackwood, *The Glass House Tapes: The Story of An Agent Provocateur and the New Police-Intelligence Complex*, Avon Books, New York, 1973.

Clark, Howard, *American Saturday*, Richard Marek Publishers, New York, 1981.

Clark, Larry D., *The Grand Jury: The Use and Abuse of Political Power*, Quadrangle Books, Chicago, 1975.

Clavir, Judy, and John Spitzer (eds.), *The Conspiracy Trial*, Bobbs-Merrill Company, Indianapolis, 1970.

Cleaver, Eldridge, *Soul on Ice*, Delta Books, New York, 1968.

_____, *Post-Prison Writings and Speeches*, Ramparts/Vintage Books, New York, 1969.

_____, *Soul on Fire*, World Books, Waco, TX, 1978.

Coates, Jim, *Armed and Dangerous: The Rise of the Survivalist Right*, The Noonday Press, New York, 1987.

Cohen, Mitchell, and Dennis Hale (eds.), *The New Student Left: An Anthology*, Beacon Press, Boston, (Revised and Expanded Edition) 1967.

Coben Stanley, *A. Mitchell Palmer: Politician*, Columbia University Press, New York, 1963.

Cohen, Stanley, and Jock Young (eds.), *The Manufacture of the News*, Sage Publications, Beverley Hills, CA, 1973.

Cohn-Bendit, Daniel, *Obsolete Communism: The Left-Wing Alternative*, McGraw-Hill Publishers, New York, 1968.

Commission of Inquiry Into the Black Panthers and the Police, *Search and Destroy*, Metropolitan Applied Research Center, New York, 1973.

Committee to End the Marion Lockdown, *Can't Jail the Spirit: Political Prisoners in the U.S.*, Chicago, 1989.

Cook, Fred J., *The Unfinished Story of Alger Hiss*, William Morrow Company, New York, 1958.

_____, *The FBI Nobody Knows*, Pyramid Press, New York, 1965.

Cooper, Lyn, Elliot Curie, Jon Frappier, Tony Platt, Betty Ryan, Richard Schauffler, Joy Scruggs and Larry Trujillo, *The Iron Fist in the Velvet Glove: An Analysis of U.S. Police*, Center for Research on Criminal Justice, Berkeley, CA, 1975.

Copeland, Vincent, *The Crime of Martin Sostre*, McGraw-Hill Publishers, New York, 1970.

Coulter, Robert K., "Federal Law and Indian Tribal Law: The Right to Civil Counsel and the 1968 Indian Bill of Rights," *Columbia Survey of Human Rights Law, Volume 3*, Deford and Company, Baltimore, MD, 1971.

Cowan, Paul, Nick Egelson, and Nat Hentoff, with Barbara Herbert and Robert Wall (eds.), *State Secrets: Police Surveillance in America*, Holt, Rinehart and Winston Publishers, New York, 1974.

Cray, Ed, *The Enemy in the Streets*, Doubleday Publishers, Garden City, NY, 1972.

Cronon, E. Davis, *Black Moses: The Story of Marcus Garvey and the United Negro Improvement Association*, University of Wisconsin Press, Madison, 1955.

Davies, Peter, *The Truth About Kent State: Challenge for the American Conscience*, Farrar, Straus and Giroux Publishers, New York, 1973.

Davis, Angela Y., *et al.*, *If They Come In The Morning*, Signet Books, New York, 1971.

Davis, David Bryan, *The Fear of Conspiracy*, Cornell University Press, Ithaca, NY, 1971.

Deloria, Vine Jr., *Custer Died For Your Sins: An Indian Manifesto*, Macmillan Publishers, New York, 1969.

_____, *We Talk, You Listen: New Tribes, New Turf*, Macmillan Publishers, New York, 1970.

_____, *Behind the Trail of Broken Treaties: An Indian Declaration of Independence*, Delta Books, New York, 1974.

Dinges, John, and Saul Landau, *Assassination on Embassy Row*, Pantheon Publishers, New York, 1980.

Dewar, Michael, *Weapons and Equipment of Counter-Terrorism*, Arms and Armour Press, London, 1988.

Divale, William Tulio, with Joseph James, *I Lived Inside the Campus Revolution*, Cowels Book Company, Los Angeles, 1973.

Draper, Theodore, *The Roots of American Communism*, Viking Press, New York, 1963.

DuBois, W.E.B., *The Autobiography of W.E.B. DuBois: A Soliloquy on Viewing My Life From the Last Decade of Its First Century*, International Publishers, New York, 1968.

Dunbar Ortiz, Roxanne (ed.), *The Great Sioux Nation: Sitting in Judgement on America*, International Indian Treaty Council/Moon Books, New York/San Francisco, 1977.

Durden-Smith, Jo, *Who Killed George Jackson? Fantasies, Paranoia and the Revolution*, Alfred A. Knopf Publishers, New York, 1976.

Editors of *Akwesasne Notes*, *BIA, I'm Not Your Indian Anymore: Trail of Broken Treaties*, Mohawk Nation via Rooseveltown, NY, 1973.

_____, *Voices From Wounded Knee, 1973*, Mohawk Nation via Rooseveltown, NY, 1974.

Editors, *The Senate Watergate Report*, Bantam Books, New York, 1975.

Editors of *Rolling Stone*, *The Age of Paranoia*, Pocket Books, New York, 1972.

Editors of *U.S. News and World Report*, *Communism and the New Left: What They're Up to Now*, Collier/Macmillan Company, London, 1969.

Elliff, John T., *Crime, Dissent and the Attorney General*, Sage Publications, Beverly Hills, CA, 1971.

Ellsberg, Daniel, *Papers on the War*, Pocket Books, New York, 1972.

Emerson, Thomas I., *The System of Freedom of Expression*, Vintage Books, New York, 1970.

Emerson, Thomas I., David Haber and Norman Dorsen, *Political and Civil Rights in the United States*, Little, Brown Publishers, Boston, 1967.

Epstein, Jason, *The Great Conspiracy Trial: An Essay on Law, Liberty and the Constitution*, Random House Publishers, New York, 1970.

Erikson, Erik H., and Huey P. Newton, *In Search of Common Ground*, W.W. Norton, Inc., New York, 1973.

Evelegh, Robin, *Peace-Keeping in a Democratic Society: The Lessons of Northern Ireland*, C. Hurst and Company, London, 1978.

Farmer, James, *Lay Bare the Heart*, Alfred A. Knopf Publishers, New York, 1985.

Ferber, Michael, and Staughton Lynd, *The Resistance*, Beacon Press, Boston, 1971.

Fernandez, Ronald, *Los Macheteros: The Wells Fargo Robbery and the Violent Struggle for Puerto Rican Independence*, Prentice-Hall Publishers, New York, 1987

Figueroa, Loida, *History of Puerto Rico*, Anaya Books, New York, 1974.

Flynn, Kevin, and Gary Gebhardt, *The Silent Brotherhood: Inside America's Racist Underground*, The Free Press, New York, 1989.

Foner, Philip S. (ed.), *The Black Panthers Speak*, J.B. Lippincott Company, Philadelphia/New York, 1970.

Foster, Julian, and Durward Long, *Protest! Student Activism in America*, Morrow Publishers, New York, 1970.

Frankfort, Ellen, *Kathy Boudin and the Dance of Death*, Stein and Day Publishers, New York, 1983.

Franklin, Bruce (ed.), *From the Movement Toward Revolution*, Van Nostrum Publishing Company, New York, 1971.

Freed, Donald, *Agony in New Haven: The Trial of Bobby Seale, Ericka Huggins and the Black Panther Party*, Simon and Schuster Publishers, New York, 1973.

Forman, James, *The Making of Black Revolutionaries*, Macmillan Publishers, New York, 1972.

Garrow, David J., *The FBI and Dr. Martin Luther King, Jr.*, Penguin Books, New York, 1981.

Gartner, Alan, Colin Greer and Frank Reisman (eds.), *What Nixon is Doing to Us*, Harper and Row Publishers, New York, 1973.

Garvey, Amy Jaques (ed.), *Philosophy and Opinion of Marcus Garvey, or Africa for Africans*, Frank Cass and Co., London, 1967.

Gavel, Senator Mike, *The Pentagon Papers: The Defense Department History of United States Decision-making on Vietnam*, (four volumes), Beacon Press, Boston, 1971.

Gid Powers, Richard, *Secrecy and Power: The Life of J. Edgar Hoover*, The Free Press, New York, 1987.

Gilbert, Ben W., *et al.*, *Ten Blocks From the White House: Anatomy of the Washington Riots of 1968*, Praeger Publishers, New York, 1968.

Gitlin, Todd, *The Whole World Is Watching: Mass Media in the Making and Unmaking of the New Left*, University of California Press, Berkeley, 1980.

_____, *The Sixties: Years of Hope, Days of Rage*, Bantam Books, New York, 1987.

Gitlin, Todd, and Nanci Hollander, *Uptown: Poor Whites in Chicago*, Harper and Row Publishers, New York, 1970.

Glessing, Robert J., The Underground Press in America, University of Indiana Press, Bloomington, 1971.

Glick, Brian, *War at Home: Covert Action Against U.S. Activists and What We Can Do About It*, South End Press, Boston, 1989.

Goldstein, Robert Justin, *Political Repression in Modern America, 1870 to the Present*, Schenckman Publishing Co./Two Continents Publishing Group, Ltd., Cambridge/London, 1978.

Goodell, Charles, *Political Prisoners in America*, Random House Publishers, New York, 1973.

Goodman, Mitchell (ed.), *The Movement Toward a New America: The Beginnings of a Long Revolution*, Knopf/Pilgrim Press, New York/Philadelphia, 1970.

Grant, Joanne, *Confrontation on Campus*, Signet Books, New York, 1969.

Grathwohl, Larry, as told to Frank Reagan, *Bringing Down America: An FBI Informer in the Weathermen*, Arlington House Publishers, New Rochelle, NY, 1976.

Gross, Bertram, *Friendly Fascism: The New Face of Power in America*, South End Press, Boston, 1982.

Gunther, Gerald, and Noel T. Dowling, *Constitutional Law and Individual Rights, 1974 Supplement*, Ford Foundation Press, New York, 1974.

Harris, William H., *Keeping the Faith: A. Philip Randolph, Milton P. Webster, and the Brotherhood of Sleeping Car Porters*, University of Illinois Press, Urbana, 1977.

Harris, Richard, *Justice*, Avon Books, New York, 1970.

Hayden, Tom, *Rebellion in Newark: Official Violence and Ghetto Response*, Vintage Books, New York, 1967.

_____, *Rebellion and Repression*, World Publishing Company, Cleveland, OH, 1969.

_____, *Trial*, Holt, Rinehart and Winston Publishers, New York, 1970.

Herman, Edward S., *The Real Terror Network: Terrorism in Fact and Propaganda*, South End Press, Boston, 1982.

Hersey, John, *The Algiers Motel Incident*, Alfred A. Knopf Publishers, New York, 1968.

Hersh, Seymour, *The Price of Power*, Simon and Schuster Publishers, New York, 1983.

Hinds, Lennox S., *Illusions of Justice: Human Rights Violations in the United States*, Iowa School of Social Work, Iowa State University, Iowa City, 1978.

Hirsch, Arthur, *The French New Left: An Intellectual History from Sartre to Gorz*, South End Press, Boston, 1981.

Hoffman, Abbie, *Revolution for the Hell of It*, Dial Press, New York, 1968.

_____, *Woodstock Nation*, Vintage Books, New York, 1969.

_____, *Soon to be a Major Motion Picture*, G.P. Putnam's Sons, Publishers, New York, 1980.

_____, *Square Dancing in the Ice Age*, South End Press, Boston, 1982.

Hoffman, Anita, and Abbie Hoffman, *To America With Love: Letters from the Underground*, Stone Hill Publishing Company, New York, 1976.

Hoffman, Paul, *Moratorium: An American Protest*, Tower Books, New York, 1973.

Holt, Len, *The Summer That Didn't End*, Morrow Publishers, New York, 1965.

Horne, Gerald, *Communist Front? The Civil Rights Congress, 1946-1956*, Fairleigh Dickinson University Press, Rutherford, NJ, 1988.

Howe, Irving, and Lewis Coser, *The American Communist Party*, Praeger Publishers, New York, 1962.

Huie, William Bradford, *Three Lives for Mississippi*, WCC Publishers, New York, 1965.

Jackson, George, *Soledad Brother: The Prison Letters of George Jackson*, Coward-McCann Publishers, New York, 1973.

_____, *Blood In My Eye*, Random House Publishers, New York, 1972.

Jacobs, Harold (ed.), *Weatherman*, Ramparts Press, San Francisco, 1970.

Jacobs, Paul, and Saul Landau (eds.), *The New Radicals*, Random House Publishers, New York, 1966.

Jaffe, Julian K., *Crusade Against Radicalism: New York During the Red Scare*, Kennikat Publishers, Port Washington, NY, 1972.

Jayko, Margaret (ed.), *FBI on Trial: The Victory in the Socialist Workers Party Suit Against Government Spying*, Pathfinder Press, New York, 1988.

Jensen, Vernon H., *The Price of Vigilance*, Rand-McNally Publishers, Chicago, 1968.

Johnpole, Bernard K., *Pacifist's Progress: Norman Thomas and the Decline of American Socialism*, Quadrangle Books, Chicago, 1970.

Johansen, Bruce and Roberto Maestas, *Wasíchu: The Continuing Indian Wars*, Monthly Review Press, New York, 1979.

Johnson, Donald, *The Challenge of American Freedoms*, University of Kentucky Press, Lexington, 1963.

Johnson, Loch, *A Season of Inquiry: The Senate Intelligence Investigation*, University of Kentucky Press, Lexington, 1985.

Johnson, R.A., *Puerto Rico: Commonwealth or Colony?* Praeger Publishers, New York, 1980.

Joseph, Paul, *Cracks in the Empire: State Politics in the Vietnam War*, South End Press, Boston, 1981.

Josephy, Alvin Jr., *Now That the Buffalo's Gone: A Study of Today's Indians*, Alfred A. Knopf Publishers, New York, 1982.

Kahn, Roger, *The Battle for Morningside Heights*, William Morrow and Company, New York, 1970.

Karenga, Maulana (Ron), *Roots of the US/Panther Conflict*, Kawaida Publications, San Diego, 1976.

Katsiaficas, George, *The Imagination of the New Left: A Global Analysis of 1968*, South End Press, Boston, 1987.

Keating, Edward M., *Free Huey! The True Story of the Trial of Huey P. Newton for Murder*, Ramparts Press, Berkeley, CA, 1971.

Kelner, Joseph, and James Munves, *The Kent State Coverup*, Harper and Row Publishers, New York, 1980.

Kempton, Murray, *The Briar Patch: The People of the State of New York v. Lumumba Shakur, et al.*, E.P. Dutton Company, New York, 1973.

Kennebeck, Edwin, *Juror Number Four: The Trial of Thirteen Black Panthers as Seen From the Jury Box*, W.W. Norton and Company, New York, 1973.

Kenniston, Kenneth (ed.), *The Young Radicals*, Harcourt, Brace and World Publishers, New York, 1968.

Kent, Rockwell, *It's Me O Lord*, Dodd-Mead Publishers, New York, 1965.

King, Coretta Scott, *My Life With Martin Luther King, Jr.*, Holt, Rinehart and Winston Publishers, New York, 1969.

King, Martin Luther Jr., *Stride Toward Freedom*, Harper and Brothers Publishers, New York, 1958.

King, Mary, *Freedom Song*, W.W. Norton Publishers, New York, 1987.

Kinshasa, Kwando, *Urban Guerrilla Warfare*, Revolutionary People's Communication Network, New York, 1969.

Kirchheimer, Otto, *Political Justice: The Use of Legal Procedure for Political Ends*, Princeton University Press, Princeton, NJ, 1969.

Kitson, Frank, *Low Intensity Operations: Subversion, Insurgency and Peace-Keeping*, Stackpole Books, Harrisburg, PA, 1971.

Klare, Michael T., and Peter Kornbluh (eds.), *Low Intensity Warfare: Counterinsurgency, Proinsurgency and Antiterrorism in the Eighties*, Pantheon Publishers, New York, 1988.

Kreuger, Thomas A., *And Promises to Keep: The Southern Conference on Human Welfare*, Vanderbilt University Press, Nashville, TN, 1963.

Lane, Mark, and Dick Gregory, *Code Name "Zorro": The Assassination of Martin Luther King, Jr.*, Prentice-Hall Publishers, Englewood Cliffs, NJ, 1977.

Larrowe, Charles P., *Harry Bridges: The Rise and Fall of Radical Labor*, Lawrence Hill Publisher, New York, 1972.

Lasch, Christopher, *The Agony of the American Left*, Random House Publishers, New York, 1969.

Lasky, Victor, *It Didn't Start With Watergate*, Dell Books, New York, 1978.

Lauter, Paul, and Florence Howe (eds.), *Trials of the Resistance*, Vintage Books, New York, 1970.

Lawrence, Ken, *The New State Repression*, International Network Against the New State Repression, Chicago, 1985.

Leamer, Laurence, *The Paper Revolutionaries: The Rise of the Underground Press*, Simon and Schuster Publishers, New York, 1970.

Lester, Julius, *Look Out Whitey! Black Power Gon' Get Your Momma*, Grove Press, New York, 1969.

Levine, Mark, *et. al.* (eds.), *The Tales of Hoffman*, Bantam Books, New York, 1970.

Levin, Murray, *Hysteria in America: The Democratic Capacity for Repression*, Basic Books, New York, 1971.

Lewis, Alfred Allan, and Herbert Leon MacDonell, *The Evidence Never Lies: The Casebook of a Modern Sherlock Holmes*, Holt, Rinehart and Winston, New York, 1984.

Lewis, David L., *King: A Biography*, University of Illinois Press, Urbana, 1979.

Lipset, Seymore M., and Sheldon S. Wolin (eds.), *The Berkeley Student Revolt*, Doubleday Publishers, Garden City, NY, 1965.

Lisio, Donald J., *The President and Protest: Hoover, Conspiracy and the Bonus Riot*, University of Missouri Press, Columbia, 1974.

Lockwood, Lee, *Conversation with Eldridge Cleaver in Algiers*, Delta Books, New York, 1970.

Long, Priscilla (ed.), *The New Left*, Porter Sargent Publishers, Boston, 1969.

López, Alfredo, *Doña Licha's Island: Modern Colonialism in Puerto Rico*, South End Press, Boston, 1988.

López, José (ed.), *Puerto Rican Nationalism: A Reader*, Editorial Coqui, Chicago, 1971.

Lowenthal, Max, *The Federal Bureau of Investigation*, Harcourt-Brace Publishers, New York, 1950.

Lucas, J. Anthony, *The Barnyard Epithet and Other Obscenities: Notes on the Chicago Conspiracy Trial*, Harper and Row Publishers, New York, 1970.

Luce, Phillip Abbott, *The New Left*, David McKay Publishers, New York, 1966.

Lynd, Staughton, and Thomas Hayden, *The Other Side*, New American Library, New York, 1966.

MacLear, Michael, *The Ten Thousand Day War: Vietnam, 1945-1975*, St. Martin's Press, New York, 1981.

Mailer, Norman, *Armies of the Night: History as a Novel, The Novel as History*, New American Library, New York, 1968.

Major, Reginald, *A Panther is a Black Cat: A Study In Depth of the Black Panther Party – Its Origins, Goals, Its Struggle for Survival*, William Morrow and Company, New York, 1971.

Manchester, William, *The Glory and the Dream*, Bantam Books, New York, 1975.

Marable, Manning, *From the Grassroots: Social and Political Essays Towards Afro-American Liberation*, South End Press, Boston, 1980.

_____, *Blackwater: Historical Studies in Race, Class Consciousness, and Revolution*, Black Praxis Press, Dayton, OH, 1981.

_____, *Race, Reform and Rebellion: The Second Reconstruction in Black America, 1945-1982*, University of Mississippi Press, Jackson, 1984.

Matthews, Thomas, *Puerto Rican Political Parties and the New Deal*, University of Florida Press, Gainesville, 1960.

Matthiessen, Peter, *In the Spirit of Crazy Horse*, Viking Press, New York, 1984.

Marine, Gene, *The Black Panthers*, New American Library, New York, 1969.

McCord, William, *Mississippi: The Long Hot Summer*, W.W. Norton Publishers, New York, 1965.

McCoy, Alfred W., with Cathleen B. Read and Leonard P. Adams II, *The Politics of Heroin in Southeast Asia*, Harper Torchbooks, New York, 1972.

McWilliams, Carey, *Factories in the Fields*, Peregrine Press, Santa Barbara, CA, 1971.

Meier, August, and Elliott Rudwick, *CORE: A Study in the Civil Rights Movement*, Oxford University Press, New York, 1973.

Meltzner, Michael, and Victor Navasky (eds.), *The "Trial" of Bobby Seale*, Priam Books, New York, 1970.

Melville, Samuel, *Letters From Attica*, William Morrow and Company, New York, 1972.

Miller, James, *"Democracy is in the Streets": From Port Huron to the Siege of Chicago*, Simon and Schuster Publishers, New York, 1987.

Mitford, Jessica, *The Trial of Dr. Spock, The Reverend William Sloan Coffin, Jr., Michael Ferber, Mitchell Goodman, and Marcus Raskin*, Vintage Books, New York, 1970.

Moody, Anne, *Coming of Age in Mississippi*, Dial Press, New York, 1968.

Moore, Gilbert, *A Special Rage*, Harper and Row Publishers, New York, 1972.

Morales Carrión, Arturo, *Puerto Rico: A Political and Social History*, W.W. Norton Publishers, New York, 1983.

Morlan, Robert L., *Political Prairie Fire: The Non-Partisan League, 1915-1922*, University of Minnesota Press, Minneapolis, 1955.

Murphy, Jim, *A Question of Race*, Center for Justice Education, Albany, NY, 1988.

Murray, Robert K., *Red Scare: A Study in National Hysteria*, McGraw-Hill Publishers, New York, 1964.

Navasky, Victor, *Kennedy Justice*, Atheneum Publishers, New York, 1971.

Nelson, Anne, *Murder Under Two Flags: The U.S., Puerto Rico and the Cerro Maravilla Cover-Up*, Ticknor and Fields Publishers, New York, 1986.

Nelson, Jack, and Ronald J. Ostrow, *The FBI and the Berrigans: The Making of a Conspiracy*, Coward, McCann and Geoghegan, Inc., New York, 1972.

Newfield, Jack, *A Prophetic Minority*, New American Library, New York, 1966.

Newton, Huey P., *Revolutionary Suicide*, Harcourt Brace Jovanovich, Inc., New York, 1973.

_____, *To Die for the People*, Vintage Books, New York, 1972.

Noggel, Earl, *Into the Twenties: The United States from Armistice to Normalcy*, University of Illinois Press, Urbana, 1974.

Obadele, Imari Abubakari, *Foundations of the Black Nation: A Textbook of Ideas Behind the New Black Nationalism and the Struggle for Land in America*, House of Songhay, Detroit, 1975.

_____, *Free the Land! The True Story of the RNA 11 in Mississippi*, House of Songhay, Washington, D.C., 1984.

Ogden, August R., *The Dies Committee*, Catholic University Press, Washington, D.C., 1945.

Oglesby, Carl (ed.), *The New Left Reader*, Grove Press, New York, 1969.

O'Reilly, Kenneth, *"Racial Matters:" The FBI's Secret Files on Black America, 1960-1972*, The Free Press, New York, 1989.

Overstreet, Harry, and Bonarao Overstreet, *The FBI in Our Open Society*, W.W. Norton Publishers, New York, 1969.

Pagán, Bolívar, *Historia de los Partidos Políticos Puertorriqueños, 1898-1956*, Tomo I, San Juan, Puerto Rico, 1972.

Patterson, James T., *Congressional Conservatism and the New Deal*, University of Kentucky Press, Lexington, 1967.

Panther 21 Defendants, *Look for Me in the Whirlwind*, Revolutionary People's Communication Network, New York, 1971.

Parenti, Michael, *Democracy for the Few*, St. Martin's Press, New York, 1980.

Peters, Charles, and Taylor Branch (eds.), *Blowing the Whistle*, Praeger Publishers, New York, 1972.

Peck, James, *Freedom Ride*, Simon and Schuster Publishers, New York, 1962.

Perkus, Cathy (ed.), *COINTELPRO: The FBI's Secret War on Political Freedom*, Monad Press, New York, 1975.

Pinkney, Alphonso, *The American Way of Violence*, Vintage Books, New York, 1972.

_____, *Red, Black, and Green: Black Nationalism in the United States*, Cambridge University Press, New York, 1976.

Porter, William E., *Assault on the Media: The Nixon Years*, University of Michigan Press, Ann Arbor, 1976.

Potter, Paul, *A Name for Ourselves*, Little, Brown and Company, New York, 1971.

Powers, Thomas, *Diana: The Making of a Terrorist*, Houghton-Mifflin Publishers, New York. 1971.

_____, *The War at Home: Vietnam and the American People, 1964-1968*, Grossman Publishers, New York, 1973.

Preston, William Jr., *Aliens and Dissenters*, Harper and Row Publishers, New York, 1966.

Priaulx, Allan, and Sanford J. Ungar, *The Almost Revolution: France – 1968*, Dell Books, New York, 1969.

Price, Monroe E., *Law and the American Indian: Readings, Notes and Cases*, Bobbs-Merrill Co., Minneapolis, 1973.

Rader, Dotson, *I Ain't Marchin' Anymore*, Paperback Library, New York, 1969.

Ribes Tovar, Federico, *Albizu Campos*, Plus Ultra Press, New York, 1971.

Richards, David, *Played Out: The Jean Seberg Story*, Playboy Press, New York, 1981.

Rockefeller, Vice President Nelson, *Report to the President by the Commission on CIA Activities Within the United States*, Manor Publishers, New York, 1975.

Roper, Arthur, F. *The Tragedy of Lynching*, University of North Carolina Press, Chapel Hill, 1932.

Rosenstone, Robert A., *Romantic Revolutionary: A Biography of John Reed*, Vintage Books, New York, 1981.

Rothschild, Mary Aikin, *A Case of Black and White: Northern Volunteers and the Southern Freedom Summers, 1964-1965*, Greenwood Press, Westport, CT, 1982.

Rowe, Gary Thomas Jr., *My Undercover Years with the Ku Klux Klan*, Bantam Books, New York, 1976.

Rubin, Jerry, *Do It!*, Simon and Schuster Publishers, New York, 1969.

_____, *Growing Up at 37*, M. Evans Publishers, New York, 1976.

Sale, Kirkpatrick, *SDS*, Random House Publishers, New York, 1973.

Schanche, Don A., *The Panther Paradox: A Liberal's Dilemma*, David McKay Publishers, New York, 1970.

Schlesinger, Arthur M., *The Crisis of the Old Order*, Houghton-Mifflin Publishers, Boston, 1966.

Schrag, Peter, *Test of Loyalty*, Simon and Schuster Publishers, New York, 1974.

Schultz, John, *No One Was Killed: Convention Week, Chicago – August 1968*, Big Table Publishing Company, Chicago, 1969.

_____, *Motion Will Be Denied: A New Report on the Chicago Conspiracy Trial*, William Morrow and Company, New York, 1970.

Scott, Peter Dale, and Jonathan Marshall, *The Politics of Cocaine: Drugs, Contras, and the C.I.A.*, Black Rose Books, Montréal, Canada, 1989.

Seale, Bobby, *Seize the Time: The True Story of the Black Panther Party and Huey P. Newton*, Vintage Books, New York, 1970.

_____, *A Lonely Rage*, Times Books, New York, 1978.

Sellers, Cleveland, and Robert Terrell, *The River of No Return: The Autobiography of a Black Militant and the Life and Death of SNCC*, William Morrow Publishers, New York, 1973.

Sentner, David, *How the FBI Gets Its Man*, Avon Books, New York, 1965.

Shakur, Assata, *Assata: An Autobiography*, Lawrence Hill Publishers, Westport, CT, 1987.

Shannon, David, *The Socialist Party of America*, Quadrangle Books, Chicago, 1967.

Smith, Geoffrey, *To Save a Nation: American Countersubversives, the New Deal and the Coming of World War II*, Basic Books, New York, 1973.

Stark, Rodney, *Police Riots*, Wadsworth Publishers, Belmont, CA, 1972.

Stavins, Ralph, Richard J. Barnet and Marcus G. Raskin, *Washington Plans an Aggressive War*, Random House Publishers, New York, 1971.

Steedman, Albert A., *Chief!*, Avon Books, New York, 1975.

Stiner, Stan, *The New Indians*, Delta Books, New York, 1968.

Stone, I.F., *The Killings at Kent State*, Vintage Books, New York, 1971.

Suarez, Manuel, *Requiem on Cerro Maravilla: The Police Murders in Puerto Rico and the U.S. Government Coverup*, Waterfront Press, Maplewood, NJ, 1987.

Sullivan, William C., with Bill Brown, *The Bureau: My Thirty Years with Hoover's FBI*, W.W. Norton Co., New York, 1975.

Sussman, Barry, *The Great Cover-Up: Nixon and the Scandal of Watergate*, Signet Books, New York, 1974.

Sutherland, Elizabeth, *Letters From Mississippi*, McGraw-Hill Publishers, New York, 1965.

Tani, E., and Kaé Sera, *False Nationalism/False Internationalism: Class Contradictions in Armed Struggle*, Seeds Beneath the Snow Publications, Chicago, 1985.

Teodori, Massimo (ed.), *The New Left: A Documentary History*, Bobbs-Merrill Company, Indianapolis, 1969.

Theoharis, Athan, *The Yalta Myths: An Issue in U.S. Politics, 1945-1955*, University of Missouri Press, Columbia, 1970.

_____, *The Seeds of Repression: Harry S. Truman and the Origins of McCarthyism*, Quadrangle Books, Chicago, 1971.

_____, *Spying on Americans: Political Surveillance from Hoover to the Huston Plan*, Temple University Press, Philadelphia, 1978.

_____, *The Truman Presidency: The Origins of the Imperial Presidency and the National Security State*, E.M. Coleman Enterprises, New York, 1982.

Theoharis, Athan, *Beyond the Hiss Case: The FBI, Congress and the Cold War*, Temple University Press, Philadelphia, 1982.

Theoharis, Athan, and Robert Griffith (eds.), *The Specter: Original Essays on the Cold War and the Origins of McCarthyism*, New View Points, New York, 1974.

Theoharis, Athan, and John Stuart Cox, *The Boss: J. Edgar Hoover and the Great American Inquisition*, Temple University Press, Philadelphia, 1988.

Thomas, William R., *The Burger Court and Civil Liberties*, King's Court Press, Brunswick, OH, 1976.

Tiger, Edith (ed.), *In Re Alger Hiss*, Hill and Wang Publishers, New York, 1979.

Tindall, George B., *The Emergence of the New South*, Louisiana State University Press, Baton Rouge, 1967.

Torres, J. Benjamin, *Pedro Albizu Campos Obras Escogodes*, (three volumes), Editorial Jelofe, San Juan, Puerto Rico, 1975.

Touraine, Alain, *The May Movement: Revolt and Reform*, Random House Books, New York, 1971.

Tully, Andrew, *The FBI's Most Famous Cases*, Morrow Publishers, New York, 1965.

Ungar, Sanford J., *The Papers and the Papers: An Account of the Legal and Political Battle Over the Pentagon Papers*, E.P. Dutton Publishers, New York, 1975.

_____, *FBI: An Uncensored Look Behind the Walls*, Little, Brown and Co., Boston, 1976.

Vincent, Ted, *Black Power and the Garvey Movement*, Nzinga Publishing House, Oakland, CA, 1987.

Von Hoffman, Nicholas, *Mississippi Notebook*, David White Publishers, New York, 1964.

Walker, Daniel, *Rights in Conflict, the Violent Confrontation of Chicago During the Week of the Democratic National Convention: A Report to the National Commission on the Causes and Prevention of Violence*, Bantam Books, New York, 1968.

Walker, Pat (ed.), *Between Labor and Capital: The Professional-Managerial Class*, South End Press, Boston, 1979.

Weather Underground Organization, *Prairie Fire: The Politics of Revolutionary Anti-Imperialism*, Bay Area Prairie Fire Organizing Committee, San Francisco, 1974.

Welch, Neil J., and David W. Marston, *Inside Hoover's FBI*, Doubleday Publishers, Garden City, NY, 1984.

Weinstein, Allen, *Perjury: The Hiss-Chambers Case*, Alfred A. Knopf Publisher, New York, 1978.

Wells, Henry, *The Modernization of Puerto Rico: A Political Study of Changing Values and Institutions*, Harvard University Press, Cambridge, MA, 1969.

Weyler, Rex, *Blood of the Land: The U.S. Government and Corporate War Against the American Indian Movement*, Vintage Books, New York, 1984.

White, Walter, *Rope and Faggot: A Biography of Judge Lynch*, Arno Press, New York, 1969.

Whitehead, Don, *Attack on Terror: The FBI Against the Ku Klux Klan in Mississippi*, Funk and Wagnall's, New York, 1970.

Wilkerson, Frank, *The Era of Libertarian Repression – 1948-1973: from Congressman to President, with Substantial Support from the Liberal Establishment*, University of Akron Press, Akron, Ohio, 1974.

Williams, Robert F., *Negroes With Guns*, Third World Press, Chicago, 1973.

Williamson, Joel, *The Crucible of Race: Black-White Relations in the American South Since Emancipation*, Oxford University Press, New York, 1984.

Winick, Charles (ed.), *Deviance and the Mass Media*, Sage Publications, Beverly Hills, CA, 1978.

Wise, David, *The American Police State: The Government Against the People*, Vintage Books, New York, 1976.

Wolfe, Tom, *Radical Chic and Mau Mauing the Flak Catchers*, Farrar, Straus and Giroux, New York, 1970.

Wolin, Sheldon S., and John H. Schaar (eds.), *The Berkeley Rebellion and Beyond*, New York Review of Books, New York, 1970.

Woodward, C. Vann, *The Strange Career of Jim Crow*, Oxford University Press, New York, (Third Revised Edition) 1974.

Wright, Nathan, *Black Power and Urban Unrest: Creative Possibilities*, Hawthorn Books, Inc., New York, 1967.

Yee, Min S., *The Melancholy History of Soledad Prison: In Which A Utopian Scheme Turns Bedlam*, Harpers Magazine Press, New York, 1973.

Zavala, Iris, and Rafaél Rodríguez (eds.), *The Intellectual Roots of Independence: An Anthology of Puerto Rican Political Essays*, Monthly Review Press, New York, 1972.

Zimmerman, Bill, *Airlift to Wounded Knee*, Swallow Press, Chicago, 1976.

Zimroth, Peter L., *Perversions of Justice: The Prosecution and Acquittal of the Panther 21*, Viking Press, New York, 1974.

Zinn, Howard, *SNCC: The New Abolitionists*, Beacon Press, Boston, 1964.

_____, *A People's History of the United States*, Harper and Row Publishers, New York, 1980.

Articles

Adam, Hussein A., "Frantz Fanon: His 'Understanding'," *Black World*, No. 21, December 1971.

Adams, J.P., "AIM and the FBI," *Christian Century*, No. 92, April 2, 1975.

_____, "AIM, the Church, and the FBI: The Douglass Durham Case," *Christian Century*, No. 92, May 14, 1975.

Allen, Robert L., "Black Liberation and the Presidential Race," *Black Scholar*, No. 4, September 1972.

Anonymous, "Unsettled Accounts," *Berkeley Tribe*, August 21, 1970.

_____, "Pine Ridge After Wounded Knee: The Terror Goes On," *Akwesasne Notes*, Early Summer 1975.

_____, "Anatomy of an Informer," *Akwesasne Notes*, Early Summer 1975.

_____, "Wounded Knee Trials Go On – The Invisible Man in Phoenix and an FBI Behind Every Mailbox," *Akwesasne Notes*, Early Summer 1975.

_____, "Who Are the Real Terrorists?" *Akwesasne Notes*, Late Fall 1976.

_____, "A Collective Dedication: Ten Years After the Murder of Fred Hampton," *Keep Strong*, December 1979/January 1980.

_____, "FBI Harassment of the Black Community," *Bilalian News*, January 1980.

Antarah, Obi, "A Blueprint for Black Liberation," *Black World*, No. 22, October 1973.

Ashley, Karen, Bill Ayers, Bernardine Dohrn, John Jacobs, Jeff Jones, Gerry Long, Howie Matchinger, Jim Mellen, Terry Robbins, Mark Rudd, and Steve Tappis, "You Don't Need a Weatherman to Know Which Way the Wind Blows," *New Left Notes*, June 18, 1969.

Bailey, Dennis, "Underground," *The Boston Globe Magazine*, March 26, 1989.

Baker, Scott, "Activists attack new women's control unit," *The Guardian*, March 23, 1988.

Bates, Tom, "The Government's Secret War on the Indian," *Oregon Times*, February-March 1976.

Beichman, Arnold, "Can Counterintelligence Come in from the Cold?" *Policy Review*, No. 15, Winter 1981.

Bendant, James R., "A Disturbing Shift in the Grand Jury's Role," *Los Angeles Times*, October 2, 1974.

Benjamin, Thomas B., and Kenneth Lux, "Solitary Confinement as Psychological Torture," *California Western Law Review*, 13(265), 1978.

Bergman, Lowell, and David Weir, "Revolution on Ice: How the Black Panthers Lost the FBI's War of Dirty Tricks," *Rolling Stone*, September 9, 1976.

Berkan, Judy, "The Crime of Cerro Maravilla," *Puerto Rico Libre*, May/June 1979.

Berman, Jerry J., "FBI Charter Legislation: The Case for Prohibiting Domestic Intelligence Investigations," *University of Detroit Journal of Urban Law*, No. 55, 1978.

Bisson, Terry, and Sally O'Brien, "Young Hostages," *The Nation*, August 5, 1985.

Blackburn, D., "Skyhorse and Mohawk: More Than a Murder Trial," *The Nation*, December 24, 1977.

Blaut, James, "Are Puerto Ricans a National Minority?" *Monthly Review*, Vol. 29, No. 5, May 1977.

Botemps, Arna, "Most Dangerous Negro in America," *Negro Digest*, September 1961.

Bubka, Tony, "The Harlan County Coal Strike of 1931," *Labor History*, No. 11, Winter 1970.

Buitrago, Ann-Mari, "Sessions' Confessions," *Covert Action Information Bulletin*, No. 31 (Winter 1989).

Butz, Tim, "Garden Plot and Swat: U.S. Police as New Action Enemy," *Counterspy*, Fall 1974.

_____, "Garden Plot: Flowers of Evil," *Akwesasne Notes*, Vol. 7, No. 5, Early Winter 1975.

_____, "Bringing Vietnam Home," *Akwesasne Notes*, Early Winter 1975.

Calhoun, Patricia, "Grand Slam," *Westword*, December 14, 1983.

Calvert, Gregory, "In White America: Radical Consciousness and Social Change," *The National Guardian*, March 1967.

Carmichael, Stokely, "What We Want," *New York Review of Books*, September 26, 1966.

_____, "A Declaration of War," *San Francisco Express Times*, February 22, 1968.

Churchill, Ward, "The Strange Case of 'Wild Bill' Janklow," *Covert Action Information Bulletin*, No. 24, Summer 1985.

_____, "Due Process be Damned: The Case of the Portland Four," *Zeta*, January 1988.

_____, "Leonard Peltier: The Struggle Continues," *Zeta*, March 1988.

_____, "Who Killed Anna Mae?" *Zeta*, December 1988.

_____, "COINTELPRO as a Family Business," *Zeta*, March 1989.

_____, "Renegades, Terrorists and Revolutionaries: The Government's Propaganda War Against the American Indian Movement," *Propaganda Review*, No. 4, April 1989.

_____, "Wages of COINTELPRO: The Case of Mumia Abu-Jamal," *New Studies on the Left*, Vol. XIV, Nos. 1-2, Spring-Summer 1989.

_____, "To Serve and Protect?" *New Studies on the Left*, Vol. XIV, Nos. 1-2, Spring-Summer 1989.

_____, "The Third World at Home: Political Prisoners in the United States, *Zeta*, June 1990.

Churchill, Ward, and Jim Vander Wall, "The FBI Takes AIM: The FBI's Secret War Against the American Indian Movement," *The Other Side*, Vol. 23, No. 5, June 1987.

_____, "Strange War on the Lakota: The Case for a Congressional Investigation of FBI Activities on Pine Ridge Reservation, 1972-1976," *Rolling Stick*, No. 14, 1987.

_____, "COINTELPRO Against the Black Panthers: The Case of Geronimo Pratt," *Covert Action Information Bulletin*, No. 31, January 1989.

Ciccione, Richard, "New peace talks set with Indians," *Rapid City Journal*, March 7, 1973.

_____, "Abernathy visits Wounded Knee; Kunstler, Berrigan plan to come," *Rapid City Journal*, March 8, 1973.

_____, "Indians seek removal of lawmen at Wounded Knee," *Rapid City Journal*, March 10, 1973.

_____, "FBI agent shot, 'sovereign state' proclaimed: Wounded Knee circumstances jury topic," *Rapid City Journal*, March 12, 1973.

_____, "Federal authorities re-establish barriers around Wound Knee," *Rapid City Journal*, March 13, 1973.

Clavir, Judy Gumbo, "Open Fire! or the FBI's History Lesson," *Crawdaddy*, November 1976.

Cleaver, Eldridge, "On Lumpen Ideology," *Black Scholar*, No. 4, November-December 1972.

Clinton, Robert N., "Development of Criminal Jurisdiction Over Indian Lands: The Historical Perspective," *Arizona Law Review*, Vol. 17, No. 4, 1975.

Cohen, Felix S., "The Erosion of Indian Rights, 1950-53: A Case Study in Bureaucracy," *Yale Law Review*, Vol. 62, Spring 1953.

Cook County (Illinois) Grand Jury, "Improper Police Intelligence Activities: A Report of the Extended March, 1975, Cook County Grand Jury," *First Principles I*, January 1976.

Cook, Fred, "Justice at Gainesville," *The Nation*, October 1, 1973.

Crewdson, John, "FBI Reportedly Harassed Radicals After Spy Program Ended," *New York Times*, March 23, 1975.

_____, "Two FBI Men Die, Indian Slain," *New York Times*, June 27, 1975.

Daniels, Stuart, "The Weatherman," *Government and Opposition*, No. 9, Autumn 1974.

Day, Susie, "Political Prisoners: Guilty Until Proven Innocent," *Sojouner: The Women's Forum*, February 1989.

_____, "Resistance Conspiracy Trial," *Zeta*, September 1989.

Debo, Dan, "COINTELPRO Lives On: The Unending Ordeal of Dhoruba Moore," *New Studies on the Left*, Vol. XIV, Nos. 1-2, Spring-Summer 1989.

Deloria, Vine Jr., "Who Knows What Violence We Can Expect?" *Los Angeles Times*, August 17, 1975.

Denniston, Lyle, "FBI Says Kennedy OKed King Wiretap," *Washington Evening Star*, June 18, 1969.

Donner, Frank J., "Theory and Practice of American Political Intelligence," *New York Review of Books*, April 22, 1971.

_____, "The *Agent Provocateur* as Folk Hero," *Civil Liberties*, September 1971.

_____, "Hoover's Legacy," *The Nation*, June 1, 1974.

_____, "Let Him Wear a Wolf's Head: What the FBI Did to William Albertson," *Civil Liberties Review*, No. 3, April/May 1978.

_____, "The Terrorist As Scapegoat," *The Nation*, No. 226, May 20, 1978.

Donner, Frank J., and Eugene Cerruti, "The Grand Jury Network," *The Nation*, January 3, 1972.

Donner, Frank J., and Richard I. Lavine, "Kangaroo Grand Juries," *The Nation*, November 29, 1970.

Dunne, Bill, "The U.S. Penitentiary at Marion Illinois: An Instrument of Oppression," *New Studies on the Left*, Vol. XIV, Nos. 1-2, Spring-Summer 1989.

Editors, "The Puerto Rican Revolution," *Soulbook*, Vol. I, No. 3, Fall 1965.

Editors, "Let Us Hold High the Banner of Intercommunalism and the Invincible Thought of Huey P. Newton," *The Black Panther*, Center Section, January 23, 1971.

_____, "COINTELPRO En Puerto Rico: Documentos Secretos FBI," *Pensamiento Critico*, Summer 1979.

_____, "The Red Squads Settlement Controversy," *The Nation*, July 11, 1981.

_____, "The Executive Order," *Covert Action Information Bulletin*, No. 16, March 1982.

_____, "Ex-FBI Agent Exposes Use of Informants to Destroy the BPP," *Freedom Magazine*, Vol. 18, No. 5, January 1985.

_____, "Once a G-Man, Now a Pacifist: A costly conversion," *Newsweek*, November 23, 1987.

_____, "Ohio 7 Minus 2: On Trial for Seditious Conspiracy," *The Insurgent*, September 1989.

Elliff, John T., "Aspects of Federal Civil Rights Enforcement: The Justice Department and the FBI," *Perspectives in American History*, No. 5, 1971.

Epstein, Edward J., "The Panthers and the Police," *New Yorker*, February 18, 1971.

Erdoes, Richard, "Crow Dog's Third Trial," *Akwesasne Notes*, Vol. 8, No. 1, Early Spring 1976.

Fine, David, "Federal Grand Jury Investigations of Political Dissidents," *Harvard Civil Rights-Civil Liberties Law Review*, No. 7, 1972.

Finman, Ted, and Stewart MacAulay, "Freedom to Dissent: The Vietnam Protests and the Worlds of Public Officials," *Wisconsin Law Review*, Summer 1966.

Franklin, Raymond S., "The Political Economy of Black Power," *Social Problems*, No. 16, Winter 1969.

Garbus, Martin, "General Haig of Wounded Knee," *The Nation*, November 9, 1974.

Gelbspan, Ross, "Documents show Moon group aided FBI," *Boston Globe*, April 19, 1988.

_____, "COINTELPRO in the '80s: The 'New' FBI," *Covert Action Information Bulletin*, No. 31, Winter 1989.

Giese, Paula, "Secret Agent Douglass Durham and the Death of Jancita Eagle Deer," *North Country Anvil*, March-April 1976.

_____, "Profile of an Informer," *Covert Action Information Bulletin*, No. 24, Summer 1985.

Gladstone, Lyn, "Custer Demonstration Canceled," *Rapid City Journal*, February 5, 1973.

_____, "Tension grows on reservation," *Rapid City Journal*, March 9, 1973.

Goldberg, Carol E., "Public Law 280: The Limits of State Jurisdiction Over Reservation Indians," *UCLA Law Review*, No. 22, 1975.

Goldstein, Robert Justin, "The FBI's Forty Year Plot," *The Nation*, No. 227, July 1, 1978.

_____, "An American Gulag? Summary Arrest and Emergency Detention of Political Dissidents in the United States," *Columbia Human Rights Law Review*, No. 10, 1978.

Goodman, Carolyn, as told to Bernard Asbell, "My Son Didn't Die in Vain!" *Good Housekeeping*, May 1965.

Gottleib, Jeff, and Jeff Cohen, "Was Fred Hampton Executed?" *The Nation*, December 25, 1976.

Gordon, Diana, "Doing Edgar Proud," *The Nation*, November 13, 1989.

Gregor, A. James, "Black Nationalism: A Preliminary Analysis of Negro Radicalism," *Science and Society*, No. 26, Fall 1963.

Halsey, Peggy, "Undue Process," *Christianity in Crisis*, Vol. 48, No. 4, March 21, 1989.

Harlan, Christi, "The Informant Left Out in the Cold," *Dallas Morning News*, April 6, 1986.

Hayden, Tom, "The Politics of the Movement," *Dissent*, January/February 1966.

Higgins, Harold, "Hot Springs meeting productive," *Rapid City Journal*, February 16, 1973.

Hill, Robert A., "The Foremost Radical of His Race: Marcus Garvey and the Black Scare, 1918-1920," *Prologue*, No. 16, Winter 1984.

Hirschorn, Michael W., "Newly Released Documents Provide Rare Look at How FBI Monitors Students and Professors," *Chronicle of Higher Education*, February 10, 1988.

Hoeffle, Paul, and Phil Garber, "Seduced and Abandoned," *Zeta*, February 1989.

Hogan, Frank, "Witness for the Prosecution: Accused murderer Gregory Clifford doesn't have any friends – except the FBI," *Westword*, Vol. 11, No. 20, January 13-19, 1988.

Horrock, Nicholas M., "Ex-Officials Say FBI Harassed Dr. King to Stop His Criticism," *New York Times*, March 9, 1978.

Jacobs, James, "An Overview of National Political Intelligence," *University of Detroit Journal of Urban Law*, No. 55, 1978.

Jaimes, M. Annette, "The Pit River Indian Land Claim Dispute in Northern California," *Journal of Ethnic Studies*, Vol. 14, No. 4, Winter 1987.

_____, "Self-Portrait of a Black Liberationist," *New Studies on the Left*, Vol. XIV, Nos. 1-2, Spring-Summer 1989.

Jaimes, M. Annette, and Ward Churchill, "Behind the Rhetoric: English-Only as Counterinsurgency Warfare," *Issues in Radical Therapy: New Studies on the Left*, Vol. XIII, Nos. 1-2, Winter-Spring 1988.

Johansen, Bruce, "Peltier and the Posse," *The Nation*, October 1, 1977.

_____, "The Reservation Offensive," *The Nation*, February 25, 1978.

Kahn, Ric, "Fed Excesses: Going too far to get the Ohio 7," *The Boston Phoenix*, July 8, 1988.

Kantner, Elliott, "The FBI Takes Aim at AIM," *Seven Days*, April 11, 1977.

Kilson, Martin, "Black Power: The Anatomy of a Paradox," *Harvard Journal of Negro Affairs*, No. 2, 1968.

King, Patricia, "A Snitch's Tale: The Killer Gang (An informer tells about his life as an 'El Rukn')," *Newsweek*, November 6, 1989.

King, Wayne, "Reagan Backs F.B.I. Surveillance: Accepts Bureau Report That There Was Solid Basis for Effort Aimed at Critics," *New York Times*, February 4, 1988.

_____, "F.B.I.'s Papers Portray Inquiry Fed by Informer," *New York Times*, February 13, 1988.

Kroese, Ron, "Material witness to testify on killings," *Rapid City Journal*, July 2, 1975.

Kuipers, Dean, "Raising Arizona," *Spin*, September 1989.

Kunstler, William, "Writers of the Purple Rage," *The Nation*, No. 227, December 30, 1978.

_____, "The Ordeal of Leonard Peltier," *Covert Action Information Bulletin*, No. 24, Summer 1985.

Lardner, George Jr., "FBI Bugging and Blackmail of King Bared," *Washington Post*, November 19, 1975.

_____, "Wilkens Denies Any Link to FBI Plot to Discredit King," *Washington Post*, May 31, 1978.

Lawson, James, "And the Character Assassination that Followed," *Civil Liberties Review*, No. 5, July-August 1978.

Leonard, Edward A., "Ninety-Four Years of Non-Violence," *New South*, No. 20, April 1965.

Levasseur, Ray Luc, "My Name is Ray Luc Levasseur: Statement to the Court, January 10, 1989," *New Studies on the Left*, Vol. XIV, Nos. 1-2, Spring-Summer 1989.

Levin, S.K., "Black Panthers Get Bittersweet Revenge," *Colorado Daily*, November 10, 1982.

Lobash, Arnold H., "316 Used by FBI in Informer Role," *New York Times*, September 5, 1976.

Luce, Phillip, Abbott, "Why I Quit the Extreme Left," *Saturday Evening Post*, May 8, 1965.

Lumumba, Chokwe, "Short History of the U.S. War on the RNA," *Black Scholar*, No. 12, January-February 1981.

Lyden, Jacki, and Paula Schiller, "The Prison that Defies Reform," *Student Lawyer*, May 1987.

Lynd, Staughton, "The New Radicalism and Participatory Democracy," *Dissent*, Summer 1965.

_____, "Toward an Interracial Movement of the Poor," *Liberation*, July 1969.

Lyons, Gene, "Letter from the Land of Opportunity," *New York Review of Books*, May 30, 1974.

McCall, Cheryl, "Life on Pine Ridge Bleak," *Colorado Daily*, May 16, 1975.

McClory, Robert, *"Agent Provocateur,"* *Chicago Magazine*, February 1979.

McKiernan, Kevin, "Indian woman's death raises many troubling questions," *Minneapolis Tribune*, May 30, 1976.

Mackenzie, Angus, "Sabotaging the Dissident Press," *Columbia Journalism Review*, March 3, 1981.

Martinez, Elizabeth, "The Perils of Pilar: What Happened to the Chicano Movement?" *Zeta*, April 1989.

Marx, Gary T., "Thoughts on a Neglected Category of Social Movement Participant: The *Agent Provocateur* and Informant," *American Journal of Sociology*, No. 80, September 1974.

Mead, Judy, "Grand Juries," *First Principles II*, September 2, 1976.

Meier, August, "The Revolution Against the NAACP," *Journal of Negro Education*, No. 32, Spring 1963.

_____, "The Dilemmas of Negro Protest Strategy," New South, No. 21, Spring 1966.

Miller, Mike, "The MFDP," *The Movement*, May 1965.

Mollan, Robert, "Smith Act Prosecutions: The Effects of the Dennis and Yates Cases," *University of Pittsburgh Law Review*, No. 1126, June 1965.

Moses, Bob, "Mississippi: 1961-1962," *Liberation*, January 14, 1970.

Murphy, Paul L., "Sources and Nature of Intolerance in the Twenties," *Journal of American History*, No. 51, June 1964.

Muzik, Edward J., "Victor L. Berger: Congress and the Red Scare," *Wisconsin Magazine of History*, No. 47, Summer 1964.

Nagel, William C., "On Behalf of a Moratorium on Prison Construction," *Crime and Delinquency*, Fall 1977.

Neufield, Russell, "COINTELPRO in Puerto Rico," *Quash: Newsletter of the National Lawyers Guild Grand Jury Project*, August/September 1982.

Ofari, Earl, "W.E.B. DuBois and the Black Power Revolt," *Black World*, No. 19, August 1970.

_____, "Black Labor: Powerful Force for Liberation," *Black World*, No. 22, October 1973.

Ogden, Don, "Ohio Seven: The Whole Truth Goes Untold," *Guardian*, September 15, 1989.

O'Leary, Jeremiah, "King Wiretap Called RFK's Idea," *Washington Evening Star*, June 19, 1969.

O'Melveny, Mary, "U.S. Political Prison: Lexington Prison High Security Unit," *Covert Action Information Bulletin*, No. 31, Winter 1989.

Oppenheimer, Jerry, "The Strange Killing of a Wounded Knee Indian," *The Washington Star*, May 24, 1976.

_____, "Questions raised about FBI's handling of Aquash case," *Rapid City Journal*, May 25, 1976.

Pahl, Thomas L., "The Dilemma of a Civil Libertarian: Francis Biddle and the Smith Act," *Journal of the Minnesota Academy of Science*, No. 34, 1967.

_____, "The G-String Conspiracy, Political Reprisal or Armed Revolt? The Minnesota Trotskyite Trial," *Labor History*, No. 8, Winter 1967.

Pyle, Christopher, "Spies Without Masters: The Army Still Watches Civilian Politics," *Civil Liberties Review*, Summer 1974.

Raines, Howell, "The Birmingham Bombing Twenty Years Later: The Case That Won't Close," *New York Times Magazine*, July 24, 1983.

Raymond, John, "Files Recently Released: FBI Spying on Black Student Union Revealed," *Common Ground*, Vol. III, No. 7, April 18, 1978.

Reuben, William A., and Carlos Norman, "Brainwashing in America? The Women of Lexington Prison," *The Nation*, June 27, 1987.

Reynolds, Diana, "FEMA and the NSC: The Rise of the National Security State," *Covert Action Information Bulletin*, No. 33, Winter 1990.

Ridgeway, James, "Spooking the Left," *Village Voice*, March 3, 1987.

Ridgeway, James, and Bill Clifford, "The Gritz Gets His," *Village Voice*, July 25, 1989.

Roberts, Gene, "The Story of Snick: From 'Freedom Rides' to 'Black Power,'" *New York Times Magazine*, September 25, 1966.

Rosenberg, Susan, "Reflections on Being Buried Alive," *Covert Action Information Bulletin*, No. 31, Winter 1989.

_____, "Growing repression of political prisoners," *Gay Community News*, November 5, 1989.

Rowan, Carl, "FBI Won't Talk about Additional Wiretapping," *Washington Evening Star*, June 20, 1969.

Rowntree, John, and Margaret Rowntree, "Youth as Class," *Midpeninsula Observer*, August 12, 1968.

Rudd, Mark, "Notes on Columbia," *The Movement*, March 1969.

Rustin, Bayard, "'Black Power' and Coalition Politics," *Commentary*, No. 42, September 1966.

Ryan, Mike, "The Stammheim Model: Judicial Counterinsurgency," *New Studies on the Left*, Vol. XIV, Nos. 1-2, Spring-Summer 1989.

Saxifrage Group, "Huey P. Newton: Tribute to a Fallen Warrior," *New Studies on the Left*, Vol. XIV, Nos. 1-2, Spring-Summer 1989.

Schwerner, Nat, "Mississippi: Whitewashing the FBI," *Rights*, April-May 1975.

Sherron, Philip, "F.B.I.'s Chief Says Surveillance Was Justified," *New York Times*, February 3, 1988.

Silverstrim, Elaine, "The Ordeal of Alejandrina," *The Witness*, Vol. 71, No. 2, February 1988.

Spain, David M., "Mississippi Autopsy," *Ramparts* (Special Edition), 1964.

Student Nonviolent Coordinating Committee, "The Basis of Black Power," *New York Times*, August 5, 1966.

Suarez, Manuel, "Ex-Puerto Rican Police Agent Guilty in Slaying of 2 Radicals," *New York Times*, March 19, 1988.

Swisher, Carl, "Civil Liberities in Our Time," *Political Science Quarterly*, No. 55, September 1940.

Tackwood, Louis E., "My Assignment was to Kill George Jackson," *The Black Panther*, April 21, 1980.

Theoharis, Athan, "Building a File: The Case Against the FBI," *Washington Post*, October 30, 1988.

Tilsen, Kenneth, "The FBI, Wounded Knee and Politics," *Iowa Journal of Social Work*, Fall 1976.

_____, "Fair and Equal Justice," *Quare*, September 1976.

Tolan, Sandy, "Tough Guys Don't Dance: How the FBI Infiltrated Earth First," *Village Voice*, July 25, 1989.

Ungar, Sanford J., "An Agenda for Rebuilding the FBI," *Washington Post*, August 21, 1977.

Viorst, Milton, "FBI Mayhem," *New York Review of Books*, March 18, 1976.

Warth, Robert, "The Palmer Raids," *South Atlantic Quarterly*, No. 48, January 1949.

Weiner, Bernard, "What, Another Conspiracy?" *The Nation*, November 2, 1970.

_____, "The Orderly Perversion of Justice," *The Nation*, February 1, 1971.

Weisman, Joel D., "About That 'Ambush' at Wounded Knee," *Columbia Journalism Review*, September-October 1975.

Whitehorn, Laura, "Counterinsurgency in the Courtroom: The 'Resistance Conspiracy Case,'" *Covert Action Information Bulletin*, No. 31, Winter 1989.

Wicker, Tom, "The Iron Curtain," *New York Times*, November 19, 1972.

Wilkens, Roy, "Whither Black Power?" *Crisis*, August-September 1966.

Williams, Robert F., "1957: The Swimming Pool Showdown," *Southern Exposure*, No. 8, Summer

1980.

_____, "USA: The Potential of a Minority Revolution," *The Crusader Monthly Newsletter*, No. 5, May-June 1964.

Wolf, Louis, "COINTELPRO Gets a New Name," *Covert Action Information Bulletin*, No. 31, Winter 1989.

Woodley, Richard, "It Will Be a Hot Summer in Mississippi,"*The Reporter*, May 21, 1964.

_____, "A Recollection of Michael Schwerner," *The Reporter*, July 16, 1964.

Worster, Terry, "FBI combing Pine Ridge," *Rapid City Journal*, June 28, 1975.

Zangrando, Robert L., "From Civil Rights to Black Liberation: The Unsettled 1960s," *Current History*, No. 62, September 1972.

Zoccino, Nanda, "Ex-FBI Informer Describes Terrorist Role," *Los Angeles Times*, January 26, 1976.

Government Documents

American Indian Policy Review Commission, *Final Report, Task Force 9: Law Consolidation, Revision and Codification*, U.S. Government Printing Office, Washington, D.C., 1977.

Canadian House of Commons, *House of Commons Debate, Canada*, Vol. 128, No. 129, 1st Session, 33rd Parliament, Official Report, Thursday, April 17, 1986.

City of New York, *Interim report prepared by the First Deputy Commissioner of Police* [Jaques Nevard]: *Arrests Made on the Complaint of Columbia University Administration of Students Trespassing in School Buildings*, New York City Police Department, May 4, 1968.

Federal Bureau of Investigation, *FBI Uniform Crime Report*, J. Edgar Hoover Bldg., Washington, D.C., 1975.

U.S. Army Training Command, *US Army Operational Concept for Low Intensity Conflict*, TRADOC Pamphlet No. 525-44, Ft. Monroe, VA, 1986.

U.S. Commission on Civil Rights, *Report – Book 5, Justice*, U.S. Government Printing Office, Washington, D.C., 1961.

_____, *Law Enforcement: A Report on Equal Protection in the South*, U.S. Government Printing Office, Washington, D.C., 1965.

_____, *Monitoring of Events Related to the Shootings of Two FBI Agents on the Pine Ridge Reservation*, Mountain States Regional Office, Denver, CO, 1975.

_____, *The Navajo Nation: An American Colony*, U.S. Government Printing Office, Washington, D.C., 1975.

_____, *Events Surrounding Recent Murders on the Pine Ridge Reservation in South Dakota*, Rocky Mountain Regional Office, Denver, March 31, 1976.

_____, *Hearing Held Before the U.S. Commission on Civil Rights: American Indian Issues in South Dakota, Hearing Held in Rapid City, South Dakota*, July 27-28, 1978, U.S. Government Printing Office, Washington, D.C., 1978.

_____, *Indian Tribes: A Continuing Quest for Survival*, U.S. Government Printing Office, Washington, D.C., 1981.

U.S. Congress, Joint Committee on Assassinations,*Hearings on the Investigation of the Assassination of Martin Luther King, Jr., Vol. 6*, 95th Congress, 2d Session, U.S. Government Printing Office, Washington, D.C., 1978.

U.S. Department of Interior, Bureau of Indian Affairs, "Analysis of Official Vote of Indian Tribes on the Wheeler-Howard Bill," (Unpublished Memorandum), Washington, D.C., June 6, 1934.

_____, *Status of Mineral Resource Information on the Pine Ridge Reservation*, BIA Report No. 12 (by J.P. Gries), Washington, D.C., 1976.

U.S. Department of Interior, National Park Service, *Memorandum of Agreement Between the Oglala Sioux Tribe of South Dakota and the National Park Service of the Department of Interior to Facilitate Establishment, Development, Administration and Public Use of the Oglala Sioux Tribal Lands, Badlands National Monument*, Washington, D.C., January 2, 1976 (unpublished).

_____, *Master Plan: Badlands National Monument*, Rocky Mountain Regional Office, Denver, 1978.

U.S. Department of Justice, *Opinion of the Attorney General*, Washington, D,C., April 25, 1821.

_____, "Prosecutive Summary," No. 1613, Washington, D.C., December 19, 1964.

_____, "Supplemental Summary," No. 1822, Washington, D.C., March 5, 1965.

_____, "Martin Luther King Report" (internal document prepared for Attorney General Edward H. Levi by Stanley J. Pottinger), Washington, D.C., April 9, 1976.

_____, *Report of the Justice Department Task Force to Review FBI Martin Luther King, Jr., Security and Assassination Investigations*, Washington, D.C., January 11, 1977.

_____, "Wiretaps," *Administrative History, Volume III*, Lyndon B. Johnson Library, Austin, TX, no date.

_____, *Report of the Task Force on Indian Matters*, Washington, D.C., 1975.

U.S. House of Representatives, Committee on the Civil Service, *Report of Investigation with Respect to Employee Loyalty and Employment Policies and Practices in the Government of the United States*, 78th Congress, 2d Session, U.S. Government Printing Office, Washington, D.C., 1946.

U.S. House of Representatives, Committee on Public Lands, *Hearings Before the Committee on Public Lands: Puerto Rican Constitution*, 81st Congress, 1st Session, U.S. Government Printing Office, Washington, D.C., 1950.

U.S. House of Representatives, Committee on Internal Security, *The Black Panther Party: Its Origins and Development as Reflected in Its Official Weekly Newspaper, The Black Panther-Community News Service*, 92d Congress, 1st Session, U.S. Government Printing Office, Washington, D.C., 1971.

_____, *Gun Barrel Politics: The Black Panther Party, 1966-1971*, U.S. Government Printing Office, Washington, D.C., 1971.

_____, *Hearings on Domestic Intelligence Operations for Internal Security Purposes, Part I*, 93d Congress, 2d Session, U.S. Government Printing Office, Washington, D.C., 1974.

U.S. House of Representatives, Committee on the Judiciary, Subcommittee on Civil and Constitutional Rights, *Hearings Before the Subcommittee on Civil and Constitutional Rights, 97th Congress, 1st Session on FBI Authorization, March 19, 24, 25; April 2, 8, 1981*, U.S. Government Printing Office, Washington, D.C., 1981.

_____, *Hearings on FBI Authorization on Indian Reservations*, (Serial No. 138), U.S. Government Printing Office, Washington, D.C., March 31 and June 17, 1982.

_____, *Break-Ins at Sanctuary Churches and Organizations Opposed to Administration Policy in Central America*, Serial No. 42, 100th Congress, 1st Session, U.S. Government Printing Office, Washington, D.C., 1988.

_____, *CISPES and FBI Counter-Terrorism Investigations*, Serial No. 122, 100th Congress, 2d Session, U.S. Government Printing Office, Washington, D.C., 1988.

U.S. Senate, Committee on Pacific Islands and Puerto Rico, *Hearings Before the Committee on Pacific Islands and Puerto Rico* (Senate Document 147), 56th Congress, 1st Session, U.S. Government Printing Office, Washington, D.C., 1900.

U.S. Senate, Committee on the Judiciary, Subcommittee on Constitutional Rights, *Army Surveillance and Civilians: A Documentary Analysis*, 92d Congress, 1st Session, U.S. Government Printing Office, Washington, D.C., 1971.

_____, *Hearings on FBI Counterintelligence Programs*, 93d Congress, 2d Session, U.S. Government Printing Office, Washington, D.C., 1974.

U.S. Senate, Committee on the Judiciary, Subcommittee on Internal Security, *Revolutionary Activities in the United States: The American Indian Movement*, 94th Congress, 2d Session, U.S. Government Printing Office, Washington, D.C., 1976.

U.S. Senate, Select Committee to Study Government Operations with Respect to Intelligence Activities, *Hearings Before the Senate Select Committee to Study Government Operations with Respect to Intelligence Activities, Volume IV: Mail Opening*, 94th Congress, 1st Session, U.S. Government Printing Office, Washington, D.C., 1975.

_____, *Hearings on Intelligence Activities, Vol. 6, The Federal Bureau of Investigation*, 94th Congress, 1st Session, U.S. Government Printing Office, Washington, D.C., 1975.

_____, *Intelligence Activities and the Rights of Americans, Book II*, 94th Congress, 2nd Session, U.S. Government Printing Office, Washington, D.C., 1976.

_____, *Final Report: Supplementary Detailed Staff Reports on Intelligence Activities and the Rights of Americans, Book III*, 94th Congress, 2d Session, U.S. Government Printing Office, Washington, D.C., 1976.

_____, *The FBI's Covert Program to Destroy the Black Panther Party*, 94th Congress, 2d Session, U.S. Government Printing Office, Washington, D.C., 1976.

U.S. Senate, Subcommittee on Internal Security, *Revolutionary Activities in the United States: The American Indian Movement*, 95th Congress, 1st Session, U.S. Government Printing Office, Washington, D.C., 1976.

U.S. Senate, *FBI Statutory Charter – Appendix to Hearings Before the Subcommittee on Administrative Practice and Procedure, Part 3*, 95th Congress, 2d Session, U.S. Government Printing Office, Washington, D.C., 1979.

U.S. Senate, Select Committee on Intelligence, *The FBI and CISPES*, 101st Congress, 1st Session, Rep. No. 101-46, U.S. Government Printing Office, Washington, D.C., 1989.

Pamphlets

Anonymous, *A Call to Resist Illegitimate Authority*, RESIST, Boston, 1967.

_____, *Breaking Men's Minds*, National Committee to End the Marion Lockdown, Chicago, 1987.

Cunningham, Dennis, and Jan Susler (eds.), *Transcript of the People's Tribunal to Expose the Crimes of the Marion and Lexington Control Units*, Committee to End the Marion Lockdown, Chicago, October 24, 1987.

Davidson, Carl, *The New Radicals and the Multiversity*, Students for a Democratic Society, Chicago, 1968.

Giese, Paula, *Anatomy of an Informer*, American Indian Movement, White Earth, MN, 1976.

Glick, Brian, *A Call for Justice: The Case of the N.Y. 3*, Committee to Support the New York Three, New York, 1985.

Haber, Alan, *Nonexclusionism: The New Left and the Democratic Left*, Students for a Democratic Society, New York, 1965.

Hayden, Tom, *Revolution in Mississippi*, Students for a Democratic Society, New York, 1962.

Levasseur, Ray Luc, *Opening Statement to the Jury*, Sedition Committee, Boston, 1985.

Lyden, Jacki, "Marion Prison: Inside the Lockdown," *All Things Considered* broadcast, October 28, 1986, produced by Paula Schiller, National Public Radio. Transcript published by Committee to End the Marion Lockdown, Chicago, 1987.

Northcott, Karen, *The FBI in Indian Communities*, American Friends Service Committee, Minneapolis, 1979.

Stevens, Don, and Jane Stevens, *South Dakota: The Mississippi of the North, or Stories Jack Anderson Never Told You*, Custer, SD, 1977.

Independent Reports

American Civil Liberties Union Prison Project, *Report on the High Security Unit for Women, Federal Corrections Institution, Lexington, Kentucky*, American Civil Liberties Union Foundation, New York, 1987.

Amnesty International, *Allegations of Inmate Mistreatment in Marion Prison, Illinois, USA*, (AI Index: AMR 51/26187), New York, 1987.

_____, *The High Security Unit, Lexington Federal Prison, Kentucky*, (AI Index: AMR 51/34/88), New York, 1988.

Anonymous, *Report on the U.S. Penitentiary at Marion*, John Howard Association, New York, 1987.

Buitrago, Ann Mari, *Report on CISPES Files Maintained by the FBI and Released Under the Freedom of Information Act*, FOIA, Inc., New York, January 1988.

Cunningham, Dennis, and Jan Susler, *A Public Report About a Violent Mass Assault Against Prisoners and Continuing Illegal Punishment and Torture of the Prison Population at the U.S. Penitentiary at Marion, Illinois*, Marion Prisoners Rights Project, Chicago, 1984.

Faculty Rights Group of Columbia University, *The Community and the Expansion of Columbia University*, Columbia University, December 1967.

Fund for the Republic, *Digest of the Public Record of Communism in the United States*, Fund for the Republic, Chicago, 1955.

Gautier, Carmen, María Teresa Blanco and María del Pilar Arguellas, *Persecution of the Puerto Rican Independence Movements and Their Leaders by the Counterintelligence Program (COINTELPRO) of the United States Federal Bureau of Investigation (FBI), 1960-71*. Unpublished, copy on file.

Glick, Brian, *G's Life and Times, 1967-1972*, for the Geronimo Pratt Defense Committee, San Francisco, 1979.

Korn, Dr. Richard, *The Effects of Confinement in HSU*, study submitted to the ACLU Foundation National Prison Project, New York, 1987.

Minnis, Jack, *Mississippi – A Chronology of Violence and Intimidation Since 1961*, Student Nonviolent Coordinating Committee (internal document), Atlanta, 1963.

Movement Support Network, *Harassment Update: Chronological List of FBI and Other Harassment Incidents*, Center for Constitutional Rights/National Lawyers Guild Anti-Repression Project, New York, (Sixth Edition) 1987.

Newton, Huey P., *War Against the Panthers: A Study of Repression in America*, (dissertation), University of California at Santa Cruz, 1980.

Nissen, D.R., *Federal Anti-Communist Legislation, 1931-41*. Unpublished dissertation.

Pratt, Geronimo Ji Jaga, *Report on the Prison Suit Pratt v. Rees*, Geronimo Pratt Defense Committee, San Francisco, 1982.

Smith, Maggie, and Valerie West, *BOS-LUC, Western Sweep and the Ohio Seven: A Case Study in Counterinsurgency*, unpublished study, 1988.

Films

Anonymous, *The Murder of Fred Hampton*, Newsreel, Chicago, 1970.

de Antonio, Emile, Mary Lampson and Haskell Wexler, *Underground*, no studio, 1975.

Landau, Saul, *Voices From Wounded Knee*, Institute for Policy Studies, Washington, D.C., 1974.

Ritz, Lan Brookes, *Annie Mae: A Brave Hearted Woman*, Brown Bird Productions, Los Angeles, 1979.

Index

About South End Press

South End Press is a nonprofit, collectively run book publisher with over 150 titles in print. Since our founding in 1977, we have tried to meet the needs of readers who are exploring, or are already committed to, the politics of radical social change.

Our goal is to publish books that encourage critical thinking and constructive action on the key political, cultural, social, economic, and ecological issues shaping life in the United States and in the world. In this way, we hope to give expression to a wide diversity of democratic social movements and to provide an alternative to the products of corporate publishing.

If you would like a free catalog of South End Press books or information about our membership program—which offers two free books and a 40% discount on all titles—please write us at South End Press, 116 Saint Botolph Street, Boston, MA 02115.

Other titles of interest from South End Press:

Agents of Repression: The FBI's Secret Wars Against the Black Panther Party and the American Indian Movement
Ward Churchill and Jim Vander Wall

War at Home: Covert Action Against U.S. Activists and What We Can Do About It
Brian Glick

Freedom Under Fire: U.S. Civil Liberties in Times of War
Michael Linfield

Toward an American Revolution: Exposing the Constitution and Other Illusions
Jerry Fresia

Marxism and Native Americans
edited by Ward Churchill

The Trial of Leonard Peltier
Jim Messerschmidt